D1049277

# PROFESSING SELVES

# PROFESSING SELVES

TRANSSEXUALITY

AND SAME-SEX DESIRE IN

CONTEMPORARY IRAN

Afsaneh Najmabadi

Duke University Press   Durham and London   2014

© 2014 Duke University Press.
All rights reserved.
Printed in the United States of America on acid-free paper ∞.
Cover design by Amy Ruth Buchanan. Book interior design
by Courtney Leigh Baker. Typeset in Scala by Tseng Information
Systems, Inc.

Library of Congress Cataloging-in-Publication Data
Najmabadi, Afsaneh.
Professing selves : transsexuality and same-sex desire in
contemporary Iran / Afsaneh Najmabadi.
pages cm
Includes bibliographical references and index.
ISBN 978-0-8223-5543-4 (cloth : alk. paper)
ISBN 978-0-8223-5557-1 (pbk. : alk. paper)
1. Transsexualism—Iran. 2. Sex change—Iran.
3. Gender identity—Iran. I. Title.
HQ77.95.I7N35 2013
306.76′80955—dc23
2013025248

FOR FARSHIDEH

**CONTENTS** *Acknowledgments* ix *Introduction* 1

## ACKNOWLEDGMENTS

This book owes an existential debt to Farshideh Mirbaghdadabadi, a dear friend for many decades who warmly embraced me into her household as I began to spend long periods of time in Tehran, my base for this research. When I returned to Tehran in 2005, I had not been there for twenty-five years. The Tehran of 2005 was a vastly different city from the Tehran of 1980. Farshideh's affectionate generosity made that return possible and delightful. She enabled me to build new connections, find friendships, and become re-embedded in the networks of a city where I had been born and lived the first two decades of my life. As important, her intellectual engagement with my research was invaluable: She listened patiently, on a regular basis, to my daily accounts of what I had observed, what had distressed, angered, and surprised me. Our conversations over tea, sangak bread, cheese, and walnuts allowed me to process my thinking and write more articulate "field notes." Her multiple social networks—she seemed to know anybody and everybody I would mention as a potential research lead—put me at the center of complicated webs of social actors to whom I needed to connect. How does one say thank you?

No less existential is the debt of this book to the trans persons, gays, and lesbians in several cities in Iran during 2006–7 who accepted me into their confidence, circles of socialization, and domains of living. This research and my understanding of practices of daily life in this realm were enabled by their generosity and trust. Several persons with whom I worked closely allowed their names to be used; many more did not. At the end, given the tight circles of socialization within which all circulated, I opted to name none and instead to use made-up names throughout this work. Should they read this book, I suspect, despite the many changes of minor specifics, they would recognize themselves and each other from the stories narrated. It is hard to find the right words to express the depth of my debt and gratitude to you all.

I also would like to thank numerous journalists and filmmakers and the medical, psychiatric, health, legal, and jurisprudential professionals who gave generously of their time and attention, in particular Dr. Arash Alaei, Dr. Yahya Behjatnia, Dr. Mehrdad Eftekhar, Mitra Farahani, Hamid Farzadi, Nazila Fathi, Hujjat al-Islam Muhammad Mahdi Karimi-nia, Negin Kianfar, Dr. Faridun Mehrabi, Dr. Bahram Mirjalali, Dr. Mohammad Reza Mohammadi, Ms. Mohseni-nia, Nahaleh Moshtagh, Dr. Behnam Ohadi, Ms. Pahlavani, Dr. Mahdi Saberi, Dr. Mehrzad Seraji, Mr. Taghizadeh, Dr. Usku'i, and Mr. Zamani.

Special mention is owed Ramyar Rossoukh. In my initial ventures into anthropological fieldwork and reflection, especially when I first arrived in Tehran, I benefited enormously from conversations with him. Other friends in Tehran who made my life pleasurable during the work of this book include Kaveh Najmabadi, Iraj Nobahari, Susan Parvar, Shahla Sherkat, and Mahdieh Zohdi. Thank you all.

The book also owes a formative debt to numerous conversations with colleagues, friends, students, and discussants who commented on various presentations of ideas related to this book: Kathryn Babayan, Claudia Castañeda, Steve Caton, Kathy Coll, Ken Cuno, Alireza Doostdar, Brad Epps, Kouross Esmaeli, Michael Fischer, Behrooz Ghamari-Tabrizi, David Halperin, Jennifer Hamilton, Valerie Hoffman, Ana Huang, Abbas Jaffer, Rebecca Jordan-Young, Natalie Kampen, Deniz Kandiyoti, Dina al-Kassim, Katherine Lemons, Heather Love, Jared McCormick, Asha Nadkarni, Mark Overmyer-Vélazquez, Jyoti Puri, Leyla Rouhi, Sahar Sadjadi, Sylvia Schafer, Cyrus Schayegh, Svati Shah, Sima Shakhsari, Pat Simons, Aisha Sobh, Mary Strunk, Susan Stryker, Banu Subramaniam, Judith Surkis, and Dror Ze'evi. Special thanks to my other colleagues and friends at Studies of Women, Gender, and Sexuality at Harvard University, working with whom makes difficult days pleasurable—Robin Bernstein, Alice Jardine, Caroline Light, Christianna Morgan, Amy Parker, Sarah Richardson, and Linda Schlossberg—and to Cory Paulsen and Janet Hatch from the history department, who were always there to help me figure out many ins and outs of the university.

Seminars at which I presented talks and papers based on various parts of this research and writing provided me with numerous occasions that helped me to clarify and articulate my arguments, and I am deeply thankful to those who extended these invitations and engaged me in the ensuing conversations: Barnard College, Columbia Law School Feminist Theory workshop, Dalhousie University, several campuses affiliated with the Greater Philadelphia Women's Studies Consortium, Harvard School of Public Health, Harvard University (Center for Middle Eastern Studies and the Humanities Center's Gender and Sexuality Seminar), Princeton University, Simon Fraser University, the *Social Research* conference, Stanford University, Tehran University, the University of Arizona, the University of California (Berkeley, Davis, Irvine, and Los Angeles), the University of Connecticut, the University of Delaware, the University of Illinois, the University of Massachusetts Amherst, the University of Michigan, the University of Pittsburgh, the University of Washington, Wellesley College, Williams College, and Yale University.

My deepest gratitude to Reza Salami for his unfailing research assistance, providing me with much of the archival material without which I could not have done this work. Likewise, I have been fortunate to have had several competent and reliable research assistants in these years: Elizabeth Angowski, Mahzad Eliasi, Mary Farag, Amirali Ghiassi, Anoushe Modarresi, Rebecca Stengel, Ali Akbar Vatandoost, and Kirsten Wesselhoeft. I am grateful also to the Kinsey Institute for Research in Sex, Gender, and Reproduction for permission to use their archives, to Farid Ghassemlou at the Library of Iran's Academy of Medical Sciences, and to members of the staff at the periodical section of the National Library of Iran.

Claudia Castañeda was enormously helpful with readings of early drafts, numerous conversations, and editorial suggestions. The final version of this book benefited enormously from the editorial work of Hope Steele. I would like to thank them as well as my editors at Duke University Press, Courtney Berger and Christine Choi. I could not have asked for better readers of my manuscript than the two selected by the Press. I received incredibly insightful and helpful commentary. Thank you. My deepest appreciation goes to Maryam Momeni for her invaluable assistance with proofreading.

I wish to thank the Harvard Historical Series for granting me a publication subvention, and Dean Michael Smith of the Faculty of Arts and Sciences at Harvard University for research support.

And now for the proverbial last but truly not least. In the years of working on this book I was facing life in the shadow of the loss of several loved ones, especially my mother, Farkhoneh Khanum Sohrabi, and my close friend, Parvin Paidar. Without the supportive affective net provided by my beloved friends and family, I would have lost my bearings in life: Naghmeh Sohrabi, Bushra Makiya, Naseem Makiya, and Kanan Makiya—thank you.

A note on transliteration: I have used the Library of Congress system as modified by *International Journal of Middle East Studies*, without diacritics except for ' (*'ayn*) and ' (*hamzah*). All translations and transliterations are mine, except when the choice of the proper name transliteration of persons could be ascertained.

# INTRODUCTION

Something happened in 2003–4: Transsexuals and transsexuality in Iran became a hot media topic, both in Iran and internationally.

The biomedical practice of sex change by means of surgery and hormonal treatment in Iran dates at least to the early 1970s; for nearly four decades the topic received occasional coverage in the Iranian press. But Iranian press coverage of the "trans" phenomenon increased sharply in early 2003, and it continued to be intense over the next five years. Concurrently, articles began to appear in the world press; television and video documentary productions followed.[1] My no-doubt-incomplete tabulation generates the following summary chart (table intro.1):

Based as I was in the United States, my first entry into this topic was as a reader of English-language reports and a viewer of early documentaries. The celebratory tone of some of these reports—welcoming the recognition of transsexuality and the permissibility of sex-change operations—was sometimes mixed with an element of surprise: How could this be happening in an Islamic state? In other, and especially later, accounts, the sanctioning of sex change became tightly linked with the illegality of same-sex practices (often equated with sodomy, an offense that carries a capital punishment), thus echoing some of the official thinking in Iran. For legal and medical authorities in Iran, sex change is framed explicitly as the cure for a diseased abnormality (gender identity disorder), and on occasion it is proposed as a religio-legally sanctioned option for heteronormalizing people with same-sex desires and practices.

TABLE INTRO.1. Coverage of sex change operations in Iran

| Type of coverage | 1999–2002 | 2003–8 | 2009–10 |
| --- | --- | --- | --- |
| Press reports in Iran | 1 + coverage in a bimonthly magazine over 12 months | 35 + coverage in a bimonthly magazine over 25 months | 3 |
| Press reports outside Iran | 3 | 6 | 0 |
| Visual productions (Iranian and foreign documentaries are grouped together because many are joint productions) | 1 | 16 | 0 |

Even though this possible option has not become state policy—because, as we will see, official discourse is also invested in making an essential distinction between the trans and the homosexual—international media coverage of transsexuality in Iran increasingly has emphasized that sex reassignment surgery (SRS) was being performed coercively on Iranian homosexuals by a fundamentalist Islamic government.[2] This narrative framing (along with those concerning the suppression of women's rights and other political and labor struggles) circulates within larger reductive and totalizing transnational discourses on Iran and Islam that equate them both with the most conservative factions of the Iranian government and with the views of the most regressive Islamists. Conservative transnational forces seem to have a common stake in ignoring the lively discourse about reform, as well as the history of progressive activism in contemporary Iran and the larger Islamicate world, which offer alternative notions of rights within an Islamic society and alternative modes of living a Muslim life.

At their best, the readings of transsexuality in Iran as legal and on the rise *because* of the impossibility of homosexuality, or—even more severely—as a government-sanctioned project with the aim of eliminating homosexuality, work with a reductive Foucauldian concept of "the techniques of domination" in which subjectivity is constituted by governmental designs and hegemonic power.[3] In this book, while I hope to remain cognizant of, and indeed map out, some of these techniques in contemporary Iran, I will lean toward highlighting how such techniques become at once productive of and transported into "the art of existence."[4] Indeed, their work of domination depends on their productivity for the art of existence.

I was lucky to be in Iran for this research in a period when much about trans lives and laws was being shaped almost daily. As de Certeau has observed, the coherence of the practices that Foucault selected and examined was "the result of a particular success. . . . Beneath what one might call the 'monotheistic' privilege that panoptic apparatuses have won for themselves, a 'polytheism' of scattered practices survives, dominated but not erased by the triumphal success of one of their numbers."[5] This book hopes to capture the polytheistic scattered practices that were a critical element in shaping trans lives and subjectivities in this period.

Back in 2005, when I first began to read the press coverage extensively, I was as much puzzled by what was going on in Iran as I was irritated by its international coverage. The discourse on sex/gender/sexuality that informed the contemporary Iranian conversations regarding transsexuality was radically different from what it had been a century earlier. How did this fundamental shift take place in such a relatively short time? Pursuing this query took me to unfamiliar domains and unexpected pleasures—beyond the fever of the archives, into practices of ethnography and oral history.

This book attempts to map out a situated "cartography of desire" in Iran that locates the contemporary discourses and practices of transsexuality in a longer historical trajectory and intersecting discursive sites, including medicine, religious doctrine, psychology, criminology, the family, trans activism, and practices of everyday life.[6] Bringing together historical archives, ethnographic fieldwork, and open-ended interviews with a wide spectrum of actors, including Iranian trans persons, gays and lesbians, psychologists, surgeons, health professionals, social workers, journalists, documentary filmmakers, theologians, and state officials, the book offers a historical and ethnographic account of the particular formation of genders and sexualities that cluster around trans- and homosexuality in contemporary Iran and provides some clues for what goes into enabling certain articulations of desire and disabling others.

What trans as a category of "human kind" means today in Iran is specific to a nexus formed not simply by transnational diffusion of concepts and practices from a Western heartland to the Rest.[7] What it means to live a trans life in today's Iran is also the product of the country's sociocultural and political circumstances over the previous half century. Today, a trans identity in Iran carries a particular set of affiliations and disaffiliations, identifications and disidentifications, that are specific to this national-transnational nexus.

In the opening chapter, I begin with the present: a moment in which the transition process works around a notion of "filtering" to determine whether an applicant is "really trans," "really homosexual," intersex, or perhaps suffers from a series of other classified psychological disorders. The complex nexus that filtering represents constitutes and authorizes a category of non-normativity as a legitimate, acceptable category, a process of subject-formation/subjection that is based partly on trans persons' own actions and narratives, and therefore also on self-cognition and self-production.

One conclusion this book proposes is that the very process of psychological filtering and jurisprudential demarcating, far from eliminating gays and lesbians (if that is indeed what the Iranian authorities had hoped), has paradoxically created new social spaces. Instead of constructing an impassable border, the process has generated a porously marked, nebulous, and spacious domain populated by a variety of "not-normal" people. To persuade some gays and lesbians ("symptomatic homosexuals") to consider transitioning bodily, and to filter out the true ("morally deviant") homosexuals, this process needs to offer a safe passage between categories. Because the filtering and sorting processes depend above all on individual self-narratives, the potential uses of this nebula are limited only by each person's creativity—a decidedly abundant resource. As a wise friend urged me back in 2005, "Don't worry, people are very creative and make their own uses." And this is what I learned: not to underestimate the real problems and challenges, and at times dangers, that trans persons, gays, and lesbians face in Iran, but also to see the productivity of the power of legal-medical-religious regulations, as well as the creativity with which trans persons, gays, and lesbians use the spaces such regulative power enables and the ways in which their active participation and struggles change things.

The distinction between the (acceptable) trans and the (deviant) homosexual has been enabled by biomedical, psychological, legal, and jurisprudential discourses that emerged between the 1940s and the 1970s in Iran. Chapter 2 traces this history, mapping out how surgical transformations of trans bodies initially emerged as a variant of a larger category of "sex-change" scientific marvels, first reported in the 1930s and 1940s, which referred to intersex bodily transformations. In the discourse of national scientific progress, trans bodies emerged as affiliated with, yet distinct from, congenital intersex bodies, and sex-change medical interventions were discussed as examples of advancements in medicine and surgery.

The discourse of the marvelous within vernacular science worked with the emerging discourse of sexuality in psychobehavioral science that was not concerned with marvels. Rather, the vernacular science incorporated all bodies into its concern with the health of the nation, the progress of its educational system, and the reform of family norms.

A growing academization of the vernacular psychology and sexology of these earlier decades resulted in the dominance of "physio-psycho-sexology" within the medical and health scientific community by the late 1960s. This dominance proved critical in disaffiliating the trans from the intersex category and affiliating it with the homosexual and the transvestite. Physio-psycho-sexology also informed the emergent criminological discourse, such that sexual deviance was diagnosed as potentially criminal. Treatises on criminal sexualities described male homosexuality as almost always violent, akin to rape, prone to turn to murder, and almost always aimed at the "underage." Of particular significance was the 1934 case of Asghar Qatil (Asghar the Murderer). Asghar Qatil's reported confessions were taken to indicate that in almost all cases murder followed sex with young male adolescents, many of them "street kids." The question of whether he was insane or criminal, which ran through the public debate of this case in 1934—along with the judicial decision that he *was* a criminal (he subsequently was executed in public)—contributed to the emerging association of sexual practices existing at the time between older men and male adolescents with deviancy/criminality. This association continues to inform dominant perceptions of male homosexuality in Iran and haunts transwomen's lives even after SRS.

The history of the modern stigmatization of homosexuality is thus a crucial part of my analysis, particularly with regard to differences between male-to-female (MtF) transitions compared with female-to-male (FtM) ones. As in many other places, in Iran conceptions of female-female sexual desire and relationships have a different historical trajectory, which only very recently and very partially have come into categorical affinity with male-male sexual desires and practices (under the rubric of homosexuality). Chapter 3 traces this recent history through a 1973 widely publicized "crime of passion," alleged to be Iran's first murder that had occurred "as a result of female homosexuality." The intense and sustained coverage of the story in a popular women's weekly, which included detailed reports, letters, photographs, interviews, and experts' roundtables, in addition to blaring headlines and news articles in the national dailies, contributed to the disarticulation of the trans from the intersex and its re-articulation with the homosexual. The coverage of the case was at the same time distinct from the story of Asghar Qatil. Framed in psychobehavioral terms, the dominant discourse in this "lesbian crime of passion" was centered on the failures of parents and educators. It was cast as a preventable murder, not inherent in the nature of the sexual desire. Moreover, the accused woman's expressed desire for sex change was projected as a missed possibility that might have averted the deadly tragedy. Drawing on this double history and on my interviews, I analyze how the "problem" of homosexuality differently configures MtF transitions from FtM ones in the Iranian context.

The 1979 revolution and the consolidation of an Islamic Republic produced a paradoxical situation for transsexuality: On the one hand, it immediately made what we would name and recognize as transgendered lives impossibly hazardous, while on the other, it led to its official sanction. In the 1970s, "woman-presenting males" (*mard-i zan-numa*) had carved themselves a space of relative acceptance in particular sites and professions (this is the subject of chapter 4). The 1979 revolution, and in particular the cultural purification campaigns of the first few years after the revolution, ruptured the dynamic of acceptability and marginalization of "the vulgar" and "the deviant" accorded by the larger society. Now, woman-presenting males not only carried the stigma of homosexuality, but they also transgressed the newly imposed regulations of gendered dressing in public.

Simultaneously, the establishment of an Islamic Republic set in motion a process of bureaucratization, professionalization, and specialization of Islamic jurisprudence and the Islamicization of the state. Among the significant effects of this shift was the way Islam as an overarching discourse of governance gained power in relation to the scientific discourses that had held sway previously. With regard to the issue of sex change, Ayatollah Khomeini had expressed his opinion as early as 1964 in his Arabic master treatise *Tahrir al-wasila*, in which he had elaborated that sex change was permissible in Islam. Twenty years later, in 1984, this time in Persian and as the supreme political authority of the new state, he reissued this earlier opinion in response to a transwoman's plea. From the late 1980s through the 2000s, legal, biomedical, and psychiatric authorities worked closely with specialized clerics to carve out legal and standardized procedures for the diagnosis and treatment of trans persons and to provide financial and social support for surgeries and care (chapter 5).

Missing from the circulating accounts of this history, in official discourse as well as most documentaries, is the critical role of trans activists in this transformation. Chapter 6 attempts to bring forth their participation. I understand trans activism in Iran not simply as a state-driven project that at most has some policy benefits for trans persons. Rather, like other domains and forms of engagement with governmental institutions, such activism forms a part of the process of state-formation itself. Iranian state-formation is an on-going, fractious, and volatile process, which—more than three decades after the 1979 revolution—continues to shape and reshape, fracture and refracture, order and reorder what we name "the state."[8] This attention to trans activism shows how the state and society also are marked by trans people.

Transsexual as a religio-state-sanctioned category bears the mark of an array of challenges. But the challenges faced by trans persons—and by lesbians and gays—in Iran do not come exclusively, or even primarily, from either state or religion; they come as well from social and cultural norms. For example, a major factor is the pressure of the pervasive "marriage imperative." Marrying constitutes an enactment of adulthood out of adolescence. While socio-economic changes have pushed the average age of first marriage for men and women alike to beyond their mid-twenties, unmarried persons live as if they are not yet adult. Male-male and female-female couples live under the severe threat of the marriage imperative, which at times contributes to the decision to consider transitioning as that which may salvage a threatened relationship. The ethnographic research in this book portrays these and other complex lived realities of some trans persons with whom I worked.

## Translations and Transplantations

From the outset, this project faced enormous challenges of translation. I started with what seemed to be two simple, coherent, research questions. First, in a cultural-legal context where same-sex desire was considered shameful and same-sex practices were illegal, but within which transsexuality, even if overwhelmingly understood as shameful, was nevertheless legal and state subsidized, how did this configuration shape sexual and gender subjectivities? Second, how did insistent state regulations and religio-cultural codes and rituals concerning proper gender conduct shape sexual desires and gender identifications? Both questions were informed by the distinctions between gender, sex, and sexuality that had shaped my thinking over three decades of teaching, research, and activism in the United States. It quickly became clear that many of the stories I heard and lives I became part of seemed incoherent, if not incomprehensible, if I were to make them responsible for answering these questions. For instance, in some early conversations I would ask a variation of the question, "How did you come to recognize yourself as a trans and not a homosexual?" Not only did the question re-enact the legal and psychological understanding and dominant categorizations; more importantly, through that re-enactment, it participated in inciting the textbook narratives that these first interactions solicited. I was putting particular demands of accountability on trans persons that depended on unstated distinctions and reproduced the dominant delineations.

The categorical distinctions shaping my questions were even more situated and contingent than I had anticipated. When it came to issues of sexual/gender identification, desire, and practices, a single concept—*jins*—linguistically and culturally kept them together.[9] Not only had no distinction between sexuality and gender emerged, but, more significantly, lives were possible through that very nondistinction.

This is not a cultural relativist proposition. The contingency of these distinctions—enabling competing claims and differing ways of crafting livable lives—is, for example, argued by David Valentine in his persuasive ethnography, *Imagining Transgender*. Moreover, over the past three decades in Iran, the distinction between sex and gender has emerged powerfully in another domain—feminist activism—as a politically enabling parsing. For the topic of this book, however, those categorical distinctions proved incoherent. The tight conjunction among sex/gender/sexuality has both enabled the work of changing the body to align its gender/sexuality with its sex and set the parameters within which these changes are imagined and enacted. It has therefore necessarily contributed to the structure of self-cognition and narrative presentation among trans persons. More specifically, the persistent pattern of a tight transition from a cross-gender-identified childhood to an adolescence marked by sexual desire for one's own peers speaks to the indistinction between gender/sex/sexuality. This indistinction regularly disrupts attempts to separate the homosexual from the trans, even as that distinction is regularly invoked.

As important, some of the conceptual distinctions among gender, sex, and sexuality within the Anglo-American context, including the distinction sometimes made between transgender and transsexual (based on surgical modifications to the body), have been shaped over the past decades by the identity politics of gender and sexuality as well as queer activism and queer critical theory.[10] Transsexuality in Iran has not been shaped by such developments. Given the different political and sociocultural contexts, to what extent were analytical categories and theoretical distinctions developed in this recent Anglo-American setting useful for understanding Iran? As Brad Epps has noted, "Gender trouble, in a global frame, needs to be at once supplemented (in the deconstructive sense) and recast as 'translation trouble' or, better yet, 'language trouble.'"[11]

A related question was, How did seemingly similar assignations carry different meanings (or not) within a different politics of sex, sexuality, and gender? For instance, many of the issues that were discussed in trans support groups in Tehran resonated with some of what I had learned from conversations and debates in the United States, such as the issue of trans people becoming a node of cultural/scientific/popular obsession, the irrelevance of etiology to the claims of rights, and so on. But even when hearing resonances of familiarity, I had to learn to hear anew these familiar soundings and understand their grammar in a different location and moment of utterance. What happens when words leave one setting and become enfolded into another?[12] For instance, as will be discussed in chapters 4, 7, and 8, when the term *gay* first appeared in Iran of the 1970s, it was largely avoided by local men who could so self-identify because it was received as the English translation of a Persian word with a highly pejorative and dishonorable load (*kuni*).[13] Some twenty years later, it began to be embraced precisely for an opposite effect: It had come to provide distance from that Persian pejorative assignation and helped those who so identified to connect to a global imagined community. The broader globalized circulation of *gay*, compared with *lesbian*, here also calls for bringing in the differential genealogies and settings not only in their "original settings" but also in their "destination."

Even the simple word *sex* cannot be taken to mean the same in both locations. Its historical trace in Iran is to *jins* as genus. But, importantly, the trace is not history. The word *jins* continues to be used as genus. The doubling of jins provides a distinct set of affiliation for sex-in-Persian that is not identical to its English chains of association, with the effect that jins is never just sex. Nor can genus be innocent of sex.

The issue of the change of concepts traveling from one history and context to another does not pertain to "just words." The current procedures of diagnosis and treatment for subjects under the domain of psychiatry and psychology, including for trans persons in Iran, is based on the *Diagnostic and Statistical Manual of Mental Disorders III* and *IV* and a number of U.S.-designed tests. The dominance of American scientific discourse, training, and procedures has transported many of these concepts globally. Because of their status as science, they arrive at their destination as dislocated, as if with no history of origin. Their re-embedding in the local Iranian context, at the particular historical moment of the past two decades (discussed in chapters 1 and 5), transforms their meaning and produces specific effects in that acquired location. When thinking about imported categories and practices, my concern is not to trace the origin of import. Rather I inquire into what the borrowing, appropriation, and embracing means for the importers. What work does the import do in its local context, in relation to the many other concepts and practices with which it becomes intertwined and that inform its meaning in the transplanted space?[14]

The destination setting includes a different concept of self. What does saying "I am trans/gay/lesbian" mean when the question of "What am I?" does not dominantly reference an I narrativized around a psychic interiorized self, but rather an I-in-presentation at a particular nexus of time and place? In a socio-cultural-historical context in which the dominant narratives of the self are formed differently from that which has become dominant in much of the domain we name the West, how does one understand the seemingly similar emergences of concepts and practices labeled gay, lesbian, or trans? What concepts of self inform the various styles of (self-)cognition and individual subjectivities, as well as the relations between individuals and their social web, including state institutions? For two young Iranian women I will discuss in chapters 7 and 8, the accidental arrival of a self-identified Iranian-American lesbian into their lives allowed them to disavow and resist the locally available designations. For one woman, same-sex-player (*hamjins-baz*) was pejorative and morally loathed; the other currently available identification, *transsexual,* did not feel quite right and seemed to be a fad to be resisted. *Lesbian* allowed her a distinct and satisfying self-cognition. Her partner became *lesbian* because of her location in relation to her. Again, as Brad Epps pointed out (see note 11),

> What is at stake if we . . . query not simply agency in language but also agency in a particular language, a specific language, . . . or, indeed, and importantly, between and betwixt specific languages, the very position, so to speak, of any number of subjects, trans or not . . . who find themselves pulled, often quite painfully but also quite pleasurably, *between* two or more languages. What, in other words, occurs when two or more languages are understood, both in accordance to the general claims about language, as sites of agency? And what occurs, moreover, when such double (or triple, or multiple) sites, such double (or triple, or multiple) agencies are in conflict?

What are the implications of recognizing these differential situated meanings of words for building alliances internationally on issues of sexual rights? The final chapter of the book engages with these questions.

The problem of conceptual translation—is analytical distinction of sex/gender/sexuality productive in Iran?—is compounded at the level of language itself when translating back/writing this book in English. Persian is among the languages that do not mark gender grammatically. Ordinarily translators do not worry about the disambiguating work of translation; people known as male are given "he" and "his"; "she" and "her" are used for known females. Yet over and over again, I had to ask myself what pronoun I ought to use for this or that person in this or that moment of life. Using the third-person pronouns that have emerged in trans literature in English was not appropriate for the resolution of this dilemma: unlike the conscious challenge that such invented pronouns signify, I had to address what difference it made that such inventions had not been necessary. In the end it became clear that no simple satisfactory solution for this dilemma can be found. I have stumbled along, sometimes

using "she (or he)," sometimes "s/he," and at times simply '*u*—the Persian pronoun used for he or she—when all else seemed to fail.

## Venturing into Ethnography

From its early moments of conception, this research was caught by an ex-
oticizing anxiety of the kind all too familiar to anthropologists. Was not my
imagination stirred up by "an almost voyeuristic curiosity," as Kandiyoti had
called it?[15] As Ramyar Rossoukh noted at the time (in conversations that constituted part of my ethnographic education), I could not escape the fact that I
too was in pursuit of the exotic. Was it possible to carry on this pursuit in ways
that could enable a de-exoticizing of my subject(s)? Would the "angel of history" or the "thick descriptions of ethnography" save me? As I mapped various sociocultural spaces within which I imagined the subject of transsexuality
was being produced—such as visual documentaries and commercial films;
press and television reports; biomedical and psychology research; books, dissertations, and articles in scientific sites; psychiatry and psychology practices
and discourses; Islamic jurisprudential writings; national and local scientific
seminars; and state-sponsored legislation and social services—it was impossible not to notice that my own research was about to carve yet another such
space of subjectivity.

As it turned out, my actual challenges were somewhat different from those
I had imagined. By the time I began my fieldwork in Iran in May 2006, the
trans community was used to being treated as objects of curiosity. They had
become actively engaged in taking charge of the process of their own production—not only in the most obvious form, as narrators of their life stories that
would enable them to get the recognition and certification they wanted, but
more pointedly through intervention in the various sites of subjectivation
to use those sites for their own purposes, sometimes on an individual level,
sometimes in terms of what might benefit their group rights.

Such interventions took numerous forms and constituted a significant element of the cartography of the subject trans. Members of the trans community
engaged with numerous organs of government and medical professions on an
almost daily basis. In the medical field, several have familiarized themselves,
in great detail, with various available surgical procedures and kept themselves
updated on relevant scientific developments. One FtM was completing his
medical education and planned to specialize in sex reassignment surgery (SRS).

They monitored each other's participation in the production of documentaries and press articles, whether as direct participants or as critics. Initially

received as welcome publicity, by the time I began my research, many trans persons had become wary of and resistant to these productions. They found the documentaries at times detrimental to their needs; they felt they had no control over a production's narrative, its dissemination, or the effects possible politicization of their cause internationally might produce in the politically volatile atmosphere in Iran. There was a deep tension verging on hostility within the larger trans/gay/lesbian community on these issues.

The trans individuals with whom I chose to work closely were focused on engaging with government institutions and changing things to be able to live more livable lives in Iran; they were critical of those who participated in the documentaries and thought (especially after the first enthusiastic wave of reports) that such films largely portrayed a terrible trans life in Iran. They were made objects of pity; this they deeply resented. Trans participants in the documentaries were thought by others in the community to take part either for monetary gain (two persons were said to have paid for their operations from the money they got from producers) or because they wanted to become notorious so that they could make a case for asylum and leave the country.

Concerns over the character of international coverage, and in particular concern about promises not kept by producers in terms of sites of screening of documentaries, had turned them into highly skeptical and resistant actors. It was I who had to answer their questions first: What good is history and ethnography for them?[16] My eventual "breakthrough" moment did not arrive until some of the trans activists decided that I could indeed be of use to them. They began to ask me to accompany them to various meetings with officials with the explicit assignment of adding my "scientific voice," with the authority of the best-known American university, to their arguments. That I was conversant in Islamic jurisprudential arguments that favored their case—something that most trans activists had no patience to learn—was an unexpectedly useful skill.

Given the amount of publicity that the topic had received and the numerous documentaries that had been produced, my research route had to deal with the challenge of a road littered with signposts. My own entry into this research had, of course, been occasioned and initiated by these very signposts. The establishment of these early signposts had produced the effect of seeing things again and again within an already-framed narrative, making it more likely to miss seeing other things, at least initially. They had set the terms of questions that were asked again and again—and questions not asked. They had created the expectation of the questions to be asked and encouraged the ready-at-hand narrative responses, already recited numerous times. I discuss some of the challenges of being defined by this prior scene and the difficulties of finding my way off the "main highway" into the vastly more complicated little side roads and sites in several chapters.

This ethnographic venture has posed challenges and opportunities for critical self-reflection on what history and historical writing is about. Some may sound naïve, but I was/am a naïve anthropologist. As a historian more comfortable with archives, with written and visual texts, I was not at ease as the maker of my own archive of interviews and field notes. Paradoxically, relief came with a deeper appreciation of how, as historians, we too produce our own archives as we select some texts and ignore others, producing relevance as we go.

An additional challenge was my differential relationship with different groups of informants,[17] in particular the ethics of interviewing trans persons. Having been trained in, and having practiced for decades, the "hermeneutics of suspicion"—skepticism toward the transparency of texts—and having learned to always suspend belief, I soon realized that when listening to trans people I needed to reflect on the meaning and effects of disbelief in this particular junction. Here were subjects who had spent their lives struggling to be believed. The whole legal-medical system has been designed to "filter the fake from the real," to catch the pretend trans subjects, so to speak. My critical skepticism toward every story I heard or read would put me precisely where hostile family/legal/medical authorities were: where any kind of empathy would become impossible. I had to learn how to listen in a way that would not feign a naïve belief in everything, yet would begin with (though not end on) suspension of disbelief.[18]

This was not an easy exercise. As any anthropologist or journalist knows well, one's interviewees tell their stories as they want you to hear them. Factual information varies depending on where you are hearing the story. The same person would tell one story in a trans support group run by activists, a somewhat different version in a trans support group held in and supervised by personnel from the Welfare Organization (on which they are dependent for partial compensation of surgery expenses and other social services), and yet another in a face-to-face private interview (actually several stories, depending on where we were conversing—in a surgeon's office, in a park, etc.).

The stories are purposefully partial and will always remain so. Indeed, this constitutes a strategic survival shield (already extensively studied in other contexts) that allows trans persons (and gays and lesbians, many of whom blend into the trans community) to get what they need from doctors, officials, psychologists, friends and families, journalists and filmmakers, and historian-anthropologists. The success of this strategy depends on giving select information or no information at all. There is a point in the production of partial ignorance. Making room for their own tenuous existence, despite legality, depends at times on being unreadable and looking ignorant, if you will, and on other occasions looking as if they are the very subject as defined by the legal/jurisprudential/medical discourse. While power produces and organizes statistics, laws, archives, and so on, living may depend, often enough, on not being included in statistics, on looking like law-abiding folks, on making sure you do not leave any archival material as traces for the paws of power. As de Certeau put it, "Innumerable ways of playing and foiling the other's game . . . that is, the space instituted by others, characterize the subtle, stubborn, resistant activity of groups which, since they lack their own space, have to get along in a network of already established forces and representations."[19]

Trans individuals (like all of us) use very different languages, and indeed perform very different personas, in different sites: for example, at the surgeon's office; with their psychologist; in the Legal Medical Board hearings that will decide whether to issue the official trans certificate that entitles them to get hormones, surgery, and the precious exemption from military service; with their close friends; or with alienated parents. Only some of these languages and stories survive for later historians, who may be able to imagine the emergence of a trans subjectivity at the knot of legal/medical/jurisprudential discourses, but with the loss of that which leaves no trace: the creative playfulness of trans individuals' self-subjectivation gets lost in the process of archivization. The "'miniscule' and quotidian" ways in which they "manipulate the mechanisms of discipline and conform to them only in order to evade them" do not make it into historical records.[20] Combined with an acute awareness of how much material we ignore and throw out, even from the historical archives, this can only intensify a historian's humility about the limits of our historiographical projects.

Although I became privy to several stories told, some of the stories would not remain in any recorded form. At critical points of the conversation interviewees often would ask me to turn off the recorder and not take any notes, which also implied a promise that I would not write on that point. I also have had to make decisions (I hope ethical ones) about what information to use and what to ignore totally, even from the material I was allowed to record. In that sense, I have been making up an archive for my work and possibly for future researchers. How does one reconcile ethical responsibility to one's profession with that toward living subjects when making decisions about selective destructions? Do I have any ethical responsibility for saving as complete a bank of information as I have at my disposal?

These questions remain unanswered in this book.

# 01

## ENTERING THE SCENE

Shortly after ten o'clock on a Wednesday morning in the autumn of 2006, Ms. Mohseni-nia, a friendly and, as I learned later, highly professional and cherished social worker, led me into a generic room with almost bare walls painted a tired greenish blue. A large, seminar-sized, rectangular table sat in the middle of the room, with several men and women seated around it. I recognized Dr. Mehrzad Seraji at the far end. She signaled me to go and sit next to her, a welcome (to my nervous state) recognition that my presence was approved.[1] From her commanding location at the table, I realized that Dr. Seraji was the head of the commission whose work she had invited me to observe.[2] A very sympathetic and competent psychiatrist, Dr. Seraji evidently enjoyed the respect of the other professionals present.

I had met Dr. Seraji a few weeks earlier to learn more about what is colloquially referred to as "filtering"—a four- to six-month period of psychotherapy that is undertaken along with hormonal and chromosomal tests, the stated goal of which is to determine whether an applicant is "really transsexual," "really homosexual," "intersex," or perhaps suffers from a series of other classified psychological disorders. The filtering process has become possible through the condensed workings of legal, Islamic jurisprudential (*fiqhi*), and biomedical/psycho-sexological discourses and through the work of various structures, the combined topography of which we often call "the state."[3] This complex authorizing nexus has made the category of transsexual intelligible and acceptable; at the same time, the process of distinguishing between "trans-" and "homo-"

in part depends on trans persons' own actions and narratives, and thus on their self-definitions and self-productions. This does not end the complexity of the story, however. The various institutions and discourses are not systematically coherent and predictable, nor are they necessarily coherently tied to each other. The discursive and institutional incoherence is often put to making livable lives possible.[4]

Before leading me into the room, Ms. Mohseni-nia, in a whisper, asked a young person in feminine attire for his/her permission for me to be in the session. At the time, I wondered how his/her total dependence on the vote of this meeting would make it possible for him/her to say no, even though Mohseni-nia gave him/her explicit assurance that s/he did not have to accept. The very request for permission, however—compared with the way clients in a surgery practice were treated, where I had been led into the surgeon's room for an interview while a client was still dressing—was a surprising relief to me.

However brief, these moments of a trans person's very different treatment in the Tehran Psychiatric Institute (TPI) and the surgeon's office suggest the complex and ambivalent status of this category in Iran. On the one hand, transsexuality has been taken up as a legitimate category of being, as evidenced by the commission's very existence. On the other, the criteria for establishing belonging in that category, and its very legitimacy as a distinct category, is a matter of considerable debate, concern, and ambivalence in multiple domains. This becomes apparent when we consider in more detail the certification process, including the commission's purpose and practices as well as its ties to other institutions and their discourses.

To approach the certification process through the commission and associated institutions and discourses is to highlight the workings of power in processes of subjection and subject formation from a dominant point of view, however critical that approach may be. Trans persons' accounts of the certification process offer a different view—one of differently staged performances of the same process. Their stories will be presented in later chapters of this book. For now, however, I will offer one example of this alternative staging. Throughout the months of supervised therapy, presumably a diagnostic process, trans persons prepare each other, especially for the final TPI Commission interview. These preparations benefit from the culture of preparing for the nationwide annual university examination—the *kunkur*—for which many high school graduates spend a year preparing. Participants in the certification process use the questions asked of one candidate to prepare another, generating a common pool of potential questions and the expected answers. This body of knowledge, produced by trans persons, is regularly used to strengthen one's case. As one female-to-male trans person (FtM) said to the commission in a meeting I attended, "When I was coming for my interview, other TSS kept giving me advice on what to say and what not, how to behave, and so on. But I am not here to fool anyone."[5]

Preparation sessions also provide occasions for laughing at the authorities and the absurdity of their perceptions about trans persons. When Mahnaz, a young woman who was thinking about sex change, walked into a well-known sex-change clinic for an initial conversation, she was interviewed by a psychiatry intern and an assistant to the surgeon. They first berated her, she recounted, for wearing a headscarf in observation of the hijab code. "What kind of man can you be looking like this?" Mahnaz did not believe in the code and had no trouble taking off the scarf, but that was just the beginning of their "diagnostic tests." Next, they wanted to see her wristwatch to see if it was a man's or a woman's watch; they checked her legs to see if they were shaved. At this point in the conversation, another trans person asked: "Did they ask you the toothpaste tube question: Do you squeeze it in the middle or from the bottom up?" This was a familiar enough question; everyone roared with laughter.[6]

## The Certification Process

At the completion of the required supervised therapy, the commission reviews the case file of a sex-change applicant. It is composed of a lead psychiatrist (in the meetings I attended, this was either Dr. Seraji or Dr. Eftekhar), a second psychiatrist (Dr. Salehi), and a supervising case psychologist (Mr. Farzadi, who at the time had an MA and was pursuing his doctorate in clinical psychology). Every commission decision must be signed by all three members. In addition to Ms. Mohseni-nia, the indispensable social worker who made the initial case report in the meetings I attended, several other young men and women — medical graduates who had chosen to do their specialization internship in psychiatry — were always present. They were rarely asked to participate in the proceedings.

Following Ms. Mohseni-nia's case report, various members of the commission would ask questions for further clarification. Farzadi was usually the one who answered these questions because he had either directly supervised or reviewed each case during the 2006–7 period of my fieldwork. Then, the applicant was called in for one last round of questions. Upon the departure of the applicant, the commission had a summary discussion and decided whether to approve the case and send it to the Legal Medicine Organization of Iran (LMOI), to require further tests and therapy, or to turn it down.

The commission's option of referring an applicant for further evaluation points to the explicitly recognized difficulty of establishing the necessary distinction between the "really trans" and other categories. But I never saw the commission exercise the option of turning down an application altogether. Indeed, there seemed to be a general attitude in the TPI, and among its affiliated therapists, that whether applicants were TS or otherwise sex/gender-variant, it was their job to find a socially acceptable "solution for the problem." If after the first few sessions the therapist concluded that the person was "really homosexual," the applicant was sent to a psychologist who worked with homosexuals. As a state-affiliated institution, the TPI itself did not provide such services, but several psychologists did work with "real homosexuals" in private practice. One therapist held separate group and family therapy sessions for each group. For "*gays* and *lesbians*," she said when I interviewed her, "my goal is to persuade both the person and his/her family to come to terms with it, to accept it."[7] This was by no means a dominant approach among the larger Iranian psychiatric and psychological community, for whom the category of trans remains relatively more acceptable at this time.

For many years, including during the initial period of my fieldwork, the scene of who had the last word (before the final hearing and decision of the LMOI) had been haphazard and sometimes treacherous. A trans applicant was referred to a psychologist for the required period of supervised therapy. For those who could not afford the more pricey, private, and usually more friendly psychologists, this was a person selected from a number of psychologists affiliated with several public hospitals that were affiliated with the Iran University of Medical Sciences (IUMS), such as Rouzbeh and Imam Husayn hospitals. Many of these professionals were known to be hostile to trans persons and opposed the very idea of legal certification. They saw their goal not as "diagnosis" but as "dissuasion" (*insiraf*). Trans activists campaigned tirelessly to put an end to this scene. By summer 2007, all applicants were sent to the TPI, known for its trans-friendly professionals, where they either saw one of two main therapists affiliated with this project (Farzadi and Pahlavani, at the time of my work), or were sent for therapy at private clinics if the TPI could not accommodate new clients.

This was only one of many significant procedural details that changed during the course of my fieldwork, making a description of trans as merely a state-approved category deceptively simplified. Indeed, during this period, the TPI itself, first established in 1977, went through many transitions. In the summer of 2006, its graduate teaching and research facilities, including the main library and the offices of its quarterly publication *Andishah va raftar* (*Thought and behavior*), were located in a clinical-research complex attached to the university-affiliated Hazrat Rasul Akram Hospital in the newer western developments of Tehran's exploding metropolis, off Sattar Khan Boulevard. At this time, the commission's monthly meetings were held in an old, dilapidated building located at the eastern end of Taleghani Avenue, which also housed the Treatment Unit of the TPI, with Nonmedical Therapy on the third floor.[8] By the summer of 2007, they all had moved to the new complex, consolidating the commission's position within Iran's contemporary medical education, which has undergone massive growth and modernization over the past four decades.[9]

The name of the TPI journal also has changed. *Andishah va raftar* began publication in the summer of 1994; in the fall of 2006 its title was changed to the *Journal of Psychiatry and Clinical Psychology*. Dr. Mehrdad Eftekhar explained that the name change was in recognition of unfamiliarity (in translation) of the old title to their international colleagues.[10] Concerns about the compatibility of scientific practices and procedures in Iran with internationally recognized ones have increased since the mid-1990s as the end of the war-decade isolation made it possible for more Iranian scientists to participate in their respective international communities.[11] For many Iranian medical professionals, the connection with, and the weight of, international scientific communities are critical for their positioning in relation to their more Islamist-oriented colleagues at home. The latter are more inclined to foster the state-supported movement for the compliance of scientific practices and paradigms with Islamic precepts.

These changes at the TPI and beyond, influenced as they have been by trans activism, national and international policies, and the tumultuous shaping of the Islamic Republic of Iran, signal the instability of any historical and ethnographic account. What I offer here, therefore, does not aim for coherence. I follow some threads that do not necessarily lead to a clear outcome or may have an importance in the future that they do not have today, while attempting to describe the formation of the category trans and what it may mean to live a trans life in Iran in the early twenty-first century.

## Around and Beyond the Commission

The requirement that applicants undergo "therapy"—perhaps more accurately called "an evaluation"—before being "diagnosed," and the TPI commission's location in a state-linked psychiatric institution, situate the process of certification in a psychological or psychiatric discourse of mental health and pathology that works together with a more explicitly legal one. When the commission decides to recommend an applicant for certification as *transsexual* to the LMOI, the Psychiatric Ward of the LMOI takes charge of the process. Ordinarily, the main duty of psychiatrists and clinical psychologists who work under the auspices of this Ward is to respond to requests from judicial authorities, such as the prosecutors and the courts, related to case files under judicial consideration. For transsexuals, it defines its task as "confirmation of affliction with gender identity disorders and issuance of permit for sex-change in case of those individuals who cannot tolerate their biologic identity as a result of this affliction."[12]

This much-sought-after certification is the legal document that opens numerous doors. Not only does the certificate authorize the permissibility of hormonal treatment and sex reassignment surgery (SRS), but it also entitles the recipient to basic health insurance (provided by the state), financial assistance (for partial cost of surgeries and for housing aid), and exemption from military service. The LMOI also instructs a special court to approve the name change of the certified person (after SRS), which entitles the person to receive new national identification papers.[13]

BEFORE SITTING DOWN next to Dr. Seraji, I look around the room. On one wall there are the jointly framed portraits of Ayatollahs Khomeini and Khamenei—a very familiar sight in all state buildings and many private businesses. On an adjacent wall is another portrait—one of Freud.

As jarring as the close proximity of these three patriarchs may be at first sight, it is precisely the coming together of politico-religious authority with the scientific authority of psychology/psychiatry—the coming together of biomedical and psycho-sexological discourses with Islamic jurisprudential (*fiqhi*) rulings after 1979—that has enabled the sorting of different categories of sex/gender-variant persons, including the filtering of trans from non-trans.[14]

While each of these discourses has its own genealogical formations, they have been brought together by the bureaucratization and institutionalization of Islam and the Islamicization of professional and civil domains in Iran after 1979.[15] In the process, fiqh has become highly specialized and acquired a disciplinary shape,[16] whereas modern state rationalization has been painted over "with Islamic green."[17] I will return to this topic more fully in chapter 5. A more immediate paternal figure for the current practices of TPI, however, is Dr. Faridun Mehrabi. Unlike many other medical, psychiatric, and legal figures, his name is always mentioned with deep respect among trans and other gender/sex-variant persons. There is also a common acknowledgment among the therapists who work closely with this population about his pioneering courage. Among other achievements, he is credited with the establishment of the Sex Clinic in the TPI in 2003. In his private practice, Dr. Mehrabi has collaborated and mentored a younger generation of psychologists to work with gender/sexual nonheteronormative persons and their families. Among trans and gay and lesbian communities, these psychologists also are generally considered to be the most friendly (but too pricey for many to afford).[18]

One of the earliest psychologists who began working closely and sympathetically with gender/sexual nonheteronormative young people in Tehran more than thirty years ago, first in the TPI and Mihrigan Hospital and later in his private clinic as well, Dr. Mehrabi talked about "facing a great deal of hostility, even after Ayatollah Khomeini's fatwa in 1985. I was teaching in the TPI at the time, we were inundated with TS people coming, and pleading for sex change. I must have given over a hundred talks at the office of the Journal [*Andishah va raftar*]."[19] In one of the earliest articles that appeared in that journal, Dr. Mehrabi presented a study based on sixty-eight cases treated in his own clinical practice between March 1989 and October 1995.[20] He also supervised one of the earliest master's theses on the subject.[21] Based on a sample of fifteen MtF and sixty "non-afflicted" persons, much of the dissertation is a summary of psycho-sexological literature from English-language sources on gender identity disorder (GID). A questionnaire "in compliance with diagnostic criteria of DSM-IV, MMPI-2, Millon Clinical Multiaxial Inventory, and Cottle Personality Inventories" and a questionnaire developed by the researcher to get information about early life developments of the subject were used.[22] Questions in the latter are focused on games the subject played, the clothes and playmates s/he preferred, her/his parents' reactions to non-gender/sex-normative childhood interests, her/his emotional relation with each parent, and so on. The dissertation is informed by the writings of Richard Green and John Money (*Transsexualism and Sex Reassignment*), Paul Kaplan (*Adolescence*), and a whole host of diagnostic tests developed and approved by American Psychiatric Association. The questionnaire on early life development has since become a prototype for questionnaires that trans applicants must complete when they begin their supervised counseling.

Hamid Farzadi, who is among the newer generation of therapists trained by Dr. Mehrabi, was the supervising therapist at the TPI during the period of my fieldwork. As such, he sat at the heart of the state-supervised certification process for trans applicants. From his commission presentations and recommendations, I expected a generally trans-friendly approach. Yet his articulations in our extended conversations challenged my assumptions about how far a person in his position might be willing to go under the conditions of a state-supervised certification process. In my mind, a state-supervised process was something akin to Foucault's panopticon, with all lights focused on bodies and psyches of trans persons. When I first began this project, I had imagined this thing we call "the state" with a very clear agenda of eliminating homosexuals. As I became more familiar with the so-called filtering process, I imagined the supervised process as one aimed at trapping trans persons to confessions of homosexuality. Farzadi's approach was unexpectedly disarming.

When I interviewed him in October 2006, Farzadi had worked for almost four years at the TPI. His responsibilities included supervising the admission of clients at the Sex Clinic, directing the certification process for trans persons all the way to the commission review stage, and writing up and sending the commission's decisions to the LMOI. To a great extent, he has been responsible for ensuring both that each applicant is supervised by a coordinated team—a therapist (at the time of my interview this was either Farzadi himself or Ms. Pahlavani, another psychotherapist) and a social worker (at the time Ms. Mohseni-nia)—and that individual information is recorded in a fashion useable for clinical data analysis. He has had to invent, through trial and error, "the structure of the transition process at the TPI, since there is no institution here that sets standards of practice," he told me. He attributed the success of the process, and the subsequent assignation of the TPI as the sole institution to which the LMOI sends trans persons, to the fact that "we are far less orthodox here, we look at it as a social and historical issue, not a moral issue. If someone is sane, if someone does not have any mental disorder, we think that person has the right to decide her/his own life. This person is not a legal minor, and does not need a guardian if it is not a case of some disorder that pushed the person to harm him/herself. If the person is logical and rational, then it is not up to us to stop her/him from sex surgery."

I reacted to this confident self-presentation, which seemed to ignore the process of filtering that had come to seem so central to the dominant view of transsexuality, with a good deal of skepticism and resistance. I asked him how he dealt with the limitations set upon an individual "to decide how to live her/his own life" when only transsexuality is legal among the possible range of sexual/gender variant lives? After all, I emphasized, within the dominant conception, the required months of supervised therapy are argued to be critical for distinguishing transsexuals from homosexuals. Initially, Farzadi responded by reiterating the familiar narrative of clinical distinction between the two categories, insisting that there was no way a homosexual person would put her/his body through the kind of somatic changes to which a transsexual aspires. Even when they report similar sexual practices, he maintained, their self-perception in these practices are distinct.

I resisted his answer, giving him the example of a woman in her mid-forties who had gone to Hujjat al-Islam Karimi-nia to ask if she was living in sin (see chapter 5). Karimi-nia's response had been to offer her the option of sex change in order to live without sin. Farzadi agreed that strong feelings about guilt and sin can be a problem and at times push people in the direction of using sex change in this way. He said,

> That is possible, but at least in Tehran that would be rare. This is a big city, it is true that homosexual acts are not legal, not accepted by religion, and are considered immoral, but homosexuals don't have any difficulty living their lives, many male homosexual couples rent the same house and live as roommates. They just can't get married! That is all. It is very unlikely that considerations of illegality would push anyone to ask for sex-change. Even if some religious leaders were to recommend this, I don't know any psychologist who would go for it. It would be highly unprofessional. Dr. Mehrabi in his workshops and classes always talked about this issue: Do you think if you dissuade a transsexual from changing sex you are serving that person? No, that is not so. You saw at the commission meeting, that woman, Zahra [an FtM, still using her female name]. She is very religious, so much so that she said if she feared her parents would curse her ['aqq-i validayn], if she feared this act was not religiously permitted, she would suffer and live with it all her life.

But he was surely familiar, I responded, with how many applicants came to these therapy sessions with prepared narratives, and he must know that many needed to get the certificate to live their lives less harassed by security and city police forces. Farzadi's response was one I had not anticipated:

> Yes, I know, but I base my work on the basis of truthfulness. In the first meeting, I tell the person: look, everything you tell me I take as true, if you lie about your life, I will take it as true, you are an individual and you have the right to do anything with your life, don't try to tell me stories to convince me, I am already convinced. If someone wants to commit suicide, that is their business. I tell the person: I am not going to say go and have surgery; that is only one option. I am not playing cops and robbers here, I am not a detective trying to trap you and catch you. I am here to help you come to terms with what you want. It is not my job to tell you what you ought to want.

My surprise at this response was generated by the fact that, as I had come to know it, the clinical practices were based in part on the desirability of dissuasion (insiraf). Both trans-friendly therapists and those hostile—who see their objective as dissuasion (insiraf)—share the pathologization of transsexuality as GID. Morally conservative currents in behavioral psychology and what is called "Islam-therapy" both aim at changing nonheteronormative "amoral" behavior. More generally, the pathologization of transsexuality as GID and the related practices of diagnostic filtering provide the ground for invoking dissuasion as therapeutic. Since one diagnostic criterion of the filtering process is that true transsexuals cannot be dissuaded, dissuasion becomes the aim of therapy as well as a key therapeutic technique. Only if a person were totally unable to be persuaded would s/he be considered a "real transsexual" candidate for sex change.

Not surprisingly, the centrality of dissuasion sets in motion various levels of distrust and skepticism, if not outright antagonism, between the therapist and the trans person. Kamran, a twenty-three-year-old FtM, for instance, had several harrowing stories about his therapist. He said the therapist always treated him roughly, once slamming the door shut as he walked in, as if he were very angry with him; another time he threatened to throw an ashtray at Kamran because he was not cooperative. But Kamran was very blasé about the whole thing. The first time the therapist was rough, he was a bit scared, he said. But then he remembered his friends had told him to expect it: This was part of being tested for his strength, for his manhood. Only women would get frightened! He had been advised to anticipate and react in a manly way.

Farzadi's narrative of not playing cops and robbers was humbling to me. It made me realize that in the initial months of my research, I had approached everyone (whether gender/sex-variant persons, surgeons, legal personnel, or therapists) with skepticism about their stories, as if I were laying traps for them to trip over the homosexual/TS line, to see how I could catch them in that game. It was totally disarming to see someone dealing with this from the exactly opposite direction, with a receptive attitude that suspended skepticism altogether. To be certain of his meaning, I asked, "You don't aim for insiraf?" "Definitely not," Farzadi said with no hesitation:

> If we want to dissuade our client, in most cases we can. We can tell them this is a sin, this will ruin your family, etc., etc. But here, we don't go for that kind of orthodoxy. I say, at the present we don't have a mujtahid higher than Imam Khomeini and he said it was okay and if our preliminary clinical investigations rule out any mental disorders and psychological problems,

why should I aim to dissuade? Some of my psychologist colleagues react emotionally to this problem. I ask them why don't you react similarly when someone is diagnosed as clinically depressed? This is a similar phenomenon . . . no, I don't act with the clients like a policing system, like a detective who is there to catch them [*muchgiri*], or to dissuade them.

Farzadi's approach also seems to be a way out of a potential ethical problem that, I speculated, was faced by many therapists who worked within the "dissuasion" paradigm. For instance, when questioning Zahra—whom Farzadi had recalled earlier in our conversation—in the meeting of the TPI commission I attended, Farzadi had asked "If you could live like a man from all points of view, would you be willing not to go for sex-change?" Zahra responded: "I will have problems with my partner, our society will not accept it, I myself cannot accept it." Zahra's response had made me wonder then about the ethical dilemma that proceeded from it: when the homosexual category is socially abject and legally troublesome, does one vote for a TS status in such a case? The same question had arisen for me in the case of an MtF candidate who went before the commission on the same day as Zahra, for whom the summary report indicated that, "From first year of middle school s/he had felt s/he was a woman, but s/he hates homosexuality, while being attracted to men. Her/his religious family thinks s/he is a homosexual. Four or five times s/he has thought of committing suicide. S/he says that s/he has not had any sexual relations. 'I can't with a woman and I can't with a man so long as I have a male body.'" In the ensuing conversation, the commission therapists indicated that they considered her/him a borderline case (between homosexual and TS); yet they felt they had to take into account that, under the circumstances, they could not withhold certification as a transsexual.

Farzadi, on the other hand, would not face a similar ethical dilemma. According to his approach, if the circumstances make a person ask for a TS status, that is the person's right and not Farzadi's business. I wondered aloud how different it would be if legal authorities and the NAJA (the police force) shared his approach. This time, Farzadi echoed what by now I had heard from professionals across the spectrum of positions on transsexuality:

What you have to understand is that in our country we have a pretty advanced medical system, [and] our religious system is relatively enlightened on this issue, but socially things are not the same. Also, there is no uniform or standard way of dealing with many issues. So I say it is a person's individual human right to go cross-dressed, but if I said this to a client, and s/he got arrested on the street tomorrow, s/he would suffer a great deal until someone could convince the police that they had the wrong person in custody. S/he could suffer in all kinds of ways in detention. S/he could come back and say: Didn't you say I could cross-dress? To convince the authorities that these people should be permitted to live fully as the other sex/gender for at least a year (once they have been certified) before undergoing their surgical operation, it takes someone as authoritative as Ayatollah Khomeini, or someone who goes after this matter as a full-time job! But even if we standardize proper legal processes, there is the society, the family, the neighbors. How could a male-bodied person dress up as female and go into all-women spaces? How is s/he going to be received? It isn't just a matter of law and religion.

While some educational workshops are said to have taken place to train the police force about transsexuality and how to interact with trans persons, many harrowing tales of rapes of MtFs continue to emerge; many police officers assume that MtFs are male sex workers, and that as such they deserve to be raped. Farzadi was skeptical about the claims of training workshops.

Farzadi's rather radical approach to transsexuality—which seems to circumvent the filtering process altogether by allowing applicants to identify themselves without question and to recognize the practical needs of trans persons undergoing transition—counters any rigid notion about how the Islamic state enacts its power in the case of transsexuals and beyond. The nature of that power is more effectively described as productive, in that it sets the limits on what criteria will be used to *approve* a person as TS. Within those limits, paradoxically conflicting and competitive approaches produce the habitable space of living for trans persons and indeed for the very categories of persons that the state is invested in allocating to the beyond of acceptability.

### Vernacular Psychology and the Brain

Among the approaches that have emerged on the edges of the certification process is the neuro-psycho-biological approach of Behnam Ohadi. Ohadi is important for my account in part because he has come to the scene of transsexuality—and of neuro-psycho-biology—from the world of popular psychology. As such, he represents yet another discursive site in which the nature of transsexuality is being constituted and contested in Iran.

Much of Ohadi's writing has been in the tradition of the mass-market vernacular psychology that emerged in the 1940s—a genre that has exploded into a national market of readers over the past several decades. Several publishers specialize in producing such books and pamphlets: in glossy paperback editions, in impressive formats that look like textbooks, and in small popular pamphlets that are light and good for subway reading. Old popular titles are reprinted and retranslated, with no saturation limit in sight.[23] As important, Islamic-inspired vernacular psychology texts have emerged as a popular genre. Several Qum publishers now publish popular short books on sexual, marriage, and parental matters for adolescents and young couples that combine ethical Islamic injunctions with modern behavioral psycho-sexological advice.

Ohadi is one of the local authors who have now joined the previously established line of translated authors in this genre. Ohadi's books cover a wide spectrum of topics,[24] but he is best known for his writings and translations on the topic of sexuality.[25] Looking for one of his titles, I went to a well-known bookseller across from Tehran University on the famous booksellers' row. Upon mentioning the name, the bookseller gave me a sarcastic look and said, "Oh, yeah, the guy who writes books by the kilo." In addition to writing psychosexual texts "by the kilo," Ohadi also regularly publishes articles on psychological and family counseling matters in magazines (such as *Psychology and Society* and *Zanan*, both now closed down by the authorities) as well as popular dailies (such as *I'timad* and *Sharq*). He also has several blogs.[26]

His most often reprinted book, *Tamayulat va raftarha-yi jinsi-i tabi'i va ghayr-i tabi'i-i insan* (Natural and unnatural human sexual tendencies and behaviors), is largely responsible for his name being associated with the topic of sexuality in a variety of media today in Iran. The book is a revised, somewhat modernized and popularized version of the sexological literature already in circulation by the 1970s. Predictable chapters cover "defining key concepts," "stages of psychosexual development," "psychology of human sexuality," "psychology of love," "psychology of sexual puberty," "criteria of natural and unnatural," "sexual dysfunction," "sexual deviations," "sexual/gender identity disorders," "homosexuality," and "sexual abuse."[27]

First published in 2000, by 2005 this book had been reprinted five times. Its central aim is to draw the important boundary between "natural and deviationist behaviors"[28] and to emphasize the importance of the scientific recognition of "natural and unnatural human sexual tendencies and behaviors" so that such behaviors are not treated as crimes but as illnesses that require cure.[29] His version of the "repressive hypothesis" has become the hallmark of Ohadi's numerous books and articles: He suggests that the suppression of the natural satisfaction of sexual desire causes Iranian society's various sexual troubles. Ohadi persistently argues that the more social control is exercised over young people's heterosexual activities, the more they turn to masturbation, homo-sexuality, and sexual deviations.[30]

Ohadi's project, centered on the necessity of "scientific and rational" treat-ment of issues of sex and sexuality (32), has taken him into empirical neuro-psycho-biological research on transsexuality. Inspired by similar psychoso-matic research carried out in the 1990s by de Vries, Zhou, Hofman, Gooren, Swaab, Green, Kruijver, and others who had reported statistically meaningful differences in particular areas of the brain between trans persons and non-transsexual control groups, in 2006 Ohadi chose to do his doctoral dissertation as a similar empirical study.[31] He published an early report about this project in *Ravanshinasi va jami'ah*; an article based on his dissertation research sub-sequently has been published.[32] According to his published resume, Ohadi is currently continuing this line of comparative research with female homo-sexuals and male homosexuals, comparing each group to nonhomosexual con-trol groups.[33]

The debates over such somatic etiological projects are well known and I do not propose to restage them here. Instead I consider the particular scene of play between science and law in Iran associated with this kind of research. In his *Ravanshinasi va jami'ah* article, Ohadi paid special tribute to Dr. Moham-mad Reza Mohammadi as chair of the Psychiatry Department at Tehran Uni-versity of Medical Sciences (TUMS) and as his dissertation supervisor for his unfailing support. The published research article, with his primary authorship, also bears several other names. In addition to Dr. Rahimian (of the MRI cen-ter where the actual brain measurements were conducted) and several TUMS professionals, the list includes Dr. Mahdi Saberi, legal psychiatrist and head of the commission at the LMOI that processes and decides on transsexual appli-cations and certifications. What these dedications and inclusions make clear is the difference between the staging of transsexuality in Tehran and in the European and American scenes: Somatic etiological research is being carried out in Iran with the support of psychiatrists who extend legal supervision over transsexual lives. There is no suggestion of concern about conflicts of interest in such a public declaration of the researcher's associations with these psy-chiatrists.

As a psychiatrist invested in Islam therapy, Dr. Mohammadi's support for such research was possibly motivated by the hope for a negative result that would further back up his contention that these "delusional states" can and should be treated by bringing people back to the "straight path" via Islam/spiritual therapy. Many transsexuals participated in Ohadi's research, hoping for some biological proof that would further consolidate their legal status and make their desired bodily changes and social practices easier to achieve. In fact, I first heard about this research from trans activists with whom I worked. Somewhat to my surprise, the same activists I had admired for their tireless lobbying and negotiation with numerous local, regional, and national government bodies to get things changed for transsexuals were recruiting transsexuals to participate in this study. Ever skeptical of the legal effects of bio-etiological arguments, I was horrified. I thought of the nightmare of official policies becoming based on some brain measurement. I explained my fears to trans activists involved. I argued vehemently that etiological, presumably scientific, research was ill conceived, that it was based on the premise that some simple causal connection could be found between something (whether fetal development, parental upbringing, or something else) and a very complex phenomenon—about which, I argued, we were better off thinking the cause was irrelevant and unknowable. People develop in infinitely different ways and that is that. How about invoking the well-known jurisprudential cautionary end of Qur'anic interpretive tradition, "God knows best"? I expressed my fear that such "scientific" results could hurt them as much as help them. I talked about one clear advantage of the current system—namely, its critical dependence on their own narratives—a dependence that they could lose should these presumably empirical experiments conclude that something in their brains could tell doctors and legal authorities what their rights ought to be.

None of them were receptive to my arguments. Given the many difficulties they dealt with, given the authority of science, given that Dr. Ohadi was considered to be one of the trans-friendly psychiatrists, they insisted they had nothing to lose from their participation. They knew they were different and the experiment would show that. Moreover, Sina (an FtM activist) argued, even the framing of transsexuality as a "disease" and the search for its etiology had important benefits: "You forget its benefits for our families. Families want to know why their kid is like this." Another important consideration on the part of trans activists for recruiting subjects for this project was the issue of acting as responsible, serious, and respectable citizens. As Houri (an MtF activist) put it, "The more we participate in such activities, the more seriously our demands will be taken. We will be seen to be respectable people. It will also teach TSS how to act as responsible people." But what if then the doctors decided on the grounds for their difference and excluded anyone whom they decided did not fit the pattern? They did not think that was something they needed to worry about. Should that be the outcome, they would find ways of getting around it.

It turned out they were perhaps more in tune than I was with the complexities of how science works (or doesn't) in Iran. Some of them were invited to the final presentation of Dr. Ohadi's research to the examining board.[34] They thought it was too ambiguous to mean much; none of them seemed to have liked the results. But it didn't matter anyway, they were sure. Alternatively, some transsexuals had already begun to use the purported results of Ohadi's research, insisting on brain differences as a way of arguing against people (such as Dr. Mohammadi) who argued that transsexuality was an "acquired" (*iktisabi*) condition and thus could be unlearned, and against those *gays* and *lesbian*s who criticized *TS*s for going this way in order to live less socially abject lives and to escape state repression.[35]

When I asked another trans-friendly psychiatrist, a key figure in the TPI and its trans-diagnosis commission, what the legal repercussions of Ohadi's findings were, he responded with a simple "nothing" and concurred with the activists that this research was of no legal consequence. In part, this is because of the many kinds of disagreements between several subgroups of psychiatrists in the medical establishment that cut in various ways. Some of the issues are simply contests over professional domains of power: The kind of sexological school that Ohadi represents is not considered scientific enough by most of the psychiatrists in the academia in Iran. Other lines of differentiation arise over the status of interaction between science and religion in the field of psychology. These are not neat and solid. Whereas Dr. Mohammadi's approach is supported by the whole "Islamization of sciences" project, trans-friendly psychiatrists have Ayatollah Khomeini's fatwa on their side—something that no doctor, and no lawmaker, would challenge.

### Points of Entry: Modes of Cognition and Experiences of Certification

A disparity between the trans experience of the certification process and that of the professionals who administer it emerges in my account of the Iranian discourse of transsexuality as it is constituted at the intersection of medicine, the law, fiqh, psychology/psychiatry, and several institutions of the Islamic Republic of Iran. It is evident, for example, in the juxtaposition of Farzadi's commitment not to play cops and robbers with certification applicants and their own *kunkur*-based strategies for outwitting what they see as a game of detection, not as a presumably scientific diagnostic process—with the therapist set to trap them in failure. Given the centrality of filtering—notwithstanding Farzadi's approach—in the process, this is hardly surprising. More important, though, the disparity between perspectives on the diagnostic process of filtering points to the fact that, although filtering shares much of the conceptual vocabulary of

Euro-American GID literature, in important ways it constitutes a perhaps less rigid grid than many professionals, invested in claims of scientific standards and its international compatibility, would like it to be.

To begin with, *tashkhis*—the Persian word for diagnosis in a medical context—has a far less pathological burden than the word *diagnosis* bears in English. While the *Oxford English Dictionary* notes that the etymology of "diagnosis" is found in the Greek root that bears similar meanings—to distinguish, to discern—the listed meanings are medical (the determination of the nature of a diseased condition) and biological (the distinctive characterization in precise terms of a genus, species, etc.). "Diagnosis" is of course currently used in other domains in English, such as diagnostic tests of cars or computers, but these seem to be later metaphoric derivatives of the biomedical meaning. A similar point pertains to the word *bimar*, patient. While the word's location in medical discourse positions it within a pathologizing dynamic, it continues to retain an active trace within other cultural domains—such as love, as in "the malady of love," *bimar-i 'ishq*—that works against its complete absorption into pathology.[36]

Beyond its psychomedical usage, tashkhis is widely used to mean perception, distinction, and discernment. For instance, a person referred to as *"mutishakhkhis"* means a person of distinction. One can be complimented for having a strong sense of tashkhis—discernment. Second, the sites of diagnosis are multiple, each with its own style of cognition. The associative chains of meaning, which affiliate tashkhis with discernment and distinction, at once enable, and are in turn confirmed by, the informal styles and various sites of (self-)discernment of a person as trans. The disparity also suggests that a purely discursive and institutionally focused account of certification, as a focal point for the wider discourses of transsexuality, does not adequately account for the much more indeterminate and varied way that these terms and the wider discourse of transsexuality actually work in relation to the certification process and trans lives. In particular, professional scientific procedures, and the religious sanction that has enabled those procedures since the 1980s, do not derive their authority simply within and from scientific and legal-religious discourses. The various sites and styles of (self-)cognition that emerge in casual party conversations, in unsolicited professional advice, in a TS support group, on a television documentary, and through media coverage of and by transsexuals all participate interactively in production of meaning of (self-)naming persons as TS or *gay* or *lesbian*.

To understand how this interaction bears on the self-identification and lives of Iranian TSs, *gays*, and *lesbians*, it is important to note that points of entry into the labyrinth of certification—whether a person begins the process by going first to a therapist, to the LMOI, to a urologist, or even to an army physician—are quite diverse and make a huge difference in how a person experiences and navigates the entire procedure. There are also different levels of entry, which affect the way one is processed. To start, the formal certification is usually preceded by years of struggle with family: some have lived years of (at least partially) double lives. In addition, some may have taken hormones for years, and may have even found willing surgeons to do early stages of surgery, such that one may get away with not even entering the formal certification until fully post-op. It is a publicly acknowledged fact that people can get hormones and even be operated upon with no permit, at which point they can go to the LMOI to begin the legal process of changing their name and official documentation.[37] While such individuals would face a great deal of resistance and hostility, the LMOI, when confronted with a changed body, has no option but to finally agree to the legal status of somatic change. Money is also a factor. As one applicant bitterly said about the commission's resistance to ratify his/her case, if s/he had money s/he wouldn't even be there, since s/he could have gotten the whole thing done without legal certification.

Figure 1.1 maps graphically the complicated labyrinth of socio-institutional sites one has to navigate. Some of these paths have already been discussed; others I will return to in chapters 5 and 6.

Points of entry also often are related to how one comes to recognize oneself, or be categorized by others, as possibly trans. The suspecting, recognizing, and categorizing agents could be one's parents and relatives; teachers and other school personnel; and therapists, doctors, and other health professionals who "notice" something different. They may also be social workers or religious scholars to whom one may turn for advice, or they may be the police cadre who, while processing nonconforming persons arrested by morality squads, may "recognize" the person not as a sex deviant but as a gender-disordered person. Other nonheteronormative persons, including other trans persons and self-identified homosexuals, may also engage in diagnosing and categorizing one another. Moments of self-cognition are at times narrated as a process of seeing oneself in terms of characters presented in media representations: newspaper reports, magazine articles, radio programs, and quite frequently satellite television programs and documentary videos.

Sites of cognition are multiple, in terms of both institutional and noninstitutional entry points. Each site has its own style of cognition, which bears differently on the (self-)discernment of a person as trans. That such discernment could occur outside state institutional domains is by no means always a

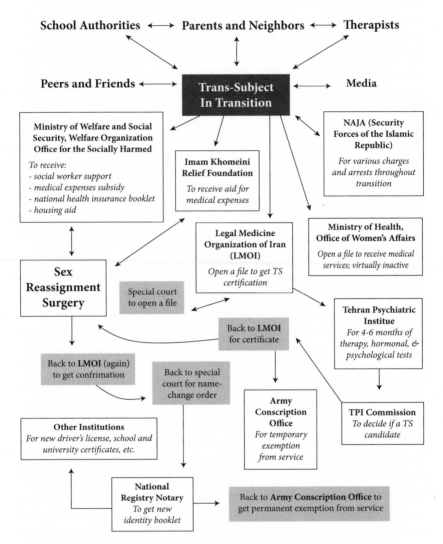

FIGURE 1.1. Finding one's way through the labyrinth of cognition and change. It is not necessarily navigated in a sharp temporal sequence.

positive thing; identification, by oneself or others, necessarily involves a level of subjection. Diagnostic discernments made from within a given community can be overbearing and at times hostile, as it was for Amin, a young, nonheteronormative male person I met at a small party of self-identified MtFs and *gay* men. Although Amin considered himself not to be masculine in the dominant cultural mode, he was not interested in being identified either as *gay* or as *TS*. But for a wide range of people his nonheteronormative male persona and gestures marked him sometimes as *gay* and sometimes as *TS*. Two gay men at the party, Muhsin and Zia, could not agree. Muhsin, who was Amin's close friend, insisted that Amin was *gay*; indeed, he hoped that they would become lovers. Zia, on the other hand, was convinced that Amin was *TS* and wanted me to listen to his life story and persuade him that he was *TS*. Amin himself was interested only in talking about literature and telling me about his aspiration of becoming a writer. When pressed by his friends on matters sexual, he said he was asexual and that he had heard about these categories only recently when he was arrested on his way to a writing workshop. The arresting officers treated him roughly and were about to book him on charges of sexual solicitation at the police station when their supervisor noticed Amin and told his men that they had misrecognized him; he must be a *TS*. He then told Amin he should go to the LMOI and get a certificate to avoid similar mix-ups in the future. Amin still did not understand what he had been labeled; his first idea was that the officer must have thought he was a prostitute and wanted him to go to the LMOI to register as such, but he was grateful to be released and miss only half the workshop!

A second example of such problematic identification comes from one of the *TS* support group's weekly Thursday afternoon meetings I attended. On this day, a young woman and her mother had come for the first time. As was the practice of the group, we began by going around and introducing ourselves. Many self-identified as *MtF*, *FtM*, *gay*, or *TS* (only rarely there were women in the meeting who identified as *lesbian*). When it came to the newcomers, the mother spoke first and explained they were there because her daughter had (sexual) problems and she had heard about this meeting from a friend. She had come to the meeting to see whether her daughter was trans. A discussion immediately ensued, with various people offering their perception/cognition of the young woman. Most suggested that she could not possibly be *TS* or even *lesbian*, since she looked very feminine in her attire and makeup. When a guest doctor, who had been invited to talk about sexual practices and HIV risks, suggested that they should let the woman decide for herself, several people disagreed: she was new, and the rest of them had a lot of experience with cognition and discernment of TS. Some of the notions of cognition offered at these meetings were based on sexual practices. For example, in another meeting where the issue arose, several MtFs insisted that those MtFs who had had prior married lives and produced children could not possibly be MtF.

It is not only in a TS support group or among TS and other nonheteronormative socializing circles, but also in many other places, that professionals as well as lay people offer cognition. Several transsexuals remembered how the acceptance of their distinct differences first happened unexpectedly, at a family party, or in a clinic, when a doctor whom the transsexual had visited for unrelated medical needs told him/her that s/he needed a sex change. The advice had been offered informally, and in this exchange of casual conversation, it was received as confirmation of the person's own prior self-identification.

Many moments of (self-)cognition also are narrated through the media. Negar, a twenty-seven-year-old MtF from Isfahan with a master's degree in mathematics, recalled that a few years ago she had read an article about trans persons in one of the newspapers that had made sense to her. Before then, she said, she had no idea that such a phenomenon existed and that it was possible to have a sex change in Iran. Her cognition had been confirmed more than a year before our conversation by one of her university roommates, who pursued a master's in psychology. He too had encouraged her to pursue the option. As a result of these encounters, she went to Dr. Majd, who diagnosed her as TS. Regardless of the narrative content of the media's intense coverage of transsexuality over the 2003–8 period, transsexuality became not only a recognized topic of social recognition, but—more importantly for trans persons—the coverage provided a medium through which they gained valuable information: where to go to get what they wanted, how to meet other trans persons, what they were entitled to ask for in various government offices. The coverage also served as a medium of self-cognition. In this sense, the meditative work gave a name to a set of feelings and desires that had long haunted a person in conflicting ways because it was not recognizable by one's parents, friends, neighbors, and school peers. I will come back to these issues more fully in the last two chapters.

Both Mahnaz and Delara—who considered themselves FtM but had not yet adopted male names, nor were they yet "in the habit"—also identified the media, specifically a popular satellite documentary program, as a factor in their self-cognition.[38] This particular program was notable in that it included an actual enactment of "diagnosis" on the air.[39] In the second part of the program, the presenter Amini and MtF Taraneh/Rima Aram (she uses both first names on this and other programs) were joined by a cast of professionals: Dr. Usku'i (a plastic surgeon who had more recently trained for SRS); Farshid Taqizadeh (at the time doing his psychiatry internship at Rouzbeh Hospital, with a focus on the study of homosexuality); and Zamani (Dr. Mirjalali's indispensable assistant, who has worked with him since 1990, first as an operating room technician for general surgery and more recently trained as an SRS technician). There was also another participant, Kia, a twenty-three-year-old, feminine-styled male, with long hair, plucked eyebrows, a very close shave, and long fingernails, who was diagnosed on the program. When discussing how doctors concluded who was a good candidate for SRS, Dr. Usku'i said that other TSs, such as Taraneh (to whom she pointed), were the best judges. "Ms. Aram herself has become a good *filter*," she said, then pointing to Kia and asking Taraneh for her diagnosis/cognition of Kia. Taraneh, with no hesitancy, pronounced Kia not *TS* but *gay*: "My opinion about our friend is that he is a complete man, but because of psychological problems, and because he hangs out with our community, the community of *trans*es and *gay*s, he has become confused about his identity. I actually think that he is not even *gay* but *bisexual*, on the basis of information that I have." Taqizadeh confirmed this diagnosis/cognition with a professional voice: Having interviewed Kia just before the program, he could say for sure that Kia was *gay*, not *TS*. Taqizadeh talked at length about his research on *homosexuals*. Invoking the power and authority of science to determine untouchable "facts" of nature, he argued that

> homosexuality is not a deviation, it is very normal, it is deep in our genes, it is embedded in the brain; we have scanned the brains of these people and it is different from the brains of *heterosexuals*. I realize that in Iran people think of it as deviation and in Islam it is a major sin, but I am saying this from a medical perspective. Since 2002, I have studied 250 true *homosexuals*, that is, not *bisexuals*, they didn't come to me out of any necessity, I visited them, I did several kinds of psychological tests and I have the results showing that these people do not suffer from sexual deviation. . . . We need to diagnose properly so that *homosexuals* are not sent to SRS. All doctors need to learn these things. . . . We need to establish a school of sexology in Iran. This is necessary, like a heart clinic. . . . Families need to learn that they ought to support their *trans* and *homosexual* children. Do they throw out their child if s/he is suffering from thalassemia?

Strikingly, Taqizadeh set a psycho-neuro-biological presentation in conversation with Taraneh's filtering knowledge that another professional, Dr. Usku'i, had called upon. At some level, this may strike us as a refreshing recognition of the limit of the medical expert's domain of knowledge production. Transsexuals often crack jokes about what they thought the real motivation of TS diagnosis was: The surgeons wanted to make a buck out of their challenges.[40] It is also indicative, once again, of the different styles of discernment and naming someone as *trans* or *gay* or *lesbian* that can traverse professional — scientific, legal, and therapeutic — as well as lay discursive domains.

I address the implications of this style of (self-)discernment/cognition for concepts of self, identification, and identity in chapter 8. For now, having mapped out a provisional nexus of the diverse cognitions of transsexuality in contemporary Iran, I ask in the next three chapters how the conceptual possibility of transsexuality, around which this nexus formed, came about. What are some of the historical emergences that have made transsexuality a thinkable category in today's Iran?

## "BEFORE" TRANSSEXUALITY

The contemporary dominant configuration of transsexuality, informed by psycho-medical and jurisprudential discourses within which practices and procedures of changing sex have operated in Iran since the 1990s, is fairly recent. In its earliest reported appearance in Iran, in the 1930s and 1940s, "changing sex" referred to intersex transformations—some reported as spontaneous—but increasingly the phrase indicated those transformations effected through surgical interventions.

These reports included cases in Iran, but they also began to include accounts of sex change in Europe and the United States that had become international news since the late 1940s, and especially since the story of Christine Jorgensen in 1953. Here, transsexual surgeries emerged as a variant of the larger scientific marvel of sex change. In popular weeklies and national dailies, such operations drew on the same fascination as other wondrous spectacles of nature and achievements of medicine, including the separation of conjoined twins and the reattachment of accidentally severed limbs. All these instances provided not only similar occasions for reflections on the wonders of nature/ creation, but also moments of national pride and celebration of Iranian scientific progress. In this discourse, transsexual bodies emerged as affiliated with, yet distinct from, intersex bodies.

A concurrent conversation pertained not to the exceptional and the marvelous, but to everyone. This was concerned with the health of the nation, the progress of its educational system, and the reform of family norms. By the

1960s, this conversation was embraced to no small degree for its possibilities regarding women's empowerment. Some of the earliest discussions of trans-sexuality appeared within texts on marital relations, scientific psycho-sexology, and sexual criminology, often serialized in the popular weeklies of the time.

These two trends had an earlier presence in the scientific discourses of academic dissertations and medical circles. However, their domain expanded enormously as they circulated in the popular magazines and radio talk shows in the 1940s through the 1960s. In the early 1970s, they converged in several sensational news stories, the coverage of which indicated, and perhaps con-tributed to, an important shift in the conceptualization of transsexuality. From its earlier affiliation with (and resemblance to) the intersex condition, trans-sexuality became repositioned in relation to sexual deviancy, more specifically homosexuality; it shifted from the physical body onto the psychosexual.

This shift was further facilitated by (and in turn contributed to) a con-solidation of the concept of sex that, by then, traveled among and connected many registers, in particular, the psychiatric diagnosis of sexual deviancy (in psycho-behavioral-sexological literature) and sexual disorder in biomedical/ endocrinological diagnostic discourse.[1]

This chapter maps out these threads and the emerging dominance of psychobehavioral sexology that set the scene of sex-change surgeries in Iran of the 1970s.

### Wonders of Nature and Marvels of Science

Reports of "spontaneous" sex change in Iran can be found in the earliest issues of national dailies.[2] For instance, Ittila'at, a daily that began publica-tion in 1926, reported that a pair of twins, Nanah-Gul and Gul-Chaman, in the village of Kamand had begun over the previous two years to wear male clothes and change their names to Gul 'Ali and 'Ali Gul.[3] The reported reason for this change was a massive growth of hair on their faces; the report noted, "male and female organs [are both present] in them: one does not dominate the other." This report had been filed not by a journalist, but by an officer of the new organization set up to issue national identification booklets (shinasnamah) for everyone. The national identification booklet remains a key documentary domain for today's transition process. Before this legal requirement, it seems that one could change from one sex/gender to another informally, almost at will! Ittila'at reported on Munirah, a woman from Tigan Tappah Afshar, who had decided that being a woman was no good.[4] She had been married but her husband did not take care of her, she said, "so I decided to resign from womanhood and become a man and earn my own living." Accordingly, Munirah had changed her clothes, haircut, manners, and name to those of a man ('Abd al-'Ali Khan) and had since worked as a manservant (*naukar*) for a local merchant.[5]

While some of these cases came to light as part of the work of a centralizing state in its attempts to document and track its subjects by requiring identification registration and a choice of family name, on other occasions more scandalous behavior "outed" trans lives. One profession that seems to have provided a topic of repeated scrutiny and anxiety was that of masseurs (*dallak*) in women's public baths. *Khvandaniha* reported that for the previous nineteen years Sayyid Turab had been known as Galin Khanum and had worked as a masseur in the women's bath of a village near Bujnurd.[6] A customer recently had become uncomfortable because of some "suspicious acts" of Galin Khanum. Her complaint led to further investigations, during which it became clear that Galin Khanum was Sayyid Turab.[7] Sex/gender changes in adult persons in other countries also were regularly reported in the Iranian press, including the story of the Czechoslovakian runner Zdenk Koubkov.[8] Other reports covered stories from Egypt, France, and Turkey.[9]

The overall frame of these reports was that of strange or wondrous (*'ajayib va gharayib*) creatures—a significant concept in the cultural cosmos of Islamicate world. As Hunsberger notes, it "came to refer to a vast genre of literature comprising travels . . . , cosmography . . . , biology . . . , and the supernatural."[10] In this paradigm, the strange and the marvelous were signs of God's power of creation, "demonstrating his existence, majesty and order for the world." By the middle decades of the twentieth century, at least in Iran, there was a perceptible shift in referentiality of the wondrous from creation to nature (though nature remained largely a sign of God's power), and thus a new emphasis on the emerging linkage of the marvelous and the strange with science. The wondrous became what science was challenged to explain and make rationally understandable. The double referentiality to God's power and to achievements of modern science positioned intersex persons and, linked with them, trans persons within the cosmos of the strange and the wondrous. It provided them with a space of appreciation and, along with scientific achievements, national celebration. They often were reported in the same pages as strange births— conjoined twins being a favorite of this genre—or peculiar quirks of nature, such as a hen that became a rooster.[11]

Surgeries to alter intersex conditions were reported in the Iranian press as early as 1930 and became more frequent in the 1940s through the 1960s. The first major case, reported in the daily *Ittila'at* (October 27, 1930), received full front-page coverage.[12] Under the title "An important surgery: a man has become woman," and a subtitle "Wondrous creation" (*khilqat-i 'ajib*), the article reported: "Last week an important surgery took place at the state hospital which is not only unprecedented in Iran, but perhaps it has not happened in this way even in the rest of the world. This surgery opens a new chapter in the medical and health history of our country and deserves to become the focus of scientists' attention and be discussed at conferences and health councils from a scientific point of view." According to the report, the Police Organization of Azarbaijan had sent a young person, eighteen years of age, from Garrus to Tehran. Tehran's Police Health Office had sent her/him to the state hospital, where s/he had demanded that her/his male organs be surgically removed and her/his female ones be completed or s/he would commit suicide. We learn of no male name for this person; apparently s/he had already chosen a female name (Kubrà) and insisted that everyone call her by that name, though in an initial letter to the hospital s/he referred to her/himself as "Kubrà, son of Tahir Sultan."[13] The report noted that not only was this person's demand strange but s/he was strange (wondrous) from the point of view of creation because s/he had both male and female organs, though her/his male organs had been more complete. While bodily s/he was dominantly masculine, the report added, from the point of view of feelings, femininity (*unasiyat*) was dominant and s/he was in love with becoming a woman. What had pushed the young person to this decision had been "great feelings of lust—lacking totally in male lust and having female lust." Note that in this description, as in later narratives by and about trans persons, sex and gender remain conceptually indistinct. Moreover, what we call sexuality in English—namely what is related to one's desire—also remains indistinct from sex/gender. Physiological signs, emotional states, and "feelings of lust" all went into the diagnostic discussion of Kubrá's sex/gender (self-)cognition.

Operated on October 24 by a team of doctors led by Dr. Khal'atbari, Kubrà was said to be recovering well and to be very happy. The report concluded, "This event is a wondrous story that speaks to Iran's medical progress and the advance of its surgical capabilities." It called for appreciation of a doctor such as Khal'atbari and congratulated the health authorities for having such specialized doctors.

While this case may have been significant for building national and state pride in the early years of Pahlavi state centralization, it did not become part of consolidation of medical knowledge and practices in Iran. That had to wait for Tehran University and its School of Medicine. Established in 1934, the school systematically cultivated professional scientific linkages between medical teaching and practice, reflected in part in an accumulation of theses written by graduating members of the school, in cases appearing in medical textbooks, and in the publication of the school's first regular academic journal in 1943.[14]

One health professional, who for the next decades served as a major link among educational, medical, and state institutions, was Dr. Jahanshah Salih (1904/5–1998[?]). An American-trained gynecologist, he made his mark on medical education and practice by publishing a comprehensive textbook in Persian on gynecology that went through many printings and revisions.[15] He was appointed Dean of Tehran University's School of Medicine in 1948 and was centrally involved in establishing its obstetrics/gynecology department and the Women's Hospital as an affiliated training hospital. He served as President of Tehran University, as Minister of Health (beginning in 1950), and as personal obstetrician to Queen Farah.[16]

A generation of obstetricians/gynecologists were selected and trained by Jahanshah Salih at the Women's Hospital. This was also the place where many intersex and trans sex surgeries were performed. Several of these surgeries became textbook cases in the expanded edition of Salih's book, which added a number of cases in the section on "double-sexedness or hermaphrodism."[17]

While the many cases reported in the press in the 1940s and 1950s were not substantively different from the one reported in 1930, their significance lay in their location and dissemination: These surgeries were performed in a teaching hospital in which interns examined the patients and observed the operations. Moreover, the patients were included as cases in Salih's important textbook, which was part of the training of generations of obstetricians/gynecologists, demonstrating an institutional consolidation of medical education and practice.[18] These textbook cases included one that was categorized as a very rare "true hermaphrodite," two male "pseudo-hermaphrodites," and one female "pseudo-hermaphrodite." All were described with full detail of the circumstances that had brought the person to hospital, physical examination, diagnostic tests, and surgical changes, along with numerous photographs of the patients' "reproductive organs" as well as microscopic images of their organ tissues and chromosomes.[19] Significantly, Salih recommended that, when deciding what operation to perform, physicians ought to take into account not only the diagnostic physical criteria of the patient's dominant sex but also his/her social circumstances and, if necessary, withhold medical information to ensure that a patient's marital life is not disturbed. Further, he emphasized that as part of the diagnostic process, the doctor must try to find out "the sexual tendencies of the patient through precise questions" (285–86). This was significantly different from classic Islamic medical treatises and jurisprudential writings in which the aim of one's sexual desire is not considered of diagnostic value for deciding on the gender/sex of a "difficult hermaphrodite." Before puberty, the main determinant of the sex of ambiguous bodies was considered to be related to the urinary orifice.[20] If that were not conclusive, it was hoped that developments at puberty would resolve the ambiguity. For Dr. Salih, the presumption of natural heterosexuality (more on this below) already had become a guide for diagnosis of the dominant genus/sex of intersex individuals. This emergent modernist affiliation of sexual desire with diagnostic procedure for disambiguating intersex people presaged the diagnostic distinctions that were to form around transsexuals in later decades.

As he revised his textbook in the early 1960s, Salih could no longer ignore what had begun to be reported in popular press as "real sex change." The "Double-sexedness or hermaphrodism" section of his text ended by stating, "completely and absolutely changing one's sex is not possible. . . . Contrary to rumors, totally void of any truth—that off and on circulate and become popular about a woman becoming a man or a man becoming a woman—such reports have no scientific validity. No man or woman can completely transform his or her sex to the opposite" (287–88). The "oppositeness" of man and woman, and what defined each category, were contested issues. What did define real (wo)manhood? Munirah's narrative, as we saw earlier, indicated that resigning from womanhood and becoming a man was about making her own livelihood as a man, which had required her to change name, attire, haircut, and manners. These changes had enabled Munirah to work and live as a man. For some medical practitioners and for some intersex and trans persons, a key criterion was/is the ability to "get married"—a phrase that often means the ability to have penile-vaginal intercourse. Salih's definition was centered on the bioscientific considerations of sex differentiation. His categorical skepticism was the opinion of many physicians in the 1960s and continues to be part of the scientific view of opponents of the permissibility of sex change. For many of these physicians, the inability to be physiologically reproductive is offered as grounds for the impossibility of true sex change.

Just as important as the entry of the intersex category into medical textbooks and the training of specialists were the multiple circulations of their stories, with increasing frequency, in the press from the 1940s onward. When a popular biweekly magazine, *Khvandaniha*, reprinted from the provincial paper *Khurasan* the story of the twenty-two-year-old Bihruz Nuri (formerly Marziah) of Gunabad—along with several pre- and postoperative photographs—the daily *Ittila'at* followed suit.[21]

*Khvandaniha* was a key circulatory site in this regard. Literally meaning "the reading worthies," under the editorship of 'Ali Asghar Amirani, it began publication in September 1940, initially as a monthly. In Amirani's words, "As it is clear from the name, *Khvandaniha* will include selected material worth reading (*khvandani*) from hundreds of different scientific, literary, social, economic, historical, health, sports and satirical writings published by the country's press, whether published in Tehran or provincial towns."[22] With the 1941 departure of Riza Shah and the sudden burst of a relatively free press on Iran's cultural and political scene, the magazine soon changed to a twice-weekly publication. In addition to reprints, the magazine published material that it commissioned as well as translations from the foreign press.[23] One of its important features was its regular serialization of translated books on such topics as marital relations and sexual lives. Many of these translations were later (and at times simultaneously with their serialization) published as books, and a number of them continue to appear in new editions and retranslations. Through these circulations, *Khvandaniha* became an important site for emergence of vernacular psychology and sexology.[24]

The reprinting of Bihruz Nuri's story in *Khvandaniha* gave national prominence to a provincial story. I know of no other case that received such lengthy coverage during this period. Much of the story is reported as a first-person narrative, apparently at Marziah's brother's initiative. During his hospital visit after Marziah's operation, he had taken a number of photographs and asked her/him to give these photos to *Khurasan* newspaper along with her/his life story so that the family would no longer be a target of people's scornful comments about Marziah.

Marziah was born in a small village (Dalu'i, part of the Gunabad township) in 1929, with ambiguous genitalia; the distressed parents immediately sought medical advice, going all the way to Mashhad's American Hospital.[25] The doctors' prognosis was that Marziah was female and that once s/he was older, a minor surgery would take care of her/his birth defect. S/he thus was given a female name and brought up as a girl. S/he recalled, however, that s/he was different from other children. From early childhood, s/he liked the military uniform and wished to enter military service like her/his older brother, who after their father's death joined the army and now served in the Gunabad gendarmerie. S/he recalled her/his childhood as a period of stress "because I was always interested in the games boys played and the kinds of activities they engaged in." But s/he was prevented from doing what s/he liked by school authorities and by her/his uncle and brother-in-law, who had taken charge of Marziah's upbringing after her/his father passed away when s/he was only two.

Unlike the narratives of later decades, however, Marziah's narrative did not insist on some strong sense of an early true gender, with the childhood interests as symptomatic of later developments. After four years of elementary school, s/he was kept at home, devoting her/his time to learning "womanly work such as weaving cloth, spinning yarn, cooking and laundry." To the surprise of all the adult women around her/him, Marziah soon excelled at these skills. Living within spaces of womanhood and doing woman-identified work made a woman out of his/her earlier "tomboyishness," she recalled. "Their habits and temperament affected me and I was left with no masculine inclinations." Once s/he reached marriageable age, life became more complicated. S/he had several persistent and socially appropriate suitors; s/he was indeed very amenable to marrying a maternal cousin, but by then s/he knew that s/he "may not be able to have a husband," that is, may not be able to engage in heterosexual intercourse. Marziah's mother had told her/him that an American doctor had said s/he needed a small operation to repair a congenital defect (no other specification is given here), but s/he lived with the uncertainty that s/he might never be able to be a suitable wife. By the time s/he had reached twenty years of age, there had been no breast development, and later s/he noticed that the shape of her/his arms and legs had become more masculine.

After much agony s/he declared that s/he intended never to get married. This decision created a good deal of family discord, and Marziah's continued refusal to consider marriage became a subject of much scornful local conversation. S/he decided to leave Dalu'i. In the spring of 1949, hearing about a position for a nurse at a new clinic in Kakhak (a nearby hamlet), Marziah volunteered to work there even though "it was considered terrible for a woman to take an office job or any employment that was considered masculine." Her/his success at work was the major source of happiness in Marziah's life. Marziah's brother's objection to her/his employment and limited social life often made Marziah think about the advice of the American doctors. Eventually s/he went to Mashhad to seek medical advice. It was then that s/he was informed that her/his congenital defect could be repaired, but in the direction of becoming male—much to Marziah's and the family's delight. At the time of the interview, the person now named Bihruz (formerly Marziah) had undergone one surgery, and two more were planned to complete the process.

As we will see in other cases, the challenge of sex-disambiguation in Marziah's narrative is linked with the ability to consummate marriage. In this case, Marziah was born with no vagina, but with a small opening through which urine passed. The doctors had assumed this was connected to a womb and could be shaped into a vagina when s/he was older. It was this uncertainty about "having a proper female organ" that had become the marriage obstacle in Marziah's eyes. While Bihruz did recall an interest in boys' games and activities and a fondness for military uniform and service, these proclivities s/he narrated as gone through socialization within the world of women. Indeed, Marziah's eventual decision to seek medical help was motivated by the desire to have the surgery that was to correct her/his problem "so that I could expediently get a husband and save myself and my family from all this humiliation and disgrace."

Similarly, Allahvardi 'Alizadah, who had lived as a man but knew he could not get married in his self-identified *khunsá* (hermaphroditic) condition, became determined to clear his ambiguity so that he could marry the girl with whom he had fallen in love.[26] Most of the cases of intersex surgeries reported in the Iranian press of this period included marriage as a central concern. Sometimes the people involved were already married but with no children, an issue that brought the person or the couple to doctors.[27] Patients and readers alike were assured that sex-disambiguated individuals were capable of having "normal marital lives."

As for Bihruz Nuri, for Allahvardi 'Alizadah another sign of full manhood was the possibility of performing military service, from which he previously had been exempt because of his khunsá condition. By the 1940s and 1950s, one generation after the introduction (in 1925) of conscription for young men, military service had become an important badge of adult masculinity.[28]

The case of the sixteen-year-old Farhad Farjadi (formerly Faridah), from Shabistar, found international attention. First reported in *Ittila'at*, Farjadi's narrative is similar to Bihruz Nuri's as far as childhood "gender misidentification" is concerned.[29] S/he too reported that since childhood s/he preferred playing boys' games. S/he also expressed delight that s/he could now enter military service. Farjadi's case was reported in *Scoop* and *Vue*.[30] The *Scoop* report categorized Farjadi's case with those of Christine Jorgensen and Ewan Forbes Semphill as one of sex change. The details provided, however, would indicate that s/he had been intersex, growing up female but at puberty noticing changes that eventually made her/his mother seek medical advice.

Reports of intersex surgery continued throughout the 1950s into the 1970s.[31] At times, their scientific import was highlighted. This was the case, for instance, where three female members of the same family from Abadan went through sex change to become males. Dr. Hisam Nahrir, a geneticist from Isfahan University, took a research interest in the family and went to Abadan to investigate.[32] On other occasions, reports continued to be framed in wondrous terms, as in the case of an adult man who went to Shahriza Hospital in Mashhad with extreme abdominal pain and delivered twins! S/he subsequently was scheduled for a sex-change operation.[33]

Not infrequently the reports provided occasions for humor. Humorous commentary on intersex surgeries in this period fell within what could be considered positive humor—in sharp contrast to the satire of the same period associated with (male) same-sex practices (as we will see in chapter 4). The humor circulating around reports of intersex (and European sex-change) surgeries indicates that at this point in time there was as yet no affiliation between sex change and anything morally apprehensible; it was a morally safe topic. The later rupture of this affiliation of intersexuality and transsexuality and the establishment of a family resemblance between transsexuality (especially MtF) and homosexuality introduced the weight of moral approbation against (male) homosexuality onto transsexuality.

An example of such morally safe, though misogynous, humor appeared in connection with the case of Batul Khanum. An article—under the headline "Wondrous mistake [ishtibah-i 'ajib]: Why did this twenty-two-year-old young person think s/he was created female whereas s/he was a man?"—reported on a surgery performed in the Women's Hospital on Batul Khanum who, around the age of sixteen or seventeen, instead of developing into a young woman, began to see male features develop.[34] She quit school and eventually decided to see a doctor at the Women's Hospital. There she became a case for medical students to examine and learn from. In addition to a bodily examination, she was asked about her attraction to women and men, an attraction that turned out to be mostly for women, apparently confirming that something was amiss! The doctors decided to operate on her and bring out her "hidden male organs." A day later, a popular magazine ran satirical verses singing praises of Dr. Salih who had such miraculous expertise as to bring a man out of a woman, unlike the men of the country who had proven themselves useless for managing the affairs of the state.[35]

In a similar vein, after the news of Fatimah 'Asgari's sex change in Abadan in 1969, Khvandaniha reprinted a cartoon from Karikatur (figure 2.1). The top line is attributed to the patient, "The Abadani girl who has become a man said, 'I am happy they call me a man.'" Underneath, the two doctors whisper, "Poor chap, he hasn't seen the hospital bill yet; that would emasculate him."[36]

During these decades, coverage of sex change abroad began to appear with increasing frequency and details. Khvandaniha printed a brief report on Christine Jorgensen, with two photographs of her as a young man and the new woman, along with the presumably surprised friend of hers, Joe, who could not believe the change.[37]

FIGURE 2.1.
Cartoon from
*Karikatur.*
Reprinted in
*Khvandaniha,*
December 20,
1969.

These reports clearly sold. An advertisement in *Ittila'at*[38] invited readers to purchase the forthcoming issue of the magazine *Asia* because it carried a report about "this astonishing creature," the French ambassador in England, who had lived forty-nine years as a man and had now been a woman for three years and was in love with an English lord. While such reports continued into the 1970s, by then interest increasingly had shifted to reports on sex-change surgeries in Iran, whether on intersex individuals or on persons who were explicitly said to have "healthy perfect bodies."

A brief report in *Kayhan*, under the bewildered title "In Shiraz a man voluntarily became a woman!" informed readers that a thirty-one-year-old man, who wished for anonymity, had been operated on in Namazi Hospital and became a woman. S/he was said to have been in every way a healthy man, but had a deep desire to become a woman, had been in women's clothes for a long time, and had taken "female hormones." S/he was from Tehran and had consulted several psychologists. The Legal Medicine Organizations of Tehran and Shiraz had declared the operation permissible. The report ended: "The former man has said that soon s/he will marry a man who knows her/his condition fully. Doctors have said that s/he is capable of marrying."[39]

The bewildered title and tone of the short report point to the near incomprehensibility of someone who is "in every way a healthy man" desiring to become a woman. Surely everyone would prefer to be a man. This cultural presumption continues to inform the differentiated reception of MtF compared with FtM transitions in contemporary Iran, as we will see in chapters 6 and 7.

By the mid-1970s, several hospitals in Tehran and at least one in Shiraz were carrying out sex surgeries.[40] A 1976 report by Dr. Kariminizhad of the Women's Hospital stated that over the previous three years, some fifty persons with transsexual tendencies had been seen at the hospital and that twenty of them had gone through sex surgery.[41] While sex-reassignment surgeries had retained their early connection to the sex-disambiguating work of science, their respectability already had begun to suffer. The source of this disrepute was the emerging dominance of behavioral psycho-sexology. Around this time, the Medical Council of Iran (MCI), a professional state-affiliated organization of physicians, began to discuss the ethics of SRS. In a 1976 decision, the MCI declared that sex-change operations, except in intersex cases, were ethically unacceptable and must be declared illegal—a ruling that was not reversed for more than a decade.

The diverse and increasing reports of sex change in Iran and internationally provided important occasions for the emerging conversation on the scientific understanding of "sex" and contributed to the production of two important and related effects. The first was the shifting of the discourse on sex change from wonders of nature/creation to scientific sexology; the second was the dislodging of sex in sex change from sex as it related to the anatomical distinction/ ambiguity between male and female to sex as it related to sexual desire and practices. The latter occasionally had been raised in the context of some intersex changes, as noted earlier, but its full configuration was shaped within the vernacular psychology of sex.

## The Science of Sex

The reports on sex change not only provoked anxiety of an emasculating type for at least some men—"What if I wake up a woman?" It also produced wild claims about the possibility of any man becoming a woman and vice versa. *Khvandaniha*'s report on Jorgensen and Semphill, for instance, was framed within a sensational article with the title: "From now on any woman can become a man and any man can become a woman!"[42] In fantastically exaggerated prose, possibly confounding intersex and trans surgeries, the article claimed that changing sex had become a certain fact of life, that in most advanced countries doctors and surgeons change girls and boys between seven and ten years of age to the other sex, and on occasion they perform these operations on adults. These operations were as easy and successful as appendix surgery. Such changes should not surprise us, the article noted, because physiologists had proven that in every human being there were both sexes present and every one of us, man or woman, could be in charge of our male and female hormones.[43]

Other articles made connections back in time and to other places. A favorite character was Le Chevalier d'Éon; ancient Greece provided a frequent destination for originary placement of non-normative desires and practices. Others made contemporary associations with transvestism, homosexuality, and sex work.[44]

This latter move overlapped with the second trend emerging in this period. Not all circulation and reception of sex change was of a positive, triumphant character. Official medical science, as in Salih's textbook, did not share the enthusiasm of vernacular science on this topic. Their discourse was formed through recent developments in endocrinology and genetics, scientific branches that increasingly crossed paths with developmental and behavioral psychology of sex/gender/sexuality. Psycho-sexology, however, was shaped in a nebulous space that included coverage of matters sexual by popular journals. There was thus a productive looping effect, a generative traffic, between the vernacular and the more academically generated knowledge within biomedical and psycho-sexological professional domains.

In the emerging psycho-sexological articulation, "changing sex" was not seen to be caused by merely physiological factors; rather the phenomenon was seen to be linked, at least in part, to "unnatural" psychological traits, abnormal sexual tendencies, and corrupt moral behavior. Dr. Ahmad Sayyid Imami issued some of the earliest warnings.[45] Noting that a desire for sex change may to some extent result from hormonal imbalance (an idea that had begun to gain wide currency in vernacular sexological literature), the rest of the article mapped out a number of arguments that became the general wisdom in this period: that in all human beings both male and female hormones existed, that the fetus in early weeks did not have differentiated sex, and that among children sometimes one observed the emergence of opposite sex behavior. Most of such changes were barely noticeable; others were temporary. But in those people for whom such changes became consolidated after puberty, one ought to look for psychological factors as well. Men who looked like women also developed womanly psychological traits. Such unnatural changes could be a result of temporary situations, for instance, among men who lived without women, such as sailors or prisoners, but as soon as they returned to society they reverted to their nature. In some of them, however, such unnatural traits became second nature. Women turned to other women because of terrible sexual experiences with men.

Sayyid Imami also was interested in how such people could be cured. If these changes were caused by changes in hormonal excretions, he regretted to say, it was difficult to do much. But those who had become unnatural as a result of habit or psychological effects, especially during adolescence, could be helped. Experiments with hormones, he noted, were currently under way; perhaps the results could be used to strengthen a young person's natural sexual tendencies and to help them overcome the unnatural tendencies. Parents, Sayyid Imami warned, played an important role in making sure that they did not bring up their children unnaturally. He followed this warning with a list of recommendations for parents.

In other articles Sayyid Imami broached the topic of same-sex desire, at times in a philosophical and ambivalent mode.[46] By the late 1960s, however, Sayyid Imami shifted more radically toward a condemnation of sex change: he now saw it as an indication of sexual deviation. In response to the coverage and popularity of the topic of sex change, he found it necessary to reach the same public through the pages of *Tandurust* and clarify matters. In an article titled, "Is sex change from woman to man and vice versa possible?," Sayyid Imami emphasized that "what you read in nonscientific press is not changing sex, but clarification of sex [*tabyin-i jinsiyat*]—that is, repairing a birth defect that can be corrected. . . . Putting such people aside, there have always been . . . those who are inclined toward their own sex/genus [*jins-i muvafiq*], and in some of them this feeling is so strong that they follow this in their behavior, clothes, and life completely. . . . These people are in fact afflicted with sexual deviancy, which is unnatural, and from a medical point of view any unnatural act must be considered an illness." He discussed various possibilities for a causal explanation—was it hereditary? was it an effect of family and school socialization? an effect of social circumstances (such as staying in boarding schools and army barracks)?—and concluded that it was not easy to arrive at a clear answer. Moreover, "It is also possible that mental and nerve-related conditions create a situation where the person has no control or will power over his/her behavior, similar to people who are addicted to alcohol, opium, and heroin. It is this latter group that is the worst. . . . They totally surrender to their lust and desire . . . and sometimes use hormones in order to facilitate their goals and professions, such as dancing boys in certain cafes who use them to make their body and voice totally feminine. These deviants should really be called 'patients.'"[47]

Over the same period, it was not only weeklies and dailies that produced and circulated sexual knowledge, but a growing body of books as well, translated from American and European sexological literature. *The Encyclopedia of Sexual Knowledge*, for instance, saw its partial translation into Persian in

1946.[48] Translated and adapted by 'Abdallah Rahnuma, this text is one of the earliest widely circulating books that introduced the concept of developmental sexuality, through a reading of Freud, to Persian readers.[49] It introduced the notion that all children were bisexual through puberty and parents should not consider the display of such a tendency with alarm or mete out punishment for its manifestations. It was only its persistence into adulthood that should be considered a sexual deviation. Men who are afflicted with sexual deviation were said to have womanly temperament and behavior, make themselves up as women, and exhibit womanly gestures and movements. It is here that a brief paragraph is devoted to the "disease of transformation of sex" in which "a person born male has psychology and temperament of a woman. . . . Some resort to all means and even castrate themselves and transplant a woman's organ into themselves."[50]

By the 1960s, books were directed at parents and educators so that they could impart correct sexual education to children and adolescents. Their pedagogical mission often had a tone of moral alarm. Puberty, for instance, is said to be "one of the most dangerous stages of life. For this reason, parents must keep their adolescents under observation and from afar keep a watch on them and prevent their socializing with inappropriate individuals, because in this stage young people are very prone to accepting bad influences, embracing improper and harmful acts, and having abnormal [ghayr-i 'adi] sexual inclinations."[51]

The pedagogical and moral vision of this genre of psych-sexological parental advice drew on the media discourse, as well as that of the scientific community, on sex change. As such, it contributed to bringing several distinct perceptions into a contested national conversation. A central concern of this sex-education literature (emerging in part out of concern with marital performance) was sexual impotence (natavani) in men and frigidity (sardmizaji) in women—a concern it shared with another popular genre: how to increase one's sexual prowess (quvvah-i bah), which connected it with "traditional" medicine. Its modernized version combined information on food with the new popularized psychosexual know-how. Pursa'id's *Cure Your Sexual Impotence with Food*, possibly from the mid-1940s, is a good example.[52] Unlike texts of the older genre, which were centered on remedies, this book began with a description of physiology of reproductive (sexual, or tanasuli) organs, centered on the "important work" of glands, in particular, men's testes. Pursa'id warned against youthful masturbation because it would lead to the loss of all sexual passion and create womanly behavior in a man, causing him "to always desire to be used like a woman." To support this proposition, Pursa'id reminded the reader of a recently reported case of a soldier from Arak who suddenly had developed womanly inclinations. Upon medical examination at the Tehran Army Hospital, it was found that the soldier's sex glands totally had ceased working, and instead his opposite-sex glands had become active, causing his womanly inclinations.

The proliferation of vernacular sexology troubled the growing body of professionally trained psychologists. They were alarmed by what they considered a dangerous spread of false information about sexual matters through the popular press and scandalous books. Scientific experts needed to ameliorate this scene. Hasan Hasuri prefaced his *Sexual Behavior on the Basis of Sexo-Physiology* by defining sexology: "Sexology is a science that speaks of sexual matters generally. This science has several branches, the most important of which are physiological sexology, psychological sexology, social sexology, and sexual criminology."[53]

Hasuri's preface critiqued much of what was purported to be scientific knowledge about sex as misleading, "superficial and unscientific and indeed instead of sexology they are pornography." He declared that even though such books bore "the ornament of introductions by one or several doctors . . . , they and their authors are no different from our famous *Raz-i kamyabi* and its famous author."[54]

Hasuri wrote as a neurology specialist (trained in the United States) and as a professor at Tehran Medical School. He defined *Sexual Behavior* as a textbook "for medical students, physicians, and allied professions." His introduction of a sexological understanding of sex into Iranian scientific discourse defined the thinking on "sexual matters" in Iran for the next generations of practitioners to the present time. Many of his explanations, including on subject of transsexuality, now circulate in texts of psychology, criminology, and sexual therapy. Written in twelve chapters and 642 pages, three of the longest chapters were devoted to "Sexual Deviance" (79 pages), "Sexual Impotence" (88 pages), and "Children's Sexual Behavior" (76 pages). His extended presentation of the notion of sexual/gender identity (*huviyat-i jinsi*) as formed by biological, psychological, and social factors framed his concept of congruence: "If there is a congruence [*tanasub*] among all the above factors in an individual, the person's sexual condition is said to be optimal."[55] Congruence/concordance has become not only the dominant thinking in medical and psychological circles, but also for theological/jurisprudential considerations of sympathetic clerics, as we will see in chapter 5.

As an example of the importance of the effects of "sex of rearing and assignment" (these words are set in English in the text next to the Persian) on the "gender role that an individual performs" and on the behavioral identity of a person, Hasuri introduced *tiransvistizm* ("transvestism," typeset in English as well) as a condition "in which physically and bodily the patients are totally natural but they display deep psychological disorder, such as considering oneself a woman in a man's outfit who is inclined [sexually] to one's own sex [hamjins] but never considered oneself a *hamjins-baz* [a same-sex-player; in parenthesis in English, 'homosexual'] as well as another psychological syndrome called *tiransiksu'alizm* [in parenthesis in English, 'transsexualism'] in which this psychological drive is so strong that the patient will go to any lengths to have a surgical operation." Such illnesses, he explained, were related to the way parents assigned a child's gender at birth and how the person was received by others and conceived his/her gender.[56]

His later discussion of "the necessity of correctly determining the sex of a newborn" was informed by the proposition (again now circulating as common sense of gender/sexual matters in the literature on transsexuality) that "the sexual/gender identity of a child becomes evident to him/her by the age of two (and perhaps earlier) and once it has become shaped, it remains almost fixed and unchangeable forever" (102). He noted the current debates on whether somatic sex-type always overwhelmed the psychological effects of the sex designated by rearing, or whether psychological sex could overcome biological and hormonal factors, referencing John Money's work at Johns Hopkins. Hasuri attributed intersexuality to hormonal causes. The difficulties of determining sex at birth and its incorrect assignment, he warned, could potentially impact the psychological growth of a person (103). His central concern, however, was how parents derail natural and normal growth:

But sometimes, even though the sex of the child is quite clear, the inappropriate behavior of parents perturbs psychological balance of the child, and corrupts and shakes the gender/sexual identity of the child. For instance, often expectant parents desire to have a son, they even choose a name for it before birth (such as Mansur, Hamid, or Sa'id) and then when against their hopes the child is a girl, they use the same name with some minor change (Mansurah, Hamidah, or Sa'idah) . . . and later they tell their daughter about their wish to have a son and put her down for being a girl. This incorrect behavior and that *nam-i daujinsi* [bisexual name—the English term is added in the original] can create psychological disorder in the child. . . . The daughter tries to have boyish behavior to please her parents—from early on, she kisses the dolls goodbye, plays with boys, and as she grows up, she dresses like boys and displays "positive tendencies" toward girls. But the main difficulty arises after puberty. Now it is difficult for the girl to deny her female-ness and pretend to be a boy. Her other female peers tell her to have girlish behavior, but if she wants to suddenly change her behavior, she would feel defeated vis-à-vis her parents (103–4).

The concern about a successful married life was a critical part of the literature on developmental growth. As we have seen already, it was often part of the nar-ratives of individuals who approached doctors about their sex/gender issues. A successful "clarification/change" of sex was defined, at least in part, in terms of ability of the person to be able to "perform in marriage" after the operation. Hasuri thus instructed his students, future doctors, about their important role:

> It is the doctor's task to discourage parents from such false ideas and un-wise behavior . . . and if a newborn has unclear genitalia, the doctor must tell the parents that regrettably their child is incomplete from a sexual point of view and that tests are necessary to determine the newborn's true sex [*jins-i rastin*] and then expediently proceed to determine the sex of the new-born following the principles that we laid out previously. The doctor should be happy that at this [early] age [of the newborn], studying psychological fac-tors [for sex determination] which is very complex is not yet an issue (104).

Parents also were given advice that has become the present commonsense guidance on this topic: Gender discordant behavior of a child must not be con-sidered funny and cute, it must not be encouraged in any form, and it must be scrutinized from early childhood. While he considered a certain level of same-sex desire in adolescent a "natural homoerotic stage," he advised close scrutiny to ensure it was "outgrown" by the early twenties (218–20).

In the book's longest chapter, "Sexual Deviancies," Hasuri revisited and dis-cussed at great length many of the issues raised in earlier chapters (476–555). He reviewed various theories regarding sexual deviance—is it hereditary?—a view he rejected after covering it in one short paragraph. Is it caused by dis-orders in growth and failure of development or regression to an earlier stage of development? While he remained distant from Freud and criticized him for not making a distinction between the sexual (*jinsi*) and the reproductive (*tana-suli*), he claimed that almost everyone agreed that the "seeds of genuine devian-cies are all sown in childhood" (477). He considered the growth environment (*sharayit-i muhit*) to be "extremely important, especially during childhood." For example, "sometimes a child learns 'same-sex-playing' ['*hamjins-bazi*'] from her/his hamjins-baz mother" (478).

Hasuri divided deviancies into two categories. The first comprises those that could be considered "a sickness genuinely caused by psychological and perhaps biological causes, in which case the afflicted person must be treated with respect and sincerity" (481). But in others deviancy was a degeneracy. "Some individuals abandon their human mission and drown themselves in an inhuman cesspool and various deviancies." He noted that "today in some books, hamjins-bazi has been taken out of domain of sexual deviancy," but he considered it a deviancy and indeed had chosen it as the exemplary deviancy to discuss in further detail. The next thirty-nine pages are devoted to the topic of homosexuality (translated into Persian as hamjins-bazi—same-sex-playing) followed by four pages on pedophilia, two and a half pages on transvestism, and then five pages on transsexuality. The chain of deviancies here, with homosexuality bordering pedophilia and then moving to transvestism and transsexuality, reflects the emergent categorization of homosexuality with crime (sex with the underage), with transvestism and transsexuality as extreme homosexuality, as neighboring afflictions, under a common shadow of criminality.

Hasuri's understanding of homosexuality is located squarely within the narrative of developmental failure. He considered one of the behavioral characteristics of (male) homosexuals to be

> the display of womanly gestures and coquetry and girlish flirtation.[57] These gestures show themselves in their facial moves, their conversational intonations, and the way they dress. Same-sex-players select female names and like others to address them with these names. If someone mistakenly calls them khanum [lady], not only are they not offended, but they become very happy. Most same-sex-players display their womanly behavior only when they are in places where same-sex-players congregate; in normal situations their movements and displays are not different from normal people" (489).

At the closure of his extended discussion of male homosexuality, he concluded that if "the desire to wear female clothes is very severe, then a secondary type of transvestism has emerged from clinical homosexuality." He considered the most important social danger of homosexuals to be their seduction of others for intercourse, which also encouraged sex work because they were willing to pay high prices for anal intercourse. He recommended that if a person was known to be a same-sex-player, the police must be informed about him. The first job of the police, Hasuri recommended, was to seek help from a psychiatrist (492). Reluctantly, and only in extreme cases, he considered sex change to be a lesser evil: "Sometimes these patients desire to have a surgical operation and 'change sex.' But the surgical operation, removing their testes and giving them estrogen, does not change a man into a woman; it turns him into a neuter person who is psychologically more balanced" (501).

As did many other authors of this period, Hasuri argued that, "Usually, society is quite lenient toward deviant behavior in women" (506). This he attributed to its lesser visibility: "unlike men, same-sex-playing women do not exhibit themselves or hang out on streets. When people see two same-sex-playing women on the street, they doubt their same-sex-playing and even if they become certain of it, they look at them derisively and tolerate their deviant behavior, whereas they express disgust and hatred toward same-sex-playing men" (507). Only in extreme cases, they became visible. He further noted that, "many same-sex-playing ladies also have a desire to become men and ask surgeons to operate on them. For example, when in 1953 C. Hamburger in Denmark declared that he was willing to do this kind of operation, many same-sex-playing women went to him and most of them wanted to marry another same-sex-playing woman after becoming a man" (509).

Hasuri argued that there was no clear border separating transvestism and transsexuality (514). Reviewing John Money's studies at Johns Hopkins Hospital, Hasuri emphasized that "The cause of this deviancy is not clear. Some consider it an illness resulting from complex psychological disorders, a kind of psychic *daujinsi* (psychic hermaphrodism) [Hasuri's parenthetical translation]." Hasuri informed his readers that H. Benjamin, a top expert on this topic, considered it to result "from combined effects of psychological, biological, and circumstantial mechanisms" (518). No other treatment, except for changing sex, was effective.

Despite Hasuri's aim of producing a clear distinction between truly scientific knowledge about sexual matters and what circulated in the media at the time, his own book worked as a trafficking text between the two domains. Although he specifically wrote it as a textbook for professionals, its general outline was simplified and produced in more popular books. One gynecologist, Muhammad Mahdi Muvahhidi, trained by Jahanshah Salih, published not only technical manuscripts, but also books for a nonspecialist audience, and wrote a regular column for the popular women's weekly *Zan-i ruz*.[58] While these columns covered diverse health topics, the overwhelming majority dealt with marital issues and reproductive/sexual health. The columns were generally very short, written for a lay readership, and addressed mostly to young women. What is remarkable is that the columns that had to do with issues of sexuality closely follow, often verbatim, Hasuri's 1968 textbook.

Like Hasuri—and unlike some of the other writers of the period who had begun to use the terms *hamjins-gara'i* (same-sex orientation) and *hamjins-*

*khvahi* (same-sex desiring)—Muvahhidi used hamjins-bazi. His column on "hamjins-bazi among women"[59] followed "the failure of development" model, arguing the widespread phenomenon of becoming another girl's "*baruni*" was quite natural at a certain age.[60] Only if it continued after seventeen years of age was it considered same-sex-playing and a sexual deviation. As a column written for the general audience of a women's weekly, it ended by emphasizing preventive measures that parents must take, such as paying attention to its possible emergence, never allowing their daughter to share a bed with another woman, keeping a close eye on her socializing milieu, and seeking help if they saw any symptom of deviation. One column covered "disorders of sexual/gender identity" (using the exact expression that Hasuri had coined) in which Muvahhidi not only followed Hasuri's arguments very closely, but he also used one of the names that Hasuri had used as examples (Mansur/Mansurah).[61]

Comparing several sections in Muvahhidi's book with Hasuri's text makes it very tempting to cry plagiarism,[62] but that is not my point here. Something more important is at stake. Hasuri was a neurologist, trained in the United States, with an interest in the "psychophysiological sexology" of his time; his text was written for professional training. Muvahhidi was an obstetrician/gynecologist trained by Jahanshah Salih. Muvahhidi's popularization of Hasuri's sexology in the pages of a women's weekly indicates the vernacularization of biomedical and psychological-neurological wisdom in Iran in the 1970s, consolidating a particular understanding of sexuality, sexual deviation, homosexuality, and transsexuality. This paradigm continues to inform the professional and popular understanding of these issues to our day. In this understanding, intersexuality is considered a congenital condition caused by prenatal chromosomal mishaps and hormonal imbalances. No longer is transsexuality considered something akin to intersexuality. While intersexual adults may symptomatically resemble transsexuals—if their condition was misdiagnosed at birth and they were brought up as the gender of their less-dominant biological sex—it was unambiguously declared to be different from transsexuality, the causes of which, as writers indicated at times, were unknown. Nonetheless, much emphasis was laid on inappropriate rearing of the child by parents, which had contributed to blockage of proper psychosexual growth and was responsible for a whole range of adult deviancies—chief among them homosexuality, transvestism, and its extreme manifestation, transsexualism.[63]

That Muvahhidi was simultaneously the author of a specialized text "on complex topics related to gynecology and obstetrics" and of popular sexology and marital know-how points to the traffic between various spaces of production of knowledge about sex/gender/sexuality—the movement of ideas between the training of experts in the universities and the education of the public in the pages of the popular press. The meaning of transsexuality was formed in the space mapped by these crossings.

## The Psychology of Sex

As we have seen, the understanding of transsexuality in Iran emerged in the 1940s within the growing literature of vernacular psychology and within popular marital and parental advice literature concerned with sexual conduct. In this literature, discussions of love, desire, sex, and marriage supplied occasions to write about gender/sex dis-identification, homosexuality, intersexuality, and sex change. From a small number of occasional books and journal articles in the 1920s, this genre spread to the wider popular press. From early on, there was a lively exchange between these articles and books and the sexological literature discussed in previous sections.

In his preface to the English edition of the *Encyclopedia of Sexual Knowledge*, Norman Haire of London's Harley Street indicated that his motivation for producing in England yet one more text about sex was "that sexual ignorance is still so general, and the mass of misery arising therefrom so enormous and so appalling, that I welcome all additions to the list of volumes offering a measure of sexual enlightenment" (vii). A similar dynamic drove the proliferation of the literature of vernacular psychology of sex in the 1940s in Iran. 'Abdallah Rahnuma, the Persian translator of that text, echoed Haire, lamenting that "ignorance of sexual matters has caused a great deal of misery and misfortune for people; not knowing marital harmony they often talk about divorce" (5). He complained that, while discussion of sexual issues was permitted in Islam, and indeed it constituted part of the tasks of religious leaders, in the modern period little scientific attention had been paid to these issues. He thus considered it "his national duty" to make this book available in Persian (7).

Modern Iranians seemed to be astonishingly ignorant of sex. How had this ignorance been produced?

Two important shifts in gender and sexual notions had emerged in the course of "achieving modernity" in Iran.[64] A process of disavowing homoerotic desire had set in motion seemingly contradictory, yet enabling, dynamics. It marked homosociality as empty of homoeroticism and same-sex practices, and by insisting on that exclusion it provided a homosocially masqueraded home for homoeroticism and same-sex practices. This masquerading move could not but affect homo- and heteroeroticism. The *amrad* (young male adolescent object of desire for adult men), for instance, had been a distinct figure, both as an object of desire and as a figure for identification. By the end of the nineteenth century, both positions of desire had become feminized. To desire to be desired by a man, or to desire a man, both became positions able to be occupied only by women. This gender-dimorphic dynamic emerged in tandem with the marking of same-sex desire as unnatural.

Yet even as these cultural transformations recoded same-sex desire as unnatural, in Iranian modernist discourse, this unnatural desire was seen to be an unfortunate effect of the social institution of gender segregation. Modernist intellectuals argued that because men socialized only with other men their natural desire for women became of necessity redirected toward beardless male adolescents who, through an error of nature, looked like women. In other words, everyone was presumed naturally heterosexual, and heterosocialization and companionate marriage based on romantic love were envisaged to enable nature to correct this social ill. By the 1930s, the "failure" of nature to produce homogeneously heterosexual modern men and women provided a sociocultural space for the reconfiguration of desire. Heterosexuality could, after all, not be taken for granted—it had to be scientifically argued for—and men and women needed to be educated in its practices. Modern men and women did not seem to know how to keep each other happy, sexually speaking.

Classic Islamic thought did not presume natural heterosexuality and thus had extensive advice for husbands on how to satisfy their wives and in particular how to ensure female orgasm (thought to be necessary for conception). The modernist presumption of natural heterosexuality had cut itself off from this earlier literature and left modern men and women to practice sex naturally, without instruction. The writing and translation of marital advice texts indicated a recognition of the "failure" of modernist optimism concerning natural heterosexuality and the need for a new kind of sexual education manual.[65] This response converged with the modernist concern over national health as mediated through familial health and in particular the health of marriage, which found more intense momentum from the late 1920s when the Pahlavi state became very invested in production of healthy nationals and servants of the state.[66]

For example, Husayn'ali Khan Misbahi Nuri, a civil servant, wrote his *Dastur-i izdivaj* "with the permission of the Ministry of Education," in "simple prose, understandable by all classes, in particular women," so that "a happy and prosperous generation emerges" (3).[67] He argued that until a man or a woman got married, neither could be considered part of society. Not only was marriage necessary for the continuation of humankind, its decline—as a result of wives' increasing expectations of their husbands—had led to men's reluctance to get married and instead to "satisfy their lust in unnatural manners" (5). In good modernist fashion, he suggested that, "In a society where women are veiled and deprived from working and employment, it is impossible to stop the spread of moral corruption" (6). He believed that this had become a serious enough problem that the government had to take responsibility, make marriage obligatory, tax unmarried men, and introduce support and encouragement for marriage, such as exempting married men from military service (7). He suggested that people needed to be educated in principles of hygiene and to learn the characteristics of a good marriage. The health of both husband and wife had to be certified, and parents of the girl in particular were instructed to ensure that the future groom was not reputed to have been "involved in disreputable acts, such as being *malut* [catamite] and *maf'ul* [passive]" (15–18). He recommended that persons known to have been malut must be forbidden to marry (20). He opposed a ban on polygyny. "Such prohibition should be introduced at least twenty years after removal of the veil" (19). The unveiling of women would at once make more lasting marriages possible, prevent men from engaging in sex with other men, and encourage them to act honorably. For the time being, women were encouraged to be patient with and tolerate their husbands' philandering behavior because such behavior would slowly decrease with the maturation of the man and the consolidation of affection between husband and wife.

Misbahi Nuri attempted to combine Islamic medical precepts and moral advice with more modern needs and concepts.[68] As a hybrid text, his book was in tune with the older type of marriage advice books, yet it saw its task as responding to concerns of modern life. Translated books, on the other hand, charted a distinctly separate path. Their structure reflected the cultural environment of their initial formation, and in their translated form they engendered a different organization of sexual knowledge.

An early text in this genre is *Rahnuma-yi shawhar-i javan dar marhalah-i izdivaj* (Guidance for young husbands for the stage of marriage), a translation of Sylvanus Stall's *What a Young Husband Ought to Know*. The book was translated in 1929 into Persian by Hidayat-allah Khan Suhrab, a major in the Shiraz Brigade. After an initial discussion of the physiognomy and psychology of men and women, the book turned to advising how young husbands should take care of their wives and be sociable, loving, and caring husbands. At least seven other titles from the same series were translated into Persian.[69]

Central to the increasing circulation of these books was the notion that troubles in modern marriages were caused by sexual ignorance. Husbands did not know how to keep their wives happy, leading to increasing frigidity among women and an alarming rise in divorce rates among the urban middle class. Ignorant parents were producing confused adolescents who turned into failed, not normal, adults. A great deal of ink was spilled over men's impotence, widespread practices of masturbation, and same-sex desire and other deviancies.

For the modernizing urban middle class, translated texts carried the additional authority of Euro-American science. Particularly successful among such translations has been *A Marriage Manual*, by Hannah and Abraham Stone. First translated and published in 1948, it has gone through numerous retranslations and reprints. One translation has been used to produce an audio version for the blind.[70]

The 1948 publication of this ever-popular marriage manual seemed rather shy of the explicit discussions and graphic illustrations included in later translations and editions. It modified the Q&A format of the English version through much condensation and elimination, sometimes of whole paragraphs and at times even whole sections and chapters. All illustrations were eliminated. Homosexuality consistently fell victim to elimination or euphemism.

For example, "There are men and women with psychopathic personalities, with serious emotional derangements, individuals with abnormal sexual tendencies, with conscious or subconscious homosexual inclinations, any of which may form a serious barrier to a harmonious marital adjustment" (from the 1935 English edition, page 5) was translated into: "It is also possible that deviations in sexual desires and mental disorders make a woman or a man unsuitable for marriage" (3–4).[71]

As already indicated, beginning in the 1940s, a vast range of periodicals ran regular columns on these topics.[72] In addition, many began to serialize books on these topics.[73] It was within this literature of marital conduct and advice that "sexual deviance" and "homosexuality" (and transsexuality, its "extreme" manifestation) often were discussed as the cause of marital discord. Sections bearing titles such as "Ikhtilal dar umur-i zanashu'i" (Disorders in marital life) argued that the disinclination of spouses to have sex with each other may be caused by same-sex experiences in adolescence that became solidified into habitual homosexuality. In this context, "women's coldness" (*sardi-i zanan*) received central attention and consistently was attributed to premarital same-sex practices.[74] Timely marriage frequently was proposed as the key life move that would help overcome adolescent same-sex tendencies.[75]

Discussion of homosexuality frequently slid into transvestism and transsexuality.[76] While homosexuality and other sexual deviancies were held responsible for marital discord, parental ignorance and wrong approaches to child rearing were said to cause these deviancies in the first place. Mothers who did not allow their sons to grow independent, blocking the son's separation from the mother and his identification with the father, produced effeminate, homosexual, and in extreme cases transvestite and transsexual males. Harsh fathers blocked the development of a daughter's heterosexuality. The endocrinological wisdom of the day—"In every male person, there are some female characteristics and in every female person some male characteristics"—combined with the notion of "failure" in developmental psychology, provided a repeating refrain in support of these two claims.[77] Parents' "deviant ideas" could cause long-term developmental harm: "[P]utting girls in boys' clothes . . . indicates that the parents desired to have a male child . . . a female child in that situation will either try to become very masculine or refuse anything to do with masculinity. In either case, her development will be derailed from its natural course . . . she will not make a good spouse for her future husband . . . worse, such a child may become afflicted with 'transvestism' [mubaddal pushi] or she may wish in adulthood to be a man."[78]

In addition to the vernacular psycho-sexological texts, there seems to have been an increase in the press runs of what the respectable middle class considered pornographic: too much explicitly sexual information was circulating and corrupting the nation. Khvandaniha's ability to balance between satisfying the "insatiable curiosity" of some readers and the "sex panic" of others is indicative of the cultural contestations of these decades. An article reprinted from newspaper Vazin bore the alarming title, "Who is accountable for why these books are being printed? A book that is all sexual instructions with provocative photographs has sold 17,000 copies and has a black market."[79] A second subtitle read, "After Mahvash's Raz-i kamyabi [Secrets of fulfillment], and Asrar-i magu [Unspeakable Secrets], here comes Ab-i zindigi [Water of Life]."[80] The cover of the book apparently was a three-color photograph of a nude woman; the book had no author, no publisher, and was all sexual instructions. Adding insult to injury, the book was "written in an old-fashioned and outdated prose." With 295 pages and tens of totally nude illustrations, priced at 80 rials (around US$1.00), the author further noted that this was not the only such book; there were many, all adorned with nude pictures of foreign actors, and all sold out of the highest print runs. Why was it, the author asked, that thousands of conditions were established for newspaper editors and the press law was revised every year, but there were no limits for books and anyone could publish anything they pleased?

More significantly, the author's outrage about the old-fashioned prose and outdated information in this text demonstrated the total parting of the ways between, on the one hand, the more traditional popular pamphleteers and

Islamic writers of "explanations of questions" concerning sexual matters, and, on the other, the respectable modernist columnists who serialized scientific psychology and sexology but for whom the old-style "sex manuals" were shameful and a reason to call for censorship. The author of this article specifically called on the Minister of Culture to take responsibility. What he did not mention (and was possibly unaware of) was that *Water of Life*, and indeed this entire genre of books, was not a 1950s phenomenon. This particular book was a reprint of a book that already had been published in 1903. What was new in 1959 was the inclusion of "nude foreign actors," which transformed it from "traditional marriage know-how" into "modern pornography."

The increasing circulation of sexual material was also something that educators found alarming. An anonymous article, "written by one of our knowledgeable women writers who is a prominent education specialist," critiqued the kind of sexual education that young children were receiving through cinema and television, inciting their too-early sexual feelings (*ihsasat-i zudras-i jinsi*).[81] No longer at issue was the importance of sexual education, but instead who was the right authority for teaching youth such vital topics: parents, schools, psychologists, educators, or the media with the kind of trashy material that was miseducating our vulnerable children? The media made no distinction, the author argued, between the basic simple facts of sexual education and "sexual crimes and deviations; thus in the name of sexual education, they expose the young and the children to problems and issues and even crimes and disasters that undoubtedly are harmful and destructive for the growth and health of their intellect, soul, and body."[82] She offered a severe critique of the popular press, noting how they covered morally offensive news in seductive ways to sell more copies. The frequent reporting of what used to be considered a great sin and cause family shame—the deviation of a daughter—has made it routine; it has removed its stigma (*qubh-i 'amal*) and its shame (*Ihsas-i khata va nidamat*).[83]

Films and visual advertisements came under particularly severe criticism. Social critic Mahmud 'Inayat proclaimed that "Tehran cinemas exceed all limits [*bidad mikunand*] in displaying sexy films."[84] Vaziri Mahabadi, in his article "Art at the service of sex and sex advertising art," focused on how "Riza'iah vodka, Zuhrah dates, Yik-u-yik lemon juice, Harir paper tissues, and Suzuki cars use sexy pictures to sell through the association of their products with sex," and how art production was taken over completely by depicting artless explicit sex, corrupting women, and leading youth to sexual deviations and decay.[85] Other commentators voiced alarm over how such acceptable public discussions and visual displays of sex was beginning to overlap with underground or even criminal activities, including production of pornographic films.[86]

By the 1970s, issues of education and alarm, scientific knowledge, and so-cial control over matters concerning gender/sex/sexuality had consolidated their shared spaces of circulation, means of dissemination, and modes of im-plementation. The mutually enabling dynamic of this literature on the neces-sity of educating the young in scientific gender/sex/sexuality (*jinsi*) matters for the sake of building a strong healthy citizenry of the modern nation-state, under the supervision of educated parents and concerned educators, on the one hand, and, on the other, the alarm over the dangers of uncontrolled, un-scientific circulation of sexual knowledge through what was seen as irrespon-sible journalism has continued to produce a vast vernacular psycho-sexological literature to the present day.

This phenomenal success of vernacular psycho-sexology has changed the meaning of desire for sex change from its early affiliation with the intersex state—both belonging to the domain of the wondrous—to that of deviation (moral) and pathology (psychological). Nowhere is this sharp shift clearer than in the body of literature named "Legal Medicine" (*pizishki-i qanuni*). As this subfield, navigating medicine and criminology, took shape and matured, sexu-ality became reiteratively categorized under chapters titled "Sexual Deviations" [*inhirafat-i jinsi*]—a category that from the start carried the burden of shading into criminality.

## Sexual Crimes, Deviants, and Disorderlies

From its beginnings in the 1930s, sexual criminology emerged as interlinked with vernacular psychology, with which it shared the pages of the popular press. Public conversations about "sexual crimes" became printable news. Some of the same authors contributed to both conversations. One story, in particular—that of Asghar Qatil [Asghar the Murderer] provided the perfect text for the traffic of ideas about perversion, psycho-sexological profiles, and criminality.

On March 8, 1934, the national newspaper *Ittila'at* broke a sensational mur-der story on its first page and devoted its entire back page to the murder. For the next four months, until Asghar Burujirdi's public execution on June 27, 1934, the story occupied center stage at *Ittila'at*. Burujirdi, who instantly ac-quired the nickname Asghar Qatil, according to what was reported to be his own voluntary confessions (upon arrest), had murdered seven male adoles-cents (ranging from thirteen to seventeen years of age) and one adult man (thirty years old), in addition to some twenty-five murders that he had com-mitted in Baghdad before he had moved to Tehran. We do not learn details about his Baghdad murders, except that he had started killing the male adolescents with whom he had sex after a few of them had persisted in harassing him and asking for more money. This apparently became the pattern of his later killings in Tehran, except for the case of the thirty-year-old man. Thinking the man had suspected him to be responsible for the disappearance of one of the murder victims, Burujirdi killed him before he could attempt to blackmail him or report him to the police.

Over these four months, as Schayegh has powerfully argued, Asghar Burujirdi provided the occasion for "an outpouring of a large number of texts . . . [which] crystallize[d] a serious concern, specific to the Iranian modern middle class. . . . [His case] illustrates how, in the interwar period, social reform and the related interpretations of human behavior drew on bio-medical scientific knowledge. . . . [Advocated social and cultural reforms] were believed to rest on the practical application of modern scientific knowledge. And yet, faith in the scientific, rational manageability of a modern society was coupled with anxieties about social pathologies."[87]

Schayegh has analyzed this case fully for its significance in working through important notions of reason, self, and humanness in the formation of modernity in Iran. Here I want to reconsider the significance of Asghar Qatil's story not as one of murder but as one of perversion—or rather perversion understood as murderous—by bringing out the subsumed almost-silent text of Asghar Qatil's sexuality. The question—"was he a madman, or was he a criminal?"—that ran through the public debates of this case in 1934 and the judicial decision that he was a criminal (and his public execution) was also a conversation and a judgment on the necessary criminality of male homosexual practices between older men and younger male adolescents that, since the late nineteenth century, had become subject to Iranian modernist assault.

Asghar Qatil served as a prototype of insane murderous perversion. He became a case of sadism in texts of psychology and criminology. Almost instantly, his story made its way into one of the earliest modern psychology texts. Titled *Amraz-i ruhi* (Diseases of the soul/psyche), the book's author was Muhammad 'Ali Tutia, a doctor who had practiced for many years in Istanbul and had published a number of books on sexual hygiene in Turkish. He had established a private clinic in Tehran in the early 1930s, which focused on combating venereal diseases; he began to rewrite and publish his books in Persian.[88] In addition to his books, he began a monthly, *Sihhat-numa-yi Iran* (*Hygieneography of Iran: A journal of medicine, health and morality*), which was regularly published over a two-year period (1933–35).

His book *Amraz-i ruhi* captured Asghar Qatil's story both as a way of explaining the importance of a science that is devoted to diseases of the soul/ psyche and his individual case as a study of sadism. The introduction of the book began in Asghar Qatil's name and banked on his fame to support Tutia's argument that "Sexual needs, similar to thirst and hunger, are part of the basic requirements of every living being. The highest and most beautiful way to satisfy this instinct is marriage. . . . But refusing this natural and moral path pushes individuals to mean habits and causes them to commit terrible deeds in order to satisfy their instinctual sexual needs and they descend into the lowest human and moral depths" (6).

Asghar Qatil reappeared in the section on sadism (11–19). After a preliminary four pages reviewing what was known from history of this "disease," Tutia invoked the authority of Lombroso and von Krafft Ebing, moving on to a subgroup of "followers of sadism" who not only killed children but also "under the influence of reproductive/sexual degeneracy [*zilalat-i tanasuliyah*], with cruelty first commit sodomy with their victims" (15). Tutia eventually concluded that Asghar Qatil "is one of the persons afflicted with this disease. Undoubtedly he is a sadist" (17).[89]

In a text (perhaps from the early 1940s), possibly titled *Zan va mard* (Woman and man),[90] in a section on sexual deviation (*inhirafat-i jinsi*) (88–100), the last two pages are devoted to famous people afflicted with sexual deviation. Along with Nero, Alfred de Musset, and Rousseau, Asghar Qatil is mentioned as being afflicted with "sadistic sexual deviancy" (99).

Similarly, in Hashimi-Fard's 1963 *Masa'il va ikhtilalat-i jinsi "dar zan va mard,"* "Asghar Burujirdi, known as Asghar Qatil who murdered children after having sex with them" provided the exemplary case profile for sadism (219). In Pursa'id's *Cure your sexual impotence with food*, again Asghar Qatil is illustrative: "Some men, who are not inclined to woman kind, have a deviant inclination/nature [*tab'-i inhirafi*], such as Asghar Qatil. . . . He had explicitly said in [his] confessions that he hated woman kind . . ." (21).

Asghar Qatil's story, combining insanity, perversion, and gruesome murder, continued to provide a perfect script for the national conversations on crime and punishment. For instance, the story of another serial killer, featured in *Khvandaniha* between April 27 and May 25, 1950, was titled "Asghar Qatil-i jadid: Chigunah 13 zan ra biqatl risandam" (The new Asghar, the murderer: How I killed 13 women). Muhammad Hadi Muravvij, accused of sodomizing and killing three children in Shiraz in 1955, was nicknamed "the second Asghar Qatil."[91]

Asghar Qatil's fame did not fade. He made several appearances in the multivolume history/memoir of Ja'far Shahri about "old Tehran," published in the

1970s through the 1980s. In this vernacular ethnography, Asghar Qatil appears in two of the volumes. In volume I (348–51), in addition to the coverage of his execution, a *bahr-i tavil* (rhymed prose) about him is reproduced. He makes a second appearance in volume VI in the chapter on the peddlers of *bamiyah*, a popular sweet sold on trays in the streets. Apparently that had been one of Asghar Qatil's many odd jobs and, at least in some accounts (including Shahri's), selling the sweets had been used as a means of luring the young male victims (143–44).

The popularity of Asghar Qatil's story is thus significant for the persistent centrality given to his sex acts with the young male adolescents whom he subsequently killed. In the original reports, little emphasis was laid on the sexual aspect of the crime—indeed, the issue is conspicuously absent. As Schayegh has demonstrated, the text of the trial, the defense, and the many articles debating the case were fully centered on whether he was mad or criminal. By the time Shahri was writing his books in the late 1970s through the 1980s, however, this silent subtext had become a repeated motif. In part this was because such a motif was well suited to the overall narrative of Shahri's Tehran: a city that became dominated by various vices as it moved from the late Qajar period into the twentieth century. Chief among these vices, as far as Shahri was concerned, were *amrad-bazi* and *bachchah-bazi*. Throughout his volumes, young males (*amrads*, *nawjavans*, etc.) are written about as prime markers of urban decay and immorality. Asghar Qatil is emphatically portrayed as an older man who seduced younger male adolescents, had sex with them, and then cruelly killed them. As I have discussed elsewhere, from the late nineteenth century onward, the very processes of older man/younger man sexual practices becoming an unnatural vice also transformed *bachchah/tifl* as a word and concept that had ranged from late childhood into adolescence into what we now name a child, and the associated sexual practices *bachchah-bazi* (sex with a *bachchah/ tifl*) became what we now call pedophilia.[92] In nineteenth-century biographical and historical sources, for instance, naming a man as lover of *amrads* was noted with little, if any, approbation. Yet the same sources severely disapproved of sexual acts with very young boys, and such practices were subject to harsh punishments.[93] By the mid-1930s, in the rhymed prose reproduced in Shahri's book, addressed to Asghar Qatil, a six-month-old infant, the martyred 'Ali Asghar, has come to stand in for adolescent teenagers.

From the beginning, then, Asghar Qatil's murderous insanity became folded into discussions of perversion. Fear of murder was mobilized to cultivate and reinforce fear of *any* sexual liaison between an older man and a male adolescent. The theme of the criminality of homosexual liaisons continued into the 1940s and later. A report in *Ittila'at* linked the murder of a taxi driver by a seventeen-year-old young man (whom the paper referred to as a *tifl*, linking the older notion of the child as a male adolescent object of older men's desire with the newer meaning of *tifl* as a legally underage child) to the reported "illicit relations" (*savabiq-i namashru'*) between the two.[94]

Fear of and anxiety over sexual liaisons between older men and younger male adolescents, now increasingly and explicitly referred to as "homosexuality" or as "same-sex-playing," was cultivated most evidently by the traffic among psycho-sexology, marital advice literature, and the emerging field of scientific criminology. In this nexus, as we saw in Hasuri's articulation, most homosexuals should be treated by psychologists as mental patients (*bimar-i ravani*). A minority of "them," however, were degenerate and deserved punishment.[95] Whether they deserved scientific psycho-biomedical treatment or legal punishment, they were to be feared. In the emerging scientific psychosexual criminology, Asghar Qatil appeared regularly as an example of the criminality of male perversion.

An important comprehensive text linking sexual deviation to criminality was Ansari's *Sexual Crimes and Deviancies*. According to its preface, "This book sets out to thoroughly discuss sexual desires and instincts. Its study is therefore absolutely necessary for anyone interested in knowing themselves better and in overcoming the weak points of their characters; . . . for parents who like to deliver healthy and strong children to society; for judges, doctors, psychiatrists, education authorities, students of medicine and law; and for members of the country's police." The book emerged from a teaching appointment the author had received at the Police Academy, the subject for which he chose as "Sexual crimes and deviations: How to know them, prevent them, and treat them."[96]

The structure of the book makes it clear that it was a translated text. It turns out to be a partial and modified translation of J. Paul de River, *The Sexual Criminal: A Psychoanalytical Study*, first published in 1949 (Springfield, IL: Charles C. Thomas Publishers).[97] Like its Persian echo, de River considered that his book was "contributing toward better understanding of this type of criminal" and his audience to be "the doctor, lawyer, law enforcement officer, social worker, and others in similar or related fields." He worked very closely with law enforcement authorities in Los Angeles for many years, from which experience all the case profiles in the book were selected out "of the many thousands" that had come under his personal scrutiny (ix). Thirteen of fifteen case studies in Ansari's book came from this source; the other two came from the local press. While de River rarely collapsed the pervert onto the criminal (except in one of the final chapters on "Pertinent Facts Relative to the Sexual Criminal"), Eugene Williams—a former Chief Deputy District Attorney with whom de River had worked closely—in his introduction to the book, had no qualms about considering "the sex pervert . . . just as much a criminal as . . . the burglar or murderer" (xiv).

Ansari shared this frame. His inspired translation selectively included some chapters and left out others. More significantly, he gave a different structure to the case studies of de River's book and similarly modified the book's title. What sense can we make of the choices he made and what were their possible effects?

Let us start with the title. The Persian translation brings out explicitly what was largely implicit in de River's book: that all perverts are not simply ill but they are all at least potential criminals. Not only has the title been changed from *The Sexual Criminal* to *Sexual Crimes and Deviancies*, but throughout the text where de River talks about "the criminal," Ansari speaks of "the criminal and the deviant." In his first chapter (which does not have an equivalent in de River), after a brief psychohistorical overview of "sexual problems in the past and in the present," he concludes: "'Sexual crimes,' in other words, are the same as 'sexual deviations'" (8).

De River's book is structured around his project of studying a particular criminal character type and its consequences for legal, criminal, and judicial processes. The book is composed of three main sections—Sadism, Masochism, and The Psychological Aspect of Criminal Investigation. It ends with a selection of articles contributed by a chief medical officer from a Florida state prison, a judge from the Criminal Division of the Los Angeles Municipal Court, the head of the Morals Division of the Metropolitan Police Department of Washington, D.C., a public defender from the County of Los Angeles, and a crime writer, and lecturer.

Ansari's text is structured differently; he uses what by then had become a common grid of classification of "sexual deviancy" in Iranian discourse. The book thus opens with a brief general chapter on "sexual problems," starting with Freud's obligatory appearance as the founding father of the modern science of sex, and proceeds to define sexual deviancy and criminality. His second section, on "Different categories of sexual deviance and their role in causing crimes," includes subsections on sadism, masochism, exhibitionism, homosexuality, voyeurism, fetishism, pedophilia, incest, urolagnia, bestiality, pyromania, necrophilia, and kleptomania, many of which categories appear in de River's book either as qualified categories only (such as "sadistic pedophilia," "homosexual sadism," and "sadistic bestiality" in the sadism section) or marginally when reportedly present in a criminal whom de River had investigated for one of the "sexual crimes" of his concern. The third and final chapter in Ansari's book, "Causes of emergence of sexual crimes and deviations: How to diagnose, prevent and cure them," largely follows the third part of de River's book.

One result of this different structure is that Ansari uses de River's cases as examples, but not necessarily in the same category as they were used in the original. For instance, a profile that in de River was used to illustrate a case of "sadistic homicide and lust murder" (123–42) is used by Ansari in his section on sadomasochism (72–97); the profile of a woman from de River's "female sadistic criminal" (168–73) is used by Ansari as an example of "a woman afflicted with sadomasochism" (97–106); the profile of a "homosexual sadist" in de River (92–98) appears as a case of "a person afflicted with homosexual deviation" in Ansari (119–29).[98] In other words, Ansari translated the sexual criminology of de River into the criminality of sexual deviation, thus confirming that "sexual crime" is the same as "sexual deviancy," as he had stated at the beginning.

Among all "sexual deviation and crimes," throughout the text Ansari emphasizes homosexuality as the most deviant. In the first chapter, he introduces a distinction between moral grounds and scientific ones for defining the line between "normal and permitted" and "criminal and deviant." He offers adultery as something considered immoral that nonetheless cannot be considered "criminal and deviant" from a scientific point of view (9). On the other hand, from a scientific point of view, "loving sexually someone of one's own sex" is a sexual deviancy and crime even though the majority of such people rarely commit seriously dangerous crimes. Within the category of "sexual deviants and criminals," and more specifically homosexuals, Ansari focused on men, who, he claimed, constituted the majority of such deviants, as women were generally passive in their sexual lives, could control their impulses better than men, and were protected by their particular sense of shame and humility (13).

In the section on the homosexual (112–29), Ansari elaborates on homosexuality as "one of the oldest" deviations, which "is still widespread in Middle Eastern countries. In Iran it has considerably decreased since women's veil was abolished" (113). In the domain of psychosexual criminology, women's unveiling would not only prevent the immorality of homosexuality, as modernists had long argued, but also should have worked as a prevention against sexual crimes. Despite the growing heterosocialization of Iranian society, Asghar Qatil's actions provided, for Ansari, a confirmation that such perversions did not simply depend on a sociological contingency, namely, the lack of possibilities for socializing with women. His actions spoke to criminality. Similar to Buffington's arguments for Mexican criminology, there is a persistent, at times explicit and at other times implicit, affinity established between criminality and male same-sex practices.[99] The murderous violence of Asghar Qatil's case was put to the work of creating "guilt by inference in which all deviants share the blame for the most atrocious of their collective crimes."[100]

While Ansari offers no evidence for his proposition that homosexuality in Iran had "considerably decreased since women's veil was abolished," he was possibly hinting at the changing sites and patterns of male-male homoerotic and sexual relationships that had made them invisible to the urban middle class for several decades. Indeed, its growing visibility in a new mode from the late 1960s and especially in the 1970s in urban life produced a great deal of anxiety and social critique, which we will see in chapter 4. In Ansari's eyes, the issue of reduced visibility of male homosexuality also emerged when he elaborated on female homosexuals. He considered this phenomenon to be more widespread symptomatically, "because women often and customarily embrace each other, stroke and kiss each other, while such behavior is less seen in men" (116).

Ansari's book, like de River's, ends on treatment and prevention. "In order to build a prosperous, strong, and happy society, sexual criminals and deviants must come under supervision and treatment, and our best means for achieving this goal is to turn to psychiatrists" (193). Sexual criminals and deviants must be treated differently, not only from other criminals, but also from other mental patients. A combined specialization is called for: psychiatrists who are also familiar with criminology and penology (198).

In Ansari's text, we witness the convergence of an emergent psychosexology with modern changes in the penal and criminal system of Iran. Before the 1979 revolution and the establishment of the Islamic Republic, this convergence already had begun to inform legal textbooks. In the 1980s and 1990s, this beginning found a fertile place to grow in the Compliance project.

Mahdi Kaynia's *Mabani-i jurm-shinasi* (Fundamentals of criminology) is noteworthy in this context.[101] Kaynia (1918–95) was a professor of law at Tehran University in the 1960s and 1970s; he authored and translated numerous texts, most of which were published by Tehran University Press and have continued to be reprinted.[102] The second part of *Mabani-i jurm-shinasi* is centered on factors that may contribute to the criminality of a person. Are there any hereditary factors? How do parental rearing practices contribute to the formation of a criminal? Does gender make a difference? Developmental psychology is used to map out the possibility and meaning of criminality in different groups. Adolescent sexuality here becomes a key focus of where things could go wrong. The looping back of vernacular psychology into an academic text is evident here in the legal domain. Kaynia's primary referential text for this section is Maurice Debesse's *L'Adolescence* in the popular series "Que sais-je."[103] Many of the titles in this series were translated into Persian from the early 1960s.[104]

Kaynia's section on adolescence offered a summary of what was by then the commonplace wisdom of psycho-sexology, tracing a trajectory of infantile sexuality, a dormant period, and the bursting out of adolescence sexuality. He further argued that disturbances in adolescent development and the resulting rise of crimes, suicide, and other youth problems the country had witnessed in recent decades were effects of urbanization and parental ignorance. In the rapidly growing cities, familial support networks had disintegrated, the age of marriage had increased, and divorce rates had gone up—a combination that, he argued, was producing a rebellious young generation adrift in a city with increasing opportunities for corruption and deviation. Like other reform voices on this topic in these decades, he advocated that the Ministry of Education had an obligation to educate the country's youth in sexual matters.

The vernacular criminal sexology that had begun to take shape in the pages of *Ittila'at* now "matured" through textbooks and in academic sites and looped back into popular magazines. In an article authored by "a scientist" (*biqalam-i yiki az danishmandan*) under the title "Scientific and Medical Investigation of Sexual Criminals in Our Age," a section is devoted to and subtitled "double-sexed-ness and sex-change" (*jinsiyat-i muza'af va taghyir-i jinsiyat*).[105] After discussing "natural double-sexed-ness" (referring to the popular notion that there is some man in every woman and vice versa), the author went on to argue that "in some people there are signs of 'unnatural double-sexed-ness.'" In still others, "who are bodily, reproductively [*tanasuli*] and chromosomally perfect, hormonal disorders may produce a psychological and social sex/gender/sexuality [*jinsiyat*] that is the opposite of their reproductive sex [*jins-i tanasuli*]. These are those same-sex-players who are inclined to dress as the opposite sex and even to change sex." After talking about Tokyo, New York, and Paris, "where such young men dress up as women and work like female prostitutes" and where some of them had gone through hormonal and eventually surgical sex change, the author observed that, "Such people have been seen in Tehran as well and they are awaiting surgery. These woman-presenting boys [*pisarha-yi zan-numa*] say that since childhood they have been inclined to men."[106] More important than the specific line of argument is its location at the heart of an article on "sexual criminals," which cataloged a series of sexual crimes and advanced the claim that the purported recent increase in sexual crimes was a terrible result of the sexual revolution. As an example, the author stated that in "1974–75 in Iran at least ten books have been written or translated on sexual matters," and reported an increase in abortions in Iran, "300, 000 illegal abortions every year" (39–41).

Unlike a number of other countries, where historians have argued that the idea of scientific criminality and the field of legal medicine occupy a central place in the formation of modernity, legal medicine as a field had a feeble start in Iran—certainly, its full expansion did not come till the 1980s and 1990s.[107] Indeed, in Iran, it is important that popular criminology—through the pages of a national newspaper such as *Ittila'at*, as discussed by Schayegh—both preceded and became a founding element of scientific criminology. From the start, the latter became intertwined with vernacular psychology and concerns of national pedagogy. The convergence of criminology, law, and medicine provided the scientific ground for the field of legal medicine; psychology and sexology contributed to what went under the umbrella of "legal psychology and psychiatry." The process is significant not only for providing the conceptual ideas to do with sexual offenses and crimes but also for consolidating and institutionalizing the Legal Medicine Organization of Iran—itself an important site for the current procedures for changing sex.

In much of this literature—psychological, legal, biomedical—the transsexual and homosexual subject remained implicitly a male body. Perhaps, as Buffington has suggested, in circumstances where politics and power are male-dominated, homoerotic-affectionate friendships and same-sex practices among men can be seen as competing with national/patriotic loyalties and bonds of community and citizenship, whereas women's similar relationships do not seem to pose similar threats.[108] While female trans/homosexuality was at times mentioned, it remained incidental. Not only was it perceived as less threatening to the larger legal-religious-cultural order of things, it was assumed to be a problem of a more marginal and numerically smaller scale. When it did become a topic of public concern and conversation, it was largely linked with modernist pedagogical projects, particularly the responsibilities of modern parenthood and enlightened schooling. That is how psychology and criminology of sex/gender/sexuality met and exploded in the story of Mahin and Zahra, to which we now turn.

# 03

## MURDEROUS PASSIONS, DEVIANT INSANITIES

On November 27, 1973, in the small northern town of Lahijan, nineteen-year-old Mahin Padidarnazar murdered her girlfriend, Zahra Amin, apparently in a fit of passionate madness. Between November 1973 and August 1974, this unusual "crime of passion," claimed as Iran's first murder that had occurred "as a result of female homosexuality," gripped the country.[1] The two national dailies, *Ittila'at* and *Kayhan*, as well as their affiliated women's weeklies, *Ittila'at-i banuvan* and *Zan-i ruz*, gave front-page headlines and substantial inside space to the story, extensively reporting and analyzing both the initial crime and the later trial.

Through this coverage, a sustained discussion of "female *homosexualité*" took place in a national space, perhaps for the first time. Its public characterization as murderous connected it with the always potentially murderous criminality of male homosexuality. Yet distinct from the psycho-sexological focus of male homosexuality—and the debates over whether it was inherited and innate—this coverage was centered on socio-pedagogical concerns: This murderous phenomenon was preventable, had parents and schools been more enlightened and recognized abnormality in some adolescent girls. The national press took on the mantle of enlighteners in its coverage. *Zan-i ruz*'s reporting of the Mahin and Zahra story was plotted around the journal's social vision. A journalistic tradition, going back to the late nineteenth century, had assigned the press the role of enlightened social and cultural educators.[2] The educational mission of *Zan-i ruz* was specific: it was in the business of crafting modern womanhood. By far the more vocal of the two women's weeklies of the 1960s and 1970s, it advocated for women's rights, carried investigative reports serving its advocacy, and provided sustained "advice literature" for modern marital and parental practices that was addressed to adults as well as adolescents. Modern womanhood, in this vision, was defined in part by living modern heterosocial lives. This required redefining female-female friendship, particularly bringing under scrutiny friendship between women that was "too close," that is, seen implicitly or explicitly in the shadow of inappropriate sexuality. *Zan-i ruz*'s narrative of the Mahin/Zahra story served all these domains of sociocultural transformative pedagogy.

Crimes of passion were stock stories of the "Events/Incidents" (*havadis*) page of the dailies, although they rarely made the front page. Indeed, only two other crime stories gained similar prominence during this period, although neither received the same level of sustained critical reporting as the Mahin/Zahra story. One was an account of the familiar spurned-lover-turned-murderer. Its prominence was due to the social class of the murdered woman, Manizheh Hijazi, who was from a well-known aristocratic Tehran family and the daughter of a (deceased) high-ranking army general. Hijazi was murdered by her violent lover, Anushirvan (Andy) Razzaq-manish. The other was an exceptionally gruesome multiple murder: Fayyaz Parhizi murdered his own wife and five children along with his brother's wife and children.

The Mahin/Zahra story, however, far overshadowed the other two. What threw the story of Zahra's murder in a small provincial town onto the front pages of national dailies and important weeklies for almost nine months was, of course, that it was a case of passionate, mad, female-female love. Yet, importantly, the other two murders not only shared temporal proximity and press space with the Mahin/Zahra story, but thematic and analytic elements of overlap among them also turned out to be significant to the ways in which the Mahin/Zahra case acquired its meaning. The shared themes, as well as the distinct differences among these three stories, mapped a particular understanding of female homosexuality. The story of this unusual crime of passion also brought this "disease of deviancy"—squarely defined as the result both of the bad upbringing of children by parents and educational authorities and of improper outdated social norms—into an affinity with transsexuality. This affinity, in turn, contributed to the loosening of the knot that had tied transsexuality to intersexuality and further consolidated its recasting as a phenomenon linked with homosexuality.[3]

The thematic overlap between the Mahin/Zahra story and the Razzaq-manish/Hijazi case was centered on passionate madness. This overlap in part formed the presentation of Mahin's love for Zahra as similar to heterosexual passion, which was assumed to be familiar to readers. That familiarity immediately highlighted its sensational dangerous difference: it was not *heterosexual* passion. The theme of madness also was raised by the lawyer for the defense in Fayyaz Parhizi's case, who pointed to his client's transsexual fantasies as symptoms of his insanity. Both Parhizi and Razzaq-manish were portrayed by prosecutors as incurable sadists—threats to society. Reports of Parhizi's gruesome multiple murders, with hints of sexual undertones, were haunted by the memory of Asghar Qatil. The death sentence was requested in all three cases and pronounced in the latter two. Mahin received a life sentence. Razzaq-manish's class, along with his mother's widely reported pleas addressed to Hijazi's mother,[4] may have saved his life (his sentence was commuted on appeal). But Parhizi, an example of a sadistic, mad, lower-class threat, was executed.[5] The complex mapping of these three cases provided the press with numerous ethical and moral lessons (*dars-i 'ibrat*) to expound for the public good.

The idea of Mahin as another spurned lover turned murderer (at times linking her case explicitly to that of Razzaq-manish) was pursued by the prosecutor, who insisted that the crime was motivated by Mahin's deviancy; she was portrayed as a heartless young woman who had been set on corrupting young female adolescents and who murdered Zahra once she learned that her beloved was turning her down. This was also the story that was built up by the press, especially by *Zan-i ruz* (and, belatedly, at the time of trial by *Ittila'at-i banuvan*), but to a different end. These magazines found it to be the perfect story for promoting their modernist agenda of advocating sexual education and more freedom for women and girls (albeit under the enlightened supervision of parents and educators). Indeed, *Zan-i ruz* repeatedly prefaced its coverage by disavowing that it was making any judicial judgment in the case. Its obligation was educational; the judge would decide the legal outcome.

To construct its educational case, *Zan-i ruz*'s extensive and at times sensational coverage sought to uncover and bring to the attention of the public (especially parents and educators) a mysterious, almost sinister, subculture of female adolescent homosexuality as providing the social space that produced the crime.

A somewhat different framing was pursued by Mahin's defense lawyers. They disavowed Mahin's "sexual deviancy." She was portrayed instead as a pitiable young woman who suffered from deviant *personality* development, with possible biological and environmental causes. She was said to have a double personality, perhaps had an extra chromosome; she was a person with a female body who had developed a masculine personality and a desire for sex change.

Not only developmentally derailed, she also was portrayed as going crazy during her short one-day menstrual periods, during which time the murder was said to have occurred. Both Mahin's and Fayyaz's stories brought forward for public scrutiny what seemed to be an intersection of madness with some vaguely known personality disorder that produced a desire for sex change. The combined effect of these multiple framings contributed to the consolidation and popular knowability of a notion of desire for sex change as a personality disorder that vaguely overlapped with potentially murderous madness and that at the same time had some family resemblance to homosexuality.

## Mahin and Zahra

From the very first moment that Zahra's murder made national front-page headlines, Mahin emerged as a sensationally strange character. *Ittila'at's* (November 28, 1973) front-page title "A girl killed a student with 15 slashes from a knife," bore the subtitle: "The accused is known among her acquaintances and neighbors as '*jahil-i mahall*' [tough guy of the neighborhood]." The fuller report appeared on page 18, on the "Events/Incidents" page of the daily, along with other reports of murder, fraud, suicide, and scuffles on a soccer field. It bore the same headline, this time large enough to occupy almost the full width of the (a2) paper. A similar subheading emphasized Mahin's strange masculinity: "The accused is a young woman who always wears men's clothes and is known among her acquaintances and neighbors as 'jahil-i mahall.'" A brief report followed, giving a few more details about the circumstances of the stabbing and later death of Zahra in the hospital, ending one more time with: "Mahin (the accused murderer) is Zahra's neighbor and always wears men's clothes and is known among her acquaintances and neighbors as 'jahil-i mahall.'" In other words, Mahin's dressing "as a man" and her tough-guy "*ma'ruf*" (notorious) reputation is repeated, in exactly the same words, between the front page and the report on page 18, no less than three times, literally framing the actual crime report and immediately projecting some mysterious connection between Mahin's gender nonconformity and the act of the crime. The daily *Ittila'at's* report on the second day similarly ended by reiterating that the accused "is much attached to wearing manly clothes; she does not consider anyone her rival in riding motorcycles and acting out in a masculine [*mardanah*] manner."[6]

This focus on her gender nonconformity continued to inform the presentation of Mahin by the press all the way to its end. During the trial, almost the

اشتباه نكنيد صاحب اين عكس كه
كتوشلوار مردانه بتن كرده پسر
نيست او خديجه‌خانم پديدارنظرمعروف
به مهين است كه متهم به قتل زهرا
امين ميباشد

زهرا امين دختر جوانى كه بـه
ضرب چاقوى دختر ديگرى بقتل‌رسيد

FIGURES 3.1 AND 3.2. Mahin and
Zahra. *Ittila'at*, November 29, 1973.

very same words were used by the publication to describe Mahin's appearance
in the court.[7] From start to finish, the dailies and weeklies also strengthened
this association visually. For instance, in *Ittila'at*,[8] a full-figure photograph of
Mahin in a suit accompanied the report, along with a more "feminine" photograph of Zahra (figures 3.1 and 3.2).

The caption for Mahin's picture read: "Don't be misled; the person in this
photo in a man's suit [*kut va shalvar-i mardanah*] is not a young man but Khadi-
jah Khanum Padidarnazar, known as Mahin, who is accused in the murder of
Zahra Amin." In contrast, the caption for Zahra's photo simply stated: "Zahra
Amin, the young girl who was knifed to death by another girl." Mahin's appearance "in a man's suit" remained a familiar refrain and a common photographic
pose. Photographs that emphasized Mahin's masculinity and Zahra's innocent
femininity worked often in pairs: in layouts their photographs were set on
facing pages. For instance, on December 8, 1973, *Zan-i ruz* ran Mahin's photo
on the right margin of page 18 facing that of Zahra on the left margin of page

FIGURE 3.3. *Zan-i ruz*, December 8, 1973.

19, visually framing the text (figure 3.3). The caption for Mahin's photo read: "Mahin, Zahra's murderer, went to the schoolyard on the day of the event in a man's suit [*kut va shalvar-i mardanah*] to kill Zahra." The caption of the photo of Zahra was innocently simple: "A picture from the album of the murdered Zahra." The pictorial framing of the big headline, "I kill you because I love you!" with a masculine Mahin and a feminine Zahra captured the story for a heteronormalized reading.

The textual and visual construction of Mahin's masculine sentiments, presentations, and practices constituted a thread that slowly translated into one of the important themes of the press coverage: Mahin's "gender" deviance was a symptom of her "sexual" deviance; both possibly had something to do with her desire for sex change.

In contrast to Mahin's masculine murderous strangeness, Zahra was systematically portrayed as an ordinary, young, feminine character who not only deserved our sympathy on the ground of her victimhood, but also comforted us by her normalcy.

Zahra's funeral provided an appropriate setting for the process of character building and social mapping that the dailies and (much more intensely) the weekly *Zan-i ruz* would pursue in months to come. Numerous mourning gatherings were reportedly held in mosques and neighborhood halls throughout the small town. Not only high school students but the whole city was mourning: a concert was cancelled; classes in the school where the murder had occurred were moved to another site; and details of the lives of Mahin, Zahra, and a larger group of young female friends began to become public.

Zahra emerged as a successful high school graduate who had been exempted from serving in the Literacy Corps[9]; she was taking English language classes to prepare for her university education abroad. In contrast, Mahin was reported to have completed her education only through the eighth grade. Later reports indicated that, because of her "troublesome" character and "corrupting influence" on young girls, she had been expelled from all Lahijan high schools. *Ittila'at* (December 1, 1973) explicitly linked Mahin's crime with deviant tendencies. "People of Lahijan accuse the murderer of having deviant tendencies and say that she took a new girlfriend every once in a while, and during the summer months would take her girlfriend on the back of a motorcycle to Ramsar and other places." While Mahin's "deviant tendencies" at this point are reported only as the hearsay of neighbors, they were transformed into a full-blown diagnosis in the coverage of *Zan-i ruz.*

With the dailies moving onto other crimes and events, *Zan-i ruz* passionately covered the situation for the next seven weeks. It assigned a whole team of reporters and photographers to the case—Pari Sekandari, Mahmud Azad, Ayyub Kalantari, and Nasir Mujarrad—and invited "expert professionals" (doctors, psychologists, and educators) to explain to its readers the sociopsychological significance of the murder. It embraced the story as a moral text of pedagogy.

Pari Sekandari was a well-known journalist. She was known particularly for her persistent, almost aggressive, style of interviewing and for her passionate interest in topics related to women's marital, family, and sexual lives. Some of her contributions in *Zan-i ruz* around the time of the Mahin/Zahra story included a series of articles and interviews with Dr. Husayn Parsa and Dr. Bahram Muhit about the problems of sexual relations among young couples and the importance of sex education before marriage.[10] Among these were an article on a court case brought by the mother of an eighteen-year-old man in love with a forty-two-year-old woman to stop their marriage; an investigative report of two Qazvini sisters who had lived all their lives in an old fort because they were against men and marriage; and several reports related to a topic much under debate in the 1970s that went under the heading "legal murder of women," which referred to the light prison sentence for men who killed a female relative for (suspected) improper sexual conduct.[11]

As a female reporter, Sekandari seems to have gained access to sources in this case (for instance, the homes of the girls and conversation with their mothers) that may have been closed to male journalists. While Sekandari and *Zan-i ruz* may have intended their coverage to draw the attention of "ignorant parents and failing educational authorities" to what they saw as a dangerous and unnoticed subculture among young girls (one that could even cause murder), the reports put into mass circulation vocabulary and concepts about female homosexuality that was unprecedented.[12] Expressions such as *barunibazi* had rarely, if ever, made it into print before these stories, and far less often into the mass-market press.

Given the murderous turn that one such case of female homosexuality had taken, Sekandari and *Zan-i ruz* opted for a bold "enlightening" project. What was hidden had to be uncovered, especially because the association between female homosexuality and murder was unusual. Unlike modern male homosexuality in Iran, which had come to live (and in important ways continues to live) under the weight of its association with pederasty, rape, and murder, female same-sex practices often had been considered largely harmless, if at times shameful. This articulation, shared by some of the parents who were quoted by the reporters, was something that had to be discredited for the issue to be taken up as a serious educational and developmental social challenge. As one report emphasized, "All of us face the danger that one day we would be told, 'your daughter had unusual and strange relations with another girl and killed her female beloved!'"[13]

*Zan-i ruz*'s opening salvo was headlined in very large letters across two pages (figure 3.3) with the subtitle "A crime of female same-sex-playing in Lahijan." The report opened by posing the situation as a window for understanding a "mental illness":

> This sad incident uncovers a mental illness that afflicts some young girls and poses the problem of female same-sex-playing and *homosexualité* for psychologists and sociologists to study. . . . Mahin, the nineteen-year-old girl who committed this murder, has a rough appearance and masculine behavior and sensibilities. She has a deep voice [*sida-yi kuluft*] and, more importantly, she is strongly attracted to friendship with young girls. Her strong love for Zahra and her disappointment about the continuation of this love caused her to commit this crime. Perhaps this is the first crime

that has been committed as a result of female *homosexualité* in Iran, and one that for the first time uncovers female same-sex-playing and poses the question: Is it not the suppressive family strictures that cause widespread same-sex-playing among young girls? This important matter must be paid attention to by sociologists and psychologists and educational lessons must be drawn to benefit female students so that the causes of moral deviancy is eradicated and sad incidents like this would not happen again. . . . But before all else, we needed to find out what the extent of the acquaintance between Mahin and Zahra was, how far their love relation had proceeded, and how the grounds for this crime had been laid.[14]

A tantalizing case was being built around the prospect of knowing the extent of their relationship as an explanatory key for understanding the crime. At the same time, the screaming headline—"I kill you because I love you!"—already informed the reader of the conclusion to come, one that proposed a logic of reading for the magazine's readers.

What is the play of same-sex-playing and *homosexualité* in the coverage of this story? Over and over again the two terms were linked together in the reports, sometimes with the additional term "same-sex-inclined." The first is a pejorative reference in Persian; its usage echoes the cultural reading of same-sex erotic attachments. As a derogatory word for an unspeakably corrupt practice, along with the other specifically female-referenced word, *baruni-bazi*, its print appearance is enabled by the second term, a transliteration of a French word, presumably offering the reader the scientific designation of the disease.[15] In that affiliation and transition, "same-sex-inclined" will emerge as the more enlightened, psycho-medicalized word for "same-sex-playing."[16]

Sekandari opted for a melodramatic, multilayered plot, telling the story several times and through different perspectives, starting with Zahra's family, Mahin's family, and neighbors and friends, and through letters exchanged between the two women. What kept these levels of story together and informed Sekandari's project was her deep conviction that this story must not be allowed to be told as a simple judicial case of murder with one person on trial. Her interviews often verged on interrogations and took a prosecutorial tone as she sought to put on trial all the individuals, families, educational authorities, and social networks and practices that she held responsible for this tragedy. In this endeavor, she presaged a narrative line that the defense would employ.

*Zahra's Family Tale: The Innocent and the Corrupt*

Sekandari started her investigative journey with a visit to Zahra's grieving family. Almost immediately she began to interrogate (and incite) the father about Mahin:

> Sekandari: Was she a bad girl?
>
> Father: She was bad, corrupt, and wicked. I always advised my daughter to stay away from her.
>
> Sekandari: Did your daughter like her?
>
> Father: Absolutely not; she was scared of her.
>
> Sekandari: Why scared?
>
> Father: Because Mahin was always threatening my daughter. . . . She behaved . . . just like a wicked man. . . .
>
> Sekandari: So why do you think Mahin wanted to kill Zahra? . . .
>
> Father: Ever since she heard I was planning to send Zahra to her brother in Germany, she suddenly became anxious and crazy.
>
> Sekandari: Anxious about what? . . .
>
> Father: She was a harasser. She harassed all the beautiful girls in town. . . . She was a deviant, full of complexes; people said many things behind her back. . . . She was a strange and out-of-the-norm girl; a girl with boyish behavior.

After several more exchanges, the father was given a break and Zahra's sister picks up the thread:

> Sister: Mahin was known as a knife-wielder [*chaqu-kish*, a word almost always used to refer to men]. . . . Once at school she drew her knife against a teacher. Everyone was scared of her. Two years ago she befriended a girl and then asked her to have dirty relations with her. The girl reported this to her family and they filed a complaint. The legal case is with the police. She was expelled from school. . . . Her only aim was to get to know beautiful girls, befriend them, and then put in action her filthy deed. . . . My sister became her next target.

Like her father, and despite the reporter's insistent suggestion that there must have been some sort of "deviant love" between the two young women, Zahra's sister insisted that Zahra had been scared of Mahin. Perhaps there had been friendship between them at the beginning, she finally conceded, but soon Zahra had pulled back. She recalled that Zahra used to say that Mahin had told her she loved her madly and could not live without her. Another family member added that the relation between the two had been terminated some two months earlier and that Zahra would not even take phone calls from Mahin.

The adjectival construction of Mahin in these exchanges included bad, corrupt, wicked, scary, threatening, just like a wicked man, harasser, rejected by society and school, jealous, agitated, deviant, strange, out of the norm, a girl with boyish behavior, knife-wielder, filthy. In contrast, Zahra is described as very good, very shy, and an excellent student. Paradoxically, Mahin's portrayal as a bad girl could undermine Sekandari's larger pedagogical project. She thus moved swiftly to guide the readers away from seeking individual character traits as causes for the tragedy to social, educational, and parental culprits, pushing the conversation toward the theme of neglectful families. Zahra's sister indicated that Mahin had purchased a present for Zahra's birthday, yet when Sekandari asked for the date, no family member seemed to remember when Zahra's birthday was. Both families were said to be "not very ordinary families."

Sekandari's critique of families was particularly targeted toward fathers. Zahra's father was reportedly more preoccupied with his (not always legal) real estate deals than with his children's upbringing. He was said to have been named in several legal cases that had arisen out of shady land deals, one of which had even involved murder. Mahin's father received particularly harsh treatment; he was portrayed as an uncaring father who thought fatherhood was just about providing bread. During the week of the trial, *Zan-i ruz* reporters went to meet Mahin's father at Abshar Hotel, which he owned and managed. Even though "he knows the prosecutor is asking for the death penalty for his daughter, and he knows that his daughter is alone in a jail cell, there is no sign of anxiety on his face; like every other night, he is entertaining clients. On stage is the orchestra and a dancer, he is talking and joking with customers as if his daughter had not been called a murderer, as if his family honor had not been dealt any blows, as if he had the acquittal and release order for his daughter in his pocket. He didn't have time to talk to us about his daughter's fate. He had to deal with his clients and the accounts and invoices. The only thing he told us was, 'See you tomorrow in court.'" In court, he was said to fall asleep in the back of the room.[17]

Sekandari further pursued the theme of neglectful families through conversations with other members of Mahin's family. But on that first day of her interviews, before going to Mahin's family, she asked one last question of Zahra's father: What punishment would he like to see Mahin suffer? He responded that Mahin's punishment was of no consequence to him, as it would not bring his daughter back to life, but the punishment of a murderer who always carried a switchblade knife and had terrorized a whole city and struck a young girl seventeen blows from a knife might send an effective message to our society.[18] When the reporter resisted the implication of Mahin merely as a mad criminal, asking "Don't you think Mahin was more a sick person than a murderer?" the father refused to accept such a diagnosis. He would not allow the "cover of illness . . . to neutralize the crime of a deviant, agitated, and wicked person."

### Mahin's Family: The Shame of It All

"I must meet her family to get to know her." Thus ended the first segment of the reportage—with a promissory note reminiscent of serialized melodramas. Sekandari headed off to meet the father and brother in Abshar Hotel on the shore of the Caspian Sea.

The title of Sekandari's second installment declared in bold huge letters: "Mahin had attempted suicide once before for Zahra's love." Smaller print marked the important points of the interviews to follow: "Doctors had told Mahin: 'You are physically a woman but have the soul of a man!'"; "In a letter Mahin had asked Zahra's hand in marriage in order to form a family together!!"; "Mahin's mother . . . told Zan-i ruz's reporter: 'Zahra had become the big idol of my daughter's life. Several times a day she would be crying for her.'"

From the first paragraph, the report constructed a narrative of the relationship with a presumed pattern of "activity" (fa'il) and "passivity" (maf'ul) in same-sex relations—a binary designation that the psychological articles would flesh out. In a parallel construction, it referred to "the two 19-year-old girls: one a murderer [qatil], the other murdered [maqtul]; one is a lover ['ashiq], the other beloved [ma'shuq]." Mahin was said to have a wicked personality that was violent, cruel, and masculine and had turned up in a female body. This was one of the first instances in which the journal began to characterize Mahin with the language of a split between body and soul.

Mahin's family spoke of Zahra as a girl "of an innocent character, kind, weak and in need of support" who had become enamored of Mahin's boldness and toughness, had begun to socialize with her and form a friendship—a friendship that slowly turned into "deviant affection and love." This relationship intensified Mahin's "homosexual desire" (hiss-i hamjins-khvahi). The crime that ensued from this love and desire, the reporter reminded the reader, was:

> a story that public opinion shall never forget, because for the first time it uncovers the deviant sexual relationship between two female students, which may indeed be a small sample of a larger pattern [musht nimunah kharvar] that exists in all corners of this country. This problem is highly significant

and important to study from the psychological, social, and family angles and must be carefully scrutinized by educators and families in order to overcome deficiencies that exist in social relations of our youth, so that innocent and inexperienced girls—and boys—do not become victims of such sad incidents. If we don't pay attention to psychological health of the youth, if we do not study and analyze their physical and mental needs realistically, the result is that Mahins and Zahras fall into the trap of deviant love, then land in murder, and injure the hearts of families.[19]

The report continued by mapping out a subculture of deviant girls, innocent victims, ignorant parents, and neglectful school authorities. It was the magazine's mission to put the responsibility for this tragic murder on all these parties rather than on Mahin as an individual criminal. Social institutions were at fault: restrictive families that did not allow natural socializing among young girls and boys. These issues, the magazine promised, would become the subject of in-depth "educational and psychological discussions." For now, it would complete the story of the love and murder. The detailed reportage of this single case would become generalized and serve as the empirical ground for the scientific analyses.

This same issue of *Zan-i ruz* also began a series of "psychological analyses" of the crime, now explicitly projected as caused by *homosexualité*. Titled *"Hamjins-gara'i!!: Humausiksualitah chist? Humausiksual kist?"* (Same-sex orientation: What is *homosexualité*? Who is a homosexual?), this was the first instance in which the magazine named the phenomenon under consideration same-sex orientation, rather than same-sex-playing. The scientific claims of this parallel "psychological" series called for the use of a less culturally marked and morally loaded term. The crux of the argument was, after all, not a moral one, but a psycho-medical and educational proposition. Running these two series in parallel set a generative reading dynamic into motion. Sekandari's reports worked on the suspense of a high-profile murder investigation. The scientific series used this interest to draw the reader into its domain of explanatory power. The power of scientific authority, in turn, underwrote the credibility of Sekandari's investigative journalism.

Like a serialized story, Sekandari's report now took up the conversation with Mahin's brother Yusif, a soft-spoken, bashful young man who felt deeply wounded and shamed by the action of his sister: "How could we look in people's eyes? How could we continue to live in this town? My sister made us lose face. I knew my sister would get us in trouble one day." Sekandari was interested in these "troubles":

Sekandari: Was it only in the past couple of years that your sister had become masculine and tough, or was she always like this?

Yusif: She was unsettled from childhood, she was wicked, . . . stubborn, wanted to always have her way. In school she would fight with
everyone. In elementary school years, my mother was called in many
times. . . .

Sekandari: Did you know that she fell in love with girls?

Yusif: No, I didn't.

Sekandari: Your "no" was uncertain and in a low voice; you must have
heard things here and there. No?

Yusif: I knew my sister was not like other girls. For a while, she cooped
herself up in the house.

Sekandari: Why?

Yusif: Because she would be teased by people when she went out; she was
looked down upon. Besides, she had been expelled from all Lahijan
high schools and she felt inferior and defeated. . . . Later she began to
go out again and then she met Zahra.

Sekandari: Who else was in her life besides Zahra?

Yusif: Previously she had relations with a girl named A'zam; it was she
who introduced Zahra to my sister.

Sekandari: But A'zam has stated that she didn't know your sister at all.

Yusif: Really! Well, we have documents that we will show when the time
comes.

Despite Sekandari's pressures to find out what these documents were, Yusif
refused to expand, hinting only that the family had letters and photographs
that would corroborate their claims and that he did not consider his sister the
only guilty party. He suggested that Zahra was playing with Mahin, encouraging her one day, rejecting her the next. He promised to persuade his mother to
talk to the reporter. Later that evening, Sekandari met Mahin's mother and a
daughter-in-law in her house. She went straight to her pursuit:

Sekandari: Do you think in this incident Zahra was at fault as well?

Mahin's mother: Yes. Of course my daughter was a very violent and bad
girl. Actually we did not dare to call her "girl." If we did, she would become angry and curse us. She hated that she was a girl. She wished
she could become a man. But Zahra was not innocent either. She used
to come and visit my daughter all the time. They would go upstairs to
Mahin's room and spend hours privately together [*khalvat mi-kardand*,
an expression with sexual undertones].

This exchange was followed by a string of questions about how long Mahin and Zahra had known each other, how long Zahra stayed when she visited, what they did in Mahin's room. To the latter question, the mother said (one imagines with annoyance): "How do I know? Mahin not only had drawn the curtains in her room, she had fixed them with pins to the walls so that no one could see through any possible cracks. . . . Besides, you think anyone in this house dared to ask anything from Mahin? She would fly into a rage. [When] I refused to give her the 100 tumans she asked me a few days ago to get a present for Zahra's birthday . . . [she] beat me up; she almost killed me."

Yusif made his mother to show Sekandari her black-and-blue bruises while the reporter relentlessly continued her interrogation, even as she noted that the battered mother was sad and distraught. Reports of Mahin's temper and violent moods were interlaced throughout the story, serving not only as a link to her ultimate violence of killing Zahra, but also as a way of constructing the masculinity of her temperament. Physical violence was woven into Mahin's masculine desire for women and constituted yet another symptom of her pathology.

Sekandari's questions now focused on Mahin's eroto-affectionate inclination toward women, set within the frame of female masculinity as something pathological.

Sekandari: When did you notice Mahin had masculine tendencies?

Mahin's mother: Many years ago. I took her to several doctors but none of them gave us a proper answer. This past summer when Mahin went to Tehran, she went to a doctor by herself and explained her abnormal [ghayr-i 'adi] situation to the doctor. The doctor had responded that she was physically and bodily a woman but mentally/psychologically [ruhan—with the soul/psyche of] a man. Mahin suffered greatly from her condition. She knew she had been born abnormal, but the doctors had repeatedly told her that she could not be changed to a man through surgery. My daughter was physically a girl, . . . but her temperament was not feminine. I always offered her words of guidance [nasihat]; I would ask her why in a small town like ours she insisted on troublesome acts; why she wore men's clothes; why she rode motorcycles, courted young girls and damaged our reputation [took away our abiru]. But she paid no attention.

Note that the mother's guidance is articulated in terms of how Mahin's actions in public affected the family's name and life, especially because they lived in a small town. The seeming condemnation thus arose out of a local habitat in which it was not possible to live unnoticed—where neighbors knew and talked, where something out of the ordinary was not accepted. It is not articulated as if something was inherently, even morally, wrong with what Mahin did. Sekandari was interested in this larger local habitat, in particular, its girls' subculture.

Sekandari: Do you know a girl named A'zam?

Mahin's mother: Of course I know her. She was very close to Mahin. The night that Mahin attempted to kill herself, A'zam stayed by her bedside all night.

Sekandari: Mahin had attempted suicide? When? How? Why?

Mahin's mother: Some time ago, about three or four months ago. She ate some opium to kill herself, but we noticed and took her to hospital . . . she told us: "Separation from Zahra is like death for me. I can't face her leaving Iran. They want to send her to Germany; let me die. . . ." That night A'zam stayed till the morning with Mahin and wept all night. And now she says she didn't know Mahin? . . . I have letters and photographs from her. . . .

Sekandari: If you knew how troubled your daughter was, why didn't you seek treatment [mu'alijah] sooner?

Mahin's mother: We did seek treatment; everyone gave a different medicine and a different advice. But my daughter was not cured. It was also the fault of the other girls; they surrounded her; some would consider her their Mecca [qiblah] and would sing her praise and flatter her.

Sekandari: But they say Zahra hated Mahin.

Mahin's mother: They are lying. I have letters from Zahra, I have photographs; she loved Mahin as a lover ['u Mahin ra 'ashiqanah dust mi-dasht]. . . .

Sekandari: Don't you think that, beginning three years ago, when you noticed that your daughter's friendship with other girls was of a deviant nature [inhiraf-alud] you should have pursued her treatment seriously and reduced her socializing with others and find a solution for her problem so that your daughter would be relieved of physical and mental deviance?

Mahin's mother: I have suffered more than my forbearance in life. What can a helpless woman do in this country? . . . I took care of these children all on my own and I have grown used to living by myself for many years now. Our house was not home to a calm and happy family. Write to people on my behalf that children growing up in dysfunctional families turn out bad.

Under Sekandari's continued unrelenting assault, the mother is reported to sob. According to Sekandari, she was quite young; forty years of age with five children; the age of her eldest would indicate that she had children at an early age. Despite moments of sympathy, Sekandari would not give up her pursuit of uncovering the mysteries of deviant female subculture.

> Sekandari: Weren't you curious to know what Zahra and Mahin did in her room?
>
> Mahin's mother: What did I know? They were two girls. What can one say about two girls being together alone? Everywhere such meetings are natural. God knows.

Sekandari was glib in the face of the mother's reluctance to open up that line of conversation; she had a feeling, readers were told, that the mother knew a lot more. Her persistent pressures kept Mahin's mother talking:

> Mahin's mother: Zahra used to call our house all the time. She used to cry for Mahin. Once, when her father had ordered her not to socialize with Mahin, she sent a letter to Mahin through A'zam in which she had written, "Mahin, for the past two days my father has imprisoned me in the room on the top floor; I cannot leave home and [come to] see you." If my daughter has committed murder, Zahra has also had her share in stoking this fire. Zahra's letters and her photographs, which she had signed on the back, show that for a long time Zahra had loved Mahin as a lover. Doctors ought to read these letters and figure out their meaning. . . .
>
> Sekandari: Where are these letters now?
>
> Mahin's mother: I have them but I will let no one to read them. They contain the secrets of this murder.

### The Mahin/Zahra Letters: A Window into the Underworld

Mahin/Zahra letters were invaluable to Sekandari's search for the truth of the social problem she sought to uncover. She could not leave without seeing them. After another two hours of patient persistence, she was triumphant; the mother allowed her to see a few pictures with Zahra's handwriting on the back, dedicating the pictures to Mahin with such phrases as "Your Zari," and "Mahin's Zari" ("Zari" is often used for "Zahra"). Sekandari also made copies of a couple of letters that were in Zahra's handwriting and selectively let the readers read a few snippets of these precious documents—these little windows into the mysterious world she was set to uncover. Even as she exposed the letters, she incited the unspeakability of the mysteries by censoring them:

> Dear Mahin, greetings to you. It is 25 minutes to 2 pm as I write this letter. It is Saturday. Gulpaygani [a popular male singer of the period] is singing "I am sad" [*dilam giriftah*] [. . .][20] on the radio; [. . .] truly I am missing you [*dilam barat giriftah*—playing on the song's title] and there is a deep void of you here. Your letter is in front of me. I have come to the section where you write: "You were the first person in front of whom I took off my blouse." Mahin, let me write to you that I was the first simple girl you found and you used my simplicity and did whatever you wanted with me. Perhaps you'd say that I too desired it. But I swear to God, I did not want it at all. [. . .] Mahin, did you want anything else? What did you want? That I'd do what you asked of me? But I am sorry. I would not do this, because it is you who is like this, not me. You have written a lot about your embarrassment/shame [*khijalat*]. Why did you not display such embarrassment about the kind of things you did to me—things that will torture me for a lifetime when I recall them. I know that it is impossible that you and I could live together for a lifetime; it is impossible that my family would give me to you. . . . (Here retelling parts of the letter would be against public decency and we omit these) . . . You tell me to believe your words. I want to accept them and believe that you love me, but when I remember what you did to me, I doubt your honesty and doubt your love. Mahin, do you remember (repeating these sentences is also outside the bounds of decency). . . . About your question—that your biggest wish is to form a family with me, and that is what you most ask of God; you plead with me to believe you—I know you do not lie to me and I know you love me, but my wishes and yours differ. But you do not consider what I want; the only thing you think about is several times a week (these sentences are also omitted).

Paradoxically, the power of the letter for the readers' imagination resided in precisely in those ". . ." and those deleted sentences; in the unspoken, unprintable details of what had gone on in Mahin's locked, tightly curtained room upstairs.

After this "strange letter," as Sekandari called it, which openly revealed the sexual and erotic love of the two girls, she read another letter in Zahra's handwriting in which Zahra expressed her deep attachment to Mahin. Sekandari did not share this letter with the readers, however, but instead took the reader through more intense conversations with the mother, who finally succumbed to her persistence and allowed her to see Mahin's room—that site of scandalously unprintable ellipses:

> A very small room on the second floor of the house, with a bed, a desk and an armchair, with yellow curtains that have been carefully pinned to the wall so that no one could see in from the outside. [. . .] There is a vase, made in Hamadan, on which a line from Khayyam has been written: "I cannot live without good wine." [. . .] Mahin's mother says Zahra had given this jug to her daughter. On the arm of the red leather armchair Zari [. . .] has been carved. [. . .] And there is a picture album with a few pictures of Zahra in it. On the back of one of them we read: "Zari-Mahin, dearest Zari I'd die for your eyes. Dearest Zari, I'd die for your look. Dearest Zari, I'd die for your lips." On several places on the wall there is engraved Mahin's Zahra, . . . Zari . . . Zahra. There is also a notebook of Mahin's in which she has written about her bitter life, full of disappointments, humiliations, and insults; her expulsions from schools, her feelings for girls, her masculine tendencies, and her deep hopelessness after her visits to doctors. In the last year of the diary, there is only one name, Zahra.

The letters were turned over to the defense team during the short trial in late July 1974. They constituted important support for the defense's argument that the relationship between the two young women had been mutual. In addition, one of Mahin's defense counsels, Ahmad Mu'tamidi, produced a notebook in which the two girls both wrote—a common practice among "best girlfriends" in high school. He read portions of this notebook to prove that there was no hint of same-sex-playing in the notebook. The relationship, as he constructed it in court, had been a deep mutual affectionate attachment. Some verses that Zari had written in the notebook, addressed to Mahin, were read aloud in court and reported widely in the press:

> No bird can tolerate a cage
> You have become captive in my love
> I know, I know, but
> You shall not remain my captive forever
> Tell me, which bird would tolerate a cage
> Yes, my dear
> You shall depart
> And will forget
> That a girl with black hair and a heart full of affection
> Poured all her life with sincerity onto your feet.[21]

Mahin's family considered these letters and memento as important evidence that Mahin was not the sole driver of this relationship gone wrong, but for Sekandari they provided windows into a subculture she had set out to bring to light.

## The Insidious World of Adolescent Girls

Rumors had been circulating quickly in the small town of Lahijan. People said that when Mahin was arrested, she was home calmly sipping a cup of tea and watching television. People said that when the morning after the murder she was told that Zahra had died, she had reacted in anger, "Couldn't those bastards save her?" But then she was said to have regained her calm and smoked a cigarette—yet another sign of her masculinity or, alternatively, a corrupt femininity. People said that she was not anxious in jail; she joked with everyone, ate well, smoked a lot, and, with no anxiety or sadness, went to bed early—as if she had murdered no one, as if the girl she had murdered had not been the dearest person to her. It was as if, Sekandari wrote, jail was working like a cure for her rebelliousness, her wickedness, and agitation—as if she were finally getting the needed supervision that her family had withheld from her. She was a sick woman who should have been cured by psychologists so that she would not commit such a terrifying crime.

In addition to reported rumors, photographs were used to configure the world of adolescent girls. In one of the earliest reports, a group photo of eight young girls at the birthday party of one of them introduced the reader to another woman, A'zam Yazdan-shinas. She was said to have been deeply implicated in the network of besotted female friends around Mahin. A'zam was said to have introduced and acted as a messenger between Zahra and Mahin when their love was going through a crisis; she was said to have had her own attraction to Mahin but had been rejected. Now married for several months and pregnant, A'zam was called in for questioning by the investigator but was not asked to testify in court—something that was noted in protest by one journalist.

In court, Mahin charged A'zam with turning Zahra against her and with inciting Mahin against Zahra on the day of the murder. In response to the judge's inquiry about details and motives of A'zam's action, Mahin suggested that she had been in love with her and had repeatedly asked for more intimate relations, which Mahin had refused on the grounds of fidelity to Zahra.[22] A'zam became revengeful and, according to Mahin's testimony in court, on the day of the crime when she, Zahra, A'zam, and another common friend Shahnaz (Fatimah) Qunu'i (A'zam's sister-in-law) were hanging out in the yard of the high school, A'zam had told Mahin off for reestablishing her relationship with Zahra, telling her that Zahra no longer loved her. A'zam provoked her (Mahin) by calling her incompetent and lacking in honor (*bighayrat*), an accusation that made Mahin mad: "I lost all sense and the next thing I remember is that I was at home." The judge challenged this account, saying that in her statement to the interrogator A'zam had denied being in any argument on that day with Mahin or Zahra. She had stated that her husband had dropped her at the school, and shortly after, Mahin and Zahra had gone to another side of the yard and that was when she had heard a scream. She had denied any friendship with Mahin, stating that her husband had forbidden her to socialize with Mahin. Mahin called A'zam a liar and stated that they all spent a great deal of time together and that A'zam was one of the friends who took letters back and forth between her and Zahra. She further accused A'zam of having dishonored two families for lust and passion (*hava va havas*). "What passion are you talking about?" the judge asked.

Mahin: She was afflicted with sexual tendencies.
Judge: A'zam was a married woman.
Mahin: Before she was married; and because of that passion she has killed two people.[23]

While A'zam did not emerge as a loveable character in this story, the central figure remained Mahin. There seemed to be a strange air of fear and hatred in the city, Sekandari wrote, toward Mahin—this girl who had long imposed herself on everyone as a boy, a wicked and harassing boy at that. The owner of the shop from which Mahin was said to have rented a motorcycle several times a week reported that Mahin would always come with several girls in tow and would then take one of them on a ride. In response to the reporter's question—what kind of a girl was Mahin?—the shop owner laughed and a few young men in the shop chimed in: "Who would dare to call her a girl; everyone was scared of her. . . . [E]ven boys were very scared of her."

A classmate of Zahra from ninth grade, Nahid Yazdan, recalled Zahra as a kind and affectionate girl. She wasn't surprised to hear that Mahin had knifed Zari—Mahin was capable of anything; but still, Nahid insisted that she did not think there was anything between them but a simple friendship. Was this aura of cultivated fear around Mahin produced by her rough, at times violent, presentation? Were her female masculinity and the common parental warnings of the dangers of becoming a "victim of baruni-bazi," if one got too close to a character known for her designs on innocent young women, at work? In this plot, Mahin was a dangerous hunter against whom one had to instruct and protect potential prey.

Another schoolmate, Mina Ajma'i, also was interviewed—or, more accurately, incited. In response to Sekandari's question, "What kind of behavior do you think Mahin had?" Mina elaborated, "She would befriend beautiful girls and had dirty expectations of them, so girls would run away from her. Her voice was deep like men's. Everyone said she always carried a knife in her socks."

Mahin herself articulated a sense of her centrality in this world of female friendship. When the judge asked her, "In Lahijan people say . . . that you had relations with several married women. Are these rumors true?" Mahin responded, "Several women wanted me to be with them, but I would not consent. First, because they were married. Second, because I loved only Zari. One of the women even pleaded with me and said that her husband could not satisfy her and wanted me to be with her a couple of hours a week!"[24]

Sekandari used the rumors circulating around A'zam to build the insidious aura of the baruni subculture. Despite the fact that A'zam's husband had banned all interviews, Sekandari persisted and eventually made her way into A'zam's house. A'zam was described as a beautiful woman, resting under a blanket, looking scared. Perhaps, according to Sekandari, fear had been put into her. To Sekandari's insistent questioning, she at first gave short denials—she had not known Mahin at all and knew Zahra only a bit. After being interrogated at length, she said that she was simply too exhausted to talk more. Dismayed, Sekandari left A'zam and joined the city procession to the graveyard to commemorate the seventh day of Zahra's death. She talked to more of Zahra's friends, soliciting their judgment: "Is it true that Mahin was in love with Zahra and that Zahra also loved Mahin in the same way?" A friend moaned and screamed that Mahin must be executed, adding "One cannot say everything . . . one cannot open one's mouth, no I can't. . . ."

Another friend butted in: "Mahin was a sexual deviant. She was madly in love with Zahra and would always say if Zahra left her, she would die of grief. She would tell everyone that she loved Zahra. I think when she heard Zahra was leaving for Germany, she went crazy." Sekandari tirelessly surveyed the neighbors, soliciting their commentary. 'Abd al-Riza Rast-ravan: "I also had heard Mahin fell in love with girls." Riza Farahpur: "I knew Zahra, she attended the remedial classes in Arya High School. She was a good looking shy girl. I knew Mahin too. No one would dare to give her a bad glance [nigah-i chap]. Even boys were scared of her. Very easily she would get into a fight and use her knife. . . . Really with this act we boys have become amazed about love.

She was Majnun and Zahra Layli. Their story was the tale of Majnun and Layli. Too bad that Majnun turned out to be a murderer."

Within this subculture, Mahin occupied a pivotal place: She was reportedly the singular masculine figure around whom the girls formed a circle of admirers and possibly curious hopeful lovers. When a Mr. Burhan testified about Mahin's designs on his daughter, Shirin, the defense lawyer, to refute the accusation that Mahin wanted to force her friendship on Shirin, produced a letter written by Shirin to Mahin, expressing her regrets that for several days they had not talked, saying even though this lack of communication perhaps might not matter to Mahin, she would die of grief if she didn't talk to her for an hour and asked her to send a response through whomever she chose. When asked in court to explain this letter, Mahin stated that Shirin did not have a good reputation and she did not want her to be part of their friendship circle (*jurgah*).[25]

This was the circle that the press repeatedly warned parents about. When the daily *Ittila'at* published excerpts from Mahin's diary[26] they were prefaced: "Even though these letters and diary entries may not be worthy for judicial purposes, they are worthy of social reflection. At the very least parents can realize from the content of these notes how a simple friendship between two female friends changes color and slowly becomes the ground for a social disaster. [Reading these letters] will enable parents to kill at conception a possible future disaster. They can observe in their child's behavior and temperament the slightest change."

The entries selected for publication began on April 23, 1973, and ended on November 7, 1973 (a mere three weeks before the murder). They went to support the notion that Mahin was madly in love with Zahra and that a good day in her life was one in which she had seen Zahra and been happy with the meeting, and a bad day was one in which she either didn't get to see her or for some reason Zahra had been angry with her. Mahin repeatedly expressed impatience with their being apart and prayed to God to make it possible for them to form a union (*bih ham birisim*, with affective and erotic connotations of union).

During the course of the trial, Mahin had reportedly named several other women who were her friends in high school. The *Zan-i ruz* reporter concluded that, "From the first sessions of the court hearings, especially from the many letters exchanged between Mahin, Zahra, A'zam, and other girls—all are available—it is clear that there was a group of girls with more or less homosexual tendencies, and they had surrounded Mahin in Lahijan. If we think of Mahin as some exceptional girl who put spells on girls and pulled them into her world of abnormal rapture, we would be deceiving ourselves. It is all too easy to lay the responsibilities of society and of families, and the clear backwardness of our educational principles and the deficiencies of our approach to the young generation, on one girl's shoulders. . . . The truth is that many of the girls who became victims of Mahin's sexual deviancy had at least some leanings toward deviancy themselves."[27]

Within this circle, Mahin's strange masculine abnormality was mapped out not simply in terms of her clothes, her watch (with a metal strap), her gestures, her cigarette smoking (like a man), her carrying a knife, and her passion for motorcycles, but also through her place within this female world and, most pointedly, in the intense passion she had developed for Zahra and the way she articulated the meaning of that relationship for reporters and the court alike. A key feature of this relationship emerged as the sense of proprietorship that Mahin exercised over Zahra's life.

When the presiding judge, Ghulamriza Shahri, asked Mahin about her last conversations with Zahra, she responded, "We discussed our running away together. But then we got into an argument because her skirt was too short." Shahri asked, "What does her short skirt have to do with you?" To which Mahin simply retorted: "Of course it is my business."

The prosecutor had prepared a case on the basis of Zahra's desperate attempts to move away from Mahin's improper designs for her, which had caused Mahin's outrage and eventual act of murder. In court, Shahri asked Mahin for further clarification:

> Judge Shahri: Zahra, in her letter of October 28, 1973, informed you that she wanted to get married. But you intervened in this decision; the kind of intervention that men make. In your response you ordered her not to marry, not even go to wedding celebrations, "don't go out at all," you wrote. Why did you write these sentences?
> Mahin: Zahra always asked my permission wherever she wanted to go.
> Judge Shahri: Were you in charge of her [*magar ikhtiardarash budi*]?
> Mahin: Almost. Even if she wanted to go to her sisters' home, she asked for my permission.[28]

The sentiment of honorable jealousy (*ghayrat*) that informed Mahin's reported articulations would evidently have been considered normal if only she had been a man; in her, it was yet another sign of strange misplaced masculinity.[29]

When the judge pointed to sections of Zahra's letters written in a more distant tone, saying that she no longer wanted to see her, Mahin explained them as regular lovers' quarrels: "Once in a while that is the way Zahra would talk, but then she would change her mind and beg me, saying that she loved me and she loved her family and couldn't choose between the two." According to

Mahin, Zahra was scared of living with her in Lahijan because of social pressures and for her family's sake, and they had planned to run away to Abadan and get married there and live together. Mahin was going to work and Zahra do the housework. Indeed, she claimed that they had a pact that if Zahra were to be forced by her family into a marriage, they would commit double suicide.[30]

## Zan-i ruz's Mission

Sekandari's early weeks of reportage on how the two young women's families, friends, and neighbors talked about them and their relationship was missing a key voice. At the time, Mahin was not allowed any visitors. Unlike Sekandari's confident diagnosis, "the prosecutor and the investigator have not yet figured out the motive in this crime," she wrote, "and across the country many families are waiting to discover the truth; they want to know what Mahin confesses in official interrogation and what she reveals from the secrets of her relationship with Zahra and other girls."[31]

Until such official clarity was obtained, the magazine would keep up its social responsibility—its guardianship of the public. In a concluding section of the second part of the reportage, subtitled "Scientific discussion of homosexuality," Sekandari observed that the little town of Lahijan had been abuzz for the previous two weeks with the love story of Zahra and Mahin and Zahra's murder. But the concern had become national:

Many families across the country are anxious [nigaran] about simple friendships of their daughters; "baruni-bazi," long widespread among girls, is now terrifying families—now that a nineteen-year-old girl is buried and another young girl is accused as a murderer and lives in a prison cell. Many think of Mahin as a violently wild and insane human being who was afflicted with deviant tendencies. Others consider her a double-personality person, a sick and pitiable person who had no control over many of her actions, tortured by her desire for girls. . . . In order to awaken the minds of families—to learn the lesson ['ibrat] of the Lahijan incident—starting with this issue, Zan-i ruz will publish a series of articles under the title of "homosexualité," or "same-sex orientation" [hamjins-gara'i], using the writings of doctors and experts so that fathers, mothers, and the young can read and become familiar with complex and important issues that have so far been left out of the press. Regrettably, under the pretext that discussion of complex issues of sexuality is prohibited or is sinful, some oppose a public conversation of the inner pain and psychological complexities of people. But in the current atmosphere of openness and curiosity in today's Iran, such educational matters must be explained in scientific language and in the words of experts so that families and youth become informed and are not led astray through ignorance.[32]

Thus began a seven-week series of articles on the topic of homosexuality. The articles presumed the naturalness of heterosexuality, which was paradoxically always haunted by homosexuality to a far greater extent than most people were said to be willing to admit. The detailed descriptions from the previous weeks of crime reportage were now interwoven into what was promised to be "one hundred percent scientific." The first installment bore such subheadings as "What factors make a young man hate women and a young woman hate men and push them to homosexuality?" and "In the mysterious world of homosexuals, what roles do two girls play and what do they feel?" The subheadings and the content of the articles continued to inflame the curiosity of readers who wanted to find out more about a mysterious subculture and to cultivate a sense of alarm in parents and educators. The promised scientific analysis was to guide a proper response. As summarized in the preface to the first article:

The horrid and sad crime in Lahijan . . . should sound the alarm for our society, for fathers and mothers, and for educational authorities, because the only obvious cause of this horrible crime was the existence of a *homosexuelle* and a homosexual relationship between the murdered and the murderer. Such relations are widespread in human societies, including our own country. We cannot permit a self-deceiving silence over them.

There are many married men and married women who innately and psychologically [*zatan va ruhan*] suffer from homosexual desires. All fathers and mothers, all teachers of elementary and high schools, and, above all, all girls and boys must know that such a danger may befall any uninformed and unaware youngster. . . . Had Mahin's father and mother . . . known more, they would have looked for a cure seriously before she took up the knife of a murderer in her hand. In the following analytical article, using the latest discoveries of the science of psychoanalysis and the most recent views of famous world sexologists, we try to explain the causes and factors of homosexuality in simple, though one hundred percent scientific, language. We hope this analysis will be a correct step toward a proper handling of and dealing with any social problem, especially the difficulties that arise in the domain of sexual problems.[33]

The article that followed did not indeed differ from what had already become the new paradigm circulating in popular journals and radio programs in the

1940s through the 1960s, as discussed in the previous chapter. But the *Zan-i ruz* series not only set this paradigm into mass circulation for possibly a different readership—the readership of the magazine, one of the two most popular women's weeklies, was largely urban women and young girls. It also marked the shift that had taken place in sources of scientific knowledge dissemination: Unlike previous coverage of such issues in a journal such as *Khvandaniha*, which had overwhelmingly depended on the translation of mostly American texts, here a roundtable of Iranian experts set the discourse. Moreover, discussions of sexuality, in particular female homosexuality, were not embedded within the popularization of Euro-American psycho-sexology texts; the series centered on female sexuality as the real and the native, as the here and now of our own adolescents. Not only had the staging of the experts—the scientists of the psyche/soul—become nativized, but the *Zan-i ruz* coverage of the Mahin/ Zahra story of love and murder had produced a native subject for female homosexuality. In this process, the unspeakable girl-on-girl playing of the old way of conceptualizing/naming was transformed into a category of modern scientific psycho-sexological taxonomy.

Ironically, this very nativizing moment of the birth of the Iranian female homosexual was an ambiguous one. Was Mahin a female *homosexuelle*? Was she a girl who desired to be a man and thus better identified as *transexuelle*? Were these distinct or shades of the same diagnostic categories? Could extreme *homosexualité* be cured by sex change? It is the ambiguity of this moment of genesis that continues to work against any simple recuperation of Mahin as a lesbian subject who awaited a name. As credibly, and indeed in today's Iran perhaps even more credibly, she could be recuperated as an FtM transsexual.

This contingent nativization, both in its temporal and its cultural paradigmatic meaning, differed importantly from that of male homosexuality. The latter was born under the shadow of Asghar Qatil; female homosexuality had the imprint of Mahin. While Mahin also had committed a murder, her murderous act was narrated as an avoidable tragedy: Had parents and other guardians of the youth been less ignorant and acted more responsibly, the disastrous outcome could have been prevented. Asghar Qatil's criminality, on the other hand, had been captured by categories of sadism, sadistic pedophilia, and homosexual sadism. Mahin's differently marked homosexuality prefigured, and continues in the present to configure, different perceptions and sociocultural reception of MtF and FtM transsexuality.

The first article in *Zan-i ruz*'s series served as an introductory overview; subsequent issues offered the transcription of the magazine's science roundtable. It began with definitions. Unlike the earlier modernist presumption of natural heterosexuality in all human beings, a notion of homosexuality as a phenomenon among a minority informs the series. The article treated the reader to a grand historical rush through time and society, including a mention of Sappho and Lesbos, the status of *homosexualité* in ancient Greece.

It quickly moved on to how "the science of psychoanalysis has clarified for us the understanding that a great number of *homosexuelles* suffer from neurosis," and thus could be treated by doctors and "cured." But "there are those who do not go to doctors and psychoanalysts" and "they are usually considered sexual deviants and perhaps their *homosexualité* is to some extent innate and inborn [*zati va fitri*]." A summary of psychoanalytical readings (through its Americanization as it came to Iran) on child development, gender and sexual differentiation, and the possible nodes of "failure" to achieve healthy heterosexuality was presented. The article concluded with the assertion that the "behavior of the father and mother in relation to each other and to their children, and the family climate, have a primary and determinative role in [producing] *homosexualité* among the youth." It further discussed what scientists considered to be some of the biological and social causes of *homosexualité*. It is within the discussion of biological factors that the journal discussed the issue of all human beings being "two-sexed [*dau-jinsi*]." As we have seen in the previous chapter, a link was claimed between the "biological causes" of *homosexualité* (lack of the balance of "masculine and feminine hormones") and transsexuality: "Some of the people who suffer from this syndrome . . . can succeed, with the help of doctors and surgical operations, to fundamentally change their sex/gender [*jinsiyat*] and we have seen many instances of such sex-changes in Iran too."[34]

Somewhat surprisingly, sex segregation was not mentioned among the social causes listed in this article, though the roundtable doctors and later magazine commentary did come back to this issue. Rather, the finger was pointed at those social types that "prey on the youth," for which reason "in the legal codes of a majority of countries any open expression of *homosexualité* is considered sexual deviance and moral corruption and faces very heavy punishment."[35]

Distinct from previous coverage of homosexuality in the popular press, *Zan-i ruz* gave more specific space to female homosexuality. The article emphasized that women who had a masculine physique and manly comportment and behavior, "despite their female appearance are innately [*zatan*] male and thus their *homosexualité* has physical and biological reasons. . . . The only solution is to take such a girl to doctors so that her sex could be changed to that of a boy through a surgical operation."

The next three issues offered the transcripts of a roundtable that the magazine had organized, inviting two psychologists (Muhammad 'Ali Sham'i and Malik Fazili) to participate in this scientific endeavor, followed by another serialized translated article (authored by a group of "world famous psychoanalysts") and culminating in a final installment: "Can the *homosexuelles* be cured?"[36]

The conversations with the psychologists largely expanded what the magazine previously had suggested to be the psychological causes of homosexuality, with a nativist bent. Fazili expressed regret that no scientific research on this topic had yet been carried out in Iran and that "people do not like to talk about such topics openly. Yet undoubtedly, such research is needed in Iran . . . in order to protect the health of people in society . . . especially because in addition to general factors that cause *homosexuel* tendencies, there are some native elements that ought to be studied separately." It was among these native elements that the issue of "the closed nature of society, especially in small towns," and restrictions on "friendly social interactions between girls and boys" were raised as a contributing cause of homosexuality in Iran, preventing a person's growth out of what Fazili considered a natural stage of adolescent same-sex tendency toward mature heterosexuality. Another native factor, he suggested, was the strong desire of parents for boys, in which case parents might treat a daughter like a son.

In these conversations, the magazine's reporter raised particular facets of Mahin's and Zahra's lives and details of the murder to elicit socio-psychological explanations. Thus not only did the series produce a "scientific analysis of female *homosexualité*," it also served the emergent psychology profession admirably. At a time when the professional domain of its practice was largely limited to small circles of the urban elite, largely in Tehran, the magic of psychologists explaining such a mysterious and complicated issue as female homosexuality, and the crime of passion that it had caused, was helpful for establishing its status as a respectable profession to which ordinary citizens needed to turn. Psychology was not simply for the mad. Parents and educators needed it as well.

The conversations also served the magazine's agenda of putting the focus on educational and parental failings. Sekandari suggested that not only Mahin and Zahra, but all the girls who were around Mahin and sometimes acted as go-betweens, came from "unbalanced families." It was astonishing that the only measure ever taken had been to expel Mahin from schools, without the school authorities noticing Mahin's deviancy. No one, including Mahin's parents and relatives, to whom reportedly other parents had complained about Mahin's behavior, had followed up on the matter.

While much emphasis was put on the transient nature of adolescent homosexual desire, the issue of "true homosexuality" remained to be resolved. How
did one tell if a homosexual was innately so and was thus incurable? Although
the psychologists agreed that there were a small number of "permanent innate *homosexuelles*," even these, they proclaimed, could be treated with proper
psychoanalytic care. The doctors who had seen Mahin, Fazili conjectured,
were most likely not trained psychologists; moreover, "Mahin seems to have
gone to them to change sex and become a man. Some *homosexuelle* girls mis-
takenly think that perhaps they were really men and decide to change their
sex." Sham'i confirmed this judgment: "They think of themselves as a man in
a woman's body or a woman in a man's body. . . . [T]hey call themselves *transexuelle*." If they were not cured, and if their desire for sex change was frustrated, they turned to crime or became suicidal—a diagnosis that fitted the
magazine's narrative about Mahin perfectly.

It is important to emphasize here the difference between notions of heterosexuality informed by the emergent psychobehavioral notions of sexuality and
those of early twentieth-century modernist moral writings. In the latter mode,
as discussed in the previous chapter, every human being was innately, totally,
naturally, and permanently heterosexual. The critique was directed solely
against the social institution of "sex-segregation," held responsible for same-
sex practices. Such practices did not mean that the practitioners suffered from
any illness, nor from the failure of achieving heterosexuality.

In contrast, the psychobehavioral notions that had emerged by the 1970s
and informed the national conversation on sex assumed the normality of
heterosexuality structured around a developmental story: children were seen
as indifferent to the sex of the object of their attachment; a degree of adolescent
homosexuality was seen as natural; and adolescent homosexual desire would
grow into normal heterosexuality. Importantly, this maturation depended on
correct parenting and proper education (and enlightened popular magazines)
to ensure the redirection of homosexual desire toward the opposite sex.

The work of heterosocialization became different in this discourse. In the
earlier modernist mapping of desire, once heterosocial practices became dominant, the natural heterosexuality of each and every human being would be en-
sured its permanent manifestation. Now heterosocialization required permanently practiced, supervised, and controlled enactment, including what was
called "healthy activities" for the young, such as the establishment of Youth
Palaces (*kakh-i javanan*) as safe spaces for young men and women to socialize
under adult supervision. Such mixed-sex socialization was needed as part of
the developmental scheme of achieving adult heterosexuality. In this model,

numerous moments presented the possibility of failing to achieve heterosexuality. Thus society, parents, educators, magazines, and radio and television all needed to contribute to the work of minimizing the possibility of failure. Ironically, despite the reiteration of the normality of heterosexuality, this scheme recognized that a great deal of social work was needed for its production.

This expert coverage in *Zan-i ruz* proved irresistible to the magazine's rival, *Ittila'at-i banuvan*, which had not covered the case in December 1973 at all. When it joined the press during the trial, it called upon its own set of experts for scientific and legal commentary.[37] The experts included Zafardukht Ardalan (a professor of social sciences), Husayn Parsa (an obstetrician and gynecologist), Katibi and Khamenei (lawyers), Sarukhani (a professor of sociology), and Ibrahim Khvajah-nuri (author and psychoanalyst).

Khvajah-nuri proclaimed that "very serious research . . . has cleared up one thing: All the teaching concerning sexual matters that has been imparted to girls and boys is completely false and harmful, creates complexes, and is psychologically unhealthy." He further argued that such ways of dealing with sexuality created feelings of guilt and fear in adolescents, especially girls, who became fearful of sex, because much social talk about men and sex was in terms of warning girls against being duped by men; thus girls grew up with negative feelings toward men and feelings of degradation (*khiffat*) about themselves. He nonetheless rejected the label of mental illness. "Not every bad habit should be called a mental illness." Furthermore, "there was the issue of sexual and love jealousy, which regrettably many people still cultivate as a normal, and even justified and admired quality." He suggested that, like other social issues, first a social consensus had to be cultivated about the social, psychological, religious, political, cultural, historical, and economic causes of the problem.[38]

Ardalan, the social science professor, believed "that such deviations among the youth, especially among girls, are a result of excess restrictions that parents impose." In response to the reporter's question of why, then, "even in advanced countries where socializing between girls and boys is permitted, some girls are inclined to same-sex-playing," Ardalan attributed the phenomenon to lack of parental love toward children. Parsa, the gynecologist, emphatically agreed that "*homosexualité* or same-sex orientation . . . is a psychological problem that is observed among people who have lacked parental love." Khamenei, a lawyer, clarified that in "our legal system, there is no punishment for homosexuality between two women, but sodomy [*liwat*] . . . is a punishable crime." Katibi confirmed that "from a legal point of view homosexuality between two girls is not a crime . . . ; it is a moral deviation and a harm to the psyche/soul [*afat-i ruhi*]."

The intense press coverage of the story of Mahin and Zahra brought out readers' response. A retired teacher living in London wrote of her observations during her twenty years of teaching in girls' high schools.[39] During these years, she had witnessed scenes that she never would have imagined she would dare to write about. She witnessed how "young girls would become gripped with abnormal passions and at times had too intimate relations with each other. At times these attachments would be redirected toward young female teachers. . . . I am embarrassed to say that some of my colleagues would stoke the fire of this abnormal and deviant passion." She expressed hope that this "bitter event would open the eyes of fathers and mothers and serve as a warning to educational authorities."

Not all readers were approving of so much "sex talk." One reader, Firuz Lutfipur, asked "Why do you speak so much of sex?"[40] This seemingly simple question gave the magazine a golden opportunity to reiterate its enlightenment project:

> Mr. Firuz Lutfipur, in a letter that has a very harsh tone, writes, "Why do you talk so much in the pages of *Zan-i ruz* of sex and sexual problems? In most of your articles, I see sexual problems discussed very openly. I accept that most of the time these articles are instructive and consciousness-raising. But I don't like their naked character. Sexual instinct, precisely because it is an instinct, exists in all human beings and there is no need to talk about it in such detail. From the time of Adam and Eve human beings have reproduced without having a teacher and an instructor in this field. Don't you think talking excessively about sexual issues creates moral corruption and shakes the foundation of society and family?"
>
> We received Mr. Lutfipur's letter in the days when two sensational and scandalous "sexual" trials, one in Tehran and one in Rasht, have made the public deeply aware of sexual problems and their impact on individuals' behavior and actions. In Tehran a man who had killed, perhaps because of sexual sadism, the daughter of one of the most well known families of Iran was sentenced to death. And in Rasht, a nineteen-year-old girl has been sentenced to life in prison for killing her dearest friend with 16 slashes of a switchblade knife, and the main motive of this crime is female same-sex-playing. There are tens of such incidents every year—incidents that have no other roots than "sex and sexual tendencies." Perhaps the writer of this letter thinks denying reality would wipe it out. Alas, that is not so. . . . Why is it fine to speak about such trivial matters as children's sneezing, coughing, and diarrhea, but one cannot speak of the child's reproductive organs, sexual activities, and sexual instincts? . . . We are willing to read tens of

books about cooking and how to make different kinds of pickles and jams, or listen to scores of conferences and lectures about insomnia, but as soon as the topic of sexual matters is raised we stuff cotton into our ears and declare that silence must be observed. . . . Where has this voluntary negligence taken us? We have prostitutes; we have violent rape; we have homosexual men and women; we have sexual dissatisfaction and frustration that is ruining families. To treat all these ills, we first must become friendly [ashti kunim] with our body and our sexual instinct. . . . Mr. Lutfipur! If physical illnesses are caused by microbes and viruses, sexual diseases are caused by ignorance and bad education.

What went unsaid in *Zan-i ruz*'s discourse was that the letter writer's presumption of the naturalness of heterosexuality and the pervasive ignorance that the magazine claimed were both effects of modernist heterosexual presumption. Not only had nature clearly failed; more importantly, the very modern practices of heterosocialization of urban life and professionalization of knowledge production had cut off the modern middle class from previous networks of sexual knowledge—whether Islamic texts, marital practice manuals, or homosocial male and female networks.

If the press needed any more dramatic performances to get its educational message to the public, the trial—in particular Mahin's last defense—amply complied.

## The Trial

The trial began on July 18, 1974, in Rasht, the provincial capital of Gilan.[41] The dailies headlined it as "one of the most clamorous [sensational, *janjali*] trials of the year."[42] The case was prepared by a Lahijan prosecutor, Mr. Zirakju. The prosecutor's case was a familiar one of vengeful, premeditated murder carried out by a disappointed, deviant woman when faced with Zahra's refusal to respond to her immoral demands. Zahra wanted to live a normal life. Mahin would not respect Zahra's wishes, threatened her repeatedly, and eventually killed her. The prosecutor demanded the death sentence.

Mahin was assigned a court-appointed lawyer, 'Abd al-Husayn Malikzadah; her father hired a private lawyer, 'Abbas Danishkhvah. A third lawyer (referred to as "the family lawyer"), Ahmad Mu'tamidi, at times contributed to the defense. These lawyers did not seem to agree on the best line to take. While one accepted Mahin's same-sex-playing as her condition but denied that it was a motive for murder (emphasizing that the murder was caused by temporary insanity), another rejected "the charge of sexual deviancy" and characterized her as suffering from physiological and mental abnormalities, resulting in a personality disorder that needed treatment. The defense team accepted that Mahin and Zahra were in an intimate relationship, but portrayed it as a deep romantic love between Mahin with a male personality and Zahra as an innocent adolescent. They emphasized it as mutual affection. On the other hand, the prosecutor emphasized it as a case of same-sex-playing, in which Mahin was the hunter and Zahra the prey, describing Mahin as a vagrant (*vilgard*) and a despicable character.

The two major dailies and their affiliated women's weeklies covered the trial extensively, emphasizing Mahin's gender/sexual nonconformity both in their textual narrativizations and their pictorial presentations. *Ittila'at* featured a photograph of Mahin (figure 3.4) displaying a mustache, a goatee, eyeglasses, and a hat, with a caption that read: "Mahin Padidarnazar . . . exhibits masculine behavior, wears masculine clothes, and has a masculine hairstyle. This is one of her last photographs, which she has changed in this way while in prison, giving herself eyeglasses, mustache, and a beard."

All printed what were purported to be verbatim questions and answers between the judge and Mahin, the defense's statements, and Mahin's own final defense. These records did not quite match, but the insistence on factual accuracy was important for the press's larger educational and scientific claims. *Ittila'at* ran excerpts from what it claimed to be its exclusive access to Mahin's diary and letters under the headline "Shocking memoir of Mahin on the verge of murdering Zari." *Kayhan* published an exclusive interview with Mahin. *Zan-i ruz* ran its own interview with Mahin and reprinted Mahin's letter to her brother in which she had asked his help to change her sex.[43]

A hyper-sensational and melodramatic style of prose worked to move the readers "interested in the faith of our young girls, these future mothers," but especially targeted the parents, who were called upon to check their children's diaries and letters to catch such problems in a timely fashion. *Ittila'at* noted that usually such notebooks were very private, reflecting one's most inner feelings, and reading them without permission would be unethical, but "in our opinion, if parents felt that their child's behavior is not natural and normal, they could, with the best intentions for their child, seek help from the child's diary to seek the reason(s) for their child's problem."[44]

Many claims of "first-ness" circulated again and again. The crime was the first of its kind; so was the trial. The scientific coverage of female homosexuality was the first. Such claims of first-ness were important for the pedagogical pursuit: Female homosexuality was presented as a novel social problem, one

FIGURE 3.4.
Mahin displaying
a masculine
appearance.
*Ittila'at*, July 21,
1974.

مهین بددارنظر که بانهام هل دوست و همشاگردی سابق خود
زهراء در رشت محاكمه میشود، رفتاری پسرانه دارد و لباس پسرانه
میپوشد وبموهایش اراییش پسرانه میدهد .
این یکی ازآخرین عکسهای مهین است که خود در زندان آن را به
این روز در آورده و برای خودش عنک وریش و سبل کشیده .

that the press argued reflected old-fashioned parental and educational habits
unsuited for a changing, modernizing society. Even though at the time of the
murder *Zan-i ruz* had already exhaustively covered many social issues, the trial
offered another occasion. The magazine folded Mahin's expressed desire for
sex change into the more familiar same-sex-playing. The narrative and numerous photographs dramatized the coverage, which verged on sensationalism:
"Mahin! You killed your friend Zahra with 16 slashes of a switchblade knife.
Do you understand? You are Zahra's murderer! . . . . In the history of criminal
trials in Iran, this is the first time that a nineteen-year-old girl is in the court
charged with murdering another nineteen-year-old girl, and that, with 16 stabs
of a switchblade knife. But even stranger ['*ajib'tar*] than all of this, is the motive
for murder: feminine same-sex-playing! Female *homosexualité*, or *lesbianism*."[45]

This opening was followed by a dramatic summary of the events of the day
of murder with such flourishes as "the heart-breaking screams of a girl . . .
broke the silence over the city of Lahijan . . . On the green grass of the schoolyard, there was a bloodied red switchblade knife. And those who got to the

body first saw in the darkness of the sunset the shadow of a man running away barefoot. . . . . But this was not a man; it was a girl, named Mahin Padidarnazar." The news spread within minutes in the small town of Lahijan and forced all families with young daughters to ask, "Why should a nineteen-year-old girl kill another nineteen-year-old girl with such cruelty?"

> But the Lahijanis already knew the painful answer to this question: All Lahijanis knew Mahin; she was a boy-presenting [*pisarnuma*] girl and always wore men's clothes, presented herself as a man, rode motorcycles, picked fights, and no man in town dared to eye her with an inappropriate glance, because she always hid a switchblade knife in her socks. . . . And even stranger: She looked at the town's beautiful girls with a different eye, the eye of a lustful man, and had abnormal and mysterious relationships with some of the town's girls. All this too was well known.

The melodramatic style continued throughout the trial reports. The prosecutor had asked for the death penalty: "death is already awaiting this girl; what a strange attraction does the look of death have." After listing the names of all legal personnel and members of Zahra's and Mahin's families, and describing the large crowd of spectators (one report claimed that people lined up in the early morning every day to get in and that every day more than two hundred people were turned away), the reporter noted: "All is ready: the lawyers, the clients, the judge, the angel of justice, and the book of law. . . . The only person absent from this spectacular scene is Zahra. It is she who should scream from her grave, 'Mahin! Why did you kill me?' but the dead have no voice. . . ."[46]

Not only did *Zan-i ruz* use melodramatic language in its reports, it also described Mahin's last defense as "a skillful defense, which was a dense summary of an exceptional and very tragic novel—a novel of which perhaps only one chapter was read in court, making everyone weep."[47] Not only Zahra's mother and her sisters, but also Mahin's family members, were described as uncontrollably sobbing at various moments during the eight-day trial. And the spectators and even the prison guards were reported to cry loudly.

Although the defense lawyers may not have agreed on how to categorize Mahin, both rejected homosexuality as the cause of crime and focused instead on temporary insanity and mental disorder. The spectators also offered both versions: some considered her guilty, some sick. Many considered Mahin's father, 'Abbas Padidarnazar, the real responsible party.

Malikzadah sought to build his defense on the basis of the mental and physiological disorder. He asked the court to invite a team of doctors to examine Mahin physically and psychologically. Mu'tamidi, another defense lawyer, similarly called his client a mental patient (*bimar-i ravani*). Through a reading of letters and notebooks, he portrayed the relationship between Mahin and Zari as intensely affectionate, but not sexual. He claimed that Mahin had committed the crime when she was menstruating. Mu'tamidi's court statement, as reported in the press, is worth quoting at length:

> Mahin was born in Lahijan and went to school at the age of six; her parents have little accurate information about her childhood. I spoke with her mother; she does not remember Mahin ever playing with dolls, she was never interested in girls' games. She was a playfully devilish [*shaytan*] girl but very intelligent and studious. She continued through the third grade in Pirbazari school in Lahijan and then was moved to another school. From the fifth grade, that is, when her puberty was setting in and her personality was shaping, her temperament and her psyche suddenly changed such that she flunked the fifth grade. . . . She failed in high school as well. . . . Her father took her to Tehran, but there too she quarreled with teachers and students and they returned to Lahijan. . . . Her nurturing environment was not a balanced one. She said her father was too busy to pay attention to the children but that she loved her mother a lot. . . . I checked with Dr. Ladan, Rasht's Legal Medical doctor. I asked him, considering Lahijan's climate, at what age girls begin to menstruate. He responded between eleven and twelve years of age. . . . But Mahin did not menstruate at ten, nor at fifteen, because her body's organism is not proper, she is ill . . . she has an extra chromosome. She told me in jail that she had something like a one-day light menstruation but even that one day put her in an insane state of mind. . . . [T]he day she committed injury with a knife, she was in the same abnormal state. . . . My client's character began to change radically; . . . at fourteen her situation ceased to be one of a woman; she began to wear male trousers and jacket, carry prayer beads [*tasbih*] and a knife, and imitate male gestures, wishing to become an army officer or a policeman on a motorcycle. Can she be considered a man then? No. . . . I say she has a masculine personality, a personality that has not been shaped properly. . . . I reject the charge of sexual deviancy and *homosexualité*. I say she has double personality. She has personality deviancy not sexual deviancy.[48]

Mu'tamidi requested that Mahin be granted a psychological examination. In support of his request, he produced a letter written by Mahin, dated April 15, 1973 (eight months before the crime), to her brother in Germany asking his help to change sex, "Help me if you can, I cannot be a woman." Mr. Mu'tamidi concluded his plea in these words: "When I ask Mahin to talk about Zahra, she speaks so eloquently and beautifully and uses such metaphors and similitude it is as if I am talking with a Victor Hugo, a Lamartine, or I am hearing the songs of Bilitis from her tongue."[49]

The presiding judge rejected Mu'tamidi's request for a new medical and psychological examination. Mahin herself went along with her lawyers, declaring herself "ill and a nervous wreck," but emphasized that after Zahra's death, life was immaterial to her and she was prepared for any punishment. On the fifth day of trial, another lawyer, 'Abbas Danishkhvah, took up the defense. His statements reportedly "made the spectators and the accused weep a great deal." He addressed Zahra's mother, "Respectable Lady, if Mahin's execution would heal your grieving heart, I am authorized to tell you that Mahin is ready to die." Then addressing Mahin, he said: "You, whose whole being is saturated with the infinite power of love, I admire your courage. If death is what is awaiting you, go to it with open arms" (severe weeping of the spectators and Mahin). Then he addressed the public prosecutor: "Your indictment is against Mahin, but the indictment of public opinion is otherwise. You ought to put on trial Zahra and her family; you ought to put on trial the owners of commercial classes, summer remedial institutes, doctors of the Legal Medical board, lawyers of the judiciary—in other words, all who in the court of public opinion are thought to be factors in this crime. Then he pointed his finger to Mahin's father. "You are the first accused person in this case, not your daughter. Someone who in Hotel Abshar . . . holds feasts every night and hosts female dancers [raqqasah-ha]." What is fault of Mahin, who has grown up under this person's supervision? . . . He then talked about Zahra's father and his real estate deals, an occupation that deprived his family and children of his supervision and education. The abnormal love letters sent by Mahin to Zahra were not one, two, or ten. Zahra's family had seen these letters and confessed that they did not pay any attention. 'Abbas Danishkhvah then addressed the spectators, "What are you doing in this court? Go back home and inspect your daughters' and sons' private papers." It is society that is guilty in this affair.[50]

In her own defense, Mahin spoke at length. She blamed her family who gave her everything she asked for but not love and care. When she was twelve, she began to feel that there was something wrong with her, but was too scared to discuss it with her family; she feared that they would laugh at her. One day she decided to take matters into her own hands and went to a doctor.

> The doctor scolded me and said, "Don't you have a mother or a father? Why are you here alone? Don't waste my time." See how my pride was wounded?
> . . . Then one day I wrote a letter to my brother asking him to find a psycholo-

gist for me. He showed the letter to my parents, . . . I became the laughing stock of the family. All our relatives now knew that Mahin fell in love with girls. . . . Who could I turn to in order to discuss my illness? . . . until November 11, 1971, when I met Zari. I felt she was exactly what I had expected all these years. I attached myself strongly to Zari. My only companion and soulmate was Zari. . . . We sought solace in each other. She gave me hope in life.

Mahin then went over the story of A'zam's love for her, her fidelity to Zahra, and her rejection of A'zam's demands. To demonstrate that the love between her and Zahra was mutual, she reported that once a forty-five-year-old man had asked for Zahra's hand in marriage. Zahra called Mahin and went over to her place in tears, saying that her family were all for this marriage. Asked by Mahin how she had responded, Zahra had sworn that if they tried to force her into marrying anyone, young or old, she would come to Mahin so that they could commit suicide together.

Mahin concluded by begging to be taken, even if only for one hour, to Zari's grave . . . which she called their joint grave. She asked for all Zari's letters, and ended by reciting a poem she had composed for Zari:

In a small town, the daughter of the king of Peris had died.
When the news of her death spread in the town, all the people of the town
   went to take sanctuary in their houses.
Each person sat in a corner in mourning.
The sky was surly [akhmu], it rained, and rained, and rained.
The sea was screaming, and wailing.
Flowers wilted away. Everyone was silent and sad.
The townspeople considered one person guilty. Each holding a stone,
   waited for her.
One day, she appeared in the town.
Everyone began hurling stones at her.
But she, paying no attention to their stones, went to the graveyard.
See, they didn't know that she was also dead.
Those unaware people were throwing stones at a dead body.
The day the daughter of the king of Peris had died, she had died with her.
They were throwing stones at a dead body.
A body that walked, but had no soul, had no heart.
Throw stones, o' people!
Throw stones, throw stones! Perhaps your hearts will be lightened.
But what is the use?
Regrets, regrets, regrets [pashimuni]![51]

Mahin reportedly could not finish her defense and began to weep uncontrollably. The trial came to a close on July 25, 1974. Mahin received a life sentence.[52]

## What Was in a Name?

"Mahin, from a sexual point, are you a girl or a boy?" Sekandari had asked Mahin. She had responded by confirming: "I swear [*baba, vallah billah*] that I am a girl."

> Sekandari: From a psychological point of view, do you consider yourself a boy or a girl?
>
> Mahin: I have always considered myself psychologically a boy. . . . It isn't my fault that nature has created me this way.
>
> Sekandari: Have you ever wished to become one hundred percent a boy through surgery?
>
> Mahin: Yes, many times . . . I took some steps in that regard as well, I went to doctors, but it didn't go anywhere. . . .
>
> Sekandari: Mahin, is it true that you are a same-sex-player? Are you a *lesbian*?
>
> Mahin: Yes I am, but it isn't my fault, I don't take pride in it, but I like girls and same-sex-playing.[53]

Mahin embraced the labels offered her by the reporters and here referred to herself as a same-sex-player, a lesbian, and as a girl-in-body, a boy psychologically. The press, however, continued to debate whether she were a same-sex-player or a *dau-shakhsiyati* (of double personality). Dau-shakhsiyati was an ambiguous category, at times used to refer euphemistically to bi-/homosexuals.[54] Faridun Farrukhzad, a popular entertainer of the period who was known for his homosexual (as well as heterosexual) relationships, was sometimes referred to as dau-shakhsiyati.[55] At the same time, this term also had begun to be used to refer to transsexuals, distinguishing them, though not always consistently, from *dau-jinsiyati*, which was a term more often used for intersex individuals.

The press ran headlines indicating no uncertainty that Mahin was a same-sex-player and, moreover, that this was the motive for the murder she committed. At the same time, and especially around the trial, they began to report on her as dau-shakhsiyati, distinguishing this category from that of same-sex-player. *Ittila'at*'s headline, for instance, ran: "Mahin is a double-personality patient not a sexual deviant."[56] It reported Mahin's letter to her brother Sirus Padidarnazar, then in Germany: "There is something I want to discuss with you, but I am embarrassed. This embarrassment has taken me close to death several times. I want to change sex. Dear Sirus, don't ridicule me. If you can, help me. I can't be a woman."

The timing mattered. In Iran of 1973–74, transsexuality was still too new a topic to constitute a taken-for-granted category upon which lawyers could build a criminal defense. Nonetheless, the previous decades' emerging psycho-medical literature on transsexuality, as well as its vernacular circulation, was well enough known for Mahin's lawyers to plot a narrative of her childhood development as a case of "gender identity disorder" and, on that basis, to plea for treatment instead of punishment.

The press was more muddled than the lawyers on whether homosexuality and transsexuality were distinct or the same phenomena. When *Zan-i ruz* ran the text of Mahin's letter to her brother in a prominent box, it was prefaced: "It has now been proven that Mahin . . . has one hundred percent homosexual tendencies and on a few occasions she has even tried to change sex."[57] In this articulation, Mahin's expressed desire for sex change simply provided evidence of her same-sex orientation. The magazine criticized the court for its unwill-ingness to open up the issue of female same-sex-playing, even though it had been raised repeatedly in the proceedings. At the same time, it took issue with the defense lawyer who had based his defense on Mahin's being "of two person-alities." More than rejecting a distinct diagnosis, however, the magazine was against the categorization of "Mahin's condition" as a biopsychological one; it insisted that the condition was caused by ignorance and the failure of parental care, the irresponsibility of school authorities, and outdated social norms.[58] Be-yond "individual treatment," it called for radical social rethinking and reform of the gender/sexual life of the country through enlightened policies, such as introducing sex education and coeducation in the country's schools.

This larger social argument was carved in part through the space that the Mahin/Zahra story shared with the other two crimes of the same months. With one of these it shared the crime-of-passion plot, with the other, deviant insanity. These three cases not only overlapped in time and shared press space, but explicit links were made among them.

As noted earlier, Mahin's trial coincided with another crime-of-passion trial, this one heterosexual. The continued bordering of the reports and pic-tures of the two cases — not only by their topical proximity but also by their spa-tial arrangement on the printed page — as well as explicit comparisons between the two, informed the construction of the Mahin/Zahra relationship and more generally that of (female) homosexuality through a heterosexual template. The opening paragraph of *Ittila'at* read: "While the trial of Anushirvan Razzaq-manish and his death sentence is still on people's tongues, another shocking trial is coming to its critical days."[59]

Razzaq-manish's case had the common element of a spurned lover turned murderer. As a heterosexual crime of passion, a crime to do with Tehran high society, the Hijazi/Razzaq-manish case had a substantively different sensationalism and a different appeal to readers. Indeed, while the Mahin/Zahra case soon drifted into obscurity and public forgetfulness, there were plans afoot to produce Hijazi/Razzaq-manish's story as a film.[60] Mahin's trial coincided with Razzaq-manish's appeal of his death sentence. On July 23, 1974, *Ittila'at* boxed both cases on its front page. On the day that Mahin's trial ended and her lawyers filed an appeal against her life sentence, Razzaq-manish's death sentence also was appealed. The two shared headlines in the "Events" pages of the dailies.[61]

As we already saw, *Zan-i ruz* drew an explicit parallel between the two cases to make its case for extensive coverage of what one reader had objected to as "too much sex." As "sexual crimes," they were treated as belonging to the same category. The murderers' criminal acts were the symptom of diseased persons: in one case, the disease of sadism, in the other, the disease of double personality/same-sex-playing. *Ittila'at-i banuvan* similarly introduced its coverage in these terms: "Mahin Padidarnazar's trial, on the heels of the Fayyaz and Razzaq-manish trials, is among the sensational [*janjali*] trials of Iran's judiciary these days."[62]

Fayyaz's case was the other story that produced surprising thematic overlaps with the Mahin/Zahra story. The first reports of Fayyaz's story appeared in the "Events" section of the dailies in mid-October 1973.[63] It was a gruesome case, in which Fayyaz Parhizi had killed his own wife and five children along with his brother Ayaz's wife and two children. Coverage of this crime was included in the reports of the Mahin/Zahra case, even though they were different in almost every respect, not simply because they were both sensational, although they certainly were. But Fayyaz's defense lawyer also based his defense on insanity. He presented to the court a long narrative about Fayyaz's life that hinted that his mental disorder was related to his brother's forcing him to get married; among his other symptoms, including his hallucinations that bordered on madness, readers were told that "he sees all the feminine qualities in himself and feels that he had become a girl."[64]

It is important to note that in both cases, although same-sex-playing was disavowed by lawyers, cross-sex/gender identification was emerging as a condition from which a defense in criminal cases could be launched publicly. This is the same period in which reports of sex change in Iran or abroad increasingly circulated in the dailies. Indeed, in the same issue of *Zan-i ruz* that ran the last part of its three-segment coverage of Mahin's trial, interspaced with that coverage, there was another noteworthy article: "Summary of an astonishing book, written by a former man, *How I became a woman*." The article featured news of Jan Morris's book ("every page of this exceptional book reveals strange secrets about dau-jinsi [two-sexed] people") and included several pages of excerpts from the book, along with numerous photographs.[65]

During the same months that *Zan-i ruz* had put female homosexuality under critical scrutiny, the rival weekly *Ittila'at-i banuvan* ran its eight-week coverage (January 9 to February 27, 1974) of the happy "wondrous, extraordinary, unbelievable but true" story of an MtF transsexual, Rashil (Rachel, formerly Sa'id) Sa'idzadeh. I will discuss Rashil's story more fully in the next chapter.

The extensive coverage of the story of Mahin and Zahra took the discussion of (female) homosexuality, linked with transsexuality, out of the little segments buried in health columns, marital advice books, and translations of popular psychology books and put it into mass circulation as never before. Terms such as *girl-on-girl-playing* and *same-sex-playing* became printable in women's weeklies, to be distinguished from a more scientifically usable coined word: *same-sex orientation (hamjins-gara'i)*—a word that has stayed with us both as a psycho-sexological categorization and as a category for self-identification. While *Zan-i ruz* and the rest of the popular press may have aspired to use this story as a text of admonishment and an occasion for the advocacy of enlightened cultural reform concerning sexuality, that disciplinary project was dependent on producing hamjins-gara'i as a popularly available knowledge—a knowing that could be appropriated by readers as well. One self-identified lesbian from a southern town, now in her early fifties, recalled, "I was about fifteen years old at the time. I read the story in *Kayhan* or *Ittila'at*, as well as other magazines. I remember the title, 'A same-sex-playing girl killed another girl.' Since I was a lesbian, I took special interest in the story and followed it closely." Some thirty-five years later, when this conversation took place in the United States where the narrator had lived for many years, she remembered much of the story, articulated through differently available categories, such as "tomboy": "This incident happened in the north, Mahin was a tomboy. She was born to a family with four brothers and this last one, Mahin, was a girl. Mahin's family was in the hotel industry. Mahin acted like boys, and fell in love with the neighbor's daughter, Zahra. The family of the girl found out and wanted to send Mahin to Germany, but she didn't want to go and when [Mahin] heard that they were marrying Zahra off, she knifed Zahra. The authorities put Mahin in jail. Mahin wanted to have a sex change."[66]

Perhaps even more importantly, beyond the scale of circulation (national dailies) and the distinct character of the readership, this story was a local, indeed provincial, story. Mahin and Zahra, along with the women's subculture that was mapped through these reports, could not even be dismissed as northern Tehrani "corruption." They came to stand for a national phenomenon — "our lesbians," not some Euro-American curiosity, not psycho-sexological cases analyzed in scientific textbooks or health pages of magazines, nor translations of "foreign" science or "alien" cultures. The Lahijan world of women's friendships, erotic attachments, and sexual relations were ours to own, understand, reform, but certainly not to deny. The Mahin/Zahra story "nativized" vernacular psycho-sexology, particularly as it pertained to (female) homosexuality. Female homosexuality was no longer about Euro-American sexual libertinism, Sappho, or peculiar hormonal imbalances with which biomedical science was concerned. It became about our own here and now, about the lives of our own female adolescents — it became locally urgent.

Framed as a story centered on Mahin's masculinity, the popularized narrative projected Mahin's desire for sex change as a possibility that might have prevented the deadly tragedy. Combined with the stories of Rashil Sa'idzadeh and other sex change reports of the period, the Mahin/Zahra coverage contributed to the consolidation of the mapping of several distinct notions about sexuality that continue to inform, to the present day, bio-psychological-ethical discourse on homo- and transsexuality in Iran.

The concept of "true homosexuality" emerged in Iran in this period. Unlike the earlier modernists' conception, this discourse did not assume heterosexuality as the only true human condition; it distinguished transient homosexual desire from true homosexuality. The former was considered part of the normal and natural process of developmental growth; its continued adult state was a symptom of developmental failure that was largely attributed to parental and family life, although occasionally homosocializing practices also were targeted as contributory causes. This failed state could be corrected with the help of psychologists. There was more mystery connected to the true homosexual, a presumably small minority who could not be treated at all. Only expert psychologists could diagnose a true homosexual. Such persons had to be taken seriously because their moral/psychic deviancy was associated with high rates of crime and suicide as well as other psychopathic behavior. It was here that some began to think of sex change as a potential remedy, though this remained a very unclear association. Nobody seemed to know what this connection might be. Yet the very concept of "true" came to inform the concept of transsexuality in later decades as well. As discussed in chapter 1, today's diagnostic and treatment practices of transsexuality are pivoted around distinguishing "true transsexuals" from others. The distinction between a transient moral/psychic deviancy and the true innate one continues to inform notions of homo- and transsexuality among both Islam-therapists and mainstream behavioral and clinical psychologists.

Although in the 1940s and 1950s transsexuality had remained largely indistinct from intersexuality, by the 1970s its transition to an affiliation with homosexuality seemed to be complete. Over the last years of the decade and then again from the early 1990s, a clearer line of differentiation between transsexuality and homosexuality would emerge; nonetheless, they were thought to have important "family resemblances," a resemblance that continues to define the parameters of discourse on transsexuality.

This realignment of transsexuality from intersexuality to homosexuality did not serve it well: From a family resemblance to an inborn congenital condition, it moved under the shadow of a stigmatized (especially for aspiring MtFs) deviant sexuality and decadent practices. Correspondingly, the subject of transsexuality shifted from medical curiosity and scientific achievement to shady lives and poor reputation. This may, in part, have contributed to the Medical Council of Iran's decision to ban sex-change operations in 1976, as we will see in the next chapter.

## "AROUND" 1979  *Gay Tehran?*

Tehran in the early 1970s offered a spectrum of overlapping conceptions of maleness and masculinities. This spectrum structured everyday practices of life with regard to nonheteronormative male gender/sexual desires, and it construed nonheteronormative maleness as being at once criminal, immoral, and theatrical. This chapter offers a preliminary mapping of that scene. It is not, and cannot be, a social history of "gay Tehran." Although the available scholarly writing on this topic agrees on the existence of an "active gay subculture"[1] in 1970s Tehran, this literature is anecdotal, and the critical archival and ethnographic research necessary to produce an informed history remains yet to be done. But I also want to argue that to name the 1970s as the decade of a *gay* Tehran obscures important in-distinctions between what is now named gay (always considered male in this context by all writers on the topic) and what is now considered MtF trans. My purpose is thus to offer an initial mapping of the complex overlaps and connections between these lives. I want to trace continuities across the "before" and "after" of the 1979 revolution, as well as note the ruptures introduced by regime change into the scene of nonheteronormative males. Simply casting the advent of the Islamic Republic as the brutal end of gay Tehran does not do justice to the complexity of the tale.

The story of "gay Tehran" in the 1970s has been articulated in at least two domains. At the time, there were a number of articles about Tehran's "gay scene" in the American gay press. Jerry Zarit's article at the end of the decade put it succinctly: "Iran was for me, and for others like me, a sexual paradise. In terms of both quantity and quality it was the most exciting experience of my life."² Not all reports shared Zarit's enthusiasm. David Reed's article was more sobering.³ By the time of its publication, the idea of "Tehran as gay paradise" must have been circulating widely; Reed was writing a tale of warning against this backdrop: ". . . legend has it that gay sex is big in Teheran. On my way overland from India last year I heard straight travelers' tales of 'queer Iranians.' After un-gay India I couldn't wait. A New York friend of mine heard similar hot tales last month while researching a Teheran job offer. He's as excited now as I was then. He shouldn't be. For his sake and for anyone else gay considering work or play among the Persians, I'll tell my tale of Teheran. In seven months there I survived rape, robbery, and what an Iranian called romance."⁴ Unlike many previous rosy pictures, Reed wrote, "Iranian homosexuals hide in their closets. Or they are hidden in prisons. . . . Iran punishes it [sodomy] with severe jail sentences. . . . Paranoia pervades what little public gay life exists in Tehe-ran."⁵ After writing at length about several bars and baths, he summarized his experience in these words: "And such is the myth of gay Iran. Hot air."⁶ Para-dise or hell, the American gay press after 1979 began to report on the extermi-nation of Tehran gay life by the Islamic Republic.⁷ There is an implicit progres-sivist dynamic to these stories: The emerging gay subculture of Tehran would have led naturally to a livelier, more open gay Tehran, except that its life was cut short by the 1979 revolution and the subsequent Islamization of society.

A second domain for the formation of the gay Tehran story has been within Iranian diasporic gay communities, some of whose members lived in Iran in the 1970s.⁸ But their recollections are narrated through later gay identifica-tion developed in their new homes, which, in the 1980s and 1990s, when much of this immigration took place, were dominated by a particular style of sexual identity politics. The Iranian gay diasporic progressivist narrative was informed by this contingent dominance. Through the lens of later identities, earlier sexual and gender subjectivities and practices began to be seen as prob-lematic and backward.

From its earliest manifestation in the diasporic press, Iranian gay iden-tity marked its emergence through a dis-identification with that past. This included a clear demarcation between *hamjins-gara'i* (same-sex inclination/orientation) and *hamjins-bazi* (same-sex-playing).⁹ The former has been em-braced as a modern form of identification that outwardly expresses a true inner self; hamjins-bazi, on the other hand, has been disavowed, perhaps because of its pejorative use by government officials, in condemnatory religious texts, in pathologizing contexts by medical professionals, or in hostile general usage within Iranian society and culture at large. This disavowal of hamjins-bazi has been articulated through turning the societal and cultural abjection back onto the concept itself: they disavow same-sex-playing due to its presumed abusive character and its being marked by disparities of age and economics. This is in contrast to same-sex-oriented relations (characterized as hamjins-gara'i) that allow for genuinely egalitarian romantic relationships among same-sex partners.[10] The differentiating move between hamjins-gara'i and hamjins-bazi thus articulates a homonormative response to an antiheteronormative project.[11]

The imagining of gay Tehran worked differently in these two domains. For the growing gay liberation movement of the 1970s in the United States, traveling to "gay Tehran," in fiction or in person, was a search for one's "own kind" beyond national borders. In that sense, it fit well with liberationist dreams of the internationalization of activism and with solidarity work based on "finding the same everywhere" (as in, "Sisterhood is Global").[12]

Within diasporic Iranian gay activist politics, imagining the gay Tehran of the 1970s provided a critical intervention in the Iranian cultural politics of denial that insisted on the foreignness of non-normative gender/sexual desires and practices. My point here is not to question the sociological existence of such non-normative desires and practices, but to suggest, rather, that imagining them and the period of 1970s as *gay* may prevent other, equally pertinent ways of thinking about the scene of male non-normative gender/sexuality during that decade. Actively un-familiarizing ourselves with what already has been read through the prism of gay Tehran would, I hope, open up the possibility of seeing differently, and asking different questions about, nonheteronormative practices of life at that time. Furthermore, the dominant narrative of the 1970s as gay Tehran has contributed to the notion of a sharp rupture with the 1980s, making the 1979 revolution into a radically transformative event, obscuring important continuities and different sorts of discontinuities.

### The Spectacle of Unmanly Males

The gay Tehran I wish to reread was part of a complex, rapidly growing urban society, in certain domains of which particular styles of nonheteronormative male lives were becoming somewhat visible. This was particularly the case in the growing entertainment industry, which ran the gamut from modern film and television shows to nightclubs that catered to a range of class-inflected tastes. "Lower class" clubs were performance venues that sustained older and more traditional forms of male dance and entertainment, while the performance of such dances in newer, more cosmopolitan nightclubs, and in film, made them more visible to a layer of the urban middle-class population that may not have been exposed to them in earlier decades; indeed, the urban middle class may well have developed its sense of modernness in part from the disavowal of such cultural enactments.

Mahin's masculinity (chapter 3) was a strange yet familiar sight. Stories of females living unusual masculine lives were told in history books and in neighborhood gossip. In the more recent period of the 1950s through the 1970s, newspapers and magazines had become another site of such stories. Females living masculine lives fascinated the public. *Khvandaniha*, under the headline, "This woman works as a porter in men's clothes in Amin al-Sultan Square," reported:

> "People who live and work there know her [Sughrá Valizadeh] as 'Abdallah and do not know she is a woman. She says that she and her sister had worked as midwives for some thirty years, but the Ministry of Health—because they were not certified—stopped them from practicing. 'After a few months of unemployment, I got myself a job in a drug den [*shirah'kishkhanah*], but then the government closed them down; thankfully I could kick the habit I had picked up there and am now healthy and strong.' She says after presenting for jobs as a woman with no success she decided to don men's clothes and started working here and no one knows that."[13]

In many of these cases, especially in the women's press of the 1960s, the stories of females living masculine lives would be rescued from the suspicion of "improper sexuality" through the affirmation of the modern marriage ideal, the failure of which had pushed women into these unusual paths. Alternatively, economic hardship and the social inhospitality of many professions to women were said to have forced the choice of masculine living (see figure 4.1 and its caption).

It is seductive to read these stories as tales of resistance against compulsory heterosexuality. Reading them through a related, but not identical, lens of the "marriage imperative" offers a different possibility. As I have suggested in the introduction and will discuss at more length in chapter 7, getting married was, and continues to be, a life-cycle social expectation, without which one does not become an adult in others' and possibly in one's own perception. The marriage imperative, when not reduced to compulsory heterosexuality, often has been discussed as a reproductive demand or a requirement of gender conformity. Tze-Ian D. Sang's perceptive and historically rich analysis, for instance, raises similar issues vis-à-vis the collapse of the marriage imperative into compulsory heterosexuality. She focuses largely on its work for the production of normative womanhood.[14] But men are as expected to get married as women. I do not

FIGURE 4.1. Guli, a young woman who has worked as a man for years "as a porter and a bus driver. . . . At the age of forty, she has not yet got married. . . . She loves her work and hates marriage. Who knows what events have made her be so skeptical about men!?" *Khvandaniha*, May 28, 1968; story based on a report in *Ittila'at-i banuvan*.

گلی دختر استو کار میکند، کاوی که خیلی از مردهااز
زیرش درمیروند، گلی نزدیک بچهل سال داردو هنوزشوهر
نکرده است . اواز سالها پیش آن بکارهای مردانه داده و
وسیله باربری و راننده گی آتوبوس امرار معاش میکند . در
ایستگاه دروازه قوجان نام گلیورد زبان همه است ،اوعاشق
کار استو ازازدواج بیزار اگس جصداند چماجرای موجب
این بدبینی او نسبت بجنس مرد شده است ؟؟

deny the workings of these other demands, but suggest that there is something more. The adulthood of everyone is bound to marriage. It is almost incomprehensible that someone would wish not to marry.

If we assume that the key imperative is not the taboo of homosexuality (compulsory heterosexuality) but rather the marriage imperative, then the pressure on women and men was/is not so much not to have sex with "their own sex" as not to become resistant to marriage, not to resist the dominant determinant of one's life plot. Many mothers, for instance, could identify with, and even take (hidden) pride in, their daughter's urge for some degree of masculine behavior. Fathers may similarly appreciate the subtext of the desirability of masculinity. All this parental tolerance, if not pride, would slowly fade into anxiety and eventually into pressure if a non-normative daughter did not grow out of these tendencies by her twenties and if the early signs of masculinity translated into a refusal to marry. To really get out of the marriage imperative, a woman would have to enact a surfeit of resistance; that is, a degree of over-performance of masculinity by a woman could let her off the hook, with the family giving up on her as a woman. This usually means losing familial protection; it means possibly being shunned and feeling forced to move away and to actually live as a man, to make a living as a man, and possibly to live in men's clothes. When the cases of females living as men could not be subsumed into dominant narratives of forced marriages, abusive husbands, or economic hardship, they would be presented as bizarre exceptions, verging on insanity. This was the case of the two sisters from Qazvin, sixty-one and sixty-five years old, who had lived the previous forty-five years of their lives in an abandoned Qajar-era fort, largely cut off from the outside world. Even in this case, they were said, as highly educated women of their time, to have opted for this life to refuse unwanted marriages.[15]

The trouble with Mahin's style of masculinity was that she had not only combined her masculinity with same-sex desire, but she also was reported to have recruited other young women to engage in non-normative sexual practices and disrupted marriages. She had pressured Zahra to refuse her family's entertainment of marriage proposals and disrupted the marital harmony of her married friends by providing them with an alternative object of desire and sexual pleasure. She had "overdone" female masculinity.

The acceptable configuration of public female non-normative gender self-styling (up to the limit of marriage disruption) did not have an equivalent for males: males who did not wish to marry or could not perform their "marital duties" could not get away from their social obligations through a surfeit of feminine performance.

In earlier times, dressing as a woman and opting for a womanly career could mean "housewifery," that is, becoming a male kept by another man.[16] By the mid-twentieth century, such behavior would have added scandalous shame to the insult and injury of refusing adult manhood. Males who wanted to *live* womanly lives tended to keep it a secret, fearing censure and punishment. Such was the fate of a male person who had worked for nineteen years as a female masseur in a women's public bath.[17] In another case, a male person who had lived and worked for the previous fifty years as a woman was forced into men's clothes, with her hair shaved off her head.[18] In yet another case, a male person refused to leave the hospital in men's clothes after her forced "disambiguating sex-surgery" and declared her intention to continue living a womanly life.[19] These reports never had any admiring or approving edge to them; rather, they were cause for apprehension and incomprehension.

A less scandalous report about "the young man who dresses and behaves in a completely contrary fashion," who wore his hair long and was a dancer, constituted an exception: He was thought to stand out like "a red bean on the surface of rice pudding." He was a spectacle. *Khvandaniha*'s lengthy account was made possible in part by displacing his contrarian self-presentation onto his "unusual background"—of an Azarbaijani father and a mother from Istanbul.[20] The report vacillated in tone, sometimes sympathetically presenting the "young man" as a philosophically oriented intellectual, at other times as a weird recluse, and sometimes as someone whose unconventional self-presentation produced unwanted social reaction: He was followed by curious street kids who made fun of him; he had been arrested twice for appearing inappropriately in public. A line drawing of his face (compared with a full-stature photograph) made his face appear more female by emphasizing his plucked eyebrows and giving him fuller hair (figures 4.2 and 4.3). The sketch performed a "distancing mimicry" that pulled him toward a woman-presenting male, imagining the "contrarian young man" as an out-of-place character and presumably explaining his street harassment.

He was said to have eventually opted for a more routine life, making his living by opening a sandwich shop on Maulavi Street in a popular southern Tehran neighborhood. His "strange" style of public self-presentation and his former chosen profession (a dancer with an Azarbaijani dance troupe) positioned him on the border of social tolerance: men as dancers or performers of female roles in theatrical and, more recently, cinematic roles.

The figure of the male performer or dancer has a long history in Iran. Anthony Shay's numerous essays offer us a rich conceptual vocabulary for understanding the cultural work of this figure and its history, not only for the Tehran of the 1970s but also into the present. Several of his propositions are pertinent here. He challenges "the romantic views that many gay men hold that the presence of male dancers and the sexual interest expressed toward them by Middle Eastern men somehow constitutes evidence for an environment accepting of homosexuality and a utopian gay paradise," and "the oft-expressed viewpoint that male dancers were imitating or parodying women. . . . The presence of male dancers, professional and nonprofessional, in public and private space requires a (re)evaluation of the meaning of these male bodies."[21] Shay argues that in the 1970s in Iran, modern choreographers attempted to eradicate traces of the earlier male choreographic tradition by creating what he calls hypermasculine styles of movement for male dancers, often within "folk dance" choreographies, "suitable to the urban Westernized male and their sensitive elite audiences."[22] As he notes, the older style of male dancers continued their performances in "the gritty underworld" of nightclubs and cafés. Indeed, "[i]n the late 1960s and early 1970s a wave of nostalgia for Qajar-era [before 1925] performing and decorative styles swept through Tehran, where a number

قیافه‌ای متفکر گریه‌والی بلنــد دارد او
میگوید دردنیا همه‌چیز دراطراف وجود
من دور میزند

FIGURES 4.2 AND 4.3. Both these images are
from *Khvandaniha*, January 29, 1955.

میگوید وقتی بااین لباس مخصوص در
خیابا؟ دراه‌میروم مردم کوچه‌ای مرا آسوده
نمیگذار ندبهمین لحاظناگزیرم همواره از
نقاط خلوت رفت و آمد کنم

of cafés sprang up in which former boy dancers, now elderly but still capable performers, appeared."[23] The sharp contrasts between the two modes of male dance performance, Shay concludes, point to "the underlying changes in attitudes toward sexuality and gender."[24]

For the emerging urban middle class, the more traditional male dancer and entertainer may have come to mark lower-class taste and were tainted with the immorality of suspected sexual availability. The male dancer and *zan-push* (woman-attired) male actors, however, not only continued to occupy the café entertainment scene and some of the more "gritty" nightclubs, but the figure of the zan-push got a new, somewhat more respectable, life in the growing cinema and theater productions.[25]

The dominant style of the zan-push was what Beeman calls "pretend mimic," that is, looking like a woman but achieving a "distance" from the female through exaggeration of clothing, makeup, the high pitch of the voice, and body movements. What cultural spaces did this "distance" provide in the 1940s and 1950s? This was a style of performance that accommodated significant traffic, even then, between the worlds of stage and screen and the ongoing public conversations about sex change.

In 1955, for example, *Khvandaniha* published in its regular "Album of Artists" page a picture of the actor 'Ali Tabish, dressed as a woman, along with a commentary entitled "Is this a man or a woman?" (figure 4.4):

> You have frequently read in the press that in such and such corner of the world, for example in Europe or America, a woman or a man was fed up with her/his own (sex!) and with a surgery her/his constitution was changed.
>
> This (twentieth-century whim) has not yet found adherents in Iran, so the man you see in this picture in women's clothes, standing with special coquettishness, is our very own famous actor 'Ali Tabish. Since he hasn't had any luck with manhood, he decided to don for a few hours the attire of (devil's apprentices), not in street and public but in the play (*Charley's Aunt*) in which he plays the role of a capricious woman.[26]

Zan-push performances were included in many films that in a later period were called "FilmFarsi." Among these are *Madmuazil Khalah* (Ms. Auntie, 1957, Amin Amini) with 'Ali Tabish playing the aunt figure; *Zalim-bala* (translated on the film posters as The Naughty Girl, 1957, Siamak Yasami); and Shabaji Khanum (1958, Sadiq Bahrami). The anxiety in the mid-1950s over waking up as the other sex also was reflected in the satirical 1959 film, *'Arus Kudumah?* (Which one is the bride?, Farrukh Ghaffari).[27]

As Beeman notes, "Sexuality is also an important undertone for the 'mi-

آلبوم هنرمندان

مرد است یا زن؟

بارها در مطبوعات خوانده‌اید
که فلان گوشه دنیا مثلا در اروپا یا
امریکا خانم یا آقائی از (جنس !)
خودش سیر شد و با یک عمل جراحی
ماهیت اورا عوض کردند .

این (هوس قرن بیستم) هنوز در
ایران طرفدار پیدا نکرده است و
آقائی را که در این عکس ملاحظه
میکنید لباس زنانه پوشیده و با ناز و
کرشمه مخصوص ایستاده مال مملکت
خودمان است ، علی تابش هنرپیشه
معروف چون از مردی خیری ندیده
بود تصمیم گرفت چند ساعتی هم جامه
(شاگردان شیطان) را در بر کند ولی
نه در اجتماع و خیابان بلکه در
نمایشنامه (خاله چارلی) که رل یک زن
هوس باز را بعهده گرفت .

FIGURE 4.4. 'Ali Tabish as Charley's aunt. *Khvandaniha*, October 1, 1955.

metic' female portrayers. . . . Since these actors, with few exceptions, claim to be fully heterosexual males, this situation can be an uncomfortable social position for them."[28] This "uncomfortable social position" was much murkier for male dancers who performed in the "gritty world" of nightclubs. Along with the more respectable reports of "Album of Artists," *Khvandaniha* (and other magazines) would also publish alarming reports, with lurid photographs, about the nightclub life of Tehran (as well as major European cities), emphasizing that these spaces were populated by men dressing up as women to exploit male clients.[29] They produced a steamy and seamy nightlife designed to rob hard-working citizens by luring them with the temptations of alcoholic drinks, entertaining music and dances, and "available" male and female singers and dancers. According to one 1954 report, there were a total of 332 cafés and restaurants in Tehran, only a dozen of which offered musical and dance performances. These were said to be largely clustered in two areas of Tehran, by this time known for their more "gritty" nightlife—Lalah-zar and the district around Shahr-i nau (Tehran's red-light district). The report further implied an overlap between sex work and the entertainment offered in these nightclubs by describing several of them as run by women named "Khanum," a designation often used, in this context, for women who bossed their own group of sex workers. The report included several photographs of performers and clients, including one of a male dancer, Baqir Namazi (figure 4.5).[30]

At times, a male dancer would attract public attention accidentally—often in the context of charges of "taking advantage" (ighfal, a word with a high sexual charge) of men or of scuffles leading to injuries and the pressing of charges, all of which worked to consolidate the association of some sort of criminality with non-normative gender/sexual presentations. Such was the case of Akbar Burzabadi, who was arrested after knifing one of a group of young men who had been harassing him on a Tehran street. Akbar was "a woman-presenting male [mard-i zan-numa] who makes himself up as a woman and works at one of Tehran's popular musical [saz-u-zarbi] café-restaurants. Yesterday evening, Akbar, with wig and heavy make-up, left home to go to work." He was followed and harassed by a group of young men and eventually attacked them with a knife, injuring one of them, who filed a complaint. The paper added, "The officers [at the police station] indicated that he had been booked several times in the past on the charge of taking advantage of men; he sits at café customers' tables, looking like a woman, and taking advantage of them."[31]

Within this context, a "distancing" style of feminine mimesis could signal particular kinds of gender/sexual desire: it could be enacted by males who wanted to present themselves as female-acting non-females (thus the need for "distancing exaggerations") who wanted to be desirable to men who desired female-presenting non-females. At the same time, some males opted for "complete" mimesis—working as female dancers and intending to be taken totally for women. This style of mimesis allowed some males to live as women.[32] Such, for instance, was the case of one café dancer known as Nargis Salihi, who was believed to be a woman and who had worked for five years before it was found out that s/he was Nasir Salihi (figure 4.6). The "outing" resulted from a café scuffle that led to Salihi's detention, along with a number of clients, at the local police station. When interrogated at the police station, Salihi explained that she had moved to Tehran from Arak (a small provincial town) five years ago. Because she "was very fond of wearing women's clothes," she explained,

باقر نمازی در چند کشور خ دنمائی کرده و باعث تفریح و شگفتی عموم شده است وی گویا اخیرا بنابدعوت یکی از کاباره‌ها خیال دارد بابانو پروانه به بیروت برود

FIGURE 4.5. Male dancer Baqir Namazi, said to have performed well in several countries. *Khvandaniha*, September 25, 1954, p. 37.

FIGURE 4.6.
Nargis Salihi at
the police station.
*Kayhan*, May 13,
1969.

"I made myself look like a young woman. I then went to the town registry in Ray [a suburb of Tehran] and declared my birth certificate lost and requested a new one in the name of Nargis Salihi. With the new birth certificate, I began a career of singing and dancing and have developed a circle of admirers."[33]

As we will see more fully in chapter 7, both styles of self-fashioning continue to inform MtF public presentations today and are often cause for tension between those who want to completely live as women, and thus argue against the exaggerated femaleness of those other MtFs, who, in their opinion, "are giving a bad name to the community."[34] In the 1970s, these two analytically distinct styles of male non-normativity existed more as a continuum, which also included a range of other strategies for males living as women. Some were individuals such as Nargis, who lived as women without undergoing any form of medicalized body modification, but a growing number of people opted for various degrees of hormonal and surgical intervention.

The world of non-normative males was visible in the 1970s not only in the "gritty world" of entertainment. The upper echelons of an expansive art world—painters, photographers, television producers, and performers—were also rumored to harbor nonmasculine males. Indeed, the two poles of the culture industry were not sealed off from each other. At elite parties catering to males who dressed as women, members of high society mingled with *khanums* who worked in menial day jobs.[35] One difference was that the very rich could dress up at home and be safely driven to such parties by their chauffeurs, whereas the less affluent had to change clothes upon arrival. These parties were the equivalent of women's nights out, *daurah* parties (women's parties that rotated among different women's homes). The more well-to-do males would throw lavish parties and invite the rest of their circles, sometimes numbering in the hundreds.

Not all men-loving men in Iran during this period opted for either of these styles, of course.[36] Many lived lives scarcely distinguishable from those of other men. They too socialized with the "more flamboyant" non-masculine-attired males.[37] These spaces of socialization acquired the label of "gay parties" or "gay bars" in international gay media coverage, as well as in collective memories of 1970s Tehran for Iranians in later decades. But males living as women who socialized through these networks did not consider themselves homosexual and defined their relationship with men in heterosexual terms. Within these intimate (*khaudi*) circles, they addressed each other by their female names. Many lived double lives; they dressed as men, went to work as men, and some were even married and had children. At night, they lived as women.[38] The parties were not a space for finding potential lovers or partners, but rather a place to dance and have fun, to exchange gossip about one's adventures, and to meet people like oneself (which by definition excluded people who were one's target of desire).

Some of these trends continue into the present. Today's "gay parties" similarly are seen to be for people of the same kind. Behzad had not been in any relationship for a while at the time of our second conversation in July 2007. All three of his previous significant relationships had broken up through the loss of his lover to marriage (with a woman). Now in his early fifties, he seemed resigned to living his life and waiting for something to just happen. When I asked him why he was not going to any gay parties to meet someone, he was puzzled: "why would I go to a party to spend time with people like myself? Years ago, in my twenties and thirties, when I was still trying to figure things out for myself, I used to go to some of these parties—they are good for the younger folk so they don't feel they are the only ones who are not like others."[39] Cyrus, another gay-identified man in his early thirties, similarly found the parties not to be where one goes to find someone: "They are for hanging out with like-minded men." He has met the last two of his partners at the gym to which he goes regularly: "The men who pick me up, they are all either married—and I move away from them as soon as I find out—or else I lose them to marriage sooner or later. It is very depressing."[40] The distinction within the party scene that Behzad and Cyrus were reporting is between those who, like Behzad and Cyrus, do not look very different from straight men and those who have more feminine—"girlie-like," Behzad called it—styles of self-presentation. But they would all be looking "out there," not in the gay parties, for potential lovers and partners.

Being like each other, then, tended (and tends) to exclude coupling as lovers. This structure of desire and identification reflects the dominance of a larger discourse in twentieth-century Iran that has transformed males and females into "opposite sexes," and which depends on the notion that "opposites attract"—a discourse that sets the parameters of sexual/gender subjectivity, whether normative or not.[41]

We have no ethnographies, nor published memoirs, that would map this culture in the 1970s. We have instead a vast circulation of rumors from the time that have since acquired the status of fact. It was said, and still often is, that Iranian television had become a safe haven for *gay* men, who enjoyed the protection of not only Reza Qotbi, the director of National Iranian Radio and Television and a cousin of Queen Farah Pahlavi, but, somewhat equivocally, of the Queen herself. When the Tehran daily *Kayhan* published a report about the purported wedding celebration of two gay men in a club, the Queen is said to have reacted negatively and asked the men involved and their friends to be-have more responsibly and avoid such excesses in the future. In their defense, the men are said to have clarified that the celebration was a birthday party and had been misreported in the press.[42] Kavus, a self-identified gay man in his late fifties in 2007, similarly recalled the public view of these marriages as misrecognition: "How could two khanums get married?" He laughed. He described these occasions as "dressing-up parties," in which at times two kha-nums would dress up as a bride and groom couple. These were carnivalesque performances, he said.[43] In real life, he added, "both of them would be inter-ested in *straight* [the word pronounced as in English] married men. Targeting married men was like a conquest, a proof of womanliness. In these parties, they would brag about who had succeeded in breaking up which marriage." If a khanum developed a special relationship with a lover, sometimes, s/he would "marry" this guy. But the occasion was not a public ritual, nor celebrated by a "wedding party." At most, for memory's sake, they would go to a photographer for a "wedding portrait," for which occasion the khanum would change to a wedding gown. A painting by Iranian artist Ghasem Hajizadeh is possibly drawn from such a photograph (see plate 1).

Painting from photographs in Iran goes back to the second half of the nineteenth century, when it began to supplement portraiture. As Layla S. Diba has observed, for Persian artists of the period, who "aspired to depict their subject as realistically as possible," photography provided the means "to produce accurate compositions."[44] In many of his paintings, Hajizadeh has ventured to connect with this earlier tradition, but he is decidedly not aspiring for realism.[45] He has produced numerous (possibly more than a hundred) paintings that seem to be based on the socializing culture of males living as women in Iran of the 1970s (see plate 2 for one such painting). Taken as a whole, these paintings constitute a visual ethnography of that scene.

Hajizadeh's deployment of the visual gap in his paintings from photographs restages the "distancing" between "body and appearance" to which woman-presenting males aspire. The very expression *mard-i zan-numa* (woman-presenting male) contains a level of linguistic double-valence that lends itself to multiple associations and incitements. The suffix -*numa* is linked with the verb *numudan* (to display, to present), making the male in mard-i zan-numa do the work of displaying womanhood. Their very enactment of presenting-like, in apparent dissonance from their body, displays a representation of womanhood. At the same time, and linked with the same root, -*numa* pulls in layers of meaning from its association with *numayish* (a show, a theatrical performance), *numayishgah* (exhibition), and *numayish dadan* (to stage an appearance, to show off). In other words, mard-i zan-numa in her/his exhibiting, showing off, mode of self-presentation as-if-a-woman performs and displays at once womanhood with a "distance" and performativity of womanhood itself.[46]

Hajizadeh's style of painting from photographs, yet distancing the painted image from the photograph, resonates with this "distancing mimesis" of womanhood performed by woman-presenting males. Photography's claim to authenticity, in particular within the earlier tradition of realistic painting in Iran, parallels the biological body's claim of some authentic sex/gender; Hajizadeh's painting from photographs enacted the "distancing mimicry" that a mard-i zan-numa presented in her/his dissonant performance of the truth of the body. The paintings retain an "as-if-photography" quality and gesture in a similar way both toward and simultaneously away from a scene of authenticity, as mard-i zan-numa does vis-à-vis "as-if-woman." Cultural recognition of the works as paintings from photographs may even incite a desire to see/

imagine what the original may have been. Similarly, a mard-i zan-numa may incite imagining what s/he would have been as a "real woman." As Brad Epps has suggested, "the painting from the photograph . . . stages, or restages, some of the tensions between the biological body and social self-presentation (self-styling), between 'being' and 'appearing.'"[47]

The effect of Hajizadeh's distancing mimicry is particularly acute in his painting of a woman-presenting male with his/her man in a composition that is reminiscent of studio wedding portraits of the period (see plate 1). The painting moves away from a presumed photograph, but within the photographic/painted text there is a second distancing as well. The "wedding" moves away from a wedding. Here two "major" acts of distancing mimicry are performed, the effects of which are further amplified in a series of "minor" distancings: the dress is not quite a wedding dress, nor is the groom quite as prepped up as a "real" groom. Unlike most studio wedding portraits of twentieth-century Iran, the bride and groom are not facing the camera frontally, but instead are turned toward each other bodily; the studio space also does not mimic the usual studio backdrops (figure 4.7).

The combined effect of the major and minor distancing mimeses keeps the viewer in suspense, in a state of unease provoked by the scandal of sex/gender uncertainty: What are we looking at? Are there two men? One man with a woman? Are they, or are they not, in a studio? Are they, or are they not, a bride and groom?

## The Shame of Unmanly Males

The emergence in the 1970s of more visible scenes of nonheteronormative maleness, along with increased knowledge of such scenes circulating in speech and print, was widely perceived as a moral corruption of Iranian culture through Westernization. The perception had class connotations: only elite society in Tehran was assumed capable of fostering such calamities. The extensive circulation of extravagant rumors about high-society circles of nonheteronormative males became part of the criticism of Pahlavi court culture, which was seen as corrupt and as encouraging further corruption. While subsequent to the establishment of the Islamic Republic and the world-wide growth of Islamist movements, one tends to associate such criticism with an "Islamist backlash"; in the 1970s, attacks against an "excess of cultural liberties" were a much more broadly voiced concern.[48] What sustained the power of nonheteronormative maleness as a sign of excessive liberty (or, as it was by then commonly called, "Westoxication")[49] was the shame and disgust associated with

FIGURE 4.7. Studio Wedding Picture, 1919, photographed by Minas Patkerhanian, 12×9 cm. Source: Parisa Dadmandan (Nafisi), *Chihrah-nigaran-i Isfahan: Gushah-'i az tarikh-i 'akkasi-i Iran.*

any public spectacle of non-masculine maleness and nonheteronormative sexuality.

What made "it"—this preferably unnamed horror—a cultural assault and moral insult was above all *not* its putative Western origin, but the shame of being *kuni*. The most derogatory word in the realm of sexuality, kuni literally means anal, but in Persian it exclusively means to be receptive of anal penetration. Young male adolescents often first become familiar with the word as that which signals the edge of abjection; for instance, when parents warn their young son to stay away from certain activities (such as dance) and from certain (ill-reputed) persons, lest they become kuni. The equivalent word for women, *baruni*, does similar disciplinary work, but its moral load is much lighter.[50]

The gut shame associated with kuni seems to have made it resistant to any measure of self-appropriation and re-signification. When the word *gay* began to arrive, some did not take to it. Behzad said he initially "disliked *gay* because in my mind I would translate it into kuni and I stayed away from it."[51] Ironically, the more recent acceptance and circulation of *gay* in Persian signifies the same aversion to kuni: the need for a word that is "not-kuni."[52]

Manifestations of shame and disgust saturate innumerable small details of personal lives. When Behzad, from the secular, educated, urban middle class, at the age of thirty felt compelled to explain to his cousin, who had been his playmate ever since childhood, that the reason for his refusal to get married was that he was "man-loving," the cousin ran to the bathroom to throw up. Just as often, the disgust was/is translated into put-down sneers and derogatory name-calling, most commonly *iva'khvahar*.[53] At the societal level, both generic humor and jokes targeting particular individuals sustain the work of anxiously warding off the threat of being "like that" oneself.

Amir 'Abbas Huvayda, Iranian prime minister from 1965 to 1978, and many members of the court and its surrounding *société* culture were regular targets of such humor.[54] A more popular target was Faridun Farrukhzad, a well-known entertainer, TV performer, and programmer.[55] He produced the popular program *Mikhak Nuqrah-'i* (Silver Coronation); he also performed in some of the more upper-echelon nightclubs and summer resorts.

My concern here is not whether Farrukhzad or Huvayda were *gay* (in whatever sense of that word); rather, I ask what cultural significance the public perception of their being "like that" may have had. What cultural labor did the public circulation of satire and mockery—rumored or printed—around their presumed effeminacy, questionable masculinity, and sexual impropriety perform? What was the relation of mockery to the regulating work of moral prohibitions and legal sanctions against sodomy, which was always assumed to be the sole meaning of such male-male relationships and was the reason for the assignation of the term *kuni*? What was the relation between these public circulations of non-normative, masculine-presenting males and the growing public visibility of woman-presenting males?

Consider, for instance, this provocative piece about Prime Minister Huvayda's trip to Qazvin. The unnamed columnist of the satirical page "Kargah-i namadmali"[56] wondered why, unlike the Prime Minister's other provincial trips—never a confidential matter—this trip was kept secret.[57] Back in 1956, when Minister of Justice Gulsha'ian had dissolved and re-formed the High Court, the daily *Kayhan* ran a satirical piece recalling that when 'Ali Akbar Davar (1885–1937), Minister of Justice, sent new judges to Qazvin who did not please Shaykh Muhammad 'Ali Sabit (the deputy from that city), the latter challenged the minister in a parliamentary session, asking if the said judges were "approved by the world [*dunyapasand*] or are they favored by Qazvinis [*Qazvini-pasand*]"? The question, the paper continued, elicited riotous laughter in the parliament, since among the members of parliament some were known to be "Qazvini-pasand." As a result of this question, Davar had cancelled those appointments. So now, *Kayhan*'s writer demanded, one wanted to be certain that the new reorganization of the judiciary would be acceptable—not simply Qazvini-pasand.[58] Other Qazvini jokes of this period played on the double meaning of *jinsi* as both sexual and in-kind. When a severe earthquake hit the area around Qazvin in 1962, a "Kargah-i namadmali" column later recalled, the popular storyteller Subhi Muhtadi, who was fundraising in a gathering for the earthquake survivors and was refused by a "good-looking young man" (on the grounds that aiding the earthquake survivors was government's responsibility), retorted by saying "This young man likes to aid his earthquake-survivor brothers in-kind [*kumak-i jinsi*]."[59]

Ethnic jokes saturate Tehrani culture. The culture of text messaging and the mass circulation of images on the Internet has increased the ubiquity of circulation of these jokes in recent years. Tehranis think Azarbaijanis (or indeed all Turkish-speaking people and others ethnically coded as Turks) are stupid ("as stupid as a donkey"); Rashtis (assumed all male) are dishonorable and don't care about the sexual transgressions of their female kin (especially their wives); Isfahanis are at once stingy and business-smart; people of Luristan are plain dumb—the list of assignations goes on, and so does the proliferation of related jokes.[60]

The jokes related to Qazvin, however, stand out as a genre of its own. Qazvinis are "well-known" among Tehranis for having a preference for *kun* (ass). Being kuni falls on the side of an "unmentionable assignation," an abomination. It provokes deep disgust; the jokes attempt to avert such provocation. The low comedy of Qazvini jokes complements the disgust-provoking unmentionability of kuni. Disgust makes things unmentionable, intensifying the spectral danger of the disgusting thing. The low comedy of Qazvini jokes works to circulate the knowability of the unmentionable in polite, enlightened company who would of course deny any such prejudicial sentiment. Because of this subtext of disgust, it is almost impossible to own the comic assignation. Iranian Turkish speakers can, and do, play with the jokes on stupidity by one-upmanship, returning the favor of stupidity to Tehranis (or more generally to Persian speakers, generically referred to as *Fars-ha*); Isfahanis can appropriate their smart economic know-how as a positive character; Rashtis can boast about their gender/sexual liberalism; even Lurs could turn their accusation of dumbness into a weapon of the weak. But what can one do with kuni? To claim the joke would put the person in a disgustingly abominable, totally abject position—unless and until the rest of one's national compatriots are willing to come to terms with *their* disgust.[61]

What does that "gut" feeling of revulsion speak to? Why does the spectral threat of being/becoming kuni seem to be so shattering to a modern (male) Iranian's sense of self? It is impossible—or, at any rate, it is not my project—to give a convincing etiology of disgust. But it is critical to ask what cultural work disgust performs. What does it do to "the disgusting"? What does it achieve for "the disgusted"? Miller asks, "Why is it that disgust figures so prominently in routine moral discourses, even more so perhaps than the idioms of other moral emotions such as guilt and indignation?"[62]

The shift from guilt and indignation to disgust that Miller discusses is a historically produced shift in idioms, possibly related to the emergence of a human-referenced sense of being in the world in which the ground for morality can no longer be as solid as divine prohibitions. In the Islamic world, in the passages of Islamic jurisprudence (fiqh) dealing with sodomy (lavat), one does not sense a sentiment of disgust. The dominant message in these passages is the enormity of the sin, of the transgression of what is referred to as *hurmat-i dubur*, the sanctity/prohibition of the anus. It is the enormity of the sin that aroused the anger of God, one is told, such that "a whole people were punished for it."[63] Whereas lavat is sinful, being kuni is disgusting. For those who have become modern, the sentiment of disgust seems to replace the work of *hurmat* and, perhaps, as Miller suggests, "acts as a barrier to satisfying unconscious desire."[64] It is this work that complements the laughing labor of the low comedy of barely disguised jokes about the Qazvinis, those infamous desirers of kunis.[65]

Other modes of comic relief about the more public circulation of images and self-presentations of nonheteronormative males in the 1970s focused on Faridun Farrukhzad (1938–92). A poet, singer, performer, actor, and television personality, in life Farrukhzad was largely a subject of gossip and approbation; in death, he has been belatedly acclaimed for his poetry and—once he was forced to leave Iran in the early 1980s—his later political activism in Europe. He was brutally murdered, it is assumed, at the instigation, if not the direct involvement, of elements within the Islamic Republic.[66] Mocked and reviled, Farrukhzad also has provided, then and now, a figure of identification for Iranian *gay* men. Pages of diasporic Iranian gay publications have articles, poetry, and celebrations of his life.[67]

Almost as soon as he began his performance career in the late 1960s, Farrukhzad became the subject of gossip columns, where he was consistently mocked for his self-presentation. He seemed to be a modernist's nightmare of the repulsions and seductions of a repressed past. What modernists had hoped to have buried in the past and in lower classes—that style of male dancing and entertaining that was deeply marked by gender/sexual inappropriateness and transgression—seemed to have found its way out not only into the more modern nightclubs but onto the national television. Farrukhzad's shows were enormously successful. The way to ward off this ghost of the past, this class-misplaced figure, this popular spectacle of a returned repressed, was to crack jokes as one watched the show and to saturate the oral and printed gossip with sexual innuendos. Responding to an article in *Sipid va siyah* in which Mas'ud Farzad had suggested "most of our poets and writers and literary luminaries are sexual deviants except for Sadiq Hidayat,"[68] the author of the satirical column "Kargah-i namadmali" argued that Sa'di's generation experienced sexual deviancy because in their time women were veiled and interactions between girls and boys were very limited. Now that this was no longer the case, people like Faridun Kar[69] and Faridun Bikar (*Kar* is a family name but also means work, labor; *bikar* is not a family name and means idle, unemployed—Farrukhzad's occupation as an entertainer was not considered real work) have no excuse for being sexual deviants and become *ankarah* ("to engage in that"—unmentionable act) when the means to be *inkarah* (to engage in this) are available.[70] Similarly, *Khvandaniha* reprinted a cartoon from the satirical weekly *Taufiq*, targeting Farrukhzad, in the tradition of a male dancer, as "available" (figure 4.8).[71]

What is remarkable in the incessant circulation and recirculation of reports about Farrukhzad was that a popular magazine such as *Khvandaniha* would at once recycle such reports and distance itself from the "gritty world" that fed

FIGURE 4.8. The top line reads: "The guy with thick mustache to the performer of 'Friday Show.'" The bottom line is meant to be a rhythmic chant to which Farrukhzad is presumably dancing: "Do you remember . . . it was night-time, it was in the plains, it was winter?!" Cartoon originally from *Taufiq*, reprinted in *Khvandaniha*, June 16, 1970.

it. For instance, in the summer of 1972, a brawl broke out during Farrukhzad's performance at the Motel Qu, a popular summer resort on the Caspian Sea, reportedly because he had made an inappropriate comment that had offended some in the audience and disturbed the family ambience of the place. Farrukhzad was beaten up, and the incident was reported in the press. The precipitating comment itself, however, is not reported, lending it the additional power of imaginative knowledge. *Khvandaniha* republished a four-page report about the episode that had appeared in *Zan-i ruz*, yet prefaced it by saying it was beneath the dignity of the journal and sensibilities of its readers for *Khvandaniha* to enter the scandalous world of what went on in the name of art, but since people took their families to these resorts, it was important for them to know to what they and their families would be exposed.[72] Farrukhzad was an irresistible topic that simultaneously fascinated, allured, and repulsed. He was well aware of this and articulated the paradox of attraction and repulsion that people felt toward him: "People love me with fear," he once said in an interview.[73]

In January 1974, Farrukhzad married for a second time. Even before the actual wedding, the press was full of gossip about the disputes between the couple and their imminent breakup.[74] His new wife was Taraneh Sunduzi, a young woman of sixteen.[75] A cover article in the April 24, 1974, issue of *Ittila'at-i banuvan* already reported marital troubles and an unhappy Taraneh. Within months of their marriage, the couple filed for divorce, which became final on June 17, 1974. Taraneh's father told reporters that when they had agreed to their daughter's marriage to Farrukhzad, "they had been unaware of some of his moral characteristics."[76] The father's vague reference to some "moral characteristics" was reported to have been articulated in more specific terms by his daughter: Taraneh was allegedly overheard telling her father, "Faridun is *dau-shakhsiyati*; no woman, even of the worst sort, could live with him. It is good we are divorced."[77]

But what did the term *dau-shakhsiyati* mean in this period? Literally a person "with two personalities," like the related expression *dau-jinsi*, a person "with two sex/genders," dau-shakhsiyati did not have a stable meaning. Both were used interchangeably to refer to persons we would name bisexual, intersex, or transgender/-sexual. Up to the present, dau-jinsi has sustained its multiple meanings—much to the dismay of trans persons who neither consider themselves to be intersex nor like the undertone of association with nonheteronormative sexuality. It was the context of its reference to Faridun Farrukhzad—a public persona already much rumored to be sexually nonheteronormative, in part defined through the cultural association of a professional male dancer with sexual availability to other men—that determined its meaning. In this sense, Taraneh, speaking from the knowing position of a former wife, explicitly stated what presumably everyone already knew.

The disturbing specter of Farrukhzad's performative persona also intersected with another source of anxiety in the 1970s; namely, that of "gender confusion." Numerous social commentators wrote essays about the current state of youth, lamenting the disappearance of manly valor and of young men with long hair whose demeanor was that of a flirtatious girl, especially when they danced to rock music—all in "blind imitations of the West."[78] For a modern Iranian masculinity that had crafted itself through hetero-gendering previously androgynous concepts of beauty, and by the adoption of more disciplined and uniform sartorial practices during the first half of the twentieth century, the new fashions and tastes of the young seemed nothing short of a threat to national honor.

Part of this gender anxiety resided in fear of the failure of sex/gender recognition and of what that misrecognition would cause. One woman wrote:

Once upon a time when we looked at men, we had no doubt that they were men. But now with these Beatle-style hair-dos and pants that show the body and high-heeled shoes and manicured nails, we are forced to look again and again to remove our doubt. In the old days, if you called a man a woman, that was an insult, but now they try to make themselves look like women. Several days ago, in Nasir Khusrau Street in Tehran, I ran into a man who had braided hair, was displaying a lot of jewelry and exactly like women had plucked his eyebrows and wore heavy make-up. It is astonishing that these men who always considered women to be beneath them and thought of themselves as the superior sex are putting themselves in women's place when it comes to dressing and make-up.[79]

Connecting such gender/sex ambiguity to sexual deviation was an easy imaginative leap. Under the bold headline, "The danger of women and men looking alike," another newspaper article cautioned against the clothing, lifestyles, and work of women and men becoming too similar. This kind of confusion "threatens today's civilization, in the same manner that two thousand years ago civilized nations such as Greece and Rome . . . were overthrown. In ancient Athens, before they were defeated by the Spartans, men had begun to make themselves up like women. . . . In ancient Rome too, similar things happened. . . . Moreover sexual deviancy, as it is today, became so prevalent that it caused their overthrow and destruction."[80] Societal destruction was not the fate of people of Lot only.

### The Hope of Gender/Sex Ambiguity

The spaces opened up by a more visible nonheteronormative maleness and by gender/sex ambiguity nevertheless offered some hopeful possibilities for women-presenting males. As I have argued in chapter 2, one significant effect of the emergence of academic and vernacular sexology and psychology was that the affiliation between transsexuality and intersexuality was severed and transsexuality was placed squarely in the spectrum of deviant sexualities, in particular as an extreme form of homosexuality. This shift transformed transsexuality from a given, created, wondrous/strange category into a diagnostic/moral one. Not only did this shift pathologize transsexuality, *im*moralize it, it also linked it to the by-then established affiliation of homosexuality with criminality. Yet such immoral and criminal inscriptions did not affect woman-presenting males overnight. At least in the first half of the 1970s, there was no homogeneously dominant sense of moral reprehensibility. The dailies and

*عجیب،حیرت‌انگیز و باور نکردنی...اما حقیقی!*

**نوزاد۲۸ساله عالم زنان!**

«سعید» که همه او را مرد بشمار می‌آوردند، حالا یک زن طناز شده است!

FIGURE 4.9. Headline of first installment of Rashil's story. *Ittila'at-i banuvan*, January 9, 1974.

popular weeklies continued to report on sex-change operations without moral apprehension. Despite some negative, at times hostile, articles by scientists and legal professionals, living nonheteronormative lives had become visibly, though precariously, more possible. Paradoxically, the affiliation of woman-presenting males with the larger world of nonheteronormative males had provided possibilities for living alternative lives, with or without surgery. As I have argued already, "gay Tehran" was inclusive of a broad spectrum of male nonheteronormativity.

The press reports of surgeries performed in Iran were particularly important in informing woman-presenting males of more affordable possibilities, which until then had seemed to be available only at great cost in Europe. The 1973 *Kayhan* report on the SRS performed in Shiraz (discussed in chapter 2), for instance, had inadvertently advertised what the process would be for any interested reader: psychological consultation and acquiring permission from the Legal Medical Board.

During the same period when *Zan-i ruz* was running various reports and articles related to the story of Zahra's murder by her jealous lover Mahin, the rival women's weekly, *Ittila'at-i banuvan*, ran the life story of Rashil (formerly Sa'id) Sa'idzadeh over eight weeks.[81] The coverage in a popular women's weekly transformed the coverage of sex change from short medical news items into a full-length, melodramatic, human interest story. In the first issue, a huge headline, running the entire width of the page, declared, "The 28-Year-Old Newborn to the World of Women." A supra-title exclaimed "wondrous, extraordinary, unbelievable . . . but true!" while a subtitle explained that "'Sa'id' whom everyone thought of as a man has now become a coquettish woman!" (figure 4.9).

Every week, the story was accompanied by photographs of her after the sex change (see figures 4.10, 4.11, and 4.12).

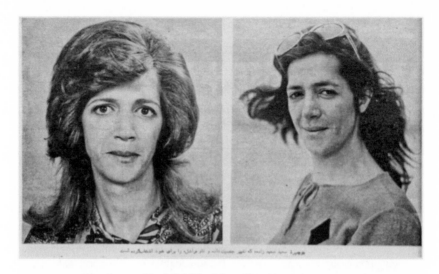

جمهوره سعید سعید زاده که شهر حسینت داده و اثر قرائی را برای خود کنظیمگیرم آمده

FIGURE 4.10. Two photos of Rashil Sa'idzadeh, *Ittila'at-i banuvan*, January 9, 1974.

FIGURE 4.11.
Another photo of
Rashil, *Ittila'at-i
banuvan*, January
16, 1974.

چهره تازه‌ای ازراشل

FIGURE 4.12. Rashil again. *Ittila'at-i banuvan*, January 30, 1974.

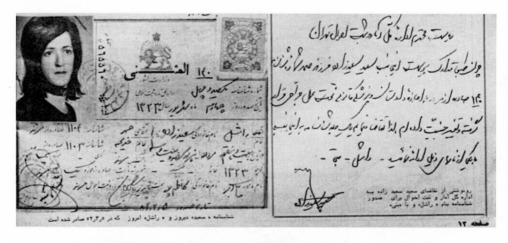

FIGURE 4.13. *Right*: Rashil's request for a new identification document with a new first name, either Rashil or Betty; *left*: her new identification document. *Ittila'at-i banuvan*, January 9, 1974.

As if "seeing was not believing"—a weight of incredulity inherited from the preoperative status of woman-presenting males as inauthentic mimicry—Rashil's various medical and legal documents were reproduced as well (figures 4.13 and 4.14).

Most important, Rashil's story was narrated as her own story and in the first person. After a long, patronizing, introductory editorial note in the first installment (as well as shorter editorials in every issue), the story unfolds in Rashil's narrative voice. The sustained narrative, serialized in the tradition of short novellas and accompanied by her postoperative photographs and legal and medical documents, fully fleshed out the story of a livable sex/gender-transitioned life. This was not a story of misery, misfit, and disorder, although all these elements were part of her story. This was instead a "sweet and interesting" story with a happy ending.

Both the editorial notes and Rashil's narrative depicted Rashil both as an intersex and a trans person. The editorial described Rashil as one of those creatures to whom nature had been cruel; s/he was born "*bilataklif*" (in a co-nundrum). It described the successful surgery as one that had transformed and transferred Rashil "who belonged physiologically to the world of men . . . but had always considered herself to belong psychologically to the world of women" to her desired womanhood. Her own narrative placed more empha-sis on sexual ambiguity. Even though she repeatedly noted that no one around her, including her mother, with whom s/he had gone to public baths through

PLATE 1. Ghasem Hajizadeh (b. 1947). © ARS. Untitled. 2009. Mixed media on paper, 33×41 cm. *Photo Credit*: Banque d'Images, ADAGP/Art Resource, NY.

PLATE 2. Ghasem Hajizadeh (b. 1947). © ARS. Untitled. 2006. Mixed media on paper, 80×90 cm. *Photo Credit*: Banque d'Images, ADAGP/Art Resource, NY.

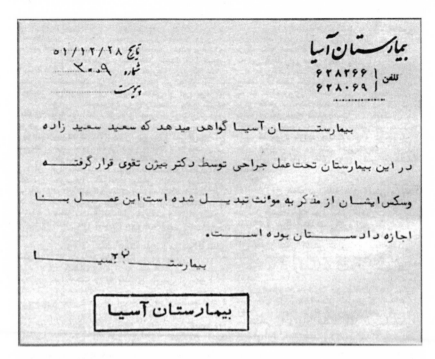

FIGURE 4.14. Hospital certification of Rashil's (then still named Sa'id) sex change from male to female. *Ittila'at-i banuvan*, January 16, 1974.

her early elementary school years, had ever noticed any unusual physical distinctions, she was convinced from early on that s/he was different from her/his brothers (s/he had six brothers and no sisters). When as a teenager s/he read a magazine article about hermaphrodites, s/he was convinced that s/he must be one, "a dau-jinsi [two-sexed], neither a boy nor a girl." This belief was strengthened when in high school s/he actually met another student, Mahdi, who had been brought up as a girl before it was decided that s/he was closer to male and a surgical operation had "clarified and fixed" his/her sex. This convinced Rashil that "even though I am apparently a boy, I am really a girl in boy's skin." The comforting self-perception was somewhat dampened when Mahdi had told her/him that there was no one in Iran who could do this operation and s/he had been sent abroad. This began Rashil's earliest surgical fantasies and later engagements with medical professionals.

Rashil's nonheteronormative gender/sex identification (and, since her/his middle school years, sexual desire) found another familiar script as well: When s/he noticed an advertisement for an acting school, s/he decided that acting would be a fitting career—s/he could play female roles. The trouble was that by the mid-1960s, a growing number of young women were already turning to these schools: "I went to the school and registered for an acting class . . . but there were enough girls there and naturally they were assigned the female roles, so after a few sessions I dropped out." Nonetheless, Rashil began to grow her/his nails and hair, pluck her/his eyebrows, use makeup, and pay attention to her/his dress style to make it more womanly—behavior that began to alarm her/his parents, especially because at this time her/his father had various employment appointments in smaller towns. Her/his father was concerned that people would begin to talk about Rashil (then Sa'id) as a "sexual deviant" and asked her/him not to make her/himself look like a woman in excess (*dar zan-numa shudan ifrat nakun*). The father also began to look for doctors from whom to seek medical advice. After several crushes (all on young men), Rashil (then Sa'id) developed a loving and caring relationship with Hushang, an electronic technician, who also encouraged her/him to seek surgical treatment, declaring that he was deeply in love with her/him and would marry her/him after surgery. Hushang died in a car accident, which devastated Rashil (then Sa'id). By this time, her/his family was transferred back to Tehran and s/he began to look for an acting job. S/he indeed got a chance to play the part of a young girl when, because of a family crisis, the assigned actress did not show up on filming day. Rashil (then Sa'id) continued to pursue acting in female roles, largely in small marginal casts. S/he met a male actor, developed a close friendship with him, and accompanied him to parties fully dressed as a woman.

What eventually pushed her/him to seek sex-change surgery was a continuous entanglement with military conscription officers who were tracing her/his absence from the army when s/he had become eligible for the two-year service. The army medical doctor diagnosed her/him as trans and began her/his legal process of transition. After a few initial tests, s/he was sent to the courts to get referred to the Legal Medical Board. There s/he was interviewed by a four-member board composed of a surgeon, a gynecologist, a psychologist, and a plastic surgeon. Several weeks of further tests and four months of psychological counseling finally took Rashil to Tehran's Asia Hospital, where Dr. Taqavi performed a series of four surgeries, the first of which occurred on February 28, 1973.

The eight-week run of Rashil's story in a popular women's weekly, which built upon previous decades of news of intersex surgeries reported as sex change as well as reports of prominent international sex-change surgeries, transformed the idea of sex change into a tangible possibility within the public imagination. Rashil's detailed life story contributed to a pattern of life narratives that would structure much of the scientific and popular writings, including autobiographical writings, about transsexuality to the present day.

As the story of Rashil Sa'idzadeh indicates, it was still possible to write, even at great length, about trans persons (especially if their gender/sexual non-normativity could be vaguely associated with a physical intersex condition) in a way that was unthinkable to write about cross-dressing males without surgical modification who were living as women. Rashil's story was framed with sympathy and at times as a form of heroism that triumphed against all odds. The woman-presenting males, on the other hand, could be laughed at, mocked, sniggered about, or tolerated in hostile silence. They could be subject to moral outrage and criminal suspicion. By the mid-1970s, however, the medical establishment, possibly alarmed at the growing rate of sex-change surgeries performed outside any norms of institutional medical supervision, transferred the moral judgment against homosexuality onto trans persons. It took the professional and disciplinary power of the MCI to bring the full weight of opprobrium associated with homosexuality to bear on the life options of woman-presenting males, thereby delineating and enforcing a kinship relationship between male homosexuality and MtF trans.

### Science Rules on Unmanly Males

Formed in 1969, the MCI established a whole series of regulations for medical practice during the first years of its operation. It also acted as the authority where complaints about medical practice could be filed and reviewed.[82] In the early 1970s, it began to produce guidelines on new medical practices, such as acupuncture. Indeed, its rulings on sex-change surgery and acupuncture were decided in the same session of the board of directors on September 28, 1976. Alarmed by the apparent increase in public awareness and the accompanying increase in the performance of sex surgeries among woman-presenting males, the MCI decided to ban sex surgeries except in the case of intersex individuals. A huge front-page headline in the daily *Kayhan* informed the public of this decision on October 10, 1976 (see figure 4.15).

The page 2 text of the report explained that the decision "meant that sex-change through surgical operations and the like, which are aimed to solely change someone's apparent condition, is no longer permitted." It quoted "an informed source" as saying that "this operation can cause psychological and physical harm and that is why the MCI has banned it. . . . From now on any doctor who performs such operations will be legally prosecuted." The paper added

FIGURE 4.15. *Kayhan*'s front page, October 10, 1976. The bold headline (on the right side of figure) announces the MCI's decision to ban sex-change surgeries.

that, "up to now some thirty sex-change operations have been performed in Iran."

The full text of the decision was not published until some three years later, in the *Newsletter of the Medical Council of Iran*. It read:

> In general, changing the apparent sex through surgical operations and the like is not possible, "neither from a psychological nor from a physiological respect." Since this type of young man—who now insistently ask that their apparent condition be changed—cannot become a perfect woman in the future and become married to a man as a woman, and since the hole that is created for them will most likely become a source of chronic infections, and since there is a high probability that they will then express enmity toward the persons who have changed their condition and their sex, or at least they will express regret under conditions that a reversal to their prior condition is not possible, therefore such persons must be considered mental patients, they

must be treated psychologically, and one cannot permit that they would be moved out of their current condition and appearance.[83]

The delay in publication perhaps indicated a level of disagreement among medical practitioners on this issue that dated back to the 1940s, when Dr. Jahanshah Salih, in his textbook, had argued strongly against the possibility, advisability, and morality of sex change (discussed in chapter 2). Indeed, this difference of opinion continues to inform conceptions and practices of sex change in Iran today.

This statement is a remarkable document on many levels. It implies that to be a "perfect woman" is to be a perfect "hole," and that surgically modified MtF trans individuals are deficient in womanhood to the extent that the surgeries they receive produce unsatisfactory holes. The concern articulated is evidently driven in part by the expressed dissatisfaction with the quality of surgery woman-presenting males were receiving. But it also was a move to put medicine's house in order, in keeping with other efforts to promote professionalization. Officially no sex change was taking place in reputable hospitals, such as Women's Hospital in Tehran; but some surgeons were carrying out sex-change operations either in smaller private clinics or by listing their clients as intersex.

A prominent gynecologist trained by Dr. Jahanshah Salih, Dr. Yahya Behjatnia—who for many years headed the Family and Infertility Clinic of the Women's Hospital—recalled that many woman-presenting males would visit him and beg him to change their sex. But because this was not a permitted practice, if they persisted, he would advise them to go abroad.[84] In some cases, by the time a woman-presenting male would come to him, he explained, s/he was dressed as a woman and looked like a woman; s/he had already obtained hormonal treatment, already had breasts, and would come for the removal of male sexual organs and vaginal construction. If there were any surgeries, he insisted, it was done surreptitiously.

Dr. Mehdi Amir-Movahedi, also a prominent gynecologist, was a highly regarded specialist in uterine surgeries, intersex surgeries, and vaginal construction for women who were born with no or very restricted vaginas.[85] He served on the Board of Directors of the MCI for several years and echoed many of the same observations as his colleague Dr. Behjatnia. He compared the situation to that of women seeking abortion. At the time, abortion was illegal except under strict certifications, such as a pregnancy threatening the mother's life. Yet with the right connections and money, many doctors would perform abortions.[86] At the Women's Hospital, Dr. Movahedi explained, "we were very strict, we would not do anything that was against regulations, nor would we train medical students for illegal surgeries. I worked there for some twenty to thirty years and I do not recall a single case of sex-change surgery. If any of our trainees performed this in their own clinic, the MCI would prosecute them. I served on the Board of Directors, we would not authorize such surgeries; it was against the law. I served eight years as the chief of the MCI court that dealt with complaints having to do with gynecological issues, and no such case was brought there." Why, then, did the MCI opt for issuing an official statement on sex change, I asked? "If there were any related complaints, they were not made when I served there. But many in the old days would do things for money and perhaps that is what happened. In my own practice, I did many vaginal constructions; but this was exclusively for intersex patients and a few times women came to me when they had marital problems and I would realize they did not have a proper vagina, just a small crevice that allowed menstrual blood flow. I would construct a vagina for them so that they could have intercourse with their husbands."

That the text of the MCI decision was not published until 1979, and that later interviews with prominent gynecologists who at the time worked in Women's Hospital insistently emphasize that no sex-change surgeries were performed by reputable surgeons in this period, lead one to speculate that, despite persistent disavowals, reputable surgeons were indeed carrying out a whole range of surgeries that began to endanger the reputability of other surgeons. The division was not a matter of differing professional opinions about the advisability of genital surgery for woman-presenting males; rather, it involved matters of moral reputation. By this time, in the dominant scientific discourse, intersex and trans persons had come to belong to distinctly different categories. The latter had become affiliated with sexual deviancy rather than birth defect. It was the morality of sex change—or rather, the moral status of the persons requesting or performing sex change—that was at issue. This was indeed at the heart of public conversations at the moment of the MCI decision against surgical sex change in 1976.

Both national dailies, *Kayhan* and *Ittila'at*, gave extensive coverage to this decision in 1976. *Ittila'at*, which was at the time viewed as the more establishment-oriented daily, ran a headline that the clerical establishment (*jami'ah-i ruhaniyat*), following the ban on sex-change surgery, called this operation a "forbidden and satanic act" (*fi'l-i haram va shaytani*).[87] Ayatallah Hajj Mirza Khalil Kamarah-'i told the paper that in the Qur'an, Satan stated that he would tempt children of Adam away from the right path and make them change their constitution. Changing one's sex is a prime example of changing one's constitution; thus sex-change surgery is a satanic act and forbidden. An "informed source" was quoted to have told the paper that if any nonintersex healthy person underwent sex-change surgery and later the person filed a complaint against the surgeon, the latter would be prosecuted on the charge of causing damage to an organ and might have his or her medical license suspended for a period. The source added that there was already one such case in front of the MCI.

Several doctors also were interviewed, including Dr. Amir-Movahedi, Dr. Husayn Parsa (at the time the director of Women's Hospital), Dr. Hasan Muhajiri, and Dr. 'Ali Asghar Pilasid. All agreed that sex-change surgeries on healthy males — males were the dominant topic of this conversation — must be forbidden, while those on intersex persons were corrective surgeries and were allowed. Several referred to healthy males who insisted on changing their sex as mental patients who should be treated psychologically.

*Kayhan*—reputedly somewhat off the establishment track—focused on doctors and interviewed woman-presenting males as well.[88] Dr. Karimi-nizhad, a well-known geneticist and the head of the Genetics and Pathology Department at Women's Hospital, spoke at length about hermaphrodites and why their operation should actually be called one of the "clarification of sex" and not "sex change." He elaborated on the importance of helping intersex individuals through these sex-clarifying surgeries. Indeed, the whole report was framed as if the MCI decision was about intersex persons, and throughout it used the word *dau-jinsi* (two-sexedness) in that sense, making no distinction between transsexuality and intersexuality. Dr. Ma'navi, a psychologist, also had taken the MCI decision to mean the banning of intersex surgeries — a decision that he found unwise and opposed. The report concluded with a section titled "individual freedoms," asking whether the issue should be considered one of individual autonomy over one's life and inviting all its readers—doctors, psychologists, geneticists, and general readers—to contribute to a discussion of these issues.

The *Kayhan* coverage included two photographs, one of an operating room, with the caption reading: "In the operating room: This may be the last patient who is on the operating table for surgery and sex-change. From now on, according to the decision of the Medical Council, no doctor is authorized to operate on 'two-sexed' persons in order to change their sex." The second (figure 4.16) showed a group of woman-presenting males, three of whom were visiting a friend who was recovering from her sex-change surgery.

With doctors, even those from Women's Hospital, and prominent psychologists unclear about the implications of the MCI decision, five days later a bulletin was issued to clarify the critical distinction that MCI was now codifying

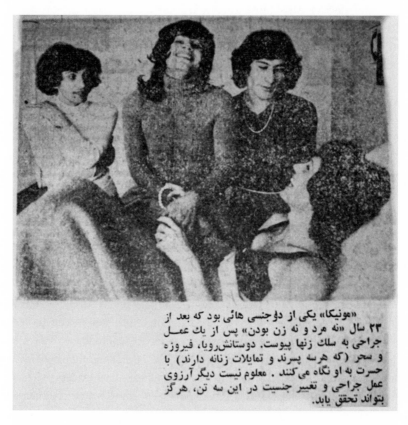

«مونیکا» یکی از دوجنسی هائی بود که بعد از
۲۳ سال «نه مرد و نه زن بودن» پس از یک عمـل
جراحی به سلک زنها پیوست. دوستانش رویا، فیروزه
و سحر (که هر سه پسرند و تمایلات زنانه دارند) با
حسرت به او نگاه می کنند . معلوم نیست دیگر آرزوی
عمل جراحی و تغییر جنسیت در این سه تن، هرگز
بتواند تحقق یابد.

FIGURE 4.16. Three woman-presenting males visiting a friend, Monica, after her surgery. The caption reads in part: "Roya, Firuzeh, and Sahar (who are all boys who have womanly inclinations) look at her enviously. It is not clear if their wish to have surgery and change sex could be fulfilled any longer." *Kayhan*, October 11, 1976.

in medical legislation. *Kayhan* ran the new MCI bulletin under the headline: "Deviant young males desire sex-change."[89]

> Pursuant to the news coverage of the decision concerning sex-change, and considering the legal responsibilities of the MCI, it has become necessary to offer some explanation in order to clarify the matter for the general public as well as for our medical colleagues. The banning of sex-change concerns those who physiologically are perfect females or males. Some of these deviant youth, either from ignorance or from whimsical desire or due to psychological disorders, want to change their sex. It must be categorically said that this is impossible. Embracing such a capricious action leads to serious side effects and difficult-to-cure diseases. From the point of view of civil law, too, there will be numerous challenges. Often such surgeries result in regret, but there is no reversal, which leads inevitably to dangerous psychological illnesses, at times ending in suicide or in murder of the surgeon.[90] Therefore, given all the issues involved and taking into account the opinion of experts and specialists in various medical fields, the MCI warns those young persons who think such operations are possible of the dangerous and ominous consequences of the operation and explicitly declares that changing one sex to the other through such operations is impossible.

The bulletin ended by emphasizing that this was different from the case of "two-sexed individuals (hermaphrodites [transliterated in Persian]) who are sexually ambiguous and exhibit a disorder of a genetic, chromosomal, or other similar nature." For such cases, after necessary tests had determined the sex of the person, surgical operations were not prohibited.

The 1976 MCI decision had paradoxical effects. It must have made some surgeons more cautious about sex-change operations, but the practice of surgical sex change continued, along with media interest in it. The medical community as well, even in the publications of the MCI itself, continued to produce articles that covered the subject of sex change in supportive terms.[91] Indeed, the MCI's insistence on the impossibility of sex change, along with the simultaneous banning of surgeries deemed impossible, combined with the prominent coverage of the decision in the national dailies, created a productive public conversation that circulated knowledge of surgical sex change on an unprecedented scale. Against the MCI's intentions, perhaps, the very possibility of such operations received broader attention.

Noushin, for example, now in her fifties, said she had no idea this operation was possible in Iran before she read these newspaper reports. In the 1970s, she was part of the socializing circle of singers and entertainers. Her/his parents had noticed her/his "incredible voice" when s/he was a teenager and encouraged her/him to take voice lessons. She became a singer and continues to be in much demand even today, though now she performs only at private parties.[92] She counted many of the famous male and female singers of the 1970s among her friends. She and another close friend, the son/daughter of a high-ranking army officer, had been planning in the mid-1970s to go to Europe for their sex-change surgeries. Her friend's father was making arrangements for them to get an appointment at a famous London clinic. The MCI decision and the newspaper coverage made them realize they could do it in Iran. Noushin and her friend visited Dr. Taqavi in Asia Hospital (the same hospital and surgeon who had operated on Rashil Sa'idzadeh). They also visited Dr. Behjatnia in the Women's Hospital. Both doctors advised them to go abroad under the current circumstances. Eventually in 1977, after a period of hormone therapy in Iran, they went abroad for their operations.[93]

Aside from going abroad or using "back-street" surgeons, the other option remained living as a woman-presenting male without surgical transformation (obtaining hormones seems to have continued to be as possible as before). Many took this latter route. One such woman-presenting male, now internationally known, was Maryam Khatun Mulk-ara (1950–2012).[94]

Born male in 1950, s/he was given the name Faridun. According to her extensive articulations of her early life, already by the time she was in her late teenage years she would go out to parties dressed as a woman.[95] When she was eighteen, during her return walk from a party, a car stopped and she noticed the occupants were "three *transsexual* males just like me." The three had the male née-names Kayvan, Umid, and Siamak, but their current names were Kati, Sharareh, and Firuzeh. The moment she joined them in the car, they designated her Faranak.

The naming marked for Mulk-ara the beginning of a new life; she referred to this accidental meeting "as the true moment of my entry into a collectivity, a group of people like myself. Anywhere in public gatherings we would go, everyone present would want to socialize with us. In those days, there was no distinction between *gay*, two-sexed people or *transsexual*s. Everyone knew these individuals existed, but no one knew exactly what the problem was. People referred to all these individuals as *'iva-khvahar'* [o'sister]" (7). Mulk-ara described these gatherings and parties as "a place where everyone was a woman, that is, even though they were known as males in social norms of recognition. . . . The ambience was just like the ambience of womanly gatherings. We talked about fashion and other women's issues."[96] In the early 1970s, she started working at the Iranian National Radio and Television, where she went to work dressed as a woman. It was there that she was first encouraged to go abroad for a sex-change operation. She spent some time in London in 1975 to learn more about herself and to look into various possibilities; it was there that she "learned about *transsexuality* and realized I was not a passive *homosexual*."[97] This moment of "learning about *transsexuality*" has become a critical node in current narratives of trans persons. In particular, learning to distinguish oneself from "a passive homosexual" has become a key moment for male-bodied persons. These interviews with Mulk-ara were carried out in 2005–7, and, as much as they provided Mulk-ara's personal narratives, they also reflected the consolidation of this distinction into contemporary discourses and practices of transsexuality I discussed in chapter 1.

Upon her return from London, Mulk-ara began to lobby various authorities to see what could be done in Iran, but everyone told her that because of the prevailing social atmosphere, the government could not do anything. By this time, of course, it was not some nebulous presumed social conservatism but an official scientific institution—the MCI—that had closed the emerging medical possibilities for SRS in Iran. This was the period in which Mulk-ara also was concerned about the implications of her practices from a religious point of view, saying, "I was in a religious conundrum" (*az lihaz-i shar'i sargardan*). She visited Ayatollah Bihbahani, who consulted the Qur'an; it opened on the Maryam chapter (a very auspicious chapter for Mulk-ara, as it is the only chapter bearing a woman's name; it was that occasion that provided her with her eventual name of Maryam). Ayatollah Bihbahani suggested that she could contact Ayatollah Khomeini on this issue, who was at the time in Najaf. Ayatollah Khomeini confirmed that "sex-change was permitted and that after surgery, she must live her life as a woman."[98] At this point, she began to plan for going to Thailand, but by then the years of revolutionary upheaval had erupted. Mulk-ara eventually did go to Thailand for her surgery, but not until 2002.

But back in the early months of 1979, once the general strikes came to an end, like most people she went back to work. It was here that her troubles began: "They asked me, who are you? Why do you look like this? When I insisted that I had a condition, they set up a meeting for me with a doctor at Day Clinic [a top private clinic]. But the doctors' treatment of me was unbelievable; it was gross. This was just the beginning of a series of arrests, questioning me over and over again. . . . Dr. Bahr al-'Ulum and the director of Sida va Sima's [the Islamic Republic of Iran Broadcasting, IRIB, previously the NIRT] health clinic threatened me, saying they would set me on fire. Eventually they forced me to take male hormones and go into male clothes. . . . This kind of treatment continued until the early 1980s; these were bad years for *gays* and dau-jinsi people. I heard several were arrested and spent time at Evin prison."

Mulk-ara was not the only woman-presenting male forced out of the NIRT/IRIB. Haideh, now in her late forties, used to teach animation classes there before she was expelled. Eventually, she opted for sex change in the late 1990s and now has her own graphic design business. Natasha, a young makeup artist, similarly was forced out of the NIRT/IRIB. For a while she tried to find jobs in private film studios, but these studios also were under increasing scrutiny for perceived immoral conduct. Eventually, she opened her own hairdressing salon and has since become quite well known in Tehran. Today, two other MtFs are employed in her salon.

In the early 1980s, as the Islamic Republic was taking shape, Maryam Mulk-ara began her persistent lobbying of various authorities to change the situation for woman-presenting males who did not wish to dress and live as men. Under the new regime, the moral purification of society became a systemic priority. Moral purification measures included closing down sites that were considered spaces of corruption, such as the businesses in the red-light district, bars, nightclubs, and many cafés and cinemas. It meant a series of horrifying public executions of women and men on charges of prostitution and sodomy. It meant intense scrutiny of all institutions, especially those such as the mass media and the universities, which were considered critical for the production of a new revolutionary Islamic culture and society but were thought to be populated by corrupt people who had to be purged. As Mulk-ara put it in her interview, these were indeed "bad years for *gays* and dau-jinsi people."

The spectrum of non-normative, male-bodied persons in the 1970s had included woman-presenting males as well as males who did not dress as or present like women. The nonheteronormativity of the latter was focused on their desire for men, while they continued to live lives largely indistinguishable—to the uninitiated—from those of normative males. These males, some of whom now name themselves *gay* or are so named by others, had shared the increased visibility of nonheteronormative males of the 1970s. That visibility became dangerous in the years after the 1979 change of regime. These men had to adopt a more circumspect style of life, something that indeed had been a way of life for many of them already.

But while the sexual politics of the new government could be warded off by some nonheteronormative males simply by living more circumspect lives, woman-presenting males faced a particular challenge in the new republic when public gender separation emerged as an important ethical project. A totally homosocial gendering of public spaces was seen as the ideal, although it was considered largely unachievable in practice. Nevertheless, strict codes of dress and gender presentation in public were put in place by a series of measures over the period of 1979–81.[99] The self-perceptions and preferred styles of living for some nonheteronormative males included, and at times critically depended on, their ability to present themselves as women and to be visibly feminine in public, but the gender norms set in place in the early days of the Islamic Republic of Iran made that nearly impossible. As Mulk-ara and others explained, many people like her felt forced to grow mustaches and beards and live, at least during the day, as men. Living a double life by presenting as a woman at night, which was practiced by many woman-presenting males even in the 1970s, suddenly became much more hazardous, to the extent that it remained possible at all.

As we have seen, in the 1970s, woman-presenting males had carved for themselves spaces of relative acceptance in particular places and professions. The more public spaces of such "acceptability," for instance, in the entertainment industry, were at once spaces of "disrepute" but also spaces in which non-normative living could be safely cordoned off and marginalized. They provided not only a measure of safety for woman-presenting males, but also for their containment and confinement from the larger society. Woman-presenting males performed the vulgar and the deviant, and the deployment of these semi-licit styles in the popular entertainment of the 1970s provided for partial tolerance of those deemed deviant.[100] The 1979 revolution, particularly the cultural purification campaigns of the first few years of the new republic, ruptured this dynamic. The vulgar, taken in the Islamist discourse (and indeed on the political Left as well) to represent the extreme embodiment of late-Pahlavi corruption, became yet another ground for massive repression of social deviance.

The enforcement of public gender codes in the years after 1979 disrupted the old continuum of male nonheteronormativity. While it was possible to be a closeted *gay* man, living openly as a woman-presenting male became increasingly impossible. Woman-presenting males not only carried the stigma of male same-sex practices, they also transgressed the newly imposed regulations of gendered dressing and presentation in public. They were always assumed to be "passive homosexuals," facing the same severe interrogations, sometimes anal rape, imprisonment, or death. Trans-dressed males walking in the streets would be arrested on charges of prostitution. Some, like Mulk-ara, were forced to take male hormones and change into male clothing and could no longer go to work looking "like that." One key effect of the policies of the early 1980s was thus the categorical bifurcation of *gay* and *transsexual*. The practices of everyday life within both categories depended on the public disavowal of homosexuality, and likewise both were predicated on the public expression of gender normativity. Given the religious sanction to sex change offered by Ayatollah Khomeini, the categorical bifurcation of nonheteronormative maleness played out quite differently in the Islamic Republic of Iran, in the years ahead, than it did in Europe and the United States. Being *transsexual*, rather than *gay*, emerged as the more socially acceptable way of being a nonheteronormative male.

## VERDICTS OF SCIENCE, RULINGS OF FAITH

As we saw in the last chapter, the years immediately after the 1979 revolution were intensely difficult for all gender/sexual nonconformists. This was an issue especially for woman-presenting males. Masculine-presenting females were targeted directly far less often, if at all, in part because they tended to be less visibly detectable.

The focus of gender regulations of the public, as far as women were concerned, was on the imposition of a dress code that was to conform to prevailing interpretations of the meaning of hijab. While many women who participated in the 1979 revolution were observant of various levels of hijab, and other women in the anti-Shah movement had donned headscarves as a gesture of solidarity with their observant sisters; for yet others the spread of the code, even before the change of regime, was a sign of discriminatory gender concepts that they resented and resisted. These acts of resistance continued after the change of regime. Indeed, it took almost three years of introducing various regulations—often tested one step at a time, locally and partially implemented, sometimes withdrawn, and then reintroduced once resistance would subside—before a stricter dress code could be put in place. The process of challenging, and juggling the limits of, the hijab code has continued to the present day. Throughout these decades, at issue was not simply a matter of Islamic modesty; what was advocated as the hijab code was articulated as the cultural contestation of what was seen as the contamination of Irano-Islamic cultural values and ways of living by "Western cultural assault." Likewise, through advocacy and the imposition of particular styles of the hijab, various Islamist forces—both before and after the change of regime—were creating and testing their power. In a similar vein, through their resistance, whether overtly or in playful turns, women opposed to compulsory veiling would insist on a different form of social power. By now, it is generally recognized that governmental forces and their supporters, as well as dissident women, have battled at every turn over the boundaries of the hijab code as an issue of power.

Today's configurations of gender-sexual identification and dis-identification continue to bear traces of the initial years after 1979. Woman-presenting males' styles of femininity marked them sharply as targets of attacks after regime change. Many were seen to engage in gravely "more exaggerated Westernized" styles of femininity than female-bodied women. Some had even adopted Western female names—such as Anna, Rachel, Monica, Sophia, and Gina—a practice that had been briefly in fashion, especially among elite urban Iranians in the 1970s, but in the case of woman-presenting males it added yet another layer to the accusation of "Westoxication." Most important, in addition to the burden of cultural inauthenticity, they were assumed to be sexual deviants; they were read as "passive" (maf'ul), "anally penetrable" (kuni) bodies. Even today, many older woman-presenting males continue to recall the terrible experiences of being picked up by morality squads, humiliated, beaten, assaulted, and at times raped (sometimes as punishment, at other times as a price for being released), and the terrifying reports that circulated.[1] Whether woman-presenting males engaged in anal sex was not the issue as far as they saw it. For them, more than fear of facing charges of sodomy, it was the daily intolerability of being forced to live as man-presenting that mattered. Almost overnight, they had been commanded to re-dress as men. Living visibly nonnormative lives became dangerously risky for male-bodied persons. Some took up more masculine-presenting appearances (growing beards and mustaches); some even got married. They all reverted to more masculine living styles in public and kept their dressing up as women to trusted private company; some pursued sex change, although some had already become inclined in that direction in the 1970s when SRS had become more available and had come to public attention.

The beginning of the Iran-Iraq war in September 1980 introduced a heightened atmosphere of scrutiny of moral conduct. Unapproved behavior, whether at the level of neighborhood knowledge or more public sites, was marked further as a betrayal of national and Islamic values at a time when the very fate of the Islamic Republic and the integrity of the national domain were seen to be under attack. Youth mobilized for the war front became warriors of public morality at home. Non-normative behavior acquired the status of insulting the blood of "the martyrs of the sacred defense." A propaganda film, made in the early 1980s, focused on showing how the rich lived carefree lives, with no concern for the war, in their northern villas by the Caspian Sea.[2] A striking segment of the documentary was an interview with two woman-presenting males—presumably the most carefree of the carefree folk. The two, Anna and Tannaz, were interrogated in the film, asked what their motivations were for dressing up as women, and if they realized that they "provoke[d]/arouse[d] [tah-rik] people and that [was] against Islamic norm and our society's ethics."[3]

Most current recollections about arrests during these early years are more horrific than this sanitized filmic vignette. But the circulation of this documentary presaged much of the later media coverage. In her report, Khaksar noted that the two woman-presenting males in this documentary were invariably received by a broad spectrum of viewers as male homosexuals, as iva-khvahar. It took another two decades before a sharp distinction between MtF and iva-khvahar became consolidated.

The pressures and hazards of daily life set into motion some of the earliest trans-lobbying activities. Mulk-ara recalled that it was in the early 1980s when she kept hearing the news of arrests of gays and daujinsi-ha (literally persons of two-sexes—until recently, a term often used to refer to trans persons) and their imprisonment in Evin Prison. When in 1982–83 she heard that yet another friend had been arrested, she called the office of the Speaker of the Parliament Hashemi Rafasanjani. She had a meeting with him in which he promised to help. Rafasanjani also introduced her to Sayyed Abdolkarim Mousavi Ardebili, then the head of the Judiciary, and to Ayatollah Jannati, who asked Ayatollah Khomeini for a directive. Khomeini's response was that in case of physiological disorders there was no problem for changing sex. Mulk-ara did not find this response satisfactory. As she put it later, "this answer was only for people who had apparently visible problems, not for transsexuals [tara-jinsiyati-ha] who have psychological challenges. . . . So one day, still in very masculine clothes, I went to Jamaran, to the household of [Ayatollah Khomeini]. . . . Also present were Ayatollahs Hashemi Rafsanjani and Ardebili. I had a brief conversation with the Imam, but the result was really satisfactory, because there and then, the Imam issued a fatwa stating that changing sex with a doctor's approval is not prohibited [bila-mani']."[4]

Mulk-ara recalled that on that day, as soon as this opinion was issued, women from the Imam's household cut her a chador—at the time, the quintessential attire of public Muslim womanhood.[5] She officially changed into the female habit. This was not only a critical moment in her narrative of personal transition; it also set a clear precedent permitting recognized trans persons to legally live trans lives before SRS. Mulk-ara, while still a male-bodied person, lived for some seventeen years as a "muhajjabah"—a woman in hijab—except on one occasion. When in 2002 she was leaving the country to have her sex-change surgery in Thailand, the passport control personnel at Tehran airport would not allow her to leave dressed as a woman. Soon after her meeting with Khomeini, Mulk-ara had received legal permission for sex change and a document instructing the authorities to change her identity documents after SRS. These papers she carried with her at all times. But her passport was still in her male name; at the airport, she was instructed that she had to look male. She told them that she would abide by their order but the sin of her dressing as a man would be on them.[6]

Mulk-ara's narrative is critically important in at least two ways. It locates insistently the originating impetus for current religiously sanctioned medico-legal transition procedures in trans activism. While her own place in that narrative was challenged by at least two other trans persons I interviewed—both MtFs in their early fifties who told stories of their own first-ness in approaching Khomeini to get religious sanction for SRS—their challenge only strengthens the agential work of trans persons in the story: Khomeini's fatwa in the mid-1980s was not issued as a result of some student-teacher exercise in theological reasoning, nor by questions sent to Khomeini by any other agent in the complicated legal and medical geography of interested parties. It was obtained by trans persons' demand put on Iran's supreme politico-religious authority.

A second narrative effect of Mulk-ara's story is to establish a temporal priority of trans persons' needs and desires over what may seem to be a consequence of the policies of the Islamic Republic. Both Mulk-ara and another MtF located their first appeal to Ayatollah Khomeini for guidance in the mid-1970s. By bridging the mid-1980s with the mid-1970s, across the rupturing event of the 1979 revolution, they establish a continuity of the later needs and desires with those embodied in persons and living styles of the earlier decade, disrupting the simplistic causal articulation that considers their desire for sex change to be a result of the persecutions of the early years of the Islamic Republic.

The fatwa and the new legal papers, however, did not end the tribulations of Mulk-ara. Like many MtFs, she often was picked up by the police on suspicion of "moral corruption and sexual deviancy." The big difference was that she would be released after she showed her papers. Papers acquired an almost totemic significance. Carrying a whole lot of "useful papers"—even a doctor's letter of introduction to TPI as a potential trans candidate—has now become a routine practice that saves days of detention and humiliation if one is arrested. While transsexuality has become a legible category, that legibility has to demonstrate itself insistently and repeatedly; it cannot be taken for granted. One cannot simply pronounce oneself trans; the truth of that designation depends on documented affirmation by some other-than-self authority. At times, papers do not match—one may be in transition or even after transition surgically, but still in transition legally. Mulk-ara's airport incident was one such mismatch. When Sina, an FtM, had stopped after a traffic accident, the disparity between his certification paper and his driving license—at the time in his female birth name—produced a humiliating conversation between him and the traffic cop who was suddenly curious about his anatomy.

Between 1983 and her eventual trip to Thailand in 2002, Mulk-ara continued to navigate various offices, including the Public Prosecutor, the LMOI, the Ministry of Health, and NAJA (the Persian acronym for Security Forces of the Islamic Republic). At every turn she faced hostile and at times threatening reception. At one point, Dr. Monafi, the Minister of Health from 1980 to 1984, called her into his office. She was delighted and hoped for some breakthrough. When she arrived, he told her to go to the warfront: "Perhaps you will get killed and your sins will be forgiven."[7] She tried to return to her job at IRIB, but only succeeded in receiving a retirement deal (replacing the previous expulsion). During Khatami's presidency (1997–2005), she finally got the breakthrough she had hoped for. "I contacted Mr. Abtahi [Vice President], . . . who sent me to Ms. Shojaei, who sent me to Dr. Kayhani-far, a vice-minister of Health and in my view Mother Teresa of Iran; for her support of *transsexuals*, she sacrificed her official position and career."[8]

As narrated in this vignette, a second set of movements—this time originating from among some medical practitioners—converged with trans activists' struggles to bring about changes. Like woman-presenting males, several doctors recalled the early 1980s as terrible years of facing these "patients" with no guidelines for acceptable action. Dr. Behjatnia recalled,

After the revolution they were in total disarray; they would come to us [gynecologists], or go to urologists, or psychiatrists. They are very insistent people, that they must change their sex. Of course, they were there before the revolution too, but I hadn't seen as many. After the revolution, in the first years, we were suddenly inundated by their visits. . . . we were wondering how we could help these patients. There was a doctor, Dr. Tahireh Labbaf, a very committed woman, one of the really good Muslims whose sole aim was to serve.[9] She was one of our residents and I had helped her through that process all the way to her board certification. So when the problem of *transsexuals* came up, I went to her and explained the problems of these patients and suggested that, since she was part of the system of power then, she ought to go after this issue and get a fatwa to resolve this problem. She worked on it, there were meetings in the Medical Council [Nizam-i Pizishki] involving gynecologists, urologists, and psychologists, and finally the process of issuing permits was worked out. . . . This was in the first years of the revolution. The whole process of working things out took a year, a year and a half.[10]

As Dr. Behjatnia's narrative indicates, in the early years after the revolution, the medical practitioners had to turn to their more Islamist-identified colleagues to introduce change. In these same years, as far as SRS was concerned, the war-time exigencies created remarkable advances in Iranian prosthetic surgical technologies that expanded training and specialization, as well as a more general acceptability, of plastic surgeries. Ironically, despite political and social pressures, transsexuals became unintended beneficiaries of these developments. Bodily modifications were no longer seen as necessarily intervening in God's design, opening a space for trans arguments that their surgeries were not elective cosmetic whims.

What set the stage for consolidation of re-conceptualizations of bodily modifications and of trans as an acceptable category of embodied personhood were the broader Islamicization of the state and society initiated in the 1980s. This process was launched in part under the title of "Compliance" (with Islam) (*intibaq*), more specifically, through Compliance of medicine (including psychiatry and psychology) with Islam.[11]

### The Compliance with Islam Project: Fatwas and Their State Effects

Before the 1979 revolution, and before the consolidation of the Islamic Republic of Iran in the 1980s, the scientific community was neither aware of nor generally concerned with Islamic rulings on medical matters.[12] By the early 1970s, its perception of transsexuality had become firmly shaped by behavioral psychology's gender-sexual dimorphism.

By the mid-1980s, however, it became clear that the biomedical and psychosexological sciences needed to present their reasoning in a different style to be able to interact with legal authorities when needed. With the establishment of the Islamic Republic of Iran, all social and cultural phenomena, from the media to the educational system and beyond, came under the critical ideological scrutiny of the new republic. Indeed, the new republic took shape through these very practices of reconstructive scrutiny. With the end of the war in 1988 and the launching of Reconstruction efforts, more concerted attention was paid to the articulation of what Compliance with Islam meant as a matter of state policy. Within the domain of medicine and psychology, this scrutiny initially was focused on problems ensuing from the mixing of women and men that transgressed rules of looking and touching (*ahkam-i nazar va lams*).

To address medical compliance with Islam, several initiatives were launched from the late 1980s, including a seminar held in Mashhad (1989) on the subject of Islamic Perspectives on Medicine, and the International Congress on Medical Ethics in Iran held in Tehran (1993). In 1994 the Ministry of Health, Healing, and Medical Education (HHME) established the High Council for Compliance of Medical Matters with Precepts of the Holy Law, which set up a scientific committee to oversee the first nation-wide Congress of Compliance. The scientific committee included eight ayatollahs, five hujjat al-Islams, and forty doctors, including Dr. Marzieh Vahid-Dastjerdi (at the time a member of the parliament and, between September 2009 and December 2012, the minister of the HHME).

On the eve of the Congress, held in Tehran in 1995, Ayatollah Khamenei addressed the members of the scientific and executive committees, emphasizing that, "What we are most afflicted by is the issue of women and men— whether in educational and scientific sectors, or in practical sectors, hospitals, clinics and the like—this is very important work that you brothers and sisters have begun."[13] Papers presented at the Congress covered various aspects of the separation of the sexes in medical practice and education so that rules of looking and touching could be observed. A few papers were devoted to discussing some of the contemporary issues that needed Islamic guidelines, such as abortion, infertility treatment, family planning and contraception, and surrogate motherhood.[14]

In the end, the scope of the actual implementation of policies and practices for ensuring compliance in medicine remained limited. In April 1998, after the second nationwide Compliance Congress (1997), Vahid-Dastjerdi helped draft a legislative proposal for the sex segregation of all medical services. The plan was vehemently opposed by doctors and health professionals and eventually was abandoned on grounds of expediency (there are not enough female doctors and not enough male nurses) and the cost of radical separation, which would include the establishment of separate hospitals for women and men.

While the congress focused on compliance in medical practice, psychological matters also were included. The topic of transsexuality was raised in a paper by the psychologist Mustafá Najafi.[15] Najafi raised the challenge of a trans person living as the other gender over a long period of time to ensure that the person could really adapt to the opposite sex/gender, as was done in other countries. He asked if this were "possible at all in our culture and in our *shar'*"[16] and concluded that psychologists faced such problems on a daily level; they needed authoritative and uniform standards for dealing with them.

The Compliance project made a significant impact on rapid growth and institutionalization of the LMOI. As we saw in chapter 2, the convergence of criminology, law, and medicine had provided not only the scientific ground for the field of legal medicine, but also for establishing the LMOI. In the early years of a new parliamentary government in Iran, in 1910 (1328 AH), a set of regulations was passed by the parliament, but it is not clear what came of it. When in the early Pahlavi period 'Ali Akbar Davar (1867–1937) was Minister of Justice, the judiciary's needs for legal medicine were taken care of by a doctor, Filsuf al-Atibba', in his own house, which was located near the Judiciary.[17] This was the pattern for the handful of physicians who would receive various requests from the Ministry of Justice in subsequent years. When in the late 1930s the new building that housed the Ministry of Justice was under construction, three rooms were allocated to legal medicine. Upon its completion in 1942, this section became officially the site of the Legal Medicine Organization.[18] A law establishing the Legal Medicine Organization of the Ministry of Justice was passed in 1952, but because of the political upheavals of the period, it is not clear what impact it had. In 1960, this organization was accommodated in "a small office in the southwestern corner of the Ministry of Justice, with a small room, with one bed, assigned to autopsy."[19] In 1965, a new law covering the responsibilities and duties of the Office of Legal Medicine was passed. In the late 1970s, with the growth of urbanization, construction of a building to house the expanding Legal Medicine Office began. This building, on the southern side of Park-i Shahr, was completed after the 1979 revolution and currently serves as the central office of the LMOI. A new law, passed in 1993, transformed the Office of Legal Medicine into an organization independent from the Ministry of Justice, although it remained under the supervision of the head of the Judiciary.[20]

While the 1979 regime change involved important revisions of legal codes and judicial structures, there were also significant continuities that consolidated, expanded, and enfolded some of the late-Pahlavi trends. A most important mediating domain in this transformation was the field of legal medicine. Here the psycho-socio-sexology of the 1970s became integrated into the Compliance project of the Islamicization of law and science and the state-centered reformation of jurisprudence.

Specifically, the penal codes were totally redone to comply with Islamic jurisprudential requirements. The legal determination of a number of punishments in the *qisas* (jurisprudentially mandated retributions) category and the exactitude of payment of *diyah* (jurisprudentially mandated compensations) for others suddenly faced the state organization with an expanded, yet uncharted, legal medical territory. As a result, the LMOI has grown enormously.

Concurrent with the emergence of the field and its infrastructures, specialized legal medicine texts began to be written and courses established in Tehran University's School of Medicine.[21] Few in number in the decades before 1979, these specialized texts increased rapidly in the 1980s and 1990s because of the need for compliance of legal codes and medical practices with Islamic jurisprudence. Faramarz Gudarzi's *Legal Medicine*, for example, started as a modest, 110-page book in 1989; by 1991, it had been expanded into 744 pages and eventually turned into a two-volume work of 1,710 pages.[22]

Gudarzi (1932–2006) is often referred to as a founding father of modern legal medicine; his texts have come to serve as basic texts of the profession. A comparison of the earlier and the latest editions of his texts demonstrates the growing integration of bio-psycho-medical discourse of sexuality with legal-fiqhi requirements of sexual practices. These growing imbrications often take the shape of enfolding various concepts and layering discourses rather than displacing one set of concepts with another. What may seem to be the coexistence of conflicting, if not incompatible, notions provides the possibility of navigating difficult challenges that the Compliance project has posed.

Gudarzi's 1991 text already had integrated sexological taxonomies, which by then had become the accepted scientific truth of sex/gender/sexuality, into its section on "Sexual problems in legal medicine" (553–616). That section's third chapter, "Sexual deviations" (568–90), categorized twenty-three "types of sexual deviation." It is not surprising that the list is virtually identical to those in psycho-sexological texts. (Equally unsurprising is Asghar Qatil's appearance under sadism.)

The two-volume 1998 edition subsumed all the material from the earlier edition and added large new sections; as a result, the same topic often is covered more than once.

In this edition, the third chapter of "Sexual problems in legal medicine," titled, as before, "Sexual deviations," is now subdivided into deviations and disorders. A new section has been added, titled "Sexual deviations from a psychic/

psychological [*ravani*] point of view," wherein the term *deviations* slips and becomes "sexual psychiatric/psychological [ravani] disorders." Transsexuality has been shifted into the disorders category, appearing under *ikhtilalat-i huviyat-i jinsi* (with "gender identity disorder" in English next to it).

The layered additive character of the text—similar to Buffington's notion of the peaceful bringing together of different theories that war in other contexts[23]—produces the seemingly conflicting categorization of transsexuality in a second instance, following the section on transvestism and as one of a series of deviations, as in earlier texts. Thus, within this monumental text, transsexualism appears at once as a gender/sexual disorder and as a sexual/gender deviation. This paradoxical situation indicates that the very definition of transsexuality in terms of its distinction from homosexuality—because of the indistinction of gender/sex/sexuality—continues to produce the concept in affinity with homosexuality. While this section follows the earlier structure, the content of the section about transsexuality has been radically revised and substantively expanded to bring it in line with the postrevolutionary legalization of transsexuality as a phenomenon that is not subject to the moral and legal prohibitions that pertain to homosexuality (1293–96). The struggling, at times conflicting, emergence of these three affiliated concepts (transvestism, transsexuality, homosexuality) brings their discussion into this text yet a third time. The fifth chapter of this part is titled, "Cognition of femaleness and maleness" (*Tashkhis-i zan ya mard budan*) (1362–69)—where both transvestism and transsexuality appear as deviations and a neighboring subsection covers persons with ambiguous genitalia.[24]

Is the desire for gender/sex change a deviation? Is it a disorder? This continues to remain a critical issue. Deviation—in its Persian expression, *inhiraf*—is associated not merely with a scientific categorization. Linguistically, culturally, and in everyday perception, inhiraf connects with a moral concept: straying from the straight path. Living the path of righteousness is not only a key concept of practice for observant Muslims, but it also informs the broader and more defuse notion of living an ethical life.[25] As we have seen, within Iranian legal medical literature there is no consistent categorization. This incoherence points to the concept's contingent formation. Initially, through psycho-sexology, transsexuality had shifted into sexological literature as an extreme case of the deviation of transvestism, itself an extreme manifestation of "passive homosexuality." Yet its permissibility in the post-1979 period made it necessary to separate, delineate, mark, and diagnose it as something *not* essentially belonging to the morally apprehensive, religiously forbidden space of inhiraf. Thus in later texts transsexuality has been shifted from deviation to the presumably more benign disorder. Significantly, this taxonomical move has taken it back to where it had started: as a disorder that now borders inter-sexuality (another gender/sex/sexual disorder).

But the question of whether transsexuality is a deviation or a disorder is by no means settled. Despite more than two decades of policy change, the social cognition of transsexuality remains a troubling elusive issue. Officials—medical personnel, Welfare Organization workers and leaders, legal practi-tioners—over and over again reiterate the by-now-familiar official line: trans-sexuality is not a deviation and should not be confused with homosexuality. In this narrative, transsexuals are variously referred to as "unfortunate crea-tures" and "patients." They are said to need family and social support as well as legal and medical assistance. That these repetitions remain necessary, points to the instability of the dividing line. Not all psychologists agree to consider it a disorder and emphasize its distinction from intersexuality. Not all clerics concur; some consider it the same as same-sex-playing, subject to the same punishments. Moreover, the contiguity of living communities of transsexual and homosexuals and the continuity of daily life patterns and practices work against the rigidness of neat taxonomical lines of separation.

Despite limited implementation, the paradigm and process of compliance brought Islamic jurisprudence and medicopsychological discourse into a pro-ductive nexus, in which the work of trans activists' lobbying from the mid-1980s would translate into procedural codification and legal consolidation of the status of transsexuality. Already on November 8, 1987, the LMOI had sent a query to the Legal Office of the Ministry of Justice asking for clarification on the legality of SRS. The ministry's response, based completely on various sec-tions of Ayatollah Khomeini's treatise *Tahrir al-wasilah*, rather than on any par-ticular article of the law, stated that sex-change surgeries were legal whether on intersex individuals or on transsexuals.[26] Over the next decades, the devel-opment of detailed legal and medical procedures for transsexuality became a celebrated showcase of achievement of compliance of medical and legal con-cepts and practices with those of fiqh.

## Specialization of Fiqh

The Compliance project—a particular instance of crafting the Islamic Republic as a modern state—necessitated and encouraged religious scholars to system-atically publish highly specialized tomes on medical matters (*masa'il-i mus-tahdisah-i pizishki*). Previously, discussion of such issues would be embedded within relevant sections of the *tauzih al-masa'il* genre (usually as appendices, when it came to specific novel issues such as artificial insemination).[27] Now fiqh became specialized and took on a "disciplinary" shape that included the publication of a large number of books dedicated to doctors and healthcare professionals. By 1999, a published bibliography of this growing literature covered 586 entries, incorporating sections on population control, abortion, insemination, sex change, genetic modifications, brain death, euthanasia, dissection, and organ transplants.[28]

When it comes to sex change, as with many other issues, there is no unanimity of opinion among Shi'i scholars who issue fatwas in Iran.[29] All consider intersex surgeries permissible because they bring out "the hidden genus" of the body. Some explicitly argue against non-intersex surgeries, while others express doubt about its permissibility or simply do not take a stand.[30] Some have changed their opinion over the years.[31]

Regardless of these differing stances, it was the overwhelming weight of Ayatollah Khomeini's fatwa that translated into law. This weight cannot be understood as a matter of religious authority; it was an authority derived from his unique position as the leader of the most massive revolution in the late-twentieth century. Here also lies the significance of the reissuance of his fatwa on the permissibility of sex change after the 1979 revolution. Unlike the earlier opinion issued in the 1960s, which largely had gone unnoticed, the mid-1980s ruling had legal ramifications. While the Iranian constitution has codified the position of the supreme *faqih* as the pinnacle of power, only Khomeini in fact had the combined religious and political authority that would translate his fiqhi opinion into law. Today, even though Ayatollah Khamenei is the Supreme Leader, the weight of his religious fatwas is no different from those of many other grand ayatollahs of similar rank. The compliance of all legislation with Islamic concepts is supervised not by him but by the Council of Guardians.[32]

Khomeini's ruling in *Tahrir al-wasilah* appears under a section on "The Examination of Contemporary Questions," within which a subsection is devoted to "The Changing of Sex."[33] In this section, in the familiar responsa style of question and answer, ten problems are covered. Questions 1 and 2 deal directly with permissibility of sex surgeries for trans and intersex persons. Subsequent questions cover particular effects of change, such as the status of a person's marriage after the change. Question (and answer) 1 reads:

> The prima facie [*al-zahir*] view is contrary to prohibiting the changing, by operation, of a man's sex to that of a woman or vice versa; likewise, the operation [in the case] of a hermaphrodite is not prohibited in order that s/he may become incorporated into one of the two sexes. Does this [sex

change operation] become obligatory if a woman perceives, in herself, the inclinations which are among the type of inclinations of a man [literally the root/origin inclinations of a man], or some qualities of masculinity; or if a man perceives, in himself, the inclinations or some qualities of the opposite sex? The prima facie view is that it [sex change] is not obligatory if the person is truly of one sex, and changing his/her sex to the opposite sex is possible (volume 2, 753–55).

The double negative in the first sentence, "contrary to prohibiting," and the concluding "not obligatory" are the critical terms that have defined the dominant views among top Iranian Shi'ite scholars and, most importantly, have defined the legal procedures for sex reassignment. From the point of view of trans persons, this conceptualization has opened up the space for acquiring the certificate of transsexuality without being required to go through any hormonal or somatic changes if they do not so wish. This continues to be hotly contested between trans persons and various state authorities. Legal and religious authorities know full well that many certified trans persons do very little, beyond living transgender lives, once they obtain their certification; at most they may take hormones. As Dr. Saberi of the LMOI put it, "These patients [trans persons] can easily draw circles around us and play games with us."[34] In his interview with me (June 2006), he was more specific: "Some of these people got their physician's recommendation and then went around and did anything they felt like. There is this fellow who eight years ago got the certification for GID [gender identity disorder], s/he got involved with the law and they brought her/him here. For eight years s/he has lived as a *homosexual* [pronounced as such in Persian] and has engaged in same-sex-playing sexual behavior [*raftarha-yi jinsi-i hamjins-bazanah*]. S/he even makes a living from this work, but hasn't operated, doesn't even cross-dress, only uses make-up, in a style that anyone who looks at her/him would recognize this person is *homosexual*." While the authorities do not like this situation, they cannot overrule Khomeini's double negative, which has now become accepted by a large number of senior scholars of fiqh. Khomeini's overwhelming and exceptional political authority has overruled even his own cautionary "prima facie."

It is important to note that some trans persons do not consider their style of living—which Dr. Saberi finds an abuse of law—an exercise of bad faith. They consider their "living as the other sex/gender" to be an enactment of their "true sex/gender." In that sense, they see their status as no different from that of an intersex person whose "true sex/gender" has been determined. Indeed, question 2 in Khomeini's *Tahrir al-wasilah* states, "For if it is known that he is a man, then that which is incumbent upon men is incumbent upon him and that which is prohibited to him is that which is prohibited to them [men] and the same is the case for women." This resonates with the sense of gender/sex within which many sex/gender-variant persons configure their relationships and practices. Maryam Khatun Mulk-ara's answer to a reporter, Hamid Riza Khalidi, about her marital life, for example, articulates this perception. Khalidi asks, "Have you been married?" "Yes, twice," she answers. "How could it be? You were still a man . . ." Mulk-ara responds: "Look, the *shar'i* rule for us in this respect is exactly similar to the rule for a woman who may face some difficulty concerning her marriage, but doesn't say anything to her fiancé or spouse until the wedding night. When on the wedding night, the husband finds out, he could divorce her or accept and live with it. We had the same situation. My first spouse knew about my situation about a year before my operation. We performed the marriage contract [*ma ba ham 'aqdi khvandim*]."[35]

Dr. Saberi, and Islamic scholars such as Hujjat al-Islam Karimi-nia, however, think the sentence that follows the one quoted above in question 2 in relation to the intersex person would not permit Mulk-ara's interpretation: "However, regarding the necessity of changing his appearance and the exposure of what is concealed, it is not obligatory unless some or all of his legal responsibilities depend on the operation and unless it is impossible for him to have prudence with regard to divine prohibitions, then the sex change is obligatory."

In other words, the double negative gives certain permissions, yet excludes any practices subject to "divine prohibitions." This same double negative creates multiple conclusions on exactly how this distinction is to be made. Dr. Saberi, for example, invokes social considerations to disallow "living as the other sex/gender":

A shar'i obstacle is one thing, a customary obstacle is another. Just imagine a place for women, let's say a hairdressing salon, where only women are there [by law, only women can work in beauty salons for women] and suddenly you notice someone there, dressed as a woman but who is a man. So this will make you upset. In our culture, this is not an acceptable customary practice, to allow someone to live cross-dressed. . . . Suppose someone notices that his daughter in university is walking with another girl, but actually that girl is a man, only looks like a woman. Well, this wouldn't be acceptable. So, we cannot issue such permits. . . . We can't just say that there is no shar'i obstacle on this issue . . . we do recommend living for a while in that frame, but only in private gatherings in places where the person is known, with people who know her/his problem.[36]

Even a brief review of the responsa literature suggests the complexity of fiqh as a source of authoritative judgment, both generally and in relation to trans persons. The designation of male and female in classical fiqh is distinctly related to the observance of topic-dependent rules. These distinctions are not identical to and do not perform the same work as biological sex taxonomies. For instance, a person of ambiguous genitalia can become assigned a "ritual gender/sex" so that s/he would follow the rules of one gender/sex.[37] In contemporary discussions, the fiqhi notion of *jins* (genus/sex) travels between two distinct registers: the classic Islamic meaning of jins as a taxonomical genus and the notion of sex (jins) in its modern sense. The transformation of the sociocultural notion of sex/gender over the past century has brought into proximity the male/female distinction of fiqh with the biological sex taxonomies and social categories of men and women. This proximity has enabled the convergence of some fiqhi thinking with the biomedical and psycho-sexological discourse about transsexuality.

Shiʻi scholars such as Karimi-nia, however, also are trained to keep these categorical distinctions apart. Karimi-nia emphasizes this point in his book *Taghyir-i jinsiyat*: "Jins in its sense of 'male and female' is something that has emerged as a secondary meaning; the primary and principal meaning of jins is not 'male and female.'"[38] The insistence on these definitional distinctions enables him to argue against those scholars who oppose sex change on the basis of opposition to changing God's work of creation. He argues that the change of male to female and vice versa is not a change in genus of a created being; it is rather a change in his/her *jinsi* apparatus.[39] As important, fiqhi thought is not invested in etiology but instead works in a problem-solving mode. Scientific problem solving has become closely connected with finding the causes of the problem; in fiqhi problem solving, the causes have no relevance. Fiqhi thought is invested in ensuring that all persons act in a manner that does not break the given rules, nor cross what it considers *hudud-allah*—the bounds set by Allah for human behavior. Thus the *sharʻi* rules are topic-dependent: when the topic changes, the rule could be different. On certain issues, changing from the category male to female (or vice versa) changes the subject and thus the rules. Indeed, that is how the gendered-ness of daily life becomes produced.

The most severe challenge that fiqhi thinking had classically faced in this domain was when the subject was completely ambiguous, as in *khunsá mushkil* (difficult hermaphrodite), for which an elaborate set of rules were worked out to deal with the unknowability of the subject's sex/gender.[40] More recently, the unanimous opinion that an intersex person may choose to go for sex-disambiguation surgery offers an alternative to such persons being assigned merely a ritual gender/sex. Such medical technologies are welcomed as technologies of transforming doubt and unknowability into certainty.[41]

A more difficult challenge, vis-à-vis "the subject of transsexuality," arises when the subject is in transition. How does one deal with "the discordant subject," with the "lack of correspondence between gender/sex of soul and body," as Karimi-nia's concept of transsexuality would have it? That is, what ritual gender/sex could be assigned to persons who are called (and often refer to themselves as) *bilataklif* (in a conundrum), or, as Karimi-nia refers to them, as those in *barzakh* (in purgatory)? Does one go by the gender/sex of the body or that of the soul? Here, trans persons insist on going by the soul. This is how many explain their daily living arrangements. It is also what enables their problematic, explicit, and often emphasized disaffiliation (we are not same-sex-players—*ma hamjins-baz nistim*) from people who engage in seemingly identical sex/gender practices but who do not consider themselves *ts*. Karimi-nia, on the other hand, wary of the intrusion of same-sex-playing that haunts fiqhi thinking on this topic, leans toward going by the gender/sex of the body. At times, however, he is more flexible. His arguments against permissibility of ritual sex/gender reassignment of in-transition persons (or those who do not desire bodily modification at all) often leans back not on fiqhi rules but, like Saberi, on what consequences such reassignment would have for public order (*nazm-i 'umumi*), public chastity (*'iffat-i 'umumi*), ethical living (*akhlaq-i hasanah*), and potential crime (*jurm*).

Understanding fiqhi thinking on this topic is further complicated by the fact that in responsa literature, within the *tauzih al-masa'il* genre written by ayatollahs, for instance, there is usually no explication of the reasoning that leads to a particular ruling. Such explication usually appears in other tomes, and more often only in the oral lessons that a scholar holds with his circle of students—future preachers and scholars. As an outsider to Islamic circles of education, I needed to craft my own circle for responsa to better understand the fiqhi reasoning on transsexuality. I headed to Qum to meet Hujjat al-Islam Muhammad Mahdi Karimi-nia, the junior scholar who has devoted much of his recent research and writing to the topic of transsexuality.[42]

## Going to Qum

The highway connecting Tehran to Qum is very straight and on a flat plain, as if it were a geospatialization of *sirat-i mustaqim*, the straight path that believing Muslim women and men are enjoined to follow in life. Its flat straightness reminded me of Zia's comment. Zia self-identifies as *gay* among friends. In the

weekly meeting of a support group for trans persons that is held at Navvab Safavi's Center for Critically Socially Harmed Groups of Welfare Organization,[43]
Zia, in the presence of a Welfare Organization social worker, suggested that
"since the culture named us all deviants [*munharif*], we possess the power to
redefine what that label might mean. Think metaphorically of driving; most
people take the straight highway to get where they want to go, but we deviate
from the straight path and take some side roads—a much more interesting
way to travel than the boring straight highway."

Like all major urban centers—perhaps even more than many, given its
new significance since 1979 as a politico-religious bastion—Qum has grown
enormously.[44] Karimi-nia's office was on the second floor of the Specialization
Center in Islamic Law and Judiciary (*Markaz-i Takhassusi-i Huquq va Qaza-yi
Islami*).[45] His education, teaching, and current research offer a prime example
of professionalization and specialization of fiqh. In 2006, having received recognition as a hujjat al-Islam through seminary education, he was completing a
doctoral dissertation in the Law Faculty of Imam Khomeini Institute in Qum
and taught at Arak University, while carrying out research at the Specialization
Center. His dissertation on transsexuality employs his Islamic jurisprudential
skills to come up with answers to the many questions concerning daily life for
transsexual persons—questions on issues of marriage, divorce, child custody,
inheritance, and so on—all of which in fiqh are structured around the gender/
sex of an individual.[46]

In between my meetings with Hujjat al-Islam Karimi-nia and afterward, I
sent him questions in e-mail messages and he patiently answered them. This
dynamic of question and answer—at times face to face, at times in virtual
space or during a telephone conversation—is no different from that which produces the responsa literature, except that I was not a theology student and was
not seeking an answer to resolve a dilemma of practice. Initially, it seemed that
the difference mattered; Karimi-nia was used to reporters and documentary
filmmakers. He received me similarly. In our first meeting, he began with the
same style of formulaic presentation of the problem, and the Islamic response
to resolution, of transsexuality that I had heard him pronounce in documentaries: that the ground for permissibility of srs is that it has not explicitly been
prohibited in the Qur'an or in the basic tenets of fiqh, unlike such matters
as drinking wine, eating pork, or same-sex-playing (*hamjins-bazi*). He further
elaborated that even for such prohibited matters, there was the provision of
*iztirar*: namely, circumstantial necessity. If you are stranded on an island and
the only thing that would save you from starvation is a pig, you are allowed to
eat its meat, but only as much as it staves off your starvation, not for pleasure

of eating. So even if some faqihs think transsexuality changes God's creation and it ought not to be allowed, they should permit it, because in many cases not permitting it leads to suicides of transsexuals.

This smoothly articulated sketch is the result of more than a decade of research and writing, as well as repeated presentations not only to journalists and documentary producers but also at numerous regional and national seminars on transsexuality. Karimi-nia's first published paper on the topic dates to 2000.[47] His first major presentation was at the first international Congress of Islamic Countries Organization for Forensic Medicine (June 24–26, 2004).[48] He began to get invitations to other seminars in Iran and was approached by national and international media for interviews. He has since become a required participant in such conversations.

Karimi-nia's article begins with a presentation of physiological (for example, chromosomal) differences of male and female bodies, then reviews the fiqhi literature on the *khunsá* (hermaphrodite), bringing the biomedical concepts into conversation with the religious discourse on this topic. He concludes that, "It seems that it is preferable to think in terms of 'reforming/correcting sex' rather than 'changing sex,' since, according to some physicians, sex-change in perfect men and perfect women who suffer from no deficiency does not exist and is impossible. The only thing that takes place in surgical operations in this field concerns the kind of khunsá who has both kinds of genitals, so that one set is eliminated and the other strengthened" (77). This is very much in line with what many physicians had insisted upon since the 1940s in Iran, as we have seen. Some still do hold this position.

Within a short few years, Karimi-nia had changed his position radically. As he became deeply invested in studying this topic, he worked closely with doctors and psychologists and, through them, began to know many transsexuals closely. Soon he became known as a trans-friendly cleric. Many practicing Muslim trans persons from all over Iran now regularly consult with him about their options.[49]

As a novice in "asking questions," I had neither a journalist's experience nor the status of a theology student. Cautiously, I started with "safe" questions, "Are trans persons permitted to live as 'the other gender/sex'?" For certified TSS, he said, "it is permitted to live trans-dressed [*mubaddal-pushi*], as long as the purpose of such cross-dressing is to cure their condition and get better, and as long as they do not engage in same-sex-playing." This is from the point of *shar'*, he emphasized. From a legal point of view, "the legal certificate is not specific, though some *transsexuals* have shown me letters giving them permission to trans-dress. The letters are meant to prevent the police from harassing them. Such permissions are transitional, to enable *transsexuals* to have a chance to reflect over their situation; the LMOI cannot give someone a permanent permit. Should a general permit be issued for living in the opposite sex's 'habit,' all hell would break loose [literally 'not a stone would stay put on another,' *sang ru-yi sang band nakhvahad shud*]."[50]

When he agreed that certified TSs are permitted to live transgendered lives in every way except having sex with someone of their own bodily sex, I used his argument of circumstantial necessity to ask if having sex with someone of their own bodily sex cannot be permitted in such cases as a matter of necessity. He categorically rejected this argument: "having sex is not a need the lack of the satisfaction of which would be life-threatening." I persisted from a different direction: "But as you know, transsexuals consider themselves to *be* the other sex." Karimi-nia was unimpressed: "In Islam, categorical sex is bodily sex, determined by the genitals. The medical sciences have other grounds as well, such as chromosomes; that may be helpful in disambiguating the intersex, but for the purposes of religious law it is the apparent sex of the body that counts." "What counts" refers to how sex/gender categories determine various fiqhi obligations—rules to live by for a pious life.

I drew an argument from a text by Ali Reza Kahani of the LMOI and his colleague Peyman Shojaei, in which they noted that in several countries, the authorities had given up trying to control and reduce "this problem" and instead had opted to change their old "sexual ethics" and treat people afflicted with GID through the satisfaction of their sexual, emotional, and psychological needs by their own sex. By changing their laws and allowing same-sex relations, they had attempted to solve this problem. Kahani and Shojaei referred to this as *jism-darmani* (soma-therapy).[51] Since he allowed cross-dressing as an expedient measure of "cure," I asked Karimi-nia why he would not authorize *jism-darmani* as a "cure." He did not believe that jism-darmani works as a cure. At this point, I expected to hear Islamic jurisprudential arguments about "the people of Lot" and their condemnation. But after a pause, instead of a fiqhi line of reasoning, Karimi-nia spoke "sociological evidence," offering the example of a woman from Shiraz who had recently come to visit him:

> She called me from Shiraz. She says she has a child from her marriage of many years ago. When her child was two years old, her husband died. She says she had always considered herself a man. I asked her how she could have considered herself a man if she got married as a woman. She says, "I thought I had an active role even in that relationship." After her husband died in an accident, she and her two-year-old started living with another

woman so that she would not be alone. They have lived together for the past twenty-three years. I asked her if they had [sexual] relations. She said, "yes, I have had relations with this woman." So you see, for twenty-three years she has been a same-sex-player and still her problem has not been solved. She had gone to Zamani [Dr. Mirjalali's assistant; Mirjalali is by far the most (in)famous sex reassignment surgeon in Iran] and he had told her that they could change her sex and this would solve her dilemma. She had talked about it with her partner who had accepted it and had said that they could then have a *shar'i* marriage. Now she wanted to know if that is permitted in *shar'*. So you see even doctors do not think same-sex relations solve a transsexual's problem.

"But then, doesn't that depend on one's concept of cure [*shafa*]?" I asked. "That way she had lived a contented life for the past twenty-three years, is that not *shafa*?" No, Karimi-nia strongly objected, "that would be condoning sinful prohibited practices as a necessity. *Transsexuals* have a disparity between their body and soul. The only *shafa* is to remove this disparity, since we cannot change people's soul, we can bring their bodies in line with their soul. This is permitted but not required. If a *transsexual* can live without committing sins, s/he doesn't have to go for bodily changes."

Karimi-nia's proposition for permitting provisional transgendered living comes under pressure not only by the "uneducated public" but also by the legal authorities who are aware that people get their certificates in order to live legally sanctioned sex/gender-variant lives. Karimi-nia shares this anxiety of the authorities. The courts, NAJA (the police force), and the LMOI have been working hard to close this loophole.

Karimi-nia insisted that permission for sex change was conditional on two points: It must be an issue of absolute necessity (*iztirar/zarurat*) and it must be real, not apparent (*haqiqi*, not *suri* or *zahiri*). This he interprets as meaning that sex change must be completed. But here fiqhi caution cannot sanction legal closure: What is permitted (*halal/mubah*) cannot be made to be required (*vajib*) short of a fatwa issued by a mujtahid who has complete hegemony over jurisprudential opinion. In Iran's recent past, only Ayatollah Khomeini enjoyed such unchallengeable politico-religious authority. Since his death, no one comes anywhere close. The many ayatollahs do not even agree on the permissibility issue, much less do they agree on turning it into a requirement.

This situation continues to allow a domain of murkiness for living nonheteronormative lives. The closest the authorities have come to an attempt at clarification is to tighten the regulations concerning the timing of issuing new name-changed *shinasnamah* (identification papers). Many trans persons, especially FtMs, apply for new identity documents after the initial operations, referred to as *takhliah*, "emptying out." They obtain letters from surgeons certifying that they have done their SRS; sometimes courts have required a bodily examination, something that trans persons find humiliating and have resisted. This also raises a problem from a fiqhi viewpoint: If a transsexual has had only a partial, "emptying out," operation, who should bodily examine him/her? In the case of a dead khunsá (hermaphrodite), for instance, Karmini-nia explained, the body has to be washed fully clothed—contrary to all other dead bodies that ought to be ritually washed naked by a person of their own sex/gender. But examination with full clothing would defeat the very aim of bodily examination of a transsexual. After strong lobbying by trans activists, the courts have now been instructed to accept physician certification.

Trans activists have also worked against the LMOI's attempt to postpone provision of new documents until the completion of reconstructive surgeries. Many, in particular many FtMs, opt not to go for reconstructive surgery at all or do so only partially. Moreover, a common concern is financial. Except for those from well-to-do and supportive families, it is simply not possible for most trans persons to have all the various needed surgeries within a short span of time; often they space it out while saving money for the next stage. The government subsidy covers only a fraction of the costs. Unless the government would be willing to cover the total cost of SRS, the legal requirement would be unenforceable. Hanging over this dispute is the fact that the government cannot be seen to enforce something with which many Islamic jurists disagree, something that can be considered neither a religious requirement nor a matter of "expediency for the state." It is this complicated imbrication of considerations of state and requirements of religion that provides negotiating and resisting spaces for trans persons.

In my third meeting with Karimi-nia, I heralded these arguments to point out to him that many trans persons cannot complete their transition speedily and their period of in-betweenness may last years; the restriction of a time period for full transition and withholding of legal changes until its completion would cause enormous hardship. He was seriously taken aback by this suggestion, as if he had not thought about it. At times I got the impression that his jurisprudential training makes him think of all matters as fiqhi problems to be solved through the learned style of fiqhi reasoning, rather than thinking through the implications for living individuals involved. After a short pause, he suggested that during the transition years, trans persons must live according to the rules of *ihtiyat* (caution) that govern the *mamsuh*—people who lack genitals. I asked what about a man who, in war or in an accident, loses his penis? That is different, he said, he can't get married of course, but since he was known to be a man, if he was already married, he does not have to annul his marriage. But an FtM without phalloplasty can live as a man but is not allowed to get married. "That is our fiqhi rule, and this is accepted by 80 to 90 percent of medical scientists as well: the criterion of sex/gender references sexual/ reproductive organ [*milak-i jinsiyat barmigardah bih alat-i tanasuli*]." When I pointed out to him that then this meant FtMs with full beards would have to dress in women's clothes and live as women and that would pose enormous hardships for them, he reflected thoughtfully and said it had to be worked out more carefully. But, at least for the moment of our exchange, he insisted that the rules of caution as applied to the *mamsuh* should apply to persons in transition. This may be a valid fiqhi position, but many trans persons simply do not care for that level of *shar'i* compliance. As one FtM put it, "Once I was diagnosed as TS, I started having sex with my girlfriend without feeling sinful." The legal authorities as well seem to act more pragmatically. A recent court case was resolved by allowing an FtM (Ardishir) to marry his long-time girlfriend (Shaqayiq). From the newspaper reports, it is not clear whether Ardishir had completed full reconstructive surgery. Shaqayiq had applied to the family court to get permission to marry Ardishir despite her father's opposition (a father's permission is legally required for a woman's first marriage). Her father stated in the court that he could not imagine his daughter's best friend as her husband. Eventually he agreed to give his permission so long as there were no medical grounds for difficulty in marriage. The case was sent to the LMOI, which confirmed that there was no medical impediment to the marriage.[52]

Karimi-nia sees his own mission on several levels. The first is to fully develop the Islamic jurisprudential arguments and provide fiqhi answers to all questions concerning transsexuality, especially in such matters as marriage, divorce, inheritance, custody rights, and so on—domains in which the categorical distinction between male and female makes a difference in rights and obligations. This he sees as a challenge in seminary circles, most of which do not know anything about this topic and are very skeptical, if not overtly hostile. His second domain of work he considers to be legal advocacy. Given the nexus of law and fiqh in the Islamic Republic of Iran, he advocates the legal consolidation of the trans person's status. In the 2005 Mashhad seminar, Karimi-nia compared the occasion to one on miscarriage and abortion held the previous year in Hamadan. He suggested that this seminar should also result in parliamentary legislation and proper legal regulations. Finally, he works to educate various authorities as well as families and individuals. As he repeated several times, the jurisprudential permissibility of sex change does not extend to so-cial circulation of knowledge, much less changing social norms (*'urf-i jami'ah*). We need, he insisted, a vast campaign of social education. "We say, for in-stance, that certified *transsexuals* can live trans-gendered lives, but the courts have to be educated, the police have to be educated, and society has to accept this. The police and the courts have some justified fears; if they allow cross-dressing in public, it will adversely affect public order. Even after all the press interviews and articles, they still call *transsexuals daujinsi!* Then even worse, at other times, they mix them with same-sex-players [*hamjins-bazan*]."[53]

Karimi-nia had repeatedly and insistently expressed his belief that "a Great Wall of China" separated trans persons from same-sex-players. The insistence at one level was counterintuitive: nowhere in fiqhi texts are transsexuals and homosexuals proximate categories requiring a separating border; transsexuals are placed in proximity with intersex persons, as we have seen in Khomeini's and other scholars' fatwas. Even Karimi-nia had begun his writings by con-founding intersex with trans persons before he moved on to conceptualizing transsexuality as sex/gender discordance between soul and body.

How then have trans persons acquired proximate status—at times ex-plicit—to homosexuals, not only in the hostile opinion among many scholars of fiqh, but also in the thinking of a trans-friendly scholar such as Karimi-nia?

This proximity has been shaped through the coming together of domains of science (in particular the notion of transsexuality as articulated in psycho-sexological literature) and fiqh. While in fiqhi thinking there may be no reason to ever connect these two categories, contemporary fiqhi thinking does not take shape in seminary-isolated spaces. Karimi-nia's thinking was shaped in part by conversations with doctors and psychologists, within whose domain of think-ing—largely based on a sexological gender-behavioral model—transsexuality and homosexuality do indeed constitute neighboring categories. The effect of various sex/gender categorical imperatives is most evident in the daily acts of hostility and violence that trans persons experience, despite the legality of their category. This is the case whether these imperatives ensue from fiqhi rules of ritual subject-hood, biomedical and psycho-sexological taxonomies, or socio-cultural paradigms that depend on gender/sex certainty. While within the fiqhi logic of "dependency of the rules on the topic" there is no necessary link be-tween *liwat* (anal intercourse), *musahiqah* (tribadism)—both beyond bounds of Allah and subject to criminal prosecution in Iran—and transsexuality, the work of these other registers contributes to the creation of a single logic of categorization, keeping all gender/sex-variant desires and practices in close proximity even within fiqhi thinking. Moreover, the sexological categorization receives visual confirmation in the self-presentation of many trans persons and possibly through often indistinct living styles of trans- and homosexuals. Ritual gender reassignment of an unoperated body would raise the specter of condoning "sexual reassignment," of providing a *shar'i hat* (*kulah-i shar'i*) for same-sex practices—something that Karimi-nia cannot afford to engage in; he must separate the categories by a "Great Wall of China."

Karimi-nia also contends that only with upholding this difference could the society become accepting of trans persons, since in his opinion there is a social consensus on condemnation of same-sex-playing. "If a person truly feels s/he is *transsexual*," he said, "we say the road is open for him/her to cross this bridge and put him/herself in the category of *transsexual*, s/he can change sex and have a healthy/uncorrupt [*salim*] life."

Paradoxically, Karimi-nia uses two seemingly contradictory metaphors. His Great Wall of China, that world's best-known example of a frontier, does what frontiers are expected to do: solidly, and against corrosions of time and force, it separates "a (legitimate) space and its (alien) exteriority."[54] Within Karimi-nia's seminary-trained fiqhi logic, *ts* and *homosexual* must be kept categorically apart. Simultaneously, and perhaps unlike many other scholars of religion, he works with actual persons who live a range of complex gender/sexual lives. In that context, he is no longer concerned with a fiqhi problem-solving exercise, but with actual dilemmas of lives. He thus offers "a bridge" to possible homosexuals to cross over to transsexuality. This bridge connects the space of legitimacy to its abject exterior—that of same-sex-playing. Karimi-nia needs a solid frontier to protect the fiqhi acceptability of sex change within the bounds of Allah, while needing to keep the bridge open for some to pass. This paradox of a wall of separation and a bridge of connection is what offers the space of living habitable lives to sex/gender-variant persons. Their story "privileges a 'logic of ambiguity' through its interaction. It 'turns' the frontier into a crossing, and the river into a bridge."[55]

I indicated to him that the international press coverage at times has presented this bridge as a "solution," perhaps even a "medical cure," for homosexuality. He vehemently denied this. "No, no, we never say that. We believe that if someone is *transsexual*, it is her/his task to prove it. If a same-sex-player makes that claim, they have to prove it; we never offer a solution for same-sex-players. . . . If someone is pursuing same-sex-playing, this is in Islam a crime, it is against social order, and if it is proven, it is punished."

During this period, there was a conversation among *gay* men, especially those who were coming to some of the trans support meetings, about whether the legibility that transsexuality had acquired in legal, scientific, and fiqhi discourses—and that had provided them with certain rights and service accessibilities—was something that could be pursued by *gay* men to similar effect. Because of different circles of socializing and styles of public presentation, *lesbian* women seemed to be less involved or interested in this conversation. To begin with, few ever came to these meetings. Moreover, they were more interested in how they could get family sanction for their arrangements for living together, even if it was a "don't ask don't tell" arrangement. When will the family stop asking when their young daughter was going to get married? That was not as much of a problem for young men. Men could reasonably postpone marriage until they were much older. In the meantime, a present burden was the social approbation of being marked as *kuni* and *iva-khvahar*, plus the ever-present danger of blackmail and legal entanglement, as well as potential accusations of sodomy (punishable by death). *Gay* men were interested in finding out if there were any biopsychological or fiqhi avenues they could open up, similar to the psychological discourse that now gave them exemption from military service.

It was with these thoughts that I began to push Karimi-nia's arguments across some potential red lines. His interest in my research provided an opportunity. In the fall of 2006, the Sociological Association of Tehran University invited me to give a talk about my research. When Karimi-nia, some months later, asked me for any writings in Persian about my work, I sent him the only Persian writing I had—the text of my talk. When I went to Qum in June 2007, to my great surprise, Karimi-nia not only had read the paper but had prepared five pages of written response to points of disagreement.[56] He spent much time going over and engaging in a seminary-style conversation with me on every point.

In my talk for the Sociological Association, I had argued that in classical Perso-Islamic thought there was no concept of natural and unnatural desire and there was no presumption of a natural heterosexuality; it was only how one acted upon desire that became subject of fiqhi rules of the prohibited or permitted. Karimi-nia's critique of these ideas was indicative of almost hegemonic modernist notions of sex and sexuality in today's Iran. He argued that "the naturalness of the mutual attraction of a man and a woman is evident and obvious . . . and that the naturalness of this desire has never been denied in Iranian or Islamic thought." Yet he departed from the modernist notion as well. In the modernist paradigm of earlier decades, gender segregation was thought to be the cause of same-sex relations: the frustration of sexual desire toward its natural objects derailed it toward unnatural ones, thus the advocacy of unveiling women and gender heterosocialization. This Karimi-nia strongly argued against and offered two examples to prove the contrary. In the story of

Lot, he said, the prophet offered his daughters to the men to marry. But despite the availability of the heterosexual option, they insisted on seeking the male guests (visiting angels). The second example was of European countries in which women and men freely socialize and yet same-sex-playing is very prevalent. He suggested that there were many issues involved in the "phenomenon of same-sex-playing," the most important one of which was lack of attention to religious and moral teachings.

In response to my insistence on using the classic Islamic distinction between desire and act, one as *ghayr-iradi* (not willful) and one as willful, and the importance of *ikhtiyar* (conscious choice) in the performance of religious obligations, his response was that, "Yes, the initial desire may be not-willed, but if the person acts on it, even if that act is simply desirous looking, that is already a willful act and is already *haram* [prohibited]. And of course if the desire is expressed, if it is acted upon, clearly all those are willful."

In great detail, he went over the story of the people of Lot and the Islamic condemnation of sex among men. When I pointed out the alternative interpretations that several Muslim gay activists have developed about that story,[57] he dismissed them as merely an inappropriate language game. While he agreed that the distinction I insisted upon between sodomy and homosexuality was accurate from the point of fiqh, he thought I was playing with words (*bazi ba lughat*). In the end, as flexible and argumentative as he was on several other issues, this was one line that he would not cross; it was his Great Wall of China, after all.

### Psyche and Soul

Karimi-nia's central perception of transsexuality as a disparity between gender/sex of body and soul is empowered by a slippage between psyche and soul that has marked the entry of "the new science of psychology" into Persian-language Iranian discourse since the early decades of the twentieth century.

The notion of psyche, in its meaning within modern psychology, was first introduced in Iran through the teaching and writings of 'Ali Akbar Siasi.[58] Siasi is rightly considered a pioneering influence in shaping the more humanist-oriented subfield of psychology in Iran (distinct from its later turn to clinical behavioral psychology and psychiatry). His autobiographical account emphasized the introduction of psychology into the curriculum of Political Science School in 1925 as a science hitherto unknown in Iran.[59] In a meeting with the then head of the Political Science School, 'Ali Akbar Dihkhuda,[60] Siasi discussed his field of specialization: pedagogical sciences and, in particular, psychology (*'ilm al-nafs*). His linking of psychology and pedagogy was informed in part by the pragmatic orientation of a generation of nationalist social scientists turned state-builders in the early decades of the twentieth century.[61]

As a result of the meeting with Siasi, Dihkhuda expressed his interest in having Siasi teach this subject in the school. In subsequent discussions with Dihkhuda, "the expression *'ravanshinasi'* was chosen for the Persian name of the new 'ilm al-nafs."[62] These linguistic choices were the result of a series of translations: Siasi translated "psyche" into the Arabic *nafs*, allowing him to claim the older notion of 'ilm al-nafs (science of nafs) as the equivalent of the new psychology—Persianizing nafs as *ravan*, and thus coining the term *ravanshinasi* to refer to the science of ravan.[63]

Siasi argued that a human being had two components: the first was material, *badaniyat* (things bodily), which was the subject of the science of life. To identify this science, he Persianized *'ilm al-hayat* as *zist-shinasi*, an expression that is now commonly used for biology. The second aspect of a human being is more properly the subject of 'ilm al-nafs or ravanshinasi. It is the combination of feelings, thoughts, actions, and reactions, referred to as *nafsiyyat*, that are attributed to one's ravan (psyche). Siasi noted that "in this book, nafs and ruh always have the same meaning and the Persian word 'ravan' will be used for them."[64] As he articulated in a later work, Siasi did not simply assume that ruh and nafs/ravan were identical concepts, but suggested that for the science of psychology the two concepts (soul and psyche) were identical and that any discussion of ruh as distinct from nafs belonged to the domain of philosophy.[65] Other intellectuals of the period continued the attempt to map the Perso-Islamic philosophical concept of soul onto the modern notion of psyche. Kazimzadeh Iranshahr's *Usul-i asasi-i ravanshinasi* (Foundational principles of psychology) is a prime example of this tendency, which became marginalized during the subsequent development of the field dominated by behavioral psychiatry.

Yet even there the matter remains open: *Andishah va raftar* (now the *Journal of Psychiatry and Clinical Psychology*), the principal Iranian psychology journal, in its regular column on equivalent vocabulary, equates ruh with soul, saving ravan for psyche. Nonetheless, an expression such as *bimariha-yi ruhi* means exactly the same as *bimariha-yi ravani* (psychological illnesses), messing up the attempt to detach psyche from a religiously embedded and philosophically informed use of ruh.

The implicit certainty of *some* kind of relationship among nafs, ravan, and ruh—despite the uncertainty over what it is—enables the contemporary traffic between "the new science of psychology" and the older sciences of religion ('ulum al-din), among healers of psyche and guardians of souls. Such murkiness allows medical professionals to present the psycho-sexological concept of transsexuality as discordance between gender/sex of psyche and body in religiously familiar language of soul and body.[66] It also enables Karimi-nia to translate the psycho-sexological concept back into gender/sex discordance between soul and body, addressing transsexuality as a psychological condition in Islamic terms. Moreover, the concept of discordance between soul and body is more benign and less pathologizing—and thus more appealing to many trans persons—than one informed by a psycho-sexological discourse of GID, especially with the heavily negative load of the term *disorder* (*ikhtilal* in Persian) compared with the more neutral weight of *discordance* (*nakhvani*).[67]

The slippage between soul and psyche thus has produced a creative space for extensive discursive and practical collaboration on the issue of transsexuality among psychiatrists, scholars of fiqh, sexologists, surgeons, and other health professionals.[68] For instance, a book by Kahani and Shojaei, both psychiatrists affiliated with the LMOI, draws on psycho-sexological and sociological literature along with the texts of several fatwas on this topic.[69] Such syncretic approaches were critical to working out the legal and administrative procedures for the certification of trans persons, since they speak to the requirements of the Compliance project. Figures from the various domains of statecraft, the psychological and psychiatric practices of biosciences, and sciences of religion also share media and educational presentations and performances on a regular basis. Dr. Mirjalali and Hujjat al-Islam Karimi-nia have appeared in numerous documentaries in which producers have interviewed both and brought them within a single narrative frame. Kahani and Saberi also have appeared in many of these productions. These figures often share the platform in scientific seminars and state-sponsored workshops and educational presentations on this topic. Major seminars, national or regional, are usually videotaped; the recorded proceedings circulate widely, similar to documentary films and videos, increasing the ripple effects of the dissemination of knowledge about transsexuality that result from these intersections. Collectively, in documentaries and in seminars, these figures have come to stand as embodiments of Science and Religion, as they draw upon and benefit from each other's domain of authority.

Like medicine, psychology was made subject to the workings of the Islamic state through the Compliance project of the 1980s. But unlike biomedical practices, in matters of daily practice psychology faced fewer challenges with regard to compliance because bodily examination and improper looking and touching usually were not involved. Therapy sessions theoretically became a challenge if an unrelated man and woman could not be in a closed room alone, but perhaps the relatively consistent gender segmentation between clients and therapists has precluded the problem.

The Compliance project has been more productive in the conceptual domain as far as psychology is concerned, bringing "sciences of religion" and "sciences of nature" into the conversation on sex/gender/sexuality. A prime example is Baqir Kajbaf's *Ravanshinasi-i raftar-i jinsi* (The psychology of sexual behavior). The book is organized in two parts: "Raftar-i jinsi az didgah-i ravanshinasi" (Sexual behavior from a psychological perspective) and "Raftar-i jinsi az didgah-i Islam" (Sexual behavior from an Islamic perspective). A preface and a conclusion bring the two parts into a reinforcing conversation. The only two areas of divergence between the two perspectives are noted to be masturbation and homosexuality.[70]

More significantly, the effect of the Compliance project on psychology has emerged in an unexpected domain: the expansion of the authority and authorship, as well as the reception and readership, of vernacular psycho-sexology (discussed in chapter 2) into a near nationally hegemonic space. This hegemony has contributed to making the conceptual divide between female/woman/feminine and male/man/masculinity into a global grid. No longer "topic dependent," as fiqhi scholars would say, the sex/gender distinction is presumed to determine virtually all differences. Small paperback books and pamphlets, with titles such as *Zanan va mardan* (Women and men), provide subway reading for young men and women who seek clarity on proper masculinity and femininity under conditions that continue to challenge both terms in the daily practices, desires, and ambitions of a new generation. Popular psychology books, largely oriented toward and marketed to young men and women couples, married (or not), advise them on how to get along with and understand "the opposite sex"—quarrel less and, above all, understand scientifically the needs and expectations of each other.[71] At the annual International Book Fair, held each May in Tehran, the largest number of displayed publishers and books is what is referred to as religious literature (*adabiyat-i mazhabi*), followed closely by spiritual and psychological literature. Specialized bookshops around Tehran University's book row are stacked with relatively cheap pamphlets on "men and women." Many dailies and weeklies run regular columns on the topic.

As before the revolutionary decades, today much is invested in this literature on delineating the presumed vast unbridgeable differences between men and women: psychological, physiological, emotional, and sexual. The ideological state pressures are too obvious to belabor. But more important is the popular belief in this vast difference—a global investment that informs gender/sex/sexuality identifications and contributes to setting the stage for an almost visceral hostility toward trans- and homosexuality. Like a male-female division, there is almost universal presumption of natural—biological and psychological—heterosexuality. Transsexuals and non-heterosexuals throw the clarity of the female and male line, coupled closely with heterosexuality, into confusion, even as many aspire to live that clarity. While there is a growing acceptance of the medico-legal-religious notion that transsexualism is not a willed (*iradi*) condition, non-heterosexuality, in contrast, continues to be seen overwhelmingly as not only unnatural but a willfully corrupt practice.

## Islam-Therapy and Its Transnational Belonging

Just as fiqh scholars have a diversity of views, psychology and psychiatry practitioners show no unanimity on the nature of transsexuality or its treatment. Some psychiatrists consider it a "delusional state" that has to be handled medically, with drugs and electroshock treatments, if needed.[72]

Another segment of the psychiatric community advocates and practices Islam-therapy, sometimes subsumed under spiritual therapy, with the explicit goal of dissuasion. In the decades of the emerging nexus between science and Islam, this school has carved its own sphere of scholarship and practice, along with institutions and scholarly publications.

Spiritual/Islamic psychology developed in affiliation with the Office of Islamic Studies in Mental Health, established in 1987 as part of the Compliance project, within the Center for Mental Health Research of the TPI. It held monthly meetings, and brief reports on the papers presented in these meetings were published regularly in *Andishah va raftar*. It took a decade for this school to establish itself at a level that could support its own nationwide seminars,[73] and another decade for the subject to become more academically mainstreamed.[74]

The papers presented at these monthly meetings centered on the relationship between religious belief and practices and a variety of psychological conditions, chief among them depression. There were also reports on clinical studies of results of religiously informed approaches to healing patients compared with the results of nonreligious therapeutic practices. A number of talks covered historical comparisons between Persian-Islamic medical texts and modern psychology and neurobiology.

In that context, the discussion of status of ruh/soul/psyche, nafs/spirit/essence, *jism*/body, and ravan/psyche were revisited. Some participants suggested reintroducing a distinction between ruh and ravan to distinguish *ma'rifat al-nafs* from ravanshinasi, re-embedding ruh within the concept of human in Islamic philosophy.[75] Dr. Mohammad Reza Mohammadi's paper, delivered on December 15, 1994, argued that in addition to the three dimensions that form the basis of our current scientific understanding of human beings—biological, psychological, and sociological—one must introduce a fourth dimension: spiritual.[76] Mohammadi's was not simply a theoretical proposition. He had been a pioneer in practicing treatment methods based on his theoretical and philosophical propositions and keenly promoted spiritual/Islam therapy as a way of treating "patients with deep character disorders." In this paper, for instance, he claimed that patients with such affliction, "for whom none of the standard medical and non-medical treatment methods had been effective, within a few limited sessions working on their spiritual dimension responded with deep changes in them and gained new outlook on life. Moreover, this method has proven effective in dealing with sexual perversions, in particular with same-sex-players. Despite the deep roots of this kind of psycho-behavioral disorder, [such patients] have taken positive steps toward growth and uplifting of their lifestyle."[77]

Mohammadi also has used this method to attempt to "cure" transsexuals who were referred to him by the LMOI and has reported the success of one case in *Andishah va raftar*.[78] Mohammadi's approach does not prevail either in the certification process or among psychology and psychiatry professionals. Few articles by spiritual therapists make it through the publication nets of *Andishah va raftar*. However, Mohammadi's continued presence as an expert who provides a religio-psychological approach consistent with the requirements of the Compliance project cannot be dismissed.

The research he presented in the jointly authored article in *Andishah va raftar* reported on a twenty-year-old male student diagnosed with gender/sexual disorder who desired sex change.[79] The paper noted that "cognitive-behavioral therapy with an emphasis on spiritual therapy" was employed in his treatment. The thirty-session moral and spiritual therapy reportedly "reduced the subject's same-sex desires and increased his participation in sex-appropriate activities, leading to his abandonment of plans to change sex."[80] The article heavily referenced many of the writings of George Rekers and his colleagues and reviewed the existing Anglo-Canadian-American research, emphasizing that, "after surgery, there is no meaningful change in such people in terms of adaptability, and that 31 percent of such people regret their action."[81] It further claimed that it had been demonstrated that "ethical therapy and spiritual and religious therapy is very effective in treating gender dysphoria in adolescents."[82]

Most importantly, the authors argued that, since under "our country's cultural particularities, it is possible that gender dysphoric disorder may not be seen as a disease and that such behavior may be considered criminal and deviational, and given that carrying out the surgical operations for sex change is not easy in our country, the main aim of this research is to identify the role of cognitive-behavioral methods with an emphasis on spiritual therapy for improvement and treatment of adolescents afflicted with gender dysphoric disorder."[83] The methods employed by the researchers are described as "self-monitoring in which the subject records daily activities," "positive thinking" involving positive feedback and encouragement for good and positive experiences, "problem-solving" to build the person's self-confidence when facing life's daily problems, "family therapy," "changing perceptions and beliefs" through helping the patient to recognize his/her perceptual errors and replace these perceptions with more realistic ones, and finally "spiritual and ethical therapy."[84] The key for understanding the latter is "to distinguish the two concepts of ravan (psyche) and ruh (spirit). In psychology reference books these two concepts are taken to be identical. . . . Spiritual therapy is based on two important principles. First, achieving soulfulness requires loving others, loving work, and loving belonging. Second, spirituality requires religious belief, belief in unity and belief in change."[85]

The work of Mohammadi and his colleagues simultaneously addresses two distinct adversarial audiences when it comes to nonheteronormative gender/sexualities, in particular transsexuality. Recall that Karimi-nia's trans-friendly Islamic jurisprudential arguments are based on the concept of transsexuality as a discordance between gender/sex of soul and body—a concept that depends on the slippage between soul and psyche. By insisting on reintroducing the distinction between ruh/soul and ravan/psyche, Mohammadi's proposition would tend to work against that grain. The distinction is also critical for crafting an autonomous discursive space for Islam-therapy, through reclaiming ma'rifat al-nafs (knowledge of soul/self) as distinct from "the new science of psychology" and establishing itself in continuity with the earlier Islamo-Persian discourse.[86]

The Andishah va raftar article provided a full case report. After a series of initial cognitive tests and a meeting with the subject and his family to explain the aims and methods of treatment, the subject was asked to keep a journal of daily reports in relation to "his real sex/gender role, that is, being a boy."[87] In individual therapy sessions, the subject was told that "there were no surgical operations that would completely and successfully transform him into a woman and that he must try to accept his real gender/sex and to engage in sex/gender appropriate activities."[88] In a subsequent session, the subject reported that while he continued to want to be a girl, he no longer desired to have sexual relations with either a man or a woman. He came to the conclusion that changing sex, completely and successfully, is not possible and that he must attempt to accept his physiological sex and become concordant with it. He was affirmed and encouraged "to practice more often male gender/sex role and avoid girlish behavior."[89] In subsequent sessions, the subject reported that contrary to earlier times, when he had enjoyed attention by men and "had enjoyed a passive womanly sex/gender role, now if a man touches me I have a bad feeling, I hate myself and feel a strong sense of inferiority and hopelessness."[90] The reports of the sessions were interwoven with what the subject was recording in his diary, indicating a progressive shift from imagining himself as, behaving as, and desiring to be a woman to slowly accepting being a man and adopting appropriate behavior, concluding with the triumphant note that the subject had finally concluded that he had wasted twenty years of his life pursuing an irrational and futile desire and now was keen to live as a man, get married, and form a family. After a year of follow-up after treatment, the authors reported, the subject had shown no sign that would indicate a return of his illness.[91]

I interviewed Dr. Mohammadi in 2006. His interest in turning to spiritual therapy, he said, went back to around 1988, when he was doing his residency in psychiatry at Tehran University. He was invited by the LMOI to attend the meetings of the trans certification commission and became one of the certifying psychiatrists. "Serving on that commission," he explained, "slowly made me realize that we give these people certification, they go and have their operations, they are happy for six months or so, and then again they are unhappy, discontented with life, and so on. I also started noticing that a lot of other people I dealt with—suicidal adolescents, others suffering from various personality disorders—I noticed that in many cases none of the current practices—psychotherapy, psycho-behavioral therapy, cognitive therapy, cognitive-psychotherapy, medical-psychiatric treatments—none work with these patients. It was then that I suggested we should bring into our program spiritual therapy."

In a summary presentation of the published paper, he explained that "We need to re-introduce the concept of *ruhi*/spiritual and *ma'navi*/contemplative/spiritual [usually used as the opposite of material, *maddi*] into our thinking and methods of working with patients. . . . I tried it in several cases. . . . The first case that responded well was with a transsexual who after twelve sessions changed his resolve and began to accept himself. It is easier to work with *homosexuals* than with trans-people."

Mohammadi was convinced that gender/sexual nonheteronormative persons could be talked into heteronormativity; they could be persuaded to accept their birth bodies and reorient their desires "properly" through spiritual therapy. I asked about the kind of conversations that he carried out with his "patients." He activated a PowerPoint presentation that he uses for training intern students and talked me through it. "It was important to introduce patients to a concept that was broader than death as the end of life. Being born is at the same time a death, the death of being part of a mother's body. Dying is similarly a new birth . . . ," he explained. "I spend a lot of time talking about what life means. . . . This allows me to discuss biologic living but also spiritual living. The biggest challenge is to get a patient to enter this conversation."

He gave two examples of people who had responded to his treatment: a person with suicidal tendencies and one with a phobia of death. I told him that I could understand the relevance of a conversation about meaning of life and death in those contexts, but how would it work with a TS person? Mohammadi explained that, in his thinking,

> a TS is just like a drug addict; wanting to satisfy what s/he desires at the moment, not thinking about the larger meaning of life. . . . The problem is teaching these people how to control their impulses. . . . I know of an FtM person who has gone through twenty-nine surgeries and is about to have a thirtieth. I asked him why he was doing that [putting in prosthetic testes]? He said because when he died he wanted the person who would wash his body to see a complete male body. I suggest to a TS applicant that we ought to discuss the long-run of life and its meaning versus the here and now. I ask, "What do you want from life?" So let's say it is a man who wants to become a woman. I ask, "What does that mean to you? Why do you want to become a woman?"

Our conversation continued:

> Najmabadi: Suppose I play that TS and tell you because I want men to accept me as a woman—many of the MtFs I have talked to say just that.
> Mohammadi: What do you want to do after you become a woman?
> Najmabadi: Well, after I am a woman, I plan to get married.
> Mohammadi: What do you know about marriage? Do you know that even two perfect people have a lot of marriage problems? In Iran, the divorce rate is around 20 percent, so even in that case one out of five

marriages break down. But you have additional problems, you will always have mental problems, so yours may break up even sooner. Look around you, most *transsexuals* are unhappy, they spend six months with one partner, it doesn't work, they move to another. You will be stuck in another impasse in life from the one you're in now. So why not think about how to get out of the current impasse. . . . It is like someone who has appendicitis, the surgeon knows that it must be operated upon; it is not a matter of you choosing what is good for you.

Caught between my skepticism about marriage in any case and a strong aversion against his authoritarian paternalism, I shifted the conversation and asked how successful his approach had been. Mohammadi explained that

most of them come for a few sessions and then stop coming. They don't want to change their minds. They are sent here by the LMOI for a six-month (to a year at most) therapy. That is not enough time. Many, after one or two sessions, realize this is not going along with what they want. There was one student from Sari [a northern city] with whom I worked for seventy sessions. First, cognitive therapy for eighteen months; no result, s/he had told her/his father that "come end of September either I have permission to operate and you pay for it or I will commit suicide." At that point I decided to introduce spiritual therapy. Now he is at a point where he is planning to marry— a girl he met at the university. It takes a long time for this method to work.

Mohammadi considered part of his challenge to be professional isolation. He complained that the majority of his colleagues did not consider his approach to be scientific and he only recently had succeeded in getting an article published in the flagship journal of the profession.[92] From the opposite direction, he said, sympathetic colleagues want him to engage in directly religious therapy—Islam therapy. "But that wouldn't work," he explained, "unless the person is a religious person. Seventy percent of people who come here are aimless in life. They don't believe in anything. First we have to deal with that problem."

Mohammadi's practices, from the point of view of trans persons who had campaigned to remove him from the list of psychologists to whom they were sent for therapy, were considered nothing short of terrifying. Two FtM activists I worked with closely had been sent to Dr. Mohammadi for their supervised therapy. Both continue to be angry about the experience, and one of them indicated that the only time in his life he came close to contemplating suicide was during those months when he was convinced Mohammadi would never send a supportive report to the LMOI. When I first met him in 2006, Sina already had undergone the first stages of his surgery, had been taking hormones for a year, and was getting his legal papers changed and planned to return to his studies in Europe. As a highly successful student, with top grades in the nationwide university entrance exams, he had received a scholarship to pursue his medical education abroad. Even though his family had been very sympathetic to his sex/gender-variant desires, he had decided to postpone any somatic changes until he had experienced life in a European country. "Maybe I would be happy as a *lesbian*," he said. Two years later, he returned to Iran to transition. He was describing the process he went through when he handed me a notebook. "Here," he said, "this is the journal that Dr. Mohammadi forced me to keep." I had read already Mohammdi's article in *Andishah va raftar* where he had explained his requirement that clients keep a journal as part of the therapy process, but never thought I would be privy to one. Like the subject reported in that article, Sina had been asked by Dr. Mohammadi to record his daily thoughts, feelings, when he felt like a man, when he felt like a woman, his immediate and long-term goals in life. At every session, Mohammadi would read the journal and engage Sina in a conversation that Sina considered hostile, at times pushing him to the edge of despair. Sina offered to let me take the notebook home and read it.

The diary starts on July 18, 2005. The top line lays out his requirements: to write about thoughts, feelings, sensibilities, important happenings in relation to being a boy or being a girl, to explain his secondary aims in life, and the ultimate aim in life. Sina's first entries record whenever he had been happy and calm: when he is mistaken for a man; when friends give him support for his eventual surgery. He also records a persistent anxiety: having abandoned for the moment his education abroad—he wanted to be finished with his transition and go back to complete his studies. By August 6, 2005, he has his first direct hostile segment against Mohammadi: "when I left your office today, I was under such physical and mental stress that my whole body was shaking," ending with: "I wonder when I will be rid of you psychologists and reach my inner goal." The next entry addresses Mohammadi directly again, contrasting his negative combative attitude to his father (who initially had rejected him but had later come around to accepting things): "unlike you, he comforts and supports me."

What is most striking is how Sina used the process to frustrate Mohammadi's project at every turn. There was little in these pages that would give Mohammadi the kind of leverage he needed to have the life and death discussions he considered the crucial point of his therapy. There were pages with

Mohammadi's underlining and question marks. There were pages where Sina explicitly expressed his anger at Mohammadi's insistent challenging of his self-perception. Sina evidently had opted to use the journal to confront him, turning the pages of the journal against his pressure rather than being pressured by the requirement of keeping a diary intended to facilitate Mohammadi's intervention against Sina's desire for sex change.

In several entries he noted that he cooked the family lunch on that day; in every case he recorded that he did so with his father, deflecting the possibility that Mohammadi would read femininity into this "fact." In a long entry (August 17, 2006), Sina writes about how he had been infuriated by men's unwanted attention to him on a street—for him a sign of his masculinity, as women are supposed to enjoy male attention—ending with a direct address to Mohammadi: "and then you keep telling me I have to stay in this gender [*jinsiyat*]. Believe me if you persist and I have to tolerate such mental ['*asabi*] pressures, I will probably do stupid things like many others who have my problem [implying suicide]." An entry two days later expresses deep anxiety over his surgery, contemplates going the illegal route since he has his family's consent and even the encouragement of psychologists such as Mehrabi, addressing Mohammadi again: "it is only you who is against it and puts obstacles in my way." He goes on for another three pages: "After so many years of struggling against myself, dealing with my family and other doctors, when as you know I have a time limitation because I must return to my studies or lose my scholarship, yet you do not issue your consent. . . . You may be able to delay things for me but will never be able to change my mind . . . it is my natural right to enjoy life and meet my needs like all other human beings."

More than a month into therapy, Mohammadi seems to have lost patience with Sina's resistance; on top of the last page of an entry, he had written the goals that he expected of these daily recordings (which clearly Sina had refused to fulfill, and less so by the day): "your thoughts, feelings, sensibilities, daily happenings, your primary and secondary goals in life." Mohammadi's injunction does not produce any difference in the entries. Sina's critical addresses to Mohammadi—bearing his underlining, and double underlining, of long passages—become a witness to a tug of war between two determined persons, a struggle over their respective ideas of Sina's manhood and Mohammadi's denial of that option. Indeed, Sina indicates in another entry that one of the reasons he hated keeping this journal was that "writing a journal is something girls do." A few entries later, Sina writes only a few sentences, indicating that he did not intend to waste his precious time writing these entries and unnecessarily lengthening his sessions as if he were not serious in his quest for sex change. He only looks forward to the end of these required sessions. He ends by saying that he is "saying all this for a final time."

Sina, however, is a hostage to the procedural frame that made his certification contingent on a recommendation by Mohammadi (who at that time was still approved as a practitioner in the certification process). In the same way that Mohammadi was set to change Sina's mind, Sina had to change Mohammadi's mind: to prove to him that there was no way he could be talk-cured out of his desire for sex change. He had no choice but to continue. Cleverly, in mid-September of 2005, he adopted Mohammadi's own approach and began to write a series of less personal, more philosophical/ethical and medical notes; it is almost as if it is Sina who is giving Mohammadi a last chance by using his own concerns and language. An October entry is more than eleven pages long; it explains at length that his condition is God's doing, but science can at least partially correct it; if God didn't make TSS, who did? If God didn't want science to figure things out, it would not have happened. Whether ironically or as a gesture of reconciliation, in the middle of this long narrative, he addresses Mohammadi as "dear Sir Dr. Mohammadi," explaining,

> When I see a young woman I am excited; I don't know why I have been created this way. It isn't under my control; science knows why; why should I be fighting myself? I think the way God has created me, this is his way of testing me. I don't know if you believe in miracles, but I do, and I have seen it in my own life. One example is how my father was turned around in his stubborn rejection of my condition. Only God could have changed his mind after four years of fighting me. I tell you: I have decided not to fight on this issue any more and will let God's way guide me forward. I know I need surgery so I am sure this is in God's plans and whether in 6 months or 600 months, this will happen. My first and last word is surgery. *wa al-salam* [an end-of-conversation expression]. I don't have time for writing more notes for you. I want to devote my time to doing useful things. I sincerely thank you for making me think about my future clearly."

Shortly after, Sina told me, he took his father with him to Mohammadi. His father threatened him with legal action if he refused to write a letter testifying that his treatment of Sina had failed to change his mind. By that time, Mohammadi had come to agree.

While Mohammadi is not currently prominent among professionals who supervise trans persons' required therapy, he remains an influential psychiatrist.[93] Of late, as we saw in chapter 1, he also has collaborated with Dr. Ohadi on a neuro-psycho-biological study of trans persons, perhaps hoping that the study would validate spiritual therapy by proving that there were no physiological differences between heteronormative and nonheteronormative brains. The collaboration illustrates the ways in which apparently disparate domains that affect transsexuality in Iran can intersect in unexpected ways.

**CHANGING THE TERMS**   *Playing "Snakes and Ladders" with the State*

On January 6, 2010, a small news item appeared on FarsNews, a semi-official news agency in the Islamic Republic of Iran. The director general of the Office for the Socially Harmed at the Welfare Organization, Mr. Hasan Musavi Chilik, announced that after two years of investigation and consultation with the Military Service Organization of Iran, it had been concluded that transgender/-sexuals (*tarajinsi-ha*),[1] who—along with gay men—previously had received exemption from military conscription under the mental disorders clause, would instead receive that exemption under the glandular disorders clause.[2] The new legislation was passed in November 2011.[3]

In the previous exemption codes, Section 33 ("Psychiatric Diseases"), Article 33.8, read: "Behavioral Disorders (psychological and nervous imbalances) and ill-conducts [*kazh-khu'i-ha*] that are in conflict with military conduct, as well as sexual and moral deviations such as transsexuals—permanent exemption." Section 30 ("Diseases of Internal Glands") included Article 30.5, which covered testicular diseases (including Klinefelter syndrome), and 30.6b, which covered hermaphrodism. The change moved transsexuality from 33.8 to 30.[4] This represented an important shift in status for trans persons, who had often referred to Section 33 exemptions as "red exemptions" because becoming marked by mental disease made one virtually unemployable. On the other hand, glandular disease exemptions are considered benign by employers.

On the face of it, one could read this announcement as one more step taken by the Iranian government to rearrange this subject population within a pathologizing taxonomy.[5] And indeed, it is that, too—although given a choice between glandular disorder and mental disease, one suspects that few would opt for the latter.[6] One comment—left after the FarsNews report was reproduced on a blog—even commended the move by saying "finally, one right move by the government." But neither condemnation nor commendation concerns me here. Over the period 2006–8, a small group of tireless trans activists had been working for this change, among numerous other policy measures. Not only the government's announcement, but also much of the current narratives about transsexuality in Iran—plotted around a governmental design, often said by the critics to be aimed at eliminating homosexuality and forcing every citizen into normative gender-sexual straight straitjackets—remain oblivious to the thousands of hours of trans-lobbying that had gone into producing this legal change. The exemption code change was above all the activists' achievement. *They* had something to celebrate.[7]

This chapter maps out how contemporary procedures for transsexuality came about in the late 1980s and the early 1990s, with a focus on trans activism, which all too often falls out of this story.

The relationship between the trans activists' work and various government offices and personnel has been the topic of many contentious conversations among trans activists in the past several years, during which a small but dedicated group of activists began to play a more visible role in lobbying, demanding, and negotiating various policies. Invariably, there were subgroups among activists with different styles and aims that sometimes clashed with each other. But the skill with which they had learned to navigate, and develop allies in, numerous committees that had been assigned various tasks related to medical, legal, and social needs of trans persons was remarkable. Similar to the state of traffic and driving habits in Tehran and Italian cities, it reminded me of de Certeau's observation, "Like the skill of a driver in the streets of Rome or Naples, there is a skill that has its connoisseurs and its esthetics exercised in any labyrinth of powers."[8] But a major difference between the labyrinth of powers in Iran and that of many other countries is that the country seems to be a site of permanent political earthquakes—sometimes on a large scale and with hundreds of casualties, sometimes in the form of small tremors, but with limited scope for those daily repetitive, routine performances that produce the effect of state coherence.[9] As Houri, an MtF in-transition activist wryly pointed out, "Do you know that game we used to play, snakes and ladders? That's what our daily lives have been like; one day we have a breakthrough in one ministry and get something put in place; then the next day, in walks someone hostile and turns all our 'woven cloth back into raw cotton,' we land at the tail of the snake, and start again."

As we saw in the last chapter, the postrevolutionary confluence of Islami-cization of governance and governmentalization of Islamic jurisprudence created the legal-scientific-bureaucratic nexus within which new concepts and practices of transsexuality became imaginable. Yet another development proved critical for the change of terms and living possibilities for trans persons. From the early 1990s, the press grew to be more independent and open; Mohammad Khatami's election as the president in 1997 further strengthened the space for investigative social reportage on previously quiet topics. New dailies and other periodicals started to appear on an exponential scale.[10] Several newspapers and magazines began to allocate space regularly to socially critical topics, such as addiction, destitute women on the streets, and runaway youth. Transsexuality emerged as one of these topics.

The broader social geography that enveloped the press coverage of trans-sexuality bordered on social vulnerability and non-conformant "disorderliness." Homosexuality and hermaphrodism were only two such categories. Trans persons also have had to deal with their border overlaps and frontier negotiations with other groups — among them cross-dressed petty thieves, usually young men clothed in women's outfits to snatch purses; young runaway girls, who usually live dressed as males in big cities and often are picked up on various charges and suspicions; more seriously, male-bodied sex workers in the case of MtFs; and, less seriously, men who have in recent years turned to nose jobs and other cosmetic experiments and are written about as men who suffer from behavioral disorders.[11]

Trans persons have shared with these groups the pages of investigative, socially conscious reporting as well as the pages devoted to "Havadis" (Happenings) — reports on urban incidents in dailies and weeklies. Indeed, several reporters and documentary producers, among them Nazila Fathi and Mitra Farahani, first were attracted to this topic as part of their attention to runaway kids and sex workers.[12]

Nor is it accidental that the first series of extensive writings about trans persons appeared in 1999 in *Rah-i zindigi*. A magazine, in the genre of general family literature and popular advice, it began publication in March 1995, first as a monthly. By December 1997 it had become bimonthly. The journal's editor, Mitra Suhayl, is a psychologist, and the magazine has a definite flavor of vernacular psychology. It was affiliated with the Rah-i Zindigi Institute, whose website, in addition to archival selections from the magazine, had a link to a set of character tests. Another link connected the site to a counseling portal, where people, especially youths, were encouraged to contact for advice about their lives. In 2007, the print run was said to be 100,000; during the summer months, the magazine increases its run to as much as 150,000.[13]

Regularly featured sections of the magazine included "For girls," "For boys," "For engaged couples," "Private lives of young couples," "Counseling on family problems," "A psychologist answers questions posed by young male and female adolescents," "A psychologist answers questions posed by young couples," "On youth," "Medical news," "Readers' contributions," "For divorcees" (literally, for those whose nests have been shattered, *ashian-pashidigan*), and, finally, "For widows."

Before the first series on trans persons, several topics had been covered as serialized reports, including one on addicts and one on mental patients. Such reports often were interwoven with in-their-own-words autobiographical narratives. The series on trans persons, titled *"man kah hastam?"* (Who am I?), began in a similar way—as the story of another "vulnerable-to-harm" group in need of social attention. It ran from February 4, 1999, through January 5, 2000. A second series ran from November 2003 through November 2005. The second series, under a new column editor, Rayhaneh Qasim Rashidi, was more openly editorialized. It usually was designated as being based on a letter from or a conversation with. . . . It also had a radically different framing. Inspired in part by Farkhundeh Aqa'i's recently published novel, *Jinsiyat-i gumshudah* (The lost gender/sexuality), the columns shared the same frame of a morality tale of caution against SRS. Aqa'i, in her introduction, indicated that sometime in the spring of 2000, she had read a report in the press about an MtF who, after SRS, had regretted what she had done.[14] The novel was presented as her hope for different life stories.[15]

In Qasim Rashidi's series, the prose is much more stylized and melodramatic. The concept of *huviyat-i gumshudah* (lost identity) occurs repeatedly. Stories are on average substantially longer (a full page instead of a quarter or half a page, which had been the rule in the earlier period) and they are much more developed, with stylistic and thematic details that become repeated from story to story. Indeed, its focus on the concept of a lost identity and of a soul trapped in the wrong body was simply not present in the earlier series. Qasim Rashidi was clearly skeptical of hormonal and surgical treatment as a solution for trans persons' demands. Unlike the first series, the narrative demand falls largely on trans persons, warning them, even aiming to educate them, against rushing to sex change, which was also the overall drive and plot of *Jinsiyat-i gumshudah*. Qasim Rashidi considered transsexuality to be a disease, "like a heart disease or kidney disease," but a disease of the soul or psyche that needed psychotherapy. This perception produced a repeated negative tone to the stories that was not even designed to evoke pity, but more a sense of alarm, a state of warning: warning parents that they must face this as a disease and get help from psychologists, warning insistent trans persons that life was not going to be rosy after surgery and that the best thing for them was to get psychotherapy to adjust to their bodies. She often included stories of trans persons who, after surgery, became disillusioned with their new lives and regretful (*pashiman*). The exceptional story of a happy trans, who objected to the published stories of miserable lives and explained that the happy trans persons became invisible,[16] in its singularity confirmed the moral lesson of the series as a whole: If you are unhappy before sex change, you will be unhappy *and* regretful afterwards.[17]

By 2003, then, it had become possible to write more openly about the public visibility of gender/sexual non-normative lives. One report noted, "In recent months, passers-by have noticed the visible though limited presence of a social group who have a manly appearance but also make themselves up as women and their movements and presentations are womanly. . . . Most people name them 'iva-khvahar,' although other labels, such as '*nar-maddah*,' '*amrud*,' '*kinig*,' and '*naukhatt*' are also used for them,[18] each with a different meaning. These people can be seen in different parts of Tehran, in places such as the Meat Market [Maydan-i Kushtargah], Park-i Shahr, Maydan-i Arya Shahr, [under] Karim Khan Overpass, the intersection of Mutahhari and Vali 'Asr [Avenues], Maydan-i Vanak. Usually they begin to appear around a couple of hours after sunset till about the hour 22 or 23."[19]

Another popular magazine, *Chilchiraq*, ran its first extensive coverage in its July/August 2003 issue; the magazine later claimed that this coverage inspired the first documentary screened in Iran, *Maria*.[20] A burst of articles in a wide range of publications on this topic exploded from early 2004 through 2008.[21] In addition to *Rah-i zindigi* and *Chilchiraq*, the topic of transsexuality was covered in the reformist women's monthly, *Zanan*, as well as in important dailies, such as *I'timad-i milli*, *I'timad*, *Hamshahri*, and *Sharq*, where long articles and interviews appeared in medical and science sections as well as in pages usually marked as "Social" or "Society." The "yellow press" also began to cover transsexuality, and for a brief period in 2004–5 gave the topic frequent full-page coverage, sometimes featuring translated articles that had appeared in the international press. This sustained coverage, despite the lean quality of the content—sometimes repeating the same story in various issues of the same journal—made transsexuality one of the stock attention-grabbing stories for the scandal sheets, along with stories about film stars' lives and various sexual and social scandals. The combination of kinds of coverage—with the dailies and science journals making transsexuality a respectable topic of social conversation, and the sensational press bringing it into popular knowledge— made transsexuality a widely recognized topic, though by no means one that was generally approved of.

There was a spiral effect to the publication and circulation of this media attention. Official seminars, such as one in Mashhad (Firdausi University, 2005) and another in Tehran (Iranshahr Hospital, 2007) were reported extensively in the dailies, and snippets would also appear as part of more sensational coverage of the yellow press. Articles appearing on network sites along with television reports—for instance, produced by the BBC—would be translated and published in Tehran. With a perceptible peak in the topic's coverage around screening such documentaries, reports in the *Guardian*, the *Independent*, the *New York Times*, the *Los Angeles Times*, and so on would pick up the topic from Iranian press reports. What intensified this spiral effect was the coincidence of these years with the spread of electronic media in Iran and the emergence of a very active weblog culture in Persian.[22] Many articles were reprinted on online magazines and weblogs. The latter included blogs set up by trans persons. Given the huge growth of electronic media in this period, public knowledge of transsexuality burst into the scene of media culture.[23]

The explosion of transsexuality into the printed and electronic media was significant in multiple ways for the emergence of a more visible group of trans activists. First, it gave them vocal leverage vis-à-vis various governmental agencies: The circulation of socially significant journalism made trans persons into subjects deserving of governmental action. Indeed, given the more open and critical atmosphere of much of the press from the mid-1990s into the first years of Ahmadinijad's first presidential term, many of the reports not only assigned themselves the task of "educating the public" but also had a critical edge, bringing under scrutiny what was seen as governmental inaction and neglect of a socially vulnerable group.

Second, the concept of transsexuality became widely knowable and a concept for (self-)cognition through the publication and circulation of these reports and documentaries. As such, they served, especially for persons outside Tehran, as the medium through which they heard about transsexuality—in terms of sex-change possibilities and its availability in Iran, and in terms of the right procedures to follow to get certification, but just as importantly in terms of self-cognition, of defining one's subjectivity. The satellite television broadcast *Yad-i yaran* was mentioned specifically by several trans persons from smaller towns as a program that made them identify themselves as *trans*. The reported rise in the number of trans applications may have been an effect of this expansion of the domain of public knowability, recognition, and self-cognition.

No basic statistics are made public on a regular basis, but the LMOI and the Welfare Organization (Bihzisti) keep records of applicants and occasionally have reported figures in seminars and interviews. One private clinic, Mirdamad, with Dr. Mirjalali as the chief surgeon, also has occasionally provided numbers. While there seems to have been a rise in numbers from the mid-1980s into the early 2000s, it also seems to have leveled off, at least for the number of applicants who go through the legal certification process. More recently, more systematic research has focused on the relative gender ratio—the frequency of MtF versus FtM applications. One doctoral dissertation's early findings indicated a steadying of the number of MtF applications but a continued rise in FtM applications.[24] One recent report has indicated that there was a jump in 2009 in the number of FtM applicants (table 6.1).[25]

Ironically, this vast public circulation of and knowledge about transsexuality also has made homosexuality a topic of public conversation, even if largely in a disavowal mode ("don't mix transsexuals with homosexuals," "we are not homosexual"). This public conversation thus enables some gender/sexual non-normative people—such as Zia and Leila, whom we will meet in the next chapter—to recognize themselves as *not* trans but as *gay* and *lesbian*.

### Does the State Matter?

While the 1979 revolution marked an important rupture in the political paradigm of rulership, on many levels this paradigmatic shift was translated into social policy through the given structures and daily practices of the existing governance. Some of these structures and practices were definitely, firmly eliminated—the institution of monarchy would be the prime example. Yet many were retained and modified in new directions.[26] The Welfare Organization—Sazman-i Bihzisti, almost always simply referred to as Bihzisti (literally, living well), which has become the central site for creating a grid of regulatory practices over the daily lives of trans persons, and which provides the net for delivery of a number of services and subsidies—is a case in point. Today Bihzisti works within the domain of the ministerial authority of the Ministry of Welfare and Social Security (MWSS). The latter was first established in 1974, when the old regime launched a number of subsidized social services in the wake of the tripling of oil prices in 1973. In 1976, the MWSS was absorbed into the Ministry of Health. In the aftermath of the revolution, Bihzisti was reestablished as an autonomous organization in 1980 and eventually came under the

Table 6.1. Reported number of trans applications and surgeries

| Date | Number of applicants and surgeries | Source |
|---|---|---|
| 1985–95 | 125 partial or full sex reassignment surgeries out of 153 applicants | Dr. Mirjalali |
| 1995–2005 | 200 surgeries out of 210 applicants | Dr. Mirjalali |
| 1987–2001<br>2001–4 | 200 males and 70 females applied to the LMOI; 214 were approved<br>Another 200 applications received | Reported in the Mashhad seminar of May 2005 and reprinted in several newspaper reports at the time |
| Applicants over the first six months of 1382 (March 21–September 22, 2004) | 27 FtM applicants and 33 MtF applicants | Reported by the LMOI in *Iran*, February 22, 2004, p. 6 |
| According to the LMOI, over the past six years (2001–6) | 422 applicants, 188 of whom pursued their application, 124 of whom received certification | *Sharq*, May 20, 2007, p. 22 |
| 1386 (March 21, 2007–March 20, 2008) | 85 permits were issued | 'Abd al-Razzaq Barzigar, Vice Chief of Clinical Medicine in the LMOI, reported by FarsNews, October 15, 2008 |
| 1381–87 (March 21, 2002–March 20, 2008) | 767 applicants, total, covered by Welfare Organization services | Hasan Musavi Chilik, Director General of the Office for Socially Harmed at the Welfare Organization, reported by FarsNews, January 20, 2010 |
| First nine months of 1388 (March 21–December 21, 2009) | 171 applicants to the Welfare Organization services, 80 percent of whom were FtM | Musavi Chilik, Director General of the Office for the Socially Harmed at the Welfare Organization, reported by *I'timad*, February 22, 2010, p. 10 |

ministerial authority of the reconfigured MWSS in 2004. Similarly, another governmental organization of relevance to the lives of trans persons, the Medical Care Insurance Organization (MCIO) (Sazman-i Bimah-i Khadamat-i Darmani), was first established in 1972 to offer medical insurance to government employees; with increased government oil revenues, in 1974 it extended its services to several other population groups, including the self-employed. The services of the MCIO were extended over the years to include the retired, the unemployed, and residents of rural areas. With the passage of the law of Universal Health Services in 1995, its coverage extended further "through a system of contributory and non-contributory insurance," and provided special coverage for "vulnerable groups."[27] Today, it is under this latter category that trans persons receive basic medical insurance coverage.

By the late 1990s, numerous governmental organizations had become involved with the life of trans persons. The dispersed and at times conflicting competition among these institutions eventually led to the formation, in 2001, of the Nationwide Committee to Supervise Sexual Disorders (Kumitah-i Kishvari-i Samandahi-i Ikhtilalat-i Jinsi). The committee was composed of representatives from the Ministries of Health, the Interior, Justice, the Supreme Court (Divan-i 'Ali-i Kishvar), the LMOI, NAJA, and Bihzisti.

According to a proposal designed by Bihzisti, a division of tasks was worked out among several government offices to create a sense of systematic attention and legal responsibility. The Nationwide Committee, by all accounts, never worked properly, possibly because of social/territorial power conflicts and budgetary competitions among some of the institutions.[28] One doctor I interviewed also suggested that the failure of the Nationwide Committee was in part "because priorities shift all the time. For a while TSs were a priority, then AIDS took over, and addiction became more important; national attention to TSs went to the back burner."[29] Since 2002, the Welfare Organization's Office for the Socially Harmed has become the key site for providing support services for trans persons. An initial budget of 20 million tumans (roughly US$20,000 at the time) soon proved inadequate and was slowly increased, with 700 million tumans allocated in 2007.[30] Over the years, a great deal of tension between the Ministry of Health and the Welfare Organization has been felt over this issue. The latter has persistently criticized the Ministry of Health for failing to live up to its responsibilities.[31] Since March 2007, a Memorandum of Understanding between the Judiciary and the Office for the Socially Harmed at the Welfare Organization has formally brought services for "persons afflicted with GID" under the latter's auspices.[32]

The initial burst of governmental and press attention during this period reportedly had been helpful in putting transsexuality on the national map; its falling out of fashion, so to speak, may have paradoxically opened the space for direct involvement, self-organization, and more grassroots activism by trans persons themselves.

While the initial intense press coverage, in Iran and internationally, had focused on stories of Mulk-ara, and to a lesser extent on Maria, the productive publicity created by the circulation of these narratives brought a number of younger trans activists into public action. Initially this occurred in direct affiliation with Mulk-ara's lobbying and her attempts to form a nongovernmental organization (NGO), but in later years it was largely autonomous. Almost all activists spoke of Mulk-ara as a pioneer to whom they owed their current social recognition, but they also had various criticisms, especially concerning her allegedly volatile and unpredictable ways of dealing with officials, which they found to be counterproductive. This younger cohort had come of age not in the harsh years of the 1980s, but in the more open sociocultural and political atmosphere of the late 1990s. They had become quite skilled in navigating their way in and out of various institutions, all the time guarding their issues from what they considered to be the hazards of politicization. They tended to be actively involved on a day-to-day basis, simultaneously pursuing different issues with several government bodies, including the LMOI, the Ministry of Health, the Welfare Organization, the Judiciary, state hospitals, and various groups of medical practitioners.

The years 2006–8 seem to have been the most intense and productive for trans activism. A small handful of activists tirelessly lobbied numerous governmental organizations to get things changed in a piecemeal, incremental fashion, and with the tempo of a "snakes and ladders game." It was sheer luck that my period of fieldwork happened to overlap with these same years, making it possible for me not only to participate in some of the meetings, but, more importantly, to observe how things changed on a day-to-day basis.

The dominant pattern of trans activist practices has not been one of translation of demands for addressing needs into a language of rights. Within the parameters of the religio-legal acceptability of transsexuality, negotiation and lobbying for needs, rather than demanding rights, has shaped trans activism. Only once, in a conversation with several trans persons in the waiting room of Mirdamad Clinic, did I hear one MtF say "we have rights like any other citizens. We should work for being recognized in the Constitution," whereupon a lot of skeptical looks turned toward her, with several people saying that speaking of constitutional rights would get them no tangible results and would turn their needs into a political football.

This attitude reflected the strong reaction, articulated by many activists, against "politicization" of their cause. They tended to work in the pattern of engaging in a "small and inconspicuous acquisition of entitlements."[33] The same word in Persian is often used both for rights and entitlements (haqq), a dual meaning that lends itself to productive ambiguities, overlaps, and possible future shifts from one meaning to another. But for the moment, trans activism in Iran has taken shape in the pattern of "incremental and fragmented actions by numerous actors," similar to what Asef Bayat has analyzed as the "logic of practice in nonmovements."[34] Unlike the "nonmovements" that Bayat analyzes, trans persons do not measure in "multimillions" but on a more numerically limited scale and localized level that is nevertheless the pattern in which trans activism has worked. Some of the actions bear a logic similar to those enacted by much larger groups, for instance, in how repeatable and repeated actions by numerous individuals come to produce the same effect as generalized policy.

A well-known example in the domain of women's rights in recent years has been to force a reluctant husband to agree to a divorce by the wife going to court and demanding immediate payment of her mahr—the contractually binding gift (in money or goods) owed by husband to wife upon marriage. While women do not have easy access to demanding a divorce, they can ask for such payment at any time after a marriage contract has been signed. The legal action brings the husband to court and often results in his granting the desired divorce instead of paying the mahr. This route now has been used repeatedly and successfully by many women and has become widely known as "getting a divorce by asking for an enforcement of mahr payment"—"mahriyah bah ijra guzashtan."

With a similar logic, trans persons have learned how to ask their physicians to write, in their letters of referral for various surgeries, hormonal, or laser treatments: "This is not an elective procedure; it is medically required." This simple phrase entitles the person to get costs covered by insurance companies or state hospitals, effectively as if it were a state-coded guidance for physicians. The success of this step has translated into the Welfare Organization publicly advocating the same. Hasan Musavi Chilik, Director General of the Office for the Socially Harmed, in a January 22, 2010, interview, explained, "A great many of TSs have no insurance coverage . . . in addition many insurance plans do not accept their responsibility to pay the cost of this surgery, since they have put it under cosmetic surgery, whereas this ailment has nothing to do with beautification and cosmetic surgeries."[35]

What does the frequent and insistent reiteration of trans activists' concern against the politicization of their issues indicate about the meaning of "the political" in contemporary Iran? While insisting that they did not wish their cause to become politicized, trans activists practiced what many other activists would consider "political engagement" (ta'amul-i siyasi) with the state. Not only did they go to various governmental offices on an almost daily basis to lobby for various needs, but they also went to the offices of the highest positions of governmental power—including the Office of the President and the Office of the Supreme Leader—to plead their case.

The one major political institution with which they were not interested in engaging was the Majlis. Not going to the Majlis speaks to the shape of trans self-formation as a body seeking entitlements, not rights. The process of change through legislation is a volatile and prolonged one, arduous and often with dubious results. Moreover, historically the Majlis has been the location of engagements for claims of rights, rather than for the acquisition of entitlements. The women's movement in Iran, for instance, in its long, fractured, and contested history of politics of engagement with "the state," has often "gone to the Majlis" rather than to other governmental institutions. Its formation through a conception of rights and its primary focus on changing laws that discriminate against women have shaped its politics of engagement (or boycott of engagement) with the state through the legislative house of the Majlis.[36] Unlike the broad shape of women's rights activism, formed around rights and shaped in terms of engagement with or opposition to institutional sites of state power, trans activists (with their need-centered pragmatics) tended to think of state-focused politics—the fractious, ever-shifting political configurations of who was in charge of which political office—as detrimental to their cause. They wanted to make sure that their access to such offices as Bihzisti, the Ministry of Health, and so on would not be affected by the political markings of the occupants of the office. Whether it was Khatami or Ahmadinijad in office, they needed to be able to go to the Presidency—"Pastaur Street," as it often was referred to. Whether it was Khomeini or now Khamenei, they needed to go to the Supreme Leader. "Not political" meant they wanted to keep their needs and entitlements guarded from the continuous vagaries of occupants of offices all the way down to ministries, judges, and lower-echelon bureaucrats. They needed to be close enough to individuals to get things done but not too closely identified with any individual.

This contrasting understanding of politics and different orientations vis-à-vis "engagement" is an effect of the legibility of transsexuality and the continued illegibility of the equality paradigm that feminists face. The legibility has made a rights-centered discourse at best unnecessary and, worse, potentially risky, because it would open up transsexual issues to the political vagaries of "the state." While Islamic rulings (e.g., Khomeini's fatwa) has been enabling for setting the parameters of social cognition and the satisfaction of needs, the Islamic rulings on women, family law, inheritance, exclusion from certain offices, and other numerous levels of discrimination make the focus on rights indispensable for women's rights advocates. The Majlis is seen as the primary seat of laws/rights. As far as trans activists are concerned, they already have received their badge of citizenship/social cognition in Khomeini's fatwa. Any other parliamentary grand document would pale in contrast. To the extent that regulations need legislation, their orientation—from a local to a larger scale, whether on military exemption or on other issues—has paid off. After all, even if a law is passed, the implementation is back to the local level, where local alliances make it work or fail.

As we have seen, it is through the category of "vulnerable" that much-needed services and entitlements have become available to transsexuals. In the process, this population has been cast as "vulnerable" to "social harm" and in need of governmental protection. And it is this same emergence that accounts for trans activists' orientation vis-à-vis the government and their avoidance of rights discourse. As Michael Fischer noted, "'Vulnerable' is a key cultural term, a legal, moral, theological, psychiatric, psychological, hormonal, medical and surgical 'switching point.' It is a legal term and category that shifts the grounds of debate from internationally defined 'human rights' language to less contested, more local and contextual, languages of welfare, justice and vulnerability. It opens up bureaucratic space using psychiatry as a procedural means of regulation and defense."[37]

"Not wishing to become political" also impacted trans activists' skepticism toward the discourse on rights. In addition to their dismissal of the usefulness of engaging with the legislative, the rights discourse had, for them, become entangled within a volatile international scene with which they had engaged for publicity in 2003–4 but of which they had grown distrustful. This was a scene over which they felt they had no control. While individual trans persons did try to use international engagement to expand their life options, as a collective body, the activists seemed to have grown increasingly wary of such entanglements.

Through the dynamic of working with and through governmental institutions, trans activists have initiated, reshaped, and brought their own agenda into play. Simultaneously, they have made themselves into subjects of governmental play. In the mid-2000s, for instance, the Welfare Organization proposed holding weekly meetings to provide consultation, organize delivery of service, and at the same time keep a more orderly eye on trans activism. Two

trans and one *gay* activist had been critical to its initial consolidation by organizing and bringing to the meetings initially reluctant trans persons. They
had consistently used the auspices of the Welfare Organization to reach other
governmental institutions to get their cases heard. The reluctance of many
trans persons indicated their resistance against coming under governmental
scrutiny. For the activists, this negotiated space of supervision was seen as the
price they paid in exchange for gaining the weight of numbers they needed for
lobbying and pressing for entitlements.[38]


## Working the State

"Do you want to come to Bihzisti with us tomorrow?" Sina asked me as we
walked down Vali 'Asr Avenue from Millat Park on a hot day in early summer 2007, after a long conversation about what he and his friends had accomplished over the previous two weeks when I had gone to Tabriz. I was processing, in silence and with admiration, his account of meetings with various
officials and what had finally been agreed upon with several ministries. He was
clearly in a great mood. But his question threw me into confusion. The regular
meetings at Bihzisti—which usually referred to the Navvab Safavi Emergency
Center of the Office for the Socially Harmed on the southeastern outskirts of
Tehran, at the end of Ahang Expressway—met on Mondays. Tomorrow would
be Wednesday. "Have the meetings changed again?" I asked, remembering
that initially Sundays had been the regular meeting day before it was changed
to Mondays. "No, I don't mean that Bihzisti. Tomorrow we are meeting with
Kian-nush again, at the main national office of the Welfare Organization, you
know the building, on the northern side of Park-i Shahr?"

I knew the area well. I had known it from my childhood days, when a dear
aunt lived in Mustaufi Alley, only blocks away, and more recently from my
visits to the LMOI, located on the southern side of the park. But still, the Welfare Organization, especially the National Office, was to me "the state." From
the first days of my research, "going to the state" had posed the hardest challenge in my work. Inevitably, my fieldwork had to take me to various institutions that had something to do with "the state." Some were literary state institutions, such as the LMOI and Welfare Organization's Emergency Center (see
figure 1.1). Others, such as Rouzbeh Hospital, the TPI, or even the Academy for
Medical Sciences (Fahangistan-i 'Ulum-i Pizishki), were more accurately state
affiliated or state sponsored to various and varying degrees. The challenge was
not facing any anticipated hurdles in these institutions. Indeed, as it turned
out, except for the reticence of the LMOI to give me any official data, I was wel-

comed and assisted in every single one. Despite these experiences, I continued to feel, over and over again, apprehension, resistance, and even almost fear in approaching state institutions. Informed by a culture of deep antistatism of earlier decades across the political spectrum, and buttressed by a social ethos of state avoidance, it was a continuous challenge for me to join trans activists in their daily, almost casual interactions, with various state institutions. I entered these sites with deep discomfort, trepidation, and sometimes fear, as if it were likely that at any moment I would be arrested and sent to Evin Prison, or at least to the Vuzara Detention Center. In the first weeks of my work, when I had gone to a Ministry of the Interior office to ask for a copy of the video recording of a recent state-sponsored scientific seminar that had covered the topic of transsexuality, I was told I needed to have permission authorizing my research. I was told to go to some office in the Central Revolutionary Court. Go to the Revolutionary Court? That was an institution that for me only carried the terrible memories of the early years of the Court's decisions that had put thousands in jail and ordered many executed. One did not walk into it voluntarily. I decided I would do without that video.

I dressed more conservatively than anyone around me—so much so that one of the activists lost his patience one day and asked me, only half joking, "Have you always made yourself this ugly?" That was the first difference I had noticed. Not only FtMs, but MtFs also came to the regular Bihzisti weekly meetings dressed more flagrantly than I could imagine "safe." I have no doubt that my body language betrayed my sense of fearful approaches and entries—a sense of "what am I doing here in this state institution?" In contrast, this new generation of activists made their way in and out of various offices, various ministries, all the way to the offices of the Supreme Leadership and the Presidency, with an ease that was as if they owned these institutions.

Even more surprising to me was how trans activists had their own way of cutting through bureaucratic barriers. Through their very daily engagements with and persistent vocal lobbying in numerous government offices, they had accumulated a great deal of social capital and clout. When I first contacted the Welfare Organization to ask about joining the trans support group's meetings, I was told I needed to be interviewed by the head of the office first. When I told Houri, who had invited me to go to the Monday meetings of the group, she said, "never mind them, come to my place and we will go together." And this is all it took: At the beginning of the meeting, the social worker in charge of the group asked who I was. Before I had a chance to respond, Houri said, "Dr. Najmabadi is a university professor, doing research. I invited her." And that was the end of that.

When on that summer day Sina invited me to join the meeting at the Welfare Organization, I reacted with my usual apprehension, though also with excitement. These were the kind of meetings I would have loved to be present at, to sit and do my "participant observations"—meetings for which I did not want to bother to get the permission letter from the appropriate state office. I told Sina that I didn't think I would be allowed to sit in. Sina frowned, took out his cell phone, and called a number, explaining to the person on the other end of the line that he was bringing with him to the meeting a professor who was doing research. There was a brief exchange, during which Sina offered some explication about my helpful knowledge for the meeting's agenda. And that was that. The next day I showed up at the entry hallway of the Welfare Organization's central office. A selected group of five activists was already there.

This was a meeting with Nastaran Kian-nush, who was at the time advisor for Women's Affairs to Dr. Faqih, then the head of the Welfare Organization. I already had heard a great deal about her from trans activists as someone very sympathetic to their needs, who was trying to do her best to help them out. I was keen to meet her. Others present were one of her assistants, Ms. Bani-Hashemi, and three journalists she had invited. Kian-nush, dressed in a stylish, brightly colored suit with a matching patterned headscarf, started the meeting. She had a friendly, relaxed, warm approach and clearly had established a respectful rapport with the activists in previous meetings. She began by emphasizing what seemed to have been a point from previous meetings: she needed them to come to her with clearly articulated issues and with plenty of solid documentation. As an example, she said, "When you tell me a student was expelled from this or that university because s/he was *trans*, I need full documentation.[39] Only then can I take up the issue with the Ministry of Education to instruct universities to be sensitive. When you say Tehran municipal should allocate housing for needy *transsexuals*, I need numbers.[40] I need to know how many people need housing, what kind of accommodation would be adequate. When you complain about this or that institution ignoring your pursuits, you need to write up your case and make a documented dossier before I could take the case to the right authorities." She asked Sina to coordinate this work. The familiar demand for documentation, for documentability, for becoming counted and accounted for, never ceased. Kian-nush's demand for documents and for numbers played out the dynamic of skepticism through which being trans was defined and experienced in so many domains of daily life. As I've already discussed, social legibility and cognition of trans-hood is critically dependent on stacks of documents. Trans persons seek and preserve these "identity papers" and at once cannot but be resentful of them—they are a continuous reminder that their recognizability is always under the terms of these papers. In the context of a meeting in a government office, there is the added discomfort and ambivalence of knowing that providing documents, necessary as they are for getting needed services, also furthers their becoming subject to governmental supervision and control.

Both Kian-nush and her assistant Ms. Bani-Hashemi persistently argued that trans activists had to learn how to do things one step at a time, using an Armenian expression common in conversational Persian, *gamas gamas*—getting one thing done in this ministry, another in that office.[41] The conversation then turned to the role of the media, apparently the main topic for the day. She introduced the three reporters, all freelancers; I had read many of their columns in dailies generally linked with reformists, *Ham-mihan*, *Sharq*, *I'timad-i milli*, and *Sarmayah*. Ihsan, an FtM, complained that the press had made them into a notorious subject and the extensive coverage did not necessarily help them. Houri disagreed; if there was some element of sensationalism, she thought this was the trans's own fault, "we don't know how to present our case." Kian-nush explained that she had selected the invited reporters based on her knowledge of their sensitivity to social issues and that she wanted the activists to trust her on this critical matter. She asked them to elect one person with whom she would consult, and asked them to let her set the timing and tone of future press coverage to coincide with moments when it would have the most constructive impact. From conversations among activists, I knew this was a point of disagreement. Both Sina and Houri were skeptical of the way several trans persons had become media stars; they felt their participation had produced at best a sense of pity for trans persons, and at worst animosity—if indeed it had not been all for private gain and fame. They were more inclined to work quietly. Ihsan was an advocate of seeking more publicity as leverage to get things done.

Kian-nush's request "to trust her" was met with measured silence; the activists were reluctant to let a government official, no matter how sympathetic and well-meaning, become a participant in their internal debates. The conversation shifted to yet another topic of contention: Ihsan had been advocating going to the Majlis. He now asked Kian-nush to facilitate a meeting with a select group of Majlis representatives. After some discussion over what they expected to get from such a meeting, Kian-nush suggested that there was some groundwork to be done before such a meeting would be useful, including what she had emphasized at the beginning of the meeting: documentation, documentation, documentation!

The last topic for the day was how Kian-nush could help them to set up an information website. This was something that had been discussed in several meetings among activists; the hope had been that a registered NGO would enable them to have a legally registered site. But the process of becoming an NGO seemed to drag on forever (discussed below). In the interim, they wanted other ways of dealing with this need. Here Kian-nush had a simple solution: She suggested that they should prepare their material and she would look into how the Welfare Organization's website could allocate a page for this topic. "In any case," she suggested, "the more material you prepare now the sooner you will be able to put things up, on your own NGO or on the Bihzisti site." She looked at Sina and added, "This should actually be part of the documentation project."

Sina's assignment as the documentation point person was not accidental. He had already prepared a massive amount of material on several occasions for various governmental institutions, including a DVD of medical information that covered and illustrated different techniques of surgery, for a high official at the Ministry of Health.[42]

As we walked out, I expected him to be pleased with yet another successful meeting. Instead he looked annoyed. Once Houri, Sina, and I sat down in a local restaurant for lunch, he suddenly blurted out, "Why didn't you say anything?" This was the last thing I had expected to hear. I had sat silent throughout, as an observer, as I had done similarly in the TPI commission meetings, especially as they had all been so articulate and conversant. Who was I to intervene? "Why do you think we wanted you to come then? It is very important for someone like Kian-nush to hear things from a respected university person." Belatedly, I realized I had been recruited into their cartography of allies and influences. I had to pull my weight in future meetings.

It was through numerous meetings like this one that activists slowly achieved some of their goals. An important such meeting was held in the summer of 2007. A delegate of activists, including Sina and Houri, went to a special meeting of the Ministry of Justice's Council for the Resolution of Conflicts. Present were representatives from the Judiciary, NAJA, the Welfare Organization (represented by Kian-nush's assistant), and the Ministries of Justice and Health. This meeting had been arranged in part because of the ongoing tension between the Ministry of Health and the Welfare Organization. The meeting concluded with recommending the formation of a special court to deal with TS's legal issues (such as change of identity papers after surgery),[43] recommending the formation of a specialized ( *fauq-i takhassusi* ) medical clinic for TSs and for sending surgeons abroad for training. Afterward Sina and Houri immediately began planning to meet with Kian-nush to ask that surgeons be brought to Iran to train a larger number of surgeons at less expense. Shortly afterward, they also learned that their demand for getting health insurance had been granted.[44]

Such trans official meetings were part of a larger scheme of social sites that worked to create relative consensus among activists on what to pursue when, and through which office, as well as to keep up pressure on government officials with whom they worked or lobbied. For instance, before the meeting with the Ministry of Justice's Council for the Resolution of Conflicts in which an agreement was reached to train more skilled specialized surgeons, the topic of the terrible quality of surgery in Iran had been discussed numerous times in trans meetings—both in the weekly meetings supervised in the Emergency Center of the Welfare Organization and in meetings with various individuals in several ministries. Through these many conversations in numerous sites a generalized knowledge of "the terrible quality of surgeries" had been produced. It had become a known and accepted fact.

The Resolution of Conflicts meeting had itself come as the culmination of a series of meetings on the initiative of the activists. Representatives from several governmental organizations had been invited to these meetings by the Welfare Organization to meet with trans activists, to respond to their questions and hear their concerns. On March 11, 2007, for instance, 'Atifah Khaushnavaz from the Women's Affairs Office at the Health Ministry and Kian-nush from the Welfare Organization were present to respond to trans concerns over medical treatments. Kian-nush had asked Khaushnavaz why the Health Ministry authorities paid no attention and did not send doctors abroad to become trained. After much discussion, Kian-nush had suggested that if the Ministry of Health could not do this, they should inform her and the Welfare Organization would take charge. Trans activists were keen to use intra-governmental competitive frictions to further their cause and had become quite skilled at this game. With it, of course, came the ever-present risk of becoming swallowed by a snake just when the end was in sight. Then one had to begin again.

Some of these meetings were reported in the press. For instance, the Iranian Students News Agency (ISNA) published a report of the April 22, 2007, meeting, which was then picked up by other publications and extended into larger social reportage.[45] The topic of this meeting—held at the Navvab Emergency Center and attended by Kian-nush, along with representatives from NAJA (Dr. Firdaus Qumashchi) and from the Judiciary—had been the absence of any central office that would coordinate the provision of the multiple services that this population needed. This meeting was followed by another in which several representatives from NAJA had come to hear in more detail how trans persons were treated by the security forces, on the streets, and in police stations.

At the end of the meeting, NAJA agreed to organize training workshops and invite trans activists to educate its members. On May 6, representatives from the Judiciary had come and activists had expressed their demand for a special court to be set up for their change of identification papers and that judges for this court be trained not to be intrusive. For instance, they should not ask for a bodily examination once the LMOI's certification, confirming that SRS had been carried out, was produced by an applicant. At this meeting, it also was announced that Bihzisti would get trans persons court-appointed attorneys or they could use Bihzisti's own legal personnel for their legal needs.

A week later (May 14, 2007), another representative from the Health Ministry came to the regular Monday meeting at the Welfare Organization. Ms. Ya'qub, in charge of the social work office at the Ministry, heard trans complaints about the high prices of their medical needs, including laser treatment for removal of facial hair for MtFs; they emphasized the need for local training of medical personnel, especially in state hospitals. In June, a representative from the Housing and Urban Development Organization attended to discuss housing needs. A critically important meeting (which eventually, in January 2010, produced the changes in military exemption law) was held on August 6, 2007. A member of the Majlis from the committee in charge of drafting the revised conscription legislation, as well as an assistant to the Defense Minister, attended this meeting. Activists explained in great detail what difficulties their current exemption code caused. The meeting ended with the Majlis deputy suggesting that the committee would look into the possibility of moving them to the glandular diseases category—a promise that was kept. This meeting also produced the proposal—now the law—that upon Bihzisti referral, trans persons in transition should be granted temporary exemption from service, an exemption that is renewable every six months upon recommendation from Bihzisti.

In August 2007, activists' demand to meet with members of the Majlis also was met. The Navvab Emergency Center of Bihzisti arranged for three activists to meet with a group of Majlis deputies. As one activist later related, "Except for one deputy, the rest had never heard about us. They looked at us with shock." At the beginning of this meeting, Dr. Faqih, then the director of the Welfare Organization, asked one of the activists to give a brief presentation about the phenomenon of transsexuality. This was largely intended to familiarize members of parliament so that when related legislation came to the floor, some deputies could speak authoritatively on the subject.

Aside from officials, sometimes trans persons who had made particularly successful transitions would be invited either by activists or by the Bihzisti. For instance, on May 27, an MtF was introduced by the social worker to the group. She was now a successful hairdresser who had been married for several years, and the Welfare Organization was helping her to adopt a child.[46] Another MtF, from a northern provincial capital, visited the group to inform them about different hormone therapy options. She was currently in Tehran to lobby the food and drug office at the Ministry of Health to import pharmaceutical needs of trans persons.

In addition to the weekly meetings at the Navvab Emergency Center of Bihzisti, for almost a year trans persons also met on their own at the office of *Ravanshinasi va jami'ah* (*Psychology and Society*) every Thursday. The use of this space had been facilitated by Dr. Ohadi, a member of the editorial board of the magazine who at the time was cultivating his relations with trans persons whom he was hoping to recruit as subjects for his doctoral dissertation project (see chapter 1). Unlike the Bihzisti meetings, here there were no officials supervising and running the meetings. Occasionally various people were invited for particular reasons; for instance, Dr. Arash Alaei was invited to run an information session on HIV/AIDS.[47] These meetings served as a place for trans persons to come together and exchange accounts of experience and information. After a few meetings, however, the more experienced people got frustrated with its repetitive character and suggested using agendas for work and keeping minutes to build from one meeting to the next. In the meeting of November 23, 2006, for instance, it was decided that the group must take charge of the collection, reproduction, and dissemination of information, until such time as they received authorization for the formation of an NGO. One activist, 'Ali, who had good access to the Internet and experience in brochure design, volunteered to download relevant information. It also was decided to go once more to the Ministry of Health to discuss the problem of surgical malpractice and demand that they either send surgeons abroad for training or bring surgeons from overseas to train people in Iran. If no results were obtained, then they would write an open letter to the president. In the following meeting, a discussion of the production of an information brochure opened up the issue of what to call themselves in Persian: No one wanted to use "tee-es" (TS), nor were they happy with "people afflicted with GID." This conversation was only a beginning that was disrupted: The magazine served them notice on that day that they were no longer welcome to hold their meetings there. Apparently other occupants of the building had complained about the presence of "immoral" people in and around the building.[48]

After losing their meeting space at the office of *Ravanshinasi va jami'ah*, Sina and Houri decided to follow through on some of the projects through the

Bihzisti meetings. In particular, by that time good work had gone into collecting information and preparing an information brochure. But they were told by Bihzisti that they "had no such right," Sina complained, and that "everything we do has to be supervised by Bihzisti. We have to show them the brochure and only if they approve can we use it, and then only among TSS. They wouldn't even give us financial support for it. 'Ali had designed the brochure, but we couldn't pursue it." Such official moves to be more in control of what activists did provided new impetus to go after the registration of an NGO.

### Iranian Society for Supporting Individuals with Gender Identity Disorder (ISSIGID)[49]

At some point in 2004, according to Maryam Mulk-ara, Hujjat al-Islam Mohammad Ali Abtahi (one of Khatami's vice presidents at the time) encouraged her to form an NGO. The process of forming and registering NGOs in Iran since the late 1990s fits well with what Ferguson and Gupta have elaborated, namely, "the outsourcing of the functions of the state to NGOs and other ostensibly nonstate agencies" as "a key feature" of the operation of states.[50] This is so not only in the case of the ISSIGID of Iran, but of many other domains as well.[51] It took another four years before ISSIGID was officially registered in mid February 2008 and its website launched in March of that year.

During Khatami's second term (2001–5), the Minister of Health Dr. Mas'ud Pizishkian, a heart surgeon, was apparently quite hostile to trans persons. Murtizá Tala'i, Tehran's Chief of Police (2000–2006), as well as Muhammad Baqir Qalibaf, NAJA's chief (2000–2005), also are said to have been particularly harsh. After years of the relaxation of harassment and arrests in the 1990s, there was a sudden surge of reported arrests. As Zia put it,

> For a while Mr. Qalibaf went around and said he wanted to separate *gays* from *trans*es, to bring *trans*es under Bihzisti coverage and punish *gays* harshly. This had a big impact, but he was opposed by Dr. Muqaddam who told him there was no way he could carry out such a scheme because *trans*es and *gays* were tightly stuck together. Nonetheless, this was a tough period; many *gays* started saying they were *trans*. It is also easier to tell your family you are *trans*. Also many therapists don't like to send people to the LMOI as *gay* [for getting the papers for military exemption], they are worried that their practice will get marked as facilitating same-sex-playing.

As Mulk-ara narrates her difficulties during this period, she was the only publicly known transsexual; she would receive phone calls day and night from other *trans*es whose friends had been taken to Evin Prison and who would beg her to intervene and get them out. Mulk-ara would turn to people in the top echelons of the government who were more sympathetic and seek their help.

It was this latter group of government personnel who finally decided something more systematic was called for. According to Mulk-ara, she was invited to a meeting to discuss the situation, and it was there that Abtahi suggested the idea of forming an NGO to facilitate dealing with trans issues. Mulk-ara had responded by saying that she knew nothing about what NGOs were and what they did. The government personnel present, especially people from the Ministry of the Interior, told her they would help her do the paperwork. Thus began years of shuttling between the Ministries of the Interior and Health. At first, Mulk-ara had wanted all founding members to be trans, but she realized that she could not find enough qualified persons (in terms of levels of university degree, with a BA being the minimal requirement for members of the board of directors). So she decided to get non-trans help. The initial founding group (*hay'at-i mau'assis*) consisted of Dr. Saberi, Dr. Riza'i, Dr. Shahmuradi, and Dr. Kahani (all from the LMOI); Dr. Ayati (a gynecological surgeon); Hujjat al-Islam Karimi-nia (an Islamic scholar); Dr. Mirjalali (a general surgeon who had become a sex reassignment surgeon over the previous two decades); Dr. Mirjalali's wife (no name given); Mr. Zamani (Mirjalali's assistant and an SRS operating room technician); an MtF trans (name withheld); an FtM trans (name withheld); Mulk-ara; and Muhammad Ab-band-kinari (Mulk-ara's husband). These people were introduced to the Ministry of the Interior, but Dr. Ayati, Dr. Mirjalali's wife, and the FtM trans later resigned. A first meeting of the founding group was held on May 13, 2006, to draft the articles of the NGO's constitution. The proposed constitution was completed and submitted to the Ministry of the Interior in the fall of 2006. It took another year and a half of frustrating navigation and lobbying before the ministry issued the permit in early January 2008.[52]

The composition of the founding board of directors reflects the initial dependency of activists on medical, legal, and religious allies to acquire a registered legitimacy. When I raised with Sina my fear that the preponderance of these figures would take their concerns out of their own control, he was dismissive: "We have a clause that the board of directors must meet every two weeks; there is also a clause that after two consecutive absences, the person will receive a warning, and after the third, their membership will lapse. None of these people will show up regularly; we will then elect our own people in their place."

Indeed, the biggest challenge has been increasing the membership. Initially given a temporary six-month permit, pending its first members' meeting, in October 2008 the permit was extended for a two-year period, during which a minimum membership of four thousand was set as a condition for issuing a permanent permit. As of May 2009, its reported membership was less than seven hundred, only some thirty of whom were said to be full members.[53] This is not surprising, though it will remain a formidable challenge. Postoperative *trans*es generally hope to disappear from any public identification. They strive to become normatively indistinguishable. In 2010, from among the very active *trans*es with whom I worked in 2006–7, one helped the new organization (behind the scenes, so to speak) to set up its website; the others have completed their transitions and have "disappeared." One is continuing his education abroad, one is married and in the process of adopting a child, two others have good jobs and are developing their careers. One recently became engaged. Except for the website manager, none are in any way involved with the new organization. This is not unexpected. As I argued earlier, trans activism in Iran is driven by need, purposefully "apolitical," and not rights oriented. Once a semiofficial NGO began to mediate responses to need, the activism of the earlier period has been replaced largely by forming local chapters of the ISSI-GID, whose primary work is to refer *trans*es to the relevant local authorities. The "mother" organization itself was virtually centralized around the person of Mulk-ara (whom numerous trans writers on the website addressed as their mother) and discouraged activism outside its own framework.

Since shortly after its formation, the ISSIGID has kept up a very active website.[54] A Qur'anic verse, in Arabic with Persian translation, serves as the top lines of the opening page (figure 6.1): "Our Lord is He who gave everything its creation, then guided it" (20: 50). Aside from links to pages that house articles, news, a collection of fatwas on transsexuality issued by various clerical leaders, and laws and regulations, there is also a link titled "Mulk-ara" that gives her personal message to the visitor.[55]

Two sections on the website showed the most activity. In "Question and Answer" questions were posed and, it seems, all answered by Mulk-ara herself or on her behalf. On certain topics—for instance, when a question was asked about identifying certain symptoms as meaning that a person was trans, or when names of physicians were asked for—her answer was to ask the person to call her on the phone for a conversation and further references. She explained this procedure in terms of avoiding any publicity for any particular doctors and the difficulty of answering some questions on the open site. Frequent questions included the quality of SRS in Iran compared with other places, how to

FIGURE 6.1. The opening page of the Persian section of the ISSIGID website, 2008–10.

deal with facial hair and a masculine vocal tone, how one's sexual pleasure was affected by the surgeries, and occasional questions posed by intersex individuals or parents with intersex children.[56]

Even more active than the Question and Answer section was the Open Forum (*tiribun-i azad*), which served as a site for conversations, including social conversations and searches for friends. This section seems to have been particularly well suited for people in smaller towns, who often left e-mails for direct correspondence. From March 2008 to January 2010, people who posted to the site were found in more than thirty different locations, including some very small towns, from all corners of the country. Besides finding friends, some posters put up extensive informational pieces on various aspects of trans lives and needs, some wrote about their own experiences (especially with hostile families and neighbors), some posted occasional poetry and what would be considered important news.[57] There were occasional playful pieces, such as one that declared, "We are masterpieces of creation."[58]

Several graduate students posted queries, explaining that they had chosen transsexuality as their dissertation topic and requested the cooperation of members; two fiction writers, a few journalists, and one filmmaker posted similar notes. Invariably, these requests met with hostile reactive posts by *transes*: go and find another topic, we won't serve as your *suzhah* (from the French *sujet*).[59]

Posters were also very quick to respond to what they considered hostile or ill-informed postings by non-*trans*es, such as the debates set off by a posting that had suggested transsexuality is an acquired condition that could be overcome.

The success of the site seems to have generated other information sites. At least two new sites have been set up since, one specifically for MtFs and the other for FtMs. These—unlike the ISSIGID site—do give information on practices and procedures, as well as names and addresses of surgeons and psychologists.[60]

This virtualization of spaces of connectivity, passing information, and engaging activists inevitably has raised the question of the website's relation to the other nonvirtual site that had come to be associated with some of the same operations, namely the weekly meetings of *trans*es at the Navvab Emergency Center of Bihzisti. The relationship between ISSIGID and Bihzisti has been a contentious one from the start. From its conceptual inception in 2004, Mulk-ara had hoped that formation of an NGO would enable her to have access to governmental funds to support what she felt she had been doing all along with no resources: help *trans*es in need but also help the government to have a structured way of working with this population. Four years later, however, Bihzisti had come to be a primary trans champion and resource center in its own name and with its own clout. With an annual budget that has grown from 20 to 700 million tumans within five years,[61] a nationwide service infrastructure, and several years of cultivated relationship with trans activists (some of whom had worked separately from Mulk-ara) and with several local and national governmental organizations and ministries, Bihzisti had developed its own domain and dynamic. Early on, in response to a question about Bihzisti subsidies posted on the site, Mulk-ara expressed hope that, "In future, all responsibilities concerning aid to *trans*es will be carried out through the Society" (April 20, 2008). This hope continued to elude Mulk-ara. The large problem of how to stabilize the society itself remained; Bihzisti is unlikely to wish to pass its supervisory powers to any NGO in any case.

While at one level ISSIGID and Bihzisti may be vying over the same resources and competing for the attention of the same population, at the same time, ISSIGID has served to routinize and bureaucratize trans activism. *Trans*es are now thought to have an official voice, although many on the site have complained that the society did little. The group of activists who lobbied so hard in 2006–8 are now almost all postop and have dispersed. As diagnostic and transition procedures have become streamlined, and as an official NGO now has a representative voice, other less formal sites have vanished. Even the group that met weekly in Bihzisti has been disbanded—among charges of the misuse of funds by one group of *transes*.[62] The creation of an NGO has resulted in a more disciplined and self-disciplining identification.

## Changing the Terms

At the end of yet another frustrating meeting, this time with a high official at the Center for Women and Family Affairs in the Office of the President, I turned to Houri and asked what she thought they had accomplished that day.

> Oh, we don't think in those terms. Nothing, if you want to know. This is the way these meetings are. We talk, answer questions, explain our needs, get some vague promises, and leave. In a month or so, we make another appointment and ask if any steps have been taken about those promises. Usually not, sometimes, there is somebody who cares—like Ms. Kian-nush at the central Bihzisti—and who takes an interest in us and tries to do things for us. But, in truth, that is not the point of these meetings. What we really get done is that a larger number of people in official positions, in as many government organizations as possible, are seeing us; they realize we are ordinary people, we don't have horns and tails [*shakh-u-dum nada-rim*—we are not monsters], we are not scary, we don't contaminate them. These meetings, above all, work against the climate of prejudice against us. Changing the prevailing stereotypes will enable us to be respected and ac-cepted as ordinary citizens.

Houri's articulation reminded me of the other campaign that was going on in the same period: the One Million Signatures campaign, in which women's rights activists had chosen to follow the strategy of what they called "Face to Face"—going door to door, in their own neighborhoods, at their workplaces, wherever they felt comfortable, to open a conversation with other women and men and ask for their signature support for a platform of women's demands.[63] But unlike the One Million Signatures campaign, trans activists had not ar-rived at their position on the basis of previous decades of rights-based activism within a spectrum of political orientations vis-à-vis the Iranian state—Pahlavi or the Islamic Republic. Their orientation had emerged pragmatically, as an exigency of daily life over the past two decades and as necessitated by civic en-titlement.

The *transes*' relation to the state is mediated not by anything to do with its "Islamic" character—that seems to be a given that one is born into and lives in. Even the engagement with religious authorities in earlier decades, critically important for the configuration and consolidation of present-day transition procedures, is now seen as history. Unlike my presumption of the need for engaging and linking with Karimi-nia's revisionary Islamic discourse, for instance, most *trans*es were uncomprehending of its usefulness. The more politically minded ones were positively hostile to the idea when I suggested it during one Thursday meeting; they thought it would be unnecessarily politicizing and provocative. It would get their issues entangled in the ideological-intellectual fights in the seminaries. The religious connection may have had some usefulness initially for getting a legal status and for establishing the credibility of *trans*es' accounts of their needs, but that was already history for almost all *trans*es with whom I talked, except a few among those who considered themselves observant Muslims. For others, the religious discourse occasionally became useful as an argument with parents. Otherwise, the concern was how to best get the state to do things.

This orientation has been largely successful in changing the terms.[64] As Hasan Musavi Chilik, Director General of the Office for Socially Harmed in the Welfare Organization, articulated in one of his interviews, "The society, authorities, and the law must accept *TS*s . . . not in terms of the corrupt, the criminal, or as mental patients, but as ordinary citizens of society. Such acceptance not only will have positive effects in terms of improving their situation; it will also make their presence in society safer, easier, and more ordinary."[65] In Musavi Chilik, *trans*es seem to have found a new state advocate.

One important indication that the status of transsexuality has acquired a certain level of ordinariness and is no longer seen as a strange or wondrous matter is that, by the end of the decade, reports on *trans*es in the press have become limited largely to news of ordinary facts, such as the change of the military exemption code. Only occasionally are more sensational items reported, such as the imprisonment and final release of an MtF trans who had blinded a man in apparent self-defense against sexual harassment[66]; the marriage of a postoperative FtM to her best girlfriend[67]; and the controversy over the presence of "bi-sexedness" among members of the Iranian National Women's Soccer Team.[68]

## What Is in a Name?

In a posting on ISSIGID site dated May 15, 2009, in answer to a question, Mulkara wrote that a trans was not a diseased person, nor did s/he suffer from any physiological ailments. This was why *trans*es should see a sexologist/psychologist to help them out. There was a quick response: "You say transsexuality is not an illness?!?!? How could I talk to my family then? They will never believe that I have a problem. They think I am acting out [*ada dar miyaram*]." Other *trans*es over and over again confirmed the same account: they continued to need the category "illness" in relation to their families. Given the continued overwhelming sociocultural identification of transsexuality with immorality — that is, with homosexuality, especially for MtFs — the language of illness continues to be critically useful.

Paradoxically, the success of becoming "more ordinary" — that is, of not being perceived as "afflicted" — continues to depend on the availability and usability of the category of affliction in contingent sites and at critical moments. Nonetheless, new possibilities have opened up for playful renamings. One *FtM* objected (in a July 18, 2009, posting) to the prevalent use of *MtF* and *FtM* among *trans*es.[69] As far as s/he was concerned, a better name for *FtM*s would be "boy-presenting girl" (*dukhtar-i pisarnuma*). Another neologism that has recently emerged is *mardan-i zan-vash* and *zanan-i mard-vash*.[70] Constructed with a suffix that means "-like" (*-vash*), these combinations would translate into "woman-like males" and "man-like females." It seems that the woman-presenting male of the 1970s has returned along with a gender/sex counterpart. The very policies that may have been intended to close the spaces for non-normative trans identifications, imaginations, and living styles have paradoxically reopened and regenerated those very spaces.

Changing the terms also has borne enormous repercussions for other categorizations. The emergence of discourse of transsexuality (*tara-jinsiyat*), the categorical naming of trans subjects, seems to assume man and woman, male and female, as already-known categories. At the same time, it has become a key part of reconfiguring natural maleness and femaleness, normal masculinity and femininity. As the decades since 1979 have struggled to define and redefine idealized and state-enforced demarcations of Islamic manhood and womanhood, today one of the key normative borders has become not-trans (and not-homosexual, for that matter).

Most significantly, to the extent that at the beginning of the 2010s there is more of a differentiation between gay men and woman-presenting males (and somewhat similarly between lesbian women and masculine-presenting females) than there had been in the 1970s, this differentiation points to a dual birth and interdependency of these categories over the past three decades. These are "coincidental" categories whose emergences were coterminous and part of reconfigurations of masculinity and femininity more generally.[71] They continue to define each other's meaning and are connected to each other in complicated ways that often resist that very differentiation, as we will see in the next chapter.

## LIVING PATTERNS, NARRATIVE STYLES

*I am the lost child of a century not yet born*
*I was born, with a body named woman*
*Why can I not love the body of another woman?*

Within minutes of our first conversation, Mahnaz, an attractive woman in her early thirties, burst into reciting her poetry. This was a long ode of desire, desire to be left alone, to love as she desired:

*I do not want that ordinary spring that others desire*
*Let me be, let me be*
*I want to hear love in a fresh blade of grass*

*No leaf will last on a tree*
*No flower will last at the bottom of a wall*
*And no wall can tell you what is in the yard*

*I do not desire modesty*
*I do not want grace*
*I shall not knock on any door, nor on any walls*

*. . .*

*I do not want that ordinary spring that others desire*
*Let me be, let me be*
*I want to cling onto love*

*. . .*

The poem was movingly performed, but I was taken aback because of the place and time of its recitation. We were sitting in the busy lobby of an up-scale Tehran hotel (where Mahnaz was staying) a day after I had met her in the offices of the Mirdamad Clinic—where I would first meet many of the trans persons who would accept my requests for interviews. She had come there from Sabzivar, a northeastern provincial city, with a friend and with cash in hand to fix the date of her SRS. In 2007, more than a year after when I last saw her, she was still weighing her options, no longer certain that she wanted to go through with SRS. She was looking into immigrating to Europe with her husband. This time, in her living room in Sabzivar, she recited the entire poem again. This was a poem that spoke her.

As I got to know Mahnaz more closely, in every encounter and in between our meetings, I was silently obsessed with the desire to name her *lesbian*. She, on the other hand, seemed to be utterly uninterested in naming herself anything. What she wanted, above all, was to be able to love women; if that could not be done in her born-female body, she would consider changing that body. Why not?[1]

The initial shape of my research questions had been informed by the emergence, in recent decades, of the field of gender and sexuality studies, in which critical analytical distinctions had formed around anatomical body significations, gender identifications, and sexual desires. This configuration had translated into the opening lines of my conversations with *trans*, *gay*, and *lesbian* people, reflecting an urge to distinguish, to make a distinction that mattered. My urge to name Mahnaz a lesbian and my way of presenting my research aims were plotted along these lines of differentiation. During the first few months of field work, I presented a variation of the same conversation opener, reproduced here from one transcript: "Well, one of the main goals of my research is to understand how a person comes to a self-understanding as *trans* and not as some other category, for instance, *homosexual*. How does a person reach identification, self-cognition, as a *transsexual*? What are some of the key memories, moments that you now remember as pivotal to this cognition?"

I am not suggesting that my opening line simply determined anyone's answer. I received incredibly varied responses. Indeed, many challenged the premise that the delineations in my question had anything to do with their process of self-cognition. As Emad, a postoperative FtM in his early thirties, put it, "The impact of these categorical distinctions is for others [other than trans persons], who are unfamiliar, and who mix up or collapse these phenomena. We, too, socialize and mix together because of the difficulties and limitations we face. The reason our families think *trans* kids are deviant is because in Iran these two groups are collapsed onto, mixed up with, each other. For us, things are clear. When an outsider comes to places we hang out, like the *Food Court* [pronounced as in English, it referred to one particular food court] on Tuesday nights, they can't tell the difference."

More problematically, my initial queries were reenacting the legal and dominant psychological understandings and categorizations that had emerged in Iran—and that my project was meant to critique. In turn, these questions tended to solicit narratives along those very lines. They tended to foreclose the possibility, at least initially, that such distinctions may not have been the dominant frame of self-cognition for my interviewees. Were not the initial "textbook" narratives that I tended to receive in early interviews elicited in part by my very frame?

Mahnaz's life story, as narrated by her, her husband, and several of her friends, was no more or less complex than the life stories I heard from many others. In all these narratives, there were patterns of similarities, especially in the stories told at the first encounter, because these often had the echo of what had been recited to doctors, friends, sometimes parents—people who had to be convinced of the veracity of one's desire. These were narratives to make one's sense of being-in-the-world intelligible to one's disbelieving audience and at the same time recalling one's sense of cognition to oneself. I was received as one more skeptic interrogator.

As Jay Prosser has noted in his work that bears the subtitle *The Body Narratives of Transsexuality*, ". . . the genre of autobiography *is* conformist and unilinear. In that its work is to organize the life into a narrative form, autobiography is fundamentally conformist. . . . In autobiography the desultoriness of experience acquires chronology, succession, progression—even causation; existence, an author. . . . transsexual autobiography is no exception to this rule of autobiographical composition."[2]

While it is the case that, in the sense pointed out by Prosser, this is a general rule of autobiographical composition, there is an important distinction to be made: Creating order and meaning out of memory fragments of a life lived out of synch with norms and normative expectations—a life pressured incessantly by "what are you?" and "why can't you be like others?"—produces a distinct narrative dynamic. Like other forms of narrative, "the end"—as both the now of recitation and the goal of recitation—is known. The journey from "as far as I remember" to this end has to end here and now. Having been marked as incoherent because of being sex/gender non-normative, the recounting of a past life, no matter how stylized, offers the possibility of coherent meaning-making through repeated recitations. Whereas the larger society and culture does not permit one's self-knowledge to be taken for granted, as granted to "the normals," "self-knowledge as a transsexual requires such narrativization."[3]

Trans- and homosexuals in Iran share a self-constituting mode: both are received skeptically by others. Self-cognition, along with its more public recitation—that is, its narrative and bodily presentations—is what makes a transsexual/homosexual re-cognized by others. As Prosser observes in a different context, "As much as transsexuality, inversion takes autobiography as its primary symptom."[4]

Moreover, even in what at times seem to be formulaic accounts—and much more in subsequent conversations—finer details of lives would emerge: one father's leather belt, another's understanding calm, one mother's vengeful scheming to stop one's surgery, a sister's protective cover, other siblings' uncaring concerns (worrying more about their own reputation among neighbors and peers), an enlightened judge, a punitive psychologist. These differences in small details I will attempt to sketch through the retelling of lives of several trans persons, as well as self-identified *gays* and *lesbians*, to map out a cartography of daily living patterns, as stories that make habitable lives possible.

MAHNAZ WAS BORN into a comfortable, middle-class family. Her parents were both professionals; she described her family as belonging to a "freer cultural" world, comparing it with her husband Taymur's family, which she described as "religious." One of the constant points of bickering and discontent with Taymur's family concerned the way she dressed and the way she did not observe proper etiquettes of male-female socializing. Taymur was two years her senior, an engineer with a very successful career. "She always wore very tight pants, and would come and sit with me, in the men's section, in family gatherings; she talked to my parents in a tone and language that was disrespectful," Taymur confirmed the disjunction in practices and expectations. He talked in the past tense. Mahnaz no longer visits his parents. He goes alone.

Although defining herself and her family as "not religious," Mahnaz practiced her own "spirituality."[5] Her spirituality was narrated as centered on her conversations with God: "I incessantly ask God to tell me what I am. I ask God, 'How is it that I have the best spouse in the world, but have no feelings for him? Why do I fall in love with women if I am a woman?'" She regularly visits a woman she considers her spiritual guide, has great faith in this woman's powers of foresight, and always consults her when faced with difficult decisions. Indeed, she chose Taymur over a much richer and more culturally compatible, though also considerably older, suitor because of this woman's advice. She narrated this story several times; it was a decision she had come to almost regret. This other suitor lived in a European country and she could have been there, not confined to the walls that she felt constricted her in a small provincial town where everyone knew each other—when she went to a court to file an initial application as an SRS candidate, the judge was a relative of her husband's and would not look at her file—and where Taymur was forever concerned about his reputation and what people might be saying about his young beautiful wife who spent her days socializing with young lads out on the streets.

"I am like that woman who went to the Prophet," Mahnaz told me in one of our early conversations. "She was married, had two kids, and went to the Prophet one day, crying and asking for help. She begged him to listen to the pain of her life, a pain that she could not tell other people, the pain that burned inside her. She told him that she had no feelings for her husband; that any time he came to and slept with her, it was torturous for her because she had no feeling of being a woman. This is exactly how I feel. Her story is exactly my story." Mahnaz stopped and was moving on to another topic, but I had never heard of a prophetic narrative like this.[6] I asked her, "How did the Prophet respond?" Mahnaz continued the story:

> He told her to go into the river nearby, immerse herself deep in water and come out. She followed his order and emerged as a complete man. The Prophet told him that s/he was no longer a woman, but a man, and could become one of the Prophet's companions and fight alongside him. After a week the husband came to the Prophet with his two kids, asking him for help in finding his missing wife. The Prophet told him that his wife would not come back and he should marry another woman. In our time, we no longer have a prophet to whom we can tell our pains and who can perform miracles to solve our problems. On the other hand, Hazrat 'Ali [the Shi'ite first Imam] has told us to move forward with time and today science proves it; when science can solve a problem, suppose your illness is cancer, some people tell us God has created you and it is sinful to interfere with God's work, but God has also created cancer in your body, he has also put the doctor to treat your cancer; God has created some people with no arm, but has also created prosthetic arms to give you hand motion; that is just like me. Science tells me that my brain is male; it gives me masculine orders.

Mahnaz's narrative resonated with many others, among trans persons and their families and friends, who came to terms with transsexuality as an act of God. It also recalls the earlier discourse on inter-/transsexuality in the 1940s and 1950s (see chapter 2), in which marvels of science began to displace wonders of creation. One day I asked Zaynab, one of Mahnaz's closest friends, a woman in her late forties who seemed to be religious in a more traditional sense, how she understood Mahnaz's situation. She was at first reluctant to answer, saying, "You'd laugh at me if I told you." But Mahnaz reassured her that it was okay to be straightforward with me. Zaynab explained that in her eyes Mahnaz was a sign of God's creative power: "I was totally amazed by God's ability to create so many differently beautiful creatures." For her, Mahnaz was truly a man, someone with a male soul who happened to have a female body. She then asked me if I had seen the television program about a creature that sang like a rooster but also laid eggs. These were all signs of God's power of creation. At this point, Mahnaz got really excited; she jumped up from the couch and asked if that were possible in humans as well? Uneasily, I offered a brief account of hermaphrodites, and mentioned the possibility of ambiguity at birth and "sex change" at puberty. Mahnaz wanted to know if she were one such case. Who could diagnose that? Has she ever observed any changing bodily signs? I asked. Has her gynecologist ever indicated something of that kind? The answer was no, but still she kept saying perhaps she was a case that hadn't become evident—yet. What mattered to her, it seemed, was that she did not want to be a woman; she wanted to be anything but a woman, including an intersex person.

Like almost all trans and other nonheteronormative identified persons I interviewed, Mahnaz's story began with tales of a "gender-discordant" childhood. These sounded like the familiar tales of liking cross-gender games, cross-gender dressing up, and so on. The important difference seemed to be that in Iran, parents and family members generally seemed to be relatively gender-flexible with young children and did not consider these childhood differences to be symptoms of future trouble; at times they even seemed to encourage daughters with "boyish" behavior and sons with "girlish" habits—something that many child psychiatrists are working hard to change.

These stories of her childhood were of course retrospective remembrances that had acquired a past significance as the foretelling of a future trans identification. Similar incidents in the childhoods of adults who did not grow up trans-identified were recounted differently: A successful female professional, in a field dominated by men, for instance, would recount her early "boyish" childhood as a foretelling of later professional achievements. Given the pervasive male societal prerogatives, recounting cross-gender childhood memories by adults who had become mainstream masculine men was less frequent.

Some *trans*es, in later years, use their recollections of their earlier years to persuade not only psychologists but also their own parents to support their trans cognition. Houri recalled that she had always thought of herself as a girl and everyone in the family had gone along with it. As she grew up and noticed other girls' bodies changing shape, she asked her mother one day why she was not like them. Her mother laughed it off, she recalled, "'Things will work out when you grow up a bit more,' she said." The critical moment for her came with the growth of facial hair:

> I almost mutilated my face trying to shave it off as hard as I could. And then it all grew back even thicker. I didn't know what to do. I went to my mother and asked for her advice. That is when I was shocked to hear, "But it is natural for a boy to grow facial hair." I said, "But girls don't grow beards and mustaches." She said, "You took the joke seriously? You are a boy." I was devastated. That was the moment I told myself, no, I don't want to become a boy; I want to stay a girl. I didn't know anything about *homosexual, transsexual*, whatever. All that mattered to me was that I had been a girl all along and I was determined to remain one.

This was by no means an exceptional narrative. Delara, a nineteen-year-old FtM, had just begun her/his transition when we met in the Mirdamad Clinic. S/he was from a relatively poor family—"*kumitah imdadi,*" as s/he put it, which means that they qualified for aid from the Imam Khomeini Relief Foundation. When I interviewed her/his back in her/his hometown, Urumiyah, a northwestern provincial capital, s/he talked about her/his family as a religious family (*khvanivadah-am mazhabiah*), some of whom had accepted her/his decision to change from female to male, while others had not. "I think what helped some of my sisters and their husbands to accept me was that there is religious ground for it. Also, I have eight sisters and no brother. So this way they will now have a brother! I am sure it would have been impossible for them to accept it were it the other way around." Initially, they had lived in a nearby village; her/his father was a shepherd, and even though they had migrated to the city, he continued to keep his herd in a place just outside the city limits and spent a lot of time there. Delara's mother took care of an elderly woman who needed someone to spend the night at her place. Delara never finished high school and had been working in various jobs to help pay for the house they built in town. First s/he cleaned houses but didn't like it and now made a much better living buying old appliances, such as refrigerators, taking them apart, extracting all the copper wires and selling them. She explained that, "Since childhood, I didn't accept that I was a girl. I knew I was a boy and acted like a boy, . . . had a lot of conflict in high school. I would tell the girl whom I loved that I was a man, and that would get me into trouble, . . . these break ups made me very sad and depressed. Then a year ago, last October, I saw that program that Mr. Amini had made for satellite television, that made me feel much better. I got the phone number from the program and followed it."[7]

Mohammad, a postoperative FtM, in his late twenties at the time of interview and a successful information technology engineer working in a government office, put it in these terms:

> Ever since I remember, I fought against accepting I was a girl, didn't want to wear girls' clothes, play girlie games. When I was young my older brother (sixteen years my senior) and his wife had problems with me but my father (my mother died when I was six) didn't notice anything. Generally in these early years, families pay no attention [to cross-gender behavior], they think at puberty, once sexual needs kick in, things will work out. But this is a big mistake. They keep silent, hoping that day will come. They say nothing to the kid, because they are scared that talking about it will further deepen the problem.

In recent years, a growing number of child psychologists and social workers have begun to write in alarming language about these childhood cross-gender tendencies and their presumed causal contribution to gender/sexual non-normativity.[8] The psychologists' narrative also informs much of the press coverage of this topic. But, at least for the moment, parents generally seem to treat these childhood playful interests as cute, as passing, rather than as worrisome.

The alarming moment for parents kicks in with adolescence and the emergence of sexual desire. Here a gender difference emerges. Girls interested in "boyish" activities and sports are sometimes warned that their femininity (often taking the form of a dubious concern with the possible rupture of the hymen) may become compromised. Parents begin to warn against very close relations with other girls that may leave one open to the charge of being someone's baruni, damaging one's reputation. In general, however, parents tend to consider girls' homosocial/-sexual relationships to be quite benign and something that eventually will be "cured through marriage." A male adolescent interested in activities considered "girlie" (such as dance, gymnastics) is warned that he could become kuni—an anally penetrated male body—if he did not wise up. Parental fear of the possibility of their son becoming kuni brings much earlier and much harsher measures to bear on the adolescent; these are the years of becoming subject to severe parental supervision, restrictions, and sometimes harsh punishments. Even after Houri had left home and moved to

Tehran, she continued to be hounded by her mother. When her parents found out that she was transitioning, they sent her a friendly invitation to come home to Damavand for a visit; when she arrived they locked her up in their house to make sure she didn't return to Tehran. She managed to escape when she was left alone with her sister; her mother eventually caught up with her back in Tehran and filed a complaint with the police, charging her with moral corruption and engaging in sex work. Houri spent a whole week in detention before she could get the judge to check her file with the LMOI and clear her name. When Tahmineh ran away from home in Abadah, her father found out where she was staying in Tehran and filed a charge of "kidnapping" against her because she was still underage and in his custody.

Arezu, an MtF in her late forties from Urumiyah, had a particularly horrific adolescence, but this was by no means completely out of the range experienced by MtFs, especially for the generation whose teenage years coincided with the 1980s. I met Arezu through Kamran, an FtM I had met at the Mirdamad Clinic. Kamran was also from Urumiyah. On my home town visit with Kamran, I had casually wondered how different the earlier generation's path of transition had been; Kamran volunteered to introduce me to Arezu, if she would agree to meet with me. Two days later, Arezu showed up at my hotel with her husband. He had accompanied her only to be sure she was safe with me, worried that this might be some journalistic stint with cameras and intrusive questioning. Soon he left us alone.

Arezu lived the life of a successful caterer, wonderful mother, and caring wife. Although based in a provincial town, her wedding planning and catering services had by now become nationally known. "I get clients from all over the country now," she said proudly. She had been married for sixteen years, had a twelve-year-old son (through adoption), and—like almost all postoperative *trans*es I had come to know—except for her husband, a few close kin, and a couple of other *trans*es, no one knew anything of her previous life.[9] "I changed my domain of social circulation completely," she explained. Her narrative began with early childhood. "When I was about three years old, I fell in love with belly dancing. I still love it." Our common passion for belly dancing went a long way toward getting the conversation rolling. "There was this Egyptian dancer, Samia Jamal.[10] They used to show her shows on television in the 1960s and 1970s. I would tie a few colorful pieces of cloth around myself and imitate her. Everyone in the family loved my performances; they laughed, clapped, and cheered me on. My father was in the army and every year on the birthday of the crown prince, there would be festivities in the Officers' Club. All the kids would line up to get gifts. I always lined up in the girls line to get a girl's toy. By the time I was ten, I had learned a lot of cooking and that is what I wanted to do professionally."

Growing up in what she described as a "strict and religious family," her first conflictive memories began in middle school, when she became friends "with another boy like myself":

> He said he had a boyfriend, we spent a lot of time together, and I learned from him how to telephone other boys and flirt with them in a girlie voice. When someone would suggest meeting me, I'd never call them back. I was too scared. But unfortunately, my friend was more willing, and one day he brought a friend of his boyfriend who wanted to have sex with me. I let it happen, but was devastated. I went home and took a whole bottle of sedatives, hoping to die. My older brother noticed and started talking with me, trying to figure out what was wrong with me. I told him I was just tired of life. Since then we have become very close. He is still my close friend and supporter. . . . In those years, I had already read articles in the magazines, or in books about men who lived as women, there was this secretary to a king, of France, or maybe England, only after his death people found out he was a man.[11] I started reading psychology books, wanted to learn more about woman-presenting males and masculine-presenting females. In these same years, my friend suggested that we should start injecting estrogen.

"You could just do that?" I asked.

> Yes, you could buy it from pharmacies and inject yourself. So we both started doing it. Both of us quickly developed womanly bodies, just as you see me right now. I used to pluck every single hair from my face. But changing sex—that was like a dream, a complete fantasy that one read about, not real. My desire to become a woman was aroused when one day in the basement I found a pile of old magazines that had articles about men who had become women. I realized this could be possible. . . . I never completed my high school education. In the first year, I was the center of other boys' attention, but even though I enjoyed it, it tormented me since I knew all they wanted was sex. I fell in love with my biology teacher and with him I experienced the pleasure of being touched, being embraced, and loved. I dropped out of high school after the first few months. These were years of feeling tormented; I enjoyed the pleasures of being desired by other young men but also felt this was inappropriate and would always feel deep regret afterward. By the time I was eighteen, I had a few friends of my own kind [hamjinsan-i khaud—in this context meaning of the same genus, males who wanted to

be women], my breasts were quite large, and I always had my hair long and very clean-shaven face. My mother had started noticing my breasts and was becoming concerned and nosy. So I decided to openly tell my family. This was also during the early post-revolutionary years. I was picked up by the *kumitahs* several times on the charge of not veiling properly [*badhijabi*], and then when they would realize I was a male, they would take me home and tell my family not to let me go on the street this way. My family, except for the brother who supported me, started treating me really harshly, my father and one of my brothers (I have four brothers) would beat me up, pull my hair and cut it with scissors, cut my nails; . . . from one of my brother's friends I learned that Dr. Mehrabi treats people like me and went to him in Tehran with one of my brothers. He was very good about it. He explained the situation, and told my brother "You have to realize you have a sister not a brother in her/him." My brother seemed to be accepting and promised to convince my father. We went back to Urumiyah. But my father was un-moving. He locked me indoors, hoping I would break down. I insisted that I wanted to be myself. After locking me up didn't work, he committed me to a juvenile correction center for a two-month stay. It was there that I was targeted by the librarian who repeatedly raped me. I used to cry at night, thinking my father sent me here so I wouldn't become a kuni, and here I was letting myself be anally penetrated to survive. Oddly that thought would give me a sense of perverse revenge pleasure. After my time was over and I came back home, one day a friend of one of my brother came to our house to see him. We met as I opened the door. He told my brother, "I met your sister and want to marry her." My brother explained my situation to him. He said it didn't matter, he would take me to Europe, pay for my sex change and we'd get married. He gave an engagement ring for me to my brother and sent his family to ask for my hand. My father blew his top; he kicked them out of the house, then bound my hands and threw me into a room, and with my older brother started beating me up. They said either change your thinking or die. I said I'd die. They gave me a packet of something and I took it. Within the hour I started vomiting violently, they took me to the bath-room and left me there, I was throwing up blood violently; by this time my mother was beside herself and intervened; but they didn't want to take me to a hospital and get into trouble. They started trying to wash my stomach, fed me milk, slapped me to keep me awake. Once my condition improved a bit, they threw me into a room and locked me in. After a week, I started thinking this wouldn't do; I have to get out of here. So I began to behave more calmly and said I would listen to them. For a month or so I played this role. Then I ran away with a bit of savings I had. I went to a nearby town, and with the help of another woman-presenting friend, I found lodging with an old woman who needed help with housework. This was a good arrangement for me. I don't know how, but my father and brother managed to find out where I was, and they came and took me away. Back to the same treatment. They started taking me to psychologists. My father took me to the Legal Medicine Organization of Urumiyah, where the doctor told him, "Why can't you understand, she is a girl, even if you kill her you can't turn her into a boy." But nothing would move him. I had another suitor who wanted to marry me. I was close friends with his sister and went to their house a lot. I used to leave our house and after a few blocks put on a chador. My father rejected him too. I ran away from home two more times, each time starting anew, and each time my father would find me. Twice more I attempted suicide. Once my father sent some *kumitah* thugs to arrest me; they took me and flogged me really hard. Another time I was picked up on the streets near a tomb I had gone to visit for *ziyarat* [visiting a saint's tomb for prayer] to feel peace. Each time, I got twenty-five lashes. That is when I decided I was going to cut my genitals myself even if that meant bleeding to death. I got some numbing medicine from a pharmacy and locked myself in the bathroom, but after a while the pain came back and I passed out, bleeding on the floor. My younger brother noticed, my mother helped and they took me to a hospital. When I gained consciousness, the first thing I touched were my genitals; I was devastated, they had stitched them right back, after all that. . . . This was my life. . . . Then they started saying either you leave this house and we never want to see you, or you agree to marry a woman and settle down. I left home when I was twenty-one and began life from zero again. . . . Sometimes I tell Kamran and a few other kids I know, you guys don't know what the hard times were like. You whine and complain if someone in Bihzisti talks rough with you. You haven't tasted the lash.[12]

There is another domain in which the legal legibility of transsexuality has improved lives: vis-à-vis parents and for parents vis-à-vis family and neighbors. When Arezu would tell her brothers and father "I am a woman," they would hear her statement to mean "I am kuni, I am a same-sex-player." In the same way, Arezu's own vocabulary for the articulation of her desire and need used cross-sex/-gender statements and practices. As she said, "In those days none of these categories, *transsexual, homosexual, GID,* etc. were known to me. I would say, 'I am a woman, you can't force me to become a man,' and my father would take out his belt and say 'I will make a man out of you.'" The wide circulation of the discourse of transsexuality and the insistent official distinction between transsexuality and homosexuality—as it comes through such statements as "parents must realize if their child is *transsexual,* s/he is not deviant"—has enabled trans adolescents to say to their parents "I am not *homosexual,* I am *transsexual.*" As Pahlavani, a therapist who worked closely with families at the TPI, put it,

> Some families would be happier if I told them their child had terminal cancer than GID; their immediate reaction is that their child is *homosexual* and that is such a shameful thing [*nang*]; the *transsexuals* themselves often talk about the intense fear they experienced when they thought they were *homosexual* and there was no way they could tell their families. It comes as a relief to them when they realize they are *transexual.* . . . Most of them are unfamiliar with the existing religious opinions sanctioning SRS . . . we need a lot of social education. It is what we achieved with addiction and with infertility. It took a lot of social education to make these issues understood as medical issues that need treatment; still a lot of families keep these issues a "family secret." This is the same thing. Like addiction and infertility, people have to learn to accept it as something that must be addressed [*zarurat*].

The religious-legal-medical discourse sanctions trans identification and discourages/prohibits same-sex desires and practices. It denies one set of auto-narratives the possibility of public cognition even as it opens up the space for the other—even if it is in the form of a sociomedical problem along the lines of addiction and infertility. It also has enabled parents to save face among family members and neighbors by presenting their "problem child" as a clinically diagnosed case, not a moral deviant. Mohseni-nia, a TPI social worker, similarly emphasized both the "ignorance of parents about religio-legal status of transsexuality," and the importance of family support to trans persons:

> These kids [*in bachchah-ha*] really want to have their families' affirmation [*ta'yid*], but instead they face denial [*inkar*]. Some just leave and say we don't want this family, how long can we wait to get their consent. It takes a long time for families to come around, especially with boys [MtFs]; it is easier with girls [FtMs], it is a cultural issue here, . . . it is really hard for families, they ask "How can we tell our neighbors that for twenty-five years we had a son, now we have a daughter?' . . . We use examples of TSs who have very successful lives after surgery. But they also hear stories of sex workers . . . so we tell them that is precisely why their support is critical. People who turn to sex work have lost their homes.[13]

At first blush, this seems to simply regenerate the completely abject position of homosexuals—and it does that, no doubt. But it also has allowed some, *gays* in particular, to have a more semi-open life by going under the mantle of *trans* (and allowing their parents to save face under that category).

Visible legibility has its paradoxical costs as well. As far as some families are concerned, so long as a son has not transitioned, "the problem" can be kept confined to the four walls of their house—or, as we have heard, locked in the four walls of a room. If an MtF is not already expelled from home, once s/he moves "into the habit," once s/he is post-transition, "the problem" becomes public—the neighborhood and the larger family will all "know" that this family has/had a "deviant son." "The problem" becomes a publicly visible scandal, no longer a containable family secret. MtFs tend to aspire to break out of the identification of their desires and practices with homosexuals. Yet, even after transition that affiliation continues to weigh on them in the eyes of many parents and the larger community of their sociality. Paradoxically, post-transition MtFs may be perceived as even more threatening and viscerally repugnant to many normalized persons since, in their eyes, they have taken on a legitimized publicly circulating face of being kuni. Homosexuals—because they tend to live under the social radar—are in a category that people could choose to not see and therefore would not have to face among their kin and neighbors (and perhaps themselves). MtFs seem to refuse invisibility. The legality and public visibility of transsexuality thus paradoxically make MtFs at times a greater threat to the normative sexual/gender order of things than homosexuals, who tend to live often unobtrusive lives. Except for occasional run ins with the morality squads, other government institutions do not concern themselves with this subgroup. As one Ministry of Health official put it, "They don't ask us for anything; we don't have to get involved with them." A trans activist confirmed the same: "They are invisible in society, they fade into the general population, unless they want to make themselves noticed [*matrah kunand*]. But *trans*es, that is a different story. Everyone says *trans*es harm society and society harms them. Sometimes, we get picked up for *badhijabi* [mal-veiling]; this is especially terrible for those who don't yet have their certification. They are taken to Vuzara station and get roughed up. By the time you prove you are in the process of getting your certification, you have spent several days in detention."

Like Mahnaz, Arezu talked about dreams and spiritual experiences; hers foretold of reaching her desired end. The night before the cleric told her she was a woman (see note 12), and could—indeed should—use the chador and *maqna'ah* at all times, she had a dream.

I was in the middle of a vast desert, I saw a large mausoleum, someone's grave; it was cubical in shape, covered with a glass container. Inside it, there was a hood, a full suit of armor, and several other battle-related objects; there was a man there, a respectable person. I told him, "I am lost, where am I?" He said, "This is Karbala." I asked "What are these objects?" He said, "They belong to the martyred Imams." Then I noticed a woman's 'abayah there. I asked "What is that?" He said "This belongs to Hazrat Zahra." I said "What a nice 'abayah." He said "This is for you to take. Do you want to wear it? It is yours, take it." I startled out of sleep. But then the next day I actually went officially into a woman's habit.

The reach of "spirituality" for self-defined "not-religious" trans persons extended, beyond dreams of transition, to old age, death, and life beyond. When I asked Yunes, an in-transition FtM, if s/he had considered the option of living as a man but without SRS, s/he said, "You know, the one thing that makes me sure I do want to do surgery, even if not immediately, is old age. When I imagine myself as elderly, I really want to be an old man not an old woman. When I die, I want something about a man to be written on my grave, not about someone who lived as a man." Imagining death had come up in several other conversations. Because the SRS operations were not of high quality, many corrective surgeries had to be performed to complete the process. Both MtFs and FtMs had explained the reason they were putting themselves through these multiple surgeries in terms of "when my body is being washed for burial, I want the washer (wo)man to see a completely (fe)male body."

The workings of religious and spiritual concepts are, of course, more complex. Zaynab's strong religious beliefs, which allowed her to see Mahnaz as a sign of God's creative powers, had its reproachful side as well. On two occasions, she was, openly and in front of Mahnaz and Taymur, disapproving. Zaynab sharply criticized Mahnaz for "looking at me with lustful eyes. She looks at me as a man would. I am a married woman. That isn't right. Only my husband has the right to look at me like that." For Zaynab, Mahnaz was simply a man. In another conversation, she quietly murmured to me, "I don't think it is right that Mahnaz continues to live with Taymur. That constitutes sodomy; that is forbidden." In her narrative, lavat/liwat (sodomy) did not index anal intercourse—whether between a husband and his wife or between two men. For Zaynab, any sexual intimacy between a man and a person of manly identification, even though Mahnaz at the time had a fully female body, constituted forbidden sex between two men. In her eyes, it was not Mahnaz's body that mattered. While religious scholars such as Hujjat al-Islam Karimi-nia may consider sex/jins of the physical body to be the final arbiter in defining a person's sex/gender as far as rules of fiqh are concerned, that primacy does not generalize into some universal Muslim belief and practice. Zaynab's spiritualized Muslim-ness takes the sex/jins of the soul as determining the sex/gender of Mahnaz.

Moreover, Zaynab's discomfort points to the dominance of the modernist narrative of marriage as a contract between "opposite sexes." With the transformation of marriage—from a passage into adulthood and a contract that created a conjugal home for licit sex and procreation into a romantic venture between a man and a woman, initially as complementary and later as opposite sexes—marriage acquired a heterosexual/-gender dynamic that has now taken over larger cultural domains.[14] The opposite positing of sexes within marriage has worked to produce men and women more generally as opposites of each other in multiple domains, such as temperament, feelings, emotional needs, and sexual drives—recall that even how one squeezes one's toothpaste tube has become genderized![15]

The binarizing dynamic works beyond the heterosexual marriage and its patterning of man/woman as opposite sexes. It works as well to sharply heterogender/heterosexual patterns of non-normative relations; the masculine-presenting female and the woman-presenting male are necessarily viewed as practicing what is considered sexually masculine and feminine.

This pervasive binarizing work of the modern conceptualization of marriage, moreover, works through and contributes to a regeneration of cultural parameters within which gender, sex, and sexuality need not become distinct categories in defining living practices or patterns of (self-)cognition. The circulation of a single word, *jins* (and its variations, such as *hamjins-khvah*, *tarajinsiyat*, etc.), keeps anatomical body significations, gender identifications, and sexual desires tightly together.[16] This tight conjunction has both enabled the reform of practices concerning the changing of body to align its gender/sexuality with its sex and has set the parameters within which these changes are imagined and enacted. It has contributed to the structure of self-cognition and narrative presentation among trans persons. The persistent pattern of a tight transition from a cross-gender-identified childhood to an adolescence marked by sexual desire for one's own genus/jins speaks to the indistinction among gender/sex/sexuality.

Mohammad's narrative on these critical years was echoed by numerous other trans persons, both FtM and MtF:

When I entered middle school, this dualism [feeling I was a boy when every-one else thought I was a girl] became much stronger for me because I started having sexual desire. I felt there was something problematic about my sexual desire. At that age, we don't know ourselves. I felt I was attracted to girls . . . but I too [like my father and older siblings] thought things would work themselves out. But these conflicts intensified. From second grade in middle school I had girlfriends . . . my relationship with my girlfriends was different from that of two ordinary girls [*dau dukhtar-i 'addi*]. In those years, because girls are restricted in their relations with boys, when there is a girl with my kind of tendency, other girls become attracted to her. For this reason, we can establish such relations very easily. At that time, I had heard that such relations are called same-sex-playing, but I believed that I was not a same-sex-player because I felt I did not accept myself as a girl, I am not a girl so I couldn't have same-sex-playing desires.

To others, however, in these difficult years Mohammad had to continue to self-present as a girl: "Sometimes I would ask older people if it were possible for two girls to get married. They would always say, 'No, that is impossible, don't even talk about it.'"

I asked: "When you say you had desire for other girls but did not consider yourself a same-sex-player, how did you reach that distinction? Was it because you thought same-sex-playing was a bad thing?"

No, no, not at all. Even what I was I thought was a bad thing. I was fear-ful; sometimes I would have nightmares about it. I was scared that if I told people I was not a girl, I would be arrested, put in jail, and killed. What was in my thinking was this: When they talk about same-sex-playing that means the desire of two people of the same sex for each other, but I didn't consider myself a girl at all, so I would tell myself I was a boy, everything about me is like a boy, so my feelings and desires were also like a boy's; that is why I would not accept being considered a same-sex-player. So my problem [for myself] was what am I then? High school years were the worst; these issues created a lot of headaches for me! I was in an all-female social space, all day every day, surrounded by girls; just imagine sending a boy into a gather-ing of girls! Imagine what he would suffer, right when from a sexual point of view his body reacts, when his sexual hormones are active . . . I started romantic relationships that after a while would lead to such places. Because I accepted myself as a boy, the other side had no problem with me. Con-trary to the people on the other side [meaning MtFs] who suffer greatly in their high school years, we have great fun in high school! Girls never leave us alone. Sometimes, I was even approached by young married women. We had to watch out for school authorities though; if they heard anything, or sensed anything, they would report to our parents and we'd get in trouble.

Indeed, the narration of high school years by MtFs depicts anything but fun. Some are tormented by the fear of possibly being a "passive male homosexual." Shahrzad, an MtF in her early thirties, had heard the word *gay* when in high school:

So I thought I was *gay*, and though at first I didn't know exactly what it meant, I thought it meant a man with feminine feelings. When I heard more explanations, and that we are also called same-sex-player or same-sex-desirer [hamjins-gara], I hated these words. I became familiar with these concepts through the news or conversations with people like myself. For instance, I heard that Elton John was *gay*, that is, he is a man who has sex with men. This thought really tortured me. The other word that really tormented me was *ivakhvahar*. In our neighborhood, there was this guy known as 'Ali Khaushgilah ['Ali the beautiful]. He was killed, perhaps by his father, or someone else, I don't know. When I was around nineteen, I heard about *transsexuals*, but there was no clear concept about it.

While some trans narratives were structured around "I always knew I was . . . ," many other narratives, whether those of MtFs or of FtMs, were focused around years of struggle for self-cognition, defined sharply by the delineating line between trans- and homosexuality. As already discussed in several chapters, this is a differentiating line generated by dominant legal, religious, and psycho-bio-sexological discourses. The grid of cognition is premised on sorting into two either/or categories—MtF or gay, FtM or lesbian—and is especially punitive over the MtF/gay distinction on the fiqhi, legal, and state levels. It informs the media coverage as well. Over and over again, well-meaning commentators, including interviews with officials of Bihzisti published in the dailies, center on how the public, but especially the families, must learn and recognize this critical difference—that transsexuality is not a moral deviation and trans persons must not be treated as "bad people." This is also why so many trans persons, at least in publicized domains, say, ever insistently, "we are not same-sex-players." It has become a grid of self-cognition through dis-identification.

Often the disavowal of homosexuality out of transsexuality verges on homophobia.[17] When the Thursday meetings at the offices of *Psychology and Society* were shut down in November 2006, it set off a new round of discussions on this issue. In a Bihzisti meeting (January 7, 2007) Sina, who had acted as the coordinator and was seen as a leader of the Thursday meetings, was criticized by several trans persons for his responsibility: He had advocated for and welcomed the presence of *gay* men and *lesbian* women to these meetings. The presence of *gay* men was held as responsible for the neighbors' complaints that caused the loss of the meeting space. Sina's explanation—that many MtFs were a lot more visibly provocative than *gay* men, who were virtually indistinguishable from "ordinary" men—was not persuasive.

Mulk-ara was said not to socialize with Houri because she was rooming with Zia, a self-identified *gay* man. On other occasions, her disavowal was articulated in more utilitarian language: "They introduce themselves as *trans* and even go and get certification in order to get military exemption and do other things, they ruin our position and have multiplied our problems." Sina, however, disagreed with this argument: "To the contrary, because they are not recognized and have to worry about threats, *homosexuals* [*bachchah-ha-yi humausikchual*] behave a lot more cautiously than *transes* [*bachchah-ha-yi tirans*]."

"We are women not same-sex-players," MtFs emphasized over and over again, at least in public pronouncements. Taraneh put it in these words (in the *Yad-i yaran* TV documentary): "A same-sex-player, even if he is maf'ul [passive], he'd never use makeup. People should know this: if a guy goes out in cross-appearance [*zahir-i mubaddal*], if he wears makeup, they should not view him through the same-sex-player lens; this guy loves to be a woman, her/his thinking is feminine, and thinking is what human character is about." This narration of a not-same-sex-player feminine male retains the continuity between MtF transsexuality and woman-presenting males of the 1970s; yet it is distinct in that it seeks to exclude any notion of homosexuality from its domain. Taraneh continued:

> This person is really a woman. It is nature's fault that s/he was born male and has to become female. The easiest criterion I can offer you for recognizing which male is a same-sex-player and which *transsexual* is to look at the person's appearance. A same-sex-player male goes for same-sex-playing with a full male appearance. But the male who uses makeup, puts on lipstick, this person is not a man. S/he is a woman. S/he has male chromosomes, so was born male, but from the point of view of subjectivity [*zihniyat*], behavior, temperament, s/he is perfectly a woman. . . . We are not same-sex-players; I personally detest same-sex-playing, even though many of my best friends are same-sex-players—this is because we understand each other.

Taraneh's emphasis on appearance is noteworthy: the difference is visible on a person's surface; one does not need to excavate it from any depth. Ironically, Kia was sitting on the same panel—he was a young man whom everyone, including Taraneh, would insist was not *trans* but *gay*, and yet aspects of his appearance Dr. Usku'i noted as feminine: his shoulder-length hair, his manicured fingernails, a touch of mascara.

While some trans persons, and others for that matter, have come to treat homosexuality as a linked, similarly pathologized, and to-be-tolerated "condition," for many, the recognition of transsexuality as a "disorder" has contributed to the further categorization of homosexuality as a "willed deviation." Mohsen, a postoperative young man with Klinefelter syndrome, put it this way: "I think same-sex desire is a moral deviation, but the desire for changing one's sex is related to one's brain, to what one thinks. People who desire sex change, even if they have sex with a woman before [sex-change] operation, never exhibit their genitals, they cannot accept having sex as a womanly body with another woman. It is not at all same-sex-playing. . . . But those who are same-sex-players are happy with their bodies." As the diagnostic discourse about transsexuality has gained near hegemony, the desire for sex change as something beyond the person's willpower is underscored: "It is not a frivolous desire, it is not a whim," one therapist emphasized in a television documentary. The implicit, and at times explicit, foil here is that same-sex desire is a frivolous desire. It is this insistent distinction and pushing of homosexuality to "willed deviation" or "frivolous desire" that has, in recent years, opened up a conversation among *gays* and *lesbians* about whether perhaps they too need to embrace the dominant narrative of transsexuality as a "born"—"not acquired"—condition for themselves.

Despite his defense of *gays*' (and *lesbians*') presence at their meetings, Sina's self-cognition narrative also was differentiated along a tight gender/sex binary: "I am not *lesbian*, I get offended if someone calls me that," Sina said. "It is fine to be a *lesbian*, it is just not me. Before I went abroad to study, a couple of doctors told me, 'go there and live as a *lesbian*.' I guess I could have. But that is not me. If I am in a relation with a girl, I want her to treat me as a man, I want her to feel she has a man in her life."

Yet the boundaries are not as clear as it would seem. In more private settings, many would agree that, before the operation, their desires and practices are not distinguishable from those of people with same-sex desires. As Sina put it, "I guess my relation with my girlfriends, before my transition, was similar to *lesbian* relations." This was a particularly vexing issue when it came to MtFs who had used hormones for many years, had a womanly body shape, and had perhaps removed their testes as a result of atrophy and its complications, but had not pursued the removal of the penis and vaginal construction. Were their sex lives homosexual or heterosexual?[18] The uncertainty made both clearly postoperative MtFs (such as Mulk-ara) and clearly *gay*-identified men very uncomfortable.

Zia attributed the whole problem to the tight gender binary in the society at large.

> You see, part of the problem is that in our society there is a big emphasis on who is a man and who is a woman. That is why sexual minorities have become limited to the two categories *gay* and *trans*. If other positions would become known and accepted, like *lady-boy, gay queen, she-boy, drag queen* [all these words were pronounced as in English], I bet you fewer people would go for surgery. Many are just like me; they like to dress up as women. But they don't know how to manage life like I do. They are incompetent, so they complain. Others, like Mulk-Ara, say so-and-so was once married and has children, so he couldn't be a *trans*; he couldn't be *gay*. But this is stupid. People used to be married off at an early age; their parents chose their spouse and married them off.

Note that Zia, like several other gay men who have become more connected with the virtual spaces and discourses of sexuality, have begun using the notion of "sexual minority." This is a recent emergence. One university student spoke of it disapprovingly: "it is an intellectual gesture, they don't want to opt for an identity and say what is the difference, *gay, trans*, whatever, we are all sexual minorities."[19]

The sex/gender/sexuality indistinction, along with its tight binarization, have made it difficult to conceive of postoperative sexuality as anything but heterosexual. When in a conversation with Sina, Zia, and Houri I sounded a dissident note by suggesting that not all postoperative transsexuals are *straight*, and gave the example of American MtFs I knew who were in relationships with women, everyone looked perplexed. Zia eventually broke the silence and said, "I don't understand. A man does SRS to become a woman so that she can pair up with a man, s/he doesn't do the operation to become a *lesbian*." Sina added, "So what was the point [of transitioning]?" and Zia added, "Probably she was one of those *trans*es who rushed into transition and later regretted it."

An often-recited marker of distinction was how one felt about one's born-body. Mehran spoke in very strong terms about disliking his former female body: "I never took a shower with my clothes off." Sina explained that over the previous few years he had developed several close relationships initiated through the Internet, but despite much emotional pain, in each case he couldn't bring himself to meet the woman in his preoperative body. Several others, both MtFs and FtMs, indicated that they could not allow their lovers to see their bodies before their transition: "When I am with my lover, s/he wants to see someone of the opposite sex next to him/her." This was a common refrain. For those born female, this often shaded into hating to be in *manteau-rusari* (long loose tunic and headscarf)—the iconic sign of public womanhood. Before transition, many wore this outfit only in high school or if they needed to go to a government office. If a female-bodied person didn't seem to have any trouble being in manteau-rusari, this was read as a sign that she was lesbian not FtM. "Women, *straight* or *lesbian*," played with the shape and color of their manteau-rusari, Sina told me. "For [pre-transition] FtMs, we don't want to waste money on it and just wear drab black ones, if we have to."

Yet the issue was not as fixed as some insisted. Cyrus—most often self-identified as *gay*, though at least twice he had considered transitioning—talked about his discomfort with his male body in his late teens. But he learned, he said, to come to terms with his body by going to classes and learning ballet and other dances, as well as engaging in what he named as "Buddhist meditation practices."

Delara, the nineteen-year-old preoperative FtM from Urumiyah, was not very strongly inclined to undergo bodily change; she knew she could live as a trans-dressed male once she had her certification. But, she said, "This is not Tehran. First, I am worried about getting a lot of street harassment; but most importantly, that would not be an option acceptable to my family, or to people around us more generally. They will all then think I am really a same-sex-player." If you are a certified *trans* and stay at that stage, not only are you thought to be abusing the legal system but you are also assumed to be "really" a same-sex-player—a conceptual weight as important for the person as for her/his family, friends, and neighbors. This issue came up repeatedly in the hearings of the commission at the TPI. When Zahra, a twenty-five-year-old FtM from Lahijan, was asked by one of the psychologists on the commission, "If you could live in a man's clothes, would that not be enough? If you could live like a man from all points of view, would you be willing not to go for sex change?" Zahra's response indicated the challenges of sustaining a space for nonoperative trans living: "I have lived in Lahijan for the past twenty years; my father is a well-known figure; my family will not accept it; I will have problems with my partner; our society will not accept it; I myself cannot accept it."

The issue of family acceptance is a critical parameter in self-cognition and transition decisions. Family severance is a very serious social issue; much of one's life is defined and made possible (or impossible) through one's location within an intricate network of extended family members, family friends, and acquaintances. Thus, severance from family often means not only emotional hardship and homelessness for prospective trans persons, but also a loss of education and job opportunities. Most significantly, in many trans narratives, it is the pain of the emotional break that remains central.[20] Many successful MtFs have gone the extra mile to reconcile even with the most hostile families. Arezu now speaks warmly and lovingly about how her family totally embraced her after all those years of punishments and final expulsion: "I am the apple of their eye now." After transition, Houri immediately used the occasion of a family wedding to reconnect with her mother. Before that moment had arrived, she was plainly distressed and in tears every time something related to her family came up in our conversations. At times, estranged families take the first step, especially if they hear that their child is in a difficult situation. When Hamideh, an MtF sex worker, was busted on a drug raid, she called her mother to plead for bail money. Her mother obliged and that broke the ice of many years of abandonment. She is now occasionally visited by her mother, brother, and sister, although she is forbidden to visit them.

Huma, a preoperative MtF, described her family as religious (mu'min); her father, a bazaar goldsmith, had known a trans person, someone who had worked as a man all his/her life and only after death people realized s/he was female. This made it easier for him to finally accept that his own son was not masculine. Huma lived at home and would leave home as a man and change and put on makeup outside, sometimes at the home of a trans friend if they were going to a party, sometimes in quiet street corners. She was not taking hormones because, being at home as a young man, she had to preserve family respectability (abiru); she had only had laser treatment for her face.

For some trans persons, the struggle to locate oneself within terms of acceptability was framed within what they had grown up to associate with religious appropriateness. Suhayla, an FtM in his early twenties, was finishing law school at the time of his hearing in the TPI commission. He talked about his family as "religious and traditional" (mazhabi and sunnati) and considered himself similarly religious. "I have struggled with deep feelings of sin, was not sure if sex change was religiously acceptable [shar'i], so I spent quite some time studying the fatwas." Like Zaynab, Suhayla indicated that he believed "in the primacy of soul [asliyat-i ruh] and have finally concluded that with a woman's body I cannot fulfill the objectives of my creation." Suhayla was married a year ago under family pressure and had "exercised *tamkin* [in this context, sexual submission] to my husband because of my religious beliefs, but it became more and more stressful." He finally decided to explain his situation to his husband, who "is very enlightened and supportive. I have come for my operation with his full emotional and financial support." More recently, he had developed an intense relationship with a girl from Isfahan and spent extended periods of time there—two weeks at a time—to be with his girlfriend. "Once I accepted myself as a *trans* I started having sex with my girlfriend without feeling sinful." He was very happy with this relationship, he said, and referred to her as "my spouse" (*hamsaram*).

For observant Muslims, a deep sense of "incommensurability" between remaining faithful and living non-shar'i lives seems to contribute to naming oneself *trans* and at times also to making a decision to transform bodily signs of sex/gender (jins). The former is closer to what Boellstorff has called "habitation of incommensurability," the latter to its resolution.[21]

Despite whether it is articulated within a paradigm of sinfulness, for many trans persons it was critical to ask that question: "For us *trans* people, the first thing we have to deal with is: 'Am I a homosexual [hamjins-gara]?'" Kamran emphasized,

> Because we don't know; we all go through that stage. In Urumiyah Bihzisti, there was this woman, a social worker, who kept preaching at me. I told her, "Look, if I wanted to live against the Shari'a [*khilaf-i shar'*], our society has so many different layers that not only you who is sitting in the Emergency Committee, but even your more senior people many times over could not find out. I do not want to live as *homosexual*." Iran has thousands of *lesbian* groups, but Iran doesn't want to face up to it. They have parties. Of course they can live a good life. But that is not what *I* want.

For some, the certainty of to which category they belong remains painfully elusive and the struggle lasts for decades. Mehran, an FtM who was thirty-nine years old, is a highly successful and well-known photographer whose work has been exhibited in international forums. For many years, he had been considering transition; part of his hesitancy stemmed from a concern over how that would affect his career. When I interviewed him, he had done a lot of asking around but had not yet taken any steps; a gynecologist had offered to do her/his breast removal and hysterectomy free, simply because she was very fond of his art work; he felt he needed to explain why it had taken him so many years to finally come to the conclusion that he was *trans*. While his "difference from others" was a key thread throughout the narrative, it seems that several key moments moved him toward a final self-cognition as *trans*—since our interviews he has completed transition and is now known under his male name.

Born into a large family with eight sisters and four brothers, all older than him/her, in the small city of Abhar in northwestern Iran, Mehran recounted a childhood of tomboyish, *shaytun* (devilishly naughty), *quldur* (tough) behavior. S/he was once bastinadoed and once beaten up (by the assistant principal, *nazim*) in school over disobedient "rabble rousing" behavior—encouraging students not to agree to do unreasonable favors either for more senior students or for teachers. S/he narrated these incidents with proud laughter. From her/his early years, s/he remembered a teacher whose daughter was a *trans*. I asked how s/he knew. "S/he always came to school in trousers not skirts." They quickly connected and became best friends. "S/he was even more exaggerated than I was. Even to parties s/he came in trouser suits and with a necktie." I asked if this friend had since undergone sRs. S/he didn't know; s/he had lost contact with her/him since moving to Tehran. "So how do you mean that s/he was *trans*?" I asked again, with my own inner urge to name his/her friend (and perhaps Mehran as well) "butch."

> Because s/he was just like me. S/he was completely manly; s/he did everything that men do. I am sure had s/he known about *transsexuality*, s/he would have changed sex. Like me, s/he was ignorant of this option. S/he used to openly bring his/her girlfriends to parties. I never did that. For one thing I was very strict with my girlfriends, I didn't want them to be flirted with by other men or *transes* like myself. I didn't want my girlfriend to be out late at night. My girlfriends asked my permission for everything, even if they wanted to go to a family party.

This latter sentiment was echoed by several other FtMs I got to know; it usually was talked about as a sign of their manly zealousness, an honorable trait. Often it was narrated closely linked with stories of *javanmardi*—a term often translated into English as "chivalry," with similarly associated attributes of generosity, courage, right-mindedness—the gender/sexual honorable temperament constituting one attribute of javanmardi.[22]

During our long conversations, Mehran several times emphasized that he never had any problem sexually speaking; he had had girlfriends ever since his middle school years. During high school, Mehran had had a very observant girlfriend and he also began to observe Muslim daily practices more regularly. That relationship lasted many years, until Mehran was pressured into marriage when s/he was twenty-four years old. The marriage lasted one night; the next day s/he moved back home. It took Mehran another year and a half to get his/her divorce. His girlfriend broke off their relationship over his agreeing to get married. "Forty days later, as if she was done mourning for me, she got married and now has grown-up kids."

Despite a string of girlfriends, Mehran said, something continued to make him unhappy. S/he completed her/his high school education by taking extension school courses (having been expelled from high school over political activism in the early 1980s) and then moved to Tehran to pursue his/her artistic interests. For the next three years, s/he went back to Abhar once a month to be with her/his girlfriend and visit family members. In Tehran, while finishing a special degree in photography, s/he began to see therapists to figure out what was up with her/himself. Soon s/he developed a very close relation with Dr. Mehrabi. Early on, he had recommended srs; this was back in the early 1990s. Why did he not pursue it?, I queried.

> I was concerned about my mother; I knew my father would accept it, he was a scientist, *up to date* [pronounced as in English]; but it would have been very difficult for my mother in a small town where everybody knows everybody. Perhaps I was immature myself, and had not reached the depth and fullness of understanding that I have about myself now. One reaches the need for change through a process. I tried everything else. Once my work became successful, in the artists' milieu here in Tehran, I had a very good male friend. We were really good together, spent a great deal of time together. He was attracted to me and at some point I thought if marriage would work for me, ever, it would be with him. So we got married, it was a disaster; I ruined a good friendship over that experiment. I even tried living with Helga, a German lesbian, who worked here for the UN for a while. We were together for over two years. It was Helga who first told me I was not a *lesbian*; she said when she had sex with me she felt she was with a man. Living with me, she said, was like living with a man, like a husband and wife, not like two women partners. She broke up the relationship over that. I tried everything before deciding on srs. I kept thinking that somehow without surgery I would be able to become happy. Finally, I came to the realization that I simply do not understand what it means to be a woman. If someone addresses me as khanum [a generic term of address for women], I am offended, as if it is a curse word. Let me tell you an incident. When I first went to become a member of the Association of Photographers, the secretary gave me a form to fill. Unthinkingly, instead of crossing out Mr. in the address box, I crossed out Ms. When the secretary asked me to correct the form, I was astonished. The break up with Helga really shook me up. We are

still very good friends, but now I had to finally know what I was; I wasn't a *lesbian*, but what was I?

Mehran's next key critical moment was when he saw the screening of 'Attari's *Sometimes It Happens*. . . . Suddenly everything fell in place for him, he said. This is what he was, should have been, wanted to become.

The screening of that documentary, in the summer of 2006, was narrated by another interviewee as an event of enormous significance. I met Leila, and her partner Minu, through Nadereh. Nadereh I knew from the United States: an Iranian-American, self-identified lesbian who had returned to Iran in 2003, working with a women's NGO that helped generate employment for women in female-headed households. Back in the states she had once told me how easy it had been for her to find other lesbian women. Now in Tehran, when I was complaining about lesbian invisibility (to me) and explaining that I had had no problem finding trans persons and gay men, but lesbian women were few and far between, she offered to connect me with a lesbian couple, one of whom was considering transitioning. She said, "Maybe your research will help her out. I really don't think she is *trans*." By then I had learned that cognition by others was a critical component of one's self-cognition and at times I would be re-cruited as a "cognizant."

Leila and Minu's neighborhood was already familiar to me. They lived in a rented apartment in a working-class area in an eastern part of Tehran. The neighborhood had changed character from a largely migrant residential area, and it was slowly being taken over by small workshop industries—carpenters, ironsmiths, automobile body shops, and so on. More settled migrants had moved on and rents were affordable; it had become an area with a lot of university students from outside Tehran sharing apartments or other nonfamily living arrangements. Its recent history of migrant housing provided a culture of transiency that allowed for almost anonymous living.

Almost. This was not a New York–style anonymity where you may not know your nearest neighbor of fifteen years until one day something out of the ordinary happened next door. Tehran's momentous urban explosion, accelerated because of the impact of the decade of war and the millions of war-displaced migrants, and its gradual spread and swallowing of the neighboring villages and small towns into its mega-metropolis shape, had resulted in a good deal of reconfiguring of neighborhoods in inner Tehran. No longer were neighborhoods based around families and neighbors who were in the same location generation after generation. All this reconfiguration had created a situation in which rental arrangements had become widespread, so renters moving and changing did not constitute suspicious activity. Nonetheless, everyone cared about who was next door. Were they respectable people? If they were young women or men, who and where were their families? Leila and Minu had rented as university students. Leila's family lived outside Tehran; it was perfectly acceptable that the two female university friends would share a rental. Moreover, both their families had visited them and the second-floor neighbors—a young couple with two small children—had met them. By now, that familiarity meant the young married couple kept a protective eye on Leila and Minu, which in their case was not a problem: almost all their visitors were other young university-age women. Homosocial safety could be assumed.

Zia and Houri's apartment was in this same neighborhood, just three blocks from Leila and Minu's address. Two other MtFs I had come to know well were not far away. Zia and Houri were living as "brother and sister" as far as the landlord and the neighbors were concerned. Both their families lived in Damavand. Houri's family did not know her whereabouts in Tehran, since her last run-in with her mother that had resulted in the week-long detention. She still visited her brother and his wife, who lived in Tehran, but no longer gave her address to any family members. Zia's mother occasionally visited Tehran, mostly for medical checkups, and then she stayed with Zia. On those occasions, Houri would move to a friend's house, as she was living as a woman (at that time she had not fully transitioned). Houri's boyfriend had been introduced to neighbors as her fiancé. All was well, except when they invited other MtFs or *gay* men to their place: Their guests would be given strict instruction about how to dress and appear outwardly so as not to make the neighbors uncomfortable and arouse their suspicions. As Zia once explained his nervousness when an invited friend was late, "this is a *khafan* [unpleasant, not up to the latest styles and fads] neighborhood." Neighbors' discomfort and eventual suspicion could become cause for eviction or a visit by the local *kumitah* if they reported morally suspect activity.

One of the reasons that Leila gave for the easier living possibilities of lesbian couples was that a woman's not using makeup and not visibly displaying a womanly appearance did not raise suspicion among the neighbors. To the contrary; especially in a working-class neighborhood, she was perceived as a decent woman, not out there to flaunt herself to seduce men. "But when two men live together and one of them looks effeminate," Leila explained, "neighbors keep them under surveillance. It is easy to tell a *gay* appearance, much easier than a *lesbian* one."

Leila and Minu had met four years previously through a common friend at

Shahrud University, where they both attended classes. By the time I met them, they had been together for almost two years. A year earlier they had made a private commitment vow and wore identical rings. They had designed their own marriage contract on the model of legal documents, with all the usual specifics, such as *mahr*. "We don't show it to anyone," Leila said, "People would laugh at us!" I asked them if they knew about vows of sisterhood. They did not. Vows of sisterhood, historically a publicly enacted and celebrated ritual between two very special female friends, seem to have become unknown in the bigger cities, such as Tehran, over the past generation.[23] Vows of sisterhood continue to be practiced in at least some provincial capital cities and smaller towns. Kamran's sister Laleh (married with two children) had a sworn sister, as did their mother. When I first visited them, they introduced a young man who had dropped in as their cousin, adding, "well, almost a cousin; he is the son of our mother's sworn sister."[24]

By the time I met Leila and Minu, their parents seemed to have come to a recognition of the special nature of their female friendship; and in the usual practice of "don't ask, don't tell," no longer pressured either to get married. Indeed, a year after I had met them, Minu's parents decided to help their young daughter and her school buddy by allowing the couple to occupy a small apartment they owned so that they need not negotiate the sky-rocketing Tehran rents. The major tension in their lives—and one of the reasons they had been eager to talk with me—was that among at least two other female couples with whom they were close friends, one of the partners was considering transitioning. Leila in particular felt under a "peer expectation" to look into sRs as a life option. Indeed, for a time she had, and still occasionally did at the time I met them.

Leila narrated a childhood of growing up gender non-normative; certainly, she thought her parents wanted her to be a boy and treated her like one, and she believed that is why they didn't have much trouble with her later life pattern.

> All my middle and high school friends were boys; I thought of myself as a boy and went by a male name among them. All those years I hung out with my father; he was a site engineer and during summer vacations I would go with him and see what he did. I used to get a crew cut during the summer months. I wore proper female outerwear only in school, until I moved to Tehran for my university education. Then my father insisted I wear the right outfit always in public to avoid getting into any police hassle.

It was during her years at the university in Tehran that she observed other young women dating boys and was puzzled by her own total disinterest in men.

I really tried; I had several very close male friends but could not imagine touching them, kissing them. I even tried wearing makeup for a while and was pleased to be noticed by men; but this didn't last long. The novelty wore off and it was a hassle to have to get up earlier every morning to have the time to make myself up. The more difficult part was that I also noticed I did actually fancy kissing girls, and then I actually enjoyed it. You know, there isn't that much social awareness about *transsexuality, lesbianism*—I had not even heard these words till a few years ago. My initial thoughts were that I was a same-sex-player; that gave me a sick feeling, it made me feel a lot of guilt, I knew this was a sin. Don't look at me now! I used to be a relatively decent Muslim; I used to do my daily prayers and my month of fasting. Now I have come to be at peace with sin [*ba gunah kinar amadah'am*]. For a while I kept fantasizing that I would move to another city and from the get-go live as a man and everyone would know me as a man and that would be my new life. With my first girlfriend, we kept talking about me waking up one morning as male. Well, this didn't happen, and my girlfriend went and married a man. This was a big blow to me. I decided I would never have another girlfriend. I couldn't imagine going through another break up. My father died just before I finished my university education. So then I moved back home for a while and became the man of the house. I have three sisters but no brother. I have very close relations with my mother. So one day I tried to explain to her my situation by saying, "I don't think I can get married." She promptly said, "I know, I will never pressure you to get married. Get married when you feel like it."

"What do you think she meant when she said, 'I know'?" I asked.

I am not sure, but she said, "I know you can't get married." This was when I had had my break up and I was putting all my energy into my career. Then I met Minu and suddenly realized I had been on the phone with her every night. In small towns, you know, people become family very quickly. Minu came and visited me once and my mother immediately treated her as family. Maybe she sensed something special was happening between us. By that time, I had decided I needed to move back to Tehran, for my work at least. My mother had always been very supportive of my career. So it all came together. My mother was quite comfortable with my move to Tehran; she actually sold her gold and put up the money I needed as advance [*sarqufli*, the "key fee"] for a rental place, and was fine with me rooming together with Minu.

Leila had finished school in architecture and then continued in interior design. She now has a very successful design firm, and relocation to Tehran was the right professional move. When they met, Minu was finishing a degree in mathematics and was planning to become a college teacher. Leila continued:

But it isn't clear if my mother really knew what the nature of our relationship was. I think she kept thinking we were just very good friends. But I thought if she were so comfortable with the whole living arrangement, maybe I could tell her we are in love, we are a couple and that is that. So one day I started talking about it with her . . . she totally lost it, she started saying, "No, I don't understand what you are talking about. Get her out of this house, the next time I come to Tehran I don't want to see her here. Her parents live in Tehran, why doesn't she live with them? Why are her parents so irresponsible and don't take care of their daughter? You are playing with her life, okay, you never want to get married, but she needs to get married and if people know about her and you, she will lose all her chances of marriage. You are ruining her life." So, for a while, the situation with my mother got really bad. I have always been so close to her that this was very upsetting to me. Then around the same time I saw Sharareh 'Attari's film [*Sometimes It Happens . . .*]. Now I totally lost it, I saw the film, I saw this hall full of *trans*es, I started thinking maybe I was a *trans*; I started remembering all my fantasies about waking up male, of moving to another city and living as a man—Wow! It was possible to become a man. For three nights I couldn't sleep, all day and night, that is what I was thinking about. I was in a complete mental mess. I kept thinking, well, it is true that for the past few years I have been focused on my career and have not thought about these issues, but suddenly I started having a lot of memories from earlier years—how I hated the maqna'ah [the required style of head-covering in schools and offices], how I had been upset when my breasts started to grow, and so on. I kept sending e-mails to a friend of mine who was abroad, explaining my thoughts and asking her what she thought I was. Then I would sit there and wait for her response! I didn't then have enough of an income to go to a therapist, and didn't dare to discuss it with my mother or anyone else. My friend would tell me, "No, no, you are *lesbian*" (I hadn't heard the word before then) and would send me some site addresses to check and find things out. That would calm me down and get me settled for a while. Then I would suddenly remember, "But how come I didn't like the doll my father had brought from Dubai and didn't play with it? And then the next year when he brought me an airplane, I loved it so much that I didn't open the box, I just wanted to keep it new forever."

I was totally divided. One day I would think: "What is wrong with you, you have Minu, you are happy together, you have a good career developing, what does it matter if you are a *lesbian* or a *transsexual*? If you undergo sex change all you have gained in your career will be for naught. Your mother will probably have a heart attack and die. At the end of the day, you want to live with a woman and you are living with a woman." Then the next day I'd hear there was another screening of the film, and I couldn't stop myself from going there again. I'd see all these *transsexual*s, *gays*, and *lesbian*s; you'd think that the hall was not located in Iran! You know, there was a period that the atmosphere was saturated with talk of sex change; everyone started thinking they were *transsexual*. In the party after the film screening, the main character, an MtF [Taraneh Aram], kept telling me she was sure I was a *trans*. The minute I took my maqna'ah off, she gave me a look and said, "Why are you wearing that? You should go out in male clothes. Let me see your nails. Hmmm. Short and no polish. I thought so. You are *transsexual*." I would come out totally conflicted. Well, she must know, I would think. What the hell am I going to do now? What catastrophe. I am a *transsexual*. What to do? This is also when some of my friends decided to transition and kept encouraging me as well. Everybody was suddenly looking at me as if I was a *trans*, not a woman. Some of my close friends started taking hormones and developed facial hair and grew mustaches. That would make me think, oh wouldn't it be nice if I had a nice mustache and a goatee? Then Minu and I could really get married. Right now every Nauruz each of us has to go to her own family. We start every New Year apart. This way we could be together at Nauruz.[25]

In the meantime, I had that big blow-up with my mother. After a few months, it was Nauruz and I went home for the occasion and to see what I could do to work things out with my mother. It was one thing for her to have somehow understood that I would never marry a man, but quite another thing to understand that I wanted to live with a woman I loved. I told her, "Listen, Mom, you think you are worried for me and my future. I am even more concerned for me and my future. You tell me I am ruining Minu's life, but I am even more concerned that I am ruining Minu's life. If you want Minu out of the house, you tell her." I was thinking, after all, she had helped me financially to get that apartment in the first place and set me up, so she was entitled to put demands on me. She burst into tears, and I burst into tears—we just cried and cried. My older sister, Marjan, was around; she started to talk to me. I thought, "Oh good, she will understand, she is knowledgeable, I will tell her I am *lesbian* and she can explain it to my mother." The word came out of my mouth, and my sister went ballistic. She said, "Stop, I would hate you if that were true." At that point I got really pissed off and said, "You know what, like everyone else when you hear *homosexual*, when you hear *lesbian*, you only think sex, you imagine what horrible sex we do. You imagine we stick our fingers in each other's ass. You can't think love, two women loving each other. If you can't understand that, stop mentioning Minu's name." That Nauruz break I really acted out my anger. Anyone in the family and especially among my married friends would ask, "Don't you want to get married?" I'd say, "No, I really am married. You know, my friend Minu and I live together, just like you and [your husband]." Some of my friends thought that was cool; others thought I had gone mad and left me alone. But things were now out. After the Nauruz break, my mother came with me to Tehran. Minu had spent the break with her family. She came back. I was really scared, but contrary to my expectations, my mother treated her nicely. Actually in the evening, she suddenly said, "I am going to visit my sister [who lived in Tehran] and will stay the night there." I blurted, "But why? You should stay here." She said, "No, you [the plural *shuma*, not the singular *tau*] be comfortable, you need to be left alone. I'll come back tomorrow." Minu and I were so taken aback, we couldn't believe things might actually work out with our families. At the end of her visit, the only thing my mother said was that she had sold her gold to help me with this apartment; if this was going to be a joint living quarter for both of us, Minu must pull her own weight. This was a bit disconcerting, but fortunately around then not only my work started doing well, but Minu also found a good job and we became totally financially independent from our families. That really did marvels. Everybody started to give us the recognition of two adults.

But this didn't end my confusion over what I was. I told myself I was a *lesbian*, but there were moments that I felt if I transitioned, my life, our lives, would get better. For instance, a few weeks ago my sister visited me. Minu was not here. I knew Marjan would use the occasion to reopen the old conversation. She wanted to set me on the right path, she said. After a while I tried a new tack, I told her I was a *transsexual*. She hadn't heard anything about that! So I explained to her that it meant my brain was male. She said, "So go and get cured." I told her, "I would have to go through these various operations, would that make you happy? Will you tell your sister-in-law that you now have a brother and call me by a male name?" She said, "Of course not." So I told her, "Why should I bother then; just accept me as I am and leave me alone." Then she thought about it and said, "How long do you think Minu will stay with you? At some point, she will leave you and get married." I didn't say anything. Since then, she seems to have made her peace with it; maybe telling her I was *transsexual* was helpful.

"Where are you yourself these days? Still torn?" I asked.

Well, if I want to be honest, I think, well this transsexuality business, it is socially very useful. Of course I'd like to have an ordinary life, I want to be in society with my true identity, I want to be able to introduce Minu as my spouse, I want my life to be a legitimate life. This is my right. When I see I have so much trouble even with my own family, it is very tempting to say I am *transsexual*, at most I'd have to do some operations, but then I'd have a new shinasnamah [identity booklet] and Minu could become my legal spouse. If I have insurance, she can be covered by it too. We will have all the rights of a husband and wife. On the other hand, I don't hate my female body, I don't dislike that I am a woman; actually I enjoy being a strong woman. It makes me feel superior! The only thing is that I don't enjoy social- izing in girlie parties. Actually, after a period when we socialized in some *trans* and *gay* groups and some *lesbian* parties, we found that neither of us liked the atmosphere there either; we now tend to live our own lives. We are friends with a couple of other *lesbian* couples, but otherwise I don't under- stand why I should socialize only with *lesbian*s and *transsexual*s. We are both so much into our work; we don't have the kind of time that lets us go to parties every night. To be honest, there are still occasions that I say I am *transsexual*; I am perhaps 70 percent *lesbian* and 30 percent *trans*. Perhaps even that is because in our country men are so much freer. Like I would love to go around the country on a bike tour. But I can't. I could if I were *trans*. I don't want to be *trans*, but on the occasions when there are a lot of *trans* people around me, like in the screening of 'Attari's film in the House of Art- ists, it appeals to me. So, now, I try not to hang out with that crowd. It is hard. Some of them are very close friends and work colleagues.

"Have you considered the possibility of going through the supervised therapy, getting the certification so that you could live as a man, in the male habit?" I asked.

"No, I wouldn't do that. I'd be too scared that I couldn't stop myself at that stage and would go through with the whole thing. I worry about losing Minu. It took a while for her to come to terms with loving me, being in love with another woman. Now, she says, she is not sure if she could love me as a man! How would her family react to my becoming a man? It is all too risky."

"So most of your consideration, when you say there are times and places that you feel *transsexual*, are socializing occasions?" I asked. "Yes," Leila responded, "but also my career and finding housing!"

'Attari's documentary, *Sometimes It Happens* . . . was not a singular event. These were years of intense media coverage that many people now recall as critical for their cognitions. Zia, who in the Bihzisti meeting had introduced himself by saying, "Maybe I am *gay*, maybe I am *trans*; I am here to find out," speaking about his own challenging years of trying to figure out what he was, said,

> I went to several therapists. The first one was sure I was a *trans*. The second therapist put me on hormones to increase my male tendencies. Another one was too busy and let an intern take my case. This woman knew nothing; she would ask the most ridiculous questions: "What color do you like?" I'd say blue. She'd put me in boy column. "Do you play soccer?" No, I hate soccer; she'd say, "Well, you like blue but not soccer, you must be *gay*." She'd ask me what pets I kept. I'd answer cats and dogs. That totally confused her. Then the main doctor took over the file; all he wanted to know was what kind of sex I liked. "Why do you like to be *bott* [pronounced as in English]?" Being *gay* to these guys only means anal intercourse. They almost made me into a neurotic before I realized this whole thing was rather stupid.

Part of the problem, he said, was that his years of indecision coincided with the years in which transsexuality had become a media topic; he kept thinking he had to make a decision. One day, he finally told himself: "'You don't want surgery anyway, so what difference would it make even if you knew whether you were *ts* or *gay*?' Perhaps the only benefit of therapy was for me to realize that whatever I am, this is what I am. I need to learn to live well as I am. Once I decided that, I realized that what I really wanted was to be in a long-term relationship with another man."

Not all families are hostile and punitive. Some find ways of at least tolerating, if not supporting, their children's living decisions. That is how Minu described her parents:

> When I first met Leila, I had a boyfriend—actually a very nice man. I had met him through the Internet and it turned out he was from Shahrud, where I was attending university. Soon we met in Tehran and I introduced him to my family, who really liked him as well. Then I met Leila; at the time, she was still suffering from her break up. It was totally illogical; I fell madly in love with her. Really! All I wanted was to spend all my time with her. I went and told my parents I wanted an independent life. I was transferring from Shah-

rud University to the Open University in Karaj [near Tehran], and wanted to live with my friend Leila. My parents knew Leila. Actually my father had met her in a professional context and liked her a lot. First they said, "Sure, this is your life. We'll help you live independently." But I think when I said I loved Leila and wanted to live with her, some alarm bells went off. "What do you mean you love Leila? You can love Leila and be friends, but have your own ordinary [ma'muli—the word has a connotation of normality] life. You can be friends with her even when you get married." They started having second thoughts about me and Leila living together. After a while, my mother started to be softer [narm-tar shud]. She had two female friends, Sa'ideh and Mansureh, who, she said, "are like the two of you. I will take you to meet them and see if they are happy." They had lived together and were such good friends that when Mansureh had to get married, she made it a condition that her friend would continue to live with her in the same house.[26] They had lived together for many years; Mansureh had two grown-up kids. Recently they had decided to live separately. My mother wanted me to see that they were not happy, and that, after many years, they finally had to separate. So I went there and listened to their story. It turned out the reason that they separated was that Mansureh's husband had started to harass Sa'ideh, trying to pressure her to have sex with him since she was living in his house. So I told my mother, "Let me have my own experience; I want to have the experience of living with Leila. If it doesn't work, I can always separate." So my parents finally said, "Okay, bism-allah, go ahead and try it." So we started to live together. My parents like Leila a lot, but they keep a polite disapproving eye on my life. At the same time, they indirectly support us. It is strange. For example, they own an apartment and if the tenant moves out, they have promised to let us live there and pay them rent. That would be so much better for us. With Leila's family as well, I now go with her and visit them in Shahrud. At the beginning, when I broke up with my boyfriend, all my relatives thought I had gone crazy. He was a really nice guy; we were going to get married in five or six months. So all my aunts thought that our break up was terrible; they keep sending new candidates my way. What can I say; they really think I must get married; they are trying to help.

Not all partners are supportive of their partner's decision not to transition. Given the pressure of the marriage imperative, it is often the other way around. In two other couple friends of Leila and Minu, the "femme" side of the couple voiced their encouragement for their partner to transition so that they could marry. Ozra was very much for Yunes's transition decision. When I met them in the summer of 2007, Yunes was already in male clothes but had not undergone surgery. Like Minu and Leila, they had met in university. At that time, Yunes had had another girlfriend, whose father was the person who introduced Yunes to the concept of transsexuality. An electronics engineer, "but well-read in psychology," as Yunes put it, when his daughter had introduced Yunes to her parents, he had soon contacted Yunes to explain to her/him that s/he was a trans person and should get a sex change, but that he would be against his daughter marrying him/her anyway. He in fact intervened to break up that relationship. By the time I met Yunes and Ozra, Yunes had already obtained her/his TPI approval, though s/he had not pursued it to the LMOI for the final certification. S/he had one more year of university education and did not want to disrupt her/his life until graduation. S/he had started taking hormones, was happy with the growth of facial hair, and "had gone into the habit," except for when s/he'd go to classes at the university. Yunes carried the TPI approval letter at all times. "It is very useful, sometimes the traffic police stop me, thinking I am an underage male driver; I have to show them my driver's license, which is in my female name. Without the TPI letter, they would immediately book me for cross-dressing."

Ozra seemed to be even more enthusiastic about Yunes's SRS than Yunes was. When I asked what she envisaged would change in their relationship after the operation, she talked about the acceptability of their relationship for her parents. "Otherwise, thinking about the complicated surgery, six hours of total anesthesia, and so on, I would probably stop him/her. Even now, I worry about it. I feel like s/he is losing some of the qualities I love since s/he has gone on hormones. I have to come to terms with certain behaviors that weren't there before. . . . s/he has become a less sensitive person, a bit more rough, some characteristics that distinguished Yunes from other men are becoming paler by the day. So now I am trying to come to terms with this new person!"

Over and over, in trans narratives, a key moment of seeking answers to the kind of question Mahnaz had addressed to God—tell me what I am—is recited as being linked with a failed relationship, a terrible break up, often losing a lover to marriage. The first time Mohammad went to a therapist, on his own initiative, was when he turned eighteen.

> I had a terrible break up when I was fifteen or sixteen. It really affected me, I became harsh, nervous, I started chewing my nails. That is what took me to a doctor, but I started talking about this issue as well. The therapist said that she had other such patients but this wasn't her field and gave me names of other therapists, and advised me to finish my education first be-

fore I went for surgery. I already knew this surgery could be done in Turkey. When I was around eleven or twelve, there was a Turkish singer whose shows we watched on satellite TV; I heard many grown-ups murmur that this person used to be a man and had become a woman. . . . Later I heard from others that this operation was performed in Turkey. So I started telling all my friends that when I was older I was going to Turkey to become a man. In the meantime, I had to pursue my education. At the time, I didn't know we were legal in Iran.[27]

Like Mohammad, Mahnaz talked about her middle and high school years as marked by intense desire for her school friends that would not go away. In high school, she said, she experienced her first serious love, a mutual romantic relationship that lasted for two years, before her lover's family pressured her to leave Mahnaz and get married. This occasioned a serious breakdown: Mahnaz had to be hospitalized, and it took her three years to get back on her feet, she said. She never finished high school and took a full-time job at a travel agency to keep occupied. That is where she met her husband Taymur. He would come day after day to just see her and soon begged her to accept his love. After several years and consulting with her spiritual guide, she finally relented. Once married, she had been introduced to Vida, one of Taymur's female cousins, who had lived with his parents since losing her own parents in a car accident when she was a child. "She was like a sister to me," Taymur said. Soon Vida and Mahnaz became inseparable friends. Over the years, that relationship made the marriage bearable to Mahnaz. "I was so happy with Vida, and if the price of that happiness was to service Taymur [meaning to have sex with him], I could tolerate it." Her relationship with Vida lasted almost ten years. Then Vida was courted and eventually decided she needed to get married "for real." Mahnaz, by all accounts, went into a rage and tried everything to break up Vida's engagement—unsuccessfully. It was only during this period that Taymur, according to his own story, realized that all the intimacies he had witnessed between Vida and Mahnaz had a different meaning than he had assumed: "They spent all their time together; either Vida was staying with us, or Mahnaz would go to her place, especially after Vida got a job in a nearby town and had her own separate place. When we were all sitting together, they always sat on the same couch and one of them had her head on the other's lap, getting caressed, etc. I never thought anything of it then." Since Vida's marriage, Mahnaz no longer accompanied Taymur on visits to his family. Taymur went alone. Vida's marriage affected Taymur and Mahnaz's marriage as well. She now found it intolerable to have sex with him.

After failing to stop Vida's marriage, Mahnaz experienced her second break-down. "For six months," Taymur recalled, "she just sat here on the living room sofa and stared aimlessly, sometimes watching satellite television." Aimless it may have been, but, according to Mahnaz, that was also the moment of her rescue: "I was watching this program, on Omid-e Iran channel, and suddenly there were doctors and others talking about sex-change surgery. Suddenly, I realized this was my solution. I realized I wasn't alone in the world, there was such an illness and there were doctors I could go to. If only I had known this earlier, I could have changed sex and married Vida myself."[28] She wrote down the telephone numbers given on the program, noted the name of the clinic, and set off for Tehran.

Marriage as a binarized heterosexualized contract thus not only has worked to define manhood and womanhood as opposite and clearly bordered categories, but it also deeply impacts one's self-configuration as a trans person. Marriage constitutes a rite of passage to adulthood; it is an expectation that everyone must fulfill to be considered fully grown. Unmarried persons are incomplete, unfinished stories, not in any simple utilitarian sense (for instance, in order to have a child or not to grow old alone). Without a child, a married person has a problem to solve, but without marriage one has failed to achieve adulthood. As Zia once put it, "We live in a society in which one is not counted as a full human being until one gets married. It is thought that human nature demands completion through marriage. Otherwise you are half a human."[29] Indeed, marriage is what it takes to stay *in* family, to secure one's status within one's natal family rather than leave it behind.[30] Over and over, marriage decisions were narrated as turning points. Two self-identified *gay* men I interviewed extensively recalled that several times they had considered transitioning—each time turned out to occur at a moment of breaking up with a lover who had decided to get married. Male-male and female-female couples live under the severe threat of, and compete with, the marriage imperative. At times, "passive" males "overact" their femininity in a desperate attempt to avert the threat of a "real" woman and the loss of their male partner to marriage. The same is true of female-female couples: There are abundant sad narratives of long-term lesbian relationships breaking apart because the "femme" partner finally opted (or finally gave in to familial and social expectation) to marry a "real" man in spite of the heroic butch performance of her lover. This same pressure for marriage informs the dominant culture's deep investment in the proper performance of masculinity and femininity and contributes to perceptions of gender-coded roles within same-sex partnerships.

This, perhaps even more than the illegality of same-sex practices and the legality of transsexuality, pushes some people, who might otherwise define themselves as butch lesbians and effeminate gays, toward transitioning. They expect transition to make marriage available to them and, in a few instances, to salvage a threatened same-sex relationship. Nevertheless, relationships involving trans persons continue to remain under the threat of inauthenticity; the postoperative body continues to be received as not *really* the opposite body, but as body manqué, as good for fun but not for serious partnership. The body that was not good enough before continues to be not good enough after; it is often dismissed as a "plastic replica." This is particularly so for MtFs for whom infertility—at the end of the day a much more serious accusation for a female—is added to sexual inauthenticity. It is generally more acceptable for couples with infertile males to adopt children or for the wife to undergo artificial insemination. Both these options are available to an FtM husband. For MtFs, a living womb is always a threat. Social pressures at times lead the partners to contemplate leaving a "fake" man or woman for a "real" one—as many postoperative break-up stories reiterate and repeat. Despite the circulation of such sad stories, the larger social pressures for marriage continue to move some people toward transitioning.

Marriage is also sometimes arranged by parents for a daughter who continues to enact non-normative gender/sexual identifications and tendencies. As adolescents, even in their late teens, female-female relationships are thought to be harmless, temporary, and would cease upon marriage. Parents pressure marriage-resistant daughters into marriage, hoping that it will "cure" them.

Emad was forced into an arranged marriage at the age of nineteen and ran away after two days. Kamran married with some misgivings. As he put it, he had always had manly qualities—his father had died when s/he was only a few months old and s/he had grown up acting as "the man of the family": "I shoveled snow, I did all the home repairs, carried heavy stuff; family members often jokingly called me by a male name, such as Ahmad Aqa. We had no man in the family." He described his misgivings about marriage not as the result of any "contrary" sexual desire, but instead because he didn't know if he could put up with a man trying to lord it over him/her. His/her marriage's almost immediate failure was indeed what made him/her convinced that he was not really a woman. This coincided with hearing about transsexuality and seeing a television program about it:

> One day we were watching this satellite program in Persian about sex change. My sister turned to me and said, "This is just like you." I got up and went online and found any and all information, I read it all from six in the

evening till six in the morning; I found Mirjalali's clinic. Then I talked with my husband and told him either to divorce me or sign the permission to let me change my sex. But he refused and it dragged to the courts. In the court, he himself said, "Our marriage is like two men being married. We are like two parallel lines that never come together at any point." But still he wouldn't divorce me. I had to get into a prolonged court battle before finally a judge divorced me. It was a very messy divorce. Eventually I had to give up all my financial claims, including shares I had in a taxi company we owned jointly.

Kamran's sister, Laleh, supported Kamran's narrative: "Everyone in the family knew he was masculine; that's why everyone accepted his sex change with no trouble. We all knew it. He had a manly mannerism and temperament all his life."

Mehran was married off reluctantly and separated from his/her first husband after a single night. But several years later, as we have already seen, when s/he was still trying to decide "what I was," s/he actually initiated her/his second marriage with a man who was a very close friend and colleague: "I ruined a good friendship before we finally gave up." "Failure in marriage" becomes proof that one is not a woman.

A few MtFs are forced into marriage as a cure. Arezu's father and brothers gave her "the option" of getting married or getting killed. She chose the latter. But I did not come across similar narratives. Most parents opt for other pressures to "make a man" out of their "errant" son. Most commonly, they press their son to go for his compulsory military service, hoping that army service will provide the masculinizing impetus. In part, the less frequent use of "the marriage cure" for MtFs stems from a fear—should the marriage not consummate, the shame of failure would mark the family. It is a "cure" that may backfire and cause more embarrassment and scandal.[31] Moreover, men's marriages can be deferred to a much later age than women's without causing much social gossip. For MtFs, the pressure of marriage takes the form of their desire to marry their lovers and live what is considered a respectable conjugal life.

Dominant notions of manhood and womanhood inform styles of (self-)cognition among trans persons on multiple levels. As Sinnott has noted in a different context, differences "between being male and being female" in the larger society matters a great deal to how sexual/gender non-normative lives shape distinctly for men and women.[32]

For Jalal, a postoperative FtM in his early twenties, signs of manhood included being actively interested in sex and not being able to accept as a serious girlfriend a girl who was taller than him. Emad, a postoperative FtM in his early thirties, stressed feelings of power, self-reliance, and self-sufficiency as characteristics that spoke to his manhood; by contrast he criticized some trans persons for being whiners. Whining was defined as womanly. He could understand why so many MtFs were whiners, but in FtMs, he found that intolerable. Aren't you a man? He also emphasized that he had always felt a sense of ownership toward his girlfriends in high school. Keeping a jealous eye on one's girlfriend was a uniformly approved masculine characteristic, although Emad, like several other trans persons, disapproved of it when it became extreme and took the form of violence or unreasonable demands (such as, it was rumored at the time, between an FtM and an MtF couple).

Sina similarly emphasized his sense of standing on his own two feet from early childhood as a sign of masculinity: "My brother is four years older, but my family always counted on me." Other memories that were recounted as indicative of early masculinity included lording it over girls: "I always told the girls in our family how to behave properly; I would tell them, don't sit like this, don't laugh like that. Other family members all considered me a *javanmard.*" But he also noted that what was considered chivalry had changed. "Older FtMs act very differently, they think being a man means you have to be really rough, almost a thug. They think FtMs like me are *susul* [effeminate]; we don't even carry a jackknife! What kind of men are we? We are more modern, and when we get into disagreements, we try to solve things with conversation and mediation not by getting into a fight."

Womanliness was marked by very different signs, including enjoying the attentions of men on the street, cooking a meal, keeping a journal, and gossiping. Taraneh criticized some MtFs for not being able to adjust their gender characteristics: Being haughtily proud, and a reluctance to be submissive, Taraneh argued, were characteristics that MtFs ought to unlearn if they wanted to succeed in their relationships.

These concepts informed some of the differences that were narrated insistently as distinctions between MtFs and FtMs. Often referred to as *in-tarafi-ha* versus *'un-tarafi-ha*—literally, those on this side versus those on the other side—this line of separation has a historic beginning. As argued in the previous chapters, the emergence of MtFs as distinct from other categories of male non-normativity was an intensively post-1979 phenomenon. A similar urgency in marking FtMs as distinct from other categories of female non-normativity was neither present, nor does it mark the distinction as sharply in today's living practices.[33] But more importantly, the general masculine gender privileges in the society at large marks FtMs' attitudes toward MtFs. As Sina put it, "People on our side are generally more successful in life. All continue their higher education because they know 'the day after tomorrow' when they take a wife, they will have to manage a family, earn the bread, and be responsible. They must have a good income. People on the other side, they focus on finding a good husband. That is much tougher."

But perhaps even more importantly, as I have already noted, MtF lives continue to be haunted by the category kuni. Initially this affects one's self-perception, but more significantly, this haunting continues its work for parents, neighbors, and the more general societal perception. At times families who expel their errant son and cut off all ties with him still move from their neighborhood to make a clean break from the shame of that past. Making a clean break from the past is indeed what most transsexuals, especially MtFs, opt for. FtMs do not escape the issue of family respectability altogether. Kamran lives with his sister Laleh for the moment; Laleh and her husband, despite their own and their families' complete support of Kamran's transition, have moved from their house to avoid neighbors' scrutiny. "What will people say?" continues to weigh heavily on many post-transition decisions. Kamran finds the issue of peer judgment one to be avoided. Even though his boss had been exceptionally supportive, among other things providing him with insurance coverage through the only private company that covers SRS and guaranteeing him his job after medical leave, he decided that it would be too stressful for him to go and socialize with the same people but as a member of "the opposite sex," to go and sit at the men's table during breaks, to go to men's part of everything, when before he had gone to women's sections. The challenge of gender-marked spatial cartographies does not cease with transition.

With new identities, with legal documents, and with or without reconciliation with parents, setting up a life that wipes out all traces of one's earlier life is the ideal goal. Especially once one gets married, the success of marriage as far as acceptance into the family of a spouse is concerned is seen to depend on ignorance of the past. This is also critical to couples with children. Arezu's biggest fear and anxiety was that one of her sisters-in-law, who knew her son was adopted, might someday inform him of that fact.

Several older-generation transsexuals I got to know have children, and their paths to parenthood have become known as options for the younger generation. Shahrzad, who transitioned some twenty-three years ago and has been married for the past eighteen years, had succeeded in officially adopting children. Arezu and her husband worked out a more elaborate scheme to take over the custody of an infant from a young woman who had become pregnant out of wedlock. Others have adopted their husband's children from an earlier marriage. Houri's best MtF friend, Anahita, had married her husband shortly after his wife had died in a car crash and became mother to his two very young children—one almost two years old, the other only a few months old at the time. Nushin, having found out that her husband had cheated on her and had contracted a temporary marriage, agreed not to seek a divorce only if he would arrange for the woman to act as a "surrogate mother" and that they would adopt the baby. Surrogate motherhood has been used more openly by other couples. Houri's husband is a divorcé; his first marriage didn't work out because he is infertile. That is good for Houri, since they can openly go for adoption with no stigma.

Both the cultural abjection of "gay"-ness, always working under the sign of kuni, and the religious-legal sanctions against various same-sex behaviors and practices, which are most heavily weighted against anal intercourse between two males, set up the paradoxical situation in which homosexuals and transsexuals (especially gay men and MtFs) are simultaneously pulled together and set apart. Whether for reasons of cognition—am I gay? Am I MtF? Am I butch? Am I FtM?—or for exigencies of living livable lives (especially acute for MtFs and gay men), people on the spectrum of non-normative genders/sexualities reach for each other's support. They live in overlapping communities and benefit from extended networks that include them all. It is indeed the exigency of these overlapping networks that at once requires inner lines of demarcation and makes clear delineation a struggle for many.

The narrative of transition from a childhood of cross-identified gender to an adolescence marked by sexual desires for one's own genus/jins is the critical loop through which a space of habitation for homosexuality has emerged. If some of the persons with same-sex desire are after all not sinning deviants, then in principle all persons with same-sex desire must be considered not-necessarily-sinning deviants. The closed question of the forbidden-ness of same-sex practices has become open to ambiguous possibilities. While this produces pressure on same-sex desirers to consider bodily transition as a possibility for living more livable lives, it simultaneously makes it possible to live in the shadowy zone of undecidability: Is s/he TS? Is s/he homosexual? An unequivocal answer to the question of identification can be deferred.

## PROFESSING SELVES    *Sexual/Gender Proficiencies*

To be honest, there are still occasions that I say I am *transsexual*;
I am perhaps 70 percent *lesbian* and 30 percent *trans*. —*Leila*

There are always critical moments in archival diggings and ethnographic hearings that become earthquakes: suddenly you are hit by something that shakes
the ground from under your project's design, analytical structure, or expected
emergences. At times, it may be so basic as to make you think you have been
asking the wrong questions all along. Leila's statement was one such moment.
What did it mean to conceive of identification as quantifiably divisible?

As I have indicated already in several chapters, what I heard from and about
trans persons and observed in their daily living practices at times seemed
familiar, in the sense that their stories resonated with what I had learned about
transsexual lives and practices in the United States. At other times, these narratives and practices were so unfamiliar that they made the familiarity of the
other moments suspect, a case of "unwarranted familiarity."[1] I do not propose
to smooth out these unmatching moments.[2] Instead, I will conclude this book
by asking, What concept of self-hood makes Leila's statement understandable?
In what contexts, and how, does the issue of identification and naming oneself
(*trans, lesbian, gay, straight*, etc.) matter at all?

Over the past several decades, literature on the concept of self in several
academic disciplines—including philosophy, intellectual and cultural history, anthropology and sociology, psychology and social psychology, and literature—has been growing.[3] Differing strands from this literature have facili-

tated my thinking here, but what I have found most useable are concepts of a narrativizing self and narratives of the self as the stories that are available and are continuously generated for configuring one's sense of being in the world.[4] I am more interested, then, in historically contextualized accounts of the emergence of the modern concept of the self.[5] Wahrman playfully names an earlier period "'before the self': indicating a time that lacked a sense of a stable inner core of selfhood like that which will emerge at the turn of the eighteenth century [in England]. This 'pre-self,' as it were, had not been contained or well represented by the spatial model of surface versus depth, which was later to become the main modern visual aid for understanding selfhood. 'The world's all face,' it will turn out, was more than a metaphor."[6] In Wahrman's historical narrative, what he calls "the *ancien régime* of identity" was characterized "by the relatively commonplace capacity of many to contemplate—without necessarily facing some inescapable existential crisis (and often the reverse)—that identity, or specific categories of identity, could prove to be mutable, malleable, unreliable, divisible, replaceable, transferable, manipulatable, escapable, or otherwise fuzzy around the edges. Conversely, it was a regime of identity not characterized by an axiomatic presupposition of a deep inner core of selfhood."[7]

Like Wahrman, I am not primarily focused on how concepts of self are articulated in the philosophical and other texts of a period. Rather, I want to understand how selves are professed and performed proficiently. For instance, when I discuss vernacular psychology's concept of self, I am interested in it because of its vast resonance as it circulates in several sites relevant to my study of transsexuality in Iran, and most particularly how the concept does (or does not) make sense through the narratives and practices of *trans*, *gay*, and *lesbian* persons I came to know.

I also work with the possibility of many such stories being available at any given time and place, even though one of them may have acquired a dominant place, such as the interiorized deep self in contemporary Euro-American societies. My adoption of a narrativizing self is not meant as a descriptive definition. I propose to use it heuristically. While previous chapters have attempted to map out the contours of state regulations, religious requirements, and societal rules that enable and necessitate living selves that profess themselves variously at different nodes of sociality, now I want to turn to narrative details that may tell us how some people in Iran, in the contemporary period, make sense of their being in the world. These narratives, I suggest, articulate a sense of self contingently constituted within particular nodes of relations, through what one does at a given conjunction of networks of affection, work, play, and other spaces of social presence. In Riley's words, "My self might be considered, tautly, as consisting of nothing more than what it does."[8]

This is not the same as "the relational self," which has its own genealogy in psychology. The relational self in that discourse still references a deep self that acquires its depth through relations with other deep selves.[9] I am attempting to grapple with a sense of self that is not necessarily and coherently perceived and experienced as anything to do with some deep inner truth about oneself, but ventures on "a profound superficiality."[10] From this viewpoint, I find de Certeau's proposition that "each individual is a locus in which an incoherent (and often contradictory) plurality of such relational determinations interact"[11] more productive: This is a concept of a networked self-in-conduct, where performances of self are situated in a space defined by numerous connections with other selves, within numerous institutional sites, the intersection of any number of which produce a contingency of located-ness, and thus a sense of self contingent to that knot—a "working conjunction," "a bundle of results, a cluster of effects and outcomes."[12]

Erving Goffman's concept of self is similarly helpful: "The self, then, as a performed character, is not an organic thing that has a specific location, whose fundamental fate is to be born, to mature, and to die; it is a dramatic effect arising diffusely from a scene that is presented, and the characteristic issue, the crucial concern, is whether it will be credited or discredited."[13] Goffman's idea would emphasize that the produced self will not be one character because its self-ness at any particular time and place will depend on a contingent scene of performance. In Butler's articulation, "it is an identity tenuously constituted in time" and "not predetermined by some manner of interior essence."[14] The place and context will differ from one performance to another, and the audience will differ from one performance to another; different selves are thus produced all the time and any requirement of coherence among all these selves would fail to take into its understanding this always-changing genesis.

Despite its central argument around the performative constitution of self, Goffman's analysis of "whether it [the self as a performed character] will be credited or discredited" at times tends to reintroduce a distinction between a self and its performances. For instance, he speaks of "the dissonance created by a misspelled word, or by a slip that is not quite concealed by a skirt" (55), or that "the impression of reality fostered by a performance is a delicate, fragile thing that can be shattered by very minor mishaps. The expressive coherence that is required in performances points out a crucial discrepancy between our all-too-human selves and our socialized selves" (56). Goffman's analysis of the many sites and possibilities of "misrepresentation," while focused on its reception, sees its risks as arising from deception—"to be duped and misled, for there are few signs that cannot be used to attest to the presence of something that is not really there" (58). While he critiques the "common-sense view," which receives a performance as "a false front" (59), in other places he marks some performances as "concealing" certain matters (67) and distinguishes between "performances that are quite false" and "ones that are quite honest" (66), although at the same time he makes the criterion of the "coming off" of a performance its reception by an audience as sincere (71). Sincerity seems to refer to what an individual performer believes it to be.[15] But surely this may be unknown and unknowable to the receiving audience who, according to Goffman, is the judge of sincerity. Agnes's successful performance of a present womanhood with an intersex history over several years persuaded a team of psychologists, psychoanalysts, and sociologists at the University of California, Los Angeles, that she had been sincere.[16] It is not accidental that Garfinkel's engagement with Goffman is carried out through a discussion of Agnes.[17] Under observance in several domains, including work, friends and family, and medical professionals, Agnes "passed" or, in Garfinkel's words, "It would be less accurate to say of her that she has passed than that she was continually engaged in the work of passing."[18] "The deception," which was reported later and has provided the central material for much subsequent contested debate, became so named as a result of information presumably provided by Agnes herself years later.

The "coming off" of any performance for the audience cannot thus reference the intentions and beliefs of the performer. Rather, it references previous performances that have produced the effect of the currently dominant script, as if it were some essential definition. Significantly, Garfinkel noted, from Agnes's performances, the performative nature of all doing of gender:

> Agnes' practices accord to the displays of normal sexuality in ordinary activities a "perspective by incongruity." They do so by making observable *that* and *how* normal sexuality is accomplished through witnessable displays of talk and conduct, as standing processes of practical recognition, which are done in singular and particular occasions as a matter of course, with the use by members of "seen but unnoticed" backgrounds of commonplace events, and such that the situation question, "What kind of phenomenon is normal sexuality?" . . . accompanies that accomplishment as a reflexive feature of it, which reflexivity the member uses, depends upon, and glosses in order to assess and demonstrate the rational adequacy for all practical purposes of the indexical question and its indexical answers. . . . Agnes was self-consciously equipped to teach normals how normals make sexuality happen

in commonplace settings as an obvious, familiar, recognizable, natural, and serious matter of fact. Her specialty consisted of treating the "natural facts of life" of socially recognized, socially managed sexuality as a managed production so as to be making these facts of life true, relevant, demonstrable, testable, countable, and available to inventory, cursory representation, anecdote, enumeration, or professional psychological assessment.[19]

Judith Butler, from a different direction and some three decades later, suggested the concept of "sedimented acts."[20] "[T]here is no preexisting identity by which an act or attribute might be measured; there would be no true or false, real or distorted acts of gender. . . . [G]ender is an 'act,' broadly construed, which constructs the social fiction of its own psychological interiority" (528). If there is an "original" script anywhere, it is performances already enacted.[21] For instance, in the context of my observations, when one MtF says reproachfully of another MtF: even real women do not walk/talk/gesticulate/use makeup like *this*, "this" is what is considered way off the current dominant script of womanhood. Yet, for some MtFs, it is that very off-the-script performance of womanhood that is aspired to in order to emphasize one's un-manhood and at the same time one's womanhood as different from the dominant presentations of womanhood.

In this context, I receive claims of authenticity, excess, and so on as regulatory scripts for proficiency of sex/gender/sexuality performances. The question, then, is no longer, for instance, what is essentially distinct between gay and lesbian identifications and trans identifications as it is sometimes articulated (in terms of the desire for bodily modifications, for example, or the lack thereof). Rather it becomes: What performative differences enable one to pronounce that X is *trans* and Y is ivakhvahar. When Sheila, an MtF, after attending the meeting with film producer Motamedian, reported to a trans support group meeting that the persons he had invited were not *trans* but ivakhvahar, she had arrived at that judgment without any knowledge of the persons' desire for bodily change one way or another. Yet based on their performative cues—what Garfinkel would call "indexical particulars"—she made a confident cognitive pronouncement. How do such pronouncements regulate the lines of demarcation, police certain presentations, and protect one community of identification that has acquired legal legibility against "intruders"? The larger society receives trans persons as a group; in Goffman's concept, as a "team of performers" (79). This group reception makes the acceptance of individual performance of trans-hood dependent "on the good conduct" of the team (82). In an important sense, however, contra Goffman, there is no "one-man team"

(85) because the meaning engendered by any performance depends on collaboration and communication with the audience for that performance, even if that audience may be oneself alone.[22] The meaning of any performance is formed only at the moment of its doing and reception.[23]

The located, contextual, and contingent character of our daily practices of the self makes any demand for coherence of the self problematic. Such coherency demands perform disciplinary and regularity work. Some subject positions are under continuous disbelief concerning their coherence; for others, coherence is taken for granted and one's proficiency in performance is assumed, thus producing what proficiency in performance of that identification means. Others' proficiency is always under the sign of deceit, passing, pretending, and inauthenticity.

With these reflections, I return to some of the narratives that I have partially presented already in this book. What are the contingent elements that make the narratives and practices I heard and observed understandable? How can we move beyond thinking of narrativization as an act of making sense of lives already lived to what makes living lives possible? Telling stories about our lives, in other words, is not significant because in hindsight it allows us to make sense of a life already lived. It is significant because through telling these stories, we live meaningfully the present moment of our lives.


IT IS OCTOBER 17, 2006, at the weekly TS support meeting of the Navvab Safavi Emergency Center of the Office for the Socially Harmed of the Welfare Organization. The meeting is led by Mr. Asadbaygi, the resident clinical psychologist. The previous week, he had talked about the importance of "knowing oneself" (*khaudshinasi*—literally "selfology"), and had asked everyone to contemplate that topic for the following week's conversation. He opens the day by asking if the group members had engaged in "knowing oneself." He is dismayed to see that his proposition had not been taken seriously. Shahla, an MtF, blurts out that she had had no time for it. What was she doing then? "I was busy with my boyfriend, cooking, making sure I make myself up in the style he likes." Asadbaygi is clearly annoyed, "Are you that dependent on him?" Shahla is not fazed, "Of course, I am really in love with him." The group takes the conversation away from Asadbaygi's agenda. Yasaman, also an MtF, who was there the previous week in a black chador but on this day has shown up in his/her army uniform, is expected by the group to explain. "Yes, I do consider myself MtF, I do want to go for SRS, but I am also prepared to take my time. Once I change sex, I won't be able to pursue some of my ambitions. In any case, when I am in masculine clothes, I enjoy doing manly things; when I am in feminine clothes, I like to do womanly things." Maryam, another MtF, asks, "You mean you live for society, and for social sake you are willing to compromise what you want? When we ask you by what name you want to be called, your male name or your female name, you say it depends; for society's sake you are willing to shift your name and clothes?" At this point, Yasaman becomes upset, "I feel the group is challenging my *trans*-ness; how are you going to invent a *trans* barometer and measure everyone's degree of *trans*-ness? I think I am more of a *trans* than many other *trans*es; perhaps my appearance doesn't show it; but one has to be smart and think that five years this way, five years that way, won't make much of a difference for my desire. One has to be flexible for important desires in one's life." Houri, an MtF, supports Yasaman's statement: "We all have to do that. I had to work as a construction worker for a while; I had to make sure my voice was as coarse as I could make it; I had to shout at some workers and order them around; I had to act manly. I hope people don't take up hostile positions against Yasaman as happened with Ghazal last week."

The conversation continues to be centered on how each person felt about being in what "gender habit." Houri explains that now she could not imagine acting like a man and being in male clothes (at the time she was preop). Parvin, a recent postoperative MtF, explains that she still lives as a man at home; it is very critical for her to remain with her family and in the neighborhood everyone knew her as a man; there was no way she could switch to being female at home. That was the compromise she had to make with her family and she would live up to it no matter what others thought of it. When she is at her boyfriend's house, she explains, she goes into female clothes. Shahla, currently in female habit, concurs, "Yeah, if my current relationship doesn't work out and I have to go back to work, I'd switch clothes to be able to get better jobs."

## Knowing Oneself

"Not having the time for 'knowing oneself'" was a remarkable statement. For Asadbaygi, this may have meant a lack of seriousness on the part of a *trans* subject. Did the *trans*es find his proposed exercise in defining their self irrelevant to their lives? I wondered. Or was the shift in the conversation an assertion of their own agenda and a defiance of the disliked Asadbaygi? In other contexts, in conversations among themselves, some *trans*es often had talked about the importance of "knowing oneself" as a critically important process. Many would emphasize that people with non-normative gender/sex identifications should not rush into *trans* self-cognition under pressure from family, peers, lovers, or the media hype. The older and more experienced *trans*es consistently encouraged more reluctant *trans*es to use the state-demanded (and usually cost-covered) four to six months of therapy as an opportunity for self-reflection and cognition. How can we, then, understand that in this meeting Asadbaygi's calling for self-knowledge immediately had produced a long conversation about clothes and names?

On first hearing, Shahla's response and the direction of the conversation among TSs after Asadbaygi's initial opening gesture may sound like willful resistance designed to ignore and go around his Alcoholics Anonymous–type exercise. Yet on another level, Shahla was performing precisely her sense of self, her enactment of "knowing oneself": to cook, to make herself beautiful, to please her boyfriend—all these constituted her sense of being/doing woman.

The following week, in the unsupervised *trans* meeting at the offices of *Psychology and Society*, Houri advised other MtFs about how to improve their doing woman. "Instead of socializing among yourselves, you should go to where *straight* [pronounced as in English] women go. Go to women's places such as hair salons and women's sections of buses; learn woman-talk, what their style of speech is, see what topics women chat about, see how they walk, how they carry themselves in public, learn what women do, like cooking, sewing, makeup skills; you are going to need these skills in life—that is how you become a woman."

These doings were also the kind of doing (wo)man that so many MtFs and FtMs narrativized and recited as cognitive moments of their growing up into (wo)manhood. Houri's recollections of her childhood centered on time spent with and around her mother, doing whatever she did. Spaces and activities that MtFs had shared with mothers, sisters, sisters' friends, brothers' wives, and neighbors' daughters were the sites and senses of developing a sense of oneself as a woman. Similarly, FtMs' sense of being men was narrativized through what they shared with fathers and other men.

As we saw in chapter 2, Munirah's narrative of sex/gender dis-identification worked around switching clothes, getting a haircut, changing manners and name, and working and living as a man. Marziah, who became Bihruz, described her/his childhood as fully gender-cross-identified: s/he liked military uniforms and wished s/he could join the army like her/his brother and father, and she/he played boys' games. Doing (wo)man also implies undoing it. Once Marziah/Bihruz dropped out of school and stayed home, learning "womanly work, such as weaving cloth, spinning yarn, cooking and laundry," women's "habits and temperament affected me and I was left with no masculine inclinations."[24]

When Sina had noted, for a day's activity in the journal he was keeping for Dr. Mohammadi, that he had cooked the family's lunch, he made sure he mentioned that he did this with his father—that was the men's day to do the meal preparation and he was emphatically not doing something womanly with his mother. His relationship with his mother was defined in terms of his looking after her needs, driving her to a doctor's appointment, moving heavy loads around the house for her—in general being the supportive son for his mother. His negative reactions to catcalls on the streets, his sense of a female relative's "inappropriate" dress or gestures, his entitlement to tell them how to behave decently—these were all cognitive signs of his manhood.[25]

As we saw in Marziah/Biruz's case, desire for military service is narrated as a proof of manhood; enjoying housework a sign of womanhood. Delara's dislike of house-cleaning jobs and taking to work extracting copper wire from appliances were integral to his account of being not-woman-but-man. For many trans persons, feeling that one is man of the house or woman of the house (*mard-i khanah, khanum-i khanah*) was what it was all about: The sense of being a (wo)man was not precisely focused as much on one's physiological body (and even less on one's genitalia) as it was on "clothes, makeup, cooking, doing what women do"—being a woman in the world meant belonging to spaces of womanhood and acting as women did.[26] These included, in early childhood, the others with whom one played and what games were preferred, but also looking like a woman and dancing like one, putting on makeup like mother, dressing up like mother—professing a woman-self through playful displays and performative presentations of womanhood. In that context, desiring men and being desired by men become performances of womanhood, given the dominant, modern, heteronormalized binary of the two opposite sexes. Alternatively, for FtMs, pursuing higher education, getting a good job, supporting one's parents, getting married, and forming a family were what being a man in the world was about.

The numerous contested conversations about "going into and staying in habit" point to the centrality of clothes to one's sense of being in the world. Mahnaz's style of outerwear and her hanging out on streets with other young men—which outraged her husband—was tied up with her sense of masculinity. Likewise, Yasaman articulated her/his related sense of doing a gender and being in its expected habit: When s/he was in masculine clothes, s/he enjoyed doing manly things; in women's clothes s/he did womanly things. Parvin lived as man, in man's clothes, using a man's name at home to remain with her/his family; at her/his boyfriend's home, s/he switched to a female habit and did womanly things. Shahla emphasized that if her/his current relation did not work, s/he would switch back to male clothes so that s/he could get better jobs.

The sense of self in habit has been intensified by governmental sartorial policies since 1979 (and in a different modality since the 1920s), which has become a thread of the effect of "clothes make a person"—at least in the field of public visibility. For FtMs, in particular, one's feeling in clothes, a matter of habit, frequently was emphasized as demarcating gender/sex. Mehran's female friend's going to school in trousers (not in skirts) was proof that s/he was a *trans*. If a female person could tolerate wearing *manteau-rusari* (overcoat and scarf), she must be a woman.[27] This public effect of identifying a (wo)man with a particular style of clothing also has contributed to the failure of governmental attempts to solidly police the trans/homosexual border and has in turn incited, as Jackson has noted, in a different context, "its own fetishisation of surface effect" and provided ample space for sartorial resisting desires—by men, women, as well as by non-normative genders/sexes/sexualities.[28]

Linked to the issue of one's "gender habit," for MtFs, was the use and style of facial makeup—a repeatedly narrated sign not only indicating not-manhood, but also proposed as a demarcation of *trans* (as distinct from *gay*) subjectivity. Recall Taraneh's contention on the *Yad-i yaran* program: "The easiest criterion I can offer you for recognizing which male is a same-sex-player and which *transsexual* is to look at a person's appearance. A same-sex-player male goes for same-sex-playing with a full male appearance. But the male who uses makeup, puts on lipstick, this person is not a man. S/he is a woman."

In numerous narratives (both in earlier accounts of the 1940s through the 1970s and those of the persons I interviewed in 2006–7), several sex/gender performance proficiencies emerged as signs of (wo)manhood. Desiring to have a husband and being desired (and asked for in marriage) by a man was a sign of womanhood; more generally, success (or failure) in heterosexual marriage (especially among female-born persons) was a sign of gender-normative correspondence (or the lack thereof). Several trans subjects, as we saw in chapter 7, turned to marriage to test themselves.

For Delara, Mahnaz, and several other born-females, falling in love with women meant they must be not-woman. Similarly, Sina's perceived *gay* teacher's falling in love with him proved that Sina was not a girl. Arezu's love of belly dancing and cooking from her early years configured her own self-perception as a girl. Not only desires for, and enacting, sex/gender marked practices of daily life defined man/womanhood, but imagining dying in a particularly sexed body ("I want to be seen as [fe]male when my body is washed for burial") was also a critical mark and a reason given for SRS.

While some persons referenced their bodily sensations as indicating their gender/sexual identification ("I can't take a shower with my clothes off"; "I can't look into a mirror naked"), others defined their bodily gender in connection to partners: "S/he wants to see a body of the opposite sex next to her/him." Not only was doing (wo)manhood most often presented as being a (wo)man, but doing also was frequently articulated in situated terms that were dependent on others. Sina articulated his own manliness in term of a relation-location: when he was with a girl, "I want her to feel she has a man in her life." As Boellstorff has noted for *warias*, ". . . the process of occupying it involves from the outset the reactions and commentary of others. Unlike gay men, *waria* never speak of 'opening themselves' . . . in terms of revealing who they are; indeed they often discover who they are because others point it out to them."[29]

Transition decisions were as frequently articulated in terms of their social effects. For some this required flexibility. Yasaman, as we saw, was willing to postpone SRS—what did five years this way or that way matter?—to pursue her/his career options. Even if one could be happy to live a trans-identified life with little bodily modification, one would transition because not doing so would be unacceptable to others, as Zahra elaborated in response to the questions, "If you could live in a man's clothes, would that not be enough? If you could live like a man from all points of view, would you be willing not to go for sex change?" Zahra's response: "I have lived in Lahijan for the past twenty years; my father is a well-known figure; my family will not accept it; I will have problems with my partner; our society will not accept it; I myself cannot accept it."

"The world" in various ways and through innumerable emotional, sociocultural, and institutional points of power tended to withhold its acceptance of such self-cognitions and insisted on reorganizing one's sense of being in these spaces and doing these activities around a focus on the body and, for some, on the genitalia. When Arezu's father and brothers could not hear her statement "I am a woman" and responded by "doing everything it takes to make you a man," she eventually risked her life and attempted to cut off her own genitalia to close off that possibility. Many of the emotional, sociocultural, and institutional locations of one's being—one's located habitus—are organized around correspondence between one's being a (wo)man and a set of bodily marks. But as Warnke asks, "Why does wrongness manifest itself as an issue of genitalia?"[30] As we have seen, for many trans persons in Iran the reorganization of this sense of "wrongness" around genitalia emerged in adolescence; more often than not, they articulated their desire for "someone of their own sex" in abject terms of same-sex-playing—as sinful or as disgustingly horrible—and thus something about that "sameness" was questioned. As Kamran put it, "Because we don't know; we all go through that stage"—that stage of being tormented by the question of, "Am I a same-sex-player? How do I know?" and "What am I then?"

Figuring out the answers to these questions does not necessarily or usually (at least in the case of gender/sexual non-normative persons with whom I worked) take shape through therapeutic self-talk. People figure out these questions, as we have seen, through living in various arrangements and relationships and by working at particularly gender-defined jobs—for MtFs, for instance, going to the army to see if they really are not manly or being the homemaker for one's boyfriend; for FtMs, pursuing careers and goals of education that are associated with men. The shift from the "selfology" of Asadbaygi's understanding to professing one's activities, choice of clothes and names, and daily doings indeed signified a sense of self that, in numerous trans narratives and practices, was reiteratively and persistently configured within located contingencies of innumerable details of daily lives. Proficient performance in these nodes was what being/doing (wo)man was about. What seemed to matter for *trans* subject-hood was articulated in terms of figuring out how to live livable lives—with families, with partners, in terms of employment, of getting medical and legal changes they wanted, and of what made them comfortable in different spaces of life. The meaning of claiming or being hailed as *trans* or *gay* or *lesbian* thus was produced in conversations in which many participated; it was not simply an inner feeling that found a name. Moreover, living livable lives, for some, called for flexibility and the ability to switch back and forth when necessary: living a (fe)male life, in (fe)male clothes with a (fe)male name, in some spaces and times, but doing the other gender/sex in other times and places.

As we have seen, the very process of naming is itself a social cognition, sometimes in private homes, sometimes in a doctor's office, sometimes in a TS support group, and even on a TV documentary. How others recognize and name one becomes an element of one's own self-constitution. As Sina (FtM) once put it,

> In high school, we had a male literature teacher whom everyone thought was ivakhvahar. He fell in love with me. A *gay* man never falls in love with a girl. Sometimes, my friends in school would joke and tell me [the teacher] was my future wife. When I was paid attention to by guys, instead of being pleased, I would become irritated. There was this guy I met in university entrance exam preparation classes. One day, he said, "Every time I talk

with you, it's not like talking with a girl, it's more like talking with my other male friends." Eventually, I had to tell him I wasn't interested in having boy-friends. It was in those years that I realized I can be and must become a man. I told my mother. I told her I wanted to become a man. My mother first thought this was because I was very ambitious, and said, "But there are a lot of successful women in the world, you can be a successful woman." So I told her, "No, you don't understand, I must become a successful *man*."

Unlike many trans persons, Mohsen did not trace any cognition of difference from his peers to a cross-gender-identified childhood: "I didn't feel differently in childhood, but in high school, I was the center of attention of my classmates. One of my classmates, a close friend, told me one day jokingly, go and change your sex and we will get married. In high school I was very well liked, though some would tell me to stay away from them, otherwise they'd get into trouble. I guess I must have been acting in a way that I was oblivious to. That is when I started feeling I must be different, but I was totally comfortable with myself."

Self-cognition navigated its emergence in relation with others, including those others who may have been identified by other social actors as the same. As we saw in chapter 7, Zia and Houri's close friendship over many years en-abled both of them to decide who was *gay* and who was *trans*. Houri narrated this at some length:

Twelve or thirteen years ago, I met Zia. At the time, I was working in an educational institute as secretary at the front desk. He was a very young teenager and had registered in a class. I am about ten years older than him. When I saw him, it was as if I saw my own persona, ten years younger. At that time, I still didn't know anything about sex change, I thought I was *homosexual*, and that bothered me a lot. Ever since my years of puberty I'd noticed I had no desire for girls. This was step number one in realizing I was different from others, different from my age cohorts. I also began to realize I had a special feeling for men. In family gatherings, in school, I looked at men with a special feeling. In eighth grade, I fell in love with my math teacher—as a result, I always did very well in math! This was my first romance.

I interrupted here, resisting: "High school crushes are very common. Every-one has them. They don't mean much about long-term tendencies. Not every-one ends up identifying as *transsexual* or even *homosexual*. Just two days ago, I heard very similar accounts from a *gay* man, now in his early fifties." "Ha!" Houri retorted triumphantly. "The difference is this: That feeling of mine then brought me to who I am in life today. So the meaning of my first love in high school is not the same as your crush or your gay friend's first love." It was impossible to argue with her retrospective reading—my narrative about my high school crushes *not* meaning transsexuality was, after all, as retrospectively defined as hers. Houri continued:

> Look, I feel a sense of peace and comfort when I am with other women; this comes from feeling the same. It works the other way around as well; my sister-in-law always said she felt totally *relaxed* [pronounced as in English] in my company but not with my other brothers. She'd even ask me to help her get dressed, fix her bra, whatever. After middle school and a couple of years of high school, I couldn't tolerate hiding my feelings from my family, but couldn't let anything out either. So I quit school and moved to Tehran, and got myself a job. At this time, I still thought I was *homosexual*. I started socializing in *homosexual* circles, but I was not happy, I didn't feel comfortable there either. For a while I tried living like a *straight* man. I took a job in a very masculine environment, thinking if I circulate only among masculine men I will change. At work, I was really good in performing my role, but at night, I would rush home to be myself, to look as I wanted, do as it pleased me. This was a torment. I even went and introduced myself to the army to do my service, thinking that would help me become a man, even though I knew from others that I could get an exemption as *homosexual*. It was also in these years that my information circle widened, through the Internet, here and there, and when I met other kids/peers [*bachchah-ha*] like myself. I met a wonderful older woman, Anahita, who had undergone sRs twenty-four years earlier. She has two kids. Her husband had a first marriage; when one of his kids was a year and a half old and the other only two months, his wife died; soon after they met and got married; both kids think Anahita is their mother. I envied her life. She helped me a great deal; I realized that is the life I wanted; not just having sex with another man; my life differs a great deal from Zia's life.

Houri had had a long-term romantic relationship for seven years, but her partner had died in a car accident. Around the same time, Zia moved to Tehran and they have been roommates for several years now. Living together gave them both a chance of seeing each other's daily practices, desires, and needs. Once Zia got his own job and life separate from his parents, he decided it was time to figure it out if he was MtF or *gay*. He went to several therapists; one told him he was trans, but he was not sure. He said that he and Houri had a lot in common; he would have been happy if he were a woman, but he didn't want it enough to go through all the surgeries; he enjoyed dressing up as a woman, and they often borrowed clothes from each other. But for him, this was a hobby to be enjoyed at home or in parties; otherwise he went to work as a man.[31]

The category of "undecided," in a conundrum, *bilataklif* in this context pointed not to confusion over "identity" that could be clarified in some way, perhaps through therapy—including Islam-therapy. Rather it referenced the challenge of deciding what overall identification would make for an optimally livable life. Most *trans*es invoked the category bilataklif to refer to the long, at times indefinite transition (or nontransition for that matter)—namely, the period in which the person had opted to live in between. For instance, many MtFs take hormones and live in habit, removing their testes only if it becomes necessary because of severe atrophy and possible infection. These styles of living also pose situational bilataklifi, such as which entrance to a shrine one ought to go through, or Zia's "I don't know what I am" pronouncement in a Bihzisti meeting. The insistent reiteration of being in an in-between position gives some *gays* the safety of semi-openness and offers more flexible (at times playful) options for social maneuvering to *trans*es.[32] Contrary to Taraneh's categorical statement that, from their appearance, one can tell who is *gay* and who is *trans*, these appearances themselves have a range of displayed (*numudan*) femininity, from fully woman-dressed and made up to milder makeup (long fingernails, but not polished, plucked eyebrows, maybe a shade of mascara), with a range of gestures and walking styles, and including more occasional displays such as Zia's dressing up in women's clothes on occasions and for parties. It is people like Kia (see chapter 1) and Zia who indeed do go through pressure of "clarifying" what they are. What "complicates" their self-cognition (and others' cognition of them) is, as Taraneh also articulated, the common socializing sites of MtFs and *gay* men. A somewhat similar pressure is at work on FtMs, but many more FtMs seem to live more private lives and to get married and melt into heteronormalized life, whereas more often MtFs, even postoperatively, remain isolated from their families, their previous boyfriends breaking up with them and going for "real" women for marriage, and new suitors turning away when they learn of their previous status.

The issue of gender/sexual performance proficiency was articulated frequently around the notion of "*suzhah shudan*." Literally meaning "becoming a subject," this concept has to do with how others talk about a person in approbation, in gossip—it is the notion of something about you that is generated by the circulation of what is said about you and by how you are seen by others. It signals willed self-scandalization, a much disapproved of state of social self-presentation; it signifies failure, incompetence, and lack of proficiency in gender/sex performance. The referentiality in becoming a *suzhah* is not to some inner truth, but to how one is positioned in the circulation of social conversations, how one is deciphered, sometimes scandalously, sometimes because they are seen to perform in excess, the excess defined by how in reception by other people—peers, NAJA, the press, a social worker, family—one is seen to be excessively womanly.[33]

Zia's judgment of others' daily troubles was formulated in terms of their competence (or lack thereof) in sexual/gender performance. What Zia termed gender/sexual incompetence cannot be seen as effects of individual failings. As discussed in several chapters, state regulation of public gender presentation in the decades after 1979 made living as a feminine male-bodied person not only extremely hazardous but also nearly impossible, and may have contributed to the desire for sex change on the part of some woman-presenting males. Correspondingly, the relative ease of passing as male possibly had worked against the need for FtM operations. MtFs insist over and over that if they wanted to live *gay*, they could. What gives them trouble is their style of clothes and makeup. Indeed, men interested in woman-presenting males often are said to lose interest in the postoperative MtF. Despite such differentiations, MtF-trans and *gay* lives continue to gain their meanings under each other's shadow.[34] A person is one largely in terms of not being the other.[35]

When Zia, for instance, referred to himself as *gay*, this self-assignation indexed certain "repudiations"—not ivakhvahar, not kuni, not MtF. It did not simply index desiring male-bodied persons. He did not desire male-bodied MtFs nor postoperative FtMs. Naming himself *gay* indexed a complicated set of demarcations: body presentations and movements, styles of makeup and dress—all were calibrated in ways that distinguished him from both "average men" and "MtFs." His boyfriend 'Ali, with whom he now lives since Houri parted after her SRS and marriage, did not emphasize *gay*ness as self-identification and was indistinguishable visually from other young men in Tehran. Indeed, as he explained, his coworkers take him as *straight*. When questioned by them—"Are you married?" "Do you have a girl friend?" "Do you want us to find you one?"—he changes the subject to avoid being seen as "not normal." Behzad and Cyrus indexed yet different styles of living *gay*. Behzad has continued to live with his family, to whom he explained his reasons for his refusal to get married and with whom he has lived a life of "don't ask, don't tell" ever since. Outwardly, his *gay*ness is invisible except to "those in the know."

Zia, Behzad, and Cyrus, unlike 'Ali, are known and want to be known as *gay* within a safe social network, which in Cyrus's case includes his work environment. Naming oneself differently also indexes one's spaces of sociality. Zia no longer goes to Bihzisti or other spaces of socialization dominated by MtFs. Once he decided that what he really wanted was to have a steady relationship with another man, his "habitat" shifted to circles of male-male couples/close friends. These varied *gay* (and *lesbian*) styles of living indicate that, unlike what at times has been assumed, especially among diasporic Iranian conversations, there is no evidence that thinking *trans* is a result of "lack of imagination," indexing an inner identity that does not know its name. Boellstorff's suggestion that individuals' options for responding to the hailings of the dominant system are not limited to identification or dis-identification, that "the influence of power systems is neither [necessarily] direct nor oppositional, but more contingent and contextual" is very pertinent,[36] especially in a context where much of the current political analysis about Iran has been centered for the past three decades on a notion of hegemonic theocratic authoritarianism and for an even longer period on "the state."[37] As Boellstorff emphasizes, "*Bahasa gay* may therefore help us see how a system of power can result in subject positions that speak neither with nor against that system, yet articulate their unexpected logics in terms of that system's grammar—literally and figuratively."[38] In the case of self-identification as *trans* in Iran, this means that in various contingent contexts, one may respond by "Yes Sir, I am a GID patient"; at others, "We are superior creatures of God"; and perhaps, even more often, "We simply ignore your hailings and live our lives and navigate through and around the social and political labyrinths *like everybody else*"—almost.[39] Once we consider other concepts of self, a sense of self that appears "devious" to the Cartesian self because "it is dispersed" and does not manifest itself through referentiality to a deep sense of being, but rather through its ways of using the many microspaces available by interstices of dominant sociocultural politico-economic structures, "subversion" need not occur either through rejection or alteration but by using "rituals, representations, and laws imposed on them [that are] something quite different from what their" doctors, psychologists, legal authorities, and Islamic jurisprudents had in mind. Such "use of the dominant social order deflect[s] its power, . . . they escape it without leaving it. The strength of their difference lay in procedures of 'consumption.'"[40]

The cognition of oneself as *trans*—and the degrees to which one transitioned—was configured in terms of a calculus of life's options. Mahnaz, whom I had first met when she had come to the Mirdamad Clinic to make an appointment for SRS, was still living as a married woman and refused to consider going to Europe through the refugee route—an option that was much discussed in *trans, gay, lesbian* circles—because she did not want to cut off the possibility of returning to her family in Iran.[41]

Often, this process sounded like a cost-benefit matrix, virtually quantifiable. Recall how Leila and Minu talked about frustrations of being denied the small pleasures of life—not being able to be together like a family at Nauruz and starting every New Year apart, or the desire to go to places "like a couple," to imagine a day they could adopt a child, and so on. It was these impossibilities that at times made Leila think if only she'd change sex. . . . But then other considerations would enter: "If I changed sex, my current acceptance in Minu's family might be jeopardized; my professional status and social capital would be ruined," and so on. The balance of this complicated calculus for Leila so far was 70 percent in favor of not changing sex, but she felt conflicted and could see herself being tempted to the contrary.

Like Leila, Yunes's self-cognition as *trans* (he has since transitioned) was a complex contingent emergence. Before s/he had ever heard the word *trans*, s/he had assumed s/he was a same-sex-player. It was his/her former girlfriend's father who had first told her/him s/he was *trans*. S/he had all but forgotten it until a friend brought her/him some published articles. The renewed interest prompted him/her to go to Dr. Mehrabi and other therapists and finally arrive at a self-cognition as *trans*. Despite being sure now that s/he was a *trans*, in the fall of 2007 s/he was still quite concerned about "going all the way." Her/his doubts were located within a similar complex matrix of costs and benefits— both in terms of social capital s/he had built up in her/his profession and its loss afterwards as well as the costs to her/his emotional network. Part of that complication was the impact of the change on Ozra and her family, the status of their relationship among their current friends, and indeed the worry about how her/his former girlfriend would react to the news.[42]

Once a *trans* self-cognition has been arrived at, previously impossible acts become imaginable: Having sex with one's partner no longer constitutes same-sex-playing, and thus little guilt, sin, or disgust is associated with it. Mahnaz's moments of cognition as *trans* similarly were related to what that would enable her: She wanted to love women, and if acquiring (self-)cognition as *trans* would enable that desire, why not?[43]

## A Genealogy of Self

But what did selfology (*khaudshinasi*) mean to Asadbaygi? The concept has a multisedimented genealogy and current location. A quick search in the online catalog of The National Archives and Library of the Islamic Republic of Iran brings up 748 items with *khaudshinasi* in their title alone.[44] The overwhelming majority of titles divide into two categories: Islamic concepts of self-knowledge and modern psychological theories. A third input into this complex comes from astrology and related knowledge.

Self-knowledge is deeply embedded in Islamic philosophical thought. It carries a particular weight in Sufism, and more recently in the writings of modernist Islamic intellectuals, such as 'Ali Shari'ati, as well. Informed by and referencing a narrative attributed to Prophet Muhammad—"Who knows himself, knows his God"—whether in mainstream Islam or more especially in Sufi Islam, cognition of God is articulated as passing through self-knowledge.[45]

A second root and route to the idea of self is through modern psychology in its Iranian variants. While in more recent decades, a whole range of concepts— from the dominant behavioral self all the way to the less-popular Freudian self-analysis (*khaudkavi*)—circulate in this domain, its earlier entry, as already discussed, was mediated, in the late 1920s, through the marital advice literature that set the stage for the flourishing of vernacular psychology of the 1940s to the present day. Today knowing oneself is considered not only critical to a good marriage, but an essential element of success and happiness in every domain of life. A vast literature, ranging from more academic writings and translations to short, popular, pocket-sized pamphlets, advises people (especially the young) on various aspects of managing the self. To facilitate such behavioral self-management, there are online tests that one can use to know one's psychological self.

Important for the subject of this book, this thread of self's genealogy, from the start, was deeply enmeshed and formed in conjunction with changing concepts of sex/gender (jins).[46] Recall that one of the earliest texts of the new genre of advice books, published in 1929, was part of a series titled *Sex and Self* in English. When I first came across Suhrab's translation of Sylvanus Stall's 1897 text—*What a Young Husband Ought to Know*—I was amused by his choice of words for the series title. In this translation, sex made its transplantational entry as *jinsiyat*, and self in the series title (*Sex and Self*) was translated as "personal directives" (*dasturat-i shakhsi*). What can one make of the difficulty of a simple translation of self in this context? Why the particular combination of "personal" and "directives" for self?

The mere linked entry of self and sex into Iranian discourse of marital conduct through translational transplantations is of course not surprising. Co-emergent with sex as "a unique signifier and as a universal signified" in nineteenth-century Europe was a sense of an interiorized self with psychic depth, a notion that has since become a dominant narrative.[47] It is this interiorized deep self that formed the subject of the emerging science of psychology and was formed by it. As Foucault suggested, and as Davidson's *The Emergence of Sexuality: Historical Epistemology and the Formation of Concepts* (Cambridge: Harvard University Press, 2001), along with the larger field of studies of sexuality over the past several decades, have more fully articulated, knowledge about this self (whether by the self or by others) centered around issues of sexuality—the truth of the self—with psychology and pedagogy as important domains for its production.

Yet, as I have already argued, what Seigel's intellectual history and Goldstein's and Wahrman's cultural histories, among other works, also make abundantly evident is this: Why should we expect "ideas of the self" to be similar from one time and context to another? Wahrman and Goldstein masterly map the radical transformation of one's sense of self for the late eighteenth through the early nineteenth centuries that occurred in Britain and France, respectively. A genealogy of the self in Iran cannot be grounded only in Iran, of course, not even in its larger immediate cultural universe. For the period of my concern—since the mid-nineteenth century—like the idea of sex, the idea of self was refashioned as part of a transnational conversation. What we need is to figure out the shaping of local emergences within the global networks and flows. Part of this story is how "the idea of the self" in one place and time (western Europe, by the nineteenth century) became a thread of the concept of self in other places—a refashioning that included the European concept read through local lenses, enunciated for vastly different effects, or ignored altogether. What transplantations were adopted, what discard and disregard were chosen, what namings and not namings occurred—these are all issues that need specific historicization.

In Iran, psychology, especially vernacular psychology, was critical to transforming jins as genus into jins as sex. One could expect that the introduction of "the new science of psychology"—as its advocates named it since the early twentieth century—would have concurrently changed the concept of self. But such a conjunction of transplantation cannot be assumed. The concept of an interiorized self, although in partial circulation, has not become a dominant narrative. As I have argued, a notion of self narrativized through "horizontal" situational conduct rather than through deep "vertical" self-referentiality tends to make better sense of many of the life stories I heard. On issues where in psychology the concept of a unified self has become a presumption of the field, the useable concept of self in everyday practice remains "horizontally segmented."[48] Even seeming similarities—the co-emergence of psychology and pedagogy, for instance—cannot be assumed to have similar meaning and cultural effects. In the same way that Davidson has argued for lexical continuity that "hides radical conceptual discontinuity,"[49] when considering transplantation of concepts, if we simply look at translations we may miss radical conceptual refashionings. The notion of self-reliant personality, for instance, that Schayegh has persuasively argued was critical to emergence of modern self in Iran in the early twentieth century,[50] had one foot in Cousin and Janet and another in Ibn Sina, as indicated by 'Ali Akbar Siasi's attempt to read Ibn Sina through "the new science of psychology." Even the seemingly simple concept of psyche, translated into Persian as ravan, turns out to have a combined genealogy that has made different possibilities available in today's figurations of gender and sexuality. Siasi, as we saw, translated psyche into nafs (an Arabic word, allowing him to claim the older notion of 'ilm al-nafs [science of nafs] as the equivalent of the new psychology), and Persianized nafs as ravan, coining ravanshinasi as the science of ravan.

In Siasi's body of writings we also see a concept of personality that departs from Ibn Sina's and earlier philosophers' concepts—a concept of layered personality begins to shape in the psychological discourse through a re-articulation of *zahir* (apparent) and *batin* (interior). In exegetical and in Sufi writings, zahir and batin referred to different levels of meaning of a concept that were available to ordinary believers and to the spiritual elite.[51] Siasi adapted these concepts while transforming them into layers of a single personality, which, according to "the new science of psychology," constituted levels of a unified character. "*Ruh* or *nafs* manifests itself in a particular shape under the influence of body's management and satisfying the bodily needs and natural, familial, and social circumstances." This manifestation Siasi called human's apparent personality—"*shakhsiyat-i zahiri-i adami*, which would be appropriate to call a theatrical personality."[52] Most importantly, he explained that the apparent manifestation and the real constituted a unified whole. "From a psychological point of view real personality and the apparent or theatrical personality . . . are the double aspects of a unified entity."[53] The unified aspect of these two levels of personality, if sustained over time, generates, he argued, what is called *huviyat* (identity).[54]

The reference to the theatrical is not accidental. In his earlier work, *'Ilm al-nafs ya ravanshinasi*, Siasi had similarly invoked the language of performance to explain the psyche, saying "psyche is like someone who is both a singer and an audience, an actor and a spectator"[55]—a notion that informs and incites a concept of self centered around conduct. Nonetheless, Siasi's move did introduce a concept of a layered self into the Iranian discourse of psychology, which navigated between a deep psyche and a notion of authenticity and sincerity. As

Siasi put it, nafs constituted the high spiritual core of one's personality; what presented itself as the presentational personality was merely its manifestation under bodily and social circumstances and necessities.[56]

In his early writings, Siasi only briefly, occasionally, and tangentially made reference to Freud and psychoanalysis and was generally dismissive of place of sexual matters in discussion of personality and psyche. When in his later work (1970) he turned to the topic of "abnormal personalities" (*shakhsiyat-ha-yi nabihanjar*), such personalities became focused on what had by then entered into Iranian discourse through psycho-sexological literature.[57] This shift in one thinker's concept of personality/self between the late 1920s and the 1970s is indicative of the dominating emergence of behavioral psycho-sexology in these decades.

Asadbaygi's project, then, is largely informed by behavioral psychology—the dominant training in Iranian universities and medical establishments.[58] From his published articles, he seems to specialize in a whole host of social problems that go under the umbrella of "social harm"—problems such as addiction, domestic violence, obsession, suicide, and prostitution.[59] His method of running the Bihzisti weekly meetings was indeed reminiscent of twelve-step Alcoholics Anonymous meetings, a style of practice that has been adopted in Iran for treating drug addiction.

The vernacular psychological concepts of self and self-knowledge also have informed the media coverage of transsexuality, as, for instance, in the series that was published in *Rah-i zindigi* under the column title "man kah hastam?" (Who am I?). This popular bimonthly magazine (see chapter 6) had covered the topic of transsexuality subsequent to its similarly framed serialized coverage of addicts and mental health patients. All such clinical practices and popular magazine reports informed by behavioral psychology share, and contribute to the recirculation of, a concept of self-in-conduct. While in that meeting on October 17, 2006, the TSs seemed resistant to following Asadbaygi's lead and reflecting on their "selves" in the way that he was demanding of them, their response was an enactment of their sense of self-in-conduct through a series of recitations of what they had done and how they did things. To the extent that a concept of "layered-ness" occasionally entered the conversation—for instance, when Kamran was addressing the social worker he had been sent to see (see chapter 7)—it is not the self but society that is described as layered. "Our society has so many different layers," as Kamran put it. One's self's layers are his/her self-presentations, selves-in-conduct, in different social sites/layers.

## Self as Contingent Conduct

To summarize, the sense of self that informs modern subjectivities in today's Iran, in many registers, is defined largely, though not hegemonically, by notions of conduct.[60] To understand the complex scene of how individuals define their sex/gender in Iran and, in particular, how some come to embrace the notion of *trans* as appropriate self-assignation, and how they decide whether, and how far, to transition is linked not only with in-distinction between gender and sex, but also with a sense of being in the world that is centered on conduct—the situated, contingent, daily performances that depend not on any sense of some essence about one's body and psyche. Rather, it is defined in terms of its specific location and temporal node at the intersection of numerous relations that define the scene of conduct of the self in that node.

What I heard on that day, when Leila made her pronouncement of percentages of identification, and what I heard from many others, were stories that spoke to a sense of being in the world that was not dominantly shaped through indexing an inner psychic self. These were narratives of a manner of being in the world that was not simply relational, but situationally enacted. The stories were not shaped by some underlying notion of "who I am"; rather there were contingent statements as if "this is me with my parents," "here at work this other way of being feels right," "there in a party, this is how I am," and so on. In other words, while one could say these narratives of a sense of being in the world was, of course, situational, relational, fractured—but what is significant is that all these operations of fracturing, relationality, and contingency worked differently than when they are presumed to work on something named identity. They did not index that presumed deep psychic sense of self that is the ground of the concept of identity.[61] A life narrative is told as one in the context of a connected and located series of moments within the sites that give meaning to one's life. This would offer us a different way of understanding trans identification, not as something necessarily arising from within one person but as something whose meaning is shaped by one's location in many (in principle, innumerable) sites. Once rethought this way, new ways of "de-medicalization" could be imagined, since the whole process no longer remains hostage to an individual's recitations in diagnostic settings.

Moreover, one's sense of self at a given junction is not only specific to the temporal-local moment; it may, or may not, carry with it some effect for one's self-in-performance in another network knot.[62] So when you are son-to-your-father, that moment of your self-in-conduct does not necessarily carry within it your sense of being *gay* in relation to your lover, which means you may not have the urge to "come out" to your father.[63] "Why would you want to tell your parents about your sex life?" Zia asked when the subject of "coming out" was once raised.[64] He added, "Every utterance has a context; every point has a site"—so goes a Persian adage. What may strike some Iranians (or non-Iranians) as hypocrisy of a "traditional" culture that encourages a split between private lives and public appearance, or a denial of one's true inner self to those who think with and live within a paradigm of deep self, for others may be a "common sense" of the adage. It makes no sense, in this paradigm, to be, look, and perform the same self in different sites and on different occasions. Here, one does not need the unconscious to have contingent selves. The source of contingency does not lie in some inner deep, inaccessible place within one's psyche; it comes instead from the contingency of self-in-conduct at these different nodes, each node (at different moments) inciting a contingent self.

Giving up the deep self as the evident cultural narrative puts under pressure the link between self and sex in the Foucauldian register, in which sexuality is proposed to have become constituted as the core of self's truth. How does one refigure the relation between sex and self, then? I suggest that one's sexual conduct, in specific relationships, is one of the many threads of located conduct that constitutes one's sense of being in the world. In this meaning, the ambiguous (in)distinction of transsexuality from homosexuality in Iran is not produced by some simple desire and the design of the medical establishment or forces of religion and the state; it is generated in part because the spaces of daily living and sexual conduct of trans persons and gays and lesbians overlap, and performances of self in these connected and overlapping spaces at times produce a sense of indeterminacy: "Am I trans? Am I homosexual?" becomes a question of not some inner truth but of figuring out and navigating one's relationship-in-conduct vis-à-vis others.

Similarly, the relation between modern power and modern selves in Iran has been dominantly in the shape of power through and over conduct, including sexual conduct. Thus the growth of state power in the twentieth century took shape through competition and collaboration between state institutions and other sources of power over conduct. In this scene, psychology, psychiatry, and related institutions and practices are far less important than institutions such as family, courts, religious leaders, and related discourses that compete and collaborate over shaping conduct and thus over a sense of being in the world. To the extent that psychology became part of this scene, it has been dominated by behavioral/conduct psychology, and it is in that domain that psychology and Islamic jurisprudential conduct literature after the 1970s have found a new merging, as we have seen.

Normative gender/sex expectations have become formed around conduct rather than identities. At times, cultural practices and codes of conduct may not be as tightly sex/gender-inflexible as they may appear at first sight. True, shared biology is assumed to somehow have something to do with a whole bundle of commonalities-in-conduct. Thus, beginning at birth, female newborns usually are given distinctively female names. But when a growing female child behaves in ways that are ordinarily considered boyish, she begins to be called by a male name in intimate circles, tongue in cheek. Over and over again, this was part of the childhood narratives of gender/sex non-normative, female-born persons. Parents, siblings, grandparents, aunts and uncles, and neighborhood playmates used a male name for a non-normatively gendered female. The renaming gives recognition that her way of being in the world, her "behavior," has, at least for the moment, overridden the cultural expectations incited by her female body and name assigned at birth; she needs to be renamed to reflect a correction of that early "mis-naming." Importantly, among the born-male persons with whom I talked and who had reported behaving like girls during childhood, and even though many reported acceptance and even encouragement (up to a certain age and within a range of generally presumed nonsexual behavior), none reported being renamed with a female name. Is this simply a reflection of a gender order of things: the superiority of the male and the shame of a superior kind lowering himself to the level of an inferior? Yet the acceptance of female behavior in a male child up to the proximity of adolescence may indicate that the fear of renaming him with a female name may have something to do with the fear that being called by a female name could contribute to his later growth into the abject sexuality of male same-sex-playing. This is not the case for girls who exhibit boyish behavior, possibly because non-normative sex for an adolescent male is received so much more badly than non-normative sex for an adolescent female.

As I emphasized in previous chapters, from the late 1970s and definitely critically so in the aftermath of establishment of the Islamic Republic in the decade of the 1980s, we have witnessed the differentiated twin birth of *gay* and MtF *trans* (and to a lesser degree of differentiation of *lesbian* and FtM *trans*). What I also want to emphasize is that the differentiation has not focused as much on bodily distinctions (definitely not a bodily distinction zeroed in on one's genitalia) as on living styles, that is, whether or not one opts generally to live as a woman-presenting born male or a masculine-presenting born female.

Boellstorff, in *A Coincidence of Desires*, writes, "Desire may feel like a product of the individual self, but it is shaped by the fields of culture, history, and power that Foucault referred to as discourses" (35). This articulation locates the contingency of the self (the desiring self) at a level beyond the person and the moment of self-presentation. Yet there is something incomplete here: the relationship between "the fields" and the contingency of an individual's sense of being in the world. To come out of the determinative tendency of certain Foucauldian analyses, to be able to think beyond being "called into being through a discourse" (36)—positively or negatively—Boellstorff proposes the notion of "coincidence of discourses." This is a powerful move that "raises the possibility of coincidental merging of discourses, wherein homosexual desire may appear as an *unexpected effect*" (36, my emphasis). In this sense, *gayness* has become shaped in part as an unexpected effect of not-*MtF*-ness in contemporary Iran. While in the 1970s, as Behzad had said, *gay* seemed to be a foreign word for *kuni*, it has become transformed through its distinction from *trans*. *Gay* has come to mean "I don't desire sex change." But even this reading needs to be attentive to the fact that the same person, in different contexts, may self-conceive the same characteristics differently. Recall Mehran's articulations— "before I had heard *trans*, before I had heard *lesbian*"—about herself, and thus the choices she made (to get married, not to pursue sex change in 1987, not even in 1997, but eventually to pursue it in 2008–9).

Indeed, as far as *gay* and *lesbian* identifications are concerned, the naming of these relationships as "same sex" remains contested. In part, the ability of naming them with non-Persian words is a move that distinguishes them from the culturally abject category of same-sex-playing and its affiliated assignations, such as kuni and baruni. Moreover, the very distinct roles within these relationships bring any notion of sameness between partners under pressure. As Johnson observed in a different context, ". . . the very notion of 'same-sex' sexuality seems highly problematic in a situation where having the same genitals apparently does not imply same sex or same gender, and where the genitals of the person one is having sex with are apparently much less important in defining gender, both theirs and one's own, than what those (same) genitals do."[65] It is this same dynamic that works against the dominant use of generalized terms (such as *homosexual*) and a strong tendency to reach for its contingent locale and time.[66] In Iran, generalized terms have taken root in scientific taxonomies and religious-legal policy considerations, but not in anything close to their ubiquitous use in Euro-American identity politics. One does not just reach for a generalizable and generalized term everywhere and at all times as if it is a universal innate sign of humanity. Yet the reach of these general categories clearly has spread beyond their initial time and locale, but not evenly, nor imperially, as it is sometimes assumed. Some may appear in medical/psychology texts, others in the legal domain, and still others in journalism. Some may overlap. And non-normative persons may use them for particular ends in specific sites to craft spaces of habitation. What one calls oneself generates possibilities for particular living arrangements. Sinnott, in the Thai context, has argued persuasively that becoming "a recognized social category—*toms*" rather than "females who are like men," a process that she dates to the past twenty-five years, has made the formation of "communities and subcultures around them possible" (63). Becoming known as *tarajinsiyati*—the newest official neologism for transsexual—has become a similar organizing category for Iranian trans persons.

At issue is not to deny that the increasing self-referential circulation of terms such as *gay*, *lesbian*, and so on among Iranians today may indicate a different and emergent conceptual mapping of sexual practices and desires; what is problematic is the privileging of this emergent naming and configuring as intrinsically superior to other modes of living nonheteronormative sex/gender lives. The current gay discourse on the Internet is saturated with such moralizing progressivist narratives, defining its own homo-normalizing contours against the foil of these "past" and/or oppressive behaviors, in particular against same-sex-playing as frivolous and necessarily exploitative.[67]

In this context, the shaping of an ambiguous nebula of overlapping and shifting assignations and (self-)cognitions—enabled by trans/same-sex/gender practices of everyday life and the legal legibility of trans as a category defined by the state, religion, or science—has had the paradoxical effect of re-inscribing the abjectness of the homosexual and at the same time providing a space of living a homosexual life within the legal shadow of transsexuality. This paradoxically productive and enabling double work does not have to acquire its resolution through disambiguation and pulling apart identity categories, separating and delineating trans from homo. While that is surely a possibility, other future configurations—in particular, living livable and loving lives within terms of ambiguity and contingent performances of selves-in-situational conduct—remains a powerfully attractive alternative.

# GLOSSARY OF PERSIAN TERMS AND ACRONYMS

*Terms*

baruni: literally means raincoat, used to refer to a woman's
    female lover/very intimate friend

baruni-bazi: girl-on-girl playing

bilataklif: in a conundrum

daujinsi: literally "of two sexes," it is the word used in contemporary
    Persian for the intersex, the fiqhi word for which is the Arabic *khunsá*.

fiqh/fiqhi/faqih: Islamic jurisprudence/jurisprudential/jurist

hamjins-gara'i: same-sex orientation

hamjins-baz, hamjins-bazi: same-sex-player, same-sex-playing

huviyat-i jinsi: gender/sexual identity

ikhtilalat-i jinsi: gender/sexual disorders

insiraf: dissuasion

intibaq: compliance (with Islam)

iva-khvahar: literally means "o'sister," used to mark male effeminacy
    in a derogatory manner

jahil-i mahall: tough guy of the neighborhood

javanmardi: chivalry

jins: genus, kind; more recently, sex/gender

kuni: literally "anal," used to refer to men presumed to be receptive
    of anal intercourse with other men

khunsá: hermaphrodite

liwat/lavat: sodomy

musahiqah: tribadism

nafs: self, psyche

ravan: psyche

ruh: soul/psyche

shinasnamah: book of identification

tara-jinsi: transsexuality

'u: pronoun used for he or she

zan-push: woman-attired male dancers and entertainers


## Iranian organizations and acronyms

Bihzisti: The Welfare Organization—Sazman-i Bihzisti, almost always simply referred to as Bihzisti (literally, "living well")

FtM: female-to-male trans person

GID: gender identity disorder

HHME: Ministry of Health, Healing, and Medical Education

ISNA: Iranian Students News Agency

IRIB: Islamic Republic of Iran Broadcasting, previously the National Iranian Radio and Television, or NIRT

ISSIGID: Iranian Society for Supporting Individuals with Gender Identity Disorder

IUMS: Iran University of Medical Sciences

LMOI: Legal Medicine Organization of Iran

MCI: Medical Council of Iran

MCIO: Medical Care Insurance Organization

MtF: male-to-female trans person

MWSS: Ministry of Welfare and Social Security

NAJA: Persian acronym for the Security Forces of the Islamic Republic

NIRT: National Iranian Radio and Television (now IRIB, Islamic Republic of Iran Broadcasting)

SRS: sex reassignment surgery

TPI: Tehran Psychiatric Institute

TUMS: Tehran University of Medical Sciences

## NOTES

### Introduction

1   The international effect of these television and video documentaries obviously deserves more than one line noting their quantity, but this is not a task I take up in this book. For a related essay, see Roshanak Kheshti, "Cross-Dressing and Gender (Tres)Passing: The Transgender Move as a Site of Agential Potential in the New Iranian Cinema." *Hypatia* 24, no. 3 (summer 2009): 158–77.

2   See, for instance, Doug Ireland, "Change Sex or Die: An Exclusive Interview with an Iranian Transgendered Activist on Iran's Surgical 'Cure' for Homosexuality." May 11, 2007, accessed March 2, 2013, http://direland.typepad.com/direland/2007/05 /change_sex_or_d.html.

3   Examples include an early short piece of mine, "Truth of Sex" (January 12, 2005, http://www.iranian.com/Najmabadi/2005/January/Sex/index.html); and, more substantively, Raha Bahreini, "From Perversion to Pathology: Discourses and Practices of Gender Policing in the Islamic Republic of Iran." *Muslim World Journal of Human Rights* 5, no. 1 (2008), http://www.bepress.com/mwjhr/vo15/iss1/art2/. For a critique of arguments that tend "to emphasize the transsexual's construction by the medical establishment . . . [in which] the transsexual appears as medicine's passive effect, a kind of unwittingly technological product: a transsexual subject only because subject to medical technology," see Jay Prosser, *Second Skins: The Body Narratives of Transsexuality* (New York: Columbia University Press, 1998), 7.

4   See Brady Thomas Heiner, "The Passions of Michel Foucault." *differences* 14, no. 1 (2003): 22–52.

5   Michel de Certeau, *The Practice of Everyday Life*, trans. by Steven Rendall (Berkeley: University of California Press, 1984), 48.

6   I borrow this concept from Gregory Pflugfelder, *Cartographies of Desire: Male-Male*

*Sexuality in Japanese Discourse—1600–1950* (Berkeley: University of California Press, 1999).

7 Ian Hacking, "The Looping Effect of Human Kinds," in *Causal Cognition: A Multi-disciplinary Debate*, edited by Dan Sperber, David Premack, and Ann James Premack, 351–94 (Oxford: Clarendon Press, 1995). The concept of "human kind" is close to Foucault's "species," as Hacking himself notes. I find Hacking's emphasis on its "looping effect" particularly attractive because it maps out more fully and actively the generativity of the processes of producing species/human kinds.

8 As George Steinmatz has put it, "Sometimes state-formation is understood as a mythical initial moment in which centralized, coercion wielding, hegemonic organizations are created within a given territory. All activities that follow this original era are then described as 'policy making' rather than 'state-formation.' But states are never 'formed' once and for all. It is more fruitful to view state-formation as an ongoing process of structural change and not as a one-time event." See George Steinmatz, ed., *State/Culture: State-Formation after the Cultural Turn* (Ithaca, NY: Cornell University Press, 1999), 8–9.

9 This is by no means unique to Iran, of course. See Lawrence Cohen, "The Pleasures of Castration: The Post-operative Status of Hijras, Jankhas, and Academics," in *Sexual Nature, Sexual Culture*, edited by Paul R. Abramson and Steven D. Pinkerton, 276–304 (Chicago: University of Chicago Press, 1995); Megan Sinnott, *Toms and Dees: Transgender Identity and Female Same-Sex Relationships in Thailand* (Honolulu: University of Hawai'i Press, 2004). In Persian academic texts as well as in mass media, jins and its various related conjugations are used for both gender and sex. See Behnam Ohadi, *Tamayulat va raftar-ha-yi jinsi-i insan* (Sexual desires and behaviors in human beings) (Isfahan: Intisharat-i Sadiq Hidayat, 2005 [2000]).

10 Within this body of literature, a zone of critical engagement has emerged between queer theory and "its evil twin," transgender studies (Susan Stryker's term). See Stryker, "(De)Subjugated Knowledges: An Introduction to Transgender Studies," in *The Transgender Studies Reader*, ed. Susan Stryker and Stephen Whittle, 1–17 (New York: Routledge, 2006).

11 Brad Epps, unpublished discussant's comments on draft of chapter 4 of this book, presented at the Harvard Humanities Center, Gender and Sexuality Seminar, September 30, 2009. See also Mieke Bal, *Travelling Concepts in the Humanities: A Rough Guide* (Toronto: University of Toronto Press, 2002).

12 See Anna Tsing's introduction to *Words in Motion*, edited by Carol Gluck and Anna Lowenhaupt Tsing, eds., 11–17 (Durham, NC: Duke University Press, 2009); and her "Adat/Indigenous: Indigeneity in Motion" in the same volume (40–64).

13 Persian words used are italicized on the first occasion only. Like Tom Boellstorff (*A Coincidence of Desires: Anthropology, Queer Studies, Indonesia* [Durham, NC: Duke University Press, 2007]), I italicize throughout words in Persian that have entered from English (though I exclude words that have entered long ago and have by now become absorbed as if Persian, such as "tiliviziun" for television) to mark their non-identicality with their English meanings. As these words enter Persian and are articulated within distinct "linkages, patterns, and discourses that give them meaning and social consequence" (Boellstorff, *A Coincidence of Desires*, 2), my writing them

back into an English text that will circulate in a different set of "linkages, patterns, and discourses" makes it important to keep that distinction visible, even at the expense of overloading this text with italics.

14 See Tani E. Barlow, "Theorizing Women: Funü, Guojia, Jiating," in *Body, Subject & Power in China*, edited by Angela Zito and Tani E. Barlow, 253–89 (Chicago: University of Chicago Press, 1994).

15 Deniz Kandiyoti, "Pink Cards Blues: Trouble and Strife at the Crossroads of Gender," in *Fragments of Culture: The Everyday of Modern Turkey*, ed. Deniz Kandiyoti and Ayse Saktanber, 277–93 (New Brunswick, NJ: Rutgers University Press, 2002).

16 Shahnaz Nadjmabadi (in "From 'Alien' to 'One of Us' and Back: Field Experiences in Iran." *Iranian Studies* 37, no. 4 [December 2004]: 603–12) discusses the problem of "native anthropologists inevitably [being] associated with government authorities. They are regarded with suspicion or else expected to act as mediators between local people and government agencies" (604). Nadjmabadi's fieldwork took place in several rural sites, largely in remote border regions, from the 1970s to the present. The kind of suspicion I faced, as a "native" arriving from the United States, was rather that of another "alien" arriving in the wake of numerous reporters and filmmakers from the other side of borders. Having arrived from "the outside"—*az kharij*—I was received as an outsider, a "foreigner"—a *khariji*. See also Mir-Hosseini, "Being From There: Dilemmas of a 'Native Anthropologist.'" In *Conceptualizing Iranian Anthropology: Past and Present Perspectives*, edited by Shahnaz R. Nadjmabadi, 180–91 (New York: Berghahn Books, 2009).

17 Despite the "nasty connotations" of this term, as Paul Rabinow notes, I am using it in the same spirit that he points out: referring to people who were critical "to give form, to be the formative principle of, to animate" my research. See Paul Rabinow, *Reflections on Fieldwork in Morocco* (Berkeley: University of California Press, 2007 [1977]), 153.

18 For a discussion of suspension of disbelief to account for belief, see Jaques Derrida, *Archive Fever: A Freudian Impression*, trans. by Eric Prenowitz (Chicago: University of Chicago Press, 1995), 94. For a critique of the demand to suspend disbelief put on anthropologists, see Rabinow, *Reflections on Fieldwork in Morocco*, 46–47. As Gayle Salamon observes in *Assuming a Body: Transgender and Rhetorics of Materiality* (New York: Columbia University Press, 2010), "one can acknowledge the ways in which this felt sense is a product of, and also subject to, cultural interpretations without disavowing or dismissing the persistent importance of this sense" (2–3).

19 de Certeau, *The Practice of Everyday Life*, 18.

20 de Certeau, *The Practice of Everyday Life*, xiv.


*Chapter 1: Entering the Scene*

1 Mehrzad, like several other names in Persian, is used both for males and females, but it is predominantly used for boys. When she saw my surprise in our first interview, she laughed and said her colleagues often told her that her interest in GID came from her given name. Dr. Seraji is a graduate of the IUMS; she is a psychiatrist who specializes in "sexual dysfunctions."

2　The commission is part of the TPI of the IUMS. It reviews all applications related to trans or intersex surgeries and makes a recommendation to the LMOI.

3　Indeed, this process has a second productive effect: "the state" itself becomes produced as an "effect," as a socio-discursive enactment of power through the competing, conflicting, and confirming work of distinct groups of persons who populate it and engage in innumerable daily practices within these domains. On production of "the effect of a state structure," see Timothy Mitchell, "The Limits of the State: Beyond Statist Approaches and Their Critics." *American Political Science Review* 85, no. 1 (March 1991): 77–96.

4　See also Tom Boellstorff, *A Coincidence of Desires: Anthropology, Queer Studies, Indonesia* (Durham, NC: Duke University Press, 2007).

5　Transsexual persons often are referred to as "*TS*" (pronounced as in English).

6　The presumption is that females are neat and press from the bottom up; males just squeeze the toothpaste tube randomly, usually from the middle.

7　The word *lesbian* is pronounced in Persian as in English. The standard transliteration would be *lizbian*, but I have opted to use the more familiar English spelling and italicize it.

8　Nonmedical therapy covered family therapy, couples therapy, group therapy, home visit, play therapy, behavior therapy, ergo therapy, cognitive therapy, hypnotherapy, and a sexology clinic, which everyone referred to as "the sex clinic." According to the guidebook of the Treatment Unit, the Nonmedical Therapy Clinic had been set up for two purposes: to offer educational services to graduate students in clinical psychology, psychiatry, speech therapy, and ergo therapy, and at the same time offer treatment services in the same fields as well as psychological tests to clients. Most of the people who go to the Treatment Unit are sent there by various state organizations, such as the LMOI, the Military Service Unit of the Army, and various medical commissions. The guidebook, prepared by Hamid Farzadi, is directed to the interns to teach them how to set up a case file and how to proceed in each case. One section of the guidebook explains the procedure for admitting a trans person. In addition to the LMOI, trans persons sometimes go directly to the Treatment Unit of the TPI, or are sent there by their private psychologists, to initiate a file and get the commission's approval for legal certification.

9　When I went there to sit in on a commission meeting in July 2007, I asked Mohseni-nia what she thought of the move. It is a nicer place, she said, but they [meaning the Sex Clinic] had lost their autonomy; "we are now part of the whole complex that deals with all kinds of problems, including drug addiction, etc."

10　Dr. Mehrdad Eftekhar, e-mail communication, August 2009.

11　See Farhad Khosrokhavar and M. Amin Ghaneirad, "Iran's New Scientific Community." *Iranian Studies* 39, no. 2 (June 2006): 253–67. There are huge ebbs and flows in the circulation of Iranian professionals with their international colleagues, following the pulse of the attitude of Iranian political leadership toward such collaborations, and the extent of the international sanctions imposed on Iran. Between the summer/fall of 2006 and summer of 2007, there was a noticeable change: Scientists who had been going to numerous international conferences and workshops had become more cautious and some withdrew from previous commitments. These were the months when Haleh Esfandiari, a scholar of the Middle East with the Wilson Woodrow Institute in Washington, D.C., and Kian Tajbakhsh, an Iranian-American social scientist and urban planner, were imprisoned on charges of fomenting internal dissension. Esfandiari was released in August 2007. Tajbakhsh was released in September 2007, but was re-arrested in July 2009 and sentenced to a twelve- to fifteen-year prison term. He was released in April 2010 but prohibited from leaving the country. For Esfandiari's account, see her book *My Prison, My Home: One Woman's Story of Captivity in Iran* (New York: Ecco, 2009).

12 For fuller elaboration, see Sayyid Mahdi Saberi and Mohammad Reza Mohammadi, *Nigarishi nau bah ravanpizishki-i qanuni* (A new look at legal psychiatry) (Tehran: Taymurzadah, 2005), 14–16; quote from page 16.

13 Once the LMOI confirms that a person has changed sex, a court ratifies that confirmation and orders the Registry (of *Ahval*, of birth and other life events such as marriage, divorce, children, and finally death) to issue a new book of identification, in which the old name is not recorded; however, there is a clause in the explanatory page of the new booklet saying this person has changed his or her name. None of these have been simply state handouts. Countless hours of lobbying by trans activists have been put into achieving every single one of these changes. Nor can any of these gains be taken for granted: Various state, medical, and religious authorities have their own agendas. At times, some of them overlap with the trans activists' agenda. At other times, there is conflict, which the activists have opted to pursue by finding allies within various government institutions and learning how to play one against the other. Trans activists have become incredibly skilled at this game. I will return to these issues in chapter 6.

14 However, the neighborly presence of Freud can be misleading. He is there more as a general respectable father (of psychology) rather than as representative of what many may associate with his name, namely psychoanalysis. Psychoanalysis has never found much resonance in Iran. The dominant subfield of psychology in Iran, reflected in the former title of its flagship journal, *Thought and Behavior*, has been behavioral psychology—an Iranian transplantation of American behavioral psychology.

15 For an insightful analysis of this double process, see Fariba Adelkhah, *Being Modern in Iran*, trans. by Jonathan Derrick. London: Hurst, 1999 [1st ed. Paris: Karthala, 1998].

16 As Adelkhah has noted, religious education, for example, has increasingly taken an academic shape. It is now more and more carried out "in buildings that are differentiated from sacred buildings, unlike the *hozeh* and *madreseh* of earlier times, and are laid out according to Western-type arrangements (classrooms, lecture and reading rooms, tables, chairs, laboratories, etc.); it lays down precise criteria for admission, for example criteria of age, marital status, military service, level of education, and often a contractual commitment; it involves regular assessment by examination; it can be given full-time, part-time, or by correspondence according to the pupils' preferences and means; it deals at the same time with Islamic matters, themselves more and more specialized, and extra-Islamic disciplines (foreign languages, sport, etc.)" (Adelkhah, *Being Modern in Iran*, 113–14). This process has important continuities

with the seminary-based educational system before 1979. For a thorough analysis of the latter, see Michael M. J. Fischer, *Iran: From Religious Dispute to Revolution* (Cambridge, MA: Harvard University Press, 1980), chapter 3.

17 Adelkhah, *Being Modern in Iran*, 38. Although I would argue that the paint-over metaphor could be misleading; much more complicated transformations have taken shape in that process, some of which Adelkhah brilliantly analyzes in her book.

18 Both Dr. Mehrabi himself and the younger cohort also have worked to produce clinically based research on sexuality. See, for instance, Masoud Ahmadzad-Asl, Mehrdad Eftekhar, Amir Jalali, Kaveh Alavi, and Morteza Naserbakht, "Gender Identity Disorder; Transsexualism in Iran: Epidemiological Aspects of Iranian Model." Unpublished paper, 2009; and Mehrdad Eftekhar and Nahaleh Moshtagh, "Transsexualism—Iran," in *The Encyclopedia of Women in Islamic Cultures*, edited by Suad Joseph, Afsaneh Najmabadi, Julie Peteet, Seteney Shami, Jackie Siapno, and Jane I. Smith (Leiden: Brill, 2007). Both Eftekhar and Moshtagh are among Dr. Mehrabi's junior colleagues. In addition to working with Dr. Mehrabi and at the TPI, Dr. Eftekhar works in several other public and private places, including the Kausar Infertility Clinic and the Sexual Dysfunction Clinic in Farmaniyah, as well as his own private practice. He also supervises graduate-level research at the TPI. Several recent dissertations have been written on transsexuality, including Reza Bidaki, "A Study of FtM Transsexuals' Perspectives on Sexuality and Sex-change"; Amir Husayn Jalali, "Determining the Prevalence of High Risk Behavior and HIV Contamination in Persons Afflicted with Gender Identity Disorder"; and Azadeh Baghaki, "A Study of Perspectives and Sexual Practices of Transsexual and Homosexual Patients of Tehran Sexual Disorders Clinic in 2007–08 [1386]," doctoral dissertations, Medical School of IUMS, 2008. For a fuller list of MA and PhD dissertations on transsexuality, see the online catalog of National Archives and Library of Islamic Republic of Iran, key word *taghyir-i jins*.

19 Interview with Dr. Faridun Mehrabi, June 2006.

20 Faridun Mehrabi. "Barrisi-i barkhi az vizhigiha-yi 'tabaddul-khvahi-i jinsi' dar bimaran-i Irani" (Some Characteristics of Iranian Transsexualists [the journal's translation]). *Andishah va raftar* 2, no. 3 (winter 1996): 6–12. The article offered a basic report of the distribution of various factors in the population under study (age, levels of literacy, categories of employment, reasons for seeking consultation, who referred them, sexual orientation, psychological profile, and structure of families); reviewed the existing literature on transsexuality; and compared some of the numerical results with similar figures from European and American studies. Not until the winter of 2004 did two more articles on transsexuals appear in this journal. The first—Hamid Reza Attar and Maryam Rasulian, "*Tashkhis-i avvaliyah-i ikhtilal-i huviyat-i jinsi*" (First Diagnosis of Gender Identity Disorder: Case Report). *Andishah va raftar* 9, no. 3 (2004): 6–11—reported on the case of one female-born, forty-year-old person who had undergone six operations between 1997 and 2000 to become a man, yet after living for the brief period of only one month as a man had returned to the LMOI and requested to be changed back to a woman. The article recommended more careful interviews and supervised therapy. The second article, in the same issue, was authored by Khodayarifard, Mohammadi, and Abedini. I will discuss this

article more fully below. Clinic-based studies have been reported in other scientific journals in later years. See, for instance, Hejazi et al., "A preliminary analysis of 12 transsexual patients with regards to their adaptation in means of role and gender identity after a sexual reassignment surgery" (in Persian). *Scientific Journal of Kurdistan University of Medical Sciences* 13 (winter 2009): 78–87.

21 Husayn Ranjbar Shayan, "Barrisi va muqayiseh-i vizhigiha-yi shakhsiyati-i afrad-i mubtala beh ikhtilal-i huviyat-i jinsi va afrad-i bihanjar" (Investigating and comparing the personality traits of persons afflicted with gender identity disorder and normal persons), MA thesis in Clinical Psychology (no. 233), TPI, IUMS and Health and Treatment Services, winter 1999.

22 The MMPI-2 questionnaire was translated, adapted, and adopted through the work of earlier master's theses. See Fereshteh Mutabi and Ali Shahrami, "Preparation and normalization of MMPI-2 questionnaire for Tehran." MA thesis, TPI (IUMS), 1995.

23 A primary example is Hannah and Abraham Stone's *A Marriage Manual*, initially published in English in 1935. First translated into Persian and published in 1948, it has undergone numerous retranslations and reprints. At least twelve different translators have retranslated this text. Each translation has been reprinted numerous times—as often as nineteen in a single decade, sometimes by different publishers. One translation has been used to produce an audio version for the blind. I will discuss these texts further in chapter 2.

24 These books include psychologically inflected analyses of literary figures such as Sadiq Hidayat and Furugh Farrukhzad.

25 The catalog of National Archives and Library of the Islamic Republic of Iran listed nine books (several into multiple printings) and fourteen articles by Ohadi on March 13, 2011.

26 The blogs include www.iranbod.com, www.1ravanpezeshk.com, www.atashgah.com, and 1sexologistonline.blogfa.com.

27 Ohadi considers himself to be a sexology pioneer. See his interview with a monthly magazine, *Firdausi*, nos. 60–61, published on his own blog: http://iranbodonline .blogfa.com/post-291.aspx. The posting date is March 10, 2008. I do not have the magazine's date.

28 From the preface to the fifth edition of *Tamayulat va raftar-ha-yi jinsi-i insan* (Sexual desires and behaviors in human beings) (Isfahan: Intisharat-i Sadiq Hidayat, 2005 [2000], 3), by Dr. Firuzeh Ra'isi, director of the Clinic for Treatment of Sexual Problems in Rouzbeh Hospital.

29 From the preface by Dr. Khalil Mu'mini, also a psychiatrist (in *Tamayulat va raftar-ha-yi jinsi-i insan* [Sexual desires and behaviors in human beings] [5th ed.], by Behnam Ohadi. Isfahan: Intisharat-i Sadiq Hidayat, 2005 [2000], 16).

30 See, for instance, Ohadi, *Tamayulat va raftar-ha-yi jinsi-i insan*, chapter 6 on the psychology of sexual puberty, 132–36.

31 For a selection of, and a critical introduction to, this literature, see Gillian Einstein, ed., *Sex and the Brain*, Section V: Dimorphisms and Identity (Cambridge, MA: MIT Press, 2007). See also Rebecca M. Jordan-Young, *Brain Storm: The Flaw in the Science of Sex Differences* (Cambridge, MA: Harvard University Press, 2010).

32 Behnam Ohadi, "Va khudavand TS ra azmun-i adam afarid" (And God created TS

to test human/Adam). *Ravanshinasi va jami'ah* (Psychology and society) 33 (June/
July 2006): 18–23; and Behnam Ohadi, "Vizhigiha-yi tasvirbardari-i maghz-i afrad-i
duchar-i ikhtilal-i huviyat-i jinsi dar muqayisah ba afrad-i salim" (Particularities of
brain images of persons afflicted with gender identity disorder in comparison with
healthy persons). *Fasl-namah-i tazah-ha-yi 'ulum-i shinakhti* (Advances in Cognitive
Science) 9, no. 3 (fall 2007): 20–25.

33  See "A Psychiatrist," http://1ravanpezeshk.blogfa.com/post-268.aspx, accessed September 12, 2009.

34  In the preliminary prepublication version of the paper (I am grateful to Dr. Ohadi
for making a copy available to me), there was an English abstract that was not included in the print version. I reproduce the abstract here without editing (only spelling errors have been corrected):

> "**Abstract**: The comparison of brain imaging characteristics between transsexuals
> and normal individuals.
> **Objective**: The aim of this study was to compare the brain imaging characteris-
> tic of transsexuals with normal individuals. **Method**: In this descriptive analyti-
> cal study 30 persons were selected by sequential sampling in two control and
> case groups that had the inclusion criteria and did not have the exclusion cri-
> teria from patients admitted to Rouzbeh Hospital and forensic medical organi-
> zation. demographic information such as height, weight, head circumference
> and BMI were obtained and brain MRI performed by 3D FSE method. collected
> data were analyzed by Analyze volumetric software (Mayo Foundation, Roches-
> ter). Red nucleus, CSF, intradural and parenchima volume and Corpus callosum
> area were analyzed statistically using T-test Pearson correlation coefficient tests.
> **Results**: Red nucleus volume difference between case and control groups were
> significant. difference of red nucleus, parenchyma and IDV volume between male
> and females were significant too. In addition there was no significant difference
> in red nucleus volume between male patients and normal females but the differ-
> ence between female patients and normal males was significant. **Conclusion**: In
> this study difference in brain anatomical structure between transsexuals and
> normal individuals observed. It seems that maybe sometime in the process of
> development and CSF differentiation in prenatal period and intrauterine life brain
> anatomical structure changed and does not follow the normal pathway consis-
> tent with one's gender. **Key word**: Gender identity disorder, transsexualism, brain
> imaging, MRI volumetry."

35  See the GID of Iran website, Open Forum section, entry dated May 24, 2009
(3 Khurdad 1388), signed by Roham. The heated discussion continued to be an important theme in the postings for several months around this period.

36  For a similar point, see Boellstorff, *A Coincidence of Desires*, 50–51.

37  For instance, Shahrzad, an MtF in her early thirties, had taken hormones on her
own for many years, had developed a female bodily shape, and lived as a woman.
She had her atrophied testes removed—all with no legal navigation. For the time
being, she had no plans for any further surgeries.

38  I use "the habit" (and "going into the habit") in the sense of clothing, of "a distinc-

tive dress or costume," as dictionaries define it. The reason for this odd translation of *libas* (and *dar libas raftan*) is to emphasize the drastic effects of the move because of the state-required, and vastly different, styles of public dress for men and women. The decision "to go into the habit" is particularly transformative of daily life experiences for MtFs who, beyond their ordinary eyebrow plucking and use of makeup, would have to wear headscarves and shift to a style of dressing in public that is always under scrutiny by "morality squads" for all women.

39 Amini, *Farzand-i bimar-i tabi'at* (Nature's sick child), a three-part special produced for the program *Yad-i yaran*, Omid-E-Iran Television (OITN, a Persian-language satellite channel) in 2005. OITN was established by Nader Rafiee, who had been a director/producer of Channel 56 in California in 1985–87. A Los Angeles–based cable TV production begun in 1995, it later acquired satellite broadcast capabilities. It produces a variety of news, entertainment, and social and current events programs (all information is from the station's website). Like the other LA-based satellite TV channel, Jaam E Jam, it enjoys a popular reception in Iran, although the government's policy of the day dictates whether or not it is jammed and how hard the government will crack down on satellite dishes. The Khatami presidency (1997–2005) generally exhibited more leniency toward such outside cultural productions, so that they were able to be seen in Iran. One indication of that leniency was that a local producer, such as Amini, was permitted to produce programs in Iran that would get beamed back to Iranian audiences via the LA-based OITN when Seda va Sima (the Iranian National Radio and Television) would not air a similar program.

40 As one transsexual said: "Any young person walking into the Mirdamad clinic is immediately welcomed as a certain *trans* needing surgery." She added, only half-jokingly, "You mean you haven't been told yet that you are really FtM? They haven't set you up with an appointment?"

## Chapter 2: "Before" Transsexuality

1 I discuss this conceptual shift more fully in "Genus of Sex or the Sexing of Jins," *International Journal of Middle Eastern Studies* 45 (2013), 211–31.

2 Before the emergence of national dailies, recordings of hermaphrodites (*khunsá*) can be found in memoirs. See, for instance, Qahriman Mirza 'Ayn al-Saltanah, *Ruznamah-i khatirat-i 'Ayn al-Saltanah*, volume 1, 704, entry dated 29 Sha'ban 1312 (February 24, 1895) and volume 4, 2970, entry dated 11 Dhihajjah 1327 (December 24, 1909).

3 "Tabdil-i zani bah mardi," *Ittila'at*, 28, September 14, 1926, 2. The title could also be translated as change of womanhood to manhood.

4 *Ittila'at*, February 2, 1930, 3.

5 Examples include Huriah Sajjadi, a young woman of eighteen, who had changed her name from Fatimah to Qudrat, considered him/herself a "perfect [*tamam 'ayar*] and zealous [*ghayratmand*] man who has beaten boys in bicycle races and boxing matches" (*Ittila'at-i banuvan*, June 17, 1963, 12, 75); of Gul Muhammad Aqa Tajiani (female name: Gulistan Burumand) in Mashhad, who twenty-five years earlier had escaped an abusive husband and had since dressed as a man and worked as a porter

and, later, as an auto mechanic and an assistant driver along the Mashhad-Chinaran bus line (*Zan-i ruz*, March 1965 special issue, 12–14). These reports usually had a positive tone, cast in terms of women's ability to live decent lives against odds. Reports on men living women's lives were cast very differently, as we will see in chapter 4.

6   *Khvandaniha*, May 4, 1948, 13–14.

7   Reports of male masseurs in women's baths continued to surface, though with less frequency, as changes in urban domestic arrangements and the introduction of showers into middle-class homes reduced the use of public baths in large cities.

8   *Mihrigan*, April 5, 1935, 11. On this case, see Joanne Meyerowitz, *How Sex Changed: A History of Transsexuality in the United States* (Cambridge, MA: Harvard University Press, 2002), 33–34. See also Anne Fausto-Sterling, *Sexing the Body: Gender Politics and the Construction of Sexuality* (New York: Basic Books, 2000). Other sports-related accounts in the Iranian press include a report about Erika/Eric Schiendler (*Zan-i ruz*, November 15, 1975, 24–25, 67), all the way to the recent case of Caster Semenya in 2009 (http://tabnak.ir/fa/pages/?cid=60452).

9   *Khvandaniha*, June 20, 1947, 19; *Khvandaniha*, August 1, 1950, 20; and *Ittila'at*, March 31, 1954, 3, respectively.

10  Alice C. Hunsberger, "Marvels." *Encyclopaedia of the Qur'ān*. General Editor: Jane Dammen McAuliffe, Georgetown University, Washington, DC. Brill Online, 2013. Reference. Harvard University. April 19, 2013 http://referenceworks.brillonline .com/entries/encyclopaedia-of-the-quran/marvels-SIM_00274. For a gender analysis of some of this literature, see Fedwa Malti-Douglas, *Woman's Body, Woman's Word: Gender and Discourse in Arabo-Islamic Writing* (Princeton, NJ: Princeton University Press, 1991), chapter 5.

11  See *Ittila'at*, November 18, 1954, 3.

12  I am grateful to Hujjat al-Islam Karimi-nia for bringing this case to my attention. He refers to this case as the "first transsexual surgery in Iran." The details of the report point to what today would be categorized as intersex. These genealogical distinctions have emerged in recent decades, both in Iran and elsewhere, as politically significant. See, for instance, Jay Prosser's discussion of Stephen of *The Well of Loneliness* as prefiguring FtM transsexuality rather than lesbianism (*Second Skins: The Body Narratives of Transsexuality* [New York: Columbia University Press, 1998]). In Iran, although the jurisprudential discourse has moved away from deriving its acceptance of trans sex change from classic rules dealing with hermaphrodites, keeping a connection remains important. While Hujjat al-Islam Karimi-nia understands transsexuality in terms of discordance between the sex/gender of the body and that of the soul (see chapter 5), against the clerical opponents of transsexuality—who connect it to "sexual deviation," thus arguing for its prohibition—keeping some connection to intersexuality continues to provide a fiqhi safeguard.

13  The law requiring all Iranians to choose a family name and register with the Office of Personal Status Registration was passed in 1925 and modified in 1928; its implementation took several years and remained very uneven, especially outside major urban centers. In Kubrà's case, for instance, no family name is specified. S/he is identified patrilineally, a common practice of the time. The expression in her/his letter is "*Kubrá, valad-i Tahir Sultan*." *Valad* literally means offspring, but usually it

is used to mean son. For daughters, other expressions, such as *sabiyah* or *bint*, were used during this period.

14　*Namah-i mahanah-i danishkadah-i pizishki* (Monthly Gazette of School of Medicine). For more details, see Moslem Bahadori and Mohammad-Hossein Azizi, "The First Medical Journal of Tehran University," in *History of Contemporary Medicine in Iran*, accessed November 16, 2007, http://www.ams.ac.ir/AIM/07103/0029.htm. On the development of modern medicine and state construction, see Cyrus Schayegh, *Who Is Knowledgeable Is Strong: Science, Class, and the Formation of Modern Iranian Society, 1900–1950* (Berkeley: University of California Press, 2009).

15　Jahanshah Salih, *Bimariha-yi zanan va pishraftha-yi 'ilmi-i nuuvin (Gynecological Diseases and New Scientific Advances)* (1960; 1st ed., n.p., 1939). Later editions bear Tehran University Press as publisher.

16　For more on Salih, see Muhammad Mahdi Muvahhidi, *Zindiginamah-i mashahir-i rijal-i pizishki-i mu'asir-i Iran* (Biographies of famous men of medicine in contemporary Iran), vol. me 1 (Tehran: Nashr-i 'Ulum va Funun, 1992), 150–216.

17　The section on "double-sexedness or hermaphrodism" appears on pages 261–91 in the 1963 edition, which I have used here. "Two-sexedness" is a translation of *dau-jinsi*. This expression itself emerged in this period to replace the more classical *khunsá* for referring to hermaphrodites and then began to be used for trans persons until very recently.

18　At least one intern, Javad Ghafurzadah, wrote his final dissertation (School of Medicine, Dissertation no. 2018) on this topic under Salih's supervision. Dr. Ghafurzadah later performed surgeries in Tus Hospital. Another intern, Dr. Yahya Behjatnia, who completed his obstetrics/gynecology specialization in 1962–63 in the Women's Hospital under Salih's supervision, became part of the team in that hospital that carried out sex surgeries in the 1970s. He recalled that what had initially drawn his attention to sex-change operations was what he had read in Salih's textbook (interview with Yahya Behjatnia, December 2007). Both Dr. Behjatnia and Dr. Amir Movahhedi (also interviewed in December 2007) stated that in the Women's Hospital only intersex surgeries took place and that trans sex surgeries were not considered legal and authorized. I will discuss this issue in chapter 4.

19　The word used in Persian for genital/sexual/reproductive is *tanasuli*. While it is most accurately close to "reproductive," in much twentieth-century medical and popular writings it is also used for "sexual" and "genital." In this section of Salih's text, for instance, it is used to refer to "reproductive glands," "reproductive differentiation of the fetus," "reproductive eminence" in cellular development, primary and secondary "reproductive characteristics," and "reproductive abnormalities." For further discussion of the work of the term *reproductive* [*tanasuli*] in the emerging concept of "sex" in this period, see Najmabadi, "The Genus of Sex."

20　The detailed instructions are covered in Cilardo, "Historical Development of the Legal Doctrine Relative to the Position of the Hermaphrodite in the Islamic Law." *The Search* 2, no. 7 (1986): 128–70; and Paula Sanders, "Gendering the Ungendered Body: Hermaphrodites in Medieval Islamic Law," in *Women in Middle Eastern History: Shifting Boundaries in Sex and Gender*, edited by Beth Baron and Nikki Keddie, 74–95 (New Haven, CT: Yale University Press, 1991).

21 *Khvandaniha*, May 7, 1951, 22–23; May 11, 6–7; May 14, 6–7; and May 18, 6. *Ittila'at*, May 14, 1951, 7. *Khurasan* was a morning daily published in Mashhad, edited by Muhammad Sadiq Tihranian (d. 1988). See Husayn Ilahi, *Ruznamah va ruznamah-nigari dar Khurasan* (Newspapers and journalism in Khurasan) (Mashhad: Firdawsi Mashhad University Press, 2001), 172–76.

22 The magazine often has been considered a Persian equivalent of *The Reader's Digest*, and indeed it occasionally carried translations of material from that publication. Amirani's initial decision to launch it, however, does not seem to have been informed by a desire to replicate that journal. The idea of publishing "the reading worthies" was suggested to him by the director of *Ittila'at*, 'Abbas Mas'udi. See Bastani Parizi, "Ittila'at-i mukhlis va mukhlis-i *Ittila'at*" (My information as a fan of *Ittila'at*). In *Ittila'at: 80 sal huzur-i mustamarr* (*Ittila'at*: 80 years of continuous presence) (Tehran: Ittila'at, 2006), 16–40.

23 For these reasons, *Khvandaniha* serves as a good window into the press of the time and its reception. It is also important that, unlike a number of other popular magazines of shorter duration (such as *Rawshanfikr*, *Tihran-i musavvar*, and *Sipid va siyah*), it was published regularly (with rare interruptions due to censorship) through 1979. Amirani was executed on spurious charges shortly after the revolution as part of the purges against the cultural elite of the old regime held responsible for the political and moral corruption of the country.

24 I owe the expression "vernacular science" to Tani Barlow. Barlow invokes the emergence of vernacular sociology in China as a field that was discursively productive for and related to how advertisements marketed a particular set of modern girl commodities. She analyzes advertisements themselves as pedagogical texts that popularized scientific notions about health and hygiene, skin care, women care, and so on. See Barlow, "Buying In: Advertising and the Sexy Modern Girl Icon in Shanghai in the 1920s and 1930s," in *The Modern Girl Around the World: Consumption, Modernity, and Globalization*, edited by Alys Eve Weinbaum et al., 288–316 (Durham, NC: Duke University Press, 2008).

25 The American Missionary Hospital in Mashhad was founded by Dr. Cook in 1916. See Sadeq Sajjadi, "Bimarestan," *Encyclopaedia Iranica*, accessed May 11, 2011, http://www.iranica.com/articles/bimarestan-hospital-.

26 *Ittila'at*, August 6, 1972, 17. Apparently 'Alizadah had a womb that was taken out during his sex-disambiguation surgery. He stated that at birth he had evident though imperfect female organs but his parents had wanted a son and thus raised him as male and no one except for the parents ever knew his khunsá condition. He expressed pride in his popularity among neighborhood girls.

27 Examples include Fatimah 'Asgari, twenty-two years old, who became male in Abadan (*Kayhan*, July 20, 1969, 15); Ihtiram Jalilian, seventeen years old, who became male in Kirmanshah (*Kayhan*, January 17, 1970, 1, 15 and January 18, 1970, 15); Fattanah (no last name), now Muhsin, who was operated on in Europe and went to court to get a divorce from a current husband (*Kayhan*, May 8, 1973, 22–23); 'Ayishah (no last name), now Ghulamriza, twenty-two years old, from Bandar 'Abbas, who was operated on in Bushihr (*Kayhan*, October 24, 1973, 18); 'Abd al-Hadi 'Asgarzadah, thirty-one years of age, became male in Abadan (*Kayhan*, April 16, 1974, 2).

28 See, for example, Fatimah (no male name selected yet), seventeen years old from Shahrud, operated on in Tehran (*Kayhan*, February 11, 1970, 12).

29 *Ittila'at*, September 5, 1953, 10.

30 *Scoop* (January 1954, 56–57) and *Vue* (June 1954, 30–31), the Library of the Kinsey Institute: "Transexualism, Vertical File 2," and "Transexualism, Vertical File 1," respectively. Joanne Meyerowitz kindly brought this case to my attention. Farjadi's case also was reported in Carroll Hotchkiss's "His or Hers" page: "Christine in Reverse: The Hush-Hush Choice 150,000 'Girls' Must Make," *Uncensored* (October 1955): 31–22, 73; the Library of the Kinsey Institute, "Transexualism, Vertical File 1."

31 Examples include "A wondrous event in Tehran," *Ittila'at*, March 30, 1955, 1, 4, and April 1, 10 (reprinted in *Khvandaniha*, April 5, 1955, 5). *Kayhan* (August 26, 1972, 9) reported on sex-disambiguating surgery performed on a forty-five-year-old woman (Salimah Ibrahim) without her/his consent. Salimah had gone to a hospital for a hernia operation, during which s/he was changed to a man (and renamed Sulayman). Upon learning of her/his new status, s/he had objected to the surgery and refused to dress as a man or cut her/his hair short, emphasizing that having lived all her/his life as a woman, s/he could not at this age return to her/his small town (near Bushihr) as a man. I have found only one report of sex-disambiguation surgery on a child, reported in *Kayhan* (January 23, 1973, 23). It is possible that the increased availability of information about intersex individuals had encouraged the parents to take initiative at an early age.

32 *Kayhan*, December 22, 1969, 15.

33 Reprinted in *Khvandaniha* (April 28, 1959, 57, from *Pars*). I have not been able to find the original report. Another report, under the column heading "From Nature's Wonders," covered the case of the man who had had an earlier married life as a woman, given birth to a son, and later changed sex. "This man has given birth to a son!" *Zan-i ruz*, April 24, 1976, 12–13.

34 *Ittila'at*, October 28, 1948, 8 (back page).

35 *Tihran-i musavvar*, October 29, 1948, 2. This satirical poem became quite popular. Almost sixty years later, Dr. Yahya Behjatnia recited several of the lines (interview, December 2007).

36 *Khvandaniha*, December 20, 1969, 12. Sex change as a trope for articulation of emasculating anxieties was used in several other stories and reports, including *Khvandaniha*, April 27, 1954, 32; and *Tihran-i musavvar*, October 22, 1954, 14–15. I am grateful to Pamela Karimi for providing me with a copy of this story.

37 *Khvandaniha*, December 23, 1952, 11. On this episode, see Christine Jorgensen, *Christine Jorgensen: A Personal Autobiography* (San Francisco: Cleis Press, 2000), 145, the veracity of which she denied. Other reports of this genre included those of Forbes Semphill (*Khvandaniha*, December 23, 1952, 10); Elizabeth Call (*Ittila'at*, March 17, 1954, 3); Charlotte McLeod (*Ittila'at*, April 17,1954, 3); Vince Jones (*Khvandaniha*, October 30, 1954, 7); Juliet (from Mexico, formerly Julius, no last name given in report, reported in *Khvandaniha*, March 22, 1955, 27); Edwin Emerton (*Khvandaniha*, December 29, 1955, 4); Robert Allen (*Khvandaniha*, January 12, 1956, 25–26, reprinted from the health journal *Tandurust*); Roberta Cowell (*Khvandaniha*, January 21, 1956, 22–23, reprinted from the women's weekly *Ittila'at-i banuvan*;

again in *Khvandaniha*, November 18, 1958, 20; again *Khvandaniha*, April 28, 1959, 14; and again in *Ittila'at-i banuvan*, May 27, 1963, 35); Rollando Cassioti (*Khvandaniha*, November 18, 1958, 18–19); April Ashley (*Khvandaniha*, July 28, 1962, 46–47, reprinted from *Sipid va siyah*); and Jeanette Jiousselot (*Khvandaniha*, December 5, 1967, 22–23).

38  November 8, 1953, 11.

39  *Kayhan*, February 17, 1973, 19. This is the earliest non-intersex sex-change surgery reported in the Iranian press that I have found. The reported involvement of the Legal Medicine Organizations of the two cities distinguishes this report from those on intersex surgeries. Because there were no professional guidelines in place at this time, it is possible that the doctors had sought permission from the LMOs to prevent any future liabilities.

40  I have not found any data on its early frequency. Nor have I come across any FtM surgeries during this period.

41  *Kayhan*, October 11, 1976, 5.

42  *Khvandaniha*, December 23, 1952, 10–12.

43  A similar narrative informed the article that framed postsurgery photographs of Roberta Cowell and Rollando Cassioti (*Khvandaniha*, "Changing women and men to the other [sex/gender] has become one of the simplest surgeries," November 18, 1958, 18–19, a translation of an article from *Home*). See also an article from *Sipid va siyah*'s (reprinted in *Khvandaniha*, July 28, 1962, 46–47, framing pre- and post-operative photographs of April Ashley). By the mid-1960s, Harry Benjamin and the Johns Hopkins Clinic had become familiar topics. See *Khvandaniha*, October 11, 1967, "Changing sex is no longer a difficult challenge!" 36–37. Reprinted from *Ittila'at-i banuvan*.

44  "Men who like to exhibit themselves as women: Louis XIV's brother was such a man," *Khvandaniha*, August 2, 1958, 26–29. This article was part of the serialization of the translation of the book *Love Without Fear: How to Achieve Sex Happiness in Marriage* by Eustace Chesser (New York: Roy Publishers, 1947). See also *Khvandaniha*, December 5, 1967, 22–24; and *Khvandaniha*, April 25, 1959, 52–54 (reprinted from *Umid-i Iran*), for a report about men and women changing sex as linked with moral decay, not "the real sex-change people" but those who do it to make a living.

45  Sayyid Imami, "Why some men have a womanly temperament and some women develop manly behavior," reprinted from *Tandurust* in *Khvandaniha*, July 30, 1951, 21–23. *Tandurust* (*The Healthy Body*), founded in 1947 by Sayyid Imami, was oriented to the educated public.

46  *Khvandaniha*, August 11, 1959, 50–51 (reprinted from *Tandurust*).

47  *Khvandaniha*, January 27, 1968, 43–44 (reprinted from *Tandurust*). See also *Khvandaniha*, February 21, 1970, 47–49. Sayyid Imami's concern over deviant sexualities reflects a larger alarmist consideration over moral laxities as society entered the early 1970s. This issue will be discussed at length in chapter 4.

48  A. Costler and A. Willy, *The Encyclopedia of Sexual Knowledge* (New York, Eugenics Publishing, 1936; 1st ed. France, 1933; Persian translation [Tehran: Intisharat-i Farrukhi, 1946]).

49  Occasional articles about Freud and the developmental view of human sexuality had

appeared in the press of the 1930s and, more frequently, in the periodicals of the 1940s. For one example, see A. Shaki, "Gharizah-i jinsi" [Sexual instinct], *Ittila'at-i haftigi*, December 26, 1941, 10, 19. I am grateful to Cyrus Shayegh for providing me with a copy of this article.

50 Costler and Willy, *The Encyclopedia of Sexual Knowledge*, 248.

51 Mir Ahmad Hashimi-Fard, *Masa'il va ikhtilalat-i jinsi dar zan va mard* (Sexual problems and disorders in woman and man) (Tehran: Chihr, 1963; reprint 1969), 11.

52 *Natavaniha-yi jinsi khaud ra ba ghaza mu'alijah kunid* (Cure your sexual impotency with food), 7–8. I have used a 1976 reprint. No publisher. First publication is unknown, but it continues to be reprinted—the seventh reprint is dated 2003.

53 Hasan Hasuri, *Raftar-i jinsi bar payah-i siksaufiziulauzhi* (Sexual behavior on the basis of sexo-physiology) (Tehran: Tahuri, 1968), v. The English title (as printed on the back cover) reads "*A Textbook of Psychophysiological Sexology.*"

54 "*Raz-i kamyabi*" refers to *Raz-i kamyabi-i jinsi* (Secrets of sexual fulfillment), written by Ma'sumah 'Azizi Burujirdi (d. 1961), better known by her stage name Mahvash, a well-known singer, dancer, and actor in popular Persian films in the 1950s. The work was published in 1957 (no publisher). See Kamran Talattof, *Modernity, Sexuality and Ideology in Iran: The Life and Legacy of a Popular Female Artist* (Syracuse, NY: Syracuse University Press, 2011); and Farzaneh Milani, *Veils and Words: The Emerging Voices of Iranian Women Writers* (Syracuse: Syracuse University Press, 1992), 220.

55 Hasuri, *Raftar-i jinsi bar payah-i siksaufiziulauzhi* (Sexual behavior on the basis of sexo-physiology), 5.

56 Hasuri, *Raftar-i jinsi bar payah-i siksaufiziulauzhi*, 7. He returns to the subject of transsexuality and homosexuality several times in different chapters, such as chapter 4, "Children's Sexual Behavior" (144–46, 176–77); and chapter 5, "Adolescent Sexual Behavior" (212, 222–25), before a full discussion in chapter 11, "Sexual Deviations."

57 In the tradition of Iranian texts of this period, he does not specify male, but his discussion indicates that the unmarked person is male. This section is followed by a section titled "female hamjins-bazi."

58 An example of the first genre is Muhammad Mahdi Muvahhidi's *Az mabahis-i pichidah-i bimariha-yi zanan va mama'i* (On complex topics related to gynecology and obstetrics) (Tehran: Shirkat-i Sahami-i Chap va Intisharat-i Kutub-i Iran, 1966); of the second is his *Danistaniha-yi zanashu'i* (Marital know-how) (Tehran: n.p., 1966), with a preface by Jahanshah Salih. First published in 1966, it went through at least twelve reprints into the 1990s. A selection of his columns in *Zan-i ruz* was published as a book, *Razha-yi salamat* (Tehran: 'Ilmi, ca. 1976).

59 Reprinted in Muvahhidi, *Razha-yi salamat*, 24–27.

60 *Baruni* (literally meaning "raincoat") is used to refer to the "active" partner in a female-female relationship. I have not been able to find its sociolinguistic genealogy. In nineteenth-century Qajar texts, the word *malhafah* (covering sheet) is used, possibly indicating the jurisprudential definition of two naked women under the same sheet. Rebecca Stengel has pointed out (personal communication) that in Pahlavi *abaruni* meant abominable and sinful. Whether the two are related needs further research.

61 In an interview reprinted in the book, Muvahhidi again reiterated Hasuri's exact arguments, this time using another one of the names Hasuri had used (Hamid/Hamidah). As a well-known case of transvestism, he referred to the reported case of a masseur in women's baths who turned out to be male after many decades of working there in exactly the same terms that Hasuri had used for this very example. Like Hasuri, he referred to Jorgensen as the first transsexual and gave exactly the same statistical information about the number of transsexuals in the United States.

62 Compare, respectively, 79–81, 244–46, and 248 in Muvahhidi's *Razha* with 102–4, 514–17, and 520 in Hasuri's work.

63 While I have focused on Hasuri and Muvahhidi to map out the intricate relationship between vernacular and academic sexology, numerous other authors and many weeklies and dailies form part of the same geography of sexual science in these decades. For another prominent example, see Ibrahim Ja'far Kirmani, *Naujavani* (Adolescence) (Tehran: Chihr, 1970).

64 For a fuller discussion of the points argued in this segment, see Afsaneh Najmabadi, *Women with Mustaches and Men without Beards: Gender and Sexual Anxieties of Iranian Modernity* (Berkeley: University of California Press, 2005).

65 In recent decades, particularly since 1979, there has been a new coming together of this vernacular psychology with Islamic writings on sexual desire, the sexual needs of youth, and marital relations.

66 See Cyrus Schayegh, *Who Is Knowledgeable Is Strong: Science, Class, and the Formation of Modern Iranian Society* (Berkeley: University of California Press, 2009).

67 Misbahi Nuri, *Dastur-i izdivaj* (Marriage prescriptions), a revised and expanded version of *Husn-i izdivaj* (Benefits of marriage) (n.p., 1925). Misbahi Nuri authored at least one other book in the same period: *Tali'ah-i nur* (The rising of light), "a collection of 25 scientific, health, historical, and ethical essays" (n.p., 1927).

68 For instance, it echoed classic Islamic medical treatises when it argued that women who had too big a clitoris were infertile and took no interest in having intercourse with men. Instead, they took women as lovers. Cutting the extra length of the clitoris was the solution (24–26). Similarly, his argument that as a result of the way some women's seed interacted with men's seed, some boys became girlish and some girls became boyish (33–41), drew on classic Islamic discourse.

69 Two were translated by Suhrab: *Rahnuma-yi mardan az nazar-i bihdasht va zanashu'i* (Guidance for men on hygiene and marriage), and *Rahnuma-yi pisaran* (Guidance for boys). More titles were translated by Nusratallah Kasimi, a physician and a publicist. These include *Anchah bayad yik javan bidanad* (What a young man ought to know) (n.p.; 1st ed. 1937, at least four reprints); *Anchah bayad har zan-i shawhardar bidanad* (What every married woman ought to know) (Tehran: Kumish, 1994 [sixth reprint]); *Anchah bayad har mard-i zandar bidanad* (What every married man ought to know) (Tehran: Shirkat-i Mu'allifan va Mutarjiman-i Iran, 1990); and *Anchah bayad har dukhtar bidanad* (What every girl ought to know) (Tehran: Kumish, 2006 [eighth reprint]; 1st ed. 1974).

70 Tarazallah Akhavan's translation (Tehran: Gulsha'i, 1997) has been reprinted at least eight times by this publisher, at least nine times by Arghun, and by two other publishers as well. I have used the 2001 edition of his translation. At least twelve dif-

ferent translators have retranslated this text. Each translation has been reprinted numerous times—as often as nineteen in a single decade, sometimes by different publishers.

71 Akhavan's translation, however, restores the full text. It uses the revised and expanded 1965 English edition, as revised by Gloria Stone Aitken and Aquiles J. Sobrero (New York: Simon and Schuster, 1965). The first English edition had appeared in 1935. All later translations were also from the 1965 edition.

72 These periodicals included *Salamat-i fikr* (Mental Health), *Masa'il-i Iran* (Iran's Problems), *Danishmand* (Scientist), *Mahnamah-i shahrbani* (Police Monthly), *Pizishk-i khvanivadah* (Family Physician), *Ravanshinasi* (Psychology), *Huquq-i mardum* (People's Rights), *Majallah-i 'ilmi-i nizam-i pizishki* (Scientific Gazette of the Medical Association), *Talash* (Struggle), *Ittila'at-i haftigi* (Weekly *Ittila'at*), *Ittila'at-i banuvan* (*Ittila'at* for Women), and *Zan-i ruz* (Today's Woman).

73 These included René LaForgue and René Allendy, *Encyclopedia of Love*, translated from French and serialized in 1953, and Chesser, *Love without Fear*, serialized translation in 1957 and 1958. Most well known were the later serializations of the two books by David Reuben, *Everything You Always Wanted to Know about Sex but Were Afraid to Ask* (New York: HarperCollins, 1969); and *Any Woman Can! Love and Sexual Fulfillment for the Single, Widowed, Divorced, and Married* (New York: David McKay, 1971), in *Khvandaniha* in its 1970–71 issues.

74 See, for instance, *Khvandaniha*'s serialization of *Love without Fear*, June 18, 1957, 28–29; June 22, 1957, 36–37; June 25, 1957, 28–30; March 15, 1958, 24–26; June 24, 1958, 26–29.

75 Homosexual desire and practices as disrupters of marital peace continued to figure prominently. *Zan-i ruz*'s column "Mushkil-gusha" (Problem-solver) regularly ran letters from readers who were concerned about their sexual inclinations—almost always framed as worries about marital performance. The male writer of a letter, for instance, published in the Nauruz 1353 (March 1974) issue of the magazine (102), was concerned that he was "afflicted by the ailment of homosexuality" and was scared that he would not perform on his wedding night, despite his desire to form a family and have children. The magazine's "problem-solver" assured him that he was only scared of being homosexual, that a certain degree of homosexual desire was natural in every person, that his fears were understandable given how girls and boys were brought up and the kinds of fears about heterosexual relations that were cultivated in them. See also *Zan-i ruz*, April 6, 1974, 70, and May 4, 1974, 66, for other performance fear–related letters.

76 See "Men who like to make themselves look like women: Louis xiv's brother was such a man," *Khvandaniha*, August 2, 1958, 26–29; "People Afflicted with Sexual Deviancy Are Not Criminals," *Khvandaniha*, June 28, 1958, 26–29; *Khvandaniha*, August 11, 1959, 50–51; and *Khvandaniha*, April 18, 1960, 42 (the latter two reprinted from *Tandurust*).

77 See articles reprinted from *Ma'rifat-i pizishki* (Medical knowledge) in *Khvandaniha*, January 19, 1956, 22–26, and January 24, 1956, 31–32.

78 *Khvandaniha*, February 12, 1963, 40–41.

79 *Khvandaniha*, September 15, 1959, 68–69.

80    See note 49 above on Mahvash's *Raz-i kamyabi*. *Asrar-i magu* was an anthology of sexually explicit jokes, apparently collected by the essayist and poet Mahdi Suhayli (1924–87).

81    *Khvandaniha*, November 16, 1963, 10–11; November 19, 1963, 10–11; November 23, 1963, 10–11, 46; November 26, 1963, 10–11, 43.

82    *Khvandaniha*, November 23, 1963, 10.

83    *Khvandaniha*, November 26, 1963, 10. For similar articles, see "Madaris va muhas-silin-i ma" (Our schools and students), *Khvandaniha*, November 30, 1963, 12; and "Madaris-i ma va digaran" (Schools: Ours and others), *Khvandaniha*, December 3, 1963, 10–11; "Azadi-i rabitah va ravabit-i azad ya harj va marj-i jinsi" (Freedom of relations and free relations or sexual chaos), reprinted in *Khvandaniha* March 30, 1971, 28–30, from *Kanun-i sardaftaran* (a publication of the Association of Heads of Notaries). Another anonymous essay objected to the teaching of *Lady Chatterley's Lover* as part of the curriculum of the English Department of Tehran University (*Khvandaniha*, November 25, 1972, 12, 47–48). While I have concentrated my read-ing through *Khvandaniha* (and what it reprinted from other magazines), this is a topic that was covered in numerous magazines and dailies in these decades. For another example, see *Tirhan-i musavvar*, which ran a regular column, "Our special doctor answers readers' questions." Its winter 1955 segments were devoted to "Over-coming sexual defects, deviations, and problems."

84    *Khvandaniha*, January 2, 1973, 11–12, reprinted from *Nigin*.

85    *Khvandaniha*, November 24, 1973, 14–15, 40, reprinted from *Ziba'i va zindigi*. See also *Khvandaniha*, December 15, 1973, 5; Muhammad 'Ali Ahmadvand, "From genu-ine and pleasant art to putrefied and vulgar [*mubtazal*] art: Artless actors and those who employ art at the service of sex and profit," in *Khvandaniha*, January 19, 1974, 17–19, 36–37, condensed and reprinted from *Farhang va hunar*.

86    See *Khvandaniha*, June 11, 1974, 4; October 26, 1974, 4; February 23, 1974, 4; April 22, 1978, 8.

87    Cyrus Schayegh, "Serial Murder in Tehran: Crime, Science, and the Formation of Modern State and Society in Interwar Iran." *Comparative Study of Society and History* 47, no. 4 (October 2005): 836–37.

88    His books included *Amraz-i zuhravi (muqaribati)* (Venereal diseases) (1931) and *Ma-lish va tamas* (Massage and touch) (Tehran, 1931); the latter on the ill consequences of "unnatural regenerative relations, such as masturbation, tribadism, and rub-bing (*tabaq-zani, musahiqah*), and Sapphism"; and another on male same-sex prac-tices (*'ubna and liwat*). For a full discussion of Tutia within the context of the estab-lishment of medical sciences and practices, see Schayegh, *Who Is Knowledgeable Is Strong*, chapter 6. For Schayegh's discussion of Tutia's use of Asghar Qatil in *Amraz-i ruhi*, see his article, "Serial Murder in Tehran: Crime, Science, and the Formation of Modern State and Society in Interwar Iran." *Comparative Study of Society and History* 47, no. 4 (October 2005): 836–62.

89    In addition to this timely publication, Tutia published the introduction of the book as an article in his monthly magazine, *Sihhat-numa-yi Iran*. See Muhammad 'Ali Tutia, "Maraz-i ruhi: Sadizm" (A disease of the soul/psyche: sadism). *Sihhat-numa-yi Iran*, 2, no. 3 (June/July 1934): 74–77.

90   My copy of this text has only a used cardboard cover. "*Zan va mard*" is the title that is handwritten in ink on the cardboard. This text is an interesting hybrid. In a brief introduction, the translator, Y. R. Y., explains that the original text had been published in England and created quite a stir in Parliament, and that, unlike most books on marital relationships, its author was a woman. This is a reference to Marie Stopes (1880–1958), a distinguished paleobotanist, writer, and activist in the birth-control movement in Britain, with a strong belief in eugenics. See Ross McKibbin's "Introduction," in *Married Love*, by Marie Stopes and edited by Ross McKibbin (Oxford: Oxford University Press, 2004), for more on her life and writings. *Married Love* was translated into Arabic by the Egyptian doctor, writer, and publisher Niqula al-Haddad, which provided the original for the Persian. The Persian translation of 103 pages has twelve photographs of skimpily covered or totally nude women in sexually suggestive poses. Like the scientific articles on sex that were often bordered with sexually suggestive female photographs, this genre of sensational science seems to have become a feature of sexological literature in these decades.

91   *Ittila'at*, June 28, 1955, 1, 10, "Diruz dar shiraz duvvumin Asghar qatil-i 'asr-i hazir bi'i'dam mahkum shud" (Yesterday in Shiraz the second Asghar, the murderer, of the current age was sentenced to death). More details of this case appeared in *Ittila'at*, December 26, 1955, 1, 4; *Ittila'at*, December 27, 1955, 1. See also *Khvanda-niha*, "Muhakimat-i pur-sar-u-sida-yi Iran: Az Asghar qatil ta Hasan Gharavi" (Iran's sensational trials: From Asghar, the murderer, to Hasan Gharavi), August 3, 1959, 6–9. The inaugural issue of the annual publication *Ittila'at-i sal* covered a selection of what had been considered significant in all the issues of *Ittila'at* published up to 1960. The one-page initial special issue of *Ittila'at*, breaking the Asghar Qatil story, was included in this selection (402–3). This same volume also included the news of Muhammad Hadi Muravvij's death sentence with the same original title, "The second Asghar the murderer was sentenced to death" (421; reprinted from the June 28, 1955, issue).

92   For further discussion of this point, see chapter 2 of my book *Women with Mustaches and Men without Beards*.

93   See my brief discussion of this distinction in "Types, Acts, or What? Regulation of Sexuality in Nineteenth-Century Iran," in *Islamicate Sexualities: Translations across Temporal Geographies of Desire*, edited by Kathryn Babayan and Afsaneh Najmabadi (Cambridge, MA: Harvard University Press, HCMES series, 2008), 275–96.

94   November 13, 1951, 8.

95   In a way this distinction echoed the old debates between the differing views of Razi and Ibn Sina on *'ubna*, although there is no indication of a familiarity with this earlier corpus in the texts of the new sexologists. See Franz Rosenthal, "Ar-Razi on the Hidden Illness." *Bulletin of the History of Medicine* 52 (1978): 45–60.

96   Mas'ud Ansari, *Jara'im va inhirafat-i jinsi* (Sexual Crimes and Deviancies) (Tehran: Gauhar/Amir Kabir, 1961); expanded and retitled as *Psychology of Sexual Crimes and Deviancies* (Tehran: Ishraqi, 1973). Quotes are from the preface (1–3), of the 1961 edition.

97   I have used the second edition of de River's book, published in 1956; two more printings of the first edition appeared in 1950 and 1951.

98  On two topics about which Ansari could not provide a case from de River, he made a reference to an example of "voyeurism" reported in *Kayhan* (131–33), without giving much detail of the case. In another case, as an example of incest, he reproduced at length the story of a young woman who had unknowingly fallen in love with a paternal uncle, as reported in the weekly *Raushanfikr* (154–58).

99  Robert Buffington, *Criminal and Citizen in Modern Mexico* (Lincoln: University of Nebraska Press, 2000). "For late-nineteenth- and early-twentieth-century Mexican criminologists, sexual deviance of any kind was unnatural, antisocial, and linked to innate criminality" (130).

100  Buffington, *Criminal and Citizen in Modern Mexico*, 133.

101  This publication appeared in four volumes: volume 1 (Tehran: Tehran University Press, 1979); volume 2, 1981 (reprinted 1991). I do not have publication dates for the other volumes.

102  These include *Criminological Sciences* in three volumes (Tehran: Tehran University Press, 1966–1967); *Introduction to Law* (Tehran: Tehran University Press, 1969); and translations from the French of three books by Raymond Gassin.

103  The French copy to which I have had access is the 9th French edition (Paris, Presses universitaires de France, 1962 [1943]).

104  First published by 'Ilmi, then taken over by Kitabha-yi Jibi and eventually by Franklin Publishers. At least seventy titles in the series *Chah midanam?* (What do I know?) were published before 1979. Many of them were reprinted over and over again, including Debesse's *L'Adolescence*, which had at least five reprints (though Kaynia's references are to the French). Some seventy-one titles have appeared since 1979.

105  *Khvandaniha* (reprinted from *Danishmand* [*The Scientist*]), August 31, 1976, 38–42. This section is on page 41. All quotes are from this section.

106  For similar arguments, see Ahmad Human (university professor and lawyer), "Three Examples of Sexual Deviation in Tehran, Tabriz, and Paris," *Khvandaniha* (reprinted from *Huquq-i mardum* [People's Rights]), April 30, 1977, 59–62; and May 7, 1977, 62–65.

107  See Buffington, *Criminal and Citizen in Modern Mexico*. Buffington argues for the significance of criminality in the imagining of modern Mexico, "the dialectic between criminality and citizenship in Mexico as manifested in the intertwined discourses of criminology, penology, and anthropology" (7). For a similar dynamic among science, class, and citizenship, with more of an emphasis on the centrality of psychopathology, in Argentina's modernity, see chapter 3 in Julia Rodriguez, *Civilizing Argentina: Science, Medicine, and the Modern State* (Chapel Hill: University of North Carolina Press, 2006).

108  Buffington has argued that, "because it lacked a strongly politicized subtext, female homosexuality was effectively marginalized." For men, "sex was politics—male politics" (*Criminal and Citizen in Modern Mexico*, 140).

### Chapter 3: Murderous Passions, Deviant Insanities

1   *Zan-i ruz*, December 8, 1973, 18–21, 97–98, 100. "Homosexuality" in this quote was in Persian a transliteration of the French "*homosexualité*." The journal used interchangeably hamjins-bazi (same-sex-playing), *humausiksualitah* (*homosexualité*), and hamjins-gara'i (same-sex orientation). Indeed, through the coverage of this story, these words, along with related slang terms such as baruni-bazi (girl-on-girl playing), found mass circulation in print that may indeed have been the first of its kind. The more commonly used hamjins-bazi and baruni-bazi had heavy derogatory loads; hamjins-gara'i was of newer vintage, a move away from that very load toward more neutral psychologically informed views. This is the term that has now become accepted as Persian translation of homosexuality. In this chapter, I will translate hamjins-gara'i into "homosexuality" or "same-sex orientation," but keep the other terms in their transliterated forms.

2   On the self-assigned role of the modern press in Iran as moral guardians, see Amin's doctoral dissertation, "The Attentions of the Great Father: Reza Shah, 'The Woman Question,' and the Iranian Press, 1890–1946." University of Chicago, 1996.

3   I have resisted, with great difficulty, comparing this story with that of Alice Mitchell and Freda Ward as analyzed by Lisa Duggan in "The Trials of Alice Mitchell: Sensationalism, Sexology, and the Lesbian Subject in Turn-of-the-Century America" (*Signs: Journal of Women in Culture and Society* 18, no. 4 [1993]: 791–814), from which I have learned a great deal. The familiar reader will note numerous similarities. One reason for avoiding a "competitive comparativism" (a term I borrow from Brad Epps, "Comparisons, Competitions, and Cross-Dressing: Cross-Cultural Analysis in a Contested World," in *Islamicate Sexualities: Transformations across Temporal Geographies of Desire*, edited by Kathryn Babayan and Afsaneh Najmabadi [Cambridge, MA: Harvard University Press, 2008], 114–60) between the two is the way each has and can be "read forward." Duggan reads that "love murder" forward to a later emergence of a lesbian identity: "Her love for other women was neither temporary nor complementary to heterosexual marriage . . . [but] seeds of a new identity" (809). It is difficult, at least as yet, to *read forward* Mahin's presentation as the "seeds of a new identity" that would, in future, emerge as a publicly visible lesbian in Iran. It presents itself and is configured by the press as a total dead end, with a possible chink that admits the possibility of sex change.

4   See, for instance, "Dau madar va yik chubah-i dar" (Two mothers and one gallows), *Zan-i ruz*, January 3, 1976, 12–13, 82.

5   Here as well, his fate and the class imbrications of that outcome were in common with those of Asghar Qatil. For a full discussion of this issue, see Cyrus Schayegh, "Serial Murder in Tehran: Crime, Science, and the Formation of Modern State and Society in Interwar Iran." *Comparative Study of Society and History* 47, no. 4 (October 2005): 836–62.

6   *Ittila'at*, November 29, 1973, 18.

7   *Ittila'at-i banuvan*, July 31, 1974. "Up there, Zari is waiting for me! In the Court that sentenced Mahin to life in prison, the shameful and abnormal details of girls' loves were revealed" (11, 82).

8   *Ittila'at*, November 29, 1973, 18.

9   The Literacy Corps was an alternative to the compulsory two-year army service for high school graduates.

10  One of these articles, provocatively titled, "Tragedy of the night of consummation and virginity!" apparently got her and the journal into deep trouble with social conservatives. Interview with Pari Sekandari, July 15, 2008.

11  These articles appeared in the following issues, respectively: October 6, 1973, 8–9, 90, 93; October 13, 1973, 8; March 9, 1974, 16–17, 102; December 22, 1973, 18–21, 98; December 29, 1973, 20, 94, 98.

12  A very anecdotal and inadequate poll of several Iranian women, now in their fifties and sixties, indicated that every one of them remembered the Mahin/Zahra story. They all agreed that this was the topic of conversation for months.

13  *Zan-i ruz*, August 3, 1974, 12.

14  *Zan-i ruz*, December 8, 1973, 18.

15  Phonetically transliterated French words have provided the vocabulary through which scientific concepts as well as many daily object words (such as telegraph, telephone, and television) have found their way into Persian since the mid-nineteenth century. In more recent decades, in particular domains such as Internet and computer-related vocabulary, English has displaced French.

16  As argued in earlier chapters, this language already had been developed in earlier decades and had entered into some popular magazines. But *Zan-i ruz*'s coverage of the Mahin/Zahra story brought a singular focus onto homosexuality for a larger, and largely female, mass readership.

17  *Zan-i ruz*, August 10, 1974, 10.

18  Mahin's carrying of a switchblade knife (chaqu-yi zamindar) became a reiterative trope that signified her wicked masculinity. It constituted a "minor detail" that provided cultural overkill and that persisted in the minds of readers. It remained one of the details remembered by an Iranian woman in her forties who had followed this case in the press as a girl of ten.

19  *Zan-i ruz*, December 15, 1973, 8.

20  For reasons of space, I have had to be selective in translating the full letter. "[. . .]" indicates my edits. For full text of the letter, see *Zan-i ruz*, August 10, 1974, 87.

21  *Kayhan*, July 23, 1974, 18. See also *Zan-i ruz*, August 10, 1974, 86.

22  *Ittila'at*, July 21, 1974.

23  Meaning Zahra and, since her death, Mahin, as a "living dead"—bodily alive, dead in spirit.

24  *Zan-i ruz*, July 27, 1974, 12.

25  *Ittila'at*, July 23, 1974, 18.

26  *Ittila'at*, July 24, 1974, 14; July 25, 1974, 15.

27  *Zan-i ruz*, August 20, 1974, 87.

28  *Ittila'at*, July 21, 1974, 54.

29  This sentiment, carried from the culture of male-female love to female-female relations in which butch lesbians pride themselves in the expression of ghayrat toward their femme partners, seems to continue to shape many lesbian relations in today's Iran, as will be discussed in chapter 7.

30   *Kayhan*, July 24, 1974, 13–14.

31   *Zan-i ruz*, December 15, 1973, 99.

32   *Zan-i ruz*, December 15, 1973, 99.

33   *Zan-i ruz*, December 15, 1973, 26.

34   *Zan-i ruz*, December 15, 1973, 27.

35   *Zan-i ruz*, December 15, 1973, 27.

36   *Zan-i ruz*, "Why does a girl, or a boy, become homosexual?" December 22, 1973, 16–17, 99–100; "Why did Mahin not run away after killing Zahra?" December 29, 1973, 16–17, 92, 103; "Knowing a homosexual girl?!: How does one know if a girl is a true *homosexuelle?*" January 5, 1974, 28–29, 98; "Why do men and women become *homosexuelle?*" January 12, 1974, 24–25, 87; "Male supremacy [*mardsalari*] is the main root of *homosexualité!*" January 19, 1974, 24–25, 80; "Can *homosexuelles* be cured?" January 26, 1974. I have not had access to this issue.

37   *Ittila'at-i banuvan*, July 24, 1974, 8, 85; July 31, 1974, 11, 82, and an article, "Why does a girl become homosexual?" (10, 83).

38   *Ittila'at-i banuvan*, July 31, 1974, 83.

39   *Zan-i ruz*, "Homosexuality in girls' schools!" January 5, 1974, 29, 98.

40   *Zan-i ruz*, August 3, 1974, 7, 86.

41   I have not had access to the court records. The following account is based on newspaper reports. For my argument concerning the mass circulation of concepts about (homo-)sexuality the court records are not critical, but for the way this case may (or may not) have gone into the later legal configuration of transsexuality, it may be pertinent. However, the radical shift in the legal system of the country in 1979—including its criminal and civil codes—would not allow for a smooth continuity of court cases into future decades.

42   *Ittila'at*, July 18, 1974, 4.

43   The excerpts from the diaries and letters and the interviews mentioned here were published, respectively, by *Ittila'at* in the July 24, 1974, 1, 14, and July 25, 1974, 15, issues; *Kayhan* on July 23, 1974, 3; and *Zan-i ruz* on July 27, 1974, 10–12, 86–88.

44   *Ittila'at*, July 4, 1974, 14.

45   *Zan-i ruz*, July 27, 1974, 10.

46   Both sets of ellipses are in the original.

47   *Zan-i ruz*, August 3, 1974, 12.

48   *Ittila'at*, July 23, 1974, 18.

49   *Ittila'at*, July 24, 1974, 4, 14.

50   *Ittila'at-i banuvan*, July 31, 1974, 82.

51   Segments of these verses were reported in several papers; the full text here is translated from *Zan-i ruz*, August 10, 1974, 86.

52   Mahin's lawyers immediately filed an appeal. Unlike Razzaq-manish's case, the press seems to have lost interest, and I have not found any reports about Mahin's appeal process. Pari Sekandari (interview, July 2008) confirmed that Mahin had served several years of her term but had committed suicide in jail. I have not found any reports of her suicide, either.

53   *Zan-i ruz*, July 27, 1971, 86.

54   I am using "bi-/homosexual" as uncomfortable shorthand. Neither of these cate-

gories was in general circulation in Iran at the time. As we have seen, homosexuality was beginning to acquire a place, but since men who had same-sex relations often would at some point marry women, the category of "two personality" worked to capture this phenomenon.

55 I will discuss Farrukhzad and the emerging "gay and transwomen" life in Tehran of the 1970s in the next chapter.

56 *Ittila'at*, July 22, 1974, 4.

57 *Zan-i ruz*, July 27, 1974, 12.

58 For a full articulation of the stance of the press on this issue, see *Zan-i ruz*, August 10, 1974, 10–11, 84, 86–88.

59 *Ittila'at*, July 21, 1974, 54.

60 *Ittila'at*, July 27, 1974, 16.

61 See, for instance, *Ittila'at*, July 27, 1974, 18, with the huge headline: "Razzaq-manish appeals his sentence" and a smaller item: "Mahin's appeal was submitted to the court."

62 *Ittila'at-i banuvan*, July 24, 1974, 85.

63 See *Kayhan*, October 16, 1973, 8. This case took up the full "Events" page on two subsequent days. Its coverage slowly received less space, but it continued for the next three days. Once the prosecutor asked for a death sentence in mid-November, it regained its news prominence.

64 *Ittila'at*, October 23, 1973, 18.

65 *Zan-i ruz*, August 10, 1973, 8–9, 83–85.

66 My thanks to Mali Kigasari for making this account, which had been reported to her, available to me. Several other self-identified lesbians, now in their late forties and early fifties, similarly recalled how this episode and the press reports had made a lasting impression on them. Another writer, twenty years old at the time of the event, wrote a barely fictionalized account with a somewhat different plot line, in which Mahin (named "Moheen" in the novel) is helped by a female lawyer who goes from Tehran to Rasht and finds out that the actual murderer was a young man who was supposed to marry Zahra. The spurned lover-turned-murderer theme is thus preserved, but with a heterosexual twist. Nonetheless, because of the corruption of the courts, Moheen is convicted, only to be rescued from imprisonment through an elaborate escape from jail. See Behjat Riza'ee, *The Moonlike* (London: Bra Books, 1991). For a review of this book, see Nilgun, *Homan*, no. 9 (November 1994): 43.

## Chapter 4: "Around" 1979

1 See, for instance, Janet Afary, *Sexual Politics in Modern Iran* (Cambridge: Cambridge University Press, 2009), 243; Firoozeh Papan-Matin, "The Case of Mohammad Khordadian, an Iranian Male Dancer." *Iranian Studies*, 42, no. 1 (February 2009): 128.

2 Jerry Zarit, "The Iranian Male—An Intimate Look," *GPU* [Gay Peoples Union] *News*, October 1979, 19–24. The quote is from page 19.

3 David Reed, "The Persian Boy Today: Sexual Politics in Teheran," *Christopher Street*, August 1978, 14–17. As the title of his report indicates, the search for a gay paradise

in Iran was informed in part by the publication and enormous popularity of Mary Renault's *The Persian Boy* (New York: Pantheon, 1972). See, for instance, Jim Kepner's review in *The Advocate*, January 31, 1973, 26.

4  Reed, "The Persian Boy Today," 15.

5  Reed, "The Persian Boy Today," 15.

6  Reed, "The Persian Boy Today," 16.

7  For reports of persecutions and executions in the early months and years of the establishment of the Islamic Republic, see *The Advocate* 266, May 3, 1979, 7; 267, May 17, 1979, 7, 12–13; 276, September 20, 1979, 17; 281, November 29, 1979, 12; 283, December 27, 1979, 8; and 293, May 29, 1980, 12. See also *Homan* 16 (spring 2000): 16–17 for Iranian newspaper clips of executions from this period on the charge of lavat (sodomy). See also Afary, *Sexual Politics*, 265. In much of such coverage, it is routinely said that Islamic law prohibits homosexuality—even though there is no notion of homosexuality in Islamic law—or that the Islamic Republic made homosexuality a capital offense and that gay men are executed in Iran on charges of or for open expressions of homosexuality. On this issue, as far as recent executions and the international campaigns are concerned, see Scott Long, "Unbearable witness: How Western activists (mis)recognize sexuality in Iran." *Contemporary Politics* 15, no. 1 (March 2009): 119–36. The slippage is important for contemporary politics of sexuality in Iran. I will come back to further discussion of this issue in the final chapter.

8  The two domains are highly interactive: Jerry Zarit's article in *GPU News* was translated and published in one of the earliest diasporic Iranian gay journals, *Homan*, published first in Sweden (the first issue dated May/June 1991) and later in the United States. See *Homan* 5 (April/May 1992): 2–5.

9  In these distinctions, what is often lost is the very modernity of hamjins-bazi itself. The nineteenth-century vocabulary of what is at times conceived of as the prehistory of modern same-sex relations—such as *amrad-bazi* ("playing" with a male adolescent), *'ubnah-'i* ("afflicted" with a desire for anal penetration), and *bachchah-bazi* ("playing" with a young person)—did not place the two sides in a single category (jins) of person, whether in a pejorative sense (same-sex player) or in its more recent recuperation as same-sex orientation. Only in the twentieth century did jins come to mean sex as well as its earlier meaning of genus, so "hamjins" became a term that doubled the sense of sameness, as "of the same kind and of the same sex." Even today, some people in same-sex relationships do not recognize themselves to be of the same kind. As Mahan, a young man in an intimate relationship with another man, reacted to hearing their relationship referred to by a self-identified gay man as hamjins-gara (same-sex oriented), "But we are not of the same jins, we are not of the same kind [*nau'*]. We are so different" (conversation with author, June 2007).

10 See, for instance, Avaz, "Tafavut-i 'hamjins-gara' ba 'hamjins-baz' va 'bachchah-baz' dar chist?" (What is the difference between the "same-sex inclined" and the "same-sex-player" and "child-player"), *Homan* 9 (October/November 1994): 27–33. Avaz seems unaware of emergence of the concept of hamjins-gara in the Iranian discourses of psychiatry and criminology of the 1960s and 1970s (as we saw in chapter 2) and suggests that hamjins-gara is a new expression of unknown origin in Per-

sian (29, 32). My point is not to criticize the adoption (consciously or otherwise) of the concept from this earlier discourse for one's own identification, but rather that the ahistorical consciousness may have contributed to the progressivist invocation of hamjins-gara against hamjins-baz and bachchah-baz. For a more recent example, see Payman, "Hamjins-gara'i ya hamjins-bazi?!" (Same-sex-orientation or same-sex-playing?!), *Neda* 19 (June 2010): 14–15.

11 See Sima Shakhsari, "From Hamjensbaaz to Hamjensgaraa: Diasporic Queer Reterritorializations and Limits of Transgression." Unpublished paper, c. 2003.

12 For a feminist critique, see Janet Jakobsen, *Working Alliances and the Politics of Difference: Diversity and Feminist Ethics* (Bloomington: Indiana University Press, 1998).

13 *Khvandaniha*, June 30, 1956, 29 (reprinted from *Payam*). For other reports of women opting to live and work as men, see *Ittila'at-i banuvan*, June 17, 1963, 12, 75; *Zan-i ruz*, special New Year's issue, March 1965, 12–14.

14 Tse-Ian D. Sang, *The Emerging Lesbian: Female Same-Sex Desire in Modern China* (Chicago: University of Chicago Press, 2003), 92–95. I thank Martha Vicinus for bringing Sang's work to my attention.

15 *Zan-i ruz*, December 22, 1973, 18–21, 98; and December 29, 1973, 20, 94, 98.

16 See chapter 2 of Afsaneh Najmabadi, *Women with Mustaches and Men without Beards: Gender and Sexual Anxieties of Iranian Modernity* (Berkeley: University of California Press, 2005) for some examples of "keeping a young man" (*amrad-dari, adam-dari*), as it was then called.

17 *Khvandaniha*, May 4, 1947, 13–14.

18 *Kayhan*, January 5, 1977, 2, and again January 6, 1977, 1.

19 See chapter 2 for further discussion of these cases.

20 *Khvandaniha*, January 29, 1955, 20–22.

21 Anthony Shay, "The Male Dancer in the Middle East and Central Asia," *Dance Research Journal* 38, no. 1–2 (2006): 137–62. Quotes are from pages 137 and 138, respectively.

22 Shay, "The Male Dancer," 139.

23 Anthony Shay, "Choreographic Hypermasculinity in Egypt, Iran, and Uzbekistan." *Dance Chronicle: Studies in Dance and the Related Arts* 31, no. 2 (2008): 211–38. The quote is from page 234.

24 Shay, "The Male Dancer," 139.

25 *Zan-push*, literally meaning "dressed in women's clothes," refers to male actors who played women's roles in traditional theatrical performances, whether in passion plays (*ta'ziah*) or in *ruhauzi* plays (literally "over the pond," because the stage was provided by covering a garden pond with planks of wood) at celebratory occasions. For an important analysis of different styles of enacting female personas in these plays, see William O. Beeman, "Mimesis and Travesty in Iranian Traditional Theatre," in *Gender in Performance: The Presentation of Difference in the Performing Arts*, edited by Laurence Senelick, 14–25 (Medford, MA: Tufts University Press, 2002). The expression zan-push has now become part of trans vocabulary for MtFs who change to female clothes. I will discuss these transplantations in chapter 7.

26 *Khvandaniha*, October 1, 1955, 37. Parenthetical asides in the original. Other issues of this journal similarly carried news and photographs of male actors in female

roles. See the October 13, 1955, issue 37 for a picture of Majid Muhsini (an actor) in women's clothes, replacing a female actress who was sick on that performance day. See also the issues of December 22, 1955 (39), for a picture of another male actor, Mr. Hushmand, in another production of the play *Charley's Aunt* in Rasht; of January 12, 1956 (39), for Tabish again as Charley's aunt; and of March 21, 1961 (98), for pictures of four male actors, Tabish, Vahdat, Qanbari, and Bahmanyar, all in female roles. The journal had similar brief reports on non-Iranian performances of male actors in female roles. See September 1, 1959, 16 (Jack Lemon and Tony Curtis trans-dressed as female musicians in *Some Like It Hot*); June 11, 1960, 19 (picture of an Italian male actor in a female role); December 19, 1961, 39 (another picture of female-dressed Tony Curtis), among many similar others.

27  For an informative history of Iranian cinema and its different genres, see Hamid Naficy, "Iranian Cinema," in *The Companion Encyclopedia of Middle Eastern and North African Film*, edited by Oliver Leaman, 130–222 (London: Routledge, 2001).

28  Beeman, "Mimesis and Travesty," 22.

29  See "Khatirat-i jalib-i yik ruznamah-nigar-i Irani: dar in shahr mardan ba libas-i zananah az hamjinsan-i khaud pazira'i mikunanad" (Fascinating memoirs of an Iranian journalist: In this city men in women's clothes entertain [people of] their own sex) for a report on West Berlin's night life, in *Khvandaniha*, August 18, 1959, 16–19; see also "Mauvazib bashid khanumi kih kinar-i shuma nishastah mard nabashad!" (Watch out, lest the woman sitting next to you is a man!), *Khvandaniha*, April 25, 1959, 52–54 (reprinted from *Umid-i Iran*).

30  'Ali Sha'bani, "Gardishi dar kafah-ha va risturanha-yi Tehran" (A tour of Tehran's cafés and restaurants), *Khvandaniha*, September 25, 1954, 22–25, 36–37. Such reports continued to appear in the 1960s and 1970s. The emphasis, however, shifted to highlighting the growth of dance clubs as part of the "cultural turn" to dance among the youth. For one example, see Gregory Lamya, "Raqqas-khanah-ha-yi zirzamini-i Tehran bazar-i garmi yaftah-and" (Tehran's underground dance dens have a heated market), *Kayhan*, January 25, 1969, 16. See also *Ittila'at*, October 6, 1976 (7) for a report on a Turkish singer appearing in women's clothes and makeup.

31  *Kayhan*, April 19, 1973, 22. For another similar report, see *Kayhan*, October 11, 1973, 22. This was the case of two young males, eighteen and nineteen years of age, "in women's clothes and make-up," who were arrested on Tehran-Saveh road and charged with fooling men and stealing their money. The men denied the charges and stated that they were music performers (*mutrib*) working in the area villages. "We make up ourselves as women and in weddings make the guests laugh and be amused by imitating women's movements." Both reports carry photographs of arrested woman-presenting males.

32  I specifically have opted not to name this category of males living as women "transwomen" because of the specific meaning of that word in today's English-speaking context.

33  *Kayhan*, May 13, 1969, 18.

34  The latter's style is seen as a signal to men who desire nonmasculine males, despite whether they are for hire. The stigma of that kind of MtF-ness is elaborated in terms of its collapse into sex work; it is assumed that an exaggerated female appearance is

*always* a sign of commercial availability. It demarcates one style of MtF-ness as virtuous, pressing the other to the outside of the domain of acceptability for community membership—this other is not seen as truly trans. It is marked by the weight of social shame associated with "passive" homosexuality. Among self-identified gay men, on the other hand, the distancing is seen as a defense against the bodily changes that would turn a gay man into a deformed woman. As one self-identified gay man explained, "I do my best to stop gay men going that way by pointing out to them that Tehran is full of beautiful lovely girls; if his lover wanted a girl, he could find thousands; he wants his partner to be a 'male girl'" (interview with Behzad, June 2006). The presumption that most, if not all, MtFs are sex workers runs through much of the literature on Iranian (and not only Iranian) MtFs. The presumption, to the extent that it could possibly be documented sociologically (and it usually is not backed up with any data at all), depends on publicly noticeable MtF life. Those who work, for instance, as tailors, hairdressers, lawyers, and graphic designers (among the occupations of those I met in Iran) are invisible to the public eye.

35 *Khanum* is a generic form of address for an adult female. I, for instance, am often addressed as "Khanum Najmabadi" in Iran. In this period, the term also was used as an insider designation for males living as women. Information presented here about this subculture of Tehran life in the 1970s is based on conversations with several men in their fifties who now identify as gay and several who now identify as MtF.

36 It is more common today, especially in middle-class urban circles, for men-loving men to self-reference themselves as *gay* (the English word pronounced exactly the same in Persian). This was rare in the 1970s.

37 One self-identified gay man reported noticing a growing presence of what he referred to as *trans* women in these gatherings (interview with Behzad, June 2006); evidently this observation was from the vantage point of 2006 within a conversation about transsexuality today.

38 For a sensitive depiction of one such life, see Farhad Rastakhiz, "Mardi dar hashiah" (A man on the margin) (in *Mardi dar hashiah* [Hamburg: Nashr.i Kalagh, n.d.]), in which the main character/narrator, Mr. Qurayshi, is an assistant principal in a high school by day and lives a lonely, womanly life at home. I am grateful to Elham Gheytanchi for bringing this story to my attention and providing me with a copy of it.

39 Interview with Behzad, July 2007; Mark Johnson, in the context of the southern Philippines, has noted, "most find repulsive the idea that one would have sex with their 'own kind'" (*Beauty and Power: Transgendering and Cultural Transformation in the Southern Philippines* [Oxford: Berg, 1997], 90).

40 Interview with Cyrus, October 2007.

41 In the 1970s, when the word *gay* was not a dominant self-reference, few would use "homosexual" (in its French pronunciation in Persian—*humausiksual*) either. The term was largely used in psycho-medical discourse. In recent decades, *gay* has become a more acceptable word, although its meaning, as the above articulations indicate, is not identical with its usage in English. Persian words often are used as in-words, which if used to refer to someone would be recognized by another knowing person, but would be safely assumed to mean something different by the unknowing audience. Because these words continue to be used in Iran today, I have

refrained from recording them here. Some of these patterns recall somewhat similar configurations in the New York world of male-male intimacy before the 1940s, as documented and analyzed in George Chauncey, "The Double Life, Camp Culture, and the Making of a Collective Identity," in *Gay New York: Gender, Urban Culture, and the Making of the Gay Male World 1890–1940* (New York: Basic Books, 1994), chapter 10.

42 Interview with Behzad, July 2007. Whatever the meaning of these rumored "gay weddings" may have been at the time, today in both Iran and the Iranian diasporic gay and lesbian communities they are considered "gay weddings" in a more recent sense and an indication of the lively "gay culture" of the 1970s. When Leila and her partner Minu (more on them in chapter 7) had gone to a dental appointment in summer 2007 and the elderly doctor had noticed their intimacy and their identical rings, he immediately began reminiscing about "the public gay marriage of the 1970s." The event narrated by Behzad is now included in a proto-official publication, Ruhallah Husaynian, *Fisad-i darbar-i Pahlavi* (Corruption of Pahlavi Court), Markaz-i Asnad-i Inqilab-i Islami (Islamic Revolution Documentation Center), Part 3. Online edition; http://www.irdc.ir/fa/content/4915/default.aspx, last accessed July 19, 2009. The same section includes a host of other named individuals, all marked as sexually corrupt because they are "hamjins-baz." This sensibility about hamjins-bazi as a singularly significant sign of political corruption of the old regime is shared by some of the post-1979 critical rethinking of the 1970s penned by the members of that elite. The memoir of Queen Farah's mother, Farideh Diba, for example, persistently talks about 'Abbas Huvayda as a *mukhannas* (effeminate man) and a hamjins-baz. She names other men around the Court in similar terms. See *Dukhtaram Farah* (My Daughter Farah), trans. Ilaheh Ra'is Firuz (Tehran: Bih-Afarin, 2000; 12th reprint 2004), 116, 295, 300, 304, 313, 314, 320, 322, 325. The circulation of hamjins-baz through these stories about the culture of the old regime is not limited to ideologically shaped proto-official histories and exiled recollections of "things gone wrong." In a recent literary history of male-male love as celebrated in Persian literature, the author suggests that "as a result of cultural growth and presence of women in society, it [the older style of male-male love] had disappeared from the customary practice of the population, until its coming to Iran in late-Pahlavi period in its foreign [European, *farangi*] form of two men marrying each other, which caused a great deal of public commotion." Sirous Shamissa, *Sodomy: Based on Persian literature* (Tehran: Firdaws, 2002), 256. (This is the way his name and book title appear in the book itself; the Persian title is *Shahidbazi dar adabiyat-i Farsi*. Translating *shahidbazi* into "sodomy" is itself a major translation problem!)

43 Martha Vicinus has suggested that these marriages are reminiscent of "what went on in the early 18th-century London molly houses" (e-mail communication, September 28, 2009). One difference, however, seems to be that the marriages in molly houses seem to have been about ceremonies for two men who would possibly be sexual partners even if for a brief time. See Alan Bray, *Homosexuality in Renaissance England* (New York: Columbia University Press, 1982), chapter 4. Marriages between two khanums seem to have excluded that possibility.

44 See Layla S. Diba's introductory note to illustrations nos. 78 and 79 in *Royal Persian*

*Paintings: The Qajar Epoch, 1785–1925*, edited by Laya S. Diba and Maryam Ekhtiar (Brooklyn: Brooklyn Museum of Art, 1998), 251. See also 262–64 for a pair of photograph/painting-from-photographs of Nasir al-Din Shah, and Maryam Ekhtiar's introductory note confirming the same point.

45 Connecting with the nineteenth-century painting tradition in Hajizadeh's work goes beyond working off photographs; several themes from Qajar paintings, particularly the lion and sun emblem, similarly find "unrealistic" reproductions in many of Hajizadeh's paintings.

46 Johnson (*Beauty and Power*) introduces the concept of "transgenderally identified men" for men whose public self-presentation seems to have a great deal in common with the mard-i zan-numa I am discussing here. I have opted to keep the notion of -*numa* (-presenting) because it retains the performativity (*numayish*) of self-presentation.

47 Brad Epps, unpublished discussant's comments on a draft of this chapter, presented at the Harvard Humanities Center's Gender and Sexuality Seminar, Cambridge, Massachusetts, September 30, 2009.

48 See, for instance, the anonymous report, "Yadi az jashn-i hunar-i Shiraz va barrisi-i iftizahat-i 'an. . . ." [Notes on the Shiraz Art Festival and its scandalous embarrassments), in which one of the criticisms is of the explicit talk of homosexuality in one of the plays (*Khvandaniha*, November 21, 1972, 13, 54–55). The Shiraz Art Festival and the many controversies it generated are covered in several oral histories, including those of Fereydun Av, Bijan Saffari, and Farrokh Ghaffari, all at the Oral History project of Foundation for Iranian Studies. For a post-1979 Islamist perspective on the Shiraz Arts Festival, see the introduction and commentaries on documents that The Center for Research of Historical Documents (Ministry of Intelligence) has published: *Jashn-i hunar-i Shiraz bah rivayat-i asnad-i* SAVAK (Shiraz Art Festival according to SAVAK documents) (Tehran: Center for Research of Historical Documents, 2003). See also a shorter and popularized version, Fatimah Shirin, *Bazichah-i Shahbanu* (The Queen's plaything) (Tehran: Center for Research of Historical Documents, 2005). For a recent appreciative overview, see Robert Gluck, "The Shiraz Arts Festival: Western Avant-Garde Arts in 1970s Iran," *Leonardo* 40, no. 1 (2007): 20–28.

49 *Gharbzadigi*, a concept that gained popularity through Jalal Al Ahmad's essay. For an English translation of that essay, see *Gharbzadegi = Weststruckness*, trans. by John Green and Ahmad Alizadeh (Lexington, KY: Mazda Publishers, 1982). For a critical discussion, see Mehrzad Boroujerdi, *Iranian Intellectuals and the West: The Tormented Triumph of Nativism* (Syracuse, NY: Syracuse University Press, 1996).

50 Another difference between baruni and kuni is that kuni is used to designate an individual man; baruni is used within the context of a relationship between at least two women, as in "so-and-so is so-and-so's baruni."

51 Interview with Behzad, July 2007.

52 The need for a word that is not derogatory but also not an in-word signifies the emergence of a broader semi-open circulation of these conversations. For that reason, circulation of *gay* also marks the space of this semi-openness. For a similar dynamic between *gay* and *bantut* in the Philippines, see Johnson, *Beauty and Power*, 89;

and between *gay* and *kathoey* in Thailand, see Megan Sinnott, *Toms and Dees: Trans-gender Identity and Female Same-Sex Relationships in Thailand* (Honolulu: University of Hawai'i Press, 2004), 6.

53  Literally "o'sister." According to Maryam Khatun Mulk-ara, this expression came from an Italian film, possibly in the 1950s or 1960s. In this film, she explained, there were two soldiers "afflicted with this problem" who called each other "iva'khva-har" (in the Persian-dubbed version, that is), which is how it became a popular designation. See the interview with Hamid Riza Khalidi in *I'timad*, May 8, 2005, 7.

54  See Abbas Milani, *The Persian Sphinx: Amir Abbas Hoveyda and the Riddle of the Iranian Revolution* (Washington, DC: Mage Publishers, 2000), in particular 186–213, 250–56.

55  Farrukhzad was also a poet, but that remained largely unacknowledged during this period, possibly because, as a poet, he was overshadowed by his more famous sister, Furugh Farrukhzad. Much of his early poetry was in German and published in Germany, where he was studying.

56  Literally "felt-making workshop." *Namadmali* also is used to imply wringing out the hidden essence of something.

57  *Khvandaniha*, June 3, 1967, 17.

58  Reprinted in *Khvandaniha*, October 13, 1956, 9.

59  *Khvandaniha*, June 15, 1974, 16. The column was occasioned by reports of aid to African famine victims. For a similar column suggesting that some television personalities could aid the African victims "in-kind," see *Khvandaniha*, June 29, 1974, 17.

60  Even a popular tour guide to Iran cannot avoid noting this phenomenon. In a boxed paragraph, appearing only on the page on Qazvin and titled "Butt of the Joke" (surely an intended pun), the authors write: "'If you drop your wallet in Qazvin, don't bend down to pick it up!' Political correctness has yet to touch the Iranian sense of humour and poor Qazvin, 'where birds fly on one wing' [the other wing folded over their anus, it is said], suffers constantly from jibes of predatory homosexuality. Other regions are equally unfairly stereotyped for jocular effect. Men from Rasht are portrayed as sexually liberal and constant cuckolds, Esfahanis as mean and cunning, Shirazis as lazy and fun-loving, Turkmen as vengeful, Kurds as hot-blooded and the Loris of Lorestan as congenitally untrustworthy. In common jokes, Azaris are supposedly slow-witted yet cash-canny, with Tabrizis surly and religious but those from Orumieh contrastingly relaxed and open-minded. Within their loose-fitting dishdasha robes, Iranian Arab men are whispered to be endowed with an especially impressive set of wedding tackle" (Andrew Burke et al., *Iran* [London: Lonely Planet Publications, 2004], 163).

61  On the interaction between humor and disgust, see William Ian Miller, *The Anatomy of Disgust* (Cambridge, MA: Harvard University Press, 1997), in particular 9.

62  Miller, *The Anatomy of Disgust*, xi.

63  The anus under consideration in such accounts is that of a male body. A woman's anus does not have the same sanctity because a husband, according to some Islamic jurisprudents (though not all), can have anal intercourse with his wife. For further discussion of this point see my essay, "Types, Acts, or What? Regulation of Sexuality in Nineteenth-Century Iran," in *Islamicate Sexualities: Translations across Temporal*

Geographies of Desire, edited by Kathryn Babayan and Afsaneh Najmabadi, 275–96 (Cambridge, MA: Harvard University Press, HCMES series, 2008), 278–80.

64 Miller, *The Anatomy of Disgust*, 109.

65 For a different reading of the significance of this kind of humor in the 1970s, see Afary, *Sexual Politics*: "While condescending and disparaging, these references suggested at least a small degree of acceptance for a gay lifestyle" (244).

66 See Mirza Aqa (Mani) 'Asgari, *Khunyagar dar khun: dar shinakht va buzurgdasht-i Faridun Farrukhzad* (Musician/singer in blood: in recognition of Faridun Farrukhzad) (Germany: Human, 2005). In addition to the book, Mani has set up an information site for Farrukhzad, http://www.farrokhzad.info/. His book has been criticized for its virtual silence on Farrukhzad's nonheteronormative sexuality; some of the ensuing debate is available on the site. In an interview with MAHA, Mani stated that he considered "homosexuality against nature and in contradiction with reproductive process," but that sexual matters were a private issue in which no government should intervene. See MAHA, no. 4 (January/February 2005): 4–11 (the quote is from pages 4–5). For another contribution, see Majid Nafisi, "Hamjinsgara'i va Faridun Farrukhzad" (Homosexuality and Faridun Farrukhzad), *Cheraq*, no. 34 (November 2007): 56–57.

67 A self-identified Iranian gay man abroad, reminiscing about when he was around twelve years of age, writes, "The other thing that I remember from this period is Faridun Farrukhzad. He is responsible for my understanding of the rightness of my deep feelings. At that time, Faridun Farrukhzad had a weekly television show. Everyone I knew would watch this show. Sometimes, in parties while watching the show, people would crack jokes about him and everyone would laugh. I did not fully understand the jokes yet. But when someone would say 'he/she is a woman her/himself, why has he/she got him/herself a wife?' or 'he/she is looking for a husband' I knew what they meant. I heard these jokes about Faridun Farrukhzad but never laughed and didn't know at the time that in four-five years I would have a conversation with him about homosexuality and he would tell me that 'what matters is to love. A man or a woman, that doesn't matter in loving. If you one day find a young man [*pisar*] who loves you as much as you love him, don't lose him.'" Qubad, "An ruzha [Those days]," *Homan*, no. 13 (summer 1998): 25–27 (the quote is from page 26).

68 Sadiq Hidayat (1903–51) is one of the most important modern writers of twentieth-century Iran. For information on his life and work see several entries in the *Encyclopaedia Iranica* (online edition); http://www.iranicaonline.org/articles/hedayat-sadeq. His sexuality has long been a subject of speculation and discussion. In more recent years, Hidayat has been appropriated as part of the literary figures with possibly homosexual orientation, in the tradition of Oscar Wilde and others. See "Girayish-i jinsi-i Sadiq Hidayat" (Sadiq Hidayat's sexual orientation), *Cekaf*, no. 30, topic number 17. *Cekaf* is an electronic journal. Their archive is available through the IRQO site (my source; accessed on July 29, 2009). This article has no author and was republished in another electronic journal, MAHA, no. 3 (January/February 2005): 18–23. See also Afary, *Sexual Politics*, 169–73.

69 Faridun Kar (b. 1928) is a poet and literary scholar.

70 *Khvandaniha*, May 11, 1968, 39–40. When Isma'il Jamshidi interviewed Farrukhzad in July 1970 and asked him about "the many pieces of gossip that circulate" about him, he did not confirm or deny any of them. He simply indicated that he was aware of these circulations and felt sorry for people who engage in their production. This interview was republished in the Iranian gay monthly literary web journal *Dilkadah*, published from December 2005 to December 2006. See no. 8 (July/August 2006): 11–13.

71 *Khvandaniha*, June 16, 1970, 58.

72 *Khvandaniha*, August 22, 1972, 12–13, 48–49.

73 *Ittila'at-i banuvan*, January 2, 1974, 81. Although we do not have any sustained research on Farrukhzad and his life, from anecdotal information it seems that the attraction-repulsion nexus was tilted differently along gender lines. His performances seem to have been a lot more popular among women who heartily would laugh at his parodies of manhood, while adult men expressed disdain and repulsion, at least in the presence of women. Behzad (interviewed in June 2006 and July 2007) talked about how his mother would defend Farrukhzad's performances every time men of the family disparaged him, a defense that Behzad perceived as her support of himself.

74 See the report in *Ittila'at-i banuvan*, December 12, 1973, 21. They were married on January 20, 1974. See *Ittila'at*, January 21, 1974, 4.

75 *Ittila'at-i banuvan*, "Yik guftigu-yi jalib ba Faridun Farrukhzad va hamsarash Taraneh: ma 'ashiq-i ham nistim!" (An interesting conversation with Faridun Farrukhzad and his spouse Taraneh: We are not in love with each other!), January 2, 1974, 13, 80–81. Taraneh Sunduzi was always referred to in the press by her first name only. This was common practice when referring to female celebrities, such as actors, performers, and poets. Furugh Farrukhzad, for instance, was usually referred to only as "Furugh." For men, there was a distinction: some, such as male singers, were usually referred to only by first name; artists who were considered "more respectable" had both their first and family names used, as was the case for male literati who usually were referred to by their full name, family name, or poetic name.

76 *Ittila'at-i banuvan*, June 25, 1974, 20. According to her father, Taraneh had already left Farrukhzad two months earlier and moved back in with her family. *Ittila'at-i banuvan*, July 3, 1974, 22.

77 *Kayhan*, June 19, 1974, 18.

78 No author, "Javanan-i ma chizi mian-i dukhtar va pisar hastand!" (Our youth are something between girls and boys!), *Khvandaniha*, March 6, 1971, 18 (reprinted from *Khurasan*).

79 Nadereh Shahram, "Men of the twentieth century?" *Zan-i ruz*, August 3, 1974, 7, 86. For another similar essay, see Mahmud 'Inayat, "Jaff al-qalam, jall al-khaliq," *Kayhan*, December 6, 1972, 5.

80 *Khvandaniha*, "Khatar-i hamrikhti-i zanan va mardan" (The danger of women and men looking alike), trans. by Dr. Kuhsar, April 6, 1973, 36–38 (no original author or source of translation is specified). Reprinted from *Danishmand*, a general science journal.

81 *Ittila'at-i banuvan*, January 9, 1974, 12–13, 81; January 16, 1974, 12–13, 80; January

23, 1974, 11, 83; January 30, 1974, 13, 79; February 6, 1974, 21; February 13, 1974, 12, 81, 83; February 20, 1974, 13, 82; and February 27, 1974, 19, 83.

82 Attempts to form an association of health professionals had a much longer history. See Schayegh, *Who Is Knowledgeable Is Strong: Science, Class, and the Formation of Modern Iranian Society, 1900–1950* (Berkeley: University of California Press, 2009), 54–60. The more recent legislation had been submitted to the Majlis in 1960, revised in 1967, and finally ratified in 1969. See *Kayhan*, June 8, 1969 (19) for the full text of the legislation and the council regulations. See also *Kayhan*, July 27, 1969 (2), for the report of the council's inaugural meeting. The MCI also published the *Journal of the Medical Council of Iran* (*Majallah-i 'ilmi*), which was focused on research articles, and a more informational newsletter (*Nashriyah-i khabari*) in which regular reports on complaint cases and decisions reached by its board of directors were published. These reports were often reprinted in more popular journals. See, for instance, *Khvandaniha*, June 23, 1970, 20–22, and April 3, 1971, 12–15.

83 *Newsletter of the Medical Council of Iran*, no. 12 (July 23, 1979): 29 (quotation marks in original).

84 Interview, December 2007. When I asked about the operation reported in the press in February 1973 that took place in Namazi Hospital of Shiraz, he thought that was a possibility since that hospital had American and American-trained doctors. Doctors trained by Dr. Salih were trained to refuse sex surgeries except for intersex ones. Information about Dr. Behjatnia in the following section is based on my December 2007 interview and on his biographical entry in Muvahhidi, *Zindigi-namah-i pizishkan-i nam-avar-i mu'asir-i Iran* (Biographies of famous contemporary Iranian physicians), Tehran: Abrun, 2000, 2: 61–64.

85 Information about Dr. Amir-Movahedi is based on my December 2007 interview and on his biographical entry in Muvahhidi, *Zindigi-namah-i pizishkan*, volume 2, 53–59.

86 Interview, December 2007. On abortion regulations, see the text of revision of Article 42, Point 3 of the Penal Code, May/June 1973, in Gholam Reza Afkhami, ed., *Women, State, and Society in Iran 1963–78: An Interview with Mahnaz Afkhami* (Bethesda, MD: Foundation for Iranian Studies, 2003), 268–69.

87 *Ittila'at*, October 11, 1976, 2. Were the clerical authorities in Iran, like doctors, ignorant of Khomeini's 1964 fatwa (on the permissibility of sex change) or did they choose to ignore it?

88 *Kayhan*, October 11, 1976, 5.

89 *Kayhan*, October 16, 1976, 2.

90 I was unable to find any reports of the murder of surgeons who performed these operations. This could very well have been "attempted murders" or even total hype.

91 See, for example, "Akhlaq-i pizishki dar barabar-i pizishki-i nuvin: masa'il-i ikhtisasi-i akhlaq-i pizishki" (Medical ethics confronting new medicine: special problems of medical ethics), *Journal of Medical Council of Iran* 6, no. 5 (March 1978): 445–47.

92 Interview, August 2007.

93 Interview, August 2007. The experience was a harrowing one; bad surgeries occurred in several countries over many years, and the process was interrupted by the revolution and the closing of borders in the early years of the Iran-Iraq War (1980–88).

94 Mulk-ara has been the subject of numerous interviews and reports in Iran and internationally, both in print and film, about Iranian transsexuals.

95 I have depended on the following sources for this sketch of Mulk-ara's life. By far, the most extensive interview with her (and the only one in which she talked at length about her life in the 1970s) appeared as part of a four-page social reportage in the daily *I'timad* (May 8, 2005, 7–10). Mulk-ara, including a picture of her at the center of page 7, was featured on pages 7 and 10 (interview by Hamid Riza Khalidi; the total page coverage was over a fourth of the full dossier). Unless noted otherwise, the quotes in this section are all from this interview. This dossier remains the most substantive and serious press coverage of transsexuality in the Iranian press, although many other newspapers and magazines have covered various aspects of the issues, as I noted in the introduction. Other sources on Mulk-ara I have used are a short interview with her that formed part of a dossier on transsexuals in the popular weekly *Chilchiraq* (May 26, 2007, 7–13, interview on page 11) and my several phone conversations with her during the summer and fall of 2006.

96 In my conversations with her, Mulk-ara spoke about two circles in which she socialized in this period: one she called *"darbariha,"* the Court circle, which according to her included the Shah's cousin, his chief of staff, and several others she named. The other circle she referred to as lower-middle-class *"zir-i mutivassit."* The two circles overlapped in that many of the women most desired in the courtly circles were from the lower-middle-class circles and would be brought to parties.

97 Interview, June 2006. The account of how and when she first identified herself, or was identified by a doctor, as a *transsexual* differed in this conversation from the accounts reported in the interviews with *I'timad* and *Chilchiraq*, in which she said she was sent to a specialist by the National Iranian Radio and Television, who diagnosed her as *transsexual* and suggested she should go for surgery.

98 "Taghyir-i jinsiyat bilamani' ast va ba'd az 'amal taklif-i yik zan bar shuma vajib ast." Noushin and two other MtFs I interviewed each claimed that it was they who had obtained the first fatwa from Ayatollah Khomeini on permissibility of changing sex (interviews, summer 2006 and 2007).

99 There is a huge literature on this period's state policies and resistance by large sections of women against it. Although successfully implemented by the early 1980s, the public dress code for women has remained a perennial source of contestation between sections of the government, dissenting women, and, at times, young male youth. See Parvin Paidar, *Women and the Political Process in Twentieth-century Iran* (Cambridge: Cambridge University Press, 1995); Minoo Moallem, *Between Warrior Brother and Veiled Sister: Islamic Fundamentalism and the Politics of Patriarchy in Iran* (Berkeley: University of California Press, 2005); and Hamideh Sedghi, *Women and Politics in Iran: Veiling, Unveiling, and Reveiling* (Cambridge: Cambridge University Press, 2007).

100 Johnson also discusses, in a different context, the paradox of the *gay/bantut* being "both celebrated as masters of beauty and style and circumscribed as deviant and vulgar" and notes "the historical significance of the beauty parlours as both the site and means for *gays'* successful occupational reinvention of themselves" (*Beauty and Power*, 146–47). One could argue that in 1970s Iran, the entertainment industry

had become such a site for performers such as Farrukhzad and others, who found a place such as NIRT to be a site of relative acceptance where their performative skills could flourish.

*Chapter 5: Verdicts of Science, Rulings of Faith*

1 Sexual harassment and assault of MtFs continues to be a common grievance. Whether in the army or at a corrective center, a police station, or sometimes even in governmental offices, MtFs report that they get propositioned, pressured for sex "favors," and at times offered quid pro quos; there is a presumptive air of their "availability." At some government offices, measures have been taken to reduce the occasion for harassment. At the LMOI, a separate waiting room has been allocated for trans persons to protect them from the hostile or otherwise scrutinizing gaze of others waiting for various services of the LMOI. Such measures fit with that official discursive thread that defines "trans" as a category of "persons vulnerable to social harm" and thus in need of governmental protection.

2 I have not been able to view this film; an old copy that I obtained is in a format that I have not been able to translate into technically accessible versions. My comments are based on a report by Ilham Khaksar, "Gharibah-ha-yi 'alam-i khilqat!: guzarishi az vaz'iyat-i taghyir-i jinsiyat dar Iran" (The strange marvels of the world of creation: A report about the situation of sex-change in Iran), *Zanan* 124 (September 2005): 2–10.

3 Khaksar, "Gharibah-ha-yi 'alam-i khilqat!," 3.

4 Maryam Khatun Mulk-ara, interviewed by Hamid Riza Khalidi, *I'timad*, May 8, 2005, 7, 10. The quote is from page 10. A copy of this fatwa, which was made available to me by Hujjat al-Islam Karimi-nia, did not bear a date. However, in his own writings, Karimi-nia dates this fatwa to 1364/1985–6. In another interview with Mulk-ara (*Chilchiraq*, no. 247, May 28, 2007, 11), the fatwa is dated to 1365/1986–7. In this interview Mulk-ara also states that in 1975 she had written a letter of query to Ayatollah Khomeini, who was then in exile in Najaf, Iraq. In response, he had instructed her, "The obligations of a woman are obligatory [*vajib*] for you." From that date, she said, until the postrevolutionary requirements set in, forcing her to revert to male clothes, she had lived in women's clothes.

5 *Chilchiraq*, no. 247, May 28, 2007, 11.

6 *I'timad*, May 8, 2005, 10.

7 *I'timad*, May 8, 2005, 10.

8 Mulk-ara, interviewed by Khalidi, *I'timad*, May 8, 2005, 10. It is unclear what negative repercussions Kayhani-far's support had produced. Ms. Shojaei refers to Zahra Shojaei, Khatami's advisor on women's affairs and the head of the Center for Women's Participation, an office created in 1997 by presidential order.

9 A very successful gynecologist, she was selected as one of the top successful women professionals in December 2008. For an interview with her on this occasion, see *Risalat*, December 4, 2008, 19.

10 Interview with Dr. Behjatnia, December 2007 [removed exact date to make the referencing of all interviews similar; mostly because in Iran I interviewed one per-

son on several days, usually within the same week and subsequently used only the month to keep record of interviews].

11 The administrative changes that concern the topic of this book include the legal reconstitution of the Ministry of Health, Healing, and Medical Education (the law was passed in 1985 and was modified in subsequent years); the legal reconstitution of the LMOI (1993); and the legal reconstitution of the MCI, renamed the Medical Council of Islamic Republic of Iran (1996). See Maziar Ashrafian Bonab, *Zaruri-yat-i pizishki-i qanuni* (Essentials of Forensic Medicine [title translation on the back page]), with introductions by Dr. Faramarz Gudarzi and Hujjat al-Islam Zikrallah Ahmadi, 278–86, 365–66, 355–60, respectively. Note the double introductions by a medical doctor and a scholar of fiqh.

12 For instance, Dr. Mehdi Amir-Movahedi—a prominent gynecologist and a highly regarded specialist in uterine surgeries, intersex surgeries, and vaginal construction for women who were born without or with very restricted vaginas—emphatically stated that no one in the medical community in Iran knew about Ayatollah Khomeini's ruling (in the early 1960s) that sex change was permissible. In the 1970s, Amir-Movahedi had served on the board of directors of the MCI, which in 1976 had ruled against the permissibility of sex surgeries, except for intersex persons, on moral and medical grounds. He said, "If we had known of this ruling, perhaps our decision would have been different" (interview, December 2007).

13 Proceedings of this congress have been published in three volumes; see Tavakkoli Bazzaz, *Majmu'ah-i maqalat-i avvalin kungirah-i sarasari-i intibaq-i umur-i pizishki ba mavazin-i shar'-i muqaddas* (Collected papers from the first nationwide congress of compliance of medical matters with precepts of the holy law) (Tehran: Taymurzadah, 1998). The Khamenei quote is from volume 1, page 2. After the first Compliance Congress, local conferences were held in several provinces, including Mazandaran, Bushihr, and Fasa. A second congress was held in Tehran in March 1997.

14 For a discussion of the productivity of science/fiqh nexus to enable the use of assisted reproductive technology (ART) to deal with the issue of childless couples, see Mohammad Jalal Abbasi-Shavazi, Marcia C. Inhorn, Hajiieh Bibi Razeghi-Nasrabad, and Ghasem Toloo. "The 'Iranian ART Revolution': Infertility, Assisted Reproductive Technology, and Third-Party Donation in the Islamic Republic of Iran." *Journal of Middle East Women's Studies* 4, no. 2 (spring 2008): 1–28. See also the *Journal of Reproduction and Infertility*, http://www.jri.ir/fa/Default.aspx. More recently, couples in which one partner is a postoperative transsexual have turned to surrogate parenthood. The Interdisciplinary Seminar on Surrogacy, October 24–25, 2007, was organized around six panels: legal, psychological, medical, fiqhi, philosophical, and sociological. Before the wider availability of these technologies, aside from adoption, some married MtFs would allow their husbands to contract temporary marriages with the condition of taking over the ensuing child for the couple. On temporary marriage, see Shahla Haeri, *Law of Desire: Temporary Marriage in Shi'i Iran* (Syracuse, NY: Syracuse University Press, 1989).

15 Mustafá Najafi, "Ravanpizishki va intibaq" (Psychiatry and compliance), in *Majmu'ah-i maqalat*, edited by Javad Tavakoli Bazzaz, volume 3, 123–27 (Tehran: Taymurzadeh, 1998).

16　Najafi, "Ravanpizishki va intibaq," 126.

17　This brief history is based on Gudarzi, *Pizishki-i qanuni* (Legal medicine) (Tehran: Intisharat-i Anishtin, 1998); Husayn Sana'i-zadah, *Pizishki-i qanuni* (Tehran: Dadgu-star, 2008); and information from the official site of the LMOI, accessed July 1, 2010, http://en.lmo.ir/index.aspx?siteid=112&pageid=2167.

18　Gudarzi, *Pizishki-i qanuni* (Legal medicine), 92–93.

19　Gudarzi, *Pizishki-i qanuni*, 33–34.

20　Sana'i-zadah, *Pizishki-i qanuni*, 12. For the text of this law, see Ashrafian Bonab, *Zaruriyat-i pizishki-i qanuni*, 365–68.

21　Gudarzi, *Pizishki-i qanuni* (Legal medicine), 41–42.

22　Tehran: Intisharat-i Anishtan, 1995.

23　Buffington discusses how "competitive" theories of European and American crimi-nology—hereditary versus environmental causes of deviancy and criminality—were subsumed into "peacefully co-existing, mutually reinforcing subdivisions. . . . gen-eral practitioners typically drew on both explanations . . . using one theory to resolve the anomalies of the other" (*Criminal and Citizen in Modern Mexico* [Lincoln: Univer-sity of Nebraska Press, 2000], 40).

24　This chapter, and the whole section, finally concludes with the reproduction of two legal documents dating to 1987 and 1996. The first is one of the earliest Ministry of Justice explications about the permissibility of sex change. The second is a sample of a psychiatric diagnostic confirmation of transsexuality and the permissibility of SRS.

25　For a thorough discussion of the concept in Islamic sources, past and present, see Dmitri V. Frolov, "Path or Way." In *The Encyclopaedia of the Qurʾān*, Jane Dammen McAuliffe, general editor. Brill Online. Harvard University, accessed July 2, 2010, http://www.brillonline.nl/; and James A. Toronto, "Astray." In *Encyclopaedia of the Qurʾān*, Jane Dammen McAuliffe, general editor, Brill Online. Harvard University, accessed July 2, 2010, http://www.brillonline.nl/.

26　This exchange of letters is reproduced in Muhammad Mahdi Karimi-nia, *Taghyir-i jinsiyat az manzar-i fiqh va huquq* (Sex-change from the perspective of fiqh and law), Qum: Intisharat-i markaz-i Fiqhi-i A'immah-i Athar, 2010, 137–38.

27　On the *tauzih al-masaʾil* genre, see the foreword by Michael M. J. Fischer and Mehdi Abedi to the English translation of Ayatollah Khomeini's *A Clarification of Questions* (*Tauzih al-masaʾil*) (Najaf: Matbaʿat al-Adab, 1967 or 1968 [1387 AH]).

28　Muhammad Hadi Tal'ati, *Maʾkhaz-shinasi-i masaʾil-i mustahdisah-i pizishki* (Biblio-graphical study of current medical questions) (Qum: Markaz-i Intisharat-i Daftar-i Tablighat-i Islami-i Hauzah-i 'Ilmiyah-i Qum, 1999).

29　The Sunni scholars' view on this subject has a different history and current con-figuration. For the Egyptian debates, see chapter 11 of Jakob Skovgaard-Petersen, *Defining Islam for the Egyptian State: Muftis and Fatwas of the Dar al-Ifta* (Leiden: Brill, 1997). For Malaysia, see Honey Tan Lay Ean, "Jeffrey Jessie: Recognising Tran-sexuals," November 17, 2005, accessed November 7, 2009, http://www.malaysinbar .org.my/gender_issues/jeffrey_jessie_recognising_transexuals_by_honey_tan_lay _ean.html. See also Karimi-nia, *Taghyir-i jinsiyat*, 2010.

30　The website of the Gender Identity Disorder Organization of Iran (http://www.gid .org.ir/main_f.htm) has a section that lists the opinion of all major top religious scholars, including Khomeini, Khamenei, Sani'i, Fazil Lankarani, Makarim Shirazi, Musavi Ardabili, Khau'i, Gulpaygani, and Tabrizi. In addition to the published *tauzih al-masa'il*–type books, many of the ayatollahs now have websites that house their writings and through which they receive questions from their followers and offer answers. For a comprehensive bibliography of top clerical figures' specialized tomes on medical queries and decrees and an extensive summary of their positions, see also Karimi-nia, *Taghyir-i jinsiyat*.

31 For instance, Ayatollah Sani'i's earlier position permitted surgeries only in the case of intersex individuals. Ayatollah Sani'i, *Istifta'at-i pizishki* (Medical questions [translation of the title from the back page]) (Qum: Intisharat-i Maysam Tammar, 2006; 1st ed. 1997), 124–25. His current website, however, has a somewhat modified position in which he does not rule out sex change for transsexuals in absolute terms, stating that in itself one cannot say that sex change is forbidden, but emphasizing that, in most cases if not in all, he would consider it forbidden "as it causes numerous problems and disorders." See http://saanei.org/?view=01,00,00,00,0#01,05,13 ,87,0, accessed September 9, 2009. In contrast to his more explicitly permissible position as reflected in the GID Organization of Iran website, there is a similar ambiguity in the published ruling of Ayatollah Khamenei, *Risalah-i ajubat al-istifta'at* (Treatise responding to questions), trans. Ahmad Riza Husayni (Tehran: Intisharat-i Bayn al-Milali-i al-Hudá, 2005; 2001), 306.

32 Even with Khomeini's unchallenged political authority, his fiqhi views are narrated in a manner that makes room for nonconforming views. In Hadi Hujjat and Muhammad Hadi Tal'ati's compilation, *Ahkam-i pizshkan va mashaghil-i marbut bah pizishki* (Islamic rules of physicians and medical matters) (Qum: Bustan-i Kitab, 2006 [1996]), after reproducing Khomeini's questions 1 and 2 (in Persian), the compilers conclude, "changing sex through surgery in either case is *prima facie* [*zahiran*] not forbidden" (47). The emphasis is in the original. The expression *zahiran*, in distinction from *mashhur*, indicates an opinion that is not dominantly shared among scholars, but it is "the immediately apparent" position. Its usage emphasizes the space for disagreement and dissent, in this case even with Khomeini. See Mottahedeh's introduction to Baqir as-Sadr's *Lessons in Islamic Jurisprudence*, trans. Roy Mottahedeh (Oxford: Oneworld, 2003). Sex change continues to be an issue for which there is a continued public debate, with seminars held in Qum, including one organized by the Research Office of the Imam Khomeini Institute (November 6, 2007) and another in Mufid University (May 8, 2008).

33 Khomeini, *Tahrir al-wasilah*, in two volumes; the contemporary questions section (*al-masa'il al-mustahdithah*) is in volume 2 (753–55). *Tahrir al-wasilah* apparently was written in 1964–65, during the first year of Khomeini's exile to Bursa, Turkey. It was published only after his move to Najaf in late 1965. I am grateful to Maryann Shenoda for the translation from Arabic of this section of *Tahrir al-wasilah*, which I have modified slightly.

34 Banafsheh Sam Gisu, "Mahkum shudigan-i farmushi: nigahi bah vaz'iyat-i bimaran-i dauchar-i ikhtilal-i huviyat-i jinsi dar Iran" (Condemned to being forgotten: a look at the patients afflicted with sex/gender identity disorder), *Sharq*, May 20, 2007, 22.

35 *I'timad*, May 8, 2005, 7, 10; the quote is from page 10. The hypothetical question

she is discussing is most likely the issue of virginity. A marriage contract, strictly speaking, does not have to be a civil registration of any kind. Two consenting adults can pronounce the appropriate phrases and that will be marriage. In a temporary marriage, the contractual vow doesn't require any witnesses; for permanent marriages witnesses are required and usually a signed written document is kept, but not required. From the government's point of view, all permanent marriages do need to be registered on one's "book of identification" through a state-registered notary office. The expression she uses here points to a private vow.

36   Interview, June 2006. The sociocultural acceptability of such gender-sex crossing is localized within sociocultural subspaces. Houri, a preoperative, in-the-habit MtF in her late twenties, has worked in a women's hairdressing salon for several years with no trouble. When in the context of an official meeting with judicial and police personnel, one of the judges asked her about her job and heard her response, about which he simply said, "I didn't hear that."

37   Paula Sanders, "Gendering the Ungendered Body: Hermaphrodites in Medieval Islamic Law," in *Women in Middle Eastern History: Shifting Boundaries in Sex and Gender*, edited by Beth Baron and Nikki Keddie, 74–95 (New Haven, CT: Yale University Press, 1991).

38   Muhammad Mahdi Karimi-nia, *Taghyir-i jinsiyat az manzar-i fiqh va huquq* (Sex-change from the perspective of *fiqh* and law) (Qum: Intisharat-i Markaz-i Fiqhi-i A'immah-i Athar, 2010), 42–43.

39   Karimi-nia, *Taghyir-i jinsiyat az manzar-i fiqh va huquq*, 46.

40   Sanders, "Gendering the Ungendered Body."

41   For a discussion of technologies that are used to cover up doubt, see Alice Dreger, *Hermaphrodites and the Medical Invention of Sex* (Cambridge, MA: Harvard University Press, 1998), 188–92.

42   While he has become internationally known for this work, he has other publications, many concerned with international comparative law, such as *Hamzisti-i musalimat-amiz dar Islam va huquq-i bayn al-milal* (Peaceful co-existence in Islam and international law) (Qum: Markaz-i Intisharat-i Mu'assisah-i Amuzishi va Pazhuhishi-i Imam Khomeini, 2004) and *Huquq-i bashar va qanun-i asasi-i jumhuri-i Islami-i Iran* (Human rights and the constitution of Islamic Republic of Iran) (Qum: Jilvah-i Kamal, 2006).

43   The "socially harmed" includes drug addicts, sex workers, and the homeless but also embraces runaway teenagers and, more recently, abused children.

44   For a sociocultural cartography of Qum in the decades before the 1979 revolution, see Michael M. J. Fischer, *Iran: From Religious Dispute to Revolution* (Cambridge, MA: Harvard University Press, 1980), chapter 4.

45   Karimi-nia was generous with his time. I met him on three different occasions there in 2006–7.

46   Karimi-nia's recently published book, *Taghyir-i jinsiyat az manzar-i fiqh va huquq*, constitutes his doctoral dissertation, even though at the time of publication he had not yet defended it (phone interview, May 2010).

47   Karimi-nia, "Taghyir-i jinsiyat az manzar-i fiqhi va huquqi" (Sex-change from the perspective of fiqh and the law), 2000.

48 *Journal of Islamic Organization of Forensic Medicine*, no. 1, n.d. Another paper presented at this conference was Karrazi, "Sex Change Operation." Two related papers were presented in the organization's second congress (Amman, Jordan, September 5–8, 2006): Arya Hejazi, "Investigation of the accordance of new sexual role & sexual identification"; and Rana Hashemi, "The comparative study of transsexualism effects in Iran and U.S.A. rights jurisdiction and from legal medicines point of view." Titles are taken from the *Journal of Islamic Organization of Forensic Medicine*, no. 2, n.d. This journal can be accessed online at http://icfmo.com/section8/page1 .aspx.

49 Karimi-nia regularly participates in seminars and workshops held in Tehran and in provincial capitals to familiarize the legal and law-enforcement authorities with transsexuality and to "make them understand that when they see someone with non-normative (*ghayr-i muti'arif*) behavior they should not judge quickly and be provoked by it. I show them the BBC documentary; their perspective on this issue changes enormously" (interview, June 2007).

50 Interview, June 2006.

51 Ali Reza Kahani and Peyman Shojaei, *Ikhtilal-i huviyat-i jinsi* (GID) (Gender Identity Disorders [GID]) (Tehran: Taymurzadah, 2002). This argument appears on page 54 and indicates that, despite previous pages that had attempted to demarcate transsexuality from homosexuality, here they are collapsed back onto each other. The book explains transsexualism as a developmental failure, in which the person's socialization into gender roles has failed to become aligned with the biological sex category. As such, it is argued, it ought to be recognized as an illness. Correspondingly, there is an emphasis on how parents' correct attitudes toward their children could be preventative (*pishgiri*) and how, if they carefully kept their children and their growth and development under observation and acted quickly when they observed something amiss, the problem could be prevented at a very early stage (52). Developmental failure has become by far the most popular explanation for transsexuality.

52 See *I'timad*, August 25, 2009 (11) and September 9, 2009 (11).

53 *Daujinsi* literally means "of two sexes." It is the word used in contemporary Persian for intersex, the fiqhi word for which is the Arabic *khunsá*.

54 Michel de Certeau, *The Practice of Everyday Life*, trans. by Steven Rendall (Berkeley: University of California Press, 1984), 126.

55 de Certeau, *The Practice of Everyday Life*, 128.

56 Indeed, in this third meeting, Karimi-nia treated me a lot more seriously. To my surprise, he closed the door—something ordinarily not done for an encounter between a single man and a woman, and something he had not done in any of our previous meetings. I read this gesture as declaration of the irrelevance of my gender to the occasion of our one-on-one interaction across his seminar table. Perhaps he was reproducing the scene of a formal lesson plan or something of that nature, after all. That I was already sixty years old at the time and he was nineteen years my junior was no doubt helpful!

57 See Scott Kugel, *Homosexuality in Islam: Islamic Reflections on Gay, Lesbian, and Transgender Muslims* (Oxford: Oneworld Publications, 2010); and Faris Malik,

"Queer Sexuality and Identity in the Qur'an and Hadith," accessed March 12, 2011, http://www.well.com/user/aquarius/Qurannotes.htm.

58 Cyrus Schayegh, *Who Is Knowledgeable Is Strong: Science, Class, and the Formation of Modern Iranian Society, 1900–1950* (Berkeley: University of California Press, 2009), 70.

59 'Ali Akbar Siasi, *Guzarish-i yik zindigi* (Narrating a Life) (London: Paka Print, 1987), volume 1, 293–95.

60 Dihkhuda's later fame is as the designer and director for the first decades of Iran's equivalent of Oxford English Dictionary, *Lughatnamah-i Dihkhuda*.

61 The subtitle of Siasi's earliest textbook on the topic, *'Ilm al-nafs ya ravanshinasi* (Science of essence/soul or psychology) (Tehran: Tehran University Press, 1962; 1st ed. Tehran: Khudkar, 1938), which was based on his lecture notes, bears the subtitle *az lihaz-i tarbiat* (from a pedagogical point of view). See also Schayegh, *Who Is Knowledgeable Is Strong*.

62 Siasi, *Guzarish-i yik zindigi*, 295.

63 Siasi's choice of words was clearly a thoughtful one. His appreciation for language and its significance shows through his writing's fluent, clear prose and his careful choice of expressions. Unlike much later writings on this subject, Siasi's prose does not read like a bad translation! Indeed, in the introduction to the first (1938) edition of *'Ilm al-nafs ya ravanshinasi*, he noted the linguistic challenges he had faced.

64 Siasi, *'Ilm al-nafs ya ravanshinasi*, 10. He linked psychology with, and distinguished it from, two other new fields of science, namely biology and sociology, noting that the new science of psychology had moved away from its previous affiliation with philosophy and entered into the empirical sciences (11–12), and that—like biology and sociology—the basic methodology of psychology was observation and empirical evidence (21).

65 'Ali Akbar Siasi, *'Ilm al-nafs-i Ibn Sina va tatbiq-i an ba ravanshinasi-i jaded* (Ibn Sina's science of essence/soul and its compliance with modern psychology) (Tehran: Tehran University Press, 1954), 22n1, 40–41. (The French translation of the title as it appears on the back cover of the book is *La psychologie d'Avicenne et ses analogies dans la psychologie modern.*) *Tatbiq* is precisely the word used today for compliance—today's compliance seekers share with this earlier generation of state-builders the desire for bringing into compliance European sciences and Islamic modalities of knowledge production, although the direction of compliance is reversed.

66 See, for instance, the interview with Dr. Shahriar Kohanzad, one of the top sex-reassignment surgeons in Iran, in the special dossier in the monthly magazine of the Welfare Organization of Iran, *Mihr-i naw* (4 [November/December 2009 (Azar 1388)]: 23–44), on transsexuality. The interview runs from page 40 to 43. The entire dossier is framed by the notion of "contradiction between soul and body" (*tazadd-i ruh va jism*).

67 The medico-pathological load of *ikhtilal* (disparity/incompatibility/dysfunction, as in *ikhtilal-i havas, ikhtilal-i hazimah*, etc.) is far more norm-centered.

68 The slippage also has generated at least one anticlerical joke: A person asks a cleric what the difference between ruh and ravan is. The cleric responds that the two are the same thing. The person says, "Then, instead of calling you *ruhani* [literally a

spiritual person, a person of soul; *ruhani* is the polite assignation for a cleric], I shall call you *ravani* [literally mental, used to refer to mentally deranged persons]."

69   Ali Reza Kahani and Peyman Shojaei, *Ikhtilal-i huviyat-i jinsi (GID): digarjinsiyat-ju-ha (TS)* (Gender identity disorders [GID]: transsexualism) (Tehran: Taymurzadah, 2002), 57–65. The English here is the book's own translation of the title.

70   Muhammad Baqir Kajbaf. *Ravanshinasi-i raftar-i jinsi* (Psychology of sexual behavior) (Tehran: Nashr-i Ravan, 2002), 189–90.

71   Engaged couples are now required to participate in education workshops before marriage. On these workshops, see Pardis Mahdavi, *Passionate Uprisings: Iran's Sexual Revolution* (Palo Alto, CA: Stanford University Press, 2009), 220–26.

72   Euphemistically referred to as "aversion therapy," advocates of treating "sexual disorders" through cognitive-behavioral methods see their research and practices as a continuation of the earlier theories and practices dominant in the United States through the mid-1960s, and before removal of homosexuality from the *Diagnostic and Statistical Manual of Mental Disorders*. The removal, they argue, was an unscientific move, carried out under political pressure of social movements, and explains the "failure of the West" in "curing" homosexuality. See Muhammad Taqi Yasami, 'Ali Muhammadi, Ja'far Kamili, Muhammad Riza Yusufi, and Sayyid Mahdi Samimi Ardistani, "Tajrubiyati az darman-i muvaffaqiyat-amiz-i hamjins-barigi-i khaudna-pazir, farabarigi (parafilia) va tabdil-khvahi-i jinsi ba ravish-ha-yi shinakhti-raftari" (Experiences with successful treatment of egodystonic homosexuality, paraphilia, and transexuality with cognitive-behavioral methods), *The Scientific Journal of Legal Medicine* 12, no. 4 (winter 2007): 222–27. See their references on 227. (The authors of this article are all psychiatrists at Shahid Beheshti Medical Sciences University.)

73   The first seminar on "The Role of Religion in Mental Health" was not held until December 15–18, 1997. In anticipation, abstracts of forty-five papers presented at the monthly meetings of the Office of Islamic Studies in Mental Health were published. See Ja'far Bu-alhari and 'Abbas Ramazani Farani, eds. *Majmu'ah-i chakidah-i 45 sukhanrani-i Daftar-i Mutali'at-i Islami dar bihdasht-i ravani: bi-munasibat-i bargu-zari-i nukhustin Hamayish-i Naqsh-i Din dar Bihdasht-i Ravan, 24–27 Azar Mah 1376* (Tehran: Mu'avinat-i Danishjuyi, Farhangi, Huquqi va Majlis, Vizarat-i Bihdasht, Darman va Amuzish-i Pizishki va Daftar-i Mutali'at, 1997). The papers presented at this first seminar were subsequently edited by Mujtabá Ihsan-manish and 'Isá Karimi Kaysami, *Majmu'ah-i maqalat-i avvalin hamayish-i sarasari-i naqsh-i din dar bihdasht-i ravan* (Collected articles of the first nationwide seminar on role of religion in mental health) and published by an Islamic publishing house in Qum (Dafter-i Nashr-i Nuvid-i Islam) in 1998. The first international seminar on "The Role of Religion in Mental Health" was held in Tehran in 2001, and its proceedings were published in two volumes: Mujtabá Ihsan-manish, ed. *Majmu'ah-i maqalat-i avvalin hamayish-i bayn al-millali-i "naqsh-i din dar bihdasht-i ravan"* (Collected papers presented at the first international seminar on "the role of religion in mental health") (Qum: Nashr-i Ma'arif, 2003). For a report of this seminar, see *Andishah va rafter* 9, no. 1 (summer 2004): 87–88. This was followed by a second nationwide seminar that took place April 21–23, 2007. The abstracts of the papers presented were edited by Ja'far Bu-alhari, who had been the director of the TPI since 1992, in *Duvvumin*

*hamayish-i sarasari-i naqsh-i din dar bihdasht-i ravan* (The second nationwide seminar on role of religion in mental health) (Tehran: Aftab Girafic, 2007). As the director of the TPI, Bu-alhari has played an important role in the mainstreaming of transition procedures for trans persons, but his ambivalence is often expressed in press interviews. See, for instance, his interview of January 28, 2001, reported on http://isna.ir/fa/news/7911-00875/, in which he emphasizes that even though he does not condone surgical operations for "GID-afflicted patients," they are not "corrupt" and ought to be given a choice in such a decision.

74  See Ahmad Riza Muhammadpur, prepared under the supervision of Ja'far Bu-alhari, *Dau dahah talash-i mustamarr bara-yi kasb-i huviyat-i mustaqill* (Two decades of persistent struggle to acquire an independent identity) (Tehran: Aftab Girafic, 2009).

75  See, for instance, Mustafá Hamdiyeh, "Tafakkur-i ilahi va bihdasht-i ravani" (Divine thinking and mental health), paper presented in the Office of Islamic Studies in Mental Health, March 10, 1993; abstract printed in Bu-alhari and Ramazani Farani, *Majmu'ah-i chakidah*, 4. See also Ahmadi Abhari, "Naqsh-i iman va i'tiqad-i mazhabi dar darman-i bimariha va mu'arrifi-i sah maurid-i darman ba ravandarmani-i mazhabi" (The role of faith and religious beliefs in healing physical and emotional disorders [the journal's translation]), *Andishah va rafter* 2, no. 4 (spring 1996): 4–11.

76  Abstract printed in Bu-alhari and Ramazani Farani, *Majmu'ah-i chakidah*, 13. See also Mohammad Reza Mohammadi and Hushmand Hashemi-Kohanzad, "Ravandarmani-i ma'navi" (Spiritual psychotherapy) *Tibb va tazkiah* (Medicine and purification) 43 (winter 2001): 104–20.

77  Bu-alhari and Ramazani Farani. *Majmu'ah-i chakidah-i*, 13.

78  Muhammad Khodayarifard, Mohammed Reza Mohammadi, and Yasaman Abedini, "Darman-i shinakhti-raftari-i tabaddul-khvahi ba ta'kid bar darman-i ma'navi" (Cognitive-behavioral therapy with emphasis on spiritual therapy in treatment of transsexualism), *Andishah va rafter* 9, no. 3 (2004): 12–21.

79  Muhammad Khodayarifard, Mohammad Reza Mohammadi, and Yasaman Abedini. "Darman-i shinakhti-raftari-i tabaddul-khvahi ba ta'kid bar darman-i ma'navi: barrisi-i mauridi" (Cognitive-Behavioral Therapy with Emphasis on Spiritual Therapy in Treatment of Transsexualism: A Case Study). *Andishah va raftar* 9, no. 3 (2004): 12–21.

80  Muhammad Khodayarifard, Mohammadi, and Abedini, "Darman-i shinakhti-raftari-i tabaddul-khvahi ba ta'kid bar darman-i ma'navi," 12.

81  Muhammad Khodayarifard, Mohammadi, and Abedini, "Darman-i shinakhti-raftari-i tabaddul-khvahi ba ta'kid bar darman-i ma'navi," 13. Rekers' books—including *Growing Up Straight: What Families Should Know about Homosexuality* (1982), *Shaping your Child's Sexual Identity* (1982), and *Counseling Families (Resources for Christian Counseling)* (1988)—and his numerous articles are well known for their argument that gender and sexual nonnormativity are "cultural constructs" that can be treated and corrected into "normality." See Judith Butler, "Undiagnosing Gender," in *Transgender Rights*, edited by Paisley Currah, Richard M. Juang, and Shannon Price Minter, 274–98 (Minneapolis: University of Minnesota Press, 2006), particularly 286–87.

82  Muhammad Khodayarifard, Mohammadi, and Abedini, "Darman-i shinakhti-raftari-i tabaddul-khvahi ba ta'kid bar darman-i ma'navi," 13.

83 Muhammad Khodayarifard, Mohammadi, and Abedini, "Darman-i shinakhti-raftari-i tabaddul-khvahi ba ta'kid bar darman-i ma'navi," 13–14.

84 Muhammad Khodayarifard, Mohammadi, and Abedini, "Darman-i shinakhti-raftari-i tabaddul-khvahi ba ta'kid bar darman-i ma'navi," 14–15.

85 Muhammad Khodayarifard, Mohammadi, and Abedini, "Darman-i shinakhti-raftari-i tabaddul-khvahi ba ta'kid bar darman-i ma'navi," 15.

86 See Hamdiyeh, "Tafakkur-i ilahi va bihdasht-i ravani."

87 Muhammad Khodayarifard, Mohammadi, and Abedini, "Darman-i shinakhti-raftari-i tabaddul-khvahi ba ta'kid bar darman-i ma'navi," 16.

88 Muhammad Khodayarifard, Mohammadi, and Abedini, "Darman-i shinakhti-raftari-i tabaddul-khvahi ba ta'kid bar darman-i ma'navi," 17.

89 Muhammad Khodayarifard, Mohammadi, and Abedini, "Darman-i shinakhti-raftari-i tabaddul-khvahi ba ta'kid bar darman-i ma'navi," 17.

90 Muhammad Khodayarifard, Mohammadi, and Abedini, "Darman-i shinakhti-raftari-i tabaddul-khvahi ba ta'kid bar darman-i ma'navi," 18.

91 Muhammad Khodayarifard, Mohammadi, and Abedini, "Darman-i shinakhti-raftari-i tabaddul-khvahi ba ta'kid bar darman-i ma'navi," 18–19.

92 See Muhammad Khodayarifard, Mohammadi, and Abedini, "Darman-i shinakhti-raftari-i tabaddul-khvahi ba ta'kid bar darman-i ma'navi."

93 Mohammadi's published papers have reported on the successful outcome of his dissuasive therapeutic approach, but several mainstream psychiatrists and psychologists I interviewed were highly skeptical of both the approach and of his claims of success. Two were planning to develop a research project that would reach out to and study all trans applicants sent by the LMOI to Mohammadi over the previous decades. This study has since been abandoned, in part because persistent complaints about Mohammadi and his treatment methods by vocal trans activists eventually streamlined the process; the LMOI discontinued referring applicants to Rouzbeh Hospital (where Dr. Mohammadi is based) and to Imam Husayn Hospital where several other trans-hostile therapists were based. They are all now sent to the TPI.

## Chapter 6: Changing the Terms

1 This phrasing is a recent neologism, coined by connecting *tara*—a prefix equivalent to *trans* (as in *tarabari* [transport])—with *jins*, meaning sex/gender.

2 See http://behzisti.ir/News/Show.aspx?id=7313, accessed April 30, 2013.

3 For text of the new law, see http://police.ir/portal/File/ShowFile.aspx?ID=362a0d 36-97c8-40f8-872f-dd32e78e8919.

4 Like many other domains of law, legal codes concerning procedures for the medical examination of persons subject to army conscription and grounds for issuing exemption from service were revised after the 1979 revolution; new legislation was passed in 1989. See Ashrafian Bonab, *Zaruriyat-i pizishki-i qanuni* (Essentials of Forensic Medicine) (Tehran: Taymurzadah, 2001), 413–29. For text of section 30, see http://www.irteb.com/nezamvazife/2.htm; for section 33: http://www.irteb.com /nezamvazife/5.htm.

5 Like James Ferguson and Akhil Gupta, my approach to the study of the Iranian state

is one in which there is an "emphasis on its productive dimension" rather than "one characterized entirely by discipline and regulation." Perhaps even more to the point: My emphasis is on the productivity of its disciplinary and regulatory work. See Ferguson and Gupta, "Spatializing States: Toward an Ethnography of Neo-Liberal Governmentality." *American Ethnologist* 29, no. 4 (2002): 981–1002. The quote is from page 989.

6 This is also reflected in the recent discussions among some gay men that they ought to learn a few things from their trans brothers and perhaps get themselves recognized by the state as "suffering from hormonal disorder."

7 The shift, from the point of view of some MtF trans activists, has the additional value of setting them further apart from male homosexuals. I will discuss this issue more fully in chapter 7.

8 de Certeau, *The Practice of Everyday Life*, trans. by Steven Rendall (Berkeley: University of California Press, 1984), 18.

9 See Timothy Mitchell, "Society, Economy, and the State Effect," in *State/Culture: state-formation after the cultural turn*, edited by George Steinmatz, 76–97 (Ithaca, NY: Cornell University Press, 1999). Recent scholarship on "the state" has productively emphasized the significance of "everyday practices" for understanding how governmentality works. As Aradhana Sharma and Akhil Gupta have put it, "The *structure* of bureaucratic authority depends on the repetitive re-enactment of everyday practices. These iterative practices are performative [Judith Butler, *Gender Trouble: Feminism and the Subversion of Identity* (New York: Routledge, 1990)] in that, rather than being an outward reflection of a coherent and bounded state 'core,' they actually constitute that very core. It is *through* these reenactments that the coherence and continuity of state institutions is constituted and sometimes destabilized." Furthermore, "everyday statist encounters not only shape people's imagination of what the state is and how it is demarcated, but also enable people to devise strategies of resistance to this imagined state" ("Introduction: Rethinking Theories of the State in an Age of Globalization," in *Anthropology of the State*, edited by Aradhana Sharma and Akhil Gupta, 1–41 [Oxford: Blackwell, 2006]). The quotes are from pages 13 and 17, respectively; emphases are in original. For the important proposition of distinguishing between the state as a nexus of practice and institutional structure and the state-idea, Philip Abrams' 1977 essay remains critical ("Notes on the Difficulty of Studying the State [1977]," *Journal of Historical Sociology* 1, no. 1 [March 1988]: 58–89). While I have found this literature extremely helpful in thinking about how to approach the working of the Iranian state, what I am trying to bring forth for further research and analysis is the question of how to approach "the anthropology of the state" under the conditions in which such daily routine practices of the mundane do not necessarily have a repetitive, predictable pattern. I find that Keshavarzian's characterization of the state of continuous shifts and fractures on the level of political elite in Iran— as "a kaleidoscope of cross-cutting and cumulative cleavages that refract politics in complex and dynamic ways. . . . Alliances are more contingent and partial than a purely ideological reading of factionalism implies but more burdened by social realities than imagined by a strictly strategic and institutionalist understanding"— pertains as much to the broader workings of the state at all levels. See Arang Kesha-

varzian, "Regime Loyalty and Bazari Representation under the Islamic Republic of Iran: Dilemmas of the Society of Islamic Coalition." *International Journal of Middle East Studies* 41 (2009): 225–46, quote from page 242. See also Schayegh, "'Seeing Like a State': An Essay on the Historiography of Modern Iran," *International Journal of Middle East Studies* 42 (2010): 37–61.

10  "In just one year, between 1998 and 1999, the Ministry of Islamic Culture and Guidance licensed 168 publications, including seven daily newspapers, 27 weeklies, 59 monthlies, 53 quarterlies and two annual publications" (Gholam Khiabany and Annabelle Sreberny, "The Iranian Press and the Continuing Struggle over Civil Society 1998–2000," *International Communication Gazette* 63, no. 2–3 [May 2001]: 203–23, quote from page 207). By 2006, the number of licensed newspapers and magazines published is reported to have reached 3,367, "the highest in the history of print media in Iran." Kamalipour, "Print Media," in *Iran Today: An Encyclopedia of Life in the Islamic Republic*, volume 2, edited by Mehran Kamrava and Manochehr Dorraj, 394–98 (Westport, CT: Greenwood Press, 2008), 397.

11  On some recent reports of woman-presenting men's extortions, see *I'timad*, July 5, 2009, 15; September 30, 2009, 11; and November 22, 2009, 11. On runaway girls who become involved with the law, see *I'timad*, October 10, 2008, 11; and *I'timad-i Milli*, December 8, 2008, 14.

12  Interview with Mitra Farahani, June 2006; see Nazila Fathi's reports in *New York Times* on runaway youth (November 5, 2000, A13) and cross-dressed girls (February 19, 2003, A9). Her report on transsexuals appeared on August 2, 2004, A3.

13  This is quite a high figure. Circulation of newspapers in 2007 ranged from 30,000 to 150,000 with the exception of the IRIB publication, *Jam-i jam*, which boasted a circulation of 450,000. See Kamalipour, "Print Media," 397. I have not been able to find circulation figures for weekly and monthly magazines. In general, however, they tend to be lower. The Institute's website does not seem to be active any longer (last accessed June 6, 2012).

14  Possibly the same story as reported in the *Guardian*, June 20, 2000, "Sex-change Iranian hates life as woman."

15  For reviews of the novel, see Natasha Amiri, in *Jahan-i kitab*, no. 121–22, April–May 2001, 28; Bihnaz 'Ali-Pur Gaskari, in *Kitab-i mah-i adabiyat va falsafah*, no. 43, April–May 2001, 68–69; Mitra Davar, in *Dauran-i imruz*, February 16, 2000, 7; Maryam Basiri, in *Payam-i zan*, no. 124, June–July 2002, 72–75 and 79; and Ahmad Parhizi, "Namauvaffaq, chira?" in *Hambastigi*, June 19, 2001, 11. There are also two reviews in *Homan*, no. 18 (winter 2002): one by Shahin (32–33) and another by Sima (34–36).

16  *Rah-i zindigi*, 166, March 6, 2004, 13.

17  Some of the stories read like fictionalized versions of cases reported in scientific journals. In issue no. 173 (July 6, 2004): 8, for instance, there is the story of one "successful therapy, after thirty sessions," which reads like the one reported by Dr. Mohammadi and his colleagues (see chapter 5 for details). Unlike all other stories, and to emphasize that other treatments do not provide a resolution, this story is titled "A Cured TS" (Yik ti is-i darman-shudah).

18  '*Nar-maddah*': male-female; '*amrud*': a variant of *amrad*, male beardless adolescent;

'kinig': an *amrad* with a strong and well-built body; and *'naukhatt'*: a poetic expression for a male adolescent with a hint of fresh growth of down over his lips—the most beautiful and desired figure in classical Persian literature.

19 Muhammad Riza Iskandari Tariqan, "Ham-jins-gara'i, ibham-i jinsi, ya . . . ?" [Homosexuality, sexual ambiguity, or . . . ?] *Andishah-i jami'ah*, no. 30 (June/July 2003), 55–59. The quote is from page 56. Excerpts from this article also were reprinted in the daily *I'timad*, July 15, 2003, and subsequently on several websites.

20 Mansur Zabitian, "Zindigi-i shinas-namah-'i, zindigi-i vaqi'i" (Life according to birth-certificate, [versus] real life), *Chilchiraq*, July/August 2003, 6–7. 'Abis Burhan, *Maria*, 35 minutes. The first screening took place at the Fajr Festival, Tehran, February 2006. Several documentaries were produced and screened before *Maria*, but none in Iran. The earliest I know of is Mitra Farahani, *Just a Woman*, 30 minutes, first screened February 6–17, 2002, at the Berlin International Film Festival.

21 Correspondingly there was vast international coverage, both in print but most importantly in television reports and documentary films, including, in addition to those already mentioned, the following: Frances Harrison, "Iran's sex-change operation," BBC *Newsnight*, January 2005 (transcripts available at http://news.bbc.co.uk/1/hi/programmes/newsnight/4115535.stm, accessed March 2, 2013); Faramarz Amini, *Yad-i yaran*, Omid-E-Iran Television (OITN, a Persian-language satellite channel), part I: 57 minutes, part II: 96 minutes part III: 81 minutes, 2005; Kouross Esmaeli, *Legacy of the Imam*, 14 minutes, 2006; Zohreh Shayesteh, *Inside Out*, 39 minutes, 2006; Daisy Mohr and Negin Kianfar, *The Birthday*, 63 minutes, 2006; Elhum Shakerifar, *Roya and Omid*, 18 minutes, 2007; Bahman Motamedian, *Khastegi* (Tedium), 76 minutes, 2008; and Tanaz Eshaghian, *Be Like Others*, 74 minutes, 2008.

22 Persian is reportedly the fourth most common language used for blogs; others have reported it as the second, tied with French. There is a growing literature on Persian-language blogs and their cultural and political significance. For an early article, see Alireza Doostdar, "'The Vulgar Spirit of Blogging': On Language, Culture, and Power in Persian Weblogestan," *American Anthropologist* 106, no. 4 (2004): 651–62; for further scholarship on this topic, see Alireza Doostdar, "Weblogs," in *Encyclopaedia Iranica*, http://www.iranica.com/articles/weblogs, accessed March 3, 2013; Mehdi Semati, "Internet," in *Iran Today: An Encyclopedia of Life in the Islamic Republic*, volume I, edited by Mehran Kamrava and Manochehr Dorraj, 245–50 (Westport, CT: Greenwood Press, 2008); John Kelly and Bruce Etling, *Mapping Iran's Online Public: Politics and Culture in the Persian Blogosphere* (Cambridge, MA: Harvard University Berkman Center, 2008); Nasrin Alavi, *We Are Iran: The Persian Blogs* (Brooklyn, NY: Soft Skull Press, 2005); and Gholam Khiabany and Annabelle Sreberny, *Blogistan: The Internet and Politics in Iran* (London: I. B. Tauris, 2010).

23 Typing *taghyir jinsiyat* (sex change) in Persian in Google (last attempted on January 19, 2010) results in 1,180,000 items in 0.33 seconds. The only domain of media that has not covered transsexuality in Iran is the IRIB, with the exception of one radio program on Radio Javan in the summer of 2007. While a few producers who work for IRIB have been involved in the production of related documentaries, these have been done as private initiatives and none have been screened by IRIB.

24  Reported in e-mail communication with Dr. Mehrdad Eftekhar, the dissertation supervisor.

25  There has been a never-substantiated presumption among some commentators that in a country such as Iran the "oppression of women" is linked with the desire for sex change among women. One study found that among a sample population of high schools (259 girls and 242 boys in Tehran), 36.6 percent of girls and 6.0 percent of boys had indicated if they were to be reborn they would have wished to be reborn as the other sex. See Razeieh Zohrevand, "Relationship of Gender Roles Perception and Gender Contentment," *Pazhuhish-i Zanan* 2, no. 2 (summer 2004): 117–25. (The English title of the article is per the translation by the journal.) Whether and how there is any connection between gender discrimination, the fantasy of being born as the other sex, and the actual desire for sex change, has never been persuasively demonstrated and I suspect it is not demonstrable.

26  As Mahmood Messkoub has noted, "These movements [for a just and equitable society] articulated certain social objectives that have been on the national agenda for decades, and they gave a remarkable continuity to social policy despite the political vicissitudes in Iran" ("Social Policy in Iran in the Twentieth Century," *Iranian Studies* 39, no. 2 [June 2006]: 227–52; quote from page 227).

27  For further details, see Messkoub, "Social Policy."

28  According to another source, in earlier years trans persons went to the Office for Women's Affairs in Ministry of Health. Subsequent to the formation of the Nationwide Committee, the Ministry of Health ceased to be actively involved. See Fatemeh Javaheri and Zaynab Kuchekian, "Ikhtilal-i huviyat-i jinsiyati va ab'ad-i ijtima'i-i an: barrisi-i padidah-i narizayati-i jinsi dar Iran" (Gender identity disorder and its social dimensions investigating the phenomenon of sexual/gender discontent in Iran), *Rifah-i ijtima'i* (Social welfare) 5, no. 21 (summer 2006): 265–92. For an English article based on the same research, see Fatemeh Javaheri, "A Study of Transsexuality in Iran," *Iranian Studies* 43, no. 3 (June 2010): 365–77. This above-mentioned issue of the *Rifah-i ijtima'i* was devoted to the topic of women's issues in Iran. "Woman" seems to act as a default category in many domains for trans persons. As we have seen, the office to which trans persons are assigned in the Ministry of Health is the Women's Affairs Office. In 2006–7, when they approached the Office of the President to receive support, they were sent to the Center for Women and Family Affairs. A feminist lawyer and welfare consultant, who usually works with women clients involved in various family disputes, was called upon to help two trans persons, one MtF and one FtM. For her and the support NGO she led, both qualified as women in need.

29  This was part of an interview in August 2006, but the interviewee did not want this segment to be attributed to him/her.

30  As reported in *I'timad*, October 21, 2007, 10.

31  Most recently, Sayyid Hasan Musavi Chilik, Director General of the Office of Socially Harmed of the Welfare Organization, reiterated this long-standing criticism: "One of the problems facing TS patients (GID) is the refusal of the Ministry of Health to cooperate, even though, according to the guidelines overseeing ['a'in-namah] support

of the patients afflicted with GID, their treatment is the responsibility of the Ministry of Health. And it is not simply the issue of treatment. Supervising treatment and surgery centers is the task of the Ministry of Health; the kind of operation, quality of surgery, medicines that these people must take for a lifetime, all are tasks of the Ministry of Health, but regrettably this ministry has washed its hands of this subject." Reported by FarsNews, January 22, 2010, accessed March 2, 2013, http://www.farsnews.net/newstext.php?nn=8810290914.

32  For the text of this memorandum of understanding, see State Welfare Organization of Iran's site, http://www.behzisti.ir/Documents/Show.aspx?id=43. Last accessed on May 3, 2013.

33  See Thomas Hansen and Finn Stepputat, eds., *States of Imagination: Ethnographic Explorations of the Postcolonial State* (Durham, NC: Duke University Press, 2001). The quote is from page 18 of the introduction.

34  See Asef Bayat, *Life as Politics: How Ordinary People Change the Middle East* (Palo Alto, CA: Stanford University Press, 2010), 19–22.

35  FarsNews, January 22, 2010, http://www.farsnews.net/newstext.php?nn=881029 0914.

36  For this long and rich history, see Parvin Paidar, *Women and the Political Process in Twentieth-century Iran* (Cambridge: Cambridge University Press, 1995); and, more recently, Osanloo, *The Politics of Women's Rights in Iran* (Princeton, NJ: Princeton University Press, 2009).

37  Michael M. J. Fischer, "Philosophia and Anthropologia: Reading alongside Benjamin in Yazd, Derrida in Qum, Arendt in Tehran," unpublished manuscript, April 2011; quote is from page 21.

38  The weekly meetings always had an official representative present. For a while, there was a male psychiatrist present; however, trans persons didn't like him and his authoritarian ways of running the meetings. They succeeded in getting him replaced by a social worker, a woman, who was said to be friendlier.

39  This was not an infrequent report. One such case was reported on the website of ISSIGID (more on this NGO below), news section, item dated April 20, 2008.

40  For a while, in 2006–7, there was a great deal of talk about Tehran Municipality renovating and allocating an old dilapidated building for the temporary housing of homeless trans persons. There was a lot of discussion and disagreement among trans activists on this subject. Although temporary housing was a vital need, there was justified concern about the ghettoizing effect of such a move, and more seriously about how it would subject their lives (including their sexual lives and what was generally referred to as *bizinis*—business, a euphemism for sex work) to round-the-clock supervision of the security forces. There was also concern that such allocation might result in the loss of the current housing subsidy, which, meager as it was, helped some to get independent rentals. The idea of temporary housing never got off the ground.

41  Both at this meeting and at several others, including the meeting at the Center for Women and Family Affairs in the Office of the President, officials took it upon themselves to give the activists advice about how to navigate various governmental institutions. For instance, at the Center, they learned that not only the Ministry of

the Interior but also the Welfare Organization had the authority to issue permits for the formation of NGOS, except that the latter's type of NGO had limited domains in which it could be active. They were encouraged to seek NGO registration through the Welfare Organization because their case was already under the latter's domain and it was far easier to get a Welfare Organization–registered NGO. This pattern of advice indicated that the state was not a homogeneous, structurally solid formation. Even state functionaries knew that getting things done required navigating a complicated labyrinth of competing offices and interests.

42 In the autumn of 2006, a series of meetings were held, upon the request of trans activists, with several key figures in the Ministry of Health, including Dr. 'Alavian, Assistant Minister of Health, Dr. Guyan, and Dr. Zia'i; these culminated in the meeting with the minister himself, Dr. Lankarani, who was the Minister of Health from 2005 to 2009. When the utter lack of actual scientific knowledge of this subject among high ministers became evident, Dr. Zia'i had requested that the Ministry be provided with educational, scientific material. It was in this series of meetings that activists submitted a series of demands, including the demand that the government bring a team of specialists from abroad to train surgeons and nurses in SRS; that a specialized centralized clinic/hospital be set up (or one of the existing state hospitals be so assigned) in which all the needs of trans persons would be met (such as psychotherapy, hormonal treatment, SRS, postoperative care, laser hair removal, vocal cord retuning, welfare needs, social workers' assistance, etc.); that basic health insurance booklets be issued; that SRS be classified as required rather than elective surgery to make it eligible for insurance payments; and that health insurance cover their prosthetics and pharmaceutical needs. Some of these demands were subsequently met. See below.

43 After surgery, a person goes back to a special court that examines the medical records and issues an order to the Notary Registry Office, which is charged with registering every individual's personal data, to produce a new *shinasnamah* (identification booklet). As is the case with other approvals of name change, there is a notation on the last page of the new booklet stating that it has been issued subsequent to a court order of such and such a date. This notation often raises questions, whether by potential employers or by the family of a partner one wants to marry. Activists have lobbied for many years for the removal of this clause. There were occasional reports that this clause was no longer included in the new trans booklets. Other reports, however, did not confirm change of policy.

44 Through the Welfare Organization, the MCIO provides health insurance for trans persons. The insurance, which is reviewed and renewed annually, covers 70 percent of the cost of office visits and 90 percent of the cost of hospitalization.

45 For the ISNA report, see http://isna.ir/fa/news/8602-01206/.

46 Children with no legal guardians are under the supervision of the Welfare Organization, which also runs a placement program for these children. Initially ratified on March 20, 1975, regulations for fostering and adoption have been under revision by the Majlis over the past several years. For current regulations, see http://behzisti.ir /News/Show.aspx?id=5341.

47 Arash Alaei is internationally recognized for his AIDS-related work. With a group

of physicians and health workers, including his brother Kamyar, they established "harm-reduction and prevention centers" in several cities to deal with sexually transmitted infections, HIV/AIDS, and drug addiction. The clinics were recognized by the World Health Organization as a best-practice model for the Middle East and North Africa. The Alaei brothers were arrested in June 2008 and charged with acting against national security and collaborating with the American government. In May 2009, Arash Alaei was sentenced to six years in prison, Kamyar to three years. For more information, see http://www.iranhumanrights.org/tag/alaei-brothers/. They were released in 2011.

48 This was the reason that the magazine management had given. Another rumor circulating was that the presence of gay men (and occasionally lesbians) in these meetings had been reported to top officials in the Ministry of Health, generating pressure on Dr. Ohadi and threats against the magazine. The move did not pay off; the magazine itself was shut down shortly after for publishing material that was considered immoral and too sexually explicit.

49 This is the site's English title. The Persian is *Anjuman-i himayat az bimaran-i mubtala bah ikhtilal-i huviyat-i jinsi-i Iran,* closer to "Iranian Society for Supporting Patients Afflicted with Gender Identity Disorder."

50 Ferguson and Gupta, "Spatializing States," 990.

51 One such case was made into the subject of a documentary by Rakhshan Bani-Etemad. In this instance, the state made some start-up money available to citizens through a newspaper advertisement. Two female friends responded and formed an NGO for the support of abused women in a poor neighborhood. The initial financial aid enabled the work of the two women; the governmental approval also facilitated their access to various governmental agencies whose help they needed. At the same time, the project took care of a social need for which the government no longer needed to allocate human and material resources. The documentary is entitled *Angels in the House of the Sun,* 53 minutes, 2009.

52 The tensions and frustrations were not only between *trans*es and the authorities. Much to the irritation of trans activists, several others—including a documentary filmmaker, an attorney, and a television program producer, all with better connections in high places—also were trying in the same period to form NGOs on behalf of this now-popular subject for social and economic attention. At least one of them was successful in obtaining a permit but did not pursue it, in part because trans activists refused to collaborate.

53 See reports in the Q&A section of the GID site, dated October 4, 2008, and May 14 and 15, 2009. Full membership is limited to transsexuals; an affiliated membership is offered to "medical professionals and other persons professionally related to GID." See the Society's constitution and by-laws on the GID website, under the Mulk-ara link.

54 The site has been fully redesigned and was launched anew in late August 2010. The following section is based on the design and content of the earlier site, since the time-frame of this book largely ends in early 2010. The Qur'anic verses have been preserved in the new design.

55 The articles section includes both English-language material—such as DSM-IV on

GID—and Persian articles, including a long interview with Hujjat al-Islam Karimi-nia. The laws and regulations section has digital images of several legal documents, including the permit issued by the Ministry of the Interior for the formation of the society.

56  Despite a voluminous Islamic jurisprudential (fiqh) literature on the subject of intersex individuals, and the affiliation of transsexuality with intersexuality in the early 1940s (see chapter 2), the more recent discourse emerging around transsexuality has not paid any attention to the intersexuality. Only recently, a full article appeared on this topic in the popular weekly *Salamat*, no. 254, January 16, 2010, 22. Obstetricians I interviewed indicated that this topic did not receive any special training in medical schools and there were no standard diagnostic or treatment protocols in place. Intersex surgery cases during adolescence or adulthood now use the same legal/administrative channels as *trans*es and are decided by the same commission at TPI, as discussed in chapter 1.

57  Examples of such brief news items include screening of the film *Tedium* in the Venice Festival (postdated September 8, 2008), and two posts related to the news of the suicide in Toronto of Sayeh—an MtF trans who had sought asylum in Canada (posts dated August 16 and September 2, 2008).

58  ISSIGID website, March 12, 2008, "Ma shahkar-i khilqatim." The sense of being a special creature of God often found its expression in trans narratives. At a particularly tense moment during a meeting with a high official at the Center for Women and Family Affairs in the Office of the President, when the official insisted on *trans*es giving her a persuasive account of the etiology of transsexualism, Houri, with her unbeatable sense of humor, said, "Well, you know what? God creates men, God creates women, he keeps doing this, but some days he gets bored and creates *trans*es." The discourse of "God created me this way" has been adopted more recently by some *gay* men as well.

59  Becoming a *suzhah* is a highly contested topic. The expression is often used in an admonishing context. MtFs are particularly prone to criticizing other MtFs for making themselves into *suzhah*, a scandalous subject of attention, by over-the-top public displays of femininity. This, they argue, is not simply an individual failing; it gives all MtFs a bad name. I will return to this issue in the final chapter.

60  See http://www.helpftm.blogfa.com/ and http://www.helpmtf.blogfa.com/. In addition to these two sites, individual *trans*es have blogs whose addresses are regularly posted on the ISSIGID website. I have seen more than twenty such addresses over the two years (March 2008–March 2010) that I followed the site closely. Not all have remained active.

61  A thousand tumans was worth roughly a dollar in this period.

62  On this issue, see the ISSIGID website, the Open Forum, postings dated August 23, September 12, September 17, and December 10, 2009.

63  For full information and the latest news of the campaign, see http://www.sign4 change.info/english/.

64  The success of this orientation has at the same time depended on a great deal of inner policing of those who spoke in the name of the group. Activists were very disciplinary in selecting who met with whom; deciding what outfits MtFs would wear

at such meetings; and how they interacted with officials, including such details as tone of voice, etiquette of introductions, and so on. In general, MtFs were often the target of criticism of "excess and exaggeration," especially by FtMs. Mohsen, an FtM activist, put it in these terms: "The kids on the other side [*bachchah-ha-yi 'untaraf*], they have more problems, the problem of *ivakhvahari* has always been there. We are more easily accepted. It is partly their own fault. They do all women's things with thick density, so everyone stares at them and realizes this person has a problem—whether it is heavy makeup, overstated gestures, walking gait—no woman acts like that. I don't understand why they make themselves such a tableau. Many make a living from sex work."

65   FarsNews, January 20, 2010, http://www.farsnews.net/newstext.php?nn=88102 71226. For a fuller explication of his views, see his interview in *Mihr-i nau*, no. 4 (November/December 2009), 30–31.

66   For reports of the initial incident and the court ruling, see *I'timad-i milli*, August 7, 2007, 18. The accused, Mitra Nidami, was sentenced first to a two-year prison term and monetary compensation for the blinded eye. His/her terrible conditions in a men's prison were what had prompted the report. His/her prison term was reduced to ten months on appeal (*I'timad-i milli*, December 2, 2007, 14). In the spring of 2008, it was reported that even though s/he had completed her/his prison term, because s/he could not afford to pay the fine, s/he was still held in jail. Her/his lawyer, Muhammad Mustafa'i, a well-known human rights lawyer and a particular champion of abolishing the death penalty, led a fundraising effort that eventually made her/his release possible on May 22, 2008.

67   The woman in this case, Shaqayiq, had gone to the family courts to get permission to marry Ardishir despite her father's opposition (the permission of a father or legal guardian is legally required for a woman's first marriage). Her father stated in the court that he could not imagine his daughter's best friend as her husband. Eventually, he agreed to give his permission so long as there were no medical grounds for difficulty in marriage. The case was sent to the LMOI, which confirmed that there was no medical impediment to the marriage. See *I'timad*, August 25, 2009 (11), and September 9, 2009 (11).

68   See the reports on August 26, 2009, at http://tabnak.ir/fa/pages/?cid=61344; September 6, 2009, at http://tabnak.ir/fa/pages/?cid=62967; and October 12, 2009, at http://tabnak.ir/fa/pages/?cid=68227, http://tabnak.ir/fa/pages/?cid=68228, and *Sarmayah*, October 13, 2009, 10. Girls' high school sports teams have long been thought of as sites of "well-known" gender/sex nonnormativity: in my time it was basketball, now it is soccer. In the fall of 2006, in a focus meeting, one FtM, who had been on the women's national soccer team, said, "Everyone on the soccer team is like this [*intauri*]. Everyone is *mushkildar* [with problem]." Surprisingly, given the nature of the group discussion, the *taur* or the *mushkil* was never named. In this meeting, several people also said that sports teachers in girls' high schools (all female) use their position to have relations with girls. Houri at this point named the "problem": "Well, they must be lesbians."

69   This is also confusing because it is often written in the Latin alphabet within a Persian sentence and it is not clear whether one is to read it left to right or right to

left; many do not use names, or it is not clear if these are at-birth names or chosen names, and it is often not clear if one is reading a posting by an *MtF* or an *FtM*.

70 *Mihr-i nau*, no. 4 (November/December 2009), 23 and 25.

71 For similar observations, see Peter Jackson, "Performative Genders, Perverse Desires: A Bio-History of Thailand's Same-Sex and Transgender Cultures." *Intersections: Gender, History and Culture in the Asian Context*, 9 (August 2003), online edition, points 88 and 103, accessed March 3, 2013, http://intersections.anu.edu.au/issue9 /jackson.html.

### Chapter 7: Living Patterns, Narrative Styles

1 The question is not as frivolously posed as it may sound at first. In the past three decades, Iran has witnessed a changing cultural (and, of course, biosurgical) scene as far as bodily modifications are concerned. This is, in part, connected with the impact of the Iran-Iraq war and the huge number of war-wounded persons that needed various bodily reparation and prosthetic surgeries. There also has been an enormous increase in cosmetic surgeries, most visibly "nose jobs," and not only among women. Men from similar class and cultural backgrounds are seen frequently with facial bandages after nose surgery. This situation has contributed to the acceptability of srs by trans persons and some of their families. The increasing spread of nose jobs as well as the use of mascara and eyebrow plucking by *straight* men could be seen as an instance of "how the lifeworlds of *gay* men are 'leaking' into . . . national culture" (Tom Boellstorff, *A Coincidence of Desires* [Durham, NC: Duke University Press, 2007], 116). For a critically insightful essay that examines the relationship between the bodily alterations demanded by transsexuals and those demanded under the category of "cosmetic enhancement," see Dean Spade, "Mutilating Gender," in *The Transgender Studies Reader*, edited by Susan Stryker and Stephen Whittle, 315–32 (New York: Routledge, 2006). For a historical grounding of the connection between health, beauty, and new conceptualizations of the individual in Iran, see Camron Amin, "Importing 'Beauty Culture' into Iran in the 1920s and 1930s: Mass Marketing Individualism in an Age of Anti-Imperialist Sacrifice," *Comparative Studies of South Asia, Africa, and the Middle East* 24, no. 1 (2004): 79–95.

2 Jay Prosser, *Second Skins: The Body Narratives of Transsexuality* (New York: Columbia University Press, 1998), 115–16.

3 Prosser, *Second Skins*, 124.

4 Prosser, *Second Skins*, 142.

5 For an insightful essay, see Amy Hollywood, "Spiritual but Not Religious," *Harvard Divinity Bulletin* 38, no. 1–2 (winter/spring 2010): 19–26.

6 I have since checked with several hadith scholars and they have not come across anything similar to this narrative in classical compendiums.

7 *Yad-i yaran*; see chapters 1 and 6 for a discussion of this program.

8 This developmental failure model, with its focus on parenting practices, is countered by several other circulating narratives, especially among trans persons themselves. Over and over again they pointed to the Iran-Iraq War decade (1980–88) as that which produced enormous stress, which in turn affected pregnant women, say-

ing "Just look around you; most of us are in our twenties. Now, what was going on twenty years ago? The war. Everyone lived *super-stressed* [English words used] lives. Pregnant women's *stress* affects fetal development. We are all children of the Imposed War."

9  The pattern of disappearing "anonymously" into the general population, especially important for MtFs, coupled with the general association of MtFs with sex work, has contributed to the perception—never verified factually—that "most MtFs work as prostitutes." See also Deniz Kandiyoti, "Pink Card Blues: Trouble and Strife at the Crossroads of Gender," in *Fragments of Culture: The Everyday of Modern Turkey*, edited by Deniz Kandiyoti and Ayse Saktanber, 277–93 (New Brunswick, NJ: Rutgers University Press, 2002).

10  Samia Jamal, 1924–1994, belly dancer and film actress. There are substantial literature and film clips available about her. See http://en.wikipedia.org/wiki/Samia _Playal, http://www.belly-dance.org/samia-playal.html, and http://images.google .com/search?q=Samia+Jamal&biw=1030&bih=766&tbm=isch.

11  This possibly refers to Le Chevalier d'Éon, which held a wide fascination in the popular journals of the late 1940s through the 1960s in Iran. See chapter 2.

12  The harsh experience of the older generation of MtFs is generally recognized by the younger activists. As Sina put it, "The older generation really suffered a great deal before they got where they wanted to get." Arezu's narrative had a happier development from here on: "I did all kinds of jobs, long story, but I gained so much experience, bad and good, I was very responsible at my jobs and eventually met some really nice people, including a couple who almost adopted me into their life, they both worked, I helped take care of their two kids. Slowly I set up my own independent life, they helped me rent a small apartment and start my business. It was in my new place that I met my husband. His parents lived on the second floor. Soon we set up home together. I still did not know I could legally change my sex. When we were living together, someone in the building became suspicious and reported us. They arrested us and took us to the *kumitah* [neighborhood surveillance committee]. We were lucky; the judge was a really nice cleric; when he heard my story, he said, "that is no problem, go to so-and-so [name withheld] and get a religious statement from him that you are a woman, then go to so-and-so [name withheld] and he will help you get a new identity booklet." I actually got my new booklet even before I had had my operation, and with that new identity booklet we got married. The cleric told me, "This is all OK, but remember that you need to still go to the doctors and pursue your sex change." That was of course my dream, my wish come true, that is why I chose the name Arezu [means wish]; the only thing was to work and save money, so it took a while, I had to do one thing at a time. My husband didn't want me to put myself through all these operations; he kept saying that we have loved each other and been happy without it; but I needed to do it. He is the most loving supportive husband. I am blessed."

13  Houri is one of the MtFs who was regularly called upon to go to the TPI and talk to panicked parents. Getting families involved and making their consent part of the legal transition process has become a double-edged sword. At one level, it has provided an arena to which therapists and social workers can bring hostile families and

help them accept their son's or daughter's desire for sex change, thus securing a familial connection for a trans person. On the other hand, in the case of harshly resisting and hostile families, it has added further obstacles to transition. A great deal of Mohseni-nia's workload had to do with complications arising in cases where families simply refused their permission, even after months of counseling. In one case, a mother had accused the TPI, its doctors, and its case workers of having accepted bribes to issue their recommendation.

14  The heteronormalizing dynamic of romantic marriage has been insightfully discussed by Boellstorff: "But perhaps the most far reaching consequence of the shift to chosen or love marriage is that this form of marriage brings sexual orientation into being as a new kind of problem. Since arranged marriages are often constructed as unions between two entire families, not just two individuals, the failure of an arranged marriage lies primarily on the family's failure to select a proper spouse. But marriage based on choice and love implies a choosing self whose choice must be a heterosexual one" (*A Coincidence of Desires*, 52). See also pages 167 and 174.

15  I would like to emphasize that while this may sound very "traditional," it is actually quite "modern." For instance, female sexual appetite, in classical Islamic thought, was generally said to overwhelm male appetite and thus needed constraints of various kinds. In modernist thinking, active and strong sexual appetite is seen as masculine. That modernity is not a linear achievement, however, is also reflected in that the concept of the female power of sexuality, perceived as a threat to men and to the social order of things, circulates and is invoked as well. Different concepts are put to work depending on a given context.

16  In a different site, that of feminist discourse, *jinsiyat* has come to serve as the term for distinguishing anatomical body from sociocultural constructs and performances—it is used emphatically as equivalent to English gender. Here sex and sexuality occupy the category jins, and *jinsiyat* is reserved for gender. In other words, in this domain there is an indistinction between sex and sexuality—something productive for feminist attempts to rid the over-signified woman's body as a site of sex and sexuality by dismissing the significance of both categories to meanings of gender (purifying gender of sex/sexuality) that is open to change through social reform. So far the two domains have remained largely on different plains. There is no indication of feminist moves within the *trans* community. Nor is there much interest among feminists about transsexuality, except to the extent that along with homosexuals and subject to similar restrictions of rights as those of women—the primary subject of feminist movement. It is within this narrative of rights that the feminist press and feminist journalists occasionally have covered the topic of transsexuality.

17  For similar trends in the late 1960s in the United States, see Joanne Meyerowitz, *How Sex Changed: A History of Transsexuality in the United States* (Cambridge, MA: Harvard University Press, 2002), 181–84.

18  Tom Boellstorff has similarly noted: "Their feminine souls and bodily presentations mean that while male *waria* sex is understood abstractly as a form of homosexuality, it is distinguished from sex 'between two men'" ("Playing back the Nation: *Waria*, Indonesian Transvestites," *Cultural Anthropology* 19, no. 2 [2004]: 168).

19  The notion of sexual minority is also invoked to critique persistent disavowal of and

expressions of animosity toward homosexuals in GID site discussions. See the Q&A subsection, entry dated May 9, 2008: "This [expression of hatred of homosexuality and homosexuals] made me very sad. In all the world, sexual minorities have fought side by side and supported each other."

20　The significance of the familial is also reflected in numerous ways in which familial designations are used to define, or present, close relationships—as in vows of sister-hood, in mother's friends and father's friends referred to as aunts and uncles, in Houri and Zia living as and considering each other "brother and sister," and in trans persons acting as next of kin for each other in a variety of contexts.

21　See Boellstorff, *A Coincidence of Desires*, 139–44 and 156–59. Boellstorff concludes, "In Indonesia there is currently no way to be publicly *gay* and seen as a pious Mus-lim, and thus it remains 'ungrammatical.' . . . *Gay* Muslims do not necessarily feel excluded from their religion . . . but they imagine a life course of incommensura-bility where they are *gay* in the *gay* world, marry heterosexually in the *normal* world, and find religious community solely in that *normal* world" (156); "what we find is a habitation, not a resolution, of incommensurability" (158).

22　On the ethos of javanmardi in contemporary Iran, see Fariba Adelkhah, *Being Mod-ern in Iran*, trans. by Jonathan Derrick (London: Hurst, 1999; Paris: Karthala, 1998).

23　For a historical analysis of this ritual in Safavid Iran, see Kathryn Babayan, "'In Spirit We Ate Each Other's Sorrow': Female Companionship in Seventeenth-Century Safavi Iran," in *Islamicate Sexualities: Translations across Temporal Geogra-phies of Desire*, edited by Kathryn Babayan and Afsaneh Najmabadi, 239–74 (Cam-bridge, MA: Harvard University Press, 2008). Anecdotally, I have known several women of my generation whose grandmothers had enacted public rituals of sworn sisterhood and whose mothers had such recognized best female friends, whom the children called "aunts," but they had not performed the ritual.

24　It is possible that the gradual disappearance of vows of sisterhood in big urban cen-ters is linked with the emergent dominance of romantic choice marriages, which demand to be, and are expected to provide, the central, if not sole, locus of affective attachment. Thus an alternative emotional investment in a sister becomes perceived as a rival and potential threat to the attachment to one's husband.

25　Nauruz, the Iranian New Year, starting at the spring equinox, is the most signifi-cant national holiday in Iran. There is a big emphasis on family unions and familial visits. It is a very festive occasion, and, regardless of when that moment of equinox may actually fall, all family members are supposed to come together to start the new year. It is often said that how one starts the new year foretells how one will live the rest of the year. Thus to start the new year in separation not only makes the start of every year a sad moment of separation for Leila and Minu—each has to be with her own family—but it is also a reminder that they are not the same as a heterosexual couple who would be with one or the other's family.

26　This kind of arrangement is not unusual. Sometimes it becomes a news story. In 1998, a man applied to a court requesting permission to take a second wife. He was a doctor and his wife was a trained midwife; they had been married for two years and both expressly emphasized that theirs was a happy marriage. The judge was puzzled why then there was a request for a second wife. The husband insisted that this was his wife's idea; the wife confirmed the statement. Finally, and very reluctantly, the woman explained that she has had a very close female friend since the first year of college; they are very attached and spend day and night together. When someone recently had asked for her friend's hand in marriage, she became so ill that her friend broke off the marriage negotiations. She immediately recovered, then realized that since she cannot tolerate losing her friend to marriage, the only solution would be for her husband to marry her friend as a second wife. The judge agreed to issue the permit. For the full report, see the *Iran Times*, July 17, 1998, 11.

27 Mohammad had met Sina through the medical information site http://forum .iransalamat.com. They became best buddies and years later, now both postop, they so remain. Forum.iransalamat has a section on "Psychology-psychiatry" that includes a subsection on "sexual difficulties and sexual identification (from a psychiatric perspective)"—see http://forum.iransalamat.com/forumdisplay.php?f=617. In this section, recent articles include "Eliminating the 'mental patient' code for military exemption of transsexuals in Iran" (January 2010); "Looking at girls' tendency to act boyish" (December 2009); "Skepticism over Caster Semenya's gender/sex, the African woman, 800-meter world champion" (December 2009); "Gender Identity Disorder Illness (*Transsexualism*)" (December 2009); and "Homosexuality" (July 2008).

28 From Mahnaz's description, the program was the second part of *Yad-i yaran*. The self-cognitive significance of this program has been mentioned in several more recent trans-autobiographical narratives. For the case of Mehrana, as narrated on the GID website, see the entry in the Open Forum subsection dated August 13, 2009.

29 Mark Johnson similarly discusses "marriage and children" as "the primary measure of socially recognized adult status" (*Beauty and Power: Transgendering and Cultural Transformation in the Southern Philippines* [Oxford: Berg, 1997], 133). For a similar but distinct meaning of formation of family to individual lives, see Lisa Rofel, *Desiring China: Experiments in Neoliberalism, Sexuality, and Public Culture* (Durham, NC: Duke University Press, 2007): "Family is the metonym for belonging, not simply to the nation-state but to Chinese culture writ large. In China ongoing discursive productions of family are indispensable sites for establishing one's humanness as well as one's social subjectivity. For gay men to establish their normality as men, they must marry, not to prove their virility but to produce heirs. Then, too, family still provides men with moral privilege and access to social power, which is not true for women and, I suspect, is the reason it has been easier for lesbians in China to renounce marriage" (100).

30 I am grateful to Steve Caton for suggesting this line of observation.

31 This is also a fear expressed by transsexuals and homosexuals when facing pressure to get married by "unknowing" parents: "I am a man on the surface [*zahiran*], thirty-four years old. I have no desire for the opposite sex and desire my own genus/sex. My family doesn't know this and insists that I get married. I think I will face problems if I get married, because I am not aroused by girls. What shall I do?" (GID site, Q&A subsection, entry dated March 30, 2008).

32 Megan Sinnott, *Toms and Dees: Transgender Identity and Female Same-Sex Relationships in Thailand* (Honolulu: University of Hawai'i Press, 2004), 70.

33 As Boellstorff notes, in a different context and with different effects, "The prior existence of recognized male transvestites has had a profound impact upon gay subject
positions, and it is a prime reason for some differences between gay and lesbian
subject positions in Southeast Asia, since nowhere in Southeast Asia did there exist
any female transgendered subject position with anything like the visibility of *waria*,
*kathoey*, *bakla*, or other male transvestite subject positions" (*A Coincidence of Desires*,
196). And further, "because the predominant female transgender and female homosexual subject positions in contemporary Southeast Asia came into being around
the same time, they are far more intertwined, conceptually and practically, than are
male transvestite and gay subject positions" (202).

## Chapter 8: Professing Selves

1 I am borrowing this expression, and much analytical work related to it, from Denise
Riley, *The Words of Selves: Identification, Solidarity, Irony* (Palo Alto, CA: Stanford University Press, 2000); the quote is from page 9.

2 Nor do I propose to draw on the very rich anthropological literature about non-U.S.,
nonheteronormative gender/sexual identifications and practices (from which I have
learned a great deal and on which I draw at times) to produce comparable transnational patterns. I find comparative analysis beyond my comfort zone.

3 These works include Suad Joseph's *Intimate Selving in Arab Families: Gender, Self,
and Identity* (Syracuse, NY: Syracuse University Press, 1999), in which she provides
a broad review and critical engagement with largely psychodynamic theories of self
and articulates, in that context, her concept of "intimate selving." Joseph has developed this concept further in much of her subsequent body of scholarship. While I
have learned a great deal from Joseph's insightful work, my focus is more on when/
if/how selving matters at all. Michael Jackson and Ivan Karp, eds., *Personhood and
Agency: The Experience of Self and Other in African Cultures* (Uppsala: Uppsala University Press, 1990), similarly offers important insights. Further afield both temporally
and culturally is Jerrold Seigel's *The Idea of the Self: Thought and Experience in Western
Europe since the Seventeenth Century* (Cambridge: Cambridge University Press, 2005);
this is an exhaustive intellectual history that emphasizes a concept of self that has
three dimensions: the bodily or material, the relational, and the reflective.

4 Seigel explicitly resists "recent writings about the self by philosophers and human-
istically inclined psychologists [who have] favored the notion that the self is a 'narrative' entity, rooted in human propensity to remember and project, in our readiness
to make sense of things in terms of continuity and change, in our nature as what
Alastair MacIntyre calls 'a story-telling animal'" and warns against jumping on the
"narrative bandwagon too quickly" (*The Idea of the Self*, 653). Given that my pursuit is
to understand when/if/how selving matters at all, contra Seigel, I find it productive
to work with the concept of a narrativizing self and narratives of self.

5 Two works that I have found particularly helpful are Jan Goldstein, *The Post-
Revolutionary Self: Politics and Psyche in France, 1750–1850* (Cambridge, MA: Harvard
University Press, 2005); and Dror Wahrman, *The Making of the Modern Self: Identity*

*and Culture in Eighteenth-Century England* (New Haven, CT: Yale University Press, 2004).

6    Wahrman, *The Making of the Modern Self*, 168. He continues: "Instead, we can visualize this eighteenth-century configuration as a set of positions within which one identified oneself—a set of coordinates, or a matrix. One's position in this matrix, which could be prescribed or adopted (thus allowing for both subordination and agency), was relational" (168).

7    Wahrman, *The Making of the Modern Self*, 198. Wahrman's book offers a historical account of "those enabling conditions and circumstances of the eighteenth century that made this particular identity regime not only possible, and plausible, but also widely resonant" (198). It would perhaps be accurate to say that Wahrman's account is not only historical but also historicist, in the sense that there is an almost inevitable "before and after," with the after virtually wiping out the before completely. As I will discuss shortly, I am skeptical of accounts in which the past narratives of the self "in the West" are taken to have been totally erased by the deep self, with no continued life or a trace within the present.

8    Riley, *The Words of Selves*, 26.

9    Dorrin Kondo (*Crafting Selves: Power, Gender and Discourses of Identity in a Japanese Workplace* [Chicago: University of Chicago Press, 1990]) makes a similar point when she argues, "the relationally defined self of American women [references Carol Gilligan, *In a Different Voice: Psychological Theory and Women's Development* (Cambridge, MA: Harvard University Press, 1982); and Nancy Chodorow, *The Reproduction of Mothering: Psychoanalysis and the Sociology of Gender* (Berkeley: University of California Press, 1978)] still remains solidly within a linguistic and historical legacy of individualism. Relationally defined selves in Japan—selves inextricable from context—thus mount a radical challenge to our own assumptions about fixed essentialist identities and provide possibilities for a consideration of cultural difference and a radical critique of 'the whole subject' in contemporary Western culture" (33). But I am cautious about making this distinction a "civilizational" one. I suspect that even in the most individualist corners and communities of "the West," the autonomous individual is not the sole narrative for living.

10   Riley, *The Words of Selves*, 17. Kondo similarly argues "that the bounded, interiorized self is a narrative convention" (*Crafting Selves*, 25), but considers that "selves which are coherent, seamless, bounded, and whole are indeed illusions" (14). I part from Kondo's approach on this latter point. The concept of "coherent, seamless, bounded, and whole" selves has provided generations of people in many communities and cultures with a powerful narrative for living their lives. At stake is not the realness of one and the illusionary nature of the other, but recognizing that different individuals and communities have worked out numerous, and changing, creative narratives for living.

11   Michel de Certeau, *The Practice of Everyday Life*, trans. by Steven Rendall (Berkeley: University of California Press, 1984), xi.

12   Riley, *The Words of Selves*, 52–53.

13   Erving Goffman, *The Presentation of Self in Everyday Life* (New York: Doubleday, 1957), 252–53.

14  Judith Butler, "Performative Acts and Gender Constitution: An Essay in Phenomenology and Feminist Theory," *Theater Journal* 40, no. 4 (December 1988): 519, 521.

15  See, for instance, *The Presentation of Self in Everyday Life*, 81–82, where Goffman discusses self-delusion and self-deception.

16  The classic source for the story of Agnes remains Harold Garfinkel, "Passing and the managed achievement of sex status in an intersexed person," in *Studies in Ethnomethodology*, chapter 5, 116–85 (Cambridge: Polity Press, 2010 [1st ed. 1967]), and the appendix to that chapter on pages 285–88. Large excerpts from both are reproduced in *The Transgender Studies Reader*, edited by Susan Stryker and Stephen Whittle (New York: Routledge, 2006); for a concise summary of the case, see the editors' introduction on page 58. Joanne Meyerowitz reviews the case for its importance in consolidation of sex surgeries in the late 1950s (*How Sex Changed: A History of Transsexuality in the United States* [Cambridge, MA: Harvard University Press, 2002], 159–61).

17  Garfinkel, *Studies in Ethnomethodology*, 164–79.

18  Garfinkel, *Studies in Ethnomethodology*, 136–37.

19  Garfinkel, *Studies in Ethnomethodology*, 180.

20  Butler, "Performative Acts and Gender Constitution," 523.

21  Garfinkel's ethnomethodology has been important in shaping analysis and theories of gender in sociological theory and in some gender and sexualities studies, including transgender studies. For instance, Suzanne Kessler and Wendy McKenna drew on Garfinkel's ethnomethodological approach to develop their gender analysis and theory (see *Gender: An Ethnomethodological Approach* [Chicago: University of Chicago Press, 1985 (1st ed. 1978)]). There is a large related literature. See, for example, Mary Rogers, "They Were All Passing: Agnes, Garfinkel, and Company," *Gender and Society* 6, no. 2 (June 1992): 169–91; critical responses by Don Zimmerman, "They Were All Doing Gender, But They Weren't All Passing," 192–98; Roslyn Bologh, "The Promise and Failure of Ethnomethodology from a Feminist Perspective," 199–206; and Rogers's rejoinder, "Resisting the Enormous Either/Or," 207–14. See also Norman Denzin, "Harold and Agnes: A Feminist Narrative Undoing," *Sociological Theory*, 8, no. 2 (autumn 1990): 198–216; and critical responses by Richard Hilbert, "Norman and Sigmund," *Sociological Theory* 9, no. 2 (autumn 1991): 264–68; Douglas Maynard, "Goffman, Garfinkel, and Games," 277–79; and Denzin's rejoiner, "Back to Harold and Agnes," 280–85. For a more recent assessment, see Leia Kaitlyn Armitage, "Truth, Falsity, and Schemas of Presentation: A Textual Analysis of Harold Garfinkel's Story of Agnes," *Electronic Journal of Human Sexuality*, volume 4, April 29, 2001, accessed May 7, 2013, http://www.ejhs.org/volume4/agnesabs.htm. For examples of how Agnes's case impacted transgender/transsexuality studies, see Dan Spade, "Mutilating Gender," in *The Transgender Studies Reader*, edited by Susan Stryker and Stephen Whittle, 315–32 (New York: Routledge, 2006), with a discussion of Agnes on pages 315–16. Jacob Hale's "Are Lesbians Women" (in *The Transgender Studies Reader*, 281–99) draws on Garfinkel's essay on Agnes (286–87). Bernice Hausman frames the presentation of key arguments of her book *Changing Sex: Transsexualism, Technology, and the Idea of Gender* (Durham, NC: Duke University Press, 1995) in the "Introduction: Transsexualism, Technology, and the Idea

of Gender" (2–19) through Agnes's story. Curiously, Agnes's story has not informed theories of gender performativity and performance studies that have emerged since the early 1990s, a genealogical lacunae possibly reflecting the disciplinary shape of academic production of knowledge and bridges that are—or in this case are not—crossed. I am grateful to conversations with Robin Bernstein and Susan Stryker on this point.

22 As Judith Butler points out, "one does not 'do' one's gender alone. One is always 'doing' *with* or for *another*, even if the other is only imaginary" (*Undoing Gender* [New York: Routledge, 2004], 1; my emphasis). One frequently underemphasized effect of this point is that one "does" gender differently depending on who one is doing it with, for, and against.

23 The importance of Goffman's work, however, is that, contra Wahrman, performative self—Wahrman's "before the self"—is not a stage (a developmental civilizational stage?) restricted, for instance, to a particular window of time in England. Despite the dominance of deep interiorized self for over a century on many levels and in many domains, the performative self continues to be analytically powerful for understanding numerous phenomena, as, for instance, articulated in Goffman's use of contemporary (mid-twentieth century) sociological studies of communities and individuals upon which he constructs his main arguments.

24 Charlotte Furth, in a different context, notes that "identifying a wife as an 'inner person' (*nei ren*) constructed her femininity via bodily location rather than biology, a spatial habitus that taught female gender in the idiom of a socially complex domain of family life" (*A Flourishing Yin: Gender in China's Medical History, 960–1665* [Berkeley: University of California Press, 1999], 6). In Barlow's articulation, "gender is accomplished . . . through the behavior of persons in specific subject positions of kin relation." She further traces a shift away from this kin-located concept of womanhood, concluding, "The career of nüxing firmly established a foundational womanhood beyond kin categories." See Barlow, "Theorizing Woman: Funü, Guojia, Jiating," in *Body, Subject & Power in China*, edited by Angela Zito and Tani E. Barlow, 253–89 (Chicago: University of Chicago Press, 1994). The quotes are from pages 280n12 and 266, respectively.

25 I hope it is clear that I am not reciting these points approvingly. I do not think, however, that it makes sense to address a feminist critique of dominant notions of gender and sexuality to trans persons any more than to the general culture. One cannot demand trans persons to be necessarily more contestive of gender/sex normativity than other people.

26 As de Certeau notes, the characteristics of speech act: "speaking operates with the field of a linguistic system; it effects an appropriation, or reappropriation, of language by its speakers; it establishes a *present* relative to a time and place; and it posits a *contract with the other* (the interlocutor) in a network of places and relations . . . [that] can be found in many other practices (walking, cooking, etc.)" (*The Practice of Everyday Life*, xiii; emphasis in original).

27 Drawing on Tom Boellstorff, "when I began learning of these two understandings of what makes someone *waria*—soul and clothing—I suspected that the sense of having a woman's soul was more central. This reflects the dominant Western conceit

that both gender and sexuality originate as internal essences that must be confessed to ever greater spheres of life to be authentic and valid" ("Playing Back the Nation: *Waria*, Indonesian Transvestites," *Cultural Anthropology* 19, no. 2 [2004]: 167).

28 Jackson, "Performative Genders, Perverse Desires: A Bio-History of Thailand's Same-Sex and Transgender Cultures," *Intersections: Gender, History and Culture in the Asian Context*, 9 (August 2003), online edition, http://intersections.anu.edu.au /issue9/jackson.html; the quote is from point 92. This also recalls Wahrman's observation about clothes as "an anchor of personal identity" (*The Making of the Modern Self*, 177) and that "dress was taken literally to 'transnature' the wearer . . . masquer-aders 'almost chang[ing] their Nature with their Habit'" (178).

29 Boellstorff, "Playing Back the Nation," 165.

30 Georgia Warnke, "Transexuality and Contextual Identities," in *"You've Changed": Sex Reassignment and Personal Identity*, edited by Laurie J. Shrage, 28–42 (Oxford: Oxford University Press, 2009), 28.

31 Since my last visit, Houri and Zia no longer share house. Houri completed her transition, reconciled with her family, and got married in the fall of 2009. Zia lives with his male partner.

32 As Valentine notes in a different context, for many of his "subjects," living as a woman did not "preclude being 'gay' when 'gay' indexes erotic desire for someone who is male-bodied" (*Imagining Transgender: An Ethnography of a Category* [Durham, NC: Duke University Press, 2007], 117).

33 The problem of "excess" visibility is usually an MtF problem. Excess for FtMs (pre-operative) tends to be marriage refusal.

34 See Anna Lowenhaupt Tsing, "Adat/Indigenous: Indigeneity in Motion," in *Words in Motion: Toward a Global Lexicon*, edited by Carol Gluck and Anna Lowenhaupt Tsing, 40–64 (Durham, NC: Duke University Press, 2009) for an insightful discussion of "shadows."

35 See Gayle Salamon, *Assuming a Body: Transgender and Rhetorics of Materiality* (New York: Columbia University Press, 2010), 23–24, for discussion of identification always already being marked by nonidentification.

36 Boellstorff, *A Coincidence of Desires*, 117.

37 See Cyrus Schayegh "'Seeing Like a State': An Essay on the Historiography of Modern Iran," *International Journal of Middle East Studies* 42 (2010): 37–61.

38 Boellstorff, *A Coincidence of Desires*, 117.

39 In the Thursday meetings of TSS held at the offices of *Psychology and Society*, the discussion would frequently begin with everyone complaining about everything they had suffered the week before. Sina and Houri, who were the de facto leaders of these discussions, often were frustrated by the unconstructive tone of self-pity that these narratives would generate. On the first day that Dr. Arash Alaei visited the group (see chapter 6), given his experience in running self-help support groups, he immediately noticed the problematic dynamic and suggested that he would write on the board a list of all the problems voiced. The list included such topics as street harassment by NAJA "morality squads," unemployment, parental supervision and demands, relationship break ups, and so on. He then went through each problem and asked if they thought the given problem was faced only by TSS. To everyone's sur-

prise, all problems seemed to be shared by many other groups in society. There was an uncomfortable silence until one MtF objected, "But it is different with us." The discussion then became focused on what those differences were and how such differences could be addressed.

40 de Certeau, *The Practice of Everyday Life*, xii–xiii.

41 Such cost-benefit considerations are of course not limited to *trans* persons. While Zia had come to name himself as *gay* with certainty and now lives with his boyfriend, he continues to contemplate the possibility of marrying a *lesbian* woman, even having a child with her, to consolidate his relationship with his parents who have been coldly distant because of his refusal to get married.

42 Quantification works also within other identity categories. Zia often referred to his *gay* friends in terms of their percentages of gayness. At first confused, I finally realized this was the way sexual practice preferences had become codified; the percentages referred to how much preference a man had for acting *bott*. When Zia was talking about the period in which there was so much talk of transing that many *gays* began to think of themselves as *trans*, he said, "Even those who are *full-top* [pronounced as in English] started thinking maybe they should go for surgery."

43 As I already pointed out in the previous chapter, asking "Why not?" may sound as though it is turning a very complicated and serious consideration into some frivolous game. But I find Laurie Shrage's question quite pertinent: "Do some changes to the self (sex, religion, job, or age) create discontinuities with earlier selves that are profound enough to be described as the emergence of a new self?" ("Introduction" in *"You've Changed": Sex Reassignment and Personal Identity*, edited by Laurie J. Shrage [Oxford: Oxford University Press, 2009], 3). How is it that our general societal reaction to changing gender/sex is often a lot more "severe" than changing other identifications, including nationality or religion? Or, as Georgia Warnke puts it, "Identities . . . are interpretations of who we are, and as such they are intelligible only as parts of particular contexts . . . transsexuality is no different from other changes of identity such as changes in nationality or sports team affiliation. Transsexuality is no more radical because sex and gender are no less context-bound" ("Transsexuality and Contextual Identities," 33). Putting it another way, our vastly different reactions to "change of religion," for instance, compared to our reactions to "sex change" indicate our continued investment in considering sex/gender as something more profound and foundational in terms of the constitution of self than religion. Asking this question also forces us to reflect that changes that would strike one's reception/cognition by oneself and by others as "profound enough" possibly are not the same across different sociocultural contexts. Why should changing sex be always expected to signal such a profound change? Related to this, Shrage asks, "So one interesting issue is why so many of us passively accept our assigned sex identity or cannot conceive of changing this identity?" (9). David Valentine pursues a similar line of argument in his essay, "Sue E. Generous: Toward a Theory of Non-Transsexuality," *Feminist Studies* 38, no. 1 (spring 2012): 185–211.

44 A Google search on March 15, 2010, in Persian (which is more inclusive than title alone and covers weblogs devoted to the topic as well) resulted in 171,000 entries in 0.20 seconds.

45 On the Sufi concept of self, see Annemarie Schimmel, *Mystical Dimensions of Islam* (Chapel Hill: University of North Carolina Press, 1975), especially chapter 4, where she also discusses the *hadith* "Who knows himself knows his God." See also F. Rahman's entry "Dhat" in the *Encyclopedia of Islam* (2nd ed.), edited by P. Bearman, Th. Bianquis, C. E. Bosworth, E. van Donzel, and W. P. Heinrichs. Brill Online, accessed March 15, 2010, http://www.brillonline.nl/subscriber/entry?entry=islam_SIM-1816; and E. E. Calverley's entry "Nafs" in the *Encyclopedia of Islam*, accessed March 15, 2010, http://www.brillonline.nl/subscriber/entry?entry=islam_SIM-1816. 'Ali Shari'ati's best-known works on this subject include *Khaudsazi-i inqilabi* (Revolutionary crafting of self) (Tehran: Daftar-i Tadvin va Tanzim-i Majmu'ah-i Asar-i Mu'allim-i Shahid Duktur 'Ali Shari'ati, 1983); *Bazgasht bah khvishtan* (Return to oneself) (Tehran: Husayniyah Irshad, n.d.); and *Insan-i bikhaud* (Empty [without self] human) (Tehran: Daftar-i Tadvin va Tanzim-i Majmu'ah-i Asar-i Mu'allim-i Shahid Duktur 'Ali Shari'ati, 1983).

46 For a discussion of transformation of jins from genus into sex/gender, see my article, "Genus of Sex or the Sexing of Jins," *International Journal of Middle Eastern Studies* 45 (2013), 211–31. Similar to jins-as-sex, *khaud*-as-self is rarely used as a stand-alone noun. It usually appears in combined words, such as in khaudkavi or khaudshinasi, or in adjectival form, as in khaudi.

47 Michel Foucault, *The History of Sexuality: Volume I — An Introduction* (New York: Random House, 1980), 154.

48 I am borrowing the concepts of horizontal segmentation and vertical fragmentation from Goldstein, *The Post-Revolutionary Self*, but do not use it in exactly the same sense.

49 Davidson, *The Emergence of Sexuality*, 139.

50 See Cyrus Schayegh, *Who Is Knowledgeable Is Strong: Science, Class, and the Formation of Modern Iranian Society, 1900–1950* (Berkeley: University of California Press, 2009), chapter 6.

51 For the classical meanings of these Islamic concepts, see the entry "zahir" by Wael Hallaq in the *Encyclopedia of Islam*, accessed August 27, 2009, http://www.brillonline.nl/subscriber/entry?entry=islam_SIM-1816. See also the entry "Sufism and the Qur'an" by Alexander Knysh in the *Encyclopedia of the Qur'an*, edited by Jane Dammen McAuliffe, Brill Online, volume 3, page 287, accessed August 27, 2009, http://www.brillonline.nl/subscriber/entry?entry=q3_SIM-00274.

52 'Ali Akbar Siasi, *Ravanshinasi-i shakhsiyat* (Psychology of personality) (Tehran: Ibn Sina, 1970), 22.

53 Siasi, *Ravanshinasi-i shakhsiyat*, 23.

54 Siasi, *Ravanshinasi-i shakhsiyat*, 43.

55 'Ali Akbar Siasi, *'Ilm al-nafs ya ravanshinasi* (Science of essence/soul or psychology) (Tehran: Tehran University Press, 1962 [1st ed., Tehran: Khaudkar, 1938]), 23.

56 Siasi, *Ravanshinasi-i shakhsiyat*, 22–23.

57 The main psychological deviations under the chapter on "abnormal personalities," for instance, are cataloged as sadism, masochism, exhibitionism, voyeurism, and homosexuality. Siasi, *Ravanshinasi-i shakhsiyat*, 198–200. Uncharacteristic of Siasi, no English or French word is noted as equivalent to *inhiraf*, which I have translated

as "deviation" here. He seems to use *inhiraf* and *ikhtilal* (at times translated as "disorder") interchangeably.

58 There is little historical study of development of psychology in Iran, so my observations remain partial and anecdotal. One thing that is worth noting is that there is a fitting correspondence between notions of self-in-conduct, the dominance of behavioral psychology, and the emergence of the idea of the unnaturalness of same-sex desire as not linked with any inner psychic-sexual truth but with a social institution. In the modernist narrative, it is understood as an effect of living within a set of life practices, namely, gender/sex homosociality, that produce desires and practices of same-sex-playing.

59 Asadbaygi's writings largely have appeared as articles in magazines and dailies: *Javan* (Youth), October 13, 1999, 6 (about tobacco addiction); *Tus* (the name of an ancient city), September 8, 1998, 5 (about obsession); *Javan*, October 8, 2000, 4 (about violence against children); *Tausi'ah* (Development), August 3, 2004, 3 (about suicide); and *Mardum-salari* (Democracy), July 16, 2004, 5 (about domestic violence). I did not have the opportunity to interview Asadbaygi. Shortly after my work began, he was replaced by a social worker and ceased to cooperate with trans persons. My entry into these weekly meetings had been facilitated by Houri and Sina; I became included in that break down of relationships.

60 Given the larger context of decades of circulation of the notion of self with psychic depth through introduction of several schools of psychology to Iran, I do not wish to counter-pose the self-in-conduct to the interiorized self as if they are uninformed by each other.

61 Lawrence Cohen, in "The Pleasures of Castration: The Post-operative Status of Hijras, Jankhas, and Academics" (in *Sexual Nature, Sexual Culture*, edited by Paul R. Abramson and Steven D. Pinkerton, 276–304 [Chicago: University of Chicago Press, 1995]), writes, "In Hindi-speaking places . . . many strolling men who like to have sex with men identify friends and prospective friends through the language of similitude—*aise* and *jaise*, like this, like these, this way—and shared play (being *khel main*, in the game). The language of *aise* and *khel* is not a label or a fixing of essential identity in the different but parallel ways the utterance of *khush* or *hijra* often demand. The 'these' of *aise*'s 'like these' is contingent, reflexive, and dialogic, pointing not to some category or class out there but to what is being enacted by the very encounter of speaker and listener together in the park at night. Thus language . . . is momentary" (280).

62 Several scholars of East Asia have made similar suggestions in analyzing the concept of "face." See Lisa Rofel, *Desiring China: Experiments in Neoliberalism, Sexuality, and Public Culture* (Durham, NC: Duke University Press, 2007); Kondo, *Crafting Selves*; and Angela Zito, "Silk and Skin": Significant Boundaries," in *Body, Subject & Power in China*, edited by Angela Zito and Tani E. Barlow, 103–30 (Chicago: University of Chicago Press, 1994). For an insightful recent work centered on Chinese lesbian culture, see Ana Huang, "On the Surface: Conceptualizing Gender and Subjectivity in Chinese Lesbian Culture," BA honors dissertation, Harvard University, 2008.

63 In the context of contemporary Indonesia, Boellstorff writes, "What is more often the case is that it is the invisibility of gay men that allows them to find spaces of

community free from direct oppression. . . . [F]or most gay Indonesians the notion of 'opening oneself to the gay world' does not imply that it is necessary or inevitable [or even desirable?] to open oneself in all domains of one's life (such as one's family or workplace). Peter Jackson's observation that 'there is comparatively little pressure for integrating one's public and private lives in Thailand' (1997: 176) is quite accurate for Southeast Asia more generally" (*A Coincidence of Desires*, 199–200). I would say that in Iran it is in fact considered inappropriate (and at times incomprehensible) that one would integrate one's self-presentation in all domains—possibly, for that matter, the same observation would apply for anywhere—including many parts of "the West" in which identity politics and sex/gender psycho-sexology have not become the dominant and determining grid of living one's life.

64 In the context of contemporary China, Rofel writes, "that gay men shy away from telling their parents that they are gay not because of an underlying antinomy of secrecy versus truth but because they fear that they will take away their family's *mianzi* [face/status], and with it their own humanity. In this regard, sexual identity is not about the existence within the self of a separate sexual domain that is a constitutive principle of the self" (*Desiring China*, 102).

65 Mark Johnson, *Beauty and Power: Transgendering and Culture Transformation in the Southern Philippines* (Oxford: Berg, 1997), 104.

66 Sinnott similarly notes, "Thais often use specific terms for homosexual or transgendered individuals, such as '*gay*,' '*tom*,' '*dee*,' '*tut*,' or '*kathoey*' rather than trying to reach for an overarching term that could encompass all these categories, such as 'homosexual,' 'third sex/gender'" (*Toms and Dees: Transgender Identity and Female Same-Sex Relationships in Thailand* [Honolulu: University of Hawai'i Press, 2004], 8).

67 See the early *Homan* article defining the "musts" of homosexual relationships (referred to in chapter 4), but this is now common discourse in many sites. For a critique, see Shakhsari, "From Hamjensbaaz to Hamjensgaraa: Diasporic Queer Reterritorializations and Limits of Transgression," unpublished paper.

# WORKS CITED

*Persian Periodicals Frequently Cited*

*Andishah va raftar* (Journal of Psychiatry and Clinical Psychology)
*Chilchiraq*
FarsNews (news agency)
*Homan*
*I'timad*
*I'timad-i Milli*
*Ittila'at-i banuvan*
*Kayhan*
*Khvandaniha*
*Mardum-salari*
*Ma'rifat-i pizishki*
*Newsletter of the Medical Council of Iran*
*Salamat*
*Sarmayah*
*Sharq*
*Sihhat-numa-yi Iran*
*Zan-i ruz*
*Zanan*


*Films and Videos*

Amini, Faramarz. Producer, *Farzand-i bimar-i tabi'at: nuqtah-i sifr* (Nature's sick child: Point Zero), three-part special produced for the program *Yad-i yaran*, Omid-E-Iran Television, 2005. Part I, 57 minutes; Part II, 96 minutes; Part III, 81 minutes.

Kouross Esmaeli, *Legacy of the Imam*, 14 minutes, 2006.
Zohreh Shayesteh, *Inside Out*, 39 minutes, 2006.
Daisy Mohr and Negin Kianfar, *The Birthday*, 63 minutes, 2006.
Elhum Shakerifar, *Roya and Omid*, 18 minutes, 2007.
Bahman Motamedian, *Khastegi* (Tedium), 76 minutes, 2008.
Tanaz Eshaghian, *Be Like Others*, 74 minutes, 2008.

## Books and Journal Articles

Abbasi-Shavazi, Mohammad Jalal, Marcia C. Inhorn, Hajiieh Bibi Razeghi-Nasrabad, and Ghasem Toloo. "The 'Iranian ART Revolution': Infertility, Assisted Reproductive Technology, and Third-Party Donation in the Islamic Republic of Iran." *Journal of Middle East Women's Studies* 4, no. 2 (spring 2008): 1–28.

Abrams, Philip. "Notes on the Difficulty of Studying the State (1977)." *Journal of Historical Sociology*, 1, no. 1 (March 1988): 58–89.

Adelkhah, Fariba. *Being Modern in Iran*, translated by Jonathan Derrick. London: Hurst, 1999 (1st ed. Paris: Karthala, 1998).

Afary, Janet. *Sexual Politics in Modern Iran*. Cambridge: Cambridge University Press, 2009.

Afkhami, Gholam Reza, ed. *Women, State, and Society in Iran 1963–78: An Interview with Mahnaz Afkhami*. Bethesda: Foundation for Iranian Studies, 2003.

Ahmadi-Abhari, Sayyid 'Ali. "Naqsh-i iman va i'tiqad-i mazhabi dar darman-i bimariha va mu'arrifi-i sah maurid-i darman ba ravandarmani-i mazhabi" (The Role of Faith and Religious Beliefs in Healing Physical and Emotional Disorders). *Andishah va raftar* 2, no. 4 (spring 1996): 4–11.

Ahmadzad-Asl, Masoud, Mehrdad Eftekhar, Amir Jalali, Kaveh Alavi, and Morteza Naser-bakht, "Gender Identity Disorder; Transsexualism in Iran: Epidemiological Aspects of Iranian Model." Unpublished paper, 2009.

Al Ahmad, Jalal. *Gharbzadegi = Weststruckness*, translated by John Green and Ahmad Alizadeh. Lexington, KY: Mazda Publishers, 1982.

Alavi, Nasrin. *We Are Iran: The Persian Blogs*. Brooklyn: Soft Skull Press, 2005.

Amin, Camron. "The Attentions of the Great Father: Reza Shah, 'The Woman Question,' and the Iranian Press, 1890–1946." Ph.D. dissertation, University of Chicago, 1996.

———. "Importing 'Beauty Culture' into Iran in the 1920s and 1930s: Mass Marketing Individualism in an Age of Anti-Imperialist Sacrifice." *Comparative Studies of South Asia, Africa and the Middle East* 24, no. 1 (2004): 79–95.

Ansari, Mas'ud. *Jara'im va inhirafat-i jinsi* (Psychology of Sexual Crimes and Deviancies). Tehran: Ishraqi, 1973 [1961].

Aqa'i, Farkhundeh. *Jinsiyat-i gumshudah* (The lost gender/sexuality). Tehran: Nashr-i Alburz, 2000.

Armitage, Leia Kaitlyn. "Truth, Falsity, and Schemas of Presentation: A Textual Analysis of Harold Garfinkel's Story of Agnes." *Electronic Journal of Human Sexuality* 4 (April 29, 2001). Accessed July 16, 2011. http://www.ejhs.org/volume4/agnes/htm.

'Asgari, Mirza Aqa (Mani). *Khunyagar dar khun: dar shinakht va buzurgdasht-i Faridun Far-*

*rukhzad* (Musician/singer in blood: in recognition of Faridun Farrukhzad). Germany (no city): Human, 2005.

Ashrafian Bonab, Maziar. *Zaruriyat-i pizishki-i qanuni* (Essentials of Forensic Medicine). Tehran: Taymurzadah, 2001.

Attar, Hamid Reza, and Maryam Rasulian. "Tashkhis-i avvaliyah-i ikhtilal-i huviyat-i jinsi: guzarish-i mauridi" (First Diagnosis of Gender Identity Disorder: Case Report). *Andishah va raftar* 9, no. 3 (2004): 6–11.

Avaz, "Tafavut-i 'hamjins-gara' ba 'hamjins-baz' va 'bachchah-baz' dar chist?" (What is the difference between the "same-sex inclined" and the "same-sex-player" and "child-player"). *Homan* 9 (October-November 1994): 27–33.

'Ayn al-Saltanah, Qahriman Mirza. *Ruznamah-i khatirat-i 'Ayn al-Saltanah,* 10 volumes, edited by Mas'ud Salur and Iraj Afshar. Tehran: Asatir, 1995–2001.

'Azizi Burujirdi, Ma'sumah (Mahvash). *Raz-i kamyabi-i jinsi* (Secrets of sexual fulfillment). 1957.

Babayan, Kathryn. "'In Spirit We Ate Each Other's Sorrow': Female Companionship in Seventeenth-Century Safavi Iran." In *Islamicate Sexualities: Translations across Temporal Geographies of Desire,* edited by Kathryn Babayan and Afsaneh Najmabadi, 239–74. Cambridge: Harvard University Press, 2008.

Bahadori, Moslem and Mohammad-Hossein Azizi. "The First Medical Journal of Tehran University." In *History of Contemporary Medicine in Iran.* Accessed November 16, 2007. http://www.ams.ac.ir/AIM/07103/0029.htm.

Bahreini, Raha. "From Perversion to Pathology: Discourses and Practices of Gender Policing in the Islamic Republic of Iran." *Muslim World Journal of Human Rights* 5, no. 1 (2008). Accessed March 2, 2013. http://www.bepress.com/mwjhr/vo15/iss1/art2/.

Bal, Mieke. *Travelling Concepts in the Humanities: A Rough Guide.* Toronto: University of Toronto Press, 2002.

Barlow, Tani E. "Theorizing Women: Funü, Guojia, Jiating." In *Body, Subject & Power in China,* edited by Angela Zito and Tani E. Barlow, 253–89. Chicago: University of Chicago Press, 1994.

———. "Buying In: Advertising and the Sexy Modern Girl Icon in Shanghai in the 1920s and 1930s." In *The Modern Girl Around the World: Consumption, Modernity, and Globalization,* edited by Alys Eve Weinbaum, Lynn M. Thomas, Priti Ramamurthy, Uta G. Poiger, Madeleine Yue Dong, and Tani E. Barlow, 288–316. Durham, NC: Duke University Press, 2008.

Bastani Parizi, Muhammad Ibrahim. "Ittila'at-i mukhlis va mukhlis-i *Ittila'at*" (My information as a fan of *Ittila'at*). In *Ittila'at: 80 sal huzur-i mustamarr (Ittila'at:* 80 years of continuous presence), 16–40. Tehran: Ittila'at, 2006.

Bayat, Asef. *Life as Politics: How Ordinary People Change the Middle East.* Stanford: Stanford University Press, 2010.

Beeman, William O. "Mimesis and Travesty in Iranian Traditional Theatre." In *Gender in Performance: The Presentation of Difference in the Performing Arts,* edited by Laurence Senelick, 14–25. Medford, MA: Tufts University Press, 2002.

Boellstorff, Tom. "Playing Back the Nation: *Waria,* Indonesian Transvestites." *Cultural Anthropology* 19, no. 2 (2004): 159–95.

——. *A Coincidence of Desires: Anthropology, Queer Studies, Indonesia*. Durham, NC: Duke University Press, 2007.

Bologh, Roslyn, "The Promise and Failure of Ethnomethodology from a Feminist Perspective," *Gender and Society* 6, no. 2 (June 1992): 199–206.

Boroujerdi, Mehrzad. *Iranian Intellectuals and the West: The Tormented Triumph of Nativism*. Syracuse, NY: Syracuse University Press, 1996.

Bray, Alan. *Homosexuality in Renaissance England*. New York, Columbia University Press, 1982.

Bu-alhari, Ja'far, ed. *Duvvumin hamayish-i sarasari-i naqsh-i din dar bihdasht-i ravan* (The second nationwide seminar on role of religion in mental health). Tehran: Aftab Girafic, 2007.

Bu-alhari, Ja'far, and 'Abbas Ramazani Farani, eds. *Majmu'ah-i chakidah-i 45 sukhanrani-i Daftar-i Mutali'at-i Islami dar bihdasht-i ravani: bi-munasibat-i barguzari-i nukhustin Hamayish-i Naqsh-i Din dar Bihdasht-i Ravan, 24–27 Azar Mah 1376*. Tehran: Mu'avanat-i Danishjuyi, Farhangi, Huquqi va Majlis, Vizarat-i Bihdasht, Darman va Amuzish-i Pizishki va Daftar-i Mutali'at, 1997.

Buffington, Robert. *Criminal and Citizen in Modern Mexico*. Lincoln: University of Nebraska Press, 2000.

Burke, Andrew, Mark Elliott, Kamin Mohammadi, and Pat Yale. *Iran*. London: Lonely Planet Publications, 2004.

Butler, Judith. "Performative Acts and Gender Constitution: An Essay in Phenomenology and Feminist Theory." *Theatre Journal* 40, no. 4 (December 1988): 519–31.

——. *Gender Trouble: Feminism and the Subversion of Identity*. New York: Routledge, 1990.

——. *Undoing Gender*. New York: Routledge, 2004.

——. "Undiagnosing Gender." In *Transgender Rights*, edited by Paisley Currah, Richard M. Juang, and Shannon Price Minter, 274–98. Minneapolis: University of Minnesota Press, 2006.

Calverley, E. E. "Nafs." In *The Encyclopaedia of Islam* (2nd ed.), edited by P. Bearman, Th. Bianquis, C. E. Bosworth, E. van Donzel, and W. P. Heinrichs. Brill Online. Accessed March 15, 2010. http://www.brillonline.nl/subscriber/entry?entry=islam_SIM-1816.

Cekaf. "Girayish-i jinsi-i Sadiq Hidayat" (Sadiq Hidayat's sexual orientation). *Cekaf* 30, topic no. 17, 112–18, reprinted in MAHA, no. 3 (February 2005): 18–23.

Chauncey, George. *Gay New York: Gender, Urban Culture, and the Making of the Gay Male World 1890–1940*. New York: Basic Books, 1994.

Chesser, Eustace. *Love Without Fear: How to Achieve Sex Happiness in Marriage*. New York: Roy Publishers, 1947.

Chodorow, Nancy. *The Reproduction of Mothering: Psychoanalysis and the Sociology of Gender*. Berkeley: University of California Press, 1978.

Cilardo, Agostino. "Historical Development of the Legal Doctrine Relative to the Position of the Hermaphrodite in the Islamic Law." *The Search* 2, no. 7 (1986): 128–70.

Cohen, Lawrence. "The Pleasures of Castration: The post-operative status of Hijras, Jankhas, and Academics." In *Sexual Nature, Sexual Culture*, edited by Paul R. Abramson and Steven D. Pinkerton, 276–304. Chicago: University of Chicago Press, 1995.

Costler, A., and A. Willy. *The Encyclopedia of Sexual Knowledge*. New York: Eugenics Publishing, 1936.

————. *The Encyclopedia of Sexual Knowledge*, translated into Persian by 'Abdallah Rah-numa. Tehran: Intisharat-i Farrukhi, 1946.

Dadmandan (Nafisi), Parisa. *Chihrah-nigaran-i Isfahan: Gushah-'i az tarikh-i 'akkasi-i Iran* (Portrait photographers of Isfahan: a fragment of history of photography in Iran). Tehran: Daftar-i Pazhuhish-ha-yi Farhangi, 1998.

Davidson, Arnold I. *The Emergence of Sexuality: Historical Epistemology and the Formation of Concepts*. Cambridge: Harvard University Press, 2001.

Debesse, Maurice. *L'Adolescence*. Paris, Presses universitaires de France, 1962 [1st ed. 1943].

De Certeau, Michel. *The Practice of Everyday Life*. Translated by Steven Rendall. Berkeley, CA: University of California Press, 1984.

Denzin, Norman. "Back to Harold and Agnes," *Sociological Theory* 8, no. 2 (autumn 1990): 280–85.

————. "Harold and Agnes: a Feminist Narrative Undoing." *Sociological Theory* 8, no. 2 (autumn 1990): 198–216.

Derrida, Jacques. *Archive Fever: A Freudian Impression*, translated by Eric Prenowitz. Chicago: University of Chicago Press, 1995.

Diba, Farideh. *Dukhtaram Farah* (My daughter Farah), translated into Persian by Ilaheh Ra'is Firuz. Tehran: Bih-Afarin, 2000.

Diba, Layla S., and Maryam Ekhtiar, eds. *Royal Persian Paintings: The Qajar Epoch, 1785–1925*. Brooklyn: Brooklyn Museum of Art, 1998.

Doostdar, Alireza. "'The Vulgar Spirit of Blogging': On Language, Culture, and Power in Persian Weblogestan." *American Anthropologist* 106, no. 4 (2004): 651–62.

————. "Weblogs." In *Encyclopaedia Iranica*, last updated March 15, 2010. Accessed March 2, 2013. http://www.iranica.com/articles/weblogs.

Dreger, Alice. *Hermaphrodites and the Medical Invention of Sex*. Cambridge: Harvard University Press, 1998.

Duggan, Lisa. "The Trials of Alice Mitchell: Sensationalism, Sexology, and the Lesbian Subject in Turn-of-the-Century America." *Signs: Journal of Women in Culture and Society* 18, no. 4 (1993): 791–814.

Eftekhar, Mehrdad, and Nahaleh Moshtagh. "Transsexualism—Iran." In *The Encyclopedia of Women in Islamic Cultures*, edited by Suad Joseph, Afsaneh Najmabadi, Julie Peteet, Seteney Shami, Jackie Siapno, and Jane I. Smith. Leiden: Brill, 2007.

Einstein, Gillian, ed. *Sex and the Brain*. Cambridge, MA: MIT Press, 2007.

Epps, Brad. "Comparisons, Competitions, and Cross-Dressing: Cross-Cultural Analysis in a Contested World." In *Islamicate Sexualities: Transformations across Temporal Geographies of Desire*, edited by Kathryn Babayan and Afsaneh Najmabadi, 114–60. Cambridge, MA: Harvard University Press, 2008.

Esfandiari, Haleh. *My Prison, My Home: One Woman's Story of Captivity in Iran*. New York: Ecco, 2009.

Fausto-Sterling, Anne. *Sexing the Body: Gender Politics and the Construction of Sexuality*. New York: Basic Books, 2000.

Ferguson, James, and Akhil Gupta. "Spatializing States: Toward an Ethnography of Neo-Liberal Governmentality." *American Ethnologist* 29, no. 4 (2002): 981–1002.

Fischer, Michael M. J. *Iran: From Religious Dispute to Revolution*. Cambridge, MA: Harvard University Press, 1980.

Foucault, Michel. *The History of Sexuality: Volume I — An Introduction*. New York: Random House, 1980.

Frolov, Dmitri V. "Path or Way." In *The Encyclopaedia of the Qur'ān*, edited by Jane Dammen McAuliffe. Brill Online. Harvard University. Accessed July 2, 2010. http://www.brillonline.nl/subscriber/entry?entry=q3_SIM-00317.

Furth, Charlotte. *A Flourishing Yin: Gender in China's Medical History, 960–1665*. Berkeley: University of California Press, 1999.

Garfinkel, Harold. *Studies in Ethnomethodology*. Cambridge: Polity Press, 2010 [1967].

Gilligan, Carol. *In a Different Voice: Psychological Theory and Women's Development*. Cambridge: Harvard University Press, 1982.

Gluck, Robert. "The Shiraz Arts Festival: Western Avant-Garde Arts in 1970s Iran." *Leonardo* 40, no. 1 (2007): 20–28.

Goffman, Erving. *The Presentation of Self in Everyday Life*. New York: Doubleday, 1957.

Goldstein, Jan. *The Post-Revolutionary Self: Politics and Psyche in France, 1750–1850*. Cambridge: Harvard University Press, 2005.

Green, Richard, and John Money, eds. *Transsexualism and Sex Reassignment*. Baltimore: Johns Hopkins University Press, 1969.

Gudarzi, Faramarz. *Pizishki-i qanuni* (Legal medicine), two volumes. Tehran: Intisharat-i Anishtan, 1998.

———. *Pizishki-i qanuni* (Legal medicine), 4th reprint. Tehran: Intisharat-i Anishtin, 1995.

Hacking, Ian. "The Looping Effect of Human Kinds." In *Causal Cognition: A Multidisciplinary Debate*, edited by Dan Sperber, David Premack, and Ann James Premack, 351–94. Oxford: Clarendon Press, 1995.

Hadi Tal'ati, Muhammad. *Ma'khaz-shinasi-i masa'il-i mustahdisah-i pizishki* (Bibliographical study of current medical questions). Qum: Markaz-i Intisharat-i Daftar-i Tablighat-i Islami-i Hauzah-i 'Ilmiyah-i Qum, 1999.

Haeri, Shahla. *Law of Desire: Temporary Marriage in Shi'i Iran*. Syracuse: Syracuse University Press, 1989.

Haire, Norman. "Introduction." In *Encyclopedia of Sexual Knowledge*. London: Eugenics Publishing Company, 1934 (copyright 1937).

Halberstam, Judith. *Female Masculinity*. Durham: Duke University Press, 1998.

Hale, Jacob. "Are Lesbians Women?" In *The Transgender Studies Reader*, edited by Susan Stryker and Stephen Whittle, 281–99. New York: Routledge, 2006.

Hallaq, Wael. "Zahir." In *The Encyclopaedia of Islam*, 2nd ed., edited by P. Bearman, Th. Bianquis, C. E. Bosworth, E. van Donzel and W. P. Heinrichs. Brill Online. Accessed March 15, 2010. http://www.brillonline.nl/subscriber/entry?entry=islam_SIM-1816.

Hamdiyah, Mustafá. "Tafakkur-i ilahi va bihdasht-i ravani" (Divine thinking and mental health). Paper presented at the Office of Islamic Studies in Mental Health, Tehran, March 10, 1993.

Hansen, Thomas Blom, and Finn Stepputat, eds. *States of Imagination: Ethnographic Explorations of the Postcolonial State*. Durham: Duke University Press, 2001.

Hashemi, Rana. "The comparative study of transsexualism effects in Iran and U.S.A. rights jurisdiction and from legal medicines point of view." Paper presented at the Second Conference of the Islamic Countries Organization for Forensic Medicine, Amman, Jordan, September 5–8, 2006.

Hashimi-Fard, Mir Ahmad. *Masa'il va ikhtilalat-i jinsi dar zan va mard* (Sexual problems and disorders in woman and man). Tehran: Chihr, 1963, reprinted 1969.

Hasuri, Hasan. *Raftar-i jinsi bar payah-i siksaufiziulauzhi* (Sexual behavior on the basis of sexo-physiology). Tehran: Tahuri, 1968.

Hausman, Bernice L. *Changing Sex: Transsexualism, Technology, and the Idea of Gender.* Durham: Duke University Press, 1995.

Heiner, Brady Thomas. "The Passions of Michel Foucault." *differences* 14, no. 1 (2003): 22–52.

Hejazi, Arya. "Investigation of the accordance of new sexual role & sexual identification between 12 transsexuals after surgery." Paper presented at the Second Conference of the Islamic Countries Organization for Forensic Medicine, Amman, Jordan, September 5–8, 2006.

Hejazi, Arya, and Zohreh Edalati Shateri, Zahra Sadat Hosseini, Monireh Razaghian, Marzieh Moghaddam, and Saeedeh Sadat Mostafavi. "A preliminary analysis of 12 transsexual patients with regards to their adaptation in means of role and gender identity after a sexual reassignment surgery" (in Persian). *Scientific Journal of Kurdistan University of Medical Sciences* 13 (winter 2009): 78–87.

Hilbert, Richard, "Norman and Sigmund." *Sociological Theory* 9, no. 2 (autumn 1991): 264–68.

Hollywood, Amy. "Spiritual but Not Religious." *Harvard Divinity Bulletin* 38, no. 1–2 (winter/spring 2010): 19–26.

Hotchkiss, Carroll. "His or Hers" page: "Christine in Reverse: The Hush-Hush Choice 150,000 'Girls' Must Make," *Uncensored* (October 1955): 31–22, 73.

Huang, Ana. "On the Surface: Conceptualizing Gender and Subjectivity in Chinese Lesbian Culture." BA honors dissertation, Harvard University, 2008.

Hujjat, Hadi, and Muhammad Hadi Tal'ati, eds. *Ahkam-i pizshkan va mashaghil-i marbut beh pizishki* (Islamic rules of physicians and medical matters). Qum: Bustan-i Kitab, 2006 [1996].

Hunsberger, Alice C. "Marvels." In *Encyclopaedia of the Qur'ān*, vol. 3, edited by Jane Dammen McAuliffe, page 287. Brill Online. Accessed June 12, 2010. http://www.brillonline.nl/subscriber/entry?entry=q3_SIM-00274.

Husaynian, Ruhallah. *Fisad-i darbar-i Pahlavi* (Corruption of Pahlavi Court). Markaz-i Asnad-i Inqilab-i Islami (Islamic Revolution Documentation Center). Accessed July 19, 2009. http://www.irdc.ir/fa/content/4915/default.aspx.

Ibn, Sina. *'Ilm al-nafs*, translated and introduced by Akbar Danasirisht. Tehran: Chapkhanah-i Bank-i Markazi, 1969 [1939, 1952].

Ihsan-manish, Mujtabá, ed. *Majmu'ah-i maqalat-i avvalin hamayish-i bayn al-milali-i "naqhs-i din dar bihdasht-i ravan"* (Collected papers presented at the first international seminar on "the role of religion in mental health"). Qum: Nashr-i Ma'arif, 2003.

Ihsan-manish, Mujtabá, and 'Isá Karimi Kaysani, eds. *Majmu'ah-i maqalat-i avvalin hamayish-i sarasari-i naqsh-i din dar bihdasht-i ravan* (Collected articles of the first nation-wide seminar on role of religion in mental health). Qum: Dafter-i Nashr-i Nuvid-i Islam, 1998.

Ilahi, Husayn. *Ruznamah va ruznamah-negari dar Khurasan* (Newspapers and journalism in Khurasan). Mashhad: Firdawsi Mashhad University Press, 2001.

Ireland, Doug. "Change Sex or Die: An Exclusive Interview with an Iranian Transgendered Activist on Iran's Surgical 'Cure' for Homosexuality." May 11, 2007. http://direland.typepad.com/direland/2007/05/change_sex_or_d.html.

Jackson, Michael, and Ivan Karp, eds. *Personhood and Agency: The Experience of Self and Other in African Cultures.* Uppsala: Uppsala University Press, 1990.

Jackson, Peter. "Kathoey/Gay/Man: The Historical Emergence of Gay Male Identity in Thailand." In *Sites of Desire/Economies of Pleasure: Sexualities in Asia and the Pacific,* edited by Lenore Manderson and Margaret Jolly, 166–90. Chicago: The University of Chicago Press, 1997.

———. "Performative Genders, Perverse Desires: A Bio-History of Thailand's Same-Sex and Transgender Cultures." *Intersections: Gender, History and Culture in the Asian Context* 9 (August 2003), http://intersections.anu.edu.au/issue9/jackson.html.

Jagose, Annamarie, and Don Kulick. "Thinking Sex/Thinking Gender." *GLQ* 10, no. 2 (2004): 211–313.

Jakobsen, Janet. *Working Alliances and the Politics of Difference: Diversity and Feminist Ethics.* Bloomington: Indiana University Press, 1998.

Javaheri, Fatemeh. "A Study of Transsexuality in Iran." *Iranian Studies* 43, no. 3 (June 2010): 365–77.

Javaheri, Fatemeh, and Zaynab Kuchekian. "Ikhtilal-i huviyat-i jinsiyati va ab'ad-i ijtima'i-i an: barrisi-i padidah-i narizayati-i jinsi dar Iran" (Gender identity disorder and its social dimensions: investigating the phenomenon of sexual/gender discontent in Iran). *Rifah-i ijtima'i* (Social welfare) 5, no. 21 (summer 2006): 265–92.

Johnson, Mark. *Beauty and Power: Transgendering and Cultural Transformation in the Southern Philippines.* Oxford: Berg, 1997.

Jordan-Young, Rebecca M. *Brain Storm: The Flaw in the Science of Sex Differences.* Cambridge, MA: Harvard University Press, 2010.

Jorgensen, Christine. *Christine Jorgensen: A Personal Autobiography.* San Francisco: Cleis Press, 2000.

Joseph, Suad. *Intimate Selving in Arab Families: Gender, Self, and Identity.* Syracuse: Syracuse University Press, 1999.

*Journal of Medical Council of Iran.* "Akhlaq-i pizishki dar barabar-i pizishki-i nuvin: masa'il-i ikhtisasi-i akhlaq-i pizishki" (Medical ethics confronting new medicine: special problems of medical ethics). *Journal of Medical Council of Iran* 6, no. 5 (March 1978): 445–47.

Kahani, Ali Reza, and Peyman Shojaei. *Ikhtilal-i huviyat-i jinsi (GID): digarjinsiyat-ju-ha (TS)* (Gender Identity Disorders [GID]: Transsexualism). Tehran: Taymurzadah, 2002.

Kajbaf, Muhammad Baqir. *Ravanshinasi-i raftar-i jinsi* (Psychology of sexual behavior). Tehran: Nashr-i Ravan, 2002.

Kamalipour, Yahya. "Print Media." In *Iran Today: An Encyclopedia of Life in the Islamic Republic,* edited by Mehran Kamrava and Manochehr Dorraj, volume II, 394–98. Westport: Greenwood Press, 2008.

Kandiyoti, Deniz. "Pink Cards Blues: Trouble and Strife at the Crossroads of Gender." In *Fragments of Culture: The Everyday of Modern Turkey,* edited by Deniz Kandiyoti and Ayse Saktanber, 277–93. New Brunswick, NJ: Rutgers University Press, 2002.

Kaplan, Paul S. *Adolescence.* Stamford, CT: Cengage Learning, 2003.

Karimi, Muhammad Riza. *Darman ba Qur'an: ravan-darmani-i Islami* (Healing with the Qur'an: Islamic psychotherapy). Isfahan: Intisharat-i Guya, 1999.

Karimi-nia, Muhammad Mahdi. "Taghyir-i jinsiyat az manzar-i fiqhi va huquqi" (Sex-change from the perspective of fiqh and the law). *Ma'rifat* 9, no. 4 (2000): 76–82.

———. "Jurisprudence and lawful evaluation of 'sex-reversing.'" Paper presented at the First Conference of the Islamic Countries Organization for Forensic Medicine, Tehran, June 24–26, 2004.

———. *Hamzisti-i musalimat-amiz dar Islam va huquq-i bayn al-milal* (Peaceful coexistence in Islam and international law). Qum: Markaz-i Intisharat-i Mu'assisah-i Amuzishi va Pazhuhishi-i Imam Khomeini, 2004.

———. *Huquq-i bashar va qanun-i asasi-i jumhuri-i Islami-i Iran* (Human Rights and the Constitution of Islamic Republic of Iran). Qum: Jilvah-i Kamal, 2006.

———. *Taghyir-i jinsiyat az manzar-i fiqh va huquq* (Sex-change from the perspective of *fiqh* and law). Qum: Intisharat-i Markaz-i Fiqhi-i A'immah-i Athar, 2010.

Karrazi, S. M. "Sex Change Operation." Paper presented at the First Conference of the Islamic Countries Organization for Forensic Medicine, Tehran, June 24–26, 2004.

Kaynia, Mahdi. *Criminological Sciences.* Tehran: Tehran University Press, 1966–7.

———. *Introduction to Law.* Tehran: Tehran University Press, 1969.

———. *Mabani-i jurm-shinasi* (Fundamentals of criminology). Tehran: Tehran University Press, 1979–81.

Kazimzadeh Iranshahr, Husayn. *Usul-i asasi-i ravanshinasi* (Foundational principles of psychology). Tehran: Shirkat-i Nisbi-i Hajj Muhammad Husayn Iqbal va Shuraka', 1958 [1937].

Kelly, John, and Bruce Etling. *Mapping Iran's Online Public: Politics and Culture in the Persian Blogosphere.* Cambridge: Harvard University Berkman Center, 2008.

Keshavarzian, Arang. "Regime Loyalty and Bazari Representation under the Islamic Republic of Iran: Dilemmas of the Society of Islamic Coalition." *International Journal of Middle East Studies* 41 (2009): 225–46.

Kessler, Suzanne, and Wendy McKenna. *Gender: An Ethnomethodological Approach.* Chicago: The University of Chicago Press, 1985 [1978].

Khaksar, Ilham, "Gharibah-ha-yi 'alam-i khilqat!: guzarishi az vaz'iyat-i taghyir-i jinsiyat dar Iran" (The strange marvels of the world of creation: A report about the situation of sex-change in Iran). *Zanan* 124 (September 2005): 2–10.

Khamenei, Ayatollah. *Risalah-i ajubat al-Istifta'at* (Treatise responding to questions), translated by Ahmad Riza Husayni. Tehran: Intisharat-i Bayn al-Milali-i al-Hudá, 2005 [2001].

Kheshti, Roshanak. "Cross-Dressing and Gender (Tres)Passing: The Transgender Move as a Site of Agential Potential in the New Iranian Cinema." *Hypatia* 24, no. 3 (summer 2009): 158–77.

Khiabany, Gholam, and Annabelle Sreberny. "The Iranian Press and the Continuing Struggle over Civil Society 1998–2000." *International Communication Gazette* 63, no. 2–3 (May 2001): 203–23.

———. "The Politics of/in Blogging in Iran." *Comparative Studies of South Asia, Africa and the Middle East* 27, no. 3 (2007): 63–79.

———. "Becoming Intellectual: The Blogestan and Public Political Space in the Islamic Republic." *British Journal of Middle Eastern Studies* 34, no. 3 (December 2007): 267–86.

———. *Blogistan: The Internet and Politics in Iran.* London: I. B. Tauris, 2010.

Khodayarifard, Muhammad, Mohammed Reza Mohammadi, and Yasaman Abedini. "Darman-i shinakhti-raftari-i tabaddul-khvahi ba ta'kid bar darman-i ma'navi: barrisi-i mauridi" (Cognitive-Behavioral Therapy with Emphasis on Spiritual Therapy in Treatment of Transsexualism: A Case Study). *Andishah va raftar* 9, no. 3 (2004): 12–21.

Khomeini, Ayatollah Ruhallah. *Tahrir al-wasilah.* Najaf: Matba'at al-Adab, 1967 or 1968 [1387 AH].

———. *A Clarification of Questions: An Unabridged Translation of Resaleh towzih al-masael,* translated by J. Borujerdi, foreword by Michael M. J. Fischer and Mehdi Abedi. Boulder, CO: Westview Press, 1984.

Khosrokhavar, Farhad, and M. Amin Ghaeirad. "Iran's New Scientific Community," *Iranian Studies* 39, no. 2 (June 2006): 253–67.

Kirmani, Ibrahim Ja'far, *Naujavani* (Adolescence). Tehran: Chihr, 1970.

Knysh, Alexander. "Sufism and the Qur'an." In *Encyclopaedia of the Qur'ān*, volume 3, edited by Jane Dammen McAuliffe, page 287. Brill Online. Accessed June 12, 2010. http://www.brillonline.nl/subscriber/entry?entry=q3_SIM-00274.

Kondo, Dorrin. *Crafting Selves: Power, Gender and Discourses of Identity in a Japanese Workplace.* Chicago: University of Chicago Press, 1990.

Kugel, Scott. *Homosexuality in Islam: Islamic Reflections on Gay, Lesbian, and Transgender Muslims.* Oxford: Oneworld Publications, 2010.

Long, Scott. "Unbearable witness: How Western activists (mis)recognize sexuality in Iran." *Contemporary Politics* 15, no. 1 (March 2009): 119–36.

Mahdavi, Pardis. *Passionate Uprisings: Iran's Sexual Revolution.* Stanford: Stanford University Press, 2009.

Mahmudi, (no first name given). "Nafs-i adami az didgah-i hikmat-i Bu'ali Sina" (Human psyche/soul from Ibn Sina's philosophical perspective). In Tavakkoli Bazzaz, *Majmu'ah-i maqalat*, volume 1, 233–45.

Malik, Faris. "Queer Sexuality and Identity in the Qur'an and Hadith." Accessed March 12, 2011. http://www.well.com/user/aquarius/Qurannotes.htm.

Malti-Douglas, Fedwa. *Woman's Body, Woman's Word: Gender and Discourse in Arabo-Islamic Writing.* Princeton, NJ: Princeton University Press, 1991.

Maynard, Douglas. "Goffman, Garfinkel, and Games." *Sociological Theory* 8, no. 2 (autumn 1990): 277–79.

McKibbin, Ross. "Introduction." In *Married Love*, by Marie Stopes, edited by Ross McKibbin. Oxford: Oxford University Press, 2004.

Mehrabi, Faridun. "Barrisi-i barkhi az vizhigiha-yi 'tabaddul-khvahi-i jinsi' dar bimaran-i Irani" (Some characteristics of Iranian transsexualists). *Andishah va raftar* 2, no. 3 (winter 1996): 6–12.

Messkoub, Mahmood. "Social Policy in Iran in the Twentieth Century." *Iranian Studies* 39, no. 2 (June 2006): 227–52.

Meyerowitz, Joanne. *How Sex Changed: A History of Transsexuality in the United States.* Cambridge, MA: Harvard University Press, 2002.

Milani, Abbas. *The Persian Sphinx: Amir Abbas Hoveyda and the Riddle of the Iranian Revolution.* Washington, D.C.: Mage Publishers, 2000.

Milani, Farzaneh. *Veils and Words: The Emerging Voices of Iranian Women Writers.* Syracuse: Syracuse University Press, 1992.

Miller, William Ian. *The Anatomy of Disgust.* Cambridge: Harvard University Press, 1997.

Mir-Hosseini, Ziba. "Being from There: Dilemmas of a 'Native Anthropologist.'" In *Conceptualizing Iranian Anthropology: Past and Present Perspectives,* edited by Shahnaz R. Nadjmabadi, 180–91. New York: Berghahn Books, 2009.

Misbahi Nuri, Husayn'ali Khan. *Dastur-i izdivaj* (Marriage prescriptions). Tehran: Kitabkhanah-i Sa'adat, 1929.

Mitchell, Timothy. "The Limits of the State: Beyond Statist Approaches and Their Critics." *American Political Science Review* 85, no. 1 (March 1991): 77–96.

———. "Society, Economy, and the State Effect." In *State/Culture: state-formation after the cultural turn,* edited by George Steinmatz, 76–97. Ithaca: Cornell University Press, 1999.

Moallem, Minoo. *Between Warrior Brother and Veiled Sister: Islamic Fundamentalism and the Politics of Patriarchy in Iran.* Berkeley: University of California Press, 2005.

Mohammadi, Mohammad Reza, and Hushmand Hashemi-Kohanzad. "Ravan-darmani-i ma'navi" (Spiritual psychotherapy). *Tibb va tazkiah* (Medicine and purification) 43 (winter 2001): 104–20.

Mottahedeh, Roy. "Introduction." In *Lessons in Islamic Jurisprudence,* by Muhammad Baqir as-Sadr, translated by Roy Mottahedeh. Oxford: Oneworld, 2003.

Muhammadpur, Ahmad Riza. *Dau dahah talash-i mustamarr bara-yi kasb-i huviyat-i mustaqill* (Two decades of persistent struggle to acquire an independent identity). Tehran: Aftab Girafic, 2009.

Mu'mini, Khalil. Preface. In *Tamayulat va raftar-ha-yi jinsi-i insan* (Sexual desires and behaviors in human beings) (5th ed.), by Behnam Ohadi. Isfahan: Intisharat-i Sadiq Hidayat, 2005 [2000].

Mutabi, Fereshteh, and Ali Shahrami. "Preparation and normalization of MMPI-2 questionnaire for Tehran," MA thesis, TPI (IUMS), 1995.

Muvahhidi, Muhammad Mahdi. *Az mabahis-i pichidah-i bimariha-yi zanan va mama'i* (On complex topics related to gynecology and obstetrics). Tehran: Shirkat-i Sahami-i Chap va Intisharat-i Kutub-i Iran, 1966.

———. *Danistaniha-yi zanashu'i* (Marital know-how). Tehran: n.p., 1966.

———. *Razha-yi salamat.* Tehran: 'Ilmi, 1976(?).

———. *Zindiginamah-i mashahir-i rijal-i pizishki-i mu'asir-i Iran* (Biographies of famous men of medicine in contemporary Iran). Tehran: Nashr-i 'Ulum va Funun, 1992.

———. *Zindigi-namah-i pizishkan-i nam-avar-i mu'asir-i Iran* (Biographies of famous contemporary Iranian physicians). Two volumes. Tehran: Abrun, 2000.

Nadjmabadi, Shahnaz. "From 'Alien' to 'One of Us' and Back: Field Experiences in Iran." *Iranian Studies* 37, no. 4 (December 2004): 603–12.

———, ed. *Conceptualizing Iranian Anthropology: Past and Present Perspectives.* New York: Berghahn Books, 2009.

Naficy, Hamid. "Iranian Cinema." In *The Companion Encyclopedia of Middle Eastern and North African Film,* edited by Oliver Leaman, 130–222. London: Routledge, 2001.

Nafisi, Majid. "Hamjinsgara'i va Faridun Farrukhzad" (Homosexuality and Faridun Farrukhzad). *Cheraq* 34 (2007): 56–57.

Najafi, Mustafá. "Ravanpizishki va intibaq" (Psychiatry and compliance). In *Majmu'ah-i
maqalat*, volume 3, edited by Javad Tavakoli Bazzaz, 123–27. Tehran: Taymurzadah, 1998.

Najmabadi, Afsaneh. *Women with Mustaches and Men without Beards: Gender and Sexual
Anxieties of Iranian Modernity*. Berkeley: University of California Press, 2005.

———. "Truth of Sex." January 12, 2005, http://www.iranian.com/Najmabadi/2005
/January/Sex/index.html.

———. "Types, Acts, or What? Regulation of Sexuality in Nineteenth-Century Iran.
"In *Islamicate Sexualities: Translations across Temporal Geographies of Desire*, edited by
Kathryn Babayan and Afsaneh Najmabadi, 275–96. Cambridge, MA: Harvard Univer-
sity Press, HCMES series, 2008.

———. "Genus of Sex or the Sexing of Jins," *International Journal of Middle Eastern Studies*
45 (2013), 211–31.

O'Donnell, Elizabeth. "Infertile in Iran." *Le Monde diplomatique*, April 2008. Accessed
March 2, 2013. http://mondediplo.com/2008/04/15iran.

Ohadi, Behnam. *Tamayulat va raftar-ha-yi jinsi-i insan* (Sexual desires and behaviors in
human beings). Isfahan: Intisharat-i Sadiq Hidayat, 2005 [2000].

———. "Va khudavand TS ra azmun-i adam afarid" (And God created TS to test human/
Adam). *Ravanshinasi va jami'ah* (Psychology and society) 33 (June/July 2006): 18–23.

———. "Vizhigiha-yi tasvirbardari-i maghz-i afrad-i duchar-i ikhtilal-i huviyat-i jinsi dar
muqayisah ba afrad-i salim" (Particularities of brain images of persons afflicted with
gender identity disorder in comparison with healthy persons). *Fasl-namah-i tazah-ha-yi
'ulum-i shinakhti* (Advances in Cognitive Science) 9, no. 3 (fall 2007): 20–25.

Osanloo, Arzoo. *The Politics of Women's Rights in Iran*. Princeton: Princeton University
Press, 2009.

Paidar, Parvin. *Women and the Political Process in Twentieth-century Iran*. Cambridge: Cambridge University Press, 1995.

Papan-Matin, Firoozeh. "The Case of Mohammad Khordadian, an Iranian Male Dancer."
*Iranian Studies* 42, no. 1 (February 2009): 127–38.

Payman, "Hamjins-gara'i ya hamjins-bazi?!" ([Same-sex-orientation or same-sex-
playing?!), *Neda* 19 (June 2010): 14–15.

Pflugfelder, Gregory. *Cartographies of Desire: Male-Male Sexuality in Japanese Discourse—1600–1950*. Berkeley: University of California Press, 1999.

Prosser, Jay. *Second Skins: The Body Narratives of Transsexuality*. New York: Columbia University Press, 1998.

"A Psychiatrist." Accessed September 12, 2009. http://1ravanpezeshk.blogfa.com
/post-268.aspx.

Pursa'id, Isma'il. *Natavaniha-yi jinsi khaud ra ba ghaza mu'alijah kunid* (Cure your sexual
impotence with food). Tehran: Farrukhi, 1976.

Rabinow, Paul. *Reflections on Fieldwork in Morocco*. Berkeley: University of California
Press, 2007 [1977].

Rahman, F. "Dhat." In *The Encyclopaedia of Islam*, Second Edition, edited by P. Bearman,
Th. Bianquis, C. E. Bosworth, E. van Donzel and W. P. Heinrichs. Brill Online. Accessed
March 15, 2010. http://www.brillonline.nl/subscriber/entry?entry=islam_SIM-1816.

Ra'isi, Firuzeh. Preface. In *Tamayulat va raftar-ha-yi jinsi-i insan* (Sexual desires and behaviors in human beings) (5th ed.), by Behnam Ohadi. Isfahan: Intisharat-i Sadiq Hidayat, 2005 [2000].

Ranjbar Shayan, Husayn. "Barrisi va muqayisah-i vizhigiha-yi shakhsiyati-i afrad-i mubtala bah ikhtilal-i huviyat-i jinsi va afrad-i bihanjar" (Investigating and comparing the personality traits of persons afflicted with gender identity disorder and normal persons). MA thesis (no. 233) in Clinical Psychology, TPI, Iran University of Medical Sciences and Health and Treatment Services, winter 1999.

Rastakhiz, Farhad. "Mardi dar hashiah" (A man on the margin). In *Mardi dar hashiah*. Hamburg: Nashr-i Kalagh, n.d.

Reed, David. "The Persian Boy Today: Sexual Politics in Teheran," *Christopher Street* (August 1978), 14–17.

Renault, Mary. *The Persian Boy*. New York: Pantheon, 1972.

Reuben, David. *Any Woman Can!: Love and Sexual Fulfillment for the Single, Widowed, Divorced, and Married*. New York: David McKay, 1971.

———. *Everything You Always Wanted to Know about Sex but Were Afraid to Ask*. New York: HarperCollins, 1969.

Riley, Denise, *The Words of Selves: Identification, Solidarity, Irony*. Stanford: Stanford University Press, 2000.

de River, J. Paul. *The Sexual Criminal: A Psychoanalytical Study*. Springfield: Charles C. Thomas Publishers, 1949.

Riza'ee, Behjat. *The Moonlike*. London: Bra Books, 1991.

Rodriguez, Julia. *Civilizing Argentina: Science, Medicine, and the Modern State*. Chapel Hill: The University of North Carolina Press, 2006.

Rofel, Lisa. *Desiring China: Experiments in Neoliberalism, Sexuality, and Public Culture*. Durham: Duke University Press, 2007.

Rogers, Mary, "Resisting the Enormous Either/Or," *Gender and Society* 6, no. 2 (June 1992): 207–14.

Rogers, Mary, "They Were All Passing: Agnes, Garfinkel, and Company," *Gender and Society* 6, no. 2 (June 1992): 169–91.

Rosenthal, Franz. "Ar-Razi on the Hidden Illness." *Bulletin of the History of Medicine* 52 (1978): 45–60.

Saberi, Sayyid Mahdi, and Mohammad Reza Mohammadi. *Nigarishi nau bah ravanpizishki-i qanuni* (A new look at legal psychiatry). Tehran: Taymurzadah, 2005.

Sajjadi, Sadeq. "Bimarestan," *Encyclopaedia Iranica*. Accessed May 11, 2011. http://www.iranica.com/articles/bimarestan-hospital-.

Salamon, Gayle. *Assuming a Body: Transgender and Rhetorics of Materiality*. New York: Columbia University Press, 2010.

Salih, Jahanshah. *Bimariha-yi zanan va pishraftha-yi 'ilmi-i nuvin* (*Gynecological Diseases and New Scientific Advances*). Tehran: Tehran University Press, 1960.

Sam-Gisu, Banafsheh, "Mahkum shudigan-i faramushi: nigahi bah vaz'iyat-i bimaran-i duchar-i ikhtilal-i huviyat-i jinsi dar Iran" (condemned to being forgotten: a look at the patients afflicted with sex/gender identity disorder), *Sharq*, May 20, 2007, p. 22.

Sana'i-zadah, Husayn. *Pizishki-i qanuni* (Legal medicine). Tehran: Dadgustar, 2008.

Sanders, Paula. "Gendering the Ungendered Body: Hermaphrodites in Medieval Islamic

Law." In *Women in Middle Eastern History: Shifting Boundaries in Sex and Gender*, edited by Beth Baron and Nikki Keddie, 74–95. New Haven, CT: Yale University Press, 1991.

Sang, Tse-Ian D. *The Emerging Lesbian: Female Same-Sex Desire in Modern China*. Chicago: University of Chicago Press, 2003.

Sani'i, Ayatollah. *Istifta'at-i pizishki* (Medical questions). Qum: Intisharat-i Maysam Tammar, 2006 [1997].

Schayegh, Cyrus. "Serial Murder in Tehran: Crime, Science, and the Formation of Modern State and Society in Interwar Iran." *Comparative Study of Society and History* 47, no. 4 (October 2005): 836–62.

———. *Who Is Knowledgeable Is Strong: Science, Class, and the Formation of Modern Iranian Society, 1900–1950*. Berkeley: University of California Press, 2009.

———. "'Seeing Like a State': An Essay on the Historiography of Modern Iran." *International Journal of Middle East Studies* 42 (2010): 37–61.

Schimmel, Annemarie. *Mystical Dimensions of Islam*. Chapel Hill: The University of North Carolina Press, 1975.

Sedghi, Hamideh. *Women and Politics in Iran: Veiling, Unveiling, and Reveiling*. Cambridge: Cambridge University Press, 2007.

Seigel, Jerrold. *The Idea of the Self: Thought and Experience in Western Europe since the Seventeenth Century*. Cambridge: Cambridge University Press, 2005.

Semati, Mehdi. "Internet." In *Iran Today: An Encyclopedia of Life in the Islamic Republic*, volume I, edited by Mehran Kamrava and Manochehr Dorraj, 245–50. Westport: Greenwood Press, 2008.

Shahri, Ja'far. *Tihran-i qadim* (Old Tehran). Tehran: Amir Kabir, 1978.

———. *Tarikh-i ijtima'i-i Tihran dar qarn-i sizdahum* (A social history of Tehran in the thirteenth [nineteenth A.D.] century). Six volumes. Tehran: Mu'assisah-i Khadamat-i Farhangi-i Rasa, 1990.

Shakhsari, Sima. "From Hamjensbaaz to Hamjensgaraa: Diasporic Queer Reterritorializations and Limits of Transgression." Unpublished paper.

Shamissa, Sirous. *Shahidbazi dar adabiyat-i Farsi* (Sodomy: based on Persian literature). Tehran: Firdaws, 2002.

Shari'ati, 'Ali. *Khaudsazi-i inqilabi* (Revolutionary crafting of self). Tehran: Daftar-i Tadvin va Tanzim-i Majmu'ah-i Asar-i Mu'allim-i Shahid Duktur 'Ali Shari'ati, 1983.

———. *Insan-i bikhaud* (Empty [without self] human). Tehran: Daftar-i Tadvin va Tanzim-i Majmu'ah-i Asar-i Mu'allim-i Shahid Duktur 'Ali Shari'ati, 1983.

———. *Bazgasht bah khishtan* (Return to oneself). Tehran: Husayniyah Irshad, n.d.

Sharma, Aradhana, and Akhil Gupta. "Introduction: Rethinking Theories of the State in an Age of Globalization." In *Anthropology of the State*, edited by Aradhana Sharma and Akhil Gupta, 1–41. Oxford: Blackwell, 2006.

Shay, Anthony. "The Male Dancer in the Middle East and Central Asia," *Dance Research Journal*, 38, no. 1–2 (2006): 137–62.

———. "Choreographic Hypermasculinity in Egypt, Iran, and Uzbekistan." *Dance Chronicle: Studies in Dance and the Related Arts* 31, no. 2 (2008): 211–38.

Shirin, Fatimah. *Bazichah-i Shahbanu: jashn-i hunar-i Shiraz* (The Queen's plaything: Shriaz Art Festival). Tehran: The Center for Islamic Revolution Documents, 2005.

Shrage, Laurie J. "Introduction." 3–10, In *"You've Changed": Sex Reassignment and Personal Identity*, edited by Laure J. Shrage. Oxford: Oxford University Press, 2009.

Siasi, 'Ali Akbar. *'Ilm al-nafs ya ravanshinasi* (Science of essence/soul or psychology). Tehran: Tehran University Press, 1962 [1st ed. Tehran: Khudkar, 1938].

———. *'Ilm al-nafs-i Ibn Sina va tatbiq-i an ba ravanshinasi-i jadid* (Ibn Sina's Science of essence/soul and its compliance with modern psychology). Tehran: Tehran University Press, 1954.

———. *Ravanshinasi-i shakhsiyat* (Psychology of personality). Tehran: Ibn Sina, 1970.

———. *Guzarish-i yik zindigi* (Narrating a Life). London: Paka Print, 1987.

Sinnott, Megan. *Toms and Dees: Transgender Identity and Female Same-Sex Relationships in Thailand*. Honolulu: University of Hawai'i Press, 2004.

Skovgaard-Petersen, Jakob. *Defining Islam for the Egyptian State: Muftis and Fatwas of the Dar al-Ifta*. Leiden: Brill, 1997.

Spade, Dean. "Mutilating Gender." In *The Transgender Studies Reader*, edited by Susan Stryker and Stephen Whittle, 315–32. New York: Routledge, 2006.

Stall, Sylvanus. *What a Young Husband Ought to Know. Sex and Self* series. Philadelphia: Vir, 1897. Translated into Persian by Hidayat-allah Khan Suhrab, n.p., 1929.

Steinmatz, George. *State/Culture: State-Formation after the Cultural Turn*. Ithaca, NY: Cornell University Press, 1999.

Stone, Hannah, and Abraham Stone. *A Marriage Manual*, translated by Tarazallah Akhavan. Tehran: Gulsha'i, 1997.

———. *A Marriage Manual*, translated by Rahim Muttaqi Irvani. Tehran: Kanun-i Ma'rifat, 1948.

———. *A Marriage Manual*. Revised by Gloria Stone Aitken and Aquiles J. Sobrero. New York: Simon and Schuster, 1965 [1935].

Stryker, Susan. "(De)Subjugated Knowledges: An Introduction to Transgender Studies." In *The Transgender Studies Reader*, edited by Susan Stryker and Stephen Whittle, 1–17. New York: Routledge, 2006.

Stryker, Susan and Stephen Whittle, eds. *The Transgender Studies Reader*. New York: Routledge, 2006.

Tal'ati, Muhammad Hadi. *Ma'khaz-shinasi-i masa'il-i mustahdisah-i pizishki* (Bibliographical study of current medical questions). Qum: Markaz-i Intisharat-i Daftar-i Tablighat-i Islami-i Hauzah-i 'Ilmiyah-i Qum, 1999.

Talattof, Kamran. *Modernity, Sexuality, and Ideology in Iran: The Life and Legacy of a Popular Female Artist*. Syracuse, NY: Syracuse University Press, 2011.

Tan Lay Ean, Honey. "Jeffrey Jessie: Recognising Transexuals." November 17, 2005. http://www.malaysianbar.org.my/gender_issues/jeffrey_jessie_recognising_transexuals_by_honey_tan_lay_ean.html.

Tariqan, Muhammad Riza Iskandari. "Ham-jins-gara'i, ibham-i jinsi, ya . . . ?" (Homosexuality, sexual ambiguity, or . . . ?) *Andishah-i jami'ah*, no. 30 (June/July 2003): 55–59.

Tavakoli Bazzaz, Javad, ed. *Majmu'ah-i maqalat-i avvalin kungirah-i sarasari-i intibaq-i umur-i pizishki ba mavazin-i shar'-i muqaddas* (Collected papers from the first nationwide congress of compliance of medical matters with precepts of the holy law). Tehran: Taymurzadah, 1998.

Toronto, James A. "Astray." In *Encyclopaedia of the Qur'an*, general editor, Jane Dammen McAuliffe, Georgetown University, Washington, D.C.: Brill, 2010. Brill Online.
Harvard University. Accessed July 2, 2010. http://www.brillonline.nl/subscriber
/entry?entry=q3_SIM-00035.

Tsing, Anna Lowenhaupt. "Introduction." In *Words in Motion: Toward a Global Lexicon*,
edited by Carol Gluck and Anna Lowenhaupt Tsing, 11–17. Durham, NC: Duke University Press, 2009.

———. "Adat/Indigenous: Indigeneity in Motion." In *Words in Motion: Toward a Global
Lexicon*, edited by Carol Gluck and Anna Lowenhaupt Tsing, 40–64. Durham, NC:
Duke University Press, 2009.

Tutia, Muhammad 'Ali. *Amraz-i zuhravi (muqaribati)* (Venereal disease). 1931.

———. *Malish va tamas* (Massage and touch). Tehran, 1932.

———. *Amraz-i ruhi* (Diseases of the soul/psyche). Tehran: Matba'ah-i Raushana'i, 1934.

———. "Maraz-i ruhi: Sadizm" (A disease of the soul/psyche: sadism). *Sihhat-numa-yi
Iran* II, no. 3 (June/July 1934): 74–77.

Valentine, David. *Imagining Transgender: An Ethnography of a Category*. Durham: Duke
University Press, 2007.

———. "Sue E. Generous: Toward a Theory of Non-Transexuality." *Feminist Studies* 38,
no. 1 (spring 2012): 185–211.

Validi, Muhammad Salih. *Huquq-i jaza-yi ikhtisasi: jarayim 'alayh-i 'iffat va akhlaq-i 'umumi
va huquq va takalif-i khvanidigi* (Private penal laws: offenses against public decency and
morality, and family rights and obligations). Tehran: Amir Kabir, 2004.

Vidal, Gore. "Number One." *The New York Review of Books*, June 4, 1970. Accessed October
18, 2008. http://www.nybooks.com.ezp-prod1.hul.harvard.edu/articles/10956.

Wahrman, Dror. *The Making of the Modern Self: Identity and Culture in Eighteenth-Century
England*. New Haven, CT: Yale University Press, 2004.

Warnke, Georgia. "Transexuality and Contextual Identities." In *"You've Changed": Sex Reassignment and Personal Identity*, edited by Laurie J. Shrage, 28–42. Oxford: Oxford University Press, 2009.

Yasami, Muhammad Taqi, 'Ali Muhammadi, Ja'far Kamili, Muhammad Riza Yusufi, and
Sayyid Mahdi Samimi Ardistani. "Tajrubiyati az darman-i muvaffaqiyat-amiz-i hamjins-
barigi-i khaudnapazir, farabarigi (parafilia) va tabdil-khvahi-i jinsi ba ravish-ha-yi
shinakhti-raftari" (Experiences with successful treatment of egodystonic homosexuality, paraphilia, and transexuality with cognitive-behavioral methods). *The Scientific
Journal of Legal Medicine* 12, no. 4 (winter 2007): 222–27.

Zarit, Jerry, "The Iranian Male—An Intimate Look," *GPU* (Gay Peoples Union) *News*, October 1979, 19–24.

Zimmerman, Don. "They Were All Doing Gender, But They Weren't All Passing," *Gender
and Society* 6, no. 2 (June 1992): 192–98.

Zito, Angela. "Silk and Skin: Significant Boundaries." In *Body, Subject & Power in China*,
edited by Angela Zito and Tani E. Barlow, 103–30. Chicago: The University of Chicago
Press, 1994.

Zohrevand, Razeieh. "Relationship of Gender Roles Perception and Gender Contentment." *Pazhuhish-i Zanan* 2, no. 2 (summer 2004): 117–25.

# INDEX

*Page numbers in italics indicate figures.*

Batul Khanum, 47

Bayat, Asef, 212

Beeman, William O., 128–29

Behjatnia, Yahya: advice for woman-presenting men, 153, 158; on *gay* and *kuni*, 300; interview of, 338n84; on popular poem, 317n35; training of, 315n18; on trans persons' difficulties, 167–68

Behzad (pseud.): on Farrukhzad, 337n73; others' disgust with, 138; on relationships and party scene, 133–34, 332n34; self-identification of, 290–91

belly dancing, 239–40. *See also* theater and music performances

Benjamin, Harry, 57, 318n43

Bihbahani, Ayatollah, 159

"bi-/homosexuals": *dau-shakhsiyati* (double personality) as reference to, 114–15, 143; use of term, 327–28n54

Bihzisti. *See* Welfare Organization

*bisexuals*: child rearing blamed for, 54–55; others' discernment of, 36

Boellstorff, Tom: on desire and context, 299–300; on "habitation of incommensurability," 254, 362n21; on heteronormalizing dynamic of marriage, 361n14; on invisibility, 371–72n63; on nonheteronormative persons, 285, 291, 361n18, 364n33, 367–68n27; terminology treatment by, 306–7n13

brain: modes of cognition in, 30–37; Ohadi's measurement studies of, 28–30, 312n34; research on homosexuals vs. heterosexuals, 36. *See also* psychology and psychiatry

Bu-alhari, Ja'far, 347–48n73

Buffington, Robert, 72, 74, 172, 324nn107–8, 342n23

Burhan, Shirin, 97

Burujirdi, Asghar (Asghar Qatil, Asghar the Murderer): crimes of, 65–66; Mahin compared with, 101; remembered, 77; significance of case, 5, 71–72, 171; subsequent texts on, 66–69

Burujirdi, Ma'sumah 'Azizi (aka Mahvash), 53, 319n54

Burzabadi, Akbar, 130

Butler, Judith, 277, 279, 367n22

"cartography of desire" concept, 3

Cassioti, Rollando, 318n43

categories of identity: clinical determination of, 15–16; impetus for distinguishing, 232; meanings of, 3; performative differences in, 279–80; "persons vulnerable to social harm" or "socially harmed," 179, 202, 205, 214, 340n1, 344n43; as quantifiably divisible, 275, 297, 369n42; taxonomies of, 101, 171, 172–73, 177, 185, 202–3, 300. *See also* filtering and sorting processes; nonheteronormative lives and social circles; self; sexual/gender identity; trans vs. homosexual and other distinctions

Center for Critically Socially Harmed Groups of Welfare Organization. *See* Navvab Safavi Emergency Center; Office for the Socially Harmed

Center for Mental Health Research (TPI), 192

Center for Women and Family Affairs (Office of the President), 228

Central Revolutionary Court (Tehran), 216

certification process: court ratification of, 309n13; development of, 167–68, 190; Farzadi's role in, 21–22; meetings for case reviews, 15, 17–18 (*see also* Commission); number of applicants, 208, 209; with or without hormonal or somatic changes, 175–76, 252; politico-religious and scientific context of, 20–21; preparation for interviews, 16–17, 30; procedural changes, 18–19; questionnaires and inventories in, 21, 311n22; sites of entry into, 31–32; therapy in, 15–17, 18, 19, 22, 23, 190–91, 197–200, 265, 282, 308n8; timing of papers in, 182–84; trans-dressed (*mubaddal-pushi*) issue and, 180–81; trans persons' vs. profes-

certification process (*continued*)
   sionals' perspectives on, 30–32, 34–37.
   *See also* diagnosis; documents and
   papers; filtering and sorting processes;
   Legal Medicine Organization of Iran;
   Medical Council of Iran; trans vs. homosexual and other distinctions
*Charley's Aunt* (play), 128, *129*, 331n26
Chesser, Eustace, 318n44, 321n73
*Chilchiraq* (magazine), 206–7, 339n95,
   339n97
children and adolescents: causes of deviancy traced in, 62–63, 72–73; exposure to sexual materials, 64–65; foster
   and adoption programs for, 355n46;
   gender-discordant experiences of,
   236–38, 259–60, 261; gender flexibility
   allowed for, 124–25, 236, 238, 239; parents blamed for deviancies of, 54–55,
   62–63, 345n51, 359–60n8; parents'
   reading of diaries of, 108; sex assignment and rearing of, 53–55; sexual deviancy seeds in, 55–56; spiritual therapy
   touted for, 193–95; of trans persons,
   273–74. *See also* parents and families;
   puberty; sex education
Chilik, Sayyid Hasan Musavi, 202, *209*,
   212, 229, 353–54n31
Chodorow, Nancy, 365n9
citizenship/social cognition, 214. *See also*
   national identification booklets; sociocultural spaces
class: entertainment offerings reflecting, 122–23, 126, 128; moral corruption
   linked to elites, 136, 138
clothing. *See* appearance
cognition: citizenship/social, 214; multi-
   ples paths and sites of, 30–32, *33*, 34–37,
   286–87. *See also* psychology and psychiatry; self-cognition
Cohen, Lawrence, 371n61
Commission (TPI): certification role of,
   15–19, 308n2; Farzadi's role in, 21–26;
   history of, 19; legal-medical location
   of, 19–20; other psychiatrists in, 195;

politico-religious and scientific context of, 20–21; questions asked by, 25;
   staying at preoperative stage issue discussed, 252; trans persons' preparations
   for interviews, 16–17, 30. *See also* certification process
compliance (*tatbiq*), 346n65
Compliance with Islam Project: con-
   gresses on, 169, 341n13; development
   of, 168–73; implementation of, 169–73;
   Islam therapy as consistent with, 193;
   psychology's daily practices and, 190–
   91; psycho-socio-sexology integrated
   into, 170–71; specialization of *fiqh* and,
   173–78
Congress of Islamic Countries Organization for Forensic Medicine (2004), 180,
   345n48
cosmetic surgeries, 359n1. *See also* sex reassignment surgery
Cottle Personality Inventories, 21
Council for the Resolution of Conflicts,
   219–20
Council of Guardians, 174
Cowell, Roberta, 318n43
creativity, 4, 14. *See also* appearance; life
   narratives; names and name changes
criminality: anal intercourse and tribadism as, 1, 105, 121, 138–39, 184, 185,
   274, 329n7; competitive theories of,
   172, 342n23; nonnormative persons
   harassed and arrested, 130, 132, *132*,
   159–60, 163, 164–65, 166, 223–24,
   331n31, 340n1. *See also* Islamic jurisprudence; judicial system; sexual criminality; sexual deviation
cultural purification campaigns, 6. *See also*
   morality
cure (*shafa*): aversion therapy and, 347n72;
   "bridge" proposed as, 186; Islamic therapy for, 192, 193–96; marriage as, 271;
   meanings of, 182; soma-therapy as, 181
*Cure Your Sexual Impotence with Food*
   (Pursa'id), 52–53, 67
Cyrus (pseud.), 134, 252, 290–91

Fahangistan-i 'Ulum-i Pizishki (Academy for Medical Sciences), 215

families. *See* parents and families

Faqih (Welfare Organization head), 217, 221

Farahani, Mitra, 204, 352n20

Farjadi, Farhad (formerly Faridah), 46

Farrukhzad, Faridun: background, 335n55; biographer of, 336n66; interviewed, 337n70; jokes about, 138, 141–42, *142*, 336n67; marriage and divorce, 142–43, 337nn75–76; murdered, 141; others' attraction-repulsion and, 142, 337n73; sexuality of, 114

Farrukhzad, Furugh, 311n24, 335n55, 337n75

FarsNews, 202–3

Farzad, Mas'ud, 141

Farzadi, Hamid: certification process and, 17, 21–26, 30; guidebook of, 308n8; as therapist, 18

*Farzand-i bimar-i tabi'at* (Nature's sick child, documentary), 313n39

Fathi, Nazila, 204

fatwas: authority of, 174, 182

fatwas on permissibility of sex change (Ayatollah Khomeini): authority of, 24, 30, 162, 214; dating of, 339n98, 340n4; impetus for, 165–66; lack of knowledge of, 21, 338n87, 341n12; Mulk-ara's meeting with, 159; reissued, 6, 174

Fazili, Malik, 103, 104

female-female friendship: adolescent subculture depicted, 77, 87, 91, 94–99; binary construction of, 86–87; husband married to both women, 362–63n26; naturalness of, 91; notebook shared, 93; parental perceptions of, 260–63, 270; redefined as dangerous, 76, 82; sworn sisterhood and, 259, 362nn23–24. *See also* homosociality

female homosexuality: adolescent subculture mapped by media, 77, 87, 91, 94–99; binary construction of, 86–87; depicted as mental illness, 76–77,

82–83; honorable jealousy (*ghayrat*) in, 98, 326n29; Mahin/Zahra letters as window into, 91–94, 97; media as enlighteners about, 75–76, 77; media's series on, 102–7; murder caused by or not, 109, 110; physical violence depicted in, 78–80, 86, 87–90; popular attention and discourse on, 117–19. See also *baruni*; female-to-male (FtM) trans persons; *lesbians*; Mahin/Zahra story

females/women: adolescent subculture depicted by media, 77, 87, 91, 94–99; bodily modifications of straight, 359n1; living masculine lives, 81, 123–25, *124* (*see also* Mahin/Zahra story); menstruation, 78, 111; orgasms of, 60; as perfect "holes," 152, 153; sexual coldness or frigidity (*sardmizaji*), 52, 61–62; sexual deviancy of, 57, 58; sexual deviancy of men vs., 71–72; sports teams of, 229, 358n68; surrogate motherhood of, 274. *See also* appearance; femininity and womanhood; women's movement

female-to-male (FtM) trans persons: excess visibility of, 368n33; harassment and discrimination against, 167, 199, 353n25; homosexuality disavowed by, 250; initial operations (*takhliah*) on, 183; Islamic therapy for, 197–200; key moments in self-cognition of, 254–57; Mahin as, 101; masculinity expected of, 271–72; MtFs compared with, 5, 49, 208, 243, 248, 272; naming of, 230; one request to reverse SRS, 310–11n20; phalloplasty for (or not), 183–84, 196; siblings as, 46; "spontaneous," 39–40, 313–14n5; use of term, 230, 358–59n69; website for, 227

femininity and womanhood: chador as symbol of, 165–66; difficulties of defining, 43; journalistic crafting of modern, 75–76; male behavior associated with, 125; marriage and cultural context of, 269–70; pattern of "passivity" (*maf'ul*) in, 86; performed and practiced daily, 282–83; popular reading about, 191–92; self-cognition informed by, 271, 272–73; self-cognition of, 41; spaces and work associated with, 45; spatial and subject positions of, 367n24; textual and visual construction of, 79, 79–81, 80. *See also* females/women

feminist discourse, 361n16, 367n25

Ferguson, James, 223, 349–50n5

FilmFarsi, 128

films and documentaries: alleged pornography of, 64; celebratory tone of, 1; derogatory term from, 335n53; discernment of self and information about TS in, 35–36, 257, 261, 262, 264, 265, 270–71, 313n39; medical information DVD, 219; on NGO for abused women, 356n51; number of, 2; openings for discussion of transsexuality in, 206, 352nn20–21; propaganda in wartime, 165; request for copies of, 216; trans community's interventions in, 11–12; *zan-push* performances in, 128. *See also* television

Filsuf al-Atibba', 170

filtering and sorting processes: authority and function of, 15–16, 22; complex nexus of, 3–4; preparations for interviews in, 16–17, 30; sites of entry into, 31–32; therapy's role in, 17, 18, 19–20. *See also* certification process; diagnosis

*fiqh. See* Islamic jurisprudence

Fischer, Michael M. J., 214

Foucault, Michel, 2, 3, 22, 294, 298, 306n7

French words, 75, 82–83, 325n1, 326n15

Freud, Sigmund: critique of work, 55; on developmental sexuality, 52, 318–19n49; limited influence of, 309n14; presence of portrait, 20; referenced, 296; self-analysis of, 293; sexual deviancy defined by, 70

Furth, Charlotte, 367n24

Garfinkel, Harold, 278–79, 366n16, 366–67n21

*gays*: confusions about trans persons vs., 265; context and meanings of, 9; dis-identification with past, 121–22; first appearance in Iran, 9, 299; hormonal disorder classification discussed among, 350n6; illegality of, 223, 274, 362n21; Lot's story interpreted by, 188; MtFs distinguished from, 120; as "not-kuni," 138; opening for, under mantle of trans, 244; others' discernment of, 34, 36; paradox of, 339–40n100; quantification of gay-ness, 275, 297, 369n42; rumored weddings of, 134, 333n42; self-identification and -cognition of, 31–32, 290–91; social spaces of, 133–34; straight path compared, 178–79; trans persons distinguished from, 120, 161–62, 248–50; transsexuality as viewed by, 186–87; use of term, 248, 300–301, 332n36, 332–33n41; visibility of, 258. *See also* diasporic gay communities; nonhetero-normative males

"gay Tehran" story: approach to studying, 120–22; ban on sex change surgery and, 49, 151–55, *152, 156,* 157–58; context as urban, 122–23; "distancing mimesis" and self-fashioning styles in, 130, *132,* 132–33, 135–36, 331–32n34; evenhanded reporting on, 144–45; females living masculine lives, 81, 123–25, *124;* Rashil's sex change story and, 145, *145, 146, 147,* 148–51, *149;* scientific decisions on unmanly males, 151–62; shame and disgust of unmanly males in, 136, 138–44; spectacle of unmanly males in, 122, 125–30, *127, 129, 131;* visual ethnography of, *plates 1 and 2,* 134–36

gender: confusion and anxieties about, 143–44; *jinsiyat* as, 361n16; performative nature of, 277–79, 367nn21–23; self and, 293–96; spatial and subject positions of, 367n24. *See also* femininity and womanhood; masculinity and manhood; self-cognition; sexual/gender proficiencies gender identity disorder (GID): anxieties about, 143–44; aversion therapy proposed for, 347n72; certification of, 20, 175; diagnostic tests of, 21; "disorder" as pejorative, 190; educating parents about, 242–44, 360–61n13; legal adaptations in relation to, 181–82; as legal defense, 116–17; Mahin's case as, 114–15; transsexuality as deviation and/or, 24, 172–73; treatment oversight, 353–54n31. *See also* Iranian Society for Supporting Individuals with Gender Identity Disorder; Office for the Socially Harmed

Gender Identity Disorder Organization of Iran, 342–43n30

gender segregation: critique of, 104; defense of, 187–88; difficulties for woman-presenting males, 160–62; moral corruption in, 61; proposed for medical services, 169; same-sex desire as effect of, 60, 71–72, 103, 105–6, 188; therapy practices and, 191

gender/sexual desire: binary construction of, 246–51; classic Islamic thought on female, 361n15; (in)distinctions in, 7–11, 41, 187; homosexual and heterosexual, linked, 76–77; males' "distancing mimesis" and self-fashioning styles in, 130, *132*, 132–33, 135–36, 331–32n34; "opposites attract" discourse in, 134; parental fear about differences in adolescents', 238–39. *See also* sex/gender/sexuality discourse; sexual/gender identity

gender/sexual nonnormative lives. *See* nonheteronormative lives and social circles

genitalia: ambiguous, 43, 44, 55, 157, 172, 177; "wrongness" around, 285–86

Ghafurzadah, Javad, 315n18

*gharbzadigi* concept, 334n49

GID. *See* gender identity disorder

glandular disorders, 63, 73, 202–3, 221, 350n6

Goffman, Erving, 277–78, 279–80, 367n23

Goldstein, Jan, 294

Green, Richard, 21

*The Guardian* (newspaper), 207

Gudarzi, Faramarz, 171–72

Gul-Chaman/'Ali Gul (FtM), 39

Guli (female living masculine life), *124*

Gupta, Akhil, 223, 349–50n5, 350–51n9

Guyan (doctor), 355n42

Hacking, Ian, 306n7

Haddad, Niqula al-, 323n90

Haideh (pseud.), 160

Haire, Norman, 59

Hajizadeh, Ghasem, *plates 1 and 2*, 134–36, 334n45

Hamburger, C., 57

Hamideh (pseud.), 253

*hamjins-gara'i*. *See* homosexuality; same-sex orientation

*Ham-mihan* (daily), 218

*Hamshahri* (daily), 206

Hashemi Rafasanjani, Ayatollah, 165

Hashimi-Fard, Mir Ahmad, 67

Hasuri, Hasan: on homosexuality, 53, 55–57; limits of, 57–58; Muvahhidi's book compared, 58–59, 320n61; on sex determination, rearing, and assignment, 53–55

health care and health of nation: cost of, 47, *48*; law for universal, 210; marital advice linked to, 60; pride in, 38–39

hermaphrodites (*khunsá*): categories and case studies of, 42–43; fiqhi thinking on, 177–78; psychic type of, 57; recordings of, 313n2; ritual washing of dead, 183; rules concerning, 314n12; self-identified case of, 46; surgeries for, 155, 180; terms for, 315n17. *See also* intersexuality; "two (or double)-sexedness"

heteronormalization: of marriage, 246, 269, 361n14; as religio-legally sanctioned option, 1–2; socialization into, 104–5; therapists focused on, 24 (*see also* Islam therapy)

heterosexuality: absence of presumption

in classical Islam thought, 60, 187; developmental view of, 104–5; diagnostic discourse on, 43; marriage as binarized contract of, 246, 269, 361n14; no longer assumed, 106–7, 118–19; postoperative sexuality as, 251–52; presumption of, 43, 60, 100, 102, 107, 192

HHME. *See* Ministry of Health, Healing, and Medical Education

Hidayat, Sadiq, 141, 311n24, 336n68

High Council for Compliance of Medical Matters with Precepts of the Holy Law, 169

hijab. *See* appearance; dress code

Hijazi, Manizheh, 76–77, 116

history writing, 13–14, 19. *See also* life narratives

HIV/AIDS, 222, 355–56n47

*Homan* (journal), 329n8, 372n67

homosexuality: call for Iranian research on, 103, 105; conundrum about, 114–15, 148, 179, 184, 257–65, 289; removed from DSM-IV, 347n72; stigmatization of, 5, 23–24; terms for, 75, 82–83, 325n1, 326n15; transsexuality distinguished from, 159, 173, 186, 243, 248–50, 299; transsexuality linked to, 76, 102, 104, 119, 151; treatment and cure for, 102–4; "true" vs. transient adolescent, 103, 104, 118–19. *See also* female homosexuality; intersex transformations; male homosexuality; same-sex desire

*homosexuals*: advice books on, 62–65, 321n75; alternatives for, 23; certification used by, 175; disavowal of, 248–51; Hasuri's understanding of, 56–57; impossibility of living as, 2, 4; invisibility of, 244; marriage in context of relationships between, 268–70; presumed to be males and sexually deviant, 65–74; scientific view of, 36; state institution's response to, 18; terminology for, 57–58; trans persons' proximate status to, 185–86; undecided about being trans person

vs., 114–15, 148, 179, 184, 257–65, 289; use of term, 332–33n41. *See also gays; lesbians; same-sex desire

homosociality: homoerotic desire distinguished from, 59–60; safety in, 257–58. *See also* female-female friendship

hormonal treatments: availability, 158; experiments in, 51; male hormones forced on MtFs, 160, 161; self-injection of, 240–41, 312n37; state-authorized, 20

hormones: disorders of, 73, 202–3, 221, 350n6; imbalances in, 50; intersexuality linked to, 54–55

hospitals and clinics: American Missionary (Mashhad), 44, 45, 316n25; Asia (Tehran), 150, 158; Day Clinic, 159; Johns Hopkins Clinic and Hospital, 54, 57, 318n43; Mirdamad Clinic, 208, 232, 237, 239, 291; Namazi (Shiraz), 338n84; Nonmedical Therapy Clinic, 19, 308n8; Rouzbeh, 18, 36, 215, 311n28, 312n24, 349n93; Shahriza (Mashhad), 46–47. *See also* Tehran Psychiatric Institute; Women's Hospital

Houri (pseud.): adoption hopes of, 274; Bihzisti weekly meetings and, 216, 222–23; current situation of, 253, 368n31; on dealing with state ministries and offices, 203, 228; on "doing woman," 282; family counseling by, 360–61n13; gender-discordant childhood, 237; kinship terminology of, 362n20; on media coverage, 218; parent's charges and arrest of, 238–39; at Resolution of Conflicts meeting, 219–20; on somatic etiological research, 29; on time for transition process, 281; in women's sociocultural space, 344n36; on women's sports teams, 358n68; Zia's relationship with, 249, 258, 287–89

Housing and Urban Development Organization, 221

Huma (pseud.), 253

humankind concept, 3, 306n7

humor: ethnic-related, 139–40, 335n60; "God created me this way," 357n58; intersex changes, 47, 48; interview questions, 17; nonheteronormative males targeted, 138–42, 142, 336n67; soul and psyche, 346–47n68; TS diagnosis, 37

Hunsberger, Alice C., 40

Huvayda, Amir 'Abbas, 138, 139, 333n42

*huviyat-i gumshudah* (lost identity), 205–6

*huviyat-i jinsi. See* sexual/gender identity

Ibn Sina, 295

identity (*huviyat*): lost, 205–6; performance and, 295–96. *See also* categories of identity; gender identity disorder; life narratives; self-cognition; sexual/gender identity

Ihsan (pseud.), 218

illness: discussions among *gays* about, 350n6; glandular disorders, 63, 73, 202–3, 221, 350n6; HIV/AIDS, 222, 355–56n47; transsexuality categorized as, 172–73, 202–3, 221, 229–30; venereal diseases, 66, 322n88. *See also* gender identity disorder; mental illness

*'ilm al-nafs. See* psychology and psychiatry

*Imagining Transgender* (Valentine), 8, 368n32

Imam Khomeini Institute (Qum), 179

Imam Khomeini Relief Foundation, 237

'Inayat, Mahmud, 64

*The Independent* (newspaper), 207

*inhirafat-i jinsi. See* sexual deviation

insanity. *See* mental illness

*insiraf* (dissuasion), 18, 24–25

insurance: classification of treatment and, 212–13, 355n42; spousal coverage, 264; for trans persons, 20, 210, 220, 355n44. *See also* Medical Care Insurance Organization

International Book Fair (Tehran), 191

International Congress on Medical Ethics in Iran (1993), 169

Internet and social media: Google searches for sex change (*taghyir jinsiyat*) on,

352n23; humor circulating via, 139–40, 335n60; ISSIGID website, 225–27, 226, 356–57n55, 356n54, 357nn57–60; MtF- and FtM-specific sites, 227; openings for transsexuality discussion in, 207; Persian weblog culture in, 207, 352n22; trans activists' website, 219

intersex transformations (pre-1980s): advice books and, 59–65; exaggerated reports on, 49–50, 318nn43–45; humor about, 47, 48; medical categories, 42–43; overview, 38–39; psychosexological view of, 50–59; sexual deviance and criminality linked in, 65–74; "spontaneous," reports of, 39–40, 313–14n5; stories circulating about, 43–49, 316n27, 317n31; surgeries for, 40–41, 314n12; *Zan-i ruz*'s series on homosexuality in context of, 100–101. *See also* Mahin/Zahra story

intersexuality: ignored in recent trans discourse, 357n56; Khomeini's view of, 175–76; Rashil's story, 148; surgeries for, 155; terms for, 114; transsexuality delinked from, 58–59, 76, 119, 144, 154, 157. *See also* hermaphrodites; "two (or double)-sexedness"

"intimate selving" concept, 364n3. *See also* self

Iranian-Islamic state: advice on navigating institutions of, 354–55n41; bureaucratization and institutionalization of, 20–21, 341n11, 349n4; everyday practices of state in, 350–51n9; legal-medical-religious regulations and productivity of power in, 4 (*see also* legal medicine field); moral purification measures, 160–62; ongoing, fractious process of formation, 6, 306n8; productive dimension of, 308n3, 349–50n5; religious dictates and expediency of state, 183; trans activists' interactions with institutions of, 203, 215–23, 228–29. *See also* certification process; Compliance with Islam Project; Islamic jurisprudence; Islamic Revolution; Mashhad; military service; Qum; Tehran

Iranian National Women's Soccer Team, 229

Iranian Society for Supporting Individuals with Gender Identity Disorder (ISSIGID): formation of, 223–25; membership types, 356n53; Persian translation of title, 356n49; state institution relations of, 227–28; trans activism routinized via, 227–28; website of, 225–27, 226, 356–57nn54–55, 357nn57–60

Iranian Students News Agency (ISNA), 220–21

Iran-Iraq War (1980–88): border closings in, 338n93; effects of stress in, 359–60n8; moral scrutiny in, 164–65; surgical developments due to, 168, 359n1

Iran Supreme Court, 210

Iran University of Medical Sciences (IUMS), 18. *See also* Tehran Psychiatric Institute

IRIB (Islamic Republic of Iran Broadcasting), 159–60, 167, 313n39, 351n13, 352n23

Islamicization: fatwas and their state effects in, 168–73; politico-religious and scientific contexts linked in, 20–21; of state, 6. *See also* Compliance with Islam Project

Islamic jurisprudence (*fiqh*): on categorical (bodily) sex, 181; differences concerning sex change and sex/gender identity in, 174–77, 343nn31–32; empowered over scientific discourses, 6; hermaphrodites as challenge to, 177–78; homosexuality concept absent in, 329n7; intersexuality in, 314n12; military exemptions, 187, 202–3; politico-religious and scientific contexts linked in, 20–21; on sodomy, 140; specialization of, 173–78, 179; style of thinking in, 183–84; trans community's deployment of, 12; "vulnerability" in, 214. *See also* Compliance with Islam Project; judicial system

Islamic Perspectives on Medicine (seminar in Mashhad), 169, 184–85, 207, 209

Islamic Republic of Iran Broadcasting (IRIB; earlier Iranian National Radio and Television [Seda va Sima]), 159–60, 167, 313n39, 351n13, 352n23

Islamic Revolution (1979): administrative changes after, 341n11, 349n4; continuities before and after, 120, 121, 122, 208, 210, 353n26; discrimination and arrests in aftermath, 159–60, 163, 164–65, 166; legal codes and judicial structures revised after, 170–71; persecutions and executions in aftermath, 329n7; republic established, 6; women's clothing during, 163

Islamic thought: self-knowledge in, 293; sexual advice for married couples in, 60–61, 320n68; *sirat-i mustaqim* (straight path) in, 178; specific prohibitions and *iztirar* in, 179–80; strange, wondrous (*'ajayib va gharayib*) creatures in, 40–41, 46, 47, 48; trans persons and acceptability within, 253–54, 362n21

Islam therapy: cure as goal of, 192, 193–94; methods, 194–97, 198; morally conservative stance in, 24; persistence of, 200–201; popular psychology and, 27; seminars on, 347–48n73; skepticism about, 197, 349n93; somatic etiological research and, 28–30, 312n34; soul and psyche in context of, 192–93; trans person's resistance to, 197–200

ISNA (Iranian Students News Agency), 220–21

ISSIGID. *See* Iranian Society for Supporting Individuals with Gender Identity Disorder

*I'timad* (daily), 206, 339n95

*I'timad-i milli* (daily), 206, 218

*Ittila'at* (daily): adolescent girls' circle depicted by, 97; annual collected articles of, 323n91; on Asghar Qatil's story, 66; Mahin/Zahra narrative of, 75, 78–79, 79, 81, 108, 109, 114; on murdered

*Kayhan* (daily): on female lover's murder, 75; on gay wedding celebration, 134; Mahin's trial covered by, 108; on men dressed as women, *132*, 331n31; satire in, 139; on sex change surgeries, 48, 145, 317n31; on sex change surgery ban, 151, *152*, 154–55, *156*, 157; on voyeurism, 324n98

Kayhani-far (doctor), 167, 340n8

Kaynia, Mahdi, 72–73

Kazimzadeh Iranshahr, Husayn, 189

Keshavarzian, Arang, 350–51n9

Khaksar, Ilham, 165

Khal'atbari (surgeon), 41

Khalidi, Hamid Riza, 176

Khamenei, Ayatollah, 20, 343n31

*khanums*: rumored marriage of, 134–35, 333n43; use of term, 130, 133, 256, 332n35

Khatami, Mohammad, 167, 204, 213, 223, 313n39, 351n10

*khaudshinasi. See* selfology

Khaushnavaz, 'Atifah, 220

Khomeini, Ayatollah: authority of, 174, 175–76, 182; Compliance Congress addressed by, 169; on dress code for MtFs, 340n4; presence of portrait, 20; spaces for disagreement in views of, 343n32; trans persons' appeals to, 165, 166; WORK: *Tahrir al-wasila*, 6, 173, 174–76, 343n33. *See also* fatwas: on permissibility of sex change

*khunsá. See* hermaphrodites; "two (or double)-sexedness"

*Khurasan* (daily), 43–45, 316n21

Khvajah-nuri, Ibrahim, 105

*Khvandaniha* (magazine): balance struck by, 63; on Farrukhzad's performance, 142; on females living masculine lives, 123, *125*; on intersex category and surgery, 43–45, 47, *48*, 49–50; on males living feminine lives, 126, *127*; publication schedule, 316n23; *Reader's Digest* compared, 316n22; satire in, 141, *142*;

on serial killer, 67; on *zan-push* performances, 128, *129*, 129–30, *131*, 331n30

Kia (pseud.), 36, 250, 289

Kian-nush, Nastaran, 215, 217–19, 220, 228

Kigasari, Mali, 328n66

Kohanzad, Shahriar, 346n66

Kondo, Dorrin, 365nn9–10

Koubkov, Zdenk, 40

Kubrà (pseud.), 40–41, 314–15nn12–13

Kumitah-i Kishvari-i Samandahi-i Ikhtilalat-i Jinsi (Nationwide Committee to Supervise Sexual Disorders), 210

*kumitahs* (neighborhood surveillance committee), 241, 242, 258, 360n12

*kuni*: *baruni* compared, 300, 334n50; ethnic jokes and, 139–40; meanings of and shame/disgust associated with, 138, 140–41, 164, 187, 273, 300; parental fear of son's being, 238–39, 241. *See also lavat/liwat*

Labbaf, Tahireh, 167–68, 340n9

Laleh (pseud.), 271, 273

Lankarani (Minister of Health), 355n42

*lavat/liwat*: assumptions about, 188, 265; Islamic jurisprudence on, 140; punishment for, 1, 105, 121, 138–39, 160, 184, 274, 329n7; religious beliefs about, 245–46; sadism linked to, 67. *See also* anus; *kuni*

*Legal Medicine* (Gudarzi), 171–72

legal medicine field: on categorical (bodily) sex, 181; criminality and sexual deviancy linked in, 65–74; founder and key texts of, 171–72; as mediating domain in state transformation, 170–71; military exemptions and, 187, 202–3, 221, 228; paradox of, 243–44; sharing among practitioners, 190; specialization of *fiqh* and, 173–78, 179; trans persons' proximate status to homosexuals in, 185–86; transsexuality as acceptable, legal, legible category in, 2, 167–68, 186–87, 213–14, 242–44, 301. *See also* trans vs. homosexual and other distinctions

Legal Medicine Organization of Iran (LMOI): cases sent to, 17, 20, 309n13; different reasons for going to, 32; growth and institutionalization of, 170–71; ideas underlying, 74; legal reconstitution of, 341n11; on number of applicants, 208, *209*; parental rejection of suggestions, 242; Psychiatric Ward of, 20; Rashil's story and published process concerning, 145, 150; separate spaces for trans persons at, 340n1; as state institution, 215; surgery authorized by, 48, 318n39; trans activists' interactions with, 211; transgendered living opposed by, 182; trans person's appeal to, 167. *See also* certification process; Commission; Nationwide Committee to Supervise Sexual Disorders; Psychiatric Ward

Legal Medicine Organization of Shiraz, 48, 318n39

Legal Medicine Organization of Tehran, 48, 318n39

Leila (pseud.): childhood and disinterest in opposite sex, 259–60, 261; confusion about identity, 257–65; on identity as quantifiably divisible, 275, 297; Minu on, 265–66; Minu's relationship with, 257–64, 292, 333n42; self-identification of, 208; transition decision of, 292

"lesbian crime of passion." *See* Mahin/ Zahra story

*lesbianism*: use of term, 109

*lesbians*: confusions about trans persons vs., 257–65; context and meanings of, 9, 198; Mahin as, 114–15; self-identification and -cognition of, 10, 31–32; trans persons distinguished from, 248–51; transsexuality as viewed by, 187; use of term, 117, 300–301, 308n7. *See also* female homosexuality

life narratives: adolescent difficulties and horrors, 238–44, 360n12; child rearing, 273–74; as configuring one's sense of being, 276–80; cultural gender expectations, 271–73; diary written for Islam therapy as, 198–200; dualism felt in, 246–48; feelings about born-body, 251–52; gender-discordant childhood, 236–38, 259–60, 261; "God created me this way" discourse, 235–36, 357n58; learning about transsexuality, 159, 270–71; originating impetus in, 165–66; parental and familial issues, 237, 252–53, 256, 260–63; patterns and characteristics, 233–34; Rashil's story as model for, 145, *145, 146, 147*, 148–51, *149*; relationship issues, 257–63, 267–71; self as contingent conduct, 297–301; self-cognition as trans vs. homosexual, 248–51, 254–57; spirituality and religious beliefs, 234–35, 240, 245–46, 253–54; transition decision, 232, 238, 256; undecided about identity, 257–65, 289. *See also* self; self-cognition; selfology

Literacy Corps, 81, 326n9

literature: English curriculum, 322n83; on gender, 191–92; history writing and, 13–14, 19; poetry performance and, 231–32; possibly homosexual writers, 336n68; on regret for SRS, 205; responsa type of, 174–75, 177, 178, 179–80; on sexual deviation and criminality, 65–74; on sexual deviation and homosexuality, 62–65; sexual knowledge disbursed in, 51–53, 59, 60–62, 311n23, 320n69, 320–21n70, 321n73; strange, wondrous (*'ajayib va gharayib*) creatures in, 40–41, 46, 47, 48; *tauzih al-masa'il* genre of, 173–74, 178, 342–43n30

LMOI. *See* Legal Medicine Organization of Iran

*Los Angeles Times* (newspaper), 207

*Love Without Fear* (Chesser), 318n44, 321n73

Lutfipur, Firuz, 106–7

*Mabani-i jurm-shinasi* (Fundamentals of criminology, Kaynia), 72–73

MacIntyre, Alastair, 364n4

*Madmuazil Khalah* (film), 128

madness. *See* mental illness

Mahan (pseud.), 329n9

Mahin/Zahra story: adolescent girls' subculture depicted in, 77, 87, 91, 94–99, 125; female homosexuality depicted as mental illness, 82–83; fictionalized account of, 328n66; "first-ness" claims in, 108–9; letters in, 91–94, 97; Mahin's family's view of, 86–91; masculinity and femininity depicted in, 78–81, *79, 80*; media narrative of, 5, 75, 76–78; other cases' linked to, 115–17; photographs, *79, 80*; readers' response to, 106–7; remembered, 117, 326n12; sex education discussed in relation to, 81–82; significance, 118–19; trial and sentencing of Mahin, 77, 93–95, 96, 97–99, 106, 107–14; urban context, 123; Zahra's family's view of, 84–86. *See also* Amin, Zahra; female homosexuality; Padidarnazar, Mahin; Sekandari, Pari

Mahnaz (pseud.): failed relationship and breakdowns of, 268–69; gender-discordant childhood, 236; initial interview of, 17; poetry of, 231–32; self-cognition of, 35, 283, 284, 292; spirituality of, 234–35, 267; transition decision of, 291–92; Zaynab's perception of, 236, 245–46

Majlis. *See* Parliament

male homosexuality: characteristics of, 56–57; coverage of female homosexuality compared, 75; criminal and deviant assumptions about, 5, 65–69, 82, 102–3, 250; disavowed by MtFs, 248–51; MtFs linked to, 242–44; young boys as objects of desire (*amrad*), 59–60, 68, 329n9, 330n16, 351–52n18. *See also* "gay Tehran" story; *kuni*; male-to-female (MtF) trans persons; nonheteronormative males

males/men: bodily modifications of straight, 359n1; cultural preference of being, 48–49, 103, 259; marital performance anxieties of, 321n75; sexual

deviancy of women vs., 71–72; sexual impotence (*natavani*), 52–53, 62, 67; unmarked person as, 319n57. *See also* masculinity and manhood; nonheteronormative males

male-to-female (MtF) trans persons: adolescent difficulties and parental abuse of, 239–44, 360n12; attacks, harassment, and arrests of, 26, 130, 132, *132,* 159–60, 163, 164–65, 166, 223–24, 331n31, 340n1; criticized for appearance, 279, 357n59; "distancing mimesis" and self-fashioning styles in, 130, *132,* 132–33, 135–36, 331–32n34; excess visibility of, 290, 368n33; FtMs compared with, 5, 49, 208, 243, 248, 272; *gays* distinguished from, 120; "going into the habit" decision, 312–13n38, 340n4 (*see also* appearance); homosexuality disavowed by, 248–51; *kuni* as haunting lives of, 273; marriage as "cure" for, 271; self-cognition of, 240–41; surgically constructed vaginas of, 152, 153; use of term, 230, 358–59n69; website for, 227. *See also* nonheteronormative males; woman-presenting males

Malikzadah, 'Abd al-Husayn, 107–8, 110–11

Ma'navi (doctor), 155

manhood. *See* masculinity and manhood

Mansureh (pseud.), 266

*mard-i zan-numa. See* woman-presenting males

*Maria* (documentary), 206, 352n20

*Markaz-i Huquq va Aaza-yi Islami* (Specialization Center in Islamic Law and Judiciary), 179

marriage: ability to "get married," 43, 45–46, 48, 55, 316n27; age for, 187; causes of discord in, 62–65, 321n75; contract and requirements for, 259, 343–44n35, 347n71; father's permission and legal case of FtM, 184, 229, 358n67; heteronormalization of, 246, 269, 361n14; hopes for, 196–97, 266–67, 273–74; imperative of, 7, 123–25, 251,

medical knowledge and practitioners: compliance with Islam, 168–70; consolidation of, 41–42; division over SRS, 154–55; founding of NGO and, 224; guidelines on (*see* Medical Council of Iran); *ikhtilal* (disparity, dysfunction) in, 346n67; intersex category in, 42–43, 357n56; letters of referral requested, 212; surgical developments in, 168, 359n1; trans activists' interactions with, 211, 212–13

Mehrabi, Faridun: referenced, 23, 256, 292; research topics of, 310–11n20, 310n18; respect for, 20–21, 199, 241

Mehran (pseud.): failed marriage of, 271; feelings about born-body, 251; key moments in self-cognition of, 254–57, 300

men. *See* males/men

mental illness: after failed relationship, 268–69; of Asghar Qatil, 5, 66, 67, 68–69; criminality vs., 66, 68–69, 86; *dau-shakhsiyati* (double personality) as, 114–15, 143; in depiction of FtMs, 125; depression, studies of, 192; desire for sex change as, 152–53, 155, 157; of Fayyaz Parhizi, 77, 116–17; female homosexuality depicted as, 76–77, 82–83; homosexuality rejected as, 105; of Mahin, 77–78, 99, 108, 110–11, 114–15; media coverage of, 114–15, 205; TS classified as glandular disorders vs., 202–3, 221

Messkoub, Mahmood, 353n26

*Mikhak Nuqrah-'i* (Silver Coronation, television program), 138

military service: alternative to, 326n9; exemptions from, 187, 202–3, 221, 288; hopes for masculinization in, 271; legal reconstitution of codes for, 349n4; requirements for, 150; as sign of adult masculinity, 46, 282, 283

Miller, William Ian, 140

Million Clinical Multiaxial Inventory, 21

Ministry of Education, 60–61

Ministry of Health, Healing, and Medical Education (HHME; formerly Ministry of Health): critique of, 353–54n31; High Council for Compliance of Medical Matters with Precepts of the Holy Law and, 169; legal reconstitution of, 341n11; medical information DVD prepared for, 219; Nationwide Committee to Supervise Sexual Disorders and, 210; Office for the Socially Harmed in, 202–3, 209, 210; Office of Women's Affairs in, 33, 220, 353n28; quality of surgeries and, 219, 220, 222; trans activists' interactions with, 211, 221, 355n42; trans person's appeal to, 167

Ministry of Justice: Council for the Resolution of Conflicts in, 219–20; Office for the Socially Harmed and, 210; SRS clarification requested from, 173; trans activists' interactions with, 211, 220–21. *See also* Islamic jurisprudence (*fiqh*); judicial system; Legal Medicine Organization of Iran

Ministry of the Interior, 216, 224

Ministry of Welfare and Social Security (MWSS), 208, 210. *See also* Welfare Organization

Minu (pseud.): on Leila, 265–66; Leila's relationship with, 257–64, 292, 333n42

Mirdamad Clinic, 208, 232, 237, 239, 291

Mirjalali, Bahram: assistant of, 36, 182; clinic, 271; professional activities, 190, 224; surgical practice, 208, 209, 224

Mirjalali, Mrs., 224

Misbahi Nuri, Husayn'ali, 60–61, 320n67, 320n68

Mitchell, Alice, 325n3

MMPI-2 (test), 21, 311n22

modernity: marital advice based in, 60–61, 320n68; marriage in context of, 246, 361n15; same-sex desire recoded as unnatural in, 59–60; same-sex playing embedded in, 329n9; womanhood in, 75–76

Mohammad (pseud.): dualism felt by, 246–48; on failed relationship and

Mohammad (pseud.) (*continued*)
therapy, 267–68; gender-discordant childhood, 238; Sina's friendship with, 363n27

Mohammadi, Mohammad Reza: author's interview with, 195–97; career, 200–201; others' skepticism about methods, 349n93; referenced, 28, 351n17; on spiritual therapy, 193–94; trans person's resistance to, 197–200; on transsexuality as acquired, 30

Mohsen (pseud.), 250, 287, 358n64

Mohseni-nia (social worker): client interactions of, 16, 22; in Commission meetings, 15, 17; on institute's changes, 308n9; parental roles and, 243, 361n13

Monafi (doctor), 167

Money, John, 21, 54, 57

morality: anxieties about, 52–53, 318n47; medical division over sex change surgeries and, 154–55; modesty and women's dress in, 163–64; purification measures of state, 160–62; wartime scrutiny of, 164–65. *See also* dress code; sexual deviation

morality squads: dress code enforced by, 313n38; nonconforming persons arrested and abused by, 32, 163, 164–65, 166, 244; trans persons' discussions of, 368–69n39. See also *kumitahs*; police and security forces

Morris, Jan, 117

Motamedian (film producer), 279

Movahhedi, Amir, 315n18

Muhajiri, Hasan, 155

Muhit, Bahram, 81

Muhsin (formerly Fattanah), 34, 316n27

Mujarrad, Nasir, 81

Mulk-ara, Maryam Khatun (formerly Faridun): activism and lobbying of, 165, 167, 211; discrimination against, 159–60; on fatwa, 165; forced to take male hormones, 160, 161; homosexuality disavowed, 249; interviews of, 339n95; on ISSIGID operations, 223–24, 225–26,

227; on *iva'khvahar*, 335n53; marital life of, 176; self-identification of, 158–59, 165–66, 339n97; sex change surgery of, 159, 166; social circles of, 339n96; on transsexuality category, 229–30

Munirah (FtM), 39–40, 43, 282

Muravvij, Muhammad Hadi, 67, 323n91

Mustafa'i, Muhammad, 358n66

Mu'tamidi, Ahmad, 93, 107–8, 110–12

Muvahhidi, Muhammad Mahdi, 57, 58–59, 319n58, 320n61

MWSS. *See* Ministry of Welfare and Social Security

Nadjmabadi, Shahnaz, 307n16

Nahrir, Hisam, 46

Najafi, Mustafá, 170

Namazi, Baqir, 130, *131*

Namazi Hospital (Shiraz), 338n84

names and name changes: beginning process of, 32; playful renamings of trans persons, 230; self-cognition as, 286–87; significance of, 158, 159; state-authorized, 20, 182–83, 309n13; use of Western, 164. *See also* national identification booklets

Nanah-Gul/Gul 'Ali (FtM), 39

narrativizing self, 276–80. *See also* life narratives; self; sexual/gender proficiencies

Natasha (pseud.), 160

national identification booklets (*shinasnamah*): advice on getting new, 360n12; date notation in, 355n43; family name in, 41, 314–15n13; importance of, 39–40, 217–18; passports vs., 166; Rashil's request and new document, *148*; state-authorization of new, 20, 182–83, 309n13, 355n43. *See also* names and name changes

Nationwide Committee to Supervise Sexual Disorders (Kumitah-i Kishvari-i Samandahi-i Ikhtilalat-i Jinsi), 210

Nauruz (Iranian New Year), 262, 362n25

Navvab Safavi Emergency Center for Critically Socially Harmed Groups of Welfare Organization: meetings at, 215, 220–22, 227; support groups at, 179, 280–81. *See also* Office for the Socially Harmed

Negar (pseud.), 35

*Newsletter of the Medical Council of Iran (Nashriyah-i khabari)*, 151–52, 338n82

*New York Times* (newspaper), 207

Nidami, Mitra, 358n66

nightclubs. *See* entertainment industry; sociocultural spaces; theater and music performances

nongovernmental organization (NGO): for abused women, 356n51; advice on formation, 354–55n41; formation of, 223–25; others' attempts to form, 356n52; trans activists' hopes for, 219. *See also* Iranian Society for Supporting Individuals with Gender Identity Disorder

nonheteronormative lives and social circles: binary construction of, 246–51; border overlaps and support among, 204, 206, 274, 351–52n18; court circle as, 339n96; demarcations in, 290–91; disruption of, 160–62; one's identity discovered in, 158–59; openings for writing about, 204–8, 351n10, 352n21; others' discernment of one's identity in, 34–35; of singers and others, 157–58; viewed as unnatural and corrupt, 191–92. *See also* "gay Tehran" story; life narratives; self-cognition; sexual/gender proficiencies

nonheteronormative males: approach to studying, 120–22; attacks, harassment, and arrests for, 130, 132, *132*, 159–60, 163, 164–65, 166, 331n31, 340n1; ban on sex change surgery and, 49, 151–55, *152*, *156*, 157–58; context as urban, 122–23; "distancing mimesis" and self-fashioning styles in, 130, *132*, 132–33, 135–36, 331–32n34; evenhanded reporting on, 144–45; marriage of, 142–43, 337nn75–76; moral purification measures and, 160–62; post-1976

advice for, 153–54; Rashil's sex change story and, 145, *145*, *146*, *147*, 148–51, *149*; shame and disgust of, 136, 138–44; as spectacle, 122, 125–30, *127*, *129*, *131*; spectrum of, 120, 132, 133–34; visual ethnography of, *plates 1 and 2*, 134–36. *See also* male-to-female (MtF) trans persons; nonheteronormative lives and social circles; woman-presenting males

Nonmedical Therapy Clinic, 19, 308n8

Notary Registration Office, 355n43. *See also* national identification booklets

Noushin (pseud.), 157–58, 274, 339n98

Nuri, Bihruz (formerly Marziah), 43–46, 282, 283

Office for the Socially Harmed (Welfare Organization), 202–3, *209*, 210

Office of Islamic Studies in Mental Health, 192

Office of Legal Medicine. *See* Legal Medicine Organization of Iran

Office of Personal Status Registration, 314–15n13. *See also* national identification booklets

Office of Women's Affairs, *33*, 220, 353n28

Ohadi, Behnam: journal association of, 222, 356n48; neuro-psycho-biological approach of, 26–30, 200–201, 312n34

Omid-E-Iran Television (OITN), 313n39

One Million Signatures campaign, 228

Ozra (pseud.), 266–67, 292

Padidarnazar, 'Abbas (Mahin's father): defense attorney's framing of, 110–12; lawyer hired by, 107; at Mahin's trial, 85, 110; neglect by, 100, 111, 112; Sekandari's critique of, 85–86, 100, 116

Padidarnazar, Mahin: adolescent circle of, 94–99, 125; appeal and alleged suicide of, 327n52, 328n61; context of, 123; death sentence demanded by prosecutor, 107, 110; diary of, 97; family story of, 86–91, 103; as FtM transsexual, 101, 104; girlfriend murdered by, 75; knife carried by, 84–86, 96, 98, 100,

Political Science School, 188–89

popular psychology. *See* vernacular psychology

pornography, 63–65

postoperative body: disappearance of, 225, 239, 360n9; dismissal of, 270; as heterosexual, 251–52; isolation of, 289; marriage and children of, 229, 341n14; photographs of, 43, 148

Prosser, Jay, 233–34, 305n3

prostitution and sex workers, 160, 243, 253, 331–32n34

psyche: concept, 188–89; soul in relation to, 189–94. *See also* soul

Psychiatric Ward (LMOI), 20

psychology and psychiatry: academization of, 4–5; Asghar Qatil's story interpreted in, 66–69; audience expanded for, 103–4; behavioral focus of, 309n14; biology and sociology linked to, 346n64; certification process and, 30–32, 34–37; childhood cross-gender tendencies in, 238; compliance with Islam, 168–70, 190–91; differences within, 30, 192; homosexuality discussed in, 102, 103–5; Iranian developmental history in, 371n58; legal medicine linked to, 171–72; pedagogy linked to, 188–89; politico-religious context linked to, 20–21; self and relational self in, 277, 293–96, 365n9; sex in books and articles, 59–65; slippage between psyche and soul in, 189–92; somatic etiological research and, 28–30, 312n34; U.S. dominance in, 9. *See also* brain; cognition; Islam therapy; sexology; vernacular psychology

Psychology and society (journal). See *Ravanshinasi va jami'ah*

psycho-sexology. *See* sexology; vernacular psychology

psychosomatic research, 28

puberty: parental advice concerning, 52–53; psychology of, 27, 50; sexual/gender identity in, 43, 46, 55, 238; sudden

changes in, 111. *See also* children and adolescents

Pursa'id, Isma'il, 52–53, 67

Qalibaf, Muhammad Baqir, 223

Qasim Rashidi, Rayhaneh, 205–6

Qazvin (city): judicial appointments and jokes about, 139–40, 335n60

Qazvini sisters, 81, 125

Qotbi, Reza, 134

queer theory, 306n10

Qum (Iran): growth of, 179; travel to, 178

Qunu'i, Shahnaz (Fatimah), 94–95

Qur'an: on circumstantial necessity (*iztirar*), 179–80, 181; quoted on ISSIGID website, 225, *226*, 356n54; on self-knowledge, 293

Rabinow, Paul, 307n17

Radio Javan, 352n23

Rafiee, Nader, 313n39

*Rah-i zindigi* (magazine), 204–5, 296, 351n13

Rah-i Zindigi Institute, 204–5

Rahnuma, 'Abdallah, 52, 59

*Rahnuma-yi shawhar-i javan dar marhalah-i izdivaj* (Guidance for young husbands for the stage of marriage), 61

rape: expected of male *homosexuals*, 5, 82; of *gay* man, 121; of MtFs, 26, 161, 164, 241

Rastakhiz, Farhad, 332n38

*ravanshinasi*. *See* psychology and psychiatry

*Ravanshinasi-i raftar-i jinsi* (The psychology of sexual behavior, Kajbaf), 191

*Ravanshinasi va jami'ah* (Psychology and society, journal): Ohadi's article in, 28, 312n34; trans persons' meetings at offices of, 222, 248–49, 282, 356n48, 368–69n39

*Raz-i kamyabi-i jinsi* (Secrets of sexual fulfillment, M. Burujirdi), 53, 63, 319n54

Razzaq-manish, Anushirvan (Andy), 76–77, 116, 327n52, 328n61

Reed, David, 121, 328–29n3

Rekers, George, 193, 348n81

religio-psychological approach. *See* Islam therapy

religious beliefs: academic education in, 309–10n16; on guilt and sin, 23; psychological terminology and, 189–93; transition decision based in, 183, 196, 245–46; trans persons and acceptability within, 253–54, 362n21. *See also* Islamic jurisprudence; Islamic thought; Islam therapy; rituals

Renault, Mary, 329n3

reproduction issues, 43, 46–47, 317n33

rights and entitlements (*haqq*), 212–13

rituals: sexual/gender identity assigned for, 177–78, 186; of sworn sisterhood, 259, 362nn23–24; of washing dead bodies, 183, 196, 245

River, J. Paul de, 69–72

Riza'i (doctor), 224

Rofel, Lisa, 363n29, 372n64 Rossoukh, Ramyar, 11

Rouzbeh Hospital, 18, 36, 215, 311n28, 312n24, 349n93

Saberi, Mahdi, 28, 175, 176, 224

Sabit, Muhammad 'Ali, 139

sadism, 66–67, 70–71, 77, 101, 106, 116

sadomasochism, 71

Sa'ideh (pseud.), 266

Sa'idzadeh, Rashil (Rachel, formerly Sa'id): other stories in context of, 117, 118, 145; sex change story of, 145, *145*, *146*, *147*, *148*–51, *149*

Sajjadi, Huriah, 313–14n5

Salamon, Gayle, 307n18

Salehi (psychiatrist), 17

Salih, Jahanshah: hermaphrodite cases of, 42–43; other writing of, 319n58; "reproductive" as used by, 315n19; on sex differentiation, 43, 47; on SRS, 42, 50, 153; textbook of and training under, 42, 50, 57, 58, 315n18, 338n84

Salihi, Nargis (Nasir), 130, 132, *132*

same-sex desire (*hamjins-khvahi*): ambiva-lence about, 51; as disrupter of marital peace, 62–63, 321n75; intensification of, 86–87; prohibition of, 243–44; sexual deviancy linked to, 71; as shameful and illegal, 7, 136, 138–44. *See also* homo-sexuality

same-sex orientation (*hamjins-gara'i*): as defense in trial or not, 107–8; desire for sex change as evidence of, 115; media's series on homosexuality and, 99–107; recent historical context, 5; recoded as unnatural, 59–60; same-sex playing dis-tinguished from, 121–22, 329–30n10; spiritual therapy touted for, 193; "true" vs. transient adolescent, 103, 104, 118–19; use of term, 57–58, 87, 117, 300–301, 325n1. *See also* homosexuality; Mahin/Zahra story

same-sex playing (*hamjins-bazi*): age for, 58; as "cure" or not, 181–82; disavowal of, 248–51; gender segregation as caus-ing, 60, 71–72, 103, 105–6, 188; identi-fier of, 284; legal cases connected by ideas about, 114–17; modernity of term, 329n9; murder motive and, 109; older man/younger man liaisons in, 66–69; pejorative and sinful associations of, 10, 83, 186, 260, 325n1; rejection of term, 247–48; same-sex orientation distin-guished from, 121–22, 329–30n10; as sign of politically corrupt regime, 333n42; use of term, 58, 82–83. *See also* Mahin/Zahra story

Sang, Tze-Ian D., 123–24

Sani'i, Ayatollah, 343n31

*Sarmayah* (daily), 218

Sarukhani (sociologist), 105

Sayyid Imami, Ahmad, 50–51

Sazman-i Bihzisti. *See* Welfare Organiza-tion

Sazman-i Bimah-i Khadamat-i Darmani (Medical Care Insurance Organization, MCIO), 210, 355n44. *See also* insurance

Schayegh, Cyrus, 66, 68, 74, 295

science: advice literature critiqued for lack

of, 63–64; belief about God and, 235–36; compliance with Islam, 168–70; highlighted in stories about intersex surgeries, 46–47; of sex, 50–59. *See also* vernacular science

scientific discourse: Anglo-American dominance in, 9, 62; endocrinology and deviancies in, 63; French words in, 326n15; Iranian compatibility with international, 19; Islamic jurisprudence empowered over, 6; marvels of sex change and the health of nation trends, 38–39; naming in, 230; on nonheteronormative maleness and srs, 151–62; Ohadi's approach in context of, 27–30; trans community's deployment of, 12. *See also* psychology and psychiatry

*Scoop* (magazine), 46

Seigel, Jerrold, 294, 364n4

Sekandari, Pari (*Zan-i ruz* reporter): adolescent girls' subculture depicted by, 94, 95–99; on anxieties about female homosexuality, 99–100; background, 81–82; controversial writings of, 326n10; on female homosexuality as mental illness, 82–83; Mahin interviewed by, 114; on Mahin's family, 86–91; Mahin's suicide confirmed by, 327n52; Mahin/Zahra letters and, 91–94; on neglectful families, 85–86, 87, 90–91, 94, 103; on Zahra's family, 84–86

self: approaches to, 9–10, 275–78, 364nn3–4, 365n7, 369n43; contexts of identification and articulation (narrativizing self), 276–80; as contingent conduct, 297–301; genealogy of, 292–96. *See also* life narratives; selfology

self-cognition: in adolescence, 237, 238–42, 248; of being trans vs. homosexual, 248–51, 254–57; binary construction in, 246–51; cultural notions underlying, 271–73; failed marriage as prompting, 270–71; family severance issue in, 252–53; others' recognition of, 234, 257, 262, 267; points of entry and styles

of, 30–32, *33*, 34–37, 286–87; public awareness of, 207–8; questions about, 232–33; subjectivities based on, 4, 8, 10; therapy's role in, 282. *See also* cognition; life narratives; *and specific individuals*

selfology ("knowing oneself," *khaudshinasi*): clothing's function in, 283–84; importance of, 281–82; meanings of, 292–96; naming in, 286–87; performed and practiced daily, 282–83, 286; relationships in, 284–85, 287–89; support group discussion of, 280–81; *suzhah shudan* notion in, 226, 289–90, 357n59; transition decisions in, 285–86, 291–92; "undecided" (*bilataklif*) in, 289

Semphill, Ewan Forbes, 46, 49

Seraji, Mehrzad, 15–16, 17, 307n1

sex: binary construction of, 246–51; concept (pre-1990s), 39; context and meanings of, 9; prepuberty determinant of, 43; psychology depicted in books and articles, 59–65; science of, 50–59; self and, 293–96

*Sex and Self* series, 293

sex change (*taghyir-i jinsiyat*): as circumstantial necessity (*iztirar*), 179–80; differences in legal thought regarding, 174–77, 343nn31–32; earliest non-intersex surgery, 318n39; evenhanded reporting on, 144–45; fear of, 264; Google searches on, 352n23; Hasuri's view of, 56–57; information sources on, 145, 157–58 (*see also* media coverage); Mahin's desire for, 77, 80, 88, 101–2, 104, 109, 111, 114–15, 117–19; as potential remedy, 118–19; reforming or correcting sex vs., 180; shifting discourse on, 49, 55, 65, 117, 262; skepticism about, 205–6; "spontaneous," reports of, 39–40, 313–14n5; transsexual surgeries as variant of, 38. *See also* certification process; fatwas: on permissibility of sex change; intersex transformations; sex reassignment surgery; sex reassignment therapy

Sex Clinic (TPI), 21, 22

sex disambiguation: 'Alizadah's story, 46, 316n26; Marziah's story, 43–46; other examples, 46–49, 316n27, 317n31. *See also* intersex transformations

sex education: calls for, 73, 105, 106–7; Mahin/Zahra story in relation to, 81–82; responsibility for, 64–65; texts for, 52–53

sex/gender/sexuality discourse: allegations of pornography in, 64–65; approach to questions about, 3; binary construction in, 246–51; openings for transsexuality discussion in, 204–8, 351n10, 352n21; sciences of religion and of nature in, 191–92; scientific truth of, 171–72; self in, 293–96; undecided about identity in, 114–15, 148, 179, 184, 257–65, 289. *See also* films and documentaries; gender/sexual desire; literature; media coverage; sex education; sexology; vernacular psychology

sexology: academic vs. vernacular, 4–5, 53–59, 320n63; on "changing sex," 50–51; compliance with Islam, 168–70; definition of, 53; homosexuality and, 56–57; marital advice books and, 51–52, 59, 61–62, 311n23, 320–21nn69–70, 321n73; neuro-psycho-biological approach to, 26–30, 200–201, 312n34; pedagogical and moral mission of, 52–53; publication site for, 44–45; on sexual deviancy, 55–56, 62–63; sexual deviancy and criminality linked in, 65–74; shift from wonders of nature to, 49; taxonomies of, 171, 172–73. *See also* vernacular psychology

sex reassignment surgery (SRS): banned by MCI (except for intersex persons), 49, 151–55, 152; cosmetic surgeries linked to, 359n1; costs and timing of, 183–84; epiphany in realizing possibilities of, 269–70; ethics of, 49; fiqhi thinking on hermaphrodites and, 177–78; first in Iran, 314n12; going abroad for, 158, 159,

338n93; historical context, 4 (*see also* intersex transformations); initial operations (*takhliah*) in, 183; international media coverage of, 1–2, 2; lack of awareness of, 240, 255, 261, 360n12; media's cautionary tales against, 205–6; number of applicants, 208, 209; one request to reverse, 310–11n20; peer expectation of, 259; phalloplasty decision, 183–84, 196; quality issues in, 219, 220, 222; questions about, 232–33, 359n1; Rashil's story of, 145, 145, 146, 147, 148–51, 149; regret for, 193, 195, 206, 310–11n20; specialization in, 11; state-authorized, 20. *See also* certification process; fatwas: on permissibility of sex change; life narratives; sex change; transition process

sex reassignment therapy: authorities' support for, 6; context and meanings of, 9; costs of, 221; formalization of processes, 227–28; forum for questions about, 225–27; increased attention to, 1–2, 2; referral letters specifying, 212–13; trans activists' meetings with Ministry of Health concerning, 355n42. *See also* certification process; hormonal treatments; sex reassignment surgery; transition process

sex segregation. *See* gender segregation

*Sexual Behavior on the Basis of Sexo-Physiology. See* Hasuri, Hasan

*Sexual Crimes and Deviancies* (Ansari), 69–72, 324n98

*The Sexual Criminal* (River), 69–72

sexual criminality: females murdered, 76–77, 116 (*see also* Mahin/Zahra story); homosexuality and, 5, 56; male adolescents murdered, 66–69 (*see also* Burujirdi, Asghar); overlapping cases of, 115–17; sexual deviancy linked to, 65–74

sexual deviation (*inhirafat-i jinsi*): abnormal personalities and, 296, 370–71n57; anxieties about, 52–53, 62; categories of, 70–71, 171–72; "changing sex" linked to, 50–51, 318n47; criminality linked to,

sociocultural spaces (*continued*)
in, 176–77; for mixed-sex socializing,
104–5; Nauruz (Iranian New Year) and,
262, 362n25; postoperative changes in,
239, 273; transition decisions in context
of, 285–87; for transsexuality discourse,
204–8. *See also* appearance; entertainment industry; gender segregation;
media coverage; nonheteronormative
lives and social circles; theater and
music performances
Sociological Association (Tehran University), 187–88
socio-pedagogical project: adolescent
girls' subculture depicted in, 77, 87, 91,
94–99; defining female homosexuality
as mental illness, 82–83; educating public about homosexuality, 99–105; "first-
ness" claims in, 108–9; journalistic view
of, 75–76; Mahin/Zahra story as lesson
in, 91–94, 97–98; neglectful and ignorant families depicted in, 85–86, 87,
90–91, 94, 115; summary, 117–19
sodomy. See *lavat/liwat*
soma-therapy (*jism-darmani*), 181
somatic etiological research, 28–30,
312n34
*Sometimes It Happens* (film), 257, 261, 262,
264, 265
soul: Asghar Qatil's story and, 66–67; as
determining sex/gender, 245–46; as
guide for trans persons, 178, 182, 188;
joke about psyche and, 346–47n68;
life/death meanings and, 196, 198; psyche in relation to, 189–94; religious
beliefs about, 253–54, 362n21; transsexuality as disparity between body
and, 178, 182, 188, 194; transsexuality
viewed as disease of, 205–6. *See also*
psyche
Specialization Center in Islamic Law and
Judiciary (*Markaz-i Huquq va Aaza-yi
Islami*), 179
speech act, 367n26. *See also* life narratives;
selfology

spiritual therapy, 192. *See also* Islam
therapy
SRS. *See* sex reassignment surgery
Stall, Sylvanus, 61, 293, 320n69
state. *See* Iranian-Islamic state
Steinmatz, George, 306n8
Stengel, Rebecca, 319n60
Stone, Hannah and Abraham, 62, 311n23,
320–21nn70–71
Stopes, Marie, 323n90
Stryker, Susan, 306n10
Subhi Muhtadi, 139
subjectivities: ethnography as space of, 11;
self-cognition in, 4, 8, 10; *suzhah* (sub-
ject) and *suzhah shudan* in, 226, 289–
90, 357n59; workings of power in for-
mation of, 16–17. *See also* life narratives
Sufism, 293
Suhayl, Mitra, 204
Suhayla (pseud.), 253–54
Suhrab, Hidayat-allah Khan, 61, 293,
320n69
Sunduzi, Taraneh, 143, 337nn75–76
*suzhah* (subject) and *suzhah shudan*, 226,
289–90, 357n59

Tabish, 'Ali, 128, 129, 331n26
*taghyir-i jinsiyat. See* sex change
Tahmineh (pseud.), 239
*Tahrir al-wasila* (Khomeini), 6, 173, 174–76,
343n33
Tajbakhsh, Kian, 309n11
Tajiani, Gul Muhammad Aqa (Gulistan Bu-
rumand), 313–14n5
Tala'i, Murtizá, 223
*Tamayulat va raftarha-yi jinsi-i tabi'i va
ghayr-i tabi'i-i insan* (Natural and un-
natural human sexual tendencies and
behaviors, Ohadi), 27–28
*Tandurust* (*The Healthy Body*, magazine), 51
Tannaz (pseud.), 165
Taqavi (surgeon), 150, 158
Taqizadeh, Farshid, 36
*tatbiq* (compliance), 346n65. *See also* Com-
pliance with Islam Project

*Taufiq* (magazine), 141, *142*

*tauzih al-masa'il* genre, 173–74, 178, 343n30

"the techniques of domination" concept, 2

*Tedium* (film), 357n57

Tehran: ethnic jokes in, 139–40, 335n60; gender/sexual nonnormative lives observed in, 206; growth and neighborhood reconfiguration in, 257–58; nightclub districts in, 130; Shahri's critique of vices, 67–68; touted as gay paradise in 1970s, 120–22. *See also* "gay Tehran" story

Tehran Psychiatric Institute (TPI): approval letters from, 267; Center for Mental Health Research of, 192; certification process of, 17–19; educating parents about GID at, 243, 360–61n13; Sex Clinic of, 21, 22; sexuality research at, 310n18; as state institution, 215; supervised therapy at, 15–17; Treatment Unit of, 19, 308n8. *See also* Commission; *Journal of Psychiatry and Clinical Psychology*

Tehran University: English curriculum, 322n83; School of Medicine, 41–42, 53, 171–72; Sociological Association of, 187–88. *See also* Women's Hospital

Tehran University of Medical Sciences (TUMS), 28

television: BBC reports translated and aired, 207; Farrukhzad's shows on, 138, 141; self-cognition gained via, 207–8, 363n28; as space for *gays*, 134. *See also* films and documentaries; Islamic Republic of Iran Broadcasting

theater and music performances: homosexual talk in, critiqued, 334n48; male dancers and *zan-push* (men dressed as females) in, 126, 128–30, *129*, *131*, 132, *132*, 330n25; social circle of singers and others, 157–58. *See also* entertainment industry

*tiransvistizm. See* transvestism

TPI. *See* Tehran Psychiatric Institute

trans activists: approach to, 6; consensus of, 220; discipline of, 357–58n64; document and name issues for, 182–84, 309n13, 355n43; effects of NGO on, 225; formalization of, 227–28; interventions in representations, 11–12; medical community working with, 167–68; meetings of, 215–23; military exemption classification changes sought, 203; originating impetus for, 165–66; patterns of, 211–12; political engagement of, 213–15; pragmatism of, 228–29; somatic etiological research and, 29–30; state interactions of, 203, 215–23, 228–29; terminology issues, 228–30. *See also* Iranian Society for Supporting Individuals with Gender Identity Disorder

transgendered living: certificates for, 180–81, *182*; trans-dressed (*mubaddal-pushi*) issue, 180–81

transgender/-sexuals (*tarajinsi-ha*): military exemption for, 202–3; use of term, 349n1

transgender studies, 306n10

transition process: decision making about, 183, 196, 198, 232, 238, 245–46, 256, 266–67, 285, 291–92; early stages in, 32, 267; family acceptance issue in, 252–53; feelings about born-body before, 251–52; fiqhi concern about persons in midst of, 178; initial operations (*takhliah*) in, 183; length of time, 182–84, 280–81; paths of cognition and change in, *33*; personality changes in, 267; phalloplasty decision in, 183–84, 196; religious beliefs and decisions on, 253–54, 362n21; social contexts of decisions, 285–87; soul vs. body as guide for, 178, 182, 188, 194; therapy in, 15–17, 18, 19, 22, 23, 190–91, 197–200, 265, 282, 308n8; "undecided" (*bilataklif*) in, 289. *See also* certification process; filtering and sorting processes; postoperative body; sex reassignment surgery; sex reassignment therapy

transsexuality delinked from, 157; transsexuality not distinguished from, 155; use of term, 42, 43, 73, 102, 117, 158, 315n17. *See also* hermaphrodites; intersexuality

*unasiyat. See* femininity and womanhood
"undecided" (*bilataklif*), 148, 178, 289. *See also* selfology
United States: Agnes's story and, 278–79, 366n16, 366–67n21; criminology text from, 69–72, 324n98; gay liberation movement in, 122; reports on Tehran as gay paradise in, 120–21
Universal Health Services Law (1995), 210
Usku'i (surgeon), 35–36, 250
*Usul-i asasi-i ravanshinasi* (Foundational principles of psychology, Iranshahr), 189

Vahid-Dastjerdi, Marzieh, 169
Valentine, David, 8, 368n32, 369n43
Valizadeh, Sughrá, 123
*Vazin* (newspaper), 63
Vaziri Mahabadi, 64
veiling. *See* appearance; dress code
vernacular psychology: authority and authorship of, 191–92; dominance of, 4–5, 276; Islamic writing and, 320n65; jins/genus/sex in, 294–96; marital advice books in, 59–65; nativization of, 101, 118; Ohadi's approach in, 26–30, 312n34; on older man/younger man liaisons, 66–69; publication site for, 44–45; sexology in, 53–59, 320n63; sexual deviancy and criminality linked to homosexuality in, 65–74. *See also* psychology and psychiatry; sexology
vernacular science: enthusiasms of, 50; the marvelous and strange in, 4, 38–41, 46, 47, 48; media's series on homosexuality as, 99–107; nativization of, 101, 118; use of term, 316n24. *See also* science; sexology
vernacular sexology. *See* sexology
Vicinus, Martha, 333n43

Vida (pseud.), 268–69
*Vue* (magazine), 46
vulnerability: legal term of, 214. *See also under* categories of identity
Vuzara Detention Center, 216, 244

Wahrman, Dror, 276, 294, 365nn6–7, 367n23, 368n28
Ward, Freda, 325n3
Warnke, Georgia, 285, 369n43
Welfare Organization (Sazman-i Bihzisti): budget, 227; on classification of treatment needed, 212–13, 355n42; foster and adoption programs under, 355n46; information oversight by, 222–23; ISSIGID's relations with, 227–28; legal representation and, 220–21; meetings at, 214–23, 249, 354n38; origins and continuity of, 208; Resolution of Conflicts meeting and, 219–20; trans activists' interactions with, 211. *See also* Nationwide Committee to Supervise Sexual Disorders; Office for the Socially Harmed
Westernization: dress code as response to, 163–64; moral corruption linked to, 136, 138, 143
*What a Young Husband Ought to Know* (Stall), 61, 293
Williams, Eugene, 70
womanhood. *See* femininity and womanhood
woman-presenting males (*mard-i zannuma*): attacks, harassment, and arrests of, 130, 132, *132*, 159–60, 163, 164–65, 166, 331n31, 340n1; gender confusion due to, 144; heterosexual desires of, 133–34; moral purification measures and, 160–62; naming of, 158; openings for (1970s), 6; post-1976 advice for, 153–54; sex change story of, 145, *145*, *146*, 147, 148–51, *149*; sex change surgery ban and, 49, 151–55, *152*, *156*, 157–58; as spectacle, 125–30, *127*, *129*, *131*; as threat to nation, 164–65; trans-genderally iden-

woman-presenting males (*continued*)
tified men compared, 334n46; visual
ethnography of, *plates 1 and 2*, 134–36.
*See also* male-to-female (MtF) trans
persons; nonheteronormative males;
*zan-push*
women. *See* females/women
Women's Hospital: number of sex surgeries at, 49; sex change surgery ban and,
153–54, 155, 157; sex disambiguation case
at, 47; sex surgery team at, 42, 315n18
women's movement: empowerment and,
39–40, 313–14n5; face-to-face strategy
of, 228; rights issues for, 212, 213–14

*Yad-i yaran* (television program), 207–8,
363n28
Ya'qub (Health Ministry representative),
221
Yasaman (pseud.), 280–81, 283, 285
Yazdan, Nahid, 95–96
Yazdan-shinas, A'zam, 88, 90, 91, 94–95,
96, 113
Youth Palaces (*kakh-i javanan*), 104–5
Yunes (pseud.), 245, 266–67, 292

Zahra (pseud.), 23, 25, 252, 285
*Zalim-bala* (film), 128
Zamani (assistant/technician), 36, 182, 224
*Zanan* (monthly), 206
*Zan-i ruz* (weekly): adolescent girls' subculture depicted by, 94, 95–99; "enlightening" project of, 75–76, 77, 82–83,
115, 117; on Farrukhzad's performance,
142; female homosexuality depicted as
mental illness by, 82–83; homosexuality
series in, 99–105; marital performance
anxieties in, 321n75; on neglectful families, 85–86, 87, 90–91, 94, 103; on
Razzaq-manish and Mahin, 116; readership, 101; readers' letters to, 106–7; sex
change reports in, 117; sexology column
in, 57. *See also* Mahin/Zahra story; Sekandari, Pari; socio-pedagogical project
*zan-push* (dressed in women's clothes):
history of, 126, 128–30, *129*, *131*, 132,
*132*; Rashil's interest in, 149–50; use
of term, 330n25. *See also* woman-
presenting males
*Zan va mard* (Woman and man, translated
text), 67, 323n90
Zarit, Jerry, 120–21, 329n8
Zaynab (pseud.), 236, 245–46
Zia (pseud.): on binary construction, 251;
current situation of, 368n31, 369n41; on
*gays*, 34, 223, 369n42; Houri's relationship with, 249, 258, 287–89; kinship
terminology of, 362n20; on marriage
imperative, 269; self-identification of,
178–79, 208, 290–91, 298; undecided
about identity, 265
Zia'i (doctor), 355n42
Zirakju (prosecutor), 107